Best of luck in everything you do, and always keep expanding your toolbox

2018

Handbook of Improving
Performance in the Workplace

Volume Two

Selecting and Implementing Performance Interventions

ABOUT ISPI

The International Society for Performance Improvement (ISPI) is dedicated to improving individual, organizational, and societal performance. Founded in 1962, ISPI is the leading international association dedicated to improving productivity and performance in the workplace. ISPI reaches out to more than 20,000 performance improvement professionals in over 40 countries through publications and educational programs.

ISPI's mission is to develop and recognize the proficiency of our members and advocate the use of Human Performance Technology. This systematic approach to improving productivity and competence uses a set of methods and procedures and a strategy for solving problems for realizing opportunities related to the performance of people. It is a systematic combination of performance analysis, cause analysis, intervention design and development, implementation, and evaluation that can be applied to individuals, small groups, and large organizations.

Website: www.ispi.org
Mail: International Society for Performance Improvement
1400 Spring Street, Suite 400
Silver Spring, Maryland 20910 USA
Phone: 1.301.587.8570
Fax: 1.301.587.8573
E-mail: info@ispi.org

**International Society for
Performance Improvement**

WHERE KNOWLEDGE
BECOMES KNOW-HOW

About Pfeiffer

Pfeiffer serves the professional development and hands-on resource needs of training and human resource practitioners and gives them products to do their jobs better. We deliver proven ideas and solutions from experts in HR development and HR management, and we offer effective and customizable tools to improve workplace performance. From novice to seasoned professional, Pfeiffer is the source you can trust to make yourself and your organization more successful.

Essential Knowledge Pfeiffer produces insightful, practical, and comprehensive materials on topics that matter the most to training and HR professionals. Our Essential Knowledge resources translate the expertise of seasoned professionals into practical, how-to guidance on critical workplace issues and problems. These resources are supported by case studies, worksheets, and job aids and are frequently supplemented with CD-ROMs, websites, and other means of making the content easier to read, understand, and use.

Essential Tools Pfeiffer's Essential Tools resources save time and expense by offering proven, ready-to-use materials—including exercises, activities, games, instruments, and assessments—for use during a training or team-learning event. These resources are frequently offered in looseleaf or CD-ROM format to facilitate copying and customization of the material.

Pfeiffer also recognizes the remarkable power of new technologies in expanding the reach and effectiveness of training. While e-hype has often created whizbang solutions in search of a problem, we are dedicated to bringing convenience and enhancements to proven training solutions. All our e-tools comply with rigorous functionality standards. The most appropriate technology wrapped around essential content yields the perfect solution for today's on-the-go trainers and human resource professionals.

Essential resources for training and HR professionals

Handbook of Improving Performance in the Workplace

Volume Two

Selecting and Implementing Performance Interventions

Edited by
Ryan Watkins and Doug Leigh

Co-Published by the International Society for
Performance Improvement

**International Society for
Performance Improvement**
WHERE KNOWLEDGE
BECOMES KNOW-HOW

Pfeiffer
A Wiley Imprint
www.pfeiffer.com

Published by Pfeiffer
An Imprint of Wiley
989 Market Street, San Francisco, CA 94103-1741

www.pfeiffer.com

For additional copies/bulk purchases of this book in the U.S. please contact 800-274-4434.

Pfeiffer books and products are available through most bookstores. To contact Pfeiffer directly call our Customer Care Department within the U.S. at 800-274-4434, outside the U.S. at 317-572-3985, fax 317-572-4002, or visit www.pfeiffer.com.

Pfeiffer also publishes its books in a variety of electronic formats. Some content that appears in print may not be available in electronic books.

Library of Congress Cataloging-in-Publication Data
Handbook of improving performance in the workplace.
    p. cm.
  "Co-Published by the International Society for Performance Improvement."
  Includes bibliographical references and index.
  ISBN 978-0-470-19068-5 (v. 1 : cloth) – ISBN 978-0-470-19069-2 (v. 2 : cloth) – ISBN 978-0-470-19067-8 (v. 3 : cloth)
 1. Performance technology.   2. Employees–Training of.   I. International Society for Performance Improvement.
  HF5549.5.P37H364 2010
  658.3'14–dc22

                                                                                        2009026946

Acquiring Editor: Matthew Davis
Marketing Manager: Brian Grimm
Production Editor: Michael Kay

Editor: Rebecca Taff
Indexer: Sylvia Coates
Editorial Assistant: Lindsay Morton
Manufacturing Supervisor: Becky Morgan

Printed in the United States of America
Printing   10 9 8 7 6 5 4 3 2 1

CONTENTS

LIST OF EXHIBITS, FIGURES, AND TABLES

EXHIBITS

FIGURES

TABLES

INTRODUCTION TO VOLUME TWO

Improving human and organizational performance is typically a worthwhile, valuable, and even valiant effort. Improvement efforts routinely bring about "bottom-line" benefits for organizations, and likewise they routinely change lives of those working within organizations in very positive ways. After all, improving performance isn't just about improving workplace productivity; it can, and should, also lead to increased job satisfaction, longer retention, improved quality of life for employees, less job-related stress, new social networks, retained knowledge within the organization, and numerous benefits that directly impact the individuals who make up organizations as much as the organization itself and the societal partners that the organization serves.

These beneficial results, nevertheless, rarely happen by chance alone. Systematic, deliberate, and continual efforts to improve human and organizational performance are required to ensure success; as a consequence, there are generally no easy solutions and no quick fixes that can accomplish the sustainable results required for organizational success. Improving performance therefore requires both the scientific knowledge of how various interventions are effectively applied within organizations, as well as the artistic understanding of the delicate relationships among people, performance, organizational results, and beneficial outcomes for societal partners (including clients, customers, and others).

The path toward improved human and organizational performance is, however, routinely unclear and challenging to navigate. From defining what results are to be accomplished to assessing the success of your efforts—and for every step in between—there are many complex decisions and tasks that shape performance, and for each there are numerous performance interventions that can be used to achieve desirable results. From six sigma and incentive programs to mentoring and on-the-job training, there are literally hundreds of individual, team, and organizational activities that are specifically designed to improve performance. Consequently, the accomplishment of significant results is not complicated by a lack of options, but rather by the multitude of possible combinations and alternatives.

Each day, nevertheless, organizations around the globe rely on single-activity solutions to accomplish their complex goals. Your organization, for instance, probably has a few dozen improvement efforts already going on; perhaps it's leadership training, performance management, or improving employee retention. Maybe there is a restructuring initiative or a new coaching program. Or it could be the outsourcing of jobs or the introduction of e-learning courses. Or maybe even a combination of these with other activities to improve performance.

Given this complexity, simply adding another discrete and disconnected program to the mix is unlikely to significantly improve results. Few single solutions have the capacity to achieve sustainable improvements in performance. People are complex, and since organizations are made up of people, they are exponentially complicated. In response, successful performance improvement efforts work to address these complexities instead of offering a variety of one-off programs that only haphazardly address the various factors (or symptoms) underlying human and organizational performance.

By *systematic*ally and *systemic*ally aligning multiple improvement activities (both those that are already being implemented, along with new ones), it's possible to accomplish sustainable improvements to performance. But before you can start to improve performance, it is necessary to gain consistency on what it is that you are trying to improve.

IMPROVING PERFORMANCE

What Is Performance?

In order to improve *performance*, you must begin with a clear definition of what performance is, and is not. This clarification of what you are trying to improve will guide and give focus to your decisions. It will delineate the goal of your efforts from the activities that you might use to achieve it, and it will distinguish your efforts from the routine processes that typically cycle through organizations in conjunction with the latest management trends.

After all, confusion about what performance is, or is not, can be a major impairment to the accomplishment of useful results. Knowing what performance is "when you see it" is not enough to accomplish desirable and sustainable improvements. Likewise, you cannot rely on defining performance by what it is not either—identifying performance problems alone is no way to achieve success. Even more dangerous can be working with the assumption that everyone has the same operational definition of *performance*.

At the most basic and perhaps most valuable level, *improving performance* is the equivalent of *improving results*. Results are, after all, the reason that people and organizations undertake activities in the first place. Too often, the focus of improvement efforts ends up being solely on implementation of specific initiatives (for instance, quality improvement, knowledge management, information technology, employee recruitment, balanced scorecards, or training) without remembering that desired results should—and must—be accomplished.

Take restructuring as an example of a process that frequently gets off-track during implementation. Most organizations decide to restructure in order to improve performance in very specific ways: increase revenue, reduce expenses, eliminate redundancies, and so forth. Nevertheless, the complexity of restructuring initiatives routinely clouds the focus on results—and the processes associated with making structural changes—such as which departments to combine, what jobs should be cut, and who will be the boss—become the focus of the effort. When this happens, organizational politics generally takes over, and the meaningful improvements are rarely achieved.

Thus, improving performance is not just about implementing new activities, trying out new management strategies, or following any set of procedures. Improving performance is only worth the time and energy if it is going to achieve desirable and useful results.

Many well-meaning efforts likewise fail to improve results when *performance* is confused with *performing*. When such improvement efforts—often focused on implementing the new management tactics or perhaps new software applications—become inattentive to the basic results that must be accomplished they usually end up as the content of dusty binders on someone's bookshelf.

A focus on performing (what people do) does not, in the end, ensure that valuable results will accomplished. From lean six sigma programs or supply-chain management to learning management systems or executive coaching, it is easy for individuals and teams to get so wrapped up with project design, implementation, and management that they lose track of why they are doing it in the first place. Therefore, we suggest that performance be defined simply as the accomplishment of desired and useful results. This will provide a focal point for your improvement efforts and guide all of the necessary decisions to accomplish significant results.

Ground your success in a definition of performance that includes the specific results you and your organization are trying to accomplish. These desired results may be a 5 percent or better increase in individual employee productivity, zero customer returns due of faulty products, 100 percent compliance with new legislation, $3 million increases in revenue, or the elimination of poverty in developing countries. No matter which results you and your organization are trying to improve, these should be the focus of your efforts rather than the procedures, processes, strategies, techniques, tools, or resources that you might use to accomplish these results.

Why Improve Performance?

Improving performance is about accomplishing desired results; as a consequence, life itself is an ongoing undertaking in performance improvement. From achieving personal goals to assisting organizations in accomplishing their strategic objectives to partnering with others to improve the quality of life in your community, these ongoing efforts to achieve desired results keep us moving ahead. This same desire to achieve results led Thomas Edison to thousands of valuable inventions and also brought an end to communism within the former Soviet Union.

The desire to accomplish significant results holds true of individuals, teams, divisions, companies, agencies, and even communities. Most of us work to improve results not out of greed or self-indulgence, but rather for the continual improvement of our life and the lives of others. We may not be striving for results that will single-handedly end poverty in the world, but we are working to achieve worthwhile results within our personal and professional realms of influence.

Frequently, our ambitions to improve performance are achieved through the organization in which we work, and at other times these ambitions are achieved through organizations with which we volunteer our time and energy. In both cases we are striving to achieve results that benefit others. Sometimes we call them customers or clients, while at other times we call them neighbors or friends.

The perceived value or worth of the results we accomplish will vary greatly depending on the diverse perspectives taken on the products, outputs, and outcomes of our efforts. This can complicate performance improvement efforts, since our perceptions of valued results (performance) may not be aligned with the perceptions of others. In response to this challenge, the practical place to begin an improvement effort is with the clear specification of the valued and desired results that are to be accomplished within your organization and delivered outside of it.

Throughout this volume of the handbook, we will refer to Roger Kaufman's Organizational Elements Model (OEM), the basis of his Mega Planning approach to improving human and organizational performance. The OEM was designed as a framework for coordinating improvement interventions with the products, outputs, and outcomes that are to be accomplished. Kaufman's model helps align all that an organization uses, does, produces, and delivers with the outcomes accomplished in the broader society. By linking internal performance with external impacts, the model offers a systemic perspective on performance improvement and a perspective that builds on the relationships of all subsystems within the larger system of society.

Systems Theory and Performance Improvement

By and large, systems theory (or more specifically, von Bertalanffy's General Systems Theory) is viewed as the foundation of the principles, models, frameworks, and best practices that guide the improvement of human and organizational performance. As Richard Swanson describes in his three-legged stool theory of performance improvement (a metaphor he also applies to human resources development), systems theory is one of the legs on which the discipline and practice of improving performance relies. Along with theories of economics and psychology, the three legs rest on a foundation of ethics within Swanson's theoretical model. And as such, systems theory plays a dual—and potentially more important—role in the model by also being the uniting theory that defines the relationships between the three legs and the mat on which they rest.

As you can see, systems theory is an essential and integral part of both understanding performance within your organizations as well as guiding efforts to improve it. General systems theory is built on several foundational concepts, or principles, that are applied whenever we strive to improve human and organizational performance; these include non-summative wholeness, control, self-regulation, and self-organization. Within this handbook, we particularly want to focus attention on the principle of general systems theory that has direct and evident influence on the selection and implementation of performance interventions specifically: the principle of equifinality.

Expanding Your Options

Equifinality—a principle from Ludwig von Bertalanffy's General Systems Theory, which put forward that in open systems, a given end state can be reached by many potential means. It emphasizes that the same end state may be achieved via many different paths or trajectories.

Based on wikipedia.org, January 2009

Equifinality challenges us to look beyond the single solutions that we may have used in the past. Perhaps most performance issues within your organization have been addressed by traditional classroom training sessions. In this case, the principle of equifinality validates what you have probably already discovered—that training by itself is not capable of addressing the complex performance issues of today's organizations.

The accomplishment of significant results (or "end states") can, after all, be achieved through any number of potential activities (or "means"). Other options should be weighed in order to determine which activities or combination of activities, as the case usually is, are best going to accomplish the desired results. This basic notion is at the core of this handbook, and it is also the basis for most, if not all, worthwhile performance improvement models.

According to the general systems theory, equifinality applies within all open systems and is therefore a characteristic of organizations as well. While mandate, habit, or even past successes may push you in the direction of one performance improvement activity or another, there will always be multiple paths toward success in the future. Examine the various interventions that we have included in this book, and explore other fields and disciplines for more examples of improvement interventions that may help you achieve results. By expanding your options and comparing across multiple interventions—or combinations of interventions—you will find the "means" that will help you accomplish your desired "end states."

How Can Performance and Success Be Measured?

The success of activities to improve performance is measured by the results achieved. Sometimes the results are immediate, such as when a product is produced or a report is distributed to clients. Other times, however, the desired accomplishments may not be visible immediately; for instance, when a high-performer retention program is created and it takes a year or more for the benefits to be realized by the organization. Regardless of whether the benefits are immediate or delayed, the success of an improvement effort is measured by the results rather than the processes.

As the saying goes, "You pay a cow for its milk, not for standing over the bucket." In the same way, individuals and organizations are most successful when their processes and procedures produce results that benefit the team, the organization, the client, and the community.

At times, measuring results seems more challenging than measuring processes. For example, you can easily count how many employees sign up for a training course or the number of hours executives spend on succession planning. Measuring the success of a performance improvement effort must, however, include a focus on results, since *performance* is all about *results*. This is not to say that activities are inconsequential; processes and procedures are critical for getting things done. They are, in other words, necessary but not sufficient for measured success. They should also be examined when you make improvements and assess your success, and they should be complemented by demonstrated results.

Consequently, performance improvement projects rely on systematic processes to ensure that desired results guide both front-end decision making and back-end evaluation—and every step in between. With the application of a systematic approach, improvement efforts can measure the success of their procedures as well as the associated results. Although direct attribution of results to a single process is generally tough—and frequently dangerous—the contribution of improvement efforts to beneficial results is the hallmark of human performance technology models, frameworks, standards, and processes.

Where to Start?

Improving performance requires more than just good intentions; things must change in order for new and desirable results to be accomplished. Change, although often challenging, is what allows individuals and organizations to move beyond today's performance capacity in order to achieve the desired results of tomorrow. Change can, however, just as easily reduce performance and lead to undesirable outcomes for the organization and the communities in which it occurs. Thus, while change has to be created in order to form the potential for improved performance, change also has to be managed.

To create and manage change, you should rely on what Jay McTigue and Grant Wiggins call "backward design." In other words, start with the end—the desired results—in mind and then work your way backward through the necessary processes and procedures for achieving those defined accomplishments. While this sounds simple and logical, most performance improvement projects still begin with a single solution or activity in mind and then go through a process of looking for problems that the intervention might solve.

How often have you heard someone say, "We need to send everyone to training on this," "We need this new software" or "We have to bring consultants in to help us implement this"? Or maybe you hear: "We can only compete if we start doing what our competitors are doing." While each of the activities suggested in these statements might bring about valuable improvements in performance, all put a possible solution ahead of the desired results. In essence, these people are prematurely selecting their tools before they even know what it is that they are trying to build.

Remember, the systems theory principle of equifinality tells us that within organizations, there are always multiple processes that can be used to accomplish a result. Therefore, selecting a process before you have adequately defined the targeted results, as well as alternative options, is not going to be your best path toward success.

Useful results are better achieved when all options for how to improve performance are weighed against the desired results to be achieved and then compared based on their effectiveness, efficiency, and other pertinent variables specific in the performance context. While these steps may slightly delay the selection of which performance interventions to implement, it provides you the opportunity to define what results must be accomplished, what criteria should be used for selecting appropriate interventions, and then to assess how well each alternative activity will do within your organization. In the end, systems of multiple interventions are most frequently found to be necessary for achieving valuable results—thus countering the single-solution focus of "we need" this or "we must do" that.

Throughout this book you will find many performance interventions that can help accomplish positive results for your organization. None of these, however, is a "silver bullet" or a "panacea." They are simply proven activities that, when used (typically in conjunction with other proven activities), have demonstrated capacity to accomplish desirable results. As such, the decisions around selecting which interventions are going to help you and your organization be successful are best made in a systematic manner, built on models and frameworks that are grounded in pragmatic theory and research.

In recognition of this, we are using John Wedman's Performance Pyramid model (or framework) as a structure for this handbook—clustering performance interventions into building blocks for accomplishing significant results. From building performance capabilities and providing a supportive environment to giving timely performance feedback to updating employee skills, each component of the Performance Pyramid model is associated with a variety of interventions that can be used to achieve results (see Figure I.1 and Chapter Three).

The Performance Pyramid model offers a whole-system perspective on performance improvement. From culture and vision to significant accomplishments and monitoring, the model illustrates the relationships among inputs, processes, and results. Interestingly, while the Pyramid at the center of the model could be considered a hierarchical tool with one building block of performance being more important than the others, within the systemic perspective of the model you can see that all of the blocks within the pyramid itself are interconnected. As a result, each of the potential performance interventions associated with the model can play an important role in achieving desired results.

As an organizational tool for classifying performance interventions, the Performance Pyramid lies at the heart of a comprehensive and results-driven model for improving performance. As such, we are using the pyramid model as a framework for the book's chapters, examining a variety of interventions associated with each component of the model to provide a systemic perspective on improving performance.

Performance Pyramid

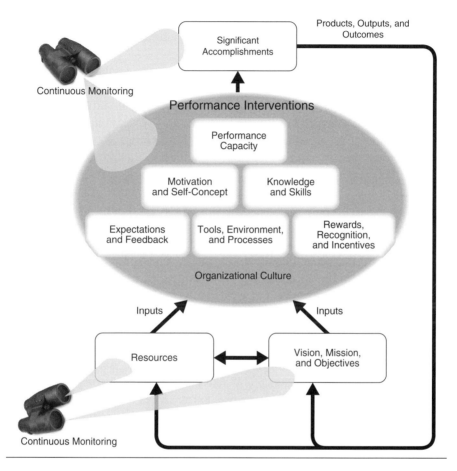

Figure I.1 The Performance Pyramid Improvement Model.

From John Wedman and Steve Graham.

In addition to the interventions included in this handbook, there are hundreds of other activities you can implement to accomplish better results. Thus, the chapters do not represent an exhaustive list, but rather a starting place. Along with the material in the chapters, we include our own discussion and descriptions of many other performance interventions—from lean six sigma to job forecasting—throughout the text.

Nevertheless, your own creativity and knowledge are the best tools you have for complementing any, or all, of these performance interventions with other activities that will work best to achieve results within your organization. For example, developing *communities of practice* can be a very effective tool—especially when paired with other interventions such as training, mentoring, and incentives—for improving individual and organizational performance. Brown-bag lunches or other informal learning opportunities, as other examples, can also be valuable additions to almost any performance improvement effort.

The consequence of having numerous and varied options when deciding which performance interventions to implement is that the decisions become increasingly challenging—just as decisions were easier when the choices were either black or black for Ford's Model T or when your options were between preparing a letter on a personal computer or a typewriter. Nevertheless while the numerous quality performance improvement activities that can be used in organizations today make decisions more challenging, our ability to improve performance and accomplish significant results make it well worth the effort. As the saying goes, "The hardest choices in life are between multiple good options."

There are, however, no easy formulas or checklists that can be used to define the "right" mix of performance interventions for your organization. Consequently, we start this handbook with a broad discussion of the models, frameworks, theories, and research findings that support the improvement of human and organizational performance (see Chapters One and Two). From there, we further introduce John Wedman's Performance Pyramid as an applicable model for organizing performance interventions and guiding improvement efforts (see Chapter Three) and introduce Roger Kaufman's Organizational Elements Model (Figure I.2) as a systemic framework for ensuring that everything your organization uses, does, produces, and delivers is aligned with beneficial results for the system in which the organization exist.

Later in the book our authors present numerous software applications that are available to assist in making improvement decisions. Nevertheless, in the end the decisions still have to be made by people—people who understand the culture of the organization, who have "power" to get things done, and who have relationships with those who will be most impacted by the changes associated with any effort to improve performance. Therefore we have also

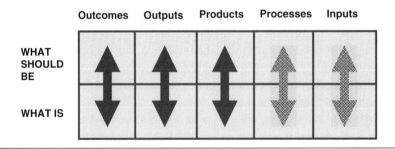

Figure I.2 Roger Kaufman's Organizational Elements Model.

included within this volume of the handbook an introduction to various individual and group decision-making techniques that can also be used to help in selecting appropriate improvement activities. From the nominal group technique and card sorts to multi-attribute utility analysis and focus groups, each of these offers a range of techniques for guiding decision making.

With Part One as its foundation, the remaining parts of the handbook are dedicated to the numerous performance interventions that you can use to accomplish results. Each chapter introduces you to an intervention, its strengths, its weaknesses, and how it could be of value to you and your organization. Use these chapters to expand your options and learn more about what can be accomplished as you work to develop systems of interventions that support the improvement of performance.

HOW TO USE THIS HANDBOOK

Our Goals

In taking on this handbook as a project, we (as editors) had to justify why this book was worth the time and energy of our authors, our publisher, and ourselves. As a result of our conversations we established four basic goals that we hope this handbook accomplishes for you, the readers:

Goal 1: The handbook should expand your perceptions of the possibilities; helping you find numerous performance interventions that can be used to improve performance.

Goal 2: The handbook should embrace performance improvement as a pragmatic science that seeks to accomplish valuable results for individuals, teams, organizations, and all of society through evidence-based practice.

Goal 3: The handbook should represent an interdisciplinary approach to improving performance, drawing on fields and disciplines that are not typically represented adequately in literature or practice.

Goal 4: The handbook should be a user-friendly guide that practitioners, students, researchers, and others can all use, regardless of their experience or academic training.

With these goals in mind, the chapters in this handbook provide both foundational knowledge on the identification and selection of valuable performance interventions, as well as useful guidelines for how to implement a variety of improvement activities within your organization. No matter whether you are reading the book from cover to cover or whether you are reading chapters that apply most directly to the current improvement opportunities within your organization, this handbook should be a valuable resource for accomplishing desirable results.

Performance Interventions

Striving to improve human and organizational performance is a worthwhile ambition; even when the path to success is uncertain. The challenges associated with improving performance are, after all, the opportunities that lead to significant improvements in individual and organizational results. Knowing which activities, or combinations of activities, will best improve performance is a demanding—and thought-provoking—part of the road to success. The processes used to make critical choices about *what to do* in order to improve performance will determine your capacity to be successful.

In this handbook we have worked to bring together a varied selection of performance interventions (also referred to as *human performance technologies* or *performance improvement activities*) that can be used to accomplish meaningful results within almost any organization. Ideally, each of these performance interventions offers a piece that can fit into the complex puzzle of improving performance within your organization. For some organizations, improved performance may require a combination of five or six integrated interventions; for other organizations, desired results may come from the introduction of just a few new activities. Each organization is unique, and each performance issue might require a different set of activities to attain desired results; thus no single performance technology—or combination of technologies—is the *right* choice for everyone or every organization.

An additional caveat is that the interventions described within the chapters of this handbook only scratch the surface of the many improvement activities that you can use to achieve desirable results. There are literally hundreds of other activities that organizations can use to improve performance and accomplish desired results; ranging from supply-chain management to ergonomics to color coding. In light of this, each part of the book also highlights numerous performance interventions that are not addressed in full chapters. These options, and others, should be considered when you are looking for the best activities to accomplish results.

Use performance interventions in various combinations whenever you or your organization is striving to accomplish valuable improvements in performance. For those improvement activities that are discussed within this handbook, apply the systematic planning, design, and development steps described by the authors. Then refer to the other parts of this handbook to ensure that you are addressing all factors underlying performance within your organization (for example, motivation, capacity, performance feedback, continual monitoring, incentives, knowledge and skills). Examine the varied activities available within each part to determine how they might also be of value in systemically improving performance, verifying that your efforts improve the entire performance system, and not just one or two elements of the system.

Parts and Chapters

In order to make heads or tails of the numerous performance improvement activities discussed throughout this handbook, we use a combination of parts and chapters to provide a guide for readers. The parts of the book mirror John Wedman's Performance Pyramid model, which he describes in detail in Chapter Three. The model provides an overarching framework for how we can examine the diverse and numerous interventions that are available to improve performance.

Within each component of the model we asked leading international experts to provide chapters on specific performance interventions and activities. For example, for Part Six (Incentives, Rewards, and Recognition) Steven Condly from the University of Central Florida contributed a chapter on incentive systems (see Chapter Eighteen), and Tahir Nisar from the University of Southampton in the United Kingdom contributed a chapter on employee and executive compensation (see Chapter Twenty). Along with the other contributions in Part Five, these authors illustrate how performance interventions can be successfully implemented to improve human and organizational performance. Numerous additional interventions that are associated with each component of the Performance Pyramid will also be discussed and included as appropriate, even when there may not be a chapter dedicated to each implementation. Hence, Figure I.3 shows the organizational framework for this book.

From mentoring and coaching to job aids and succession planning, we have organized the various interventions into the elements of the Performance Pyramid where they are most frequently applied. This isn't to say, however, that they could not be of value in supporting performance from other perspectives. Coaching, for example, shows up in both Part Four (Expectations and Feedback) as well as in Part Eight (Knowledge and Skills). In the same way, mentoring, needs assessment, appreciative inquiry, and other activities can also be applied in numerous beneficial ways within an improvement effort. Therefore, it is less important to focus on which intervention is associated with which element of the model, and more important to ensure that you are addressing all components of the Performance Pyramid.

Together, the parts and chapters of this handbook provide you with a complete framework for how you can build performance improvement systems that include multiple activities some activities will be ones that your organization is already doing, and others might be new ones that you want to add to the mix. In the end, we know that organizations should not implement single solutions or quick fixes, because these are rarely successful strategies for

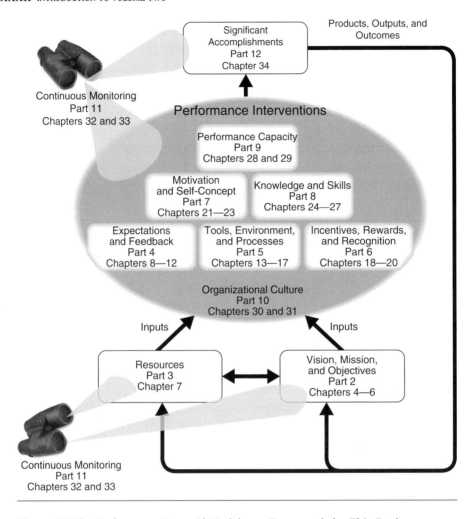

Figure I.3 The Performance Pyramid Model as a Framework for This Book.

accomplishing sustainable results. Therefore, we want to create systems of performance activities that together can achieve far more success than any single performance intervention on its own can.

Handbook Feature: Introductory Chapters

In addition to the chapters focused on specific performance interventions, in Part One we have included several chapters that provide context and direction for the selection of appropriate performance interventions. These chapters offer examples of different theories, models, and frameworks that can guide the improvement of human and organizational performance. The components in these chapters vary from those of the intervention-focused chapters, but they also provide practical and useful guidance on the given topics.

Handbook Feature: Editorial Connections

Systems that improve human and organizational performance rely on interconnected activities to support the accomplishment of significant and sustainable results. Thus, throughout this handbook we continually emphasize the importance of building improvement systems that examine all components of the Performance Pyramid model. In order to illustrate the valuable relationships to be found between the topics covered, we have written commentary at the end of each part and chapter.

Our *Editorial Connections* between chapters and our *Introductions* at the beginning and *Discussions* at the end of each part are intended to strengthen the relationships found between the individual performance interventions. These features will commonly refer you to other topics that are closely related, as well as relate the chapter content back to the overarching models that we are using to structure this book and guide your decisions about how to improve performance (Wedman's Performance Pyramid and Kaufman's Organizational Element Model). These features also move this handbook from being a collection of chapters to being a tightly integrated series of readings that together provide a support structure for improving human and organizational performance.

Handbook Feature: Expanding Your Options

Because the material in the chapters in this handbook only scratch the surface of the total number of interventions available for improving performance, throughout the handbook we have added descriptions of alternative interventions and other topics that should also be considered. Use these short descriptions to expand the variety of optional activities that you consider for each component of the Pyramid Model (or part of this handbook). For example, if you are looking for options beyond the five chapters we have included on Expectations and Feedback systems, the Expanding Your Options features in Part Three of this handbook offer short descriptions of more than fifteen other options that you might consider. Most of the short descriptions are based on current Wikipedia articles; therefore, if you want to learn more about activities from these features, Wikipedia may a good place to begin your exploration.

Chapter Components

The topics in this handbook are diverse—from coaching to job aids, from needs assessment to succession planning—and therefore each chapter is distinct. Nevertheless, as editors we did not want the handbook to be a collection of individual and disparate chapters. Our goal, rather, was to offer both distinct chapters that can be read independently and a single compilation that can be read from beginning-to-end. To achieve these goals, we have applied several organizational structures in the chapters to improve consistency and ensure that you obtain enough information to apply the interventions in your work. We have included a fair amount of content to provide transitions between the chapters, expand on important topics alluded to within chapters, and describe related interventions that you may want to consider.

The chapters included in Part One: Introduction (Chapters One, Two, and Three) are probably the most diverse of the collection, as they do not describe specific performance interventions, but rather provide the basis for relating and using the interventions that follow. Because of this, we allowed these contributing authors a fair degree of liberty to organize and structure their works.

Within the other eleven parts of the volume, we used the Performance Pyramid to provide structure, and in turn asked authors to use a defined structure. Specifically, we asked the authors to address the following components:

- *Introduction:* A short abstract of what, where, when, why, and how to use the intervention to improve performance.

- *Description:* An introduction to the intervention describing the types of results that can be expected, when the intervention could be part of an improvement system, and the primary characteristics of its successful application.

- *What We Know from Research:* A brief review of the scientific literature on the intervention and its application in organizations.

- *When to Apply:* A discussion of when the intervention is appropriate for accomplishing desired results.

- *Strengths and Criticisms:* A bulleted list describing the advantages and disadvantages of the performance intervention.

- *Recommended Design, Development, and Implementation Process:* A step-by-step guide for how to successfully implement the performance intervention in an organization.

- *Critical Success Factors:* Descriptions of the factors (social, political, economic, legal, and technological) that must be in place for the intervention to be successful.

- *Summary:* A short review of the chapter.

- *Notes:* A section to guide readers to more information on the performance intervention. These are not presented as endnotes but rather as bulleted lists of additional ideas for consideration.

- *References:* A guide to the references cited in the chapter.

- *Recommended Readings and Websites:* A guide to readings or websites that the author recommends to readers but did not reference specifically in the chapter.

- *Author Bios:* Short descriptions of the authors' backgrounds, recent works, and contact information are provided at the end of the volume.

While a few chapter topics did not lend themselves to including all of these components, in most cases the chapters do include each of these recommended elements.

Interviews with the Authors

Working with colleagues at the University of Missouri, authors who contributed chapters to the handbook were given the opportunity to discuss their topics in a podcast interview. The interviews explore the implementation of performance interventions and offer case studies of how the authors have successfully implemented the interventions within organizations. You can listen to any (or all) of these interviews at hpt.needsassesment.org

ACKNOWLEDGEMENTS

We would like to express our appreciation and gratitude for the encouragement, contributions, and patience that we have received from our wives throughout the development of this handbook. We would especially like to thank our families for their support: Christina Gee, Hillary Leigh, Jordan Gee, Doug and Judi Watkins, and Dewey and Dee Leigh.

This handbook, of course, would not exist without the tremendous contributions of all our authors. Working with us as their editors could not have been easy, so we are indebted to them both for their creativity in putting together very practical and useful chapters that are also based in research as well as for their patience. In addition, we would like to acknowledge the important contributions of John Wedman in assisting us in the development of this book. Without his help the chapters would simply be a collection of ideas rather than a valuable resource for readers. Along with Elliott McClelland and Judy Richey, John has also orchestrated the development of podcast interviews with the contributing authors (available at hpt.needsassessment.org).

We are also grateful for the many colleagues and students who have participated in the development of the concepts, models, and ideas that have formed this book, including the online students of the Educational Technology Leadership program at the George Washington University; doctoral students within Pepperdine University's Graduate School of Education; Mike Corry, Diane Atkinson, Bill Robie, Natalie Milman, Mary Futrell

(George Washington University); Bob Paull, Farzin Madjidi, Tehniat Mirza (Pepperdine University); Roger Kaufman (Florida State University); Lya, Jan, and Yusra Visser (Learning Development, Inc.); and Atsusi Hirumi (University of Central Florida).

Last, we would like to acknowledge all of those at Pfeiffer and the International Society for Performance Improvement (ISPI) who have contributed to the success of the book, including April Davis, Matt Davis, Lindsay Morton, Brian Grimm, Michael Kay, and Rebecca Taff.

PART ONE

INTRODUCTION

Before selecting and implementing any variety of performance interventions, it is important to consider the foundations on which the interventions will be built. Just as a shiny red sports car is only as fast as the engineering and design that went into it, the value created by improvement interventions is wholly dependent on the processes you use to design, develop, and implement them. From the initial planning that defines the strategic results to be accomplished to the final evaluations of performance and impact, performance improvement initiatives are best built on a solid foundation of systematic design.

Like other applied disciplines, performance improvement relies on a variety of models, theories, scientific processes, frameworks, taxonomies, and other building blocks to create this foundation. As a social science, performance improvement doesn't have a single theory, model, or framework that can be applied in all situations; people are just too complex and unpredictable. Therefore, it's necessary to put the pieces of the puzzle together for yourself each and every time you work to improve performance. Through (1) the application of procedural models derived on years of professional experience, (2) the use of pragmatic frameworks and taxonomies, and (3) the integration of scientific theories and findings, it's possible to create systems that improve individual and organizational performance in a sustainable manner.

This type of improvement effort does not, however, lend itself well to quick-fixes or one-off solutions. Systemic improvements in performance are rarely the result of activities that focus either on just one element of the performance system (for example, isolating only the knowledge and skills of employees, the setting of expectations, or the use of targeted incentives) or on pre-selected solutions (be it training, coaching, or new software). Rather, it's necessary to know first what results must be accomplished. Complex performance challenges of today's organizations are not improved by disjointed or unconnected efforts.

Similarly, no single performance improvement theory, taxonomy, model, or research finding is going to do it all for your organization. It is therefore vital for professionals to identify and, as appropriate, apply multiple, varied models. Wile's Synthesized Human Performance Technology (HPT) Model (see Figure 1.6), for instance, may provide a useful diagnostic tool for your situation. In addition, you might also want to use a procedural model, such as the traditional HPT process (see Figure 1.8), to guide your performance improvement activities. Then again, next year a new performance improvement opportunity may require that you apply different classification, diagnostic, or process models in order to accomplish sustainable results.

WHAT'S COMING UP

In Chapter One, HPT Models: An Overview of the Major Models in the Field, Frank Wilmoth and his colleagues provide an overview of numerous models, frameworks, and taxonomies for improving individual and organizational performance. Their chapter, first published in *Performance Improvement Journal*, illustrates the variations in approaches used to improve performance, the commonalities that help define performance improvement as a discipline, as well as the value of taxonomies for classifying the numerous performance interventions that are available to professionals when applying any model within their organizations.

The chapter explores the models of performance improvement by grouping them around (1) the models developed by ''pioneers'' in the discipline, (2) classification models, (3) diagnostic models, (4) process models, and (5) holistic models. This provides you a structure for comparing, contrasting, and identifying which combinations might be useful in differing situations. The models, frameworks, and taxonomies included in the chapter do not represent an exhaustive list. Rather, the authors provide an introduction to models that should drive performance improvement initiatives as a starting place that you can use to define your own approach to improving performance. In the Editorial Connections feature that follows the chapter, we highlight a few additional models and frameworks that can further guide your improvement efforts.

With quality models, frameworks, and taxonomies as your foundations, sensible decisions can be made about which performance interventions to select and implement to accomplish desired results. Sometimes it may require a little of one model and a lot of another, while at other times it may be a mix of four or five models that creates sustainable results within your organization. To say the least, determining the correct mix of models, frameworks, and taxonomies to guide your improvement effort can be challenging.

To place the models described in Chapter One in context for the purposes of this handbook, it is also useful to explore how performance improvement models are differentiated from those of other disciplines. In an article entitled "Trendspotter: RSVP+," Carol Haig and Roger Addison identify four essential characteristics of HPT (a term often used synonymously with performance improvement) that can be applied when examining the many models described in the following chapters. To Haig and Addison, HPT should focus on results, systems, value, and partnerships:

- HPT (and thus the models that define its processes) is focused on *Results*. Results are what organizations measure. When we begin a performance improvement project by specifying the *Results* and then work backward to determine what we can do to better achieve them, we have a powerful formula for successful performance improvement.

- HPT takes a *Systems* viewpoint. Every organization is a *System* with interdependencies within and across functions and among levels. Alignment among these elements is critical for any performance improvement initiative to become embedded in an organization's culture.

- HPT adds *Value*. Performance improvement is focused on delivering "valued results." Any solution's success must be tied to the success of the individual worker, the work or processes, and the workplace or organization.

- HPT establishes *Partnerships*. No performance consultant succeeds alone. Our work entails developing collaborative relationships with clients and other project stakeholders, often a great many people.

Characteristics such as these provide a structure that can be used to compare, contrast, and apply the various models, frameworks, and taxonomies included in Chapter One. In addition, you can use these "RSVP" characteristics to examine models of other disciplines, such as management, organization development, psychology, and human resources management, to see which of them will work within the context of your organization. Although models and frameworks from other disciplines, such as balanced scorecards or cash-flow analysis, provide useful tools for improving performance, their application must adhere to the results, systems, value, and partnership principles above in order to accomplish significant results. Therefore, when it comes time to implement any models or taxonomies, stay focused on these principles throughout. It is far too easy to start out with such ideals in mind only to lose focus when the implementation processes begin.

CHAPTER ONE

HPT Models

An Overview of the Major Models in the Field

Frank S. Wilmoth
Christine Prigmore
Marty Bray

As the field of human performance technology (HPT) begins to gain more mainstream attention in the eyes of those charged with improving organizational efficiency, questions arise about how to put these concepts and theories into practice. Several recent articles (Chevalier, 2000; Langdon, 2000) have described how HPT can be used in an organization. This article aims to identify the major models in the field and examine the ideas and beliefs that have lead to their conception, development, and acceptance.

For the purposes of this article, HPT is defined as a systematic approach to improving productivity and competence, through a process of analysis, intervention selection and design, development, implementation, and evaluation designed to influence human behavior and accomplishment (International Society for Performance Improvement, 2000). The article will focus on HPT as a process that bridges the gap between what is and what should be in human performance systems (Applied Performance Improvement Technology, 2000).

HPT MODELING

Modeling has traditionally been an integral part of the instructional design process. Because many of the early practitioners of HPT came from the field of instructional technology, it is not surprising that HPT process modeling has migrated and evolved from those principles. Gustafson and Branch (1997) state that "the role of models in instructional design is to provide us with conceptual and communication tools that we can use to visualize, direct, and manage processes" (p. 18). The key concept here is the ability of the individual, when looking at any complex activity, to conceptualize a myriad of causal relationships and chart them in some manner that can be communicated to others. A given model's criterion must enable HPT analysts to accurately conceptualize a suspected performance problem in a given business environment. The ability to visualize and then communicate the process logic to others will be the true measurement of any HPT model's effectiveness and suitability for use.

Stolovitch and Keeps (1992) report that early HPT practitioners attempted to use linear instructional design models to describe performance technology processes. These linear models did not always accurately describe the environment or inter-relationships in sophisticated, multifaceted business processes. As a result, the early pioneers in the HPT field began to develop their own unique models. The diversity and complexity of the analyzed environments, coupled with different perspectives and backgrounds of the profession's pioneers, have created a large number of models, many of which are still emerging and evolving.

HPT PIONEERS

The works of Gilbert, Harless, Mager, and Rummler became the principles of the foundations for performance analysis and HPT modeling theory (Rosenberg, Coscarelli, & Hutchinson, 1992). Many have acknowledged Thomas Gilbert to be the "father of performance technology" (Dean, 1998). Gilbert felt that improving the performance of people must begin with identifying and resolving the environmental barriers, thus enabling the people (performers) to achieve maximum performance (Dean, 1997).

Another performance technology pioneer who continued with Gilbert's diagnostic approach was Joe Harless. Harless believed that understanding the cause of a problem should drive any solution (Ripley, 1997). This belief would eventually become the process of front-end analysis as reflected in his first performance technology process model (Figure 1.1). This model had a clear focus on the early determination of goals and performance during the analysis phase. Later, Harless revised his original model so that it included the four phases of analysis, design, development and testing, and implementation and evaluation, which became well known by its abbreviation, ADDIE (Figure 1.2). Harless proposed to the performance technology disciples that a partnership and business focus should exist in order to apply the most cost-effective intervention.

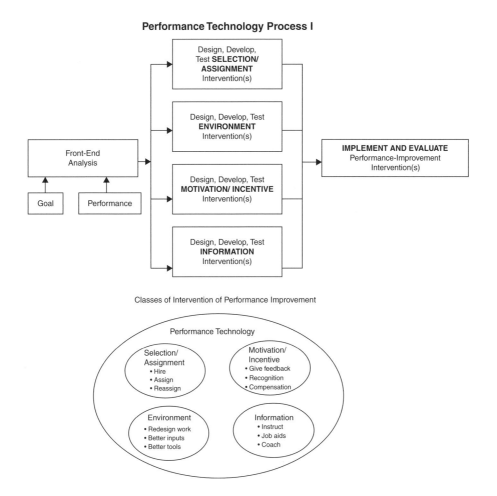

Figure 1.1 Early HPT Model.

Source: Ripley, 1997

West (1997a) reports that Robert Mager's book, *Preparing Instructional Objectives*, written in 1984 and later revised in 1997, revolutionized instructional design and performance improvement and is considered to be the standard for the instructional design profession. Mager introduced the notion that instructional designers should move beyond determining what instructors should teach; rather, they should focus on understanding what learners should be able to do as a result of the instruction. His work began to move the HPT field toward human performance objectives. His model breaks down performance objectives into three components: performance, conditions, and criterion (Table 1.1). Mager felt that the performance element is what the learner should be able to do; the conditions element comprises the situations

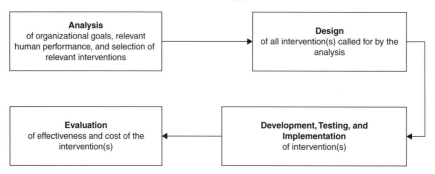

Figure 1.2 Later HPT Model.

Source: Ripley, 1997

under which performance will occur, and the criterion element is the standards or levels of acceptable performance. This model helped to shift analysis away from the instruction process itself and toward the results of instruction that lead to a change in learner performance. It also introduces the notion that human performance must have clear, measurable standards applied within definable conditions.

Table 1.1 Components of Performance Objectives

Performance	What the learner is to be able to do
Conditions	Important conditions under which performance occurs
Criterion	Quality or level of performance considered acceptable

In addition to his model for instructional objectives, Mager also developed a flow chart for analyzing performance problems (Mager & Pipe, 1984). In his model, Mager presents a series of steps that can help identify and correct performance problems. Mager cautions that the model should not be interpreted literally but should be used as a guideline for identifying and solving perform-ance problems (Figure 1.3).

Finally, there are the multiple contributions advanced by Geary Rummler. West (1997b) purports that Rummler likened organizations to ecosystems in which every component is interrelated and linked together. Rummler felt that analysis should account for the fact that organizational performance and individual performance are unique and require different solutions (Rosenberg, Coscarelli, & Hutchinson, 1992). He believed that organizational performance is as important as individual performance.

In Rummler's nine performance variables model (Figure 1.4), the organiza-tional analysis has three levels: the organizational level, the process level, and the job/performer level. Rummler maintained that the three levels are inter-related across different functions within the organization (West, 1997b). The three performance levels must be simultaneously considered and addressed before the organizational performance problems can be solved. Rummler details nine performance variables under the categories of goals, design, and management. At the job/performance level, a linear logic begins with input to the performer, who then performs thus creating output, which results in consequences. A feedback loop communicates consequences back to the performer. Rummler has identified six factors that affect human performance: performance specification, task support, consequences, feedback, skills/ knowledge, and individual capacity. Rummler's thorough consideration of these human performance factors establishes a solid foundation of logic for others to build on.

The work of these early pioneers in making a distinction between a training gap and a performance gap laid the groundwork for future practitioners to construct and test new models. In addition, their establishment of the link between individual performance and organizational performance helped to cement the acceptance and credibility of HPT solutions.

CLASSIFICATION OF MODELS

The diversity in content and structure of the various HPT models allows for a number of different classification schemes. One might be able to identify the general orientation or focus for a given set of models—for instance, those that focus on individual performance versus the performance of the organization. Another might be based on the process flow of the model, such as linear versus

Performance Analysis Flow Diagram

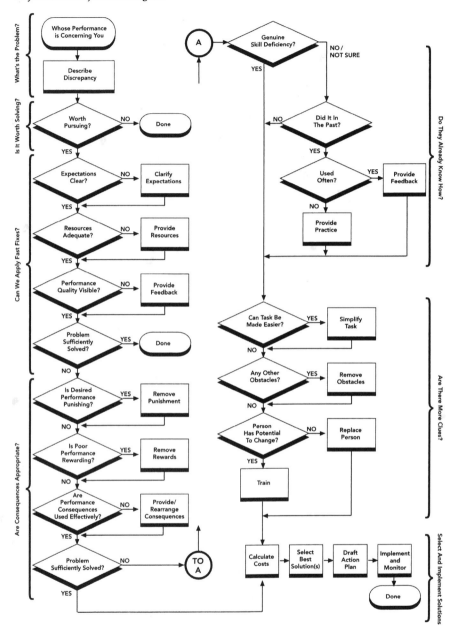

© 1997 The Center for Effective Performance

Figure 1.3 Mager's Performance Analysis Flow Chart.

Source: Mager and Pipe, 1997

Nine Performance Variables

Performance Levels	Performance Needs		
	GOALS	**DESIGN**	**MANAGEMENT**
Organizational Levels	Organizational Goals	Organizational Design	Organizational Management
Process Level	Process Goals	Process Design	Process Management
Job/Performer Level	Job Goals	Job Design	Job Management

Factors Affecting Human Performance

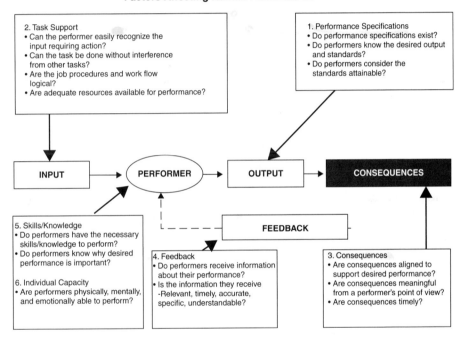

Figure 1.4 Rummler's Nine Performance Variables.

Source: West, 1997b

nonlinear. This analysis will follow the lead of Rosenberg, Coscarelli, and Hutchinson (1992) and begin with the categories of diagnostic and process models.

According to Rosenberg, Coscarelli, and Hutchinson (1992), the diagnostic model informs the performance analyst where HPT can be applied, and the process model instructs the performance analyst on how HPT can be applied. These groupings provide a clear categorization for most of the models studied; however, it became clear that another was necessary. A third category of holistic models is appropriate. The integrated approach taken by models in this last category seems to warrant a separate group. With these general categories as a starting point, we can see how the various HPT models align.

DIAGNOSTIC MODELS

Diagnostic models tell the performance analyst where HPT can be applied. Harless, with his attention focusing on early determination of goals and performance, seems to subscribe to this modeling direction. Rummler carried the diagnostic analysis to its fullest range, with separate organizational and individual performance domains that require separate solutions. Later diagnostic models followed in the footsteps of these pioneers.

The HPT model developed by William Deterline (Whiteside, 1998) focuses on the individual human element of performance, which Deterline calls the performer (Figure 1.5). The performer is potentially influenced by multiple factors, both personal and organizational. These factors are often unconnected forces that are rarely working together to improve individual performance. The challenge for the performance analyst in this environment is to effectively identify and communicate these unconnected influences to the decision-makers within the organization.

David Wile's (1996) synthesized HPT model (Figure 1.6) is a representative example of recent diagnostic models. It employs an innovative approach by

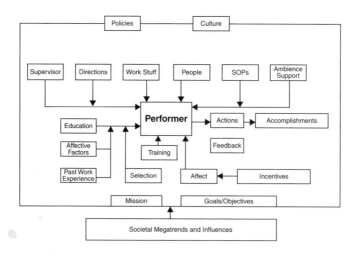

Figure 1.5 A Performer-Centered HPT Model.

Source: Whiteside, 1998

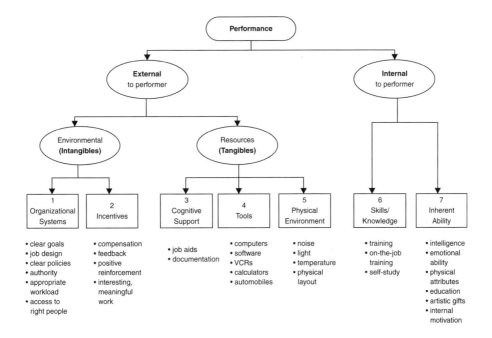

Figure 1.6 Wile's Synthesized HPT Model.

Source: Wile, 1996

presenting two separate domains and paths of analysis to use when examining human performance. Wile stays true to the diagnostic model's early supporters by focusing on elements both external and internal to the performer. He further subdivides the external domain into the categories of intangibles and tangibles, noting that each requires specific interventions. The model is unique in that it offers concrete solutions to varying performance problems and discriminates between interventions that are training solutions and those that are not. The simplicity of the diagnostic flow in this model makes it easy for the analyst to take the first steps in solving a performance problem.

The model presented in Table 1.2 moves beyond the individual performer models previously discussed. This model, advanced by Tosti and Jackson (1997), has many similarities to Rummler's HPT model. Like Rummler, Tosti and Jackson examine a performance problem at multiple levels, including organization, people, and work. Their organizational scan model (Chapter Five) plots these levels against the criteria domains of conditions, process, and outcomes to show the performance influences in each of the nine areas of the matrix (Tosti & Jackson, 1997). There are three characteristics that make this model an effective tool: it is systematic and comprehensive; it is manageable in terms of the number of areas analyzed; and it is easily communicated to the client.

Table 1.2 Tosti and Jackson's Multiple Levels

	Conditions	*Process*	*Outcomes*
Organization	Strategy, Structure: mission strategy, external business drivers, functional grouping, budget/ decision authority	Systems: degree of centralization, consistency of operations, flexibility	Organizational Results: satisfaction of investors, satisfaction of societal stakeholders, measures of success, goal alignment with/ mission
People	Climate Practices: company/individual values, management/ leadership, team norms, ethics, integrity	Performer Requirements: skills, knowledge, job aids/ references, selection, conference	Motivation: feedback, satisfaction of employees, frequency, timing, rewards and recognition, expectations
Work	Environment, Resources: physical environment, tools, materials, information, support personnel/services, accessibility of resources, workload, demands	Methods: allocation of functions, process, procedures, workflow, duplications/gaps	Products, Services: satisfaction of customers, productivity levels, standards/criteria, quality of product delivery

Danny Langdon designed the last diagnostic model we will examine. Langdon's Language of Work model (Figure 1.7) is designed to be accessible to novices who have an understanding of the knowledge and skills of their performers, yet are unable to express this knowledge systematically. The model describes performance as flowing from input, moving through processes and output to consequences. It employs a feedback loop that reminds the analyst that outside factors, called conditions here, affect the input and process. Whiteside (1998) claims that the simplicity of Langdon's model allows it to be used to examine performance at four levels: the business unit, the core process, the workgroup, and the individual. As in the previous models, the emphasis is on diagnosing the location of the performance problems.

For certain performance problems, the analyst may only require a model that helps to identify where the problems are located. In those cases, one of the

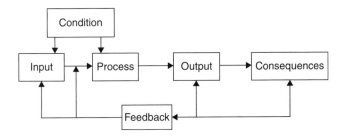

Figure 1.7 The Language of Work Model.

Source: Whiteside, 1998

models described above may be sufficient and could stand alone to address the problem. In other cases, the analyst might desire to know how to apply an HPT solution to solve a performance problem. This process approach might be used in conjunction with, or in place of, one of the models described above.

PROCESS MODELS

When we consider process models, we are considering those models that go beyond the diagnostic activities of determining where to look for performance problems and begin to show us how to examine the problem itself. Rosenberg, Coscarelli, and Hutchinson (1992) note that the origins of this type of systems analysis are in early models, such as Harless's ADDIE model. They further report that these early process models tended to be linear in nature and included the process of identifying specific solutions to the performance problems. The application of systems analysis and linear logic is a consistent trait of process models.

There are five general characteristics that help to identify process models. As stated above, most models in this group are linear or sequential. In addition, they often have phased or grouped activities, are driven by a gap analysis, are intervention oriented, and usually contain a feedback mechanism. All five characteristics will not be present in every process model, but all of the models will have some of these traits in common. The International Society for Performance Improvement (ISPI) model (ISPI, 2000) pictured in Figure 1.8 includes all these characteristics and is an appropriate example of a process model.

The next descriptive characteristic is the use of phased or grouped activities. Most process models detail a number of related activities that achieve a unified goal that represent one step in the process. For instance, there are often a number of activities that fall under the headings "Performance Analysis" and "Intervention Selection." This is the case in the ISPI and

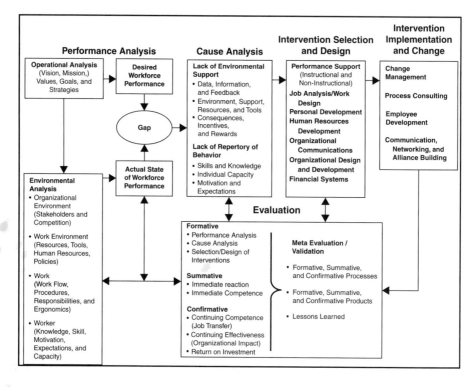

Figure 1.8 Traditional HPT Process.

Source: ISPI, 2000

the human performance model, which is displayed in Figure 1.9 (Atkinson & Chalmers, 1999). The steps in the process that the authors of these models choose to group together vary widely from model to model, but what many models have in common is the clear detailing of those groupings.

While most process models are linear in nature, authors of each model often follow different paths to achieve their end result. A number of models begin with organizational mission analysis, then do a gap analysis between the desired and actual human performance states; this is followed by cause analysis, intervention selection, implementation of interventions, and finally some form of feedback or evaluation.

Gap analysis, another important characteristic, is central to many process models. The performance gap is the difference between them in terms of performance (Robinson & Robinson, 1995). As seen in Figure 1.10, the ISPI and human performance model identify gap analysis as a step in their process (Human Performance Technologies, 2000). All these models represent the gap as the difference between the desired and actual states of performance. Rarely does a process model focus solely on human performance; instead, most seek to

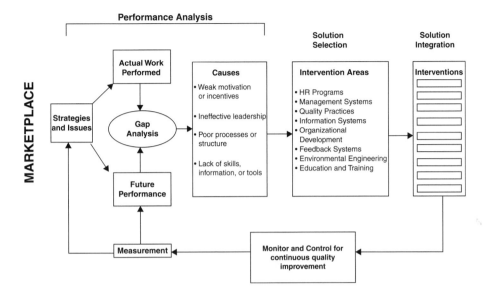

Figure 1.9 Human Performance Model.

Source: Atkinson and Chalmers, 1999

identify both organizational and individual performance gaps. Of the process models discussed so far, only the human performance model focuses solely on individual performance.

Many process models focus on performance interventions as a crucial step in the HPT process. Silber (1992) asserts that HPT interventions have a wide and varied range, beginning at the individual performer level and extending to the more complex organizational level. Rarely do performance problems require a singular intervention. Therefore, most process models describe different forms and arrangement of interventions that may be considered when deciding how best to close the performance gap. The ISPI and human performance models show a direct cause-and-effect relationship between a performance problem and the intervention.

The final characteristic that many process models have in common is the existence of a feedback loop, where the results of implementation are observed, evaluated, and reported. In most HPT models, the result of this evaluation can be the restarting of the process at one of the first steps in the model.

In summary, process models advance HPT activities beyond the discovery of where to look for performance problems and into the activities of how to analyze performance problems. The models studied have many similar characteristics; they were linear, had phased or grouped activities, sought out performance gaps, considered multiple intervention possibilities, and evaluated results with an appropriate feedback loop.

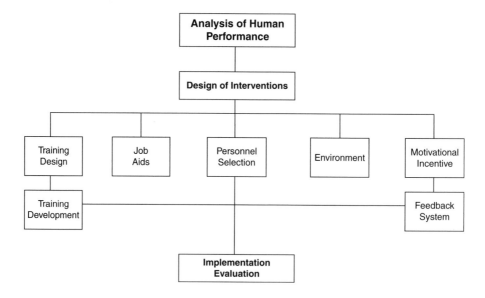

Figure 1.10 The Peak Performance System.

Source: Human Performance Technologies, 2000

Many analysts seeking solutions to their human performance problems will find that a diagnostic model, a process model, or some combination thereof will meet their needs. At other times, either the situation, or the preference of the analyst, demands a different approach.

HOLISTIC MODELS

Holistic models are categorized as such because of their nonlinear form and unique modeling characteristics. These models are often represented by overlapping domains that exist separately, but that form an ideal performance zone when combined.

As pictured in Figure 1.11, the HPT model uses three interlocking circles to represent people, processes, and organization (Advancia Consulting, 2000). These circles form the domains that symbolize the core activities of the model. Acting as outside influences on the core processes are the external activities of instructional technology, business process analysis, training systems, solution delivery, and modeling and simulations. These activities work together to develop integrated solutions for the domains of people, processes, and organization.

As seen in Figure 1.12, the three-dimensional HPT model (Stock, 1996) resembles Rummler's models in general diagnostic design. It shows three

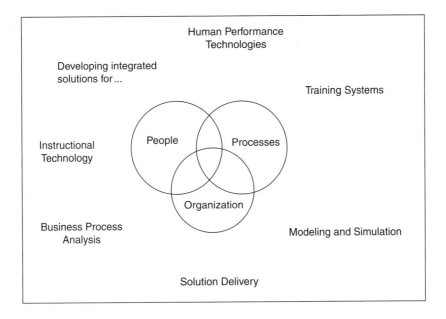

Figure 1.11 A Holistic Model.

Source: Advancia Consulting, 2000

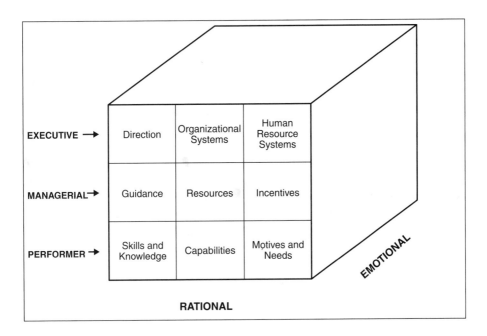

Figure 1.12 A Three-Dimensional HPT Model.

Source: Stock, 1996

dimensions of influence over performance, emotion, rationale, and executive, managerial, or performer. The latter two intersect to form nine performance factors within an organization. According to Stock, this model attempts to target the individuals who have the most influence over the organization. Stock's model is unique in its addition of a third dimension that considers the emotional intelligence of the individual when assessing the factors influencing human performance. Stock contends that human emotions have a much greater role in human performance than previously considered in the HPT field. He argues for a new approach and the increased use of emotional intelligence analysis in future HPT modeling. Stock admits that he has had varied success when trying to add intelligence analysis to actual performance problems, but encourages further study and experimentation. In that regard, Stock's HPT model is making a significant contribution to the human performance technology field.

These holistic models are generally explained with less detail than the diagnostic and process models discussed earlier. Thus, HPT practitioners with greater experience feel more comfortable using them than beginners. However, that should not discourage novices from evaluating them when deciding which model best fits their needs.

A SINGLE MODEL?

There is no single HPT model that can be universally applied to all business environments and problems. This struggle to identify and define the root causes of performance problems, while attempting to place some logical framework around the reasons for these performance gaps, has defined and advanced the field of HPT.

The traditional path in the early years of the HPT movement was to follow the ADDIE model in the instructional design process. This model's linear focus addressed performance problems that required a training solution but ignored non-training causes of poor performance. The application of training-focused solutions for non-training problems caused clients to lose both money and confidence in those who were hired to solve their performance problems. This dissatisfaction, coupled with Skinner's work in behavioral sciences and operant conditioning, opened the door for the early HPT pioneers. Former instructional design practitioners, including Harless, Mager, and Rummler, began to apply varied sciences and disciplines to the newly emerging field of HPT. Early work in the field sought to explain performance problems by placing heavy emphasis on the importance of the individual and his or her work environment and by focusing on the analysis portion of the HPT process. Today we see the continued expansion and evolution of the HPT modeling process. The models presented here, while different in their reasoning and approaches, all appear to be having some measure of success.

In addition to summarizing and categorizing the major HPT models in the field, this examination has identified three keys to success for analysts undertaking the HPT process: front-end analysis, measurement, and experience.

Harless first promoted the important concept of *front-end analysis*. His belief that the understanding of the cause of a problem should drive the solution has remained prominent in our field. Included within the front-end analysis process is an analysis of the gap between the desired and actual states of performance. Harless contributed another idea that remains crucial to HPT success, the notion of a partnership between the client and the performance analyst. Ideally, this partnership begins during the front-end analysis phase and continues throughout the life of the project. Surprisingly, this important ingredient is missing from many of the models discussed here.

Mager championed the next important concept, that of *measurability*. He introduced the idea that performance objectives must be applied under definable conditions and criteria. Analysts must have the ability to measure performance gaps and, eventually, performance gains to judge the effectiveness of given interventions. In addition, the existence of measurable performance objectives strengthens the communication between the performance analyst and the business client. Business clients want tangible methods to both quantify and justify their investments. Most of the models examined here followed Mager's lead when creating their structure, and therefore support performance objective-based measurement options.

Finally, HPT models demand *experience* and a wide range of talents from the performance analyst. The range and depth of knowledge required to use any of the models is extensive. There are few individuals who have the background to do a complete and thorough analysis entirely on their own. Because of this, teams of experts usually undertake the HPT process. Most of this expertise is needed only for limited periods and limited purposes. Selection of an HPT model should include a determination of the qualifications needed to perform the complete analysis.

CONCLUSION

In conclusion, the HPT models examined here appear to be both functional and logical efforts to analyze and communicate performance problems to clients. Selecting the best HPT model can be a daunting task. The challenge for all concerned parties is to select the best model that can be applied or adapted to address and resolve the client's problem. If there is no single HPT model capable of this task, then the performance technology analyst must have a range of HPT models from which to choose to find the best fit for the problem at hand.

References

Advancia Consulting. (2000). *Human performance technologies* [Online] Available: http://www.advancia.com/solut3.htm.

Applied Performance Improvement Technology. (2000). *A PIT stop definition* [Online]. Available: http://www.apitstop.com/general/whatis.htm.

Atkinson, V., & Chalmers, N. (1999). Performance consulting: Get your credit from your clients. *Performance Improvement, 38*(4), 14–19.

Chevalier, R. (2000). HPT: The power to change. *Performance Improvement, 39*(1), 23–25.

Dean, P. J. (1997). Thomas F. Gilbert, Ph.D.: Engineering performance improvement with or without training. In P. J. Dean & D.E. Ripley (Eds.), *Performance improvement pathfinders: Models for organizational learning systems* (Vol. 1) Silver Spring, MD: International Society for Performance Improvement.

Dean, P. J. (1998). Allow me to introduce Thomas Gilbert. *Performance Improvement, 37*(6), 13–44.

Gustafson, K. L., & Branch, R. M. (Eds.). (1997). *Survey of instructional models* (3rd ed.) Syracuse, NY: Clearinghouse on Information and Technology.

Human Performance Technologies. (2000). *The peak performance system: An accomplishment-based approach to human performance* [Online]. Available: http://www.hptonline.com/HPT_Chart.html.

International Society for Performance Improvement. (2000). What is HPT? [Online]. Available: http://www.ispi.org.

Langdon, D. (2000). Taking the h out of HPT. *Performance Improvement, 39*(1), 5–8.

Mager, R. F. (1997). *Preparing instructional objectives: A critical tool in the development of effective instruction.* Atlanta, GA: Center for Effective Performance.

Mager, R. F., & Pipe, P. (1984). *Analyzing performance problems: Or you really oughta wanna* (2nd ed.). Belmont, CA: Lake Publishing Company

Ripley, D. E. (1997). Joe Harless, Ed.D.: An ounce of analysis. In P. J. Dean & D. E. Ripley (Eds.), *Performance improvement pathfinders: Models for organizational learning systems* (Vol. 1) Silver Spring, MD: International Society for Performance Improvement.

Robinson, D. G., & Robinson, J. C. (1995). *Performance consulting.* San Francisco: Berrett-Koehler.

Rosenberg, M. J., Coscarelli, W. C., & Hutchinson, C. S. (1992). The origins of the field. In H. Stolovitch & E. Keeps (Eds.), *Handbook of human performance technology: A comprehensive guide for analyzing and solving performance problems in organizations* (pp. 14–31). San Francisco: Pfeiffer.

Silber, K. H. (1992). Intervening at different levels in organizations. H. Stolovitch & E. Keeps (Eds.), *Handbook of human performance technology: A comprehensive guide for analyzing and solving performance problems in organizations* (pp. 50–65) San Francisco: Pfeiffer.

Stock, B. (1996). Getting to the heart of performance. *Performance Improvement*, *35*(8), 6–8.

Stolovitch, H., & Keeps, E. (Eds.). (1992). What is performance technology? *Handbook of human performance technology: A comprehensive guide for analyzing and solving performance problems in organizations* (pp. 3–13). San Francisco: Pfeiffer.

Tosti, D., & Jackson, S. D. (1997). The organizational scan. *Performance Improvement*, *36*(10), 22–26.

West, J., (1997a). Robert Mager, Ph.D.: Learner-centered instruction. In P. J. Dean & D. E. Ripley (Eds.), *Performance improvement pathfinders: Models for organizational learning systems* (Vol. 1) Silver Spring, MD: International Society for Performance Improvement, 84–91.

West, J. (1997b). Geary Rummler, Ph.D.: Managing performance in the white spaces. In P. J. Dean & D. E. Ripley (Eds.), *Performance improvement pathfinders: Models for organizational learning systems* (Vol. 1) Silver Spring, MD: International Society for Performance Improvement.

Whiteside, K. S. (1998). Models, mayhem, and mystery. *Performance Improvement*, *37*(2), 47–53.

Wile, D. (1996). Why doers do. *Performance Improvement*, *35*(2), 30–35.

EDITORIAL CONNECTIONS

As Chapter One illustrates, abundant models, frameworks, and taxonomies can be used to improve performance. However, the chapter does not present an exhaustive list of those available for improving individual and organizational performance. One especially valuable model that was not included is Roger Kaufman's Organizational Elements Model (OEM), shown in Figure 1.13. Kaufman, a pioneer in the discipline of performance improvement, stands with Bob Mager, Joe Harless, and Tom Gilbert among the progenitors of HPT.

From a pragmatic perspective, the OEM is a useful diagnostic model that can both be applied in a needs assessment (see Chapter Thirty-Two) as well as used as an informative classification model when you align accomplishments with performance interventions. We believe the OEM to be an indispensible model for this handbook and for the improvement of performance.

The model expands on traditional perspectives of performance results, adding a system perspective that aligns results beyond the boundaries of the organization. While many models consider all results to be equivalent, the OEM identifies three distinct types of interrelated accomplishments. The first are *outcomes*, with the primary beneficiary being society as a whole. The second are *outputs*, with the primary beneficiary being the organization itself. Last are *products*, with the primary beneficiary being the individuals and teams within an organization.

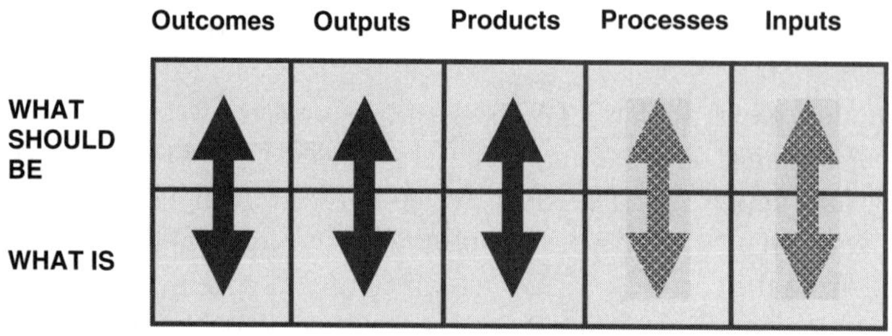

Figure 1.13 Roger Kaufman's Organizational Elements Model.

The improvement of results requires that the three types of results be closely associated and linked together. However, no one type of results is more important than another; to improve performance you must have them all.

In the same way, the three types of results must be linked to the *processes* used to achieve results and the *inputs* (or resources) used within those processes. The OEM provides you with an approach for ensuring that all five link together within your improvement system: inputs, processes, products, outputs, and outcomes. Together, these five elements provide a system perspective that aligns what is used, what is done, what results are produced, and what outputs are delivered to clients with the long-term benefits of those outcomes for our shared society.

To complete the model and apply it in improving performance, the OEM examines each of the five elements according to What Is (the current situation) and What Should Be (the ideal or desired situation). The gaps—or discrepancies—between What Is and What Should Be are needs that can drive your decisions about which interventions will best accomplish desired results. Figure 1.13 illustrates the complete OEM model, providing a valuable tool for assessing needs, analyzing performance problems, aligning performance interventions, and subsequently evaluating your results.

The OEM helps address, align, and improve performance at all levels of an organization. Performance issues do, after all, have distinct—yet closely linked—characteristics at all levels of organizational performance. From individual performance issues (such as productivity, timeliness, accuracy, or readiness), to team performance issues (such as outputs, efficiency, or relationships), to organizational performance issues (such as deliverables, return on investment, client satisfaction, or supply-chain breakdowns), and all the way to societal performance issues (such as quality of life, safety and well-being, or sustainability), the holistic perspective facilitated by Kaufman's model gives your improvement effort the broad reach to accomplish significant and long-lasting results.

Given all of the choices in models presented in Chapter One, the last thing you want to do is simply choose "the one" to be indiscriminately applied in any and all situations. While one process model may be appropriate for improving performance in customer service, another set of procedures may be better when working to improve manufacturing performance. Indeed, don't limit yourself just to models created within the discipline of performance improvement (or human performance technology). Rather, use these as guides for understanding, adapting, and applying the theory, models, and tools of various disciplines. Perhaps you can achieve desired results within your organization by using a taxonomy from the organization development (OD) literature, combined with a process model from human resource management (HRM) literature.

In this handbook we have selected John Wedman's Performance Pyramid Model and Roger Kaufman's Organizational Elements Model as frameworks for organizing and guiding our decisions related to interventions for improving human and organizational performance. While neither of these was included in Chapter One, each can be used independently or integrated with other performance models to guide your improvement efforts. As appropriate, use any or all of these models, taxonomies, or frameworks in your decision-making. You can always return to the Performance Pyramid (with its comprehensive examination of the components that support the accomplishment of significant results) and the Organizational Elements Model (with its expansive description of systemic performance that includes both internal and external factors) as foundational guides.

Any of these models can be a valuable resource when selecting and implementing useful performance interventions. Choosing the "right" model is, of course, more complicated than "pin the tail on the donkey." While logic and common sense do play roles in selecting models for guiding improvement efforts, knowledge of the theories and philosophical perspectives that underlie each model so that the model you select is a productive match for you (and your organization). The models you apply should both match the values and culture of your organization (Chapter Thirty) and also complement the other activities within the organization, thereby strengthening the theoretical perspectives that provide the foundation for decisions.

Performance improvement relies on what has been learned and applied across many related fields. From psychological research that demonstrates the essential characteristics of human behavior to the theories of cognitive science that reveal how the human brain learns and remembers, the foundations of improving performance are embedded in countless disciplines. The models and frameworks of these diverse disciplines can be used as practical guides for improving performance.

WHAT'S COMING UP

In Chapter Two, Yonnie Chyung and Shelley Berg survey the relationship between theory and practice within the context of improving human and organizational performance. The chapter weaves together the essential relationships that guide (either conscientiously or unintentionally) the many decisions required to improve individual and organizational performance. Going beyond a survey of theories that underlie the improvement models described in Chapter One, the authors examine how the practice of performance improvement (or human performance technology) is an applied science that integrates many theoretical perspectives.

From psychology and engineering to communications and information sciences, the domains of knowledge that flow into the improvement of individual and organizational performance stretch from the social sciences to the physical sciences. Because of this, performance improvement is a quintessential interdisciplinary profession. The benefits of being an interdisciplinary profession are both numerous—and challenging.

CHAPTER TWO

Linking Practice
and Theory

Seung Youn Chyung
Shelley A. Berg

INTRODUCTION

The study of human performance technology (HPT) is an applied science. Its goal is to improve human performance in organizations, using systemic (holistic, all-encompassing) and systematic (step-by-step, methodical) problem-solving approaches. Practitioners often accumulate knowledge and skills based on their own experiences; however, one's professional knowledge should also be grounded in the eclectic foundations of the field, including theories and research findings. Doing so can improve one's intuition in sensing performance problems, enable inductive and deductive reasoning, and guide the generation of cost-effective solutions. This chapter was written with the goal of connecting HPT practices to their theoretical foundations. To help practitioners learn and apply appropriate theory to their practice, we introduce a hypothetical scenario about an HPT practitioner, Susan. As her story unfolds, possibilities for decision-making based on theories and research findings are illustrated.

Case Study
Susan is an HPT consultant for a national retail chain. The retail chain has grown rapidly over the past three years, and continued growth is anticipated. This has resulted in an increase in management staff at the regional level; however, those who were recently promoted to regional management positions have taken significantly longer to get "ramped up" in their positions than new regional managers have in past years. Susan has been charged with figuring out how to bring these newly promoted managers up to speed more quickly.

SYSTEM THINKING

A characteristic that differentiates professionally trained HPT practitioners from others is having a solid theoretical base for their practice, which enables them to produce more valid and reliable long-term results. For instance, Richard Swanson (1999), with a three-legged stool illustration, has proposed three main theoretical foundations for HPT practitioners: (1) economics, (2) psychology, and (3) system theory. Although each theory has uniquely and equally contributed to the development of performance improvement practice, *system theory* is particularly important during the initial performance analysis phase.

General System Theory

The use of system-related theories and models during the performance analysis phase helps to establish alignment among various intertwined factors involved in performance improvement practice. Fundamental principles of system theory stem from general system theory (GST), which von Bertalanffy, an Austrian-born biologist, proposed more than half a century ago. Based on GST, a system is often characterized as a holistic, open, and ever-changing organism. Holism is the opposite of elementarism: it adopts Gestalt psychology's view that the whole is more than the sum of its parts, whereas in elementarism, the total is the sum of its parts. GST rejected the traditional closed-system view of organizations and facilitated open-system thinking for understanding organizational operations and alignment.

GST is vital to the study of social systems, focusing on the hierarchical elements of an organization such as organizational structure, teams, and individual performers. GST also provides HPT practitioners with the fundamental principle that inputs, processes, outputs, and feedback operate in a continuous loop. It prompts practitioners to ask questions about three fundamental items: (1) the purpose of the system, (2) the elements of the system, and (3) the relationships among the elements. This mental model helps HPT practitioners avoid treating various elements or subsystems within an organization as silos (which can potentially lead to suboptimization) and encourages them to accept that organizations function as *adaptive* systems that run through a continuous performance improvement loop. It also facilitates the management of the relationships or *interfaces* among subsystems, which performance consultants Geary Rummler and Alan Brache refer to as the management of the *white space* of an organization in their book, *Improving Performance: How to Manage the White Space on the Organization Chart*. Therefore, system thinking means thinking of issues with the concepts and characteristics of a system in mind.

System Thinking and Strategic Alignment

New performance models for analyzing organizational systems and practices were developed out of the fundamental principles of GST. Those performance models provide frameworks for understanding performance as a *system*. For example, Dale Brethower, Professor Emeritus at Western Michigan University, proposed a Total Performance System that combines systems analysis with feedback systems. In this system, performance process can be understood according to six basic components: (1) inputs, (2) a processing system, (3) outputs, (4) processing system feedback, (5) receiving system feedback, and (6) a receiving system. Within an *adaptive* system, if the goal changes, so too does performance; if performance does not meet the goal, then the performance is modified. Performance models such as this can help practitioners think of performance as a systemic issue with performance problems solved through system thinking. They guide both the development of organizational strategies and tactics as well as the management of an organization's complexity.

Because system thinking facilitates expanded and integrated understandings of the patterns and organization of any entity, as Ithaca College communications professor Gordon Rowland points out, it serves as a guiding force in organizational development, human resources, management sciences, and related fields. Ryan Watkins, a George Washington University professor, advocates that practitioners should analyze performance problems through a systemic lens to evaluate the extent to which the performance issue in question is aligned with the strategic directions of the organization. Assessing strategic alignment provides an opportunity to analyze other important issues, such as whether the performance problem is worth solving, what relationship the performance issue has with other parts and functions of the organization, and what resources are available to solve the problem.

Case Study

Before moving forward, Susan worked to understand how closing the performance gap with the regional managers fits into the bigger picture of the organization, that is, if and how it connects to the organization's vision, mission, values, and business objectives. For example, one responsibility of the regional managers is to research specific aspects of their local markets. Some of the newer regional managers have fallen behind schedule on their research activities, and that has led to ill-informed decisions, which in turn have negatively impacted revenue in those regions. Therefore, it was clear to Susan that improving the new regional managers' performance would directly impact the revenue in those regions. She knows that building a strong business case for her project is critical not only to demonstrating the importance of the project, but also to securing the resources and stakeholder buy-in necessary to make it successful.

GAP AND CAUSE ANALYSES

An important aspect of performance analysis is identifying the performance gap that needs to be addressed. In other words, it is important to understand how the current state of a performance issue compares to what the desired performance should "look like." The difference between current and desired performance is known as the *performance gap*. It is often prudent to conduct an analysis of the costs and benefits for closing such gaps in order to make a convincing business case for moving forward with the project. In working through this process, one can draw from the works of various theorists and practitioners such as Thomas Gilbert's work in engineering worthy perform-ance, Joe Harless's front-end analysis, Roger Kaufman's organizational ele-ments model, Robert Mager's goal analysis, Allison Rossett's training needs assessment and performance analysis, as well as Belle Witkin and James Altschuld's needs assessment guide. The work of Thomas Gilbert, especially his "leisurely theorems" for engineering worthy performance, is particularly helpful for gaining foundational concepts and methods for conducting gap and cause analyses. Gilbert's work is unique in that he developed *theories* for engineering behaviors and improving performance, whereas others provided *models and strategies* that intend to guide practitioners' actions.

Producing Worthy Performance

Influenced by the father of scientific management, Frederick Taylor, German-born psychologist Kurt Lewin, and American psychologist B.F. Skinner, Gil-bert's work is considered to be foundational to the HPT field (Dean, 1997). His theory begins with defining performance as consisting of both behavior and accomplishment. Gilbert suggests that behavior is a *means*, while accomplish-ment is the *end*. When determining how to improve employee performance, it is necessary to identify two components: (1) the valuable accomplishment that the employees need to produce and (2) how to help them change their behaviors to make it happen. In his book, *Human Competence*, Gilbert explains his first leisurely theorem with the following formula, which helps practitioners concep-tualize the relationship of costs to benefits in the process of improving a specific performance outcome:

$$\text{Worth of performance} = \text{Value of accomplishment} \div \text{Costs for changing behavior}$$

The ultimate goal of worthy performance is ensuring that the value of the projected accomplishment outweighs the costs associated with changing the corresponding behavior. When the costs of changing the behavior outweigh the expected value of the accomplishment, the performance improvement effort is likely to be unworthy of the investment.

Case Study

While reviewing company records, Susan noticed that many projects managed by the new regional managers did not meet their project completion deadlines and that the overall employee satisfaction toward their leadership had declined as well. Using Gilbert's first leisurely theorem, Susan clearly differentiated the regional managers' behaviors from their accomplishments before attempting to help improve their performance. The use of certain managerial techniques defined the behavior desired from them, while meeting the project deadlines and improving employee satisfaction levels defined the accomplishments desired from them. In one region, Susan determined that the cost of missed deadlines was nearly $25,000 for the year. After further analysis, she estimated that the right combination of properly targeted interventions could substantially reduce or even eliminate this cost. In fact, Susan anticipated that the benefit would likely be even greater, given the potential impact on other regions as well.

Gap Analysis: Identifying the Potential for Improving Performance

Gilbert's second leisurely theorem is used to determine the magnitude of a performance gap. Gilbert refers to this gap as "the potential for improving performance (the PIP)." Although he conceptualized the gap as a ratio between the exemplary level of performance and the level of typical performance, a performance gap can also be measured by the ratio of typical performance level and exemplary performance level.

In Susan's situation, two gaps were identified and addressed: (1) the gap between the *desired* project completion rate and the *current* project completion rate and (2) the gap between the *desired* employee satisfaction with the regional managers' leadership and the *typical* employee satisfaction level. The first performance gap can be defined by a simple calculation as follows: (a) desired state: 100 percent project completion rate, (b) current state (hypothetical): 75 percent project completion rate, and (c) gap: 25 percent (or more specifically, the ratio is 1.33 since $4 \div 3 = 1.33$). The second gap can be identified by using Gilbert's PIP. Table 2.1 presents a hypothetical dataset of employee satisfaction scores. The historically best (exemplary) performance level is 8.1 (when 10 is the highest and 1 is the lowest), while the average (typical) performance level is 5.6. Susan now sees an *opportunity* to help improve the average regional managers' performance from 5.6 up to 8.1 or better; therefore, the PIP is ratio is 1.5 since $8.1 \div 5.6 = 1.5$ (for other examples of measuring the PIP, see Gilbert, (1988)). All things being equal, individuals or groups with lower PIPs are more competitive than those with higher PIPs.

Table 2.1 An Example of Exemplary Performance Versus Typical Performance

Region	A	B	C	D	Average
Employee Satisfaction Scores on Regional Managers' Leadership	6.8	7.6	8.1	6.5	
	6.8	7.4	7.4	5.6	
	6.5	7.1	7.4	5.6	
	6.1	6.5	7.2	5.3	
	5.8	6.3	6.3	4.7	—
	5.5	6.3	5.9	4.6	
	5.2	5.4	5.4	4.4	
	5.2	5.1	4.7	4.2	
	4.0	4.7	3.2	3.8	
	2.9	4.2	3.2	3.5	
Average	5.5	6.1	6.0	4.8	*5.6*

Cause Analysis: Profiling Behavior with the Behavior Engineering Model

Gilbert's third leisurely theorem is known as the behavior engineering model (BEM). The BEM is a methodical framework for identifying the probable causes of a performance gap and determining cost-effective solutions for reducing the gap. It contains six factors that influence performance, three of which are grouped into a category of environmental supports (data, instruments, incentives), with the other three being categorized as a person's repertoire of behavior (knowledge, capacity, motives) (see Table 2.2). Consistent with general systems theory, Gilbert posits that all six factors are interdependent and that changing one factor would likely have an impact on changing other factors. Additionally, a performance improvement initiative related to one factor is unlikely to be sufficient to produce the desired result unless the conditions of the other factors are also positioned to support that initiative.

In determining potential causes of the new regional managers' performance gap, Susan should, for example, examine conditions related to each of the six factors in the BEM. In doing so, she would likely generate a list of questions to measure the current conditions of the six factors. In his article, "A Question of Performance," Gilbert describes this process as *profiling behavior* (PROBE, in short). Table 2.3 provides examples of the types of PROBE questions Susan might use for each factor.

Table 2.2 The Behavior Engineering Model

	S^d Information	R Instrumentation	S_r Motivation
Environmental supports	Data: Relevant and frequent feedback about the adequacy of performance; Descriptions of what is expected of performance; Clear and relevant guides to adequate performance.	Instruments: Tools and materials of work designed scientifically to match human factors	Incentives: Adequate financial incentives made contingent upon performance; Non-monetary incentives made available; Career-development opportunities
Person's repertory of behavior	Knowledge: Scientifically designed training that matches the requirements of exemplary performance; Placement	Capacity: Flexible scheduling of performance to match peak capacity: Prosthesis; Physical shaping; Adaptation; Selection	Motives: Assessment of people's motives to work; Recruitment of people to match the realities of the situation

From *Human Competence: Engineering Worthy Performance* (p. 88) by T. F. Gilbert. Copyright © 2007 by the International Society for Performance Improvement. Reprinted with permission of John Wiley & Sons, Inc.

Table 2.3 An Example of PROBE Questions Within the BEM Framework

Environmental Supports	Data (directional and confirmational)	• Are the employee satisfaction survey results communicated to the new regional managers? • Are good models of leadership and managerial behavior available to the new regional managers? • Are performance standards for the position clearly stated? • Are those performance standards accepted as reasonable? • Are the new regional managers receiving timely and specific feedback on their progress?

(Continued)

Table 2.3 (*Continued*)

	Instruments (tools, procedures, and resources)	• Do the new regional managers have access to all the materials, resources, and computer systems needed to do their jobs and to effectively communicate with employees? • Do all of these resources function properly? • Are their work environments comfortable and free from distractions? • Are the processes and procedures for their positions clearly defined?
	Incentives (consequences for good and poor performances)	• Are meaningful incentives available for good performance? • Are there consequences for poor performance? • Are those consequences carried out? • Is there an absence of hidden punishment for performing well? • Is there an absence of hidden incentives for performing poorly?
Personal Repertoire	Knowledge (concepts, skills, training)	• Do the new regional managers have the knowledge and skills needed to manage a project? • Do they know specific managerial techniques they can use to lead their project teams? • Is training designed in a way that prepares them to perform as expected on the job?
	Capacity (physical, mental, or emotional)	• Do the newly promoted regional managers have enough experience to learn the new skills required for the job? • Do the new managers have the necessary aptitude or personality to be effective leaders? • Are the new managers free from emotional limitations that would interfere with performance?

	Motives (intrinsic, commitment)	• Are the new regional managers willing to work under the conditions provided by the organization? • Do the new regional managers desire to be effective leaders? • What do the employee satisfaction scores mean to them? • What motivates them to perform better?

LINKING CAUSES TO INTERVENTIONS

As discussed further in Chapter Three, the Performance Pyramid can be used as a tool for identifying possible performance interventions once the causes of a performance gap have been determined. In that chapter, University of Missouri professor John Wedman points out that Gilbert's work provided the foundation for his Performance Pyramid; therefore, if HPT practitioners opt to use Gilbert's BEM as a cause analysis tool, they might find the Performance Pyramid helpful as an intervention selection tool. The following sections will explore various performance improvement solutions and the theoretical frameworks that support those practices.

Case Study

After identifying probable causes of the performance gaps, Susan began considering a variety of potential interventions that could be used to address the causal factors and to close the gaps. As is often the case with HPT projects, Susan identified a combination of interventions from across the Performance Pyramid.

Clear Expectations and Timely Feedback, with Appropriate Tools and Processes

The practice of HPT is considered relatively new. According to Jim Pershing, editor of the third edition of the *Handbook of Human Performance Technology*, it was started by a number of academics and professionals in the United States in the 1950s and 1960s. However, as society had been dealing with human performance issues in organizations for some time, several performance engineering principles were formed during the era of the industrial revolution. Frederick Taylor, for example, was a pioneer of the systematic use of goal-setting and feedback, process improvement, and task-appropriate tools to improve workplace performance in the late 19th century.

Frederick Taylor's Scientific Management. In his work at Midvale Steel in Philadelphia, Taylor observed that it was primarily the workers who determined how to do their work and how much to do, with little management influence in this area. Consequently, the workers tended to accomplish as little as possible in a day's work, thinking that working more productively would result in fewer jobs. In his effort to change this inefficient system, Taylor sought to redesign the work based on scientific principles of management, which came to be known as *scientific management*.

One of Taylor's first tasks was to determine the most efficient process for getting the workers' jobs done. To do this, he conducted a series of "time and motion" studies with workers in order to determine how to redesign the process in a way that would eliminate wasted movements while reducing workers' fatigue. The time and motion studies also provided Taylor with data upon which he could identify expectations for the workers. To complement this, Taylor designed a feedback mechanism in which each worker received a summary of his performance for the previous day. This prompted workers to increase their productivity to meet the stated expectations. With these and other performance improvement interventions in place, the reported return on investment was substantial. After nearly a century since Taylor's work, his scientific management methods are still commonly applied in a variety of contexts, such as manufacturing and office settings. These methods are evident in initiatives related to redesigning work processes to eliminate bottlenecks and increase efficiency, conducting job and task analyses to systematically set goals and train performers, and conducting performance appraisals and providing incentives to motivate performers.

The Role of Goal Setting. As shown in Taylor's work, providing clear expectations to workers helps them recognize the desired performance goals to accomplish. Incentives, monetary or non-monetary, are often used to reinforce workers' intention or commitment to fulfilling the goals. This commitment is the *sine qua non* of goal setting, as it generates a clear direction of behavior, a sufficient level of efforts, and persistence. This cognitive and perceptual model of human behavior and functioning is further supported by goal-setting theory.

An important tenet of the goal-setting theory advanced by Edwin Locke of the University of Maryland and Gary Latham of the University of Toronto is that specific and explicit goals (akin to having clear expectations) tend to produce higher levels of performance. Inviting workers into the goal-setting process also helps to make the goal more meaningful to them. Whether a goal is self-set, collaboratively set, or assigned, incentives can help increase commitment to a goal if they are directly tied to the goal, are seen as contingent on performance, and are viewed as equitable.

Another aspect of the theory addresses the difficulty of a goal. Research based on goal-setting theory has revealed that a challenging goal prompts workers to produce higher levels of performance (Pinder, 1998). However, when people do not believe that they can achieve the given level of performance specified in a goal, both their commitment to the goal and performance in pursuit of it are low, according to Locke and Latham.

The Role of Feedback. HPT practitioners should recognize not only the importance of setting clear expectations to guide performance, but also the impact that quality feedback can have on one's performance. The role of feedback in guiding performance is emphasized in behavioral psychology. One of the early behavioral psychologists, E. L. Thorndike, states in his law of effect that behaviors that are followed by an effect that is satisfying are likely to be repeated, while behaviors that are followed by an unpleasant effect are not. Similarly, B. F. Skinner, in his theory of operant conditioning, used the word "operant" to emphasize "the fact that the behavior *operates* upon the environment to generate consequences" (1953, p. 65). He proposed a basic framework for shaping behavior: that the reinforcing stimulus is synonymous with feedback (in Driscoll, 2005). Written formulaically, it is:

$$S^d(\text{discriminative stimulus}) \rightarrow R(\text{operant response})$$
$$\rightarrow S_r(\text{contingent or reinforcing stimulus})$$

This formula for changing behavior is applied within Gilbert's behavior engineering model as well. That is, provide performers with adequate data for performing job tasks (S^d) $\rightarrow$ supply adequate instruments to help them produce performance (R) $\rightarrow$ provide them with incentives contingent upon performance (S_r). Research has also shown that a combination of goal-setting and timely feedback can lead to the improved effectiveness and efficiency of performance in the workplace (Stansfield & Longenecker, 2006).

Case Study

Susan realized that the theoretical concepts of providing feedback and setting goals or expectations are intertwined in practice. She noticed in the employee satisfaction survey results that several regional managers' direct reports felt that some of the expectations were not clearly communicated to them and that they were not receiving timely feedback on the projects assigned to them. In reviewing Wedman's Performance Pyramid, Susan was able to identify several interrelated performance interventions that together could improve results in her organization. They included coaching, providing timely performance feedback, as well as new communication strategies. Susan decided to coach the regional managers to include brief updates that highlight the goals and status of the current projects during weekly meetings with direct reports. When the direct reports at the weekly meetings showed interest in these updates by asking questions or commenting on how to affect their teams' performance, this served as feedback to the regional managers and reinforced this changed managerial approach as a desirable behavior to repeat in the future.

Fair Recognition and Incentives to Improve Self-Concept and Motivation

Behavioral psychology has provided HPT practitioners an insight as to how hidden incentives and consequences influence human motivation and behavior. Robert Mager and Peter Pipe said it well in their famous book, *Analyzing Performance Problems*, "one of the most common reasons why people don't do what we'd like them to do is that the desired 'doing' is seen as punishing by the performers" (p. 44). Similarly, workers might choose not to engage in a desired behavior because an alternative behavior is more rewarding for them. However, human motivation is a complex phenomenon that requires an in-depth study. In developing employee recognition programs and incentives, HPT practitioners should go to lengths ensuring that workers perceive such programs and the rewards associated with them as meaningful, fair, and relevant to them. The importance of these practices is supported by a variety of motivational theories.

Taxonomies of Motivational Factors. A number of human needs and satisfaction theories help practitioners understand various factors that influence motivation, and those factors are often explained either in hierarchical order or in a cluster. The hierarchy of needs proposed by Abraham Maslow posits that human needs must be met in a certain order; thus, higher-level needs such as social needs would unlikely become the main driving force of behavior until lower-level needs such as safety and physiological needs are met. On the other hand, David McClelland's theory of needs suggests that people are motivated by three dominant needs, which are not in any hierarchical order: the need for achievement, the need for affiliation, and the need for power. Jonathan Bradshaw also adds that needs can be normative, felt, expressed, or compared among one another. Similar to needs theories, Frederick Herzberg proposed a two-factor theory, with a dichotomy of job satisfaction and dissatisfaction factors. Herzberg asserts that there two types of factors that influence workplace motivation: motivators, which function to *satisfy* workers (such as recognition, responsibility, and advancement); and "hygiene factors," which can function to *dissatisfy* workers if not preserved and well-managed (such as compensation, job security, and interpersonal relations). Herzberg posits that in order for motivators to be fully effective, hygiene factors must be well managed; otherwise, the dissatisfaction that results from hygiene factors will trump the impact of motivators.

Based on these theories, HPT practitioners can better understand the different types of needs that can be satisfied by different monetary and non-monetary workplace incentives, such as recognition, increased responsibility, job re-assignment, team-building strategies, and advancement and promotion opportunities. Also, using an incentive (such as a stretch assignment, which addresses the worker's needs for achievement and esteem) might not realize its motivational potential unless the worker's lower-level needs and hygiene factors (such as adequate compensation or a positive relationship with supervisors or co-workers) are satisfied.

Self-Concept and Motivation. Theories and research findings in human motivation also help HPT practitioners understand how positive self-concepts can influence human behavior and performance. For instance, experimental studies conducted at the Western Electric Company's Hawthorne Works between 1924 and 1932 revealed several unexpected results, well documented by organizational behavior pioneers F. J. Roethlisberger and William Dickson in their book, *Management and the Worker*. In particular, they relate the work of Elton Mayo, a researcher from the Harvard Business School, who conducted a series of studies with a small number of female operators in the relay assembly test room. Through his studies of these women, he revealed that it was not the experimental conditions, but rather the fact that the workers recognized that they were a special study group, that motivated them to improve performance. This phenomenon is well known today as the Hawthorne Effect. The Pygmalion Effect (also known as the self-fulfilling prophesy) suggests a similar idea, but is different in the sense that it calls for the *right* kind of attention. The Pygmalion Effect suggests that, if a manager expects that workers will display exemplary performance, they will perform at a high level if they internalize the manager's expectation. Likewise, if a manager expects poor performance from workers, that is the level of performance that they are likely to produce. Also tied to self-concept, James Adams' equity theory suggests that workers will compare their contributions and their consequent rewards to those of their colleagues. If workers perceive this relationship as unfair (for example, a peer received greater rewards for doing less work), then they might intentionally decrease work productivity to compensate for the inequity gap or might remain less productive and come to believe themselves unworthy of better rewards.

Case Study

In her analysis of the situation, Susan found out that many regional managers had a high level of need for accomplishment. She also discovered that the more competent the regional managers were, the more responsibilities and projects they had been assigned to complete. However, those who were less successful in completing their projects tended to receive fewer assignments, even though they continued to receive recognition and rewards similar to those of their more successful peers. Thus, the organization was inadvertently punishing desired performance and rewarding poor performance. Susan recognized that this would likely cause an inequity tension among the regional managers and anticipated recommending a performance-based incentive plan.

Adequate Capacity to Acquire Job Knowledge and Skills

Frederick Taylor's work with scientific management was described earlier in this chapter in relation to expectations and feedback, tools, and processes. Taylor was also a pioneer in addressing workers' capacity for performance and providing systematically designed training to improve work skills.

Human Capacity for Performance. During his work at Bethlehem Steel Company, Taylor selected high-performing workers based on physical strength and personal characteristics and used the high performance level as a standard. What Taylor did not address at that time but has gained increasing attention among HPT practitioners in recent years is how psychological status, such as emotional intelligence, affects human capacity. As Gilbert explained through his behavior engineering model, human capacity is one of the main indicators for performance potential. To this point, Daniel Goleman, who popularized emotional intelligence, describes it as "the capacity for recognizing our own feelings and those of others, for motivating ourselves, and for managing emotions well in ourselves and in our relationships" (p. 317). Emotional intelligence (EQ) is clearly part of human capacity; it refers to emotional abilities different from, but complementary to, cognitive abilities, often measured by IQ. Furthermore, research findings have connected emotional intelligence to effective leadership abilities, as well as to strong work performance (for example, Carmeli & Josman, 2006; Cross & Travaglione, 2003; Deeter-Schmelz & Sojka, 2003; Dulewicz, Young, & Dulewicz, 2005, Stein & Book, 2006).

Principles and Practices of Instructional Design. Capacity can affect an individual's ability to assimilate new knowledge, skills, and attitudes. For that reason, Frederick Taylor emphasized using a systematic method to select capable workers first and then to train them with explicit instruction. He used a scientific *task analysis* to design effective instruction.

During the last century, a wide array of theory and research has contributed to the development of a knowledge base of effective instructional design principles. Ralph Tyler introduced the importance of establishing instructional objectives and providing guidelines for writing objectives in the 1930s. Following in Tyler's footsteps, educational psychologist Benjamin Bloom led the effort for developing a taxonomy of educational objectives, which helps instructional designers recognize that learning opportunities should be sequenced in a systematic way. Instruction designed based on the hierarchical order of the cognitive domain of the taxonomy would help workers become competent in such a step-by-step fashion as: (1) acquire job-related information (knowledge and comprehension), (2) use appropriate information to successfully complete the job (application and analysis), and (3) manage multiple tasks toward the same goal (synthesis and evaluation).

B. F. Skinner's development of behavioral analysis and feedback systems has also provided a wide range of applications to instructional design in both educational and industrial settings. The fundamental design principles that Skinner used in the development of programmed instruction are still applicable to, and widely used in, the design of e-learning programs. In instructional design, Robert Mager's method of writing instructional objectives with three specific elements (performance, conditions, and criteria) is widely practiced. Robert Gagné's work is also noted for his contributions to synthesizing various principles of human learning and performance into the development of instructional theories and models. For example, in his development of nine events of instruction, Gagné adopted and combined principles of behavioral learning (operant conditioning), strategies of cognitive information processing theory (for example, gain attention from learners before helping them encode new knowledge), and the principle of *transfer of learning* that Thorndike addressed a century ago. The contributions of these theorists continue to shape today's training and instructional design practices.

Learning Through Communities of Practice. HPT practitioners should understand that learning-oriented solutions can also be non-instructional in nature. One example that has received quite a bit of attention is communities of practice. This concept, initially introduced by social learning theorist Etienne Wenger, is described as bringing people together with a shared interest in a subject to collaborate, share ideas, and learn from one another. This concept stems from the theory of situated cognition, which emphasizes the influence that interaction with one's environment has on learning (Driscoll, 2005). Recent researchers have credited communities of practice as an effective means for transferring tacit knowledge and improving performance (for example, Johnson, 2007; Lesser & Storck, 2001).

Case Study

In her analysis concerning the regional managers' project completion rates, Susan discovered that, while all managers had project management experience, they differed in their approaches. Since all had general project management knowledge, Susan decided to prepare them to focus on the higher levels of Bloom's taxonomy of objectives in the subject. She also plans to support the development of a community of practice among the regional managers to encourage them to exchange ideas and learn from one another. Throughout this process, Susan has found that it is necessary to recommend multiple performance interventions to address the performance gaps. She has also found her knowledge of theoretical foundations to be key in making informed recommendations. Without such knowledge, Susan might simply have recommended the latest quick-fix or fad solution.

Intervention Selection and Change Management

Systemic thinking should be applied throughout the process of an HPT project. In selecting an intervention, it is important to assess the potential impact that decision may have on other aspects of the affected job and organization.

Achieving the Greatest Leverage Through Diffusion of Effect. Gilbert's leisurely theorems provided helpful guidance for intervention selection from an *engineering* perspective:

1. There is no way to change one condition of behavior without changing another condition of the behavior, which Gilbert called "diffusion of effect";

2. Changing one condition of behavior can have either a positive or negative impact on changing other conditions; and

3. The greatest leverage can be achieved by changing the condition(s) that would have the most positive impact on multiple areas.

Gilbert's theory of diffusion of effect implies that the "matching-causes-to-solutions" method is not always necessary. In other words, it is not advisable to develop a separate solution for every individual cause that is identified for a performance issue. It is the HPT practitioner's responsibility to analyze and select a small number of solutions that would generate the most cost-effective results. Figure 2.1 illustrates the matching-causes-to-solutions method used in a hypothetical situation.

With the diffusion of effect in mind, a practitioner might instead select only two solutions from Figure 2.1: (1) a solution to rearrange the office environment, which could have not only a positive direct impact on work processes and workers' performance capacity, but also positive side effects on providing job information and data in a timely manner and increasing workers' motivation; and (2) a training solution that would not only close the knowledge gap, but also serve as a motivator as it would allow workers to improve performance

Figure 2.1 Selecting Solutions with the Matching-Causes-to-Solutions Method.

and provide an opportunity to receive performance-based incentives. This is illustrated in Figure 2.2.

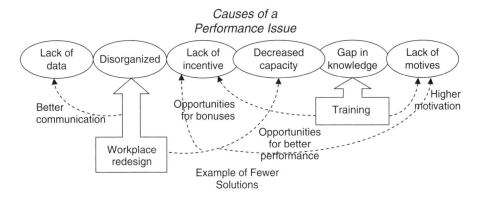

Figure 2.2 Selecting Fewer, Cost-Effective Solutions with Diffusion of Effect in Mind.

Managing Driving and Restraining Forces toward Changes. In order to better ensure that selected interventions are implemented as smoothly as possible, they should be designed with a change management strategy in mind. A basic component of change management involves identifying factors that will likely help drive the initiative and factors that might work against the initiative (see Figure 2.3). This common practice, often referred to as force-field analysis, is derived from Kurt Lewin's field theory. Field theory is a theory of social interaction that suggests that there are forces that attract an individual to a group (driving forces) and forces that repel an individual from a group (restraining forces). The same principle can be applied to any changes in an organization. For example, workplace redesign might be a cost-effective solution and may generate positive support from stakeholders. However, there might be resistance to this change due to its up-front costs, the difficulty in meeting the current projects' deadlines during the office move, and so on. These factors should be carefully analyzed and effectively managed.

Figure 2.3 Driving and Restraining Forces Toward a Change.

Case Study

Next, Susan plans to determine the most effective and feasible solutions for addressing the regional managers' performance gaps. She also understands that it involves developing change management strategies to ensure successful implementation of the solutions proposed. Susan plans to continuously monitor the stakeholders' reactions through ongoing interactions with them and careful analyses of other data while implementing her initiatives.

SUMMARY

As presented in this chapter, many of the basic HPT practices today are grounded in theory. While this chapter is not intended to provide an exhaustive list of theories that guide HPT practitioners' work, it is intended to demonstrate the significance of the practice-theory connection. Table 2.4 summarizes the practices described in this chapter, the part of this handbook in which they are discussed, and the corresponding theoretical frameworks that support those practices.

Table 2.4 Common HPT Practices Connected to Supporting Theoretical Frameworks

Common HPT Practices	Supporting Theoretical Frameworks
Establishing project alignment to ensure that HPT initiatives meet strategic goals (see Part Two)	System theories, such as general systems theory (von Bertalanffy, 1968); total performance system (Brethower, 1972); the management of the white space of an organization (Rummler & Brache, 1995)
Gap and cause analyses (see Part Eleven)	Examples include engineering worthy performance with behavior engineering model (Gilbert, 2007); front-end analysis (Harless, 1973); organizational elements model (Kaufman, 1983); goal analysis (Mager, 1984); performance analysis (Rossett, 1999); needs assessment (Witkin & Altschuld, 1995, 2000)
Interventions related to expectations and feedback (see Part Four), tools, environment, and processes (see Part Five)	Examples include scientific management (Taylor, 1911/1998); goal-setting theory (Locke & Latham, 1990); law of effect (Thorndike, 1927); Skinner's operant conditioning (Skinner, 1953)

Interventions related to incentives, rewards, and recognition (see Part Six), motivation and self-concept (see Part Seven)	Examples include understanding hidden incentives and consequences (Mager & Pipe, 1997); hierarchy of needs (Maslow, 1943); three needs theory (McClelland, 1988); two-factor theory (Herzberg, 1968); Hawthorne effect (Mayo, 1960); Pygmalion effect (Pinder, 1998); equity theory (Pinder, 1998)
Interventions related to performance capability (see Part Nine), knowledge and skills (see Part Eight)	Examples include scientific management (Taylor, 1911/1998); emotional intelligence (Goleman, 1998); instructional objectives (Mager, 1997; Tyler, 1949); taxonomy of educational objectives (Bloom, Engelhart, Furst, Hill, & Krathwohl, 1956); instructional theories (Gagné, 1985); situated cognition (Driscoll, 2005)
Systemic thinking in intervention selection/force-field analysis in change management	Examples include diffusion of effect (Gilbert, 2007); field theory (Lewin, 1948)

References

Adams, J. S. (1965). Inequity in social exchange. *Advances in Experimental Social Psychology*. *62*, 335–343.

Altschuld, J. W., & Witkin, B. R. (2000). *From needs assessment to action: Transforming needs into solution strategies*. Thousand Oaks, CA: Sage.

Bloom, B. S., Engelhart, M. D., Furst, E. J., Hill, W. H., & Krathwohl, D. R. (1956). *Taxonomy of educational objectives: The classification of educational goals (Handbook I: Cognitive domain)*. New York: David McKay.

Bradshaw, J. (1972). A taxonomy of social need. In G. McLachlan (Ed.), *Problems and progress in medical care, 7th Series* (pp. 69–82). London: Oxford University Press.

Brethower, D. (1972). *Behavioral analysis in business and industry: A total performance system*. Kalamazoo, MI: Behaviordelia Press.

Carmeli, A., & Josman, Z. E. (2006). The relationship among emotional intelligence, task performance, and organizational citizenship behaviors. *Human Performance, 19*(4), 403–419.

Cross, B., & Travaglione, A. (2003). The untold story: Is the entrepreneur of the 21st century defined by emotional intelligence? *The International Journal of Organizational Analysis, 11*(3), 221–228.

Dean, P. J. (1997). Thomas F. Gilbert, Ph. D.: Engineering performance with or without training. In P. J. Dean, & D. E. Ripley (Eds.), *Performance improvement pathfinders: Models for organizational learning systems* (Vol. 1, pp. 45–64). Silver Spring, MD: The International Society for Performance Improvement.

Deeter-Schmelz, D. R., & Sojka, J. Z. (2003). Developing effective salespeople: Exploring the link between emotional intelligence and sales performance. *The International Journal of Organizational Analysis*, *11*(3), 211–220.

Driscoll, M. P. (2005). *Psychology of learning for instruction* (3rd ed.). Upper Saddle River, NJ: Pearson Education.

Dulewicz, C., Young, M., & Dulewicz, V. (2005). The relevance of emotional intelligence for leadership performance. *Journal of General Management*, *30*(3), 71–86.

Gagné, R. M. (1985). *The conditions of learning* (4th ed.). New York: Holt, Rinehart and Winston, Inc.

Gilbert, T. F. (1982, September). A. question of performance. Part I: The PROBE model. *Training and Development Journal*, *36*(9), 20–30.

Gilbert, T. F. (1988, July). Measuring the potential for performance improvement. Training, 49–52.

Gilbert, T. F. (2007). *Human competence: Engineering worthy performance* (Tribute edition). Silver Spring, MD: The International Society for Performance Improvement.

Goleman, D. (1998). *Working with emotional intelligence*. New York: Bantam Books.

Harless, J. H. (1973). An analysis of front-end analysis. *Improving Human Performance: A Research Quarterly*, *4*, 229–244.

Herzberg, F. (1968). One more time: How do you motivate employees? *Harvard Business Review*, *46*(1), 53–63.

Kaufman, R. (1983). A holistic planning model: A system approach for improving organizational effectiveness and impact. *Performance and Instruction*, *22*(8), 3–12.

Johnson, H. (2007). Communities of practice and international development. *Progress in Development Studies*, *7*(4), 277–290.

Lesser, E. L., & Storck, J. (2001). Communities of practice and organizational performance. *IBM Systems Journal*, *40*(4), 831–841.

Lewin, K. (1948). *Resolving social conflicts* (G. W. Lewin Ed.). New York: Harper & Brothers.

Locke, E. A., & Latham, G. P. (1990). *A theory of goal setting & task performance*. Englewood Cliffs, NJ: Prentice Hall.

Mager, R. F. (1984). *Goal analysis* (2nd ed.). Belmont, CA: Lake Management and Training.

Mager, R. F. (1997). *Preparing instructional objectives* (3rd ed.). Atlanta, GA: The Center for Effective Performance, Inc.

Mager, R. F., & Pipe, P. (1997). *Analyzing performance problems* (3rd ed.). Atlanta, GA: The Center for Effective Performance, Inc.

Maslow, A. H. (1943). A theory of motivation. *Psychological Review*, 50, 370–396.

Mayo, E. (1960). *The human problems of an industrial civilization*. New York: The Viking Press.

McClelland, D. C. (1988). *Human motivation*. Cambridge, MA: Cambridge University Press.

Pershing, J. A. (2006). Human performance technology fundamentals. In J. A. Pershing (Ed.), *Handbook of human performance technology* (3rd ed., pp. 5–34). San Francisco: Pfeiffer.

Pinder, C. C. (1998). *Work motivation in organizational behavior*. Upper Saddle River, NJ: Prentice Hall.

Roethlisberger, F. J., & Dickson, W. J. (1939). *Management and the workers: An account of a research program conducted by the Western Electric Company, Hawthorne Works, Chicago*. Cambridge, MA: Harvard University Press.

Rossett, A. (1999). *First things fast: A handbook for performance analysis*. San Francisco: Pfeiffer.

Rowland, G. (1999). *A tripartite seed: The future creating capacity of designing, learning and systems*. Cresskill, NJ: Hampton Press.

Rummler, G. A., & Brache, A. P. (1995). *Improving performance: How to manage the white space on the organization chart* (2nd ed.). San Francisco: Jossey-Bass.

Skinner, B. F., (1953). *Science and human behavior*. New York: Macmillan.

Stansfield, T. C., & Longenecker, C. O. (2006). The effects of goal setting and feedback on manufacturing productivity: A field experiment. *International Journal of Productivity & Performance Management*, 55(3), 346–358.

Stein, S. J., & Book, H. E. (2006). *The EQ edge: Emotional intelligence and your success*. Mississauga, ON: John Wiley & Sons Canada, Ltd.

Swanson, R. A. (1999). Foundations of performance improvement and implications for practice. In R. J. Torraco (Ed.), *Performance improvement: Theory and practice* (Advances in Developing Human Resources, No. 1, pp. 1–25). Baton Rouge, LA: The Academy of Human Resource Development.

Taylor, F. (1998). *The principles of scientific management*. Mineola, NY: Dover Publications. (Original work published 1911).

Thorndike, E. L. (1927). A fundamental theorem in modifiability. *Proceedings of the National Academy of Sciences*, 13, 15–18.

Tyler, R. W. (1949). *Basic principles of curriculum and instruction*. Chicago: The University of Chicago Press.

von Bertalanffy, L. (1968). *Organismic psychology and systems theory*. Worcester, MA: Clark University Press.

Watkins, R. (2006). Aligning human performance technology decisions with an organization's strategic direction. In J. A. Pershing (Ed.), *Handbook of human performance technology* (3rd ed., pp. 191–207). San Francisco: Pfeiffer.

Wenger, E. (1998). *Communities of practice: Learning, meaning, and identity.* Cambridge, MA: Cambridge University Press.

Witkin, B. R., & Altschuld, J. W. (1995). *Planning and conducing needs assessments: A practical guide.* Thousand Oaks, CA: Sage.

Recommended Readings

Cyung, S. Y. (2008). *Foundations of instructional and performance technology.* Amherst, MA: HRD Press.

Dean, P. J., & Ripley, D. E. (Eds.). (1997). *Performance improvement pathfinders: Models for organizational learning systems* (Vol. 1) Silver Spring, MD: The International Society for Performance Improvement.

Gilbert, T. F. (2007). *Human competence: Engineering worthy performance* (Tribute edition). San Francisco: ISPI and Pfeiffer.

Saettler, P. (1990). *The evolution of American educational technology.* Englewood, CO: Libraries Unlimited, Inc.

 # EDITORIAL CONNECTIONS

The accomplishment of reliable, sustainable, and valuable results through the improvement of individual and organizational performance relies on (1) scientific theories from many disciplines, (2) valid and reliable findings from empirical research, and (3) the pragmatic experience of professionals. As an applied science, performance improvement relies on the relationship of these three foundations, although none of the three is exclusively the domain of human performance. Chapter Two illustrates how the principles, theories, and research of multiple disciplines can be used to guide the improvement of performance. From psychology to physics, improving human and organizational performance draws on the diverse experiences of many fields.

Nevertheless, this breadth and variation of theoretical foundations can become an albatross that weighs down researchers from finding a focus and discourages practitioners from using these foundations in their daily practice. Don't be discouraged by the depth of the theoretical foundations that are the underpinnings of human performance technology. While you may question "How does Theory X or research finding Y really impact on what we do here on a daily basis?," the reality is that you are already applying many HPT theories—often indirectly and without conscious effort—in your current activities.

The relevance of theory, research, and experience are found in their daily application, whether, for example, you apply general system theory to informally guide the analysis of organizational needs or use Locke and Latham's goal-setting theory to mentor your staff. Use the theories and research findings discussed throughout this book to both inform and challenge what you do in practice. At times, you will want to rely on the foundations that have brought you and your organization success in the past. At other times, however, you will want to challenge the underlying theories being used within your organization to determine whether alternatives may be more useful in accomplishing desired results.

To achieve valuable results in today's complex organizations requires grounding oneself in more than one theoretical foundation. For instructional designers, as an example, grounding in either "behaviorism" or "constructivism" as the sole basis for guiding their decisions is not likely to improve human performance in varied performance context. They must be able to apply the correct theory or mix of theories that will achieve results within the performance context of their organization. Some days this may draw on their understanding of B.F. Skinner's theory of operant conditioning, while on others it may require the application of principles from Jerome Bruner's constructivist theory.

In the practice of performance improvement, and specifically in the selection and implementation of performance interventions, it is important to recognize and apply the appropriate theoretical foundations to guide your decisions. Relying solely on gut instincts or the same solutions you've used in the past is not likely to achieve sustainable and valuable results. Use theoretical foundations, scientific research, and your experience to identify and implement the right mix of performance interventions to achieve desired results.

It is often valuable to consider the *worth of performance* when making these decisions. Approximating the *worth of performance* can help you determine the appropriate size, scope, budget, and other characteristics of your improvement effort. As described in Chapter Two, Thomas Gilbert proposed that, while *worth* is commonly defined differently in many contexts, when improving performance, you can define the *worth* of the effort by the value of the accomplishments (results) divided by the costs of changing behavior.

Worth of Performance = Value of accomplishment/Costs for changing behavior

Within this definition of *worth*, the *value of accomplishment* should be determined in both direct and indirect terms, stretching across all levels of Kaufman's Organizational Elements Model: outcomes, output, and products. Also, the *costs for changing behavior* should be broad, including both the costs associated with changing behavior and the costs associated with doing nothing (or the costs of not improving performance). It is often easiest to approximate these based in financial terms, although you should continue to recognize that many benefits and costs associated with improving performance are not adequately represented in purely financial terms.

WHAT'S COMING UP

Throughout the remaining parts of this handbook, you will find numerous performance interventions that can improve human and organizational performance. Each offers opportunities to accomplish significant results, and each has associated costs that should be considered when making decisions about how, when, and in combination with what other interventions they should be used. While the value of individual performance activities can be approximated, your decisions about what to do in order to improve performance are routinely complicated by the relationships among multiple activities throughout your organization. As a consequence, the numerous performance interventions covered in this handbook are classified in systemic framework, the Performance Pyramid model, to illustrate their close relationships and interdependence.

In Chapter Three, John Wedman describes his comprehensive model, guiding performance improvement initiatives by building on both the foundational pyramid framework that is at the center and examining the supporting components that form a performance system—inputs, processes, and results. The result is a useful model for systemically accomplishing significant results. You can use the Performance Pyramid to analyze current performance problems within your organization and to assess the various interventions as option-making improvements. In the same way, it can be used—along with Kaufman's OEM (see Figure I.2), Mager's Performance Analysis Model (see Figure 1.3), and other models described in Chapter One—to develop a comprehensive system for improving human and organization performance.

CHAPTER THREE

The Performance Pyramid

John Wedman

INTRODUCTION

The Performance Pyramid is a conceptual framework for analyzing performance problems and a tool for identifying (albeit at a high level) performance improvement interventions. First introduced in 1998, the pyramid has evolved from three contributing factors (vision, resources, and support system) and one outcome factor (significant accomplishments) to a more elaborate framework, a small set of diagnostic tools, and a high-level methodology for implementation. Created to provide a simple yet comprehensive framework for driving needs assessment and performance improvement processes in a systemic direction, the pyramid serves as the organizing framework for this book.

DESCRIPTION

Several years ago Robert Mager was giving a keynote speech at an ISPI conference. As always, his speech was timely and compelling, bringing a clear focus to a problem many were wrestling with, the name of the organization. As many readers are aware, ISPI started in the early 1960s as the National Society for Programmed Instruction (NSPI). Several years later, ''programmed instruction'' gave way to ''performance and instruction.'' Later still, ''national'' was replaced with ''international,'' with both name changes reflecting changes in the organization's scope. But some, including Mager, were still not satisfied with the name.

Mager commented that being named the International Society for Performance and Instruction was like being named the ''International Society for

Transportation and Bicycles." When the laughter subsided, he went on to argue for the name the organization carries today: International Society for Performance Improvement (ISPI).

About that same time, ISPI offered a workshop dealing with Thomas Gilbert's (1978) seminal book, *Human Competence: Engineering Worthy Performance.* The workshop involved lively discussions and the occasional argument about some of Gilbert's equations, their interpretation, and their implications for professional practice. Throughout it all, it was clear that something more fundamental than ISPI's name had changed.

While performance improvement as a concept was clear, performance improvement as a process was still emerging and ill-defined. For this writer and perhaps others new to performance improvement, the challenge was to translate the concept into processes that could be applied in professional practice. Mager's 1970 book *Analyzing Performance Problems* was helpful as far as it went, but it fell short in certain areas (such as lacking guidance regarding organizational culture). And even though he cautioned against it, Mager's performance analysis flow chart implied a way of thinking that seemed a bit too linear. On the other extreme, Gilbert's work was comprehensive and holistic, but it was relatively complex, making it less accessible for some practitioners.

The Performance Pyramid was developed to provide a simple, yet comprehensive perspective for analyzing performance problems and improving the performance of individuals, groups, and organizations. The pyramid draws heavily on the work of Gilbert and other scholars, as well as a host of performance improvement practitioners and customers. It has evolved over the last decade and will continue to evolve while heeding the "simple, yet comprehensive" mantra.

The pyramid is based on one *Basic Observation* that seems to hold true regardless of context.

Basic Observation: In order to accomplish something of significance, three factors must be in place: vision, resources, and support system.

Reading from bottom to top, Figure 3.1 shows resources combined with vision to fuel and direct the elements of the support system. When resources, vision, and support system are aligned (that is, working together), significant accomplishments will result.

As shown in Figure 3.2 and detailed in Table 3.1, the support system area has been elaborated within the Performance Pyramid model, with six elements playing out in the context of the organizational culture. Each element has multiple considerations that must be accounted for, both individually and collectively. (*Note:* The complete Performance Pyramid model is described at the end of this chapter.)

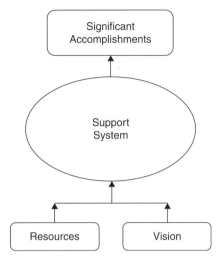

Figure 3.1 Basic Observation.

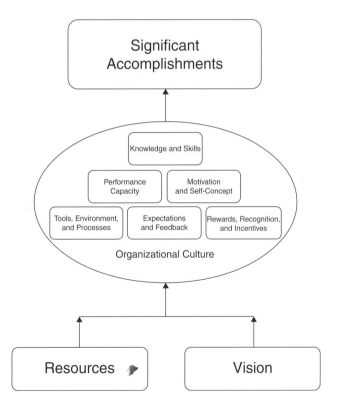

Figure 3.2 Performance Pyramid—Support System Detail.

Table 3.1 Support System Elements

Support System Elements	Considerations Include . . .
Tools, Environment, and Processes	Do the performers have the tools to do the job well? Does the work environment enable the desired performance? Are the processes effective and efficient?
Expectations and Feedback	Do the performers know what to do (and why)? Do they know how well they are doing?
Rewars, Recognition, and Incentives	Is good performance rewarded and recognized? Are incentives offered to drive changes in performance?
Performance Capability	Are the performers mentally, socially, and physically able to meet expectations?
Motivation and Self-Concept	Are the performers self-motivated; do they want to meet expectations? Do they consider themselves to be competent?
Knowledge and Skills	Do the performers have the knowledge and skills required to meet expectations?

As shown in Table 3.1, the support system consists of six elements. Each element has multiple considerations that must be accounted for, both individually and collectively.

A premise of the Performance Pyramid is that accomplishments will suffer if one or more of the performance support elements are missing or inadequate, if the elements are not aligned (that is, not compatible) with each other, or if they are incompatible with the organizational culture (see Chapter Thirty). This premise yields several *Operational Principles* summarized in Table 3.2.

Applications

The pyramid can be used throughout the needs assessment and performance improvement process, beginning with initial analysis of the performance situation, continuing through planning and implementing performance improvement interventions, and concluding with summative evaluation. A small set of data collection tools based on the model have been used in a wide variety of settings, including industry, K–12 and higher education, and non-profit organizations. When used successfully, the pyramid framework helps ensure that needs assessments are comprehensive and performance improvement interventions are systemic.

Table 3.2 Operational Principles

Operational Principles	Comments
The support system elements are inter-related; a change in one element can have implications for other elements.	For example, if a new tool is introduced, training may be required to address changes in knowledge and skill requirements, expectations regarding tool usage may need to be to communicated, and so on.
The support system elements are constrained by resources availability.	While this principle holds for all types of resources, it is most evident in terms of financial resources. Better tools, bigger rewards, and higher-skilled workers all cost money.
Collectively, the support system elements must be adequate to enable the desired performance.	A shortfall in one area (for example, limited knowledge and skills) can sometimes be made up for in another area (for example, improved tools).
The support system elements should be aligned with each other and with the vision.	For example, if the vision is to have "a cell phone in every pocket" but the sales staff are rewarded more for repeat customers than new customers, the reward system is out of alignment.
The support system elements must be compatible with the organizational culture.	Performance improvement efforts that are incompatible with the prevalent culture are doomed to failure. For example, in a culture that values consistency, efforts to increase innovation are less likely to be successful.
For any given performance situation, some support system elements are more or less important, more or less expensive, etc.	Needs assessment data will help determine importance in a given situation. The scope and sophistication of the performance improvement interventions are directly related to cost.
The support system elements are not hierarchically related but rather are presented as a cluster of equally relevant influences on performance.	For any given situation, different relationships may exist among the elements. At the risk of using a building metaphor: it doesn't matter where the blocks are as long as the overall structure is stable.

(Continued)

Table 3.2 (*Continued*)

Operational Principles	Comments
The value derived from the accomplishments must be greater than the cost of enabling the accomplishments.	If the support system consumes resources faster than they are replenished by the accomplishments, then: (1) the resources must be replenished from other sources or (2) the support system must be reduced and the vision made more achievable. In the long run, drawing resources from other sources may create performance problems for the sources.

WHAT WE KNOW FROM RESEARCH

As with any high-level framework, the Performance Pyramid is informed by a vast amount of literature, in this case the research and theory related to performance improvement. Beyond the content presented in this book, interested readers are directed to the 2006 edition of the *Handbook of Human Performance Technology: Principles, Practices, and Potential* and a growing number of scholarly journals (such as *Performance Improvement Quarterly*) and books. Focusing more on the challenge at hand—providing a framework for organizing this book—the literature is surprisingly helpful, albeit somewhat limited.

Scott Schaffer's review of organizational and human performance frameworks defined frameworks as "system-oriented representations of the flow or linkages of resources, inputs, processes, goals, and results within and external to an organization" (2000; p. 220). Thinking of a framework as "a starting point for assessment, diagnosis, or analysis of organizational problems or opportunities" (p. 222), the Purdue University professor argued performance improvement frameworks should:

- Visually communicate the nature and complexity of performance improvement;
- Frame discussion of the components to be analyzed;
- Guide the selection of data collection and analysis approaches;
- Identify key structures, forces, relationships, and interdependencies; and
- Define strategic results and targets to be accomplished.

Schaffer's examined eleven frameworks (including the Performance Pyramid), using five different perspectives: (1) change orientation, (2) theoretical basis, (3) organizational results level, (4) unit of analysis, and (5) performance analysis. Schaffer noted that, for the purpose of his review, the unit of analysis and organizational results levels should be considered one and the same. Along with five other frameworks, the pyramid was placed in the Performance Systems Architecture category (see Table 3.3).

Table 3.3 Performance Systems Architecture: Example Frameworks

Frameworks Schaffer Reviewed	Source
Balanced Scorecard	Kaplan and Norton (1996)
Behavioral Engineering Model	Gilbert (1978)
Model of Performance Technology	Deterline (1993)
Organizational Scan	Vanguard Consulting (1996)
Performance Diagnostic Matrix	Swanson (1994)
Performance Pyramid	Wedman and Graham (1998)

Source: Schaffer, 2000

When considering the pyramid from a change orientation perspective, Schaffer concluded that the pyramid was more concerned with incremental change than systemic change. And while acknowledging that it was "extremely difficult to identify a clear theoretical base for each of the frameworks" (p. 230), he concluded that the pyramid was consistent with "performance engineering" and "management" on a theoretical basis.

Schaffer found all the frameworks he reviewed, including the pyramid, addressed the micro (job/performer) and macro (organizational) levels to some degree, and concluded that the pyramid focused primarily on individuals and teams as the unit of analysis. In term of the performance analysis process, the pyramid was seen as having a formal focus on the analysis of "what is" and an informal focus on "what should be" and "cause analysis."

As a note, Schaffer's review was based on an earlier version of the Performance Pyramid. In recent years the pyramid has evolved to include the role of organizational culture in the needs assessment and performance improvement process. Also, as noted at the end of this chapter, the visual representation has been changed to reflect more of a systems representation. It is likely that Schaffer's review would have been altered by these recent refinements in the pyramid framework.

While the pyramid was created more for practicing professionals than for scholars, it has been used in at least two studies reported in the literature. In 2001 Wedman and Diggs used the pyramid framework to identify barriers to technology-enhanced learning environments in a teacher education program. Schaffer and Richardson conducted a similar study in 2004, examining performance support for the use of educational technology in a teacher education system. These two studies were consistent with Watkins and Wedman's recommendation that the pyramid be used to: (1) help performance consultants ensure that assessment and analysis data are being used and (2) protect against the tendency to select from among solutions that are well known and comfortable.

WHEN TO APPLY

Experience shows that the pyramid is particularly helpful in the early stages of the needs assessment and performance improvement processes. For example, during the planning stage, the pyramid provides a holistic perspective, presenting a wide range of potential issues for consideration. While decision-makers may opt to focus only on certain issues, the comprehensive nature of the pyramid helps ensure a narrower view is an intentional decision and not an accidental oversight.

The pyramid and the associated tools, consisting of an interview protocol and a survey template, are helpful for collecting high-level needs assessment data and crafting broad-stroke recommendations based on the findings. As mentioned earlier, the pyramid has served well in numerous needs assessment projects in a wide range of contexts. Also, as observed by Schaffer, a key feature of the pyramid is "its simplicity and visual appeal which combine to make it a useful tool when communicating the concept of performance to individuals within an organization" (2000; p. 241).

After needs assessment data have been analyzed and attention turns to designing performance improvement interventions, the pyramid can be useful for helping maintain a systemic perspective. For example, several years ago a large utility company introduced a new device (pyramid element: tool) for opening manhole covers (most likely the results of increased workers' compensation insurance claims). Fortunately, the company also addressed several other pyramid elements:

- *Expectations and Feedback.* Workers were told to use the device and supervisors were responsible for monitoring it use.

- *Knowledge and Skills.* Workers received training in how to use the device.

- *Capability.* An increasing number of workers were not capable of opening the manholes without injury.

Unfortunately, the company failed to consider other pyramid elements: self-concept and rewards, recognition, and incentives. The popular name for the device was "Sissy Bar." No doubt, the organizational culture was also at work. The pyramid serves as a constant reminder that all the elements are related and need to be considered concurrently.

All that said, the pyramid is not intended to assist with in-depth assessments of performance problems and opportunities. For example, if knowledge and skills are identified as lacking, the pyramid offers no assistance in terms of conducting a task and content analysis. If rewards, recognition, and incentives are found to be a performance barrier, the data generated by the pyramid tools may not reveal the core problems in the organization's compensation program. The myriad sub-elements associated with each pyramid element have their own body of literature and practice that provide the tools and precision necessary for detailed diagnosis and targeted interventions. An excellent collection of such resources can be found in the remainder of this book.

STRENGTHS AND CRITICISMS

The strengths and criticisms of the pyramid are described below, followed by a comparison to Gilbert's work.

First, the pyramid offers a comprehensive and systemic framework for guiding needs assessment and performance improvement efforts. It can promote an organic orientation that recognizes and values the inter-relatedness of individual and collective effort, social context, and valued accomplishments.

In most situations, individuals carry out their work in the context of groups, and groups operate in the context of organizations. The pyramid includes individual, group, and organizational factors that contribute to performance. With the addition of organizational culture, the reach of the pyramid extends beyond the individual and team to include the organization.

The pyramid is grounded in Gilbert's seminal work. Its value is in trying to make Gilbert's work a bit more accessible without watering down his contributions. The pyramid also emphasizes alignment and adequacy of all factors and elements, providing a holistic perspective. This emphasis is consistent with a common view of a system: a configuration of related parts.

The simplicity and visual appeal of the pyramid make it useful when introducing organizations to the concept of performance improvement. With all due respect to Gilbert, equations are not typically well received by managers who are looking to understand and resolve a performance problem.

The pyramid is an evolving framework. One of its strengths is its openness to new, previously unconsidered, factors and elements. If an organization's application of the pyramid does not change every few years, it is likely that it has either been abandoned due to lack of interest, discontinued due to lack of support, or superseded by another framework.

Further criticisms of the pyramid are that the term "Performance Pyramid" and associated visual representation imply a hierarchy of elements to many, an all-too-common misconception that has been difficult to dislodge. A similar problem appears to have been encountered by Mager in popularizing his flowchart. As early as 1970 he cautioned, "The flow diagram makes it look as if everything is neatly welded into place and that each step leads inevitably to the next. *Don't be deceived by appearances. The formula is not rigid*" (p. 2). The website supporting the pyramid at needsassessment.missouri.edu includes animations illustrating the non-hierarchical relationship among the elements. Unfortunately, such animations are not possible within traditional books, articles, and other print-based technology.

The pyramid and its associated tool set do not possess the precision necessary for detailed analysis. Fortunately, such tools and methods are readily available from many other sources, this book included.

Although the pyramid "unpacks" the support system factor into ten distinct elements, the other two factors—resources and vision/mission/objectives—are not elaborated upon within the current model. In addition, the pyramid recognizes the influence of organizational culture on performance and performance improvement strategies, but does not specifically address performance issues at the organization level (for example, organizational structure).

In its current form, the pyramid is a closed system and does not overtly consider external factors. For example, federally mandated compliance requirements in the banking industry have a major impact on how loans are processed, confidentially is maintained, and various other considerations. These requirements change periodically and must be addressed by the organization. Changes in the marketplace, disruptive technologies, and other external factors are not specified within the current version of the pyramid.

The pyramid framework requires empirical validation. Even though practical experience has shown the pyramid to be helpful when conducting needs assessments and planning performance improvement interventions, no scientific research into the framework has been conducted. Marra, Howland, Jonassen, and Wedman (2003), however, suggest means by which such a model might be validated.

RELATIONSHIP TO PERFORMANCE ENGINEERING

Gilbert's work in performance engineering provided the foundation of, and need for, the pyramid. The discussion below highlights selected similarities and differences between Gilbert's human competence framework and the pyramid, starting with relationships noted in Schaffer's review.

Schaffer's 2003 Comparison

As summarized in Table 3.4, the only distinction between the pyramid and Gilbert's framework is in the areas of performance analysis and cause analysis. If a phase was included in a framework, it was rated as either "informally" or "formally" addressed. Schaffer concluded that Gilbert did not address the "what should be" phase, where current or anticipated deficiencies are examined. As noted earlier, Schaffer's review was based on an earlier version of the pyramid, prior to the inclusion of "organizational culture" and the notion that the "accomplishments" should "replenish" the resources consumed by the support system. These additions might have influenced Schaffer's view of the unit of analysis and organizational results level.

Table 3.4 Schaffer's Comparisons of Pyramid and Gilbert

Comparison Point	Pyramid	Gilbert
Broad Category	Performance Systems Architecture	Performance Systems Architecture
Change Orientation	Formal approach to improving current system; Biased more toward incremental change	Formal approach to improving current system; Biased more toward incremental change
Theoretical Basis	Performance Engineering; Management	Performance Engineering; Management
Unit of Analysis and Organizational Results Level	Individual and Team	Individual and Team
Performance and Cause Analysis		
What Should Be	Informally Addressed	Not Addressed
What Is	Formally Addressed	Formally Addressed
Cause Analysis	Informally Addressed	Informally Addressed

Variables Impacting Performance

When the pyramid and Gilbert are compared in terms of the variables impacting performance, many similarities can be noted, along with a few key differences. Table 3.5 summarizes this comparison.

Table 3.5 Pyramid's and Gilbert's Variables

Pyramid Variable	Gilbert Variable	Comparison
Expectations and Feedback	Information	Same variable
Tools, Environment, and Processes	Instrumentation	Same variable
Rewards, Recognition, and & Incentives	Incentives	Same variable
Knowledge and Skills	Knowledge	Same variable
Capability	Capacity	Same variable (different label)
Motivation and Self-Concept	Motives	Pyramid focuses on performer's internal motivation to perform and the performer's self-efficacy; Gilbert focuses on internal motivation, but does not consider self-efficacy

Relationships Among Variables

Gilbert suggested an optimal ("most efficient") sequence for diagnosing behavior deficiencies, claiming that "improper guidance and feedback are the single largest contributors to incompetence in the world of work" (p. 91) and argued the diagnosis should look in this area first. Later he softened this position when he talked about the "unitary nature of behavior."

The pyramid makes no recommendation in terms of a diagnostic sequence. When using the pyramid as a guide to needs assessment, the goal is to collect data across all performance-impacting variables, allowing patterns and relationships to emerge. Also, the pyramid does not claim any one variable is necessarily the largest contributor to performance problems. Instead, needs assessment data will inform this determination on a case-by-case basis. A large-scale empirical study, across multiple contexts, is needed to resolve this difference.

Organizational Culture

How do the pyramid and Gilbert approach organizational culture: the assumptions, values, mores, and artifacts of an organization's members? Gilbert argued that culture could be engineered and claimed that a culture that does not work well "was designed by a manager who did not begin with careful analysis of its goals and values'' (p. 103). Gilbert seemed to view culture as a variable to be controlled primarily at the outset, built into the design, rather than a variable to be considered during needs assessment and performance improvement interventions.

The pyramid does not purport to be a framework for designing an organization or changing an organization's culture. Rather, it starts from the assumption that an organization, and the organizational culture, already exists, with the culture having a direct and observable influence on performance. While an organization's culture may require change, the pyramid is not designed to facilitate this extraordinary task.

Scope

In one sense, Gilbert's work is much broader in scope than the pyramid. In the preface to *Human Competence*, Gilbert claimed his theory ''illustrates matters as diverse as how to teach kids the multiplication tables and how to manage a factory; as different as how to design a school curriculum and how to make economic decisions about industrial training'' (p. vi). While the pyramid has been applied in school, corporate, and non-profit organizations, it is intended to guide organizational rather than micro-level performance analysis.

In another sense, Gilbert and the pyramid are similar in scope in that both deal with accomplishments, support systems, resources, and other variables impacting performance. The pyramid also serves the same purpose as Gilbert's model: ''It helps us to observe behavior in an orderly fashion and to ask the 'obvious' questions (the ones we so often forget to ask) toward the single end of improving human competence'' (Gilbert, 1978, p. 95). As a reminder, the pyramid had one additional purpose: to provide a comprehensive and simple framework for considering vision, resources, and support system.

Overall Approach

The most striking difference between Gilbert and the pyramid is in the approach. Engineers and designers can approach their work very differently. Gilbert, for example, used a highly analytic approach, relying heavily on equations to show relationships. In contrast, the pyramid's approach attempts to be more holistic, employing visual representations to illustrate relationships.

There is no doubt that there is a great deal more theoretical underpinning to Gilbert's work than the pyramid; after all, the pyramid benefits from standing on Gilbert's shoulders. Gilbert's work is extremely precise, and for those with engineering backgrounds, probably intuitive. This, however, brings up what may be a fundamental question related to the efficacy of either model: *Is the process of identifying, measuring, and creating human competence best approached from an engineering perspective or a design perspective?*

RECOMMENDED DESIGN, DEVELOPMENT, AND IMPLEMENTATION PROCESS

This section provides an overview of how to implement the Performance Pyramid. Additional details and resources are available at needsassessment.missouri.edu.

Layered Approach to Implementation

Using the pyramid is more organic than mechanistic, with many simultaneous sub-processes. The pyramid is best implemented using a "layers" approach (see Figure 3.3), with successive layers providing more information and allowing for more targeted interventions, albeit at the cost of more resources and time. Each layer consists of four inter-related activities: finding, collecting, and analyzing information and deciding what needs to be done.

At the lowest layer, the process is extremely simple, if not simplistic, relying on very limited data, perhaps nothing more than an interview with a major stakeholder who has identified a performance problem. The stakeholder is interviewed; the interview is analyzed; a performance improvement intervention is planned and implemented; and the results are monitored. While this layer may fly in the face of

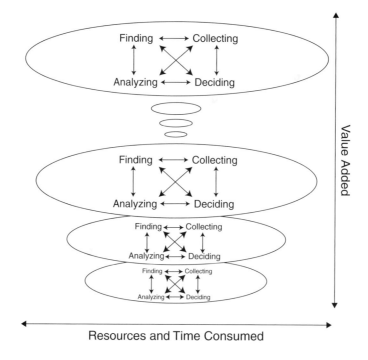

Figure 3.3 Layered Approach

best practices, the reality is that this limited approach happens every day—in the form of a direct order from a superior to "fix it and fix it now."

Assuming more time and resources are available, more in-depth assessments and targeted interventions can be brought to bear on the situation, presumably adding greater value to the performance improvement effort. For example, additional stakeholders can be interviewed, performers can be surveyed and observed, and extant data can be examined. The findings can be triangulated internally and benchmarked externally, leading to more targeted and sophisticated interventions.

In effect, the pyramid's layered approach helps address the "better-cheaper-faster" dilemma by highlighting the tradeoffs on the front end of a needs assessment and performance improvement project. Put another way, this approach helps manage customer expectations and mitigates the impact of limited resources and time. Interested readers can find out more about how a layered approach works in the area of instructional design and development in the Wedman and Tessmer (1993) and Tessmer and Wedman (1992) articles referenced at the end of this chapter.

Given the layered approach, applying the pyramid is similar to other needs assessment processes. Data sources are found, data are collected and analyzed, and intervention decisions are made. However, as mentioned earlier, these four sub-processes are not linear. Data analysis can lead to more questions requiring additional data finding, collecting, and subsequent analysis. Preliminary decisions are often reconsidered in light of new findings, especially findings that surface early in the intervention process where surprises, oversights, and failed assumptions are the norm. The overall process is highly iterative, holistic, and integrative.

Stakeholder Buy-In

Professionals experienced in working with the pyramid have found it helpful to set the stage before actually applying the model. Stage setting involves talking with high-ranking stakeholders to get their buy-in on the model as well as the activities that will ensue. This conversation should include:

- Getting to know the organization from the stakeholders' perspective(s);
- Understanding the performance problem from their perspectives;
- Helping them understand the business reasons for conducting a needs assessment;
- Showing how the pyramid model is simple, compatible with their thinking, and makes sense;
- Explaining the data collection and analysis processes; and
- Exploring hypothetical findings and their implications.

Simply put, without stakeholder buy-in before beginning the needs assessment and performance improvement process, it is highly unlikely to be gotten later, especially if the results indicate changes are warranted in the stakeholders' work.

Pyramid Implementation Tools

Following stakeholder buy-in on the idea of a systemic approach to performance improvement, the pyramid can be used to guide needs assessment activities. Two data collection tools—an interview protocol and a survey template—have been developed based on the pyramid elements. Sample items from both tools are provided in Tables 3.6 and 3.7.

Table 3.6 Sample Pyramid Interview Questions

Vision	What do you think your group (organization) is trying to accomplish? What do you wish it would accomplish?
Expectations	What is your role in working toward this accomplishment? What do you believe you are expected to do? What would you like to be doing?
Feedback	How will you know when you are meeting your performance expectations? What is a good way for you to find out how well you are meeting expectations?

As with any comprehensive needs assessment process, the pyramid can produce an enormous amount of data, and potentially create more confusion than clarity. However, a bigger risk is assuming all important data have been collected. The Pyramid Data Job Aid (see Figure 3.4) helps organize what is known and keep track of what is yet to be explored.

Table 3.7 Sample Pyramid Survey Statements

Statement	T(rue)	— U(nsure) —	F(alse)
I have received explicit expectations about [insert contextual information here].	T	— U —	F
I received regular and helpful feedback about how well I am [insert contextual information here].	T	— U —	F

The interview protocol, survey template, data job aid, and other pyramid resources are available at needsassessment.missouri.edu free of charge, with update notifications sent out periodically.

Directions:

Step 1. For each *Pyramid Element* (Column 1), indicate:

- *What you know* (2) about the performance improvement situation
- *What you don't know* (3) about the situation
- *How will you find out?* (4) what you don't know (conduct a survey of managers, interviews customers)
- Which *Performance Improvement Actions* (5) you will recommend IF you verify *What You Know* (2)

Step 2. Carry out the data collection activities listed in *How Will You Find Out?* (4). As the data are analyzed, add your findings to the *What You Know* column (2) and cross off the corresponding entry in the *What You Don't Know* column (3).

Continue to update all columns until: (1) you are about to run out of time or money or (2) your data collection is not generating anything new. At that point, begin writing your needs assessment report.

	If you verify	or learn		. . . then you will recommend
Pyramid Element (1)	*What You Know (2)*	*What You Don't Know (3)*	*How Will You Find Out? (4)*	*Performance Improvement Actions (5)*
Vision, Mission, Objectives				
Resources				
Organizational Culture				
Tools, Environment, and Processes				
(Job aid continues with other pyramid elements.)				

Figure 3.4 Pyramid Data Job Aid.

CRITICAL SUCCESS FACTORS

Before discussing the factors that are critical to successful implementation of a pyramid approach, it seems timely to address the question: "What are the *indicators* of a successful implementation?" Three success indicators readily surface.

> *Success Indicator 1.* Successful application of the pyramid optimizes all performance-impacting factors, leading to improved performance that, in turn, results in significant accomplishments. The accomplishments are considered significant if two conditions hold:
>
> - The accomplishments are manifestations of the vision, allowing the vision to advance by reaching further into the future.
>
> - The accomplishments generate more resources than are consumed by the support system, providing a positive return on investment.
>
> *Success Indicator 2.* Successful application of the pyramid changes how the organization views and approaches performance problems in the future. Put another way, not only should use of the pyramid change performance, but it should also change how performance is viewed.
>
> *Success Indicator 3.* Successful application of the pyramid refines and improves the model while heeding the "simple, yet comprehensive" mantra. Akin to an "after action review," this reflective process is grounded in the practical experiences and professional insights of pyramid users. The value of such efforts cannot be overstated.

Several factors have direct impact on successful implementation. Most of these factors are important to any needs assessment and performance improvement effort; a few are particularly important when using the pyramid model. While the following list is not comprehensive, the factors that are included have played out in actual projects, sometimes in the form of pitfalls to avoid.

Success Factor 1

Stakeholders must understand and buy-in to the systemic nature and comprehensiveness of the Performance Pyramid. Several years ago the training director at a Fortune 50 company hired my consulting group to conduct a performance assessment and make recommendations for improving how the company's corporate customer sales representatives (CCSRs) positioned the company's products against its competitors' products. We used the pyramid interview protocol to collect data from CCSRs across the country and issued a preliminary report. Not surprisingly, the report included several non-training issues (for example, the database containing information about competing products was poorly structured and yielded information that was sometimes out-of-date or simply incorrect). The training director took one look at the report, said we were "out of scope," and told us to restrict our assessment to identifying issues with training solutions; end of conversation.

Success Factor 2

The duration of a needs assessment or performance improvement project has a non-linear relationship to its value. While more time can make it possible to add more value (as suggested in the layered approach), at some point consumption costs associated with this may outweigh the value being added. Since some projects are extremely time sensitive, with time overruns having dire consequences, the reduced return on investment can be extreme.

Success Factor 3

Organizational culture has a preeminent impact on performance, and must be considered when collecting and interpreting needs assessment data, and planning and implementing performance improvement interventions. As Elson Floyd, former president of the University of Missouri system, is famous for having said, "Culture eats strategy for lunch every day of the week."

Success Factor 4

The utility of the pyramid model is directly related to the fidelity of implementation. This begins with the *Basic Observation* implicit within the pyramid that in order to accomplish something of significance, vision, resources, and a support system must be in place, extends through the *Operational Principles* summarized in Table 3.2 and includes the best practices associated with any needs assessment and performance improvement project.

Success Factor 5

The systemic nature of analysis guided by the pyramid can uncover numerous social, political, economic, intercultural, and legal factors. Navigating these waters is treacherous at best and can quickly turn a well-intentioned effort to help into a quagmire.

Both the success indicators and success factors listed above are based on professionals' observations of the pyramid being used over a ten-year span. However, these observations are not based on empirical evidence derived from professional practice. For information about how success factors and success indicators can be empirically established, see the two articles by Klimczak and Wedman (1996, 1997) referenced at the end of this chapter.

Example of Successful Implementation

Context

In the late 1990s the leadership team from a regional provider of electrical power decided it was time to address the "leadership and communication" problems it felt were plaguing the operation of one of its power plants. Annually, this plant produced enough electricity to power more than 750,000 average households, and it was recognized as a national leader in both performance and safety. However, there were signs that the work environment was deteriorating. Labor and management were increasingly being bogged down in extended and sometimes heated meetings about such topics as parking space allocation, shoe policies in non-mechanical work areas, and drinking non-alcoholic beer with lunch. A three-person consulting team was hired to analyze the situation and make recommendations. The team consisted of a business communication and decision-making expert, a leadership expert, and a performance technologist.

Process

The consulting team conducted a series of one-on-one interviews with upper- and mid-level managers, technicians, and foremen. The interviews were based on the Performance Pyramid, using an interview protocol customized for the power plant. In addition, extant data consisting of policy manuals, after-action-review reports, and training manuals were reviewed. Observations were conducted in the control room, power generation area, management work area, training areas, and the lunch room. Particular attention was dedicated to work-flow, communication patterns, and decision making. The results were compiled, analyzed for trends, and potential problem spots identified.

Findings

Rewards, Recognition, Incentives. The majority of people working in the plant had been with the provider for over ten years. They were well-paid for their expertise, with salaries commensurate with industry averages and well above the average salary of all workers in the region. The technicians were unionized and were paid based on the labor/management contract.

Vision, Mission, and Objectives. Across the board, management and technicians shared the same vision for the plant: provide a consistent flow of electrical power in a safe and efficient manner.

Tools, Environment, and Processes. Work processes were highly refined and reviewed on a regular basis. The equipment was considered to be state-of-the-art, and routine maintenance was standard operating procedure. An elaborate system of sensors alerted technicians whenever variations (for example, the temperature of a power flow switch) were outside of acceptable ranges. When problems did arise, the on-duty team of technicians would analyze the problem, determine the appropriate course of action, and immediately implement the appropriate corrective measures.

While relatively rare, unfamiliar problems were resolved with the solution being documented for future reference should it occur again. One manager observed, "The plant is getting smarter, and problems are increasingly less likely to occur."

Knowledge and Skills. Training being provided included a mix of classroom lecture/ demos, typically focusing on technical content. In addition, a lifelike simulator control room with computer-generated problems was used to sharpen technicians' problem-solving skills. The "problems" typically challenged the technicians to respond as a team. While the training materials were inconsistent in terms of design, this was not identified as an impediment to individual or team performance.

Organizational Culture. In spite of the above indicators, there was widespread recognition that something was "not right at the plant." The first insight into the source of the problem came during one interview with a technician who said, "I wish we could work as well when things are going good as we do when things go bad." When asked to elaborate, the technician said, "It's like we have two companies. When we have a big problem, everyone works to solve it. But when we don't have a problem, we end up sniping at each other." Subsequent interviews confirmed the technician's observations. One technician went so far as to say, "I just hope our pettiness doesn't trip us up the next time we have an emergency."

*Significant Accomplishment*s. From a Performance Pyramid perspective, the initial diagnosis of a "leadership and communication" problem was symptomatic of the core problem—Organizational Culture—or, more accurately, two organizational cultures: a "routine culture" and an "emergency culture." Fortunately for the power plant customers, but unfortunately for the technicians, the plant operated at such a high level of efficiency that power production problems occurred with decreasing frequency. Whereas the emergency culture directly contributed to the power plant's accomplishment (a consistent flow of electrical power in a safe and efficient manner), the routine culture was a threat to the accomplishment.

Self-Concept. Technicians' self-concept exacerbated the problems associated with the routine culture. They would often spend extended time periods watching gauges that stayed in the safe range, viewing output reports that were no different from the previous day's reports and carrying out other routine tasks. As one technician lamented, "They hire us because we know how to deal with high-risk technical problems, pay us a lot of money, and then expect us to sit around and do pretty much nothing all day." Another said, "We are problem solvers; if we don't have problems to solve, we manufacture them." Parking space allocation, shoe requirements, and lunch beverage options appeared to be such manufactured problems. The technician went on to say that no one would ever intentionally endanger the plant, but he just didn't like going to work anymore because of "negativity." He concluded by offering, "We need to work together when things are working, so we can be sure we will work together when things aren't."

Organizational Culture. The consulting team recommended changes in how managers and technicians approached non-technical problems, such as that of parking space allocations. In the past, when such problems were identified, the normal course of action was for the technicians to report the problem to the shop steward, who would raise the issue with the plant managers. The managers would examine the problem in light of the union contract and render a decision. Often the response was "That's not covered by the agreement," and that would be the end of the discussion.

The consulting team recommended that the plant implement a cross-functional team approach to resolve non-technical problems. In addition, the team recommended the plant adopt agreed-on data-collecting and decision-making processes (for example, Delphi, multi-voting) that could be used as part of the overall problem-solving process. Recognizing that these strategies would require a cultural change, the consultants recommended that management capitalize on the general dissatisfaction with the routine culture and widespread support for the emergency culture. For example, since the emergency culture valued moving quickly, working in teams, relying on data, and documenting solutions, the non-technical problems should be approached in the same way. Finally, the consulting team recommended that a "change management" position be created, with full responsibility for facilitating non-technical problem-solving processes.

Short-Term Results

As would be expected, initial implementation was uneven. While some cross-function teams were successful in terms of resolving their assigned problem (a decision-making process for problem assignment was created and adopted), other teams met only once, likely falling victim to the routine culture. When the consulting team disengaged, the general sentiment from managers and technicians alike was the plant had no choice but to change, but that the change would not be easy.

FINAL REMARKS

The complete Performance Pyramid Model is provided in Figure 3.5. As in the simplified version used earlier, the complete pyramid model shows that resources (money, people) combine with vision, mission, and objectives to fuel and direct the elements of the support system (Knowledge and Skills, Expectations and Feedback). The support system elements play out in the context of the organizational culture.

In the complete model, "continuous monitoring" is added to ensure the factors and elements work in concert to produce the desired outcomes (significant accomplishments). Also, the complete model illustrates an additional relationship between significant accomplishments, resources, and vision, mission, and objectives. Ideally, accomplishments replenish resources, perhaps in the form of a net profit. Over time, these accomplishments enable the organization to extend or recast its vision, mission, and objectives.

Performance Pyramid

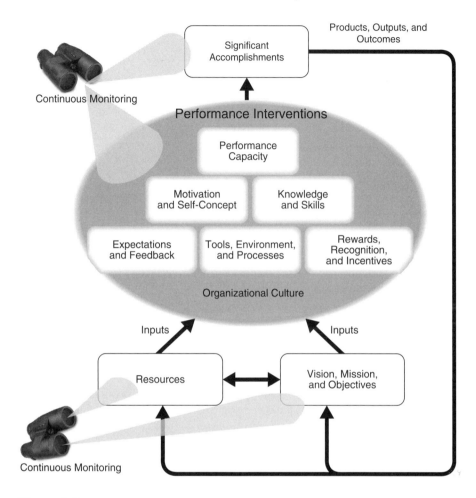

Figure 3.5 Complete Performance Pyramid.

References

Deterline, W. A. (1993, April). Looking for things to fix. *Performance and Instruction*, pp. 1–6.

Floyd, E. (2004). Keynote Address. Apple Digital Campus. University of Missouri, Columbia, MO.

Gilbert, T. F. (1978). Human Competence: Engineering Worthy Performance. New York: McGraw-Hill.

Kaplan, R. S., and Norton, D. P. (1996). *The Balanced Scorecard: Translating Strategy into Action*. Boston: Harvard Business School Press.

Klimczak, A. K., & Wedman, J. F. (1997). Instructional design project success factors: An empirical basis. *Educational Technology Research & Development, 45*(2), 75–83.

Klimczak, A. K., & Wedman, J. F. (1996). Instructional design project success indicators: An empirical basis. *Performance Improvement Quarterly, 9*(4), 5–18.

Mager, R. F., & Pipe, R. (1970). Analyzing performance problems (2nd ed.), Belmont, CA: Pitman Learning.

Marra, R. M., Howland, J., Jonassen, D. H., & Wedman, J. (2003). Validating the technology learning cycle: In the context of faculty adoption of integrated uses of technology in a teacher education curriculum. *International Journal of Learning Technology. 1*(1), 63–83.

Pershing, J. A. (2006). *Handbook of human performance technology* (3rd ed.). San Francisco: Pfeiffer.

Schaffer, S. P. (2000). A review of organizational and human performance frameworks. *Performance Improvement Quarterly, 13*(2), 220–243.

Schaffer, S., & Richardson, J. (2004). Supporting technology integration within a teacher education system. *Journal of Educational Computing Research, 31*(4), 423–435.

Swanson, R. A. (1994). *Analysis for improving performance: Tools for diagnosing organizations and documenting workplace expertise.* San Francisco: Berrett-Koehler.

Tessmer, M., & Wedman, J. F. (1992). Decision-making factors and principles for selecting a layer of instructional development activities. *Performance & Instruction, 31*(4), 1–6.

Vanguard Consulting, Inc. (1996). *Organizational Scan: A performance analysis model.* Unpublished manuscript.

Wedman, J. F., & Diggs, L. (2001). Identifying barriers to technology-enhanced learning environments in teacher education. *Computers in Human Behavior 17*: 421–430.

Wedman, J. F., & Graham, S. W. (1998). Introducing the concept of performance support using the performance pyramid. *Journal of Continuing Higher Education, 46*(3), 8–20.

Wedman, J. F., & Tessmer, M. (1993). Instructional designers' decisions and priorities: A survey of design practice. *Performance Improvement Quarterly, 6*(2), 43–57.

Watkins, R., & Wedman, J. (2003). Assessing, analyzing, and answering: A process for aligning performance improvement resources and strategies. *Performance Improvement, 42*(7), 9–17.

 # EDITORIAL CONNECTIONS

The Performance Pyramid, both as an organizational framework for the chapters of this handbook and as a holistic performance improvement model, illustrates the close relationships among the many building blocks in the successful accomplishment of results. Chapter Three offers a useful guide for how the models, frameworks, taxonomies of Chapter One—as well as their underlying scientific theories and research findings described in Chapter Two—can be used to make the challenging decisions of which performance interventions are best going to accomplish valuable results.

As a framework for this handbook, you can see how the Performance Pyramid model both utilizes and integrates the many performance interventions that are described in the following parts of the book. From needs assessment and data collection to future searches and electronic performance support systems, the model uses each of these as interventions that can, together, accomplish significant results: societal outcomes, organizational outputs, and individual or team products.

Models, frameworks, and taxonomies alone, however, are not enough to make the challenging decisions about what do in order to improve human and organizational performance. There are no formulas for determining which interventions will achieve desired results within your organization. The Performance Pyramid is no exception; it does not tell you which interventions to use for improving performance. Nor does it define which combinations of interventions work best within the context of your organization. It does provide a map for analyzing where performance systems within your organization may be failing, determining what options are available to you, and ensuring that all elements of your improvement system are contributing to the accomplishment of significant results.

While the first challenge is frequently to recognize and assess the many performance intervention options that are available for addressing performance challenges, the next challenge is to make useful decisions about which interventions to implement and how to ensure their successful application. As no one-size-fits-all solution exists, you will have to apply practical decision-making tools (such as nominal group technique, multi-attribute utility analysis, and card sorts) to guide your decision making or facilitate the decision making of others. Use these, and other, decision-making tools and techniques to guide your efforts.

Many tools and techniques can be used to determine which performance interventions are the "right" choice to improve performance within your context. The following pages include a sample of decision-making tools and techniques that you should consider to guide your decisions or facilitate the decision making of a group. These include some of the most commonly applied tools, starting with group decision-making techniques and ending with a few of the more quantitative techniques that can guide your decisions.

NOMINAL GROUP TECHNIQUE (NGT)

In response to an open-ended question, participants individually brainstorm and prioritize their own ideas before sharing them with others in the group in a round-robin format during which each participant offers ideas or opinions. After discussion the group members anonymously vote on the prioritization of the ideas listed by the group members.

Use the NGT when you are working with medium to large groups of partners in making decisions about how to improve performance. The round-robin format offers all partners the opportunity to give input to the decision, but the technique effectively moves the group toward specific decisions.

DELPHI TECHNIQUE

This technique helps groups to reach consensus by asking a small group of experts on the topic to give their input through a survey. Results of the survey are then tabulated and re-circulated to the experts for additional input and prioritization. Several rounds of surveys may be required in order to reach consensus among the experts on the prioritized topics that should be addressed in the focus group or community meeting.

The Delphi technique offers an excellent decision-making process for large groups. Using technologies such as e-mail and online surveys, the technique is especially useful for facilitating group decisions when partners are in many different locations. By utilizing multiple rounds of surveys, the Delphi process attains input from all partners and systematically moves the group toward a decision.

SWOT ANALYSIS

Focusing on the *s*trengths, *w*eaknesses, *o*pportunities, and *t*hreats (SWOTs) related to a performance problem or opportunity can guide the discussion of a focus group. Further, SWOTs can then be assessed for the relative amount of control that exists over each factor as well as the net value they add or subtract from performance. See Chapter Five for more details.

A SWOT analysis can be used for individual or group decisions by examining the context in which the results of the decision will be implemented. When selecting performance interventions, each of the SWOT factors can play a significant role in the successful achievement of desired results. Use a SWOT analysis to better understand the context of the decisions.

TABLETOP ANALYSIS

Tabletop analyses are used in a wide variety of settings to identify performance gaps and select interventions to improve performance. Tabletop analyses are discussion-based activities that you can facilitate with your decision-making partners. Using a systematic and collaborative problem solving approach, the tabletop analysis examines the performance problem and context to identify a detailed, sequential list of tasks to be performed in improving performance.

Use a tabletop analysis when working with a small group of experts on the performance challenges and the organizational context. Ideally, the same experts will participate throughout the analysis to ensure consistency and consensus building.

CARD SORTS

Card sorts is a technique that can be used to get input for defining and rank ordering desired results or for rank ordering optional performance interventions. Typically, a card sort begins with listing fifteen to thirty items on 3-by-5 index cards with a number or code written on the reverse side. After shuffling the cards, individuals or teams can then rank order, sort by category, or generate categories for the cards. Participants may also be instructed to use blank index cards to note any item they feel was erroneously not included in the stack.

Use a card sort when there are multiple options to select among, be they results to be accomplished or potential interventions for improving performance. Card sorts can be done with individuals or teams and are quite effective for making performance-based decisions.

MULTI-ATTRIBUTE UTILITY ANALYSIS (MAUA)

This analysis-based technique, borrowed from engineers making decisions about materials selection, provides a systematic process of assigning and weighing quantitative (or numeric) values to a variety of potential performance improvement programs and projects. As such, it supports your development of a justifiable process for determining what actions should be taken. MAUA is a worthwhile tool for comparing potential improvement activities, which can be particularly beneficial in organizations that especially value quantitative and systematic comparisons of alternatives (such as financial, manufacturing, aviation, construction, etc.). To complete a MAUA analysis, start by identifying the key attributes necessary to improve performance and then work with partners to weight to each of those attributes, since some will be more critical to success than others. After identifying the attributes and their respective weights, score each potential performance intervention on their ability to meet the required attributes of each successful solution in order to determine a ranking of your options (see Table 3.8).

Table 3.8 MAUA Example

	Attribute 1 Weight .15	Attribute 2 Weight .20	Attribute 3 Weight .15	Attribute 4 Weight .20	Attribute 5 Weight .30	Utility Score Sum of Weighted Ratings
Alternative 1	Rating = 7 $7 \times .15 = 1.05$	Rating = 7 $7 \times .2 = 1.4$	Rating = 4 $4 \times .15 = .6$	Rating = 5 $5 \times .2 = 1$	Rating = 8 $8 \times .3 = 2.4$	6.45
Alternative 2	Rating = 9 $9 \times .15 = 1.35$	Rating = 5 $5 \times .2 = 1$	Rating = 5 $5 \times .15 = .75$	Rating = 4 $4 \times .2 = .8$	Rating = 9 $9 \times .3 = 2.7$	6.6
Alternative 3	Rating = 4 $4 \times .15 = .6$	Rating = 3 $3 \times .2 = .6$	Rating = 6 $6 \times .15 = .9$	Rating = 2 $2 \times .2 = .4$	Rating = 9 $9 \times .3 = 2.7$	5.2
Alternative 4	Rating = 6 $6 \times .15 = .9$	Rating = 9 $9 \times .2 = 1.8$	Rating = 9 $9 \times .15 = 1.35$	Rating = 7 $7 \times .2 = 1.4$	Rating = 5 $5 \times .3 = 1.5$	6.95

Use MAUA when you have identified multiple performance interventions that can be used to improve performance. MAUA provides a systematic tool for identifying key attributes of performance interventions and then weighing your options based on those attributes. You can use the simple multi-attribute ranking technique (SMART) as a less intensive tool for applying the principles of MAUA.

Use a variety of decision-making tools and techniques to determine which interventions will best improve individual and organizational performance. Since no single intervention will improve all performance problems, nor will sustainable improvements in performance usually result from just one improvement activity, you will want to use multiple decision-making tools to prioritize your options and justify your decisions. For example, you may want to use a card sort to work with partners to reduce the number of interventions to be considered when addressing the performance issue. Then a MAUA analysis can be done to systematically compare the multiple interventions options you have for improving performance.

ELECTRONIC SUPPORT SYSTEMS FOR HPT

In addition to the tools introduced above, several online and software-based systems can assist you in improving performance. Some of these systems provide guidelines for identifying performance problems, while others help you in managing the implementation of performance interventions. Table 3.9 provides a sample listing of online and software-based support systems that may be of value to your next performance improvement initiative.

Table 3.9 Examples of Electronic Support Systems for HPT.

Software	Website
Proofpoint	www.proofpoint.net/
Advisor PI	www.professional-learning.com/advisor.htm
BNH Advent	www.bnhexpertsoft.com/english/products/advent/overview.htm
TapRoot	www.taproot.com/software.php
List of root cause analysis software	www.rootcauselive.com/Library/Software.htm

EDITORS'
DISCUSSION

Sustainable improvement of individual and organizational performance is best built on a foundation of useful models and frameworks that are derived from scientific theory and research, as well as practical experience. There is no single "right" model or process for improving performance and achieving desired results in every organization; nor does any framework or taxonomy work in all situations within the same organization. As a consequence, it is the essential task of professionals to be prepared with a variety of approaches that can be applied, as appropriate, when performance challenges are identified. Use the models presented in Chapter One as a starting place for expanding the foundations of your approach to improving performance.

The improvement of performance is an interdisciplinary field that draws on the scientific theories and research of many fields. Accordingly, it is the responsibility of performance improvement professionals to use these as foundations of their decisions. You should use scientific theory and research to justify your decisions, whether it be from the work of von Bertalanffy, Kaufman, Gagné, Skinner, Mager, and others discussed in Chapter Two. Whether your decisions concern how to resolve performance problems or the implementation strategies to be applied when performance interventions are selected, the application of scientific findings to support your decisions will distinguish your improvement efforts and better ensure the accomplishment of useful results.

While numerous performance interventions are available for any performance challenge, the Performance Pyramid offers a particularly useful model for illustrating the relationships among your options. In addition to being an organizational structure for this handbook, the Performance Pyramid also offers a comprehensive improvement model that is presented in Chapter Three. The Performance Pyramid model can be used to analyze and understand the important relationships that lead to sustainable improvements in performance. At the same time, we advise that you avoid focusing exclusively on just one or two components of the model (for example, incentives, feedback, motivation, or knowledge/skill development). The value of a systemic approach to performance is lost if all elements of the system are recognized and addressed appropriately.

Last, with so many performance interventions to choose from, it is important to apply valuable decision-making tools and techniques to determine the "right" choices for your situation. Many tools and techniques are available that you can use to collect information and facilitate quality decision making. From the nominal group technique to group interviews, and multi-attribute utility analysis to straw votes, use a variety of techniques to ensure that your decisions about which performance interventions to implement are well informed.

As the remaining chapters of this handbook will illustrate, there are an abundance of performance interventions that should be considered when making decisions about how to improve individual and organizational performance. Making these decisions, therefore, requires a systematic and comprehensive analysis of your options. Use the contents of this handbook to identify your options, their characteristics, and their strengths and weaknesses; then apply useful decision-making tools and techniques in order to determine which combination of interventions will best accomplish the desired results.

References and Resources from Editorial Contributions to Part One

Haig, C., & Addison, R. (2008). TrendSpotters: RSVP+. Retrieved January 10, 2009, at http://www.performancexpress.org/0710/.

Kaufman, R. (2006). *30 seconds that can change your life: A decision-making guide for those who refuse to be mediocre.* Amherst, MA: HRD Press.

Kaufman, R. (2006). *Change, choices, and consequences: A guide to mega thinking and planning.* Amherst, MA: HRD Press.

Kaufman, R., Oakley-Brown, H., Watkins, R., & Leigh, D. (2003). *Strategic planning for success: Aligning people, performance, and payoffs.* San Francisco: Jossey-Bass.

Swanson, R. A. (1999). The foundations of performance improvement and implications for practice. In R. Torraco (Ed.), *Performance improvement theory and practice* (pp. 1–25). San Francisco: Berrett-Koehler.

Tosti, D. (2008). It is time to dump the behavioral engineering model and most other taxonomies. Retrieved January 10, 2009, at http://www.performancexpress.org/0710/.

von Bertalanffy, L. (1968). *General system theory: Foundations, development, applications.* New York: George Brazillier.

Watkins, R. (2007). *Performance by design: The systematic selection, design, and development of performance technologies that produce useful results.* Amherst, MA: HRD Press.

Watkins, R., & Wedman, J. (2003). A process for aligning performance improvement resources and strategies. *Performance Improvement Journal, 42*(7), 9–17.

Wedman, J., & Graham, S. W. (1998, Fall). The performance pyramid. *The Journal of Continuing Higher Education 46*(3), 8–20.

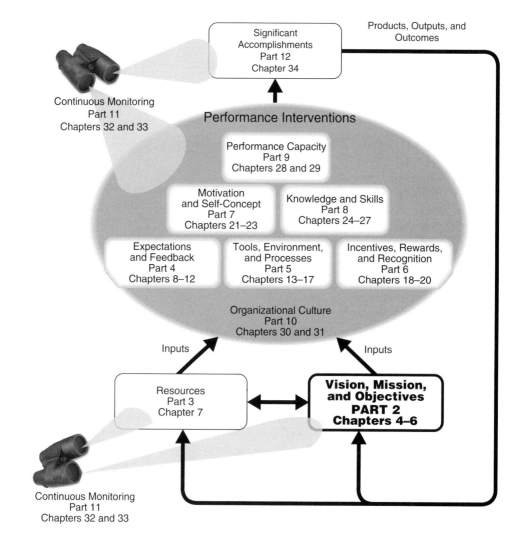

Significant
Accomplishments
Part 12
Chapter 34

Products, Outputs, and
Outcomes

Continuous Monitoring
Part 11
Chapters 32 and 33

Performance Interventions

Performance Capacity
Part 9
Chapters 28 and 29

Motivation
and Self-Concept
Part 7
Chapters 21–23

Knowledge and Skills
Part 8
Chapters 24–27

Expectations
and Feedback
Part 4
Chapters 8–12

Tools, Environment,
and Processes
Part 5
Chapters 13–17

Incentives, Rewards,
and Recognition
Part 6
Chapters 18–20

Organizational Culture
Part 10
Chapters 30 and 31

Inputs

Inputs

Resources
Part 3
Chapter 7

Vision, Mission,
and Objectives
PART 2
Chapters 4–6

Continuous Monitoring
Part 11
Chapters 32 and 33

PART TWO

VISION, MISSION, AND OBJECTIVES

From company slogans to specific performance targets, objectives take on many different forms within organizations. Many are stated overtly on posters, signs, or annual reports, while others represent the private ambitions of individuals, teams, and organizations. Yet, in all of their many forms, objectives play an essential role in the achievement of performance and the accomplishment of results.

Simply put, objectives define the desired future and provide a sense of direction in what could otherwise be unguided efforts, challenging us to stretch beyond the status-quo, giving us hope for the future. Within organizations, the development of objectives routinely takes form within annual reports, providing information on last year's performance and then offering performance objectives for the future. Similarly, at the individual employee level, training plans provide objectives and guidance to what could otherwise be a mish-mash of fragmented professional development experiences. Likewise, performance targets for sales teams frequently put forth objectives that challenge individuals to do just a little better this month than they did the month before. Objectives keep us moving ahead, looking to accomplish desired results.

Objectives do, nevertheless, require guidance. Organizational objectives must, for example, be informed by—and aligned with—the objectives of customers, clients, partners, and the broader society in which they operate; ensuring that the results of the organization contribute to the achievements of others. In the same way, guidance from organizational ambitions is essential to the objectives of individual employees, teams, divisions, or units within the organization. Alignment of objectives is therefore a fundamental characteristic of systemic performance improvement and is most clearly illustrated through the application of Kaufman's Organizational Elements Model (see the Introduction to the handbook for more information).

Expanding Your Options

Strategic planning—involves determining the direction an organization should take in the immediate future (during the following year or more) and deciding how to allocate its resources (both capital and people) appropriately to pursue its strategy. The process is usually organization-wide, or focused on a major function such as a division, department, or other major function.

Based on wikipedia.org and managementhelp.org/ definitions (January 2009)

Alignment does not, however, imply that objectives should be dictated or used as a tool for managerial control. Objectives do not come in just one color or shape, nor do they have to be derived through a top-down management approach. They can be strategic, operational, or tactical or they can be long-term or short-term, shared or private, written or verbal, pragmatic or idealistic, grass-roots or top-down. Objectives can present a vision of the organization in ten years, or they can represent that daily performance targets that are posted on a call-center's whiteboard.

As a consequence of this variety, objectives are everywhere within organizations, which often means that they are also nowhere at the same time. After all, it is easy to forget about our objectives when making numerous decisions throughout the day. We often get so busy trying to improve performance through various activities and interventions that we forget what results we are trying to accomplish . . . and why.

To improve results in measurable and long-lasting ways, it is therefore important to focus on the alignment of objectives, that is, to know and understand the objectives of your organization, as well as those of all the partners who are going to help you achieve those objectives. From the objectives of your suppliers and clients to those of individual team members and those of your organization, aligning your decisions with performance objectives allows you to link together the long-term ambitions and short-term targets. Relating strategic objectives (such as increasing market share or reducing environmental waste) with tactical ones (such as quarterly sales targets or project deadlines) can connect the objectives of the organization, its partners, and the individuals who will achieve immediate results. In many cases, this alignment between objectives turns out to be more critical to successful performance improvement than the content of the objectives themselves.

Too often, efforts to improve performance focus too narrowly on a single performance objective (for instance, increasing productivity in the manufacturing unit) without taking a broader look at the many interdependent systems (such as marketing, sales, clients, supply chains, and so forth) that will be impacted by any changes resulting from the improvement effort. Including the objectives of suppliers, subcontractors, staff, clients, and community groups when making decisions about how to improve performance helps develop broad-based support for your decisions.

Suboptimization—when improvement in one area of an organization leads to declining performance in other areas—is always a threat when you are attempting to improve individual and organizational performance. It is often tempting to focus attention solely on the performance problem within one unit of an organization without recognizing its relationships with other systems that the organization relies on, such as suppliers, internal clients, or external clients. To avoid this problem, use a systemic approach to performance improvement to reduce the odds of suboptimization.

Expanding Your Options

Scenario planning—with its roots in military intelligence, scenario planning is a strategic planning method. It is used to make flexible, long-term plans within organizations in the presence of uncertainty. A scenario in this context is an account of a plausible future. Scenario planning consists of using a few contrasting scenarios to explore the uncertainty surrounding the future consequences of a decision.

Based on www.wikipedia.org entry (January 2009)

Systemic processes, as opposed to systematic processes, take into account the many systems that make up today's complex organizations. Many of the systems operate as departments within organizations, including human resources, marketing, finance, and so forth. Other systems are informal and not found on organizational diagrams. These systems are the relationships that are built among the people who work together. For example, you may have figured out over time how to tap into the informal system of administrative staff members who process travel reimbursements. By accessing this informal system, making a few phone calls, and asking for a few favors, you can frequently get your travel reimbursement more quickly than if you stayed within the formal procedures.

Systemic performance improvement examines both the formal and informal systems within the organization to assess the relationships between the systems and the performance at the focus of the improvement effort. As a consequence, systemic improvements require the participation of many individuals and groups both within and outside the organization. For instance, if you want to improve customer service performance, all of the systems that interact with customer service should be examined: those of clients, technical support, human resources, billing, and others.

Roger Kaufman's Organizational Elements Model (OEM) provides a framework for relating and aligning all that an organization uses, does, produces, and delivers with the societal outcomes of those efforts. The model also offers a useful way to link together the strategic, tactical, and operational objectives of the many partners who have a stake in the achievement of desired results. When improving performance, refer back to the five levels of the OEM (outcomes, outputs, products, processes, and inputs) as a taxonomy for relating the numerous performance interventions that can be used to create strategic alignment.

WHAT'S COMING UP

You may, for example, want to use the Future Search technique described in Chapter Four with a large group of partners in the improvement effort to ensure that everyone is in agreement on the strategic results (or outcomes) to be accomplished. In addition, examining workforce planning and forecasting documents—often available through the human resource department—can provide information at the operational (or inputs) level that is essential to making well-informed decisions related to the impact of future trends and the results to be achieved within the organization. All of these, as well as other performance interventions for establishing strategic alignment, create the foundation for improving performance by linking and aligning the resources to be used, the processes to be applied, and the results to be accomplished (see the figure at the beginning of this introduction).

As a foundation for systemic performance improvement, Part Two of this handbook focuses on the alignment of strategic, tactical, and operational objectives within all of the related systems. This ensures that any and all performance improvement activities contribute to the accomplishment of valuable results for all partners and that suboptimization is avoided.

Lacking the ability to reliably predict the future, performance improvement projects rely on proactive techniques for defining desired results and then applying appropriate performance interventions to the accomplishment of those objectives. The chapters in Part Two of this handbook focus on performance interventions that you can use to identify, create, and align the objectives of your organization and its partners in order to guide the many decisions you will have to make in order to improve performance. Separately, together, and with a variety of other performance interventions, the material in these chapters can help you build a solid foundation that will guide in the selection and implementation of other performance interventions.

Future Search, as a starting place, is a practical and proven method for establishing a shared vision of the results to be achieved through improvement activities. A principles-based approach, Future Search provides multiple and diverse stakeholder groups with opportunities to shape the strategic alignment of an organization, division, unit, or improvement project. Building on the initial work of Fred Emery, Future Searches are task-focused activities that allow participants to collaboratively define objectives—stretching beyond the limitations of most other strategic planning exercises. In Chapter Four, Marvin Weisbord and Sandra Janoff examine Future Search as a performance intervention for building strategic alignment.

CHAPTER FOUR

Future Search

Marvin Weisbord
Sandra Janoff

INTRODUCTION

Future Search is a principle-based planning method that has been tested and refined since 1982. It has been employed with social, technological, and economic issues in North and South America, Africa, Australia, Europe, India, and South Asia. Participants find they can go beyond problem solving to make systemic improvements in their communities and organizations in a relatively short time, even when there is conflict and uncertainty. Large diverse groups can achieve four simultaneous outputs from a single meeting: shared values, a plan for the future, concrete goals, and committed implementation.

Future search relies on well-researched principles for helping people collaborate despite differences of culture, class, gender, age, race, ethnicity, language, and education. So long as the principles are honored, the method works equally well with business firms, communities, schools, hospitals, churches, government agencies, foundations and NGO's. Because future search is not tied to any one culture, requiring only that participants share their experiences, it has helped thousands of people carry out action plans they once considered impossible.

Weisbord described the context for the emergence of future search in his 1987 book *Productive Workplaces*. Tracing the evolution of modern managing and consulting back one hundred years to Frederick Taylor's principles of scientific management, Weisbord imagined two axes moving through time, one related to *who* did the coordinating and controlling, and *what* it was they actually did. He showed the way in which *who* evolved from experts doing the work toward including everybody concerned with a system. The *what* evolved from problem solving toward whole systems improving, making the whole better through dynamic shifts in peoples' capacity for cooperating and innovating.

Thus, the "learning curve" (see Figure 4.1) started in the 19th century with expert problem solving, evolved with the discovery of group dynamics into participative problem solving, then added expert systems analysis based on general systems theory in the mid-20th century. Finally, as a new millennium approached, people were learning to "get everybody improving whole systems." The evolution was cumulative, each milestone adding new potential without diminishing the strengths of earlier processes. *Productive Workplaces* set out an ambitious strategic goal: finding methods equal to the values implicit in getting everyone in an organization or a community understanding and taking responsibility for the whole. Future search was one way to do that.

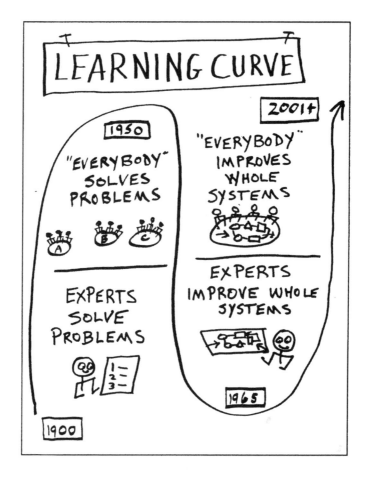

Figure 4.1 The Learning Curve.

Source: Productive Workplaces Revisited, Copyright 2004 by Marvin Weisbord, used by permission.

DESCRIPTION

We now think of future search in three related ways:

First, future search describes a *principle-based action meeting.* Indeed, the underlying principles, which can be used to design other kinds of meetings, matter more than the techniques. These principles are supported by research that we will document below. A future search usually involves sixty to eighty people or more, many of whom have never met. The typical length is four to five sessions of half a day each, spread across three days to allow for "soak time." The phases—Past, Present, Future, Common Ground, Action Planning—are simple and designed to accommodate all learning styles. People work both in functional groups ("stakeholders") and in mixed groups (a cross-section of the whole), with each person having a chance to speak and listen. The meeting is managed so that the entire group can be in dialogue at each stage. Within a few hours each person experiences the whole of the organization or community in ways that none ever has before. The key techniques are time lines re-creating the past, a "mind map" of present trends affecting everyone, the dramatization of preferred future scenarios, the confirming of common ground (those propositions agreed on by all), and action commitments based on the common ground.

Second, future search facilitators employ a specific *philosophy of facilitation,* a hands-off approach that enables people to take responsibility for themselves. This philosophy holds that all participants are doing the best they can with what they have. A meeting manager's job is to create conditions whereby people can work together despite their differences, concerns, prior experience, training, and personal quirks. Those who adopt this orientation invite people to work from their own experience and to decide for themselves what they will say and do. Participants need no special knowledge, "inputs," or prior training to succeed. The meeting manager's objective is to accept people as they are, not as he or she might wish them to be. Those who practice this philosophy do not prompt, correct, or reinterpret people. They work with whatever people bring into the room. Rather than try to change people, they seek to alter the conditions under which people interact.

Expanding Your Options

Critical thinking—the act of processing information by analyzing the structural components of a problem with the goal of reaching an optimal solution.

In that sense, future search is based on structural rather than behavioral principles. People discover opportunities for dialogue and action that they never had before; thus they often make constructive new choices without being told they should.

Finally, future search constitutes a *global change strategy*. What makes it so are three related phenomena:

1. Most of the world's work is carried out one meeting at a time. Most people say they hate meetings and spend too much time in them.

2. Future search, by contrast, provides a meeting structure, process, and positive outcomes that have been replicated by thousands of people in many of the world's cultures.

3. Those who internalize the future search principles can make constructive ripples in society without having to occupy seats of power or undergo years of study. To practice future search is to cut down the cynicism and frustration by seeking to change the world one meeting at a time. Typically, people do in a few days what once took months or could not be done at all. They nearly always form new coalitions and build relationships that often persist for years. They often develop a shared perspective on their own systems that no one person had prior to the meeting. They usually devise attractive future scenarios. In many instances they achieve dramatic results.

The method is especially useful in uncertain, fast-changing situations. It can be used to (1) start a new program or project, getting everyone aligned before action is undertaken; (2) implement an existing vision or action plan stalled for lack of understanding and/or commitment; (3) redirect a strategy beset by conflicts or paralyzed by indecision; (4) help a good organization become even better; (5) as an ongoing strategy to course correct as markets, technologies, and political cross-currents change. Several case examples are presented below.

WHAT WE KNOW FROM RESEARCH

The future search methodology was derived from a synthesis of research and theory going back to the late 1930's under the aegis of social psychologist Kurt Lewin. The principles can be summarized as follows:

First principle. Get the "whole system" in the room (defined by us as stakeholders who collectively have among them *authority to act, resources, expertise, information*, and *need*).

Second principle. Explore the whole system before seeking to fix any part of it (also framed as "think globally, act locally").

Third principle. Focus on the common ground and desired future, treating problems and conflicts as information, not action items.

Fourth principle. Have people self-manage their own small groups and take responsibility for action.

How we came to these principles is documented at length by us in the book *Future Search* and by Weisbord in *Productive Workplaces Revisited.* The seeds were planted in 1938–1939 by Kurt Lewin with graduate students Ronald Lippitt and Ralph White at the State University of Iowa. Working with local boys' clubs, they demonstrated the superiority of democratic over autocratic and laissez faire leadership behavior. They coined the term "group dynamics" to describe the effect of leader behavior on group satisfaction and performance. This opened the door to a "leadership style" industry that continues to this day.

Lippitt went on to develop sophisticated techniques for group problem solving. In the 1950s, using audiotapes collected with the help of MIT professor Douglas McGregor (author of *The Human Side of Enterprise*), Lippitt concluded that group problem solving depresses people. To stimulate positive energy, he devised methods to elicit "images of potential." Instead of asking what was wrong and how to fix it, Lippitt asked what people saw as the potential for action and who was willing to act. His insights became the precursor of preferred futuring, visioning, and appreciative methods of inquiry that became widely adopted decades later.

In the 1970s Lippitt and Eva Schindler-Rainman, a community development consultant, ran eighty-eight large workshops, the results of which they documented in *Building the Collaborative Community.* These events had two unique features. First, they involved a cross-section of the entire community, as many as three hundred people each time. Second, they focused on the future, rather than present problems. They discovered that having "everybody" involved in planning his or her own future led to many innovative, long-lasting programs. From the Lewin/Lippitt/Schindler-Rainman work we derived the principle supporting future focus and common ground as superior frameworks for system-wide action compared to conflict managing and problem solving. We also got from them the principle that a "whole system" in which face-to-face dialogue greatly increases everyone's potential for committed action.

Two other principles date back to the early days of World War II. The social scientist Eric Trist, another exponent of Lewin's work, teamed up with psychiatrist Wilfred Bion to create an innovative selection process for British Army field officers. They placed candidates in small leaderless groups and posed field problems requiring skill in balancing self-interest and group interest. They demonstrated the power of self-managed groups when people had a clear task requiring cooperation. Their finding was reinforced when in the late 1940s Trist's student, Kenneth Bamforth, visited a coal mine where he had once worked. He saw teams of multi-skilled miners working underground in self-supervised teams. By every measure, they were more productive than those in old fragmented systems where miners were closely supervised and specialized only in one job. This validated the potential of broad, general knowledge and self-management.

In the 1950s Trist partnered with the Australian social scientist Fred Emery to apply the lessons learned in coal mines to business strategy planning. In a historic conference with the newly formed Bristol-Siddeley aircraft engine company, they learned that having executives experience their work in relation to global and industry trends before making local plans reduced potential conflict, led to high commitment, and indeed resulted in a new, more efficient aircraft engine. They called their new meeting method a "Search Conference." They drew heavily on "conditions for dialogue" from the research of social psychologist Solomon Asch. He showed that, when people talk about a world that includes all their realities, they are more likely to accept each other and make more inclusive action plans. The Emery/Trist stream of research, theory, and practice led us to two additional principles: having people talk about the same world—one that includes all their perceptions—and having them self-manage their own small groups and take responsibility for action.

Thus the name "Future Search" honors these pioneers, "future" referring to the Lippitt and Schindler-Rainman collaborative futures conferences, "search" to the pioneering efforts of Emery and Trist. These stories are retold in greater detail in *Productive Workplaces Revisited* and *Discovering Common Ground.*

Applications Research

There is a great deal of anecdotal and case study evidence on the uses of future search since 1982. There also have been several formal studies. As a result, the conditions for success and failure are widely known. As no two groups, contexts, or situations are ever the same, however, studies comparing future search with other methods would neither be valid nor reliable. We cannot speculate on what would have happened had a given system used any of the more than sixty other large group methods described in Holman, Devane, and Cady's *Change Handbook.* We only know what has actually happened in hundreds of future searches around the world.

In Southern Sudan, for example, a future search led to the demobilization of more than 2,500 child soldiers and the construction of new schools and hospitals. In Milwaukee, Wisconsin, a series of future searches led to unprecedented cooperation among healthcare professionals, community leaders, and inner city families to reduce infant mortality. In Berrien County, Michigan, nine future searches sponsored by Whirlpool Foundation established a new spirit of inter-racial cooperation among citizens, leading to economic development in Benton Harbor and cooperative citizens organizations for youth, the arts, and civic engagement.

Whole Foods Markets, the world's largest natural foods supermarket chain, has used future searches every five years since 1988 to involve a cross-section of employees in strategic planning. Haworth Corporation, the global furniture manufacturer, compressed months of strategic planning into less than three days, including in the meeting both customers and suppliers, a feat that, according to chairman Richard Haworth, few imagined could be done. IKEA, the global furniture retailer based in Sweden, used future search to rethink its world-wide supply chain, resulting in a restructuring of corporate staff functions, involvement of customers in new product design, and reduction by several months of the time from drawing board to point of sale.

There have been disappointments too, notably with non-interdependent groups and in meetings with fuzzy goals and weak leadership. At the same time, many people report breakthroughs in planning they did not believe were possible. As a result of uses in many cultures, a great deal more was known by 2008 about optimizing the probability for success than when Future Search Network, our vehicle for community service and collaborative learning on effective practices, began in 1993.

Future Search Literature: A Synopsis

Weisbord's first article on future search appeared in *Planning Review* in 1984. This was followed by a chapter in the 1987 edition of *Productive Workplaces* that stimulated many practitioners to take up the method. Their many successes led in 1992 to *Discovering Common Ground,* which brought together work by thirty-five co-authors from around the world, highlighting effective practices and outlining conditions for success. We published *Future Search: An Action Guide* in 1995 and updated both the design and case studies in a second edition in 2000.

We started future search training workshops in 1991 and by 2008 had trained more than 3,500 people on five continents. Many others have now replicated the model, experimented with variations, improved the design, and validated the principles. Future Search Network (FSN) was founded in 1993 as a voluntary collaborative dedicated to service to society and shared learning. Its members have published thirty-four issues of the newsletter *FutureSearching* (formerly *SearchNEWS*), edited since 1997 by Larry Porter, a veteran OD consultant, trainer, and editor. This publication includes dozens of articles from around the world on future searches in business, community, government, education, the arts, and so on. Members discuss what they did, what they learned, and the impact they are having on society. All issues can be accessed in a searchable archive at www.futuresearch.net. In addition, scores of articles, book chapters, and case studies had been published. Some key ones are listed in the bibliography at the end of this chapter.

In 2005, Network members Rita Schweitz, Kim Martens, and Nancy Aronson edited a book of sixteen future search case studies from school districts in the United States and Canada documenting the positive impact on educational practices. Authors include not just consultants but school administrators, board members, and teachers. The cases deal with such diverse issues as district mergers, healing racial divisions, curriculum reform, school/community partnerships, and district-wide strategic plans. The book includes districts in big cities, small towns, and rural areas. It describes pitfalls, dilemmas, and the range of issues—social, political, economic, demographic, and philosophical—that make planning meetings in schools a challenge. Both notable successes and unmet aspirations add useful information to the dialogue about when, where, and how to use a future search.

Thesis Research

Of the many master's and doctoral theses written on Future Search, we have looked at findings from ten doctoral dissertations. Seven were based on a single conference, one (by Oels) on two, one (by Jimenez-Guzman) on three, and one (by Granata) on a nine-conference comparative study. Of these twenty conferences, fourteen followed the Future Search Model similar to our 1995 book, and six were based on the Search Conference Model, from which future search was partly derived.

The conferences studied by Secor, McDonald, Starodub, Jimenez-Guzman, Pickus, Concepcion, Pagano, and Granata (with one exception) met their goals. Those studied by Oels and Polyani fell short. The latter researchers attributed failures in large part to the meeting design. It should be noted that successful cases were based on similar designs. This suggests that other factors noted by the researchers, such as clarity of goals, matching participants to the task, and facilitator flexibility in working with large groups might play a role. In one of the conferences Oels studied, for example, she noted at the outset that the community fell short of having the right people for their purposes. Thus, the researcher was stuck with analyzing a meeting where failure could be predicted from the start. She also noted one facilitator's rigidity in pushing ahead with the agenda despite participants' wanting more time. This behavior might better be attributed to the meeting leader's inexperience than to flaws in the design.

Elaine Granata's dissertation uniquely was based on a comparative study of multiple conferences rather than single examples. Thus, her thesis offers useful insights for success that can be generalized. Granata investigated nine conferences, six in the Future Search and three in the Search Conference mode (on which future search is partly based). From these she developed a systematic model of effectiveness. Indeed, Granata's findings help illuminate the "design flaws" noted by some researchers in individual cases. For example, she noted these predictable outcomes when the core principles and design requirements were observed:

- The meeting sponsor's objectives were met.
- People exhibited high affect and energy that continued after the conference.
- Common ground became the impetus for change.
- People engaged in dialogue that led to mutual understanding.

Nearly always new networks formed, although these did not necessarily lead to action planning (a finding supported by Oels). For her part, Granata identified two criteria central to an effective conference, without which success is unlikely:

- Getting the right people ("whole system") in the room and
- Agreeing to work only on issues for which there is common ground.

Most importantly, in conferences judged "highly effective," people reported their desired future was being realized long after the conference ended.

Granata found no evidence to support or refute a belief held by many consultants that a democratic conference structure empowers participants who have little power to begin with. A single conference cannot be expected to change power, status, hierarchy, and other structural arrangements. However, we should point out that Future Search has been used to decentralize and redistribute power within an organization when restructuring was the meeting's stated goal, as in the IKEA case we facilitated and reported on. Granata also found that credible conference sponsors who believe in collaboration were more likely to stimulate ongoing action groups. In cases where key people were missing, there was much less sustained action after the meeting, a finding confirmed by Whitaker and Hutchcroft. The one sponsor in Granata's study who did not believe in collaboration had an ineffective conference that probably should not have been held.

"Polarization," she reported, "decreased as predicted by theory when people discover they can be united by some common ground. That does not mean that differences are gone; in fact they are not. They are isolated, recognized, acknowledged and put aside so that work on common ground can take place." (p. 5) The risk is that people will agree only at a high level of abstraction and end up doing relatively minor, non-controversial projects. This happened in the conference on repetitive strain injury studied by Polanyi in which deep value conflicts between employers and union members proved irreconcilable in a three-day Future Search.

Four studies are worth noting for the added dimensions they highlight. Lujan Alvarez Concepcion compared two similar Mexican communities concerned with sustainable forestry planning. One used a Search Conference, the other did not. Based on surveys, interviews, direct observation, and follow-up studies, Concepcion found significant statistical differences between the two. Not surprisingly, the intervention community showed greater awareness of development needs and positive attitude change compared to the static community. More, the intervention community embraced participative planning and created its own strategic plan.

Jimenez-Guzman, also working in Mexico, sought to introduce participative planning into a provincial university, a rural community, and a university school. He modified the Search Conference model to fit the Mexican culture, calling the variation a Reflection and Design Conference (RDC). He concluded that participation enhances development, enabling people to make the best of the resources they have, and that RDCs produced ongoing participation. How long this might continue remained a question mark, depending on external and internal factors beyond a researcher's (or consultant's, for that matter) control.

Pickus, by contrast, set out to study strategic planning methods used by non-profit organizations. She made the focus of her study participatory strategic planning (PSP) and its influence on personal behavior. She chose an organization using Future Search, and did a longitudinal study using surveys before, just after, and six months following the conference. She used the term "social capital formation" to describe the partnerships, collaborations, and increased trust that emerged. She concluded that personal action following the conference was partly explained by these phenomena, a finding that parallels Granata's.

Pagano based his thesis on Weisbord's 1987 "Learning Curve." He sought to move the New York City archeological resource management community from an expert problem-solving model toward an orientation whereby all concerned parties participate in improving the whole system. He used Future Search to involve a broad cross section of the city's archeological community in designing their own collaborative community for managing the city's resources in the 21st century. Action plans were made for funding, exhibits, theory and method, legislation, education, site preservation, and increased community involvement. Pagano considered the meetings' main achievement a consensus developed among organizations and entities outside the formal structures of any of them.

The most problematic uses of Future Search seem to be in highly charged political situations. Where elected officials must be relied upon for action, the potential for follow-up goes down. Multiple pressures and constituencies make it very difficult for the peoples' representatives to participate in meetings wherein they don't control the dialogue. Oels, in addition to the meeting design, also attributed inaction after the two conferences she studied (on implementing Local Agenda 21 sustainability initiatives in Germany and England) in part "to factors like the withdrawal of champions after the conference event, the cultural and institutional gap between representative and deliberative (participative) democracy, and in the limited decision-making power of municipalities in multi-level governance."

She concluded that what happens during and after a Future Search is best understood "in relation to the political context that nourishes or fails to nourish it." (p. 354) She also stipulated that "there is a lot more to facilitating effective local change than optimizing the participation tool," (p. 354) a statement we strongly support. Nonetheless, she proposed useful design modifications based on her experience, most of which already were incorporated into designs that neither she nor the facilitators she studied and the critics she quoted were familiar with in the late 1990s.

WHEN TO APPLY

People have used Future Search to make good organizations better, in times of crisis when things seemed hopeless, to consummate organizational mergers, to create networks of agencies doing similar work, to create visions and action plans where none existed, and to implement existing visions for which no action plans had worked. Some examples reveal unlimited opportunities (all examples are from FSN files and many have been reported in *FutureSearching*).

- Kansas City Consensus had input from two thousand people and agreement on wanting their city to be the "child opportunity capital." Nobody knew how to implement this vision, however. In two Future Searches some 120 people devised major new initiatives, among them the inclusion of teens in strategic planning for the hospital, neighborhood associations and schools.

- The Alliance for Employee Growth and Development, a joint venture of AT&T and its major unions, had as its mission helping people displaced by technology to find new careers. Their Future Search brought common ground, clarity, and committed action plans to a complex mission even while the parties struggled at the bargaining table.

- Alcan Smelters & Chemicals Ltd. (SECAL), a division of Alcan Aluminum Company, used Future Search to identify how its smelting facilities should be organized in the next century. Action ideas included steps for realigning corporate headquarters and specialized staff roles, continuous training, and a zero accident work environment.

- County Fermanagh, Northern Ireland, held a Future Search to create an integrated economic development plan while in the midst of sectarian struggles. They came together as a community, created a comprehensive plan that eventually involved over one thousand people in 150 implementation meetings in the following year and continued to guide action for years after.

- Ramsey County, Minnesota, created one of the first comprehensive welfare-to-work programs, integrating all needed services such as daycare, career counseling, car pooling, job training, and employment into neighborhood centers. The plan was conceived in a joint Future Search by government, social agencies, business people, and families on welfare working together.

- 3M Company's St. Paul Area Plant Engineering organization ran a Future Search as part of an ongoing effort to improve work methods, morale, quality of work life, productivity, and management practices. Despite historic union/management tensions, they produced a joint vision of a workplace redesigned around customer needs. Plant Engineering then undertook a cooperative work redesign effort that included hundreds of employees.

- In Orange County, California, St. Joseph's Health System, joined by the OC Board of Supervisors and Bank of America, organized a Future Search on housing for families earning below $10 an hour. A coalition was formed linking housing developers, low-income residents, advocates, local and state policymakers, business, labor, and health and human service providers to devise joint housing programs. Within a year the coalition had 250 members.

- In Indonesia, the Ministry of Education, the Ministry of Religion, and UNICEF co-sponsored a Future Search to develop an infrastructure for decentralizing education. The follow-up included training forty local facilitators who then ran Future Search in communities throughout the country where local leaders and citizens created strategic action initiatives.

- The heaviest concentration of ethnic Hawaiians lived in Ko'olau'loa Loa on Oahu's north shore. Queen Emma Foundation funded a Future Search to help people reconnect with traditional values of wholeness and cooperation in all areas of local life. People joined to sponsor annual community get-togethers, improve signage and awareness of highway safety on the road, cutting traffic deaths from eight per year to two, restore a daycare center, address literacy and drug abuse problems, and to initiate courses in Hawaiian culture in the high school and local branch of Brigham Young University.

Table 4.1 provides a synopsis of the differences between Future Search and other planning methods with which practitioners were not achieving hoped-for results.

Table 4.1 Future Search vs. Consultant-Centered Planning Methods

Future Search is . . .	Rather than . . .
A whole system in dialogue	Consultant researched and interviewed
Three days in length	Three or more months in length
An incorporation of everyone's thinking	Synthesis/perceptions only of a consultant
A commitment at all levels	Commitment only at the top
Rapidly implemented	Problematically implemented

When Not to Use Future Search

- When people in the room do not need each other to accomplish the task (for example, they are individual contributors or autonomous professionals).
- When leaders delegate the meeting to subordinates and show up only at the beginning and/or the end.
- When the meeting's goal is fuzzy or irrelevant to most participants.
- When the task is abstract and likely to lead to talk without action.
- When key people can't or won't come.
- If the sponsor seeks to squeeze the work into two days. They can do it, but people will be action planning late on the second day when they are dead tired and overloaded.

STRENGTHS AND CRITICISMS

There are strong reasons to consider Future Search:

- The game is won or lost in the planning, not the meeting itself. If planners can get the right people for the task and accept the time commitment, they are likely to have a successful meeting.
- Participants need only agree to show up. Pre-work may be desirable but is rarely needed.
- The structure brings together those who collectively could act if they chose.

- Ownership among participants is high and action more likely because people do all their own data assembly, analysis, dialogue, and planning.
- Two consultants or managers can lead groups of up to one hundred or more easily because the structure puts half the participants in leadership roles at all times.

Future Search also has been criticized for a variety of reasons:

- Key people may not be willing to commit three days.
- The search for common ground may lead people to sit on strong negative feelings.
- Not enough time is given to action planning.
- Some people see certain aspects of the design, such as the review of the past or the "prouds" and "sorries," as irrelevant to the objectives.

While all of the above can be valid criticisms, none is a reason for giving up a Future Search. Those who stick to the principles and plan with a local steering group greatly optimize the probability for success. Many people fail to invite key people because they believe "they won't come." We can cite dozens of cases where the right stakeholders did come. If the task is not important enough, don't hold the meeting. We agree that some people sit on strong, negative feelings, even in meetings where conflict is the norm. In Future Search we encourage people to bring up whatever they wish. The design does not require that anything be buried, only that action be directed toward common ground. We also believe people should be responsible for themselves. They have a right to hold back and to accept the consequences.

As for action planning, in early versions of our design we recommended up to three hours, having found that to be enough time when people know what they want to do. If after twelve hours of intense dialogue, people still are not sure what they want, more action planning is not likely to help. Still, we and our colleagues aim for flexibility. Often, adding two hours on the third day (going until 3 p.m. instead of 1 p.m., for example) provides whatever additional time is needed. This is a steering committee decision. The risk is not in too little time for action, it's in too little time spent in dialogue to get everybody on the same page.

In regard to the design, we see it as a projection screen onto which people put their experiences, visions, and aspirations. Nobody tells them what to think or steers them toward a particular conclusion. Because learning styles vary, so do reactions to each activity. After twenty-five years of applications in multiple cultures by hundreds of people who have tried dropping and adding to every phase, most facilitators agree that the revised generic design from our 2000 book holds up most of the time. We are preparing a third edition that will document further refinements.

RECOMMENDED DESIGN, DEVELOPMENT, AND IMPLEMENTATION PROCESS

Step 1: Planning

Schedule at least two days of meetings with a steering committee. The ideal size is six to eight people who have among them the credibility and connections to get all the other participants to come. In the first meeting, orient participants to the four principles listed above and solicit their expectations for the process. Do a brief review of the generic meeting design, for example, four or five half-day sessions devoted to the past, present, future, common ground, and action planning. Explore the conference purpose, stakeholders, and time horizons. Many issues surface as a prelude to the larger meeting. Use these meetings to identify who the "right people" are for the conference task the group has chosen. These will be a mix of those with authority, resources, expertise, information, and need. These "stakeholders" will be organized into groups that share a functional relationship to the task. (In a school conference, for example, the groups might be teachers, administrators, students, parents, support staff, etc.) Often planners make a demographic matrix to insure participation by gender, race, age, ethnicity, function, place of residence, or other relevant criteria. They also devise an invitation strategy for getting people to commit to the entire two-and-a-half-day meeting. All design and logistics decisions are made in these meetings.

Step 2: Design

Adapt the design to fit the community or organization's purposes. Usually this means choosing past and future dates to bound the exploration, and making sure the questions and task assignments are understood. Present this design to the steering committee at its second meeting. This is the time to check on how the invitation list is shaping up. One pitfall to avoid is the "they won't come" dialogue. For decades we have heard a long list of people some planners consider allergic to three-day meetings: doctors, farm workers, engineers, teachers, teenagers, diplomats, and on and on. The dialogue goes like this:

"Are the [name of stakeholder group] important to you?"

"Yes."

"Have you invited them yet?"

"Oh, no. *They* won't come."

"Why do you say that?

"Because they never have."

"Have you ever asked them?

"No. Never."

"Why?"

"Because everyone knows they won't come."

In fact, they nearly always come once they know the importance of the task and who else is coming. (If the task is not important, there is no point to the meeting.)

This is a good time to check the meeting room. We visit in advance if feasible. We like square rooms, a minimum of twelve hundred square feet for sixty-four people, no tables, plenty of wall space, *and* windows to the outside. We insist on windows. Perhaps some day someone will do the research needed to prove our suspicion that people do much better work when they can look out and see the sky.

Step 3: The Future Search Conference

Participants work on the following tasks:

Day 1: Afternoon

Task 1: Focus on the PAST. People note personal, global, and local milestones they have experienced over a period of time (set during planning, the default being thirty years) on time lines on the wall. *Mixed groups*, each a cross-section of stakeholders, review and describe the trends and patterns among the milestones noted. This gets everybody talking about the same world.

Task 2A: Focus on Present—External Trends. The *whole group* contributes to a "mind map" of current trends in the world having an impact on their lives and system. Everybody hears each person's observations, from which the group draws implications for the present and the future. This establishes the context for all work that follows. People place colored dots on the trends they consider essential to the meeting. The colors identify stakeholder groups.

Day 2: Morning

Task 2A: Focus on Present—External Trends Continued. Key trends highlighted by the colored dots the day before are confirmed with the *whole group.* Then *stakeholder groups,* those whose members share a similar function, review and report the trends important to them, what they are doing now and what they want to do in the future.

Task 2B: Internal Present. Each *stakeholder* group next makes lists of "prouds" and "sorries" in their relationship to the Future Search topic. All groups' lists are viewed as "current reality," not as problems to be solved.

Day 2: Afternoon
Task 3: Focus on the Future. *Mixed* groups prepare ideal future scenarios. They travel into the future and present their scenarios concretely as if they were happening in the present. People create new structures, programs, policy, and procedures that support the future they prefer. They tell how they overcame barriers along the way.

Task 4A: Identify Common Ground Agenda. Before closing for the day, *mixed* groups note common themes that show up in all scenarios. Common themes are identified by each group and merged by groups working together to post related items on the wall. People group similar items as they post them. Usually there is 80 percent or more overlap.

Day 3: Morning
Task 4B, Continued: Confirm Common Ground Agenda. The *whole group* in dialogue confirms their common ground values, propositions, and program ideas. If people cannot agree on a value or feature, the item is recognized as supported by some but not all and put on a "not agreed" list." As a result, everybody knows where others stand with regard to the common ground.

Task 4C: Write Statements that Capture Common Ground Commitments. Volunteers write complete statements that capture the spirit of each theme and would be understood by those not present.

Task 5: Action Planning. *Stakeholder and/or volunteer groups* make short- and long-range action plans for implementing the preferred future. People have a chance to "put a stake in the ground" and work with others who have energy for a particular project or theme. The goal is to translate common ground into policies, programs, and projects. They use existing structures or create new ones. They report to the conference before closing, and make plans for disseminating the outcomes. The conference closes between noon and 3 p.m. on Day 3.

KEEPING THE TASK FRONT AND CENTER

The Future Search conference puts people in a paradoxical spot. They have little "data" at hand to deal with other than what they produce themselves, have available as handouts, or may have read in advance. They have no speakers or consultants telling them what to think or what to do with their discoveries. They have little choice except to fight, run away, or deal with each other in a new way. Our goal in running this meeting is to hold the task front and center. Fred Emery, a pioneer of this work, held that when two people work on a common task outside of themselves they are more likely to improve their relationship than if they confront one another's habits, styles, and quirks directly in the absence of any other task.

Cutting loose old ways of relating is no small feat. It opens doors to new experiences. When people give up trying to reduce uncertainty by sticking to simple problems, they free themselves to make more creative choices. They often find themselves on common ground none knew existed. This trip into unknown territory can be made because everyone works on tasks of mutual concern. When people accept the conference task, they can work together despite their skepticism, gloomy predictions, blind faith in leaders and experts, and other "shadows" that hound many meetings.

CRITICAL SUCCESS FACTORS

Future Searches work best when they are championed by a leader with an "itch to scratch." Clearly, the search must have compelling purpose (business case, goal, mission, quest), and this purpose should be valued by all. In addition to leveraging interdependence among participants, the key principles of a Future Search must exist: the "whole system" must be in the room; the whole should be explored before seeking to fix any part; common ground and future action ought be put first (with problems and conflicts as background information); and participants themselves should be responsible for self-managing and taking action (rather than having the process be consultant-driven).

WHAT TO AVOID

The three factors most likely to undermine a Future Search are these:

- Key actors are left out, meaning the meeting will be inconclusive with a hard sell ahead to those who did not participate;
- Not enough time is allowed for exploring all facets before moving to decisions, solutions, and action; and
- People fight, flee, or freeze in the face of differences instead of keeping the dialogue alive.

In addition, avoid windowless rooms. Resist the temptation to add long expert presentations before or during the meeting on the task of the meeting. Finally, a caveat for those who may have inordinate faith in the power of participation to overcome all human failings: do not expect committed action planning from people who have little or no need for one another. We advise against doing a Future Search when common ground and implementation of action plans are not key objectives requiring cooperation by diverse parties.

SUMMARY

In summary, those who want the techniques without the philosophy and personal commitment are likely to disappoint themselves. Future Search best serves those who believe good planning requires vision, attractive goals, collaboration, commitment, hard work, sufficient time, involvement of all parties, and continual re-visiting. Most users find the rewards, in a world of non-stop change and increasing diversity, well worth the effort.

References

Asch, S. (1952). *Social psychology*. New York: Prentice-Hall.

Concepcion, L. A. (1997). Strategic planning for sustainable community forestry in Chihuahua, Mexico. Doctoral Dissertation. New Mexico State University.

Flower, J. (1995, May/June). A conversation with Marvin Weisbord: Future search—A power tool for building healthier communities. *Healthcare Forum Journal, 38*(3).

Granata, E. C. (2005). An assessment of search conferences: Citizen participation and civic engagement in turbulent times. Doctoral Dissertation. University of Colorado at Denver.

Holman, P., Devane, T., & Cady, S. (2007). *The change handbook*. San Francisco: Berrett-Koehler.

Janoff, S. (2003, Fall). Preparing for the future begins with today's youth: A future search with 50 teenagers in a rural county in SW Michigan, USA. *FutureSearching, 27*.

Janoff, S., & Weisbord, M. (2003). Three perspectives on future search: Meeting design, theory of facilitating, global change strategy. *Scandinavian Journal of Organizational Psychology, 13*.

Jimenez-Guzman, J. (2005). Participation and development in Mexico. Doctoral Dissertation, University of Pennsylvania.

Lewin, K. (1948). *Resolving social conflicts: Selected papers on group dynamics* (G.W. Lewin, Ed.). New York: Harper & Row.

McDonald, K. L. (1998). The future of school counseling and guidance in Washington state: A future search conference. Doctoral Dissertation. Seattle University.

McGregor, D. (1960). *The human side of enterprise*. New York: McGraw-Hill.

Oels, A. (2003). *Evaluating stakeholder participation in the transition to sustainable development: Methodology, case studies, policy implications.* Münster: Litverlag.

Oels, A. (2002). Investigating the emotional roller-coaster ride: A case study-based assessment of the future search conference design. *Systems Research and Behavioral Science, 19,* 347–355.

Pagano, D. N. (1993). Systems design of a collaborative community to manage New York City's archaeological resources. Doctoral Dissertation. Saybrook Institute.

Pickus, K. N. (2001). Participatory strategic planning in nonprofit organizations: The roles of social capital and collaboration in explaining changes in personal actions. Doctoral Dissertation, University of California, Irvine.

Polanyi, M. F. D. (2002). Communicative action in practice: Future search and the pursuit of an open, critical and non-coercive large-group process. *Systems Research and Behavioral Science, 19,* 357–366.

Polanyi, M. F. D. (2000). A qualitative analysis and critique of a future search conference: Reframing repetitive strain injuries for action. Doctoral Dissertation, York University (Canada).

Schindler-Rainman, E., & Lippitt, R. (1980). *Building the collaborative community: Mobilizing citizens for action.* Riverside, CA: University of California Press.

Schweitz, R., Martens, K., & Aronson, N. (Eds.). (2005). *Future search in school district change.* Lanham, MD: Rowman and Littlefield.

Secor, J. H. (1999). Advancing women as leaders: An intergenerational, multicultural future search conference for activist women. Doctoral Dissertation, Seattle University.

Starodub, L. A. S. (2001). Facilitating whole-system methods across cultures: A case study of a future search conference on the future United Nations in Pakistan. Doctoral Dissertation, The Union Institute.

Trist, E. L., & Emery, F. E. (1960, July 10–16). Report on the Barford Conference for Bristol/Siddeley Aero-Engine Corp. Document No. 598. London: Tavistock.

Weisbord, M. (1984, July). Future search: Innovative business conference. *Planning Review,* pp. 16–20.

Weisbord, M. R. (2004). *Productive workplaces revisited: Dignity, meaning, and community in the 21st century.* San Francisco: Jossey-Bass.

Weisbord, M., & Janoff, S. (1999). Future search. In P. Holman & T. Devane (Eds.), *The change handbook.* San Francisco: Berrett-Koehler.

Weisbord, M., & Janoff, S. (1999, April/June). Future search: Global change strategy. *Training matters: Promoting human potential development across Asia.*

Weisbord, M., & Janoff, S. (1999, May/June). Speaking with the ancients. *Healthcare Forum Journal.*

Weisbord, M., & Janoff, S. (2000). *Future search: An action guide to finding common ground in organizations and communities* (2nd ed.). San Francisco: Berrett-Koehler.

Weisbord, M., & Janoff, S. (2000). Zukunftskonferenz: Die gemeinsame Basis finden und handeln. (translated into German). In R. Konigswieser & M. Keil (Eds.), *Das Feuer Grosser Gruppen*. Stuttgart: Klett-Cotta.

Weisbord, M., & Janoff, S. (2001, Fall). Future search: Finding and acting on common ground: How future search is being used in Northern Ireland to build the women's sector, create an integrated economic development plan in County Fermanaugh, and build the arts and culture sector.'' *Nonprofit Quarterly*, *8*(3), l.

Weisbord, M., & Janoff, S. (2003). Future search: Finding and acting on common ground. In P. Kumar (Ed.), *Organisational learning for all seasons*. Singapore: National Community Leadership Institute.

Weisbord, M., & Janoff, S. (2005). Facilitating the whole system in the room: A theory, philosophy, and practice for managing conflicting agendas, diverse needs, and polarized views. In S. Schuman (Ed.), *The IAF handbook of group facilitation*. San Francisco: Jossey-Bass.

Weisbord, M., & Janoff, S. (2005). Faster, shorter, cheaper may be simple: It's never easy. *The Journal of Applied Behavioral Science*, *41*(1), 70–82.

Weisbord, M., & Janoff, S. (2006). Clearing the air: The FAA's historic ''Growth Without Gridlock'' conference. In B. Bunker & B. Alban (Eds.), *The handbook of large group methods*. San Francisco: Jossey-Bass.

Weisbord, M., & Janoff, S. (2007). Future search: Common ground under complex conditions. In P. Holman, T. Devane, & S. Cady (Eds.), *The change handbook*. San Francisco: Berrett-Koehler.

Weisbord, M. R., & 35 Co-Authors. (1992). *Discovering common ground*. San Francisco: Berrett-Koehler.

Whittaker, J., & Hutchcroft, I. (2002). The role of future search in rural regeneration: Process, context and practice. *Systems Research and Behavioral Science*, *19*, 339–345.

Wilcox, G., & Janoff, S. (2000, Spring). I dream of peace: A future search for the children of Southern Sudan. *FutureSearching*, 18.

ADDITIONAL RESOURCES

The following DVDs are available at www.futuresearch.net or by emailing fsn@futuresearch.net:

DVD 1 (contains three stories)

''The Children of Southern Sudan.'' A thirty-minute Blue Sky Productions video documenting UNICEF-sponsored Future Searches with Sudanese children and adults to address the crisis of losing a generation of children to the turmoil of a brutal civil war, led by Sandra Janoff.

"Discovering Community: A Future Search as a Springboard for Action in Santa Cruz County." A thirty-minute Blue Sky Productions video documenting a Future Search on affordable housing conducted by Sandra Janoff and Marvin Weisbord in Santa Cruz, California. Includes eighteen-month follow-up.

"Future Search in Action." A twelve-minute Blue Sky Productions video that shows an overview of five community and five corporate examples.

DVD 2 (contains three stories)

"Haworth Corporation–Finding the Heart of Haworth." A fifteen-minute case study of a global corporation using Future Search to launch their strategic planning process.

"Guiding the Future of Alcohol, Tobacco and Other Drugs Field." A twenty-five-minute case study in which ATOD professionals create a set of principles for their field. Sponsored by Robert Wood Johnson Foundation.

"Capacity Development for Disaster Risk Reduction." A thirty-minute video made for the United Nations Development Program showing a Future Search in which eighty-five people from thirty-five countries create a shared umbrella to guide their disaster mitigation work around the globe.

 EDITORIAL CONNECTIONS

Establishing a shared strategic vision of the results an organization seeks to accomplish is a critical element in the foundation for improving human and organizational performance. While most organizations have developed a strategic plan of some variety, too often these are developed by executive teams, becoming little more than dust-covered binders that sit on managers' shelves. Alternatively, Future Search is a performance intervention that can assist you in generating an agreeable plan for the future that guides decisions rather than gathers dust.

In addition, the principles of Future Search also provide valuable guidance to the many decisions that are required to achieve sustainable improvements to performance. From getting diverse input into decisions and taking a systemic (or "whole system") perspective on defining results, to starting with common ground rather than differences and allowing people to take responsibility for their actions, the four principles underlying the Future Search technique can (and should) be applied to many decisions related to improving human and organizational performance.

The value of these four principles applies not only at the strategic level at which long-term outcomes are defined, but equally at the tactical and operational levels, where the interim results delineate the results necessary for strategic accomplishments. As a consequence, the four principles of Future Search should be applied to the performance interventions you select for implementation—aligning the tactical and operational objectives that will lead to strategic success. Future Search has broad applications in performance improvement and can become a cornerstone of improvement efforts.

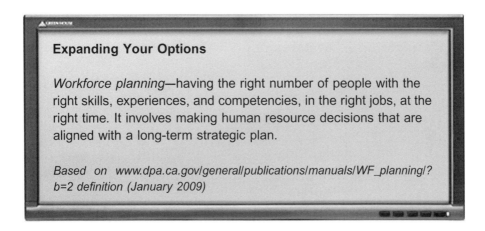

Expanding Your Options

Workforce planning—having the right number of people with the right skills, experiences, and competencies, in the right jobs, at the right time. It involves making human resource decisions that are aligned with a long-term strategic plan.

Based on www.dpa.ca.gov/general/publications/manuals/WF_planning/? b=2 definition (January 2009)

WHAT'S COMING UP

While a Future Search provides an essential component in building a solid foundation of strategic direction, the implications of these decisions are also closely tied to the context of the organization and the improvement effort. In Chapter Five, SWOT (strengths, weaknesses, opportunities, and threats) analysis is discussed as a tool for identifying, relating, and making performance improvement decisions within context. SWOT analysis has been used by organizations for many years, and its applicability as a performance intervention for developing strategic direction sustains it as a valuable tool within HPT.

In the chapter, Doug Leigh expands on the procedures of traditional SWOT analysis to include steps that ensure that analysis can lead to useful guidance for decision making. In a traditional SWOT analysis, contextual factors are classified and discussed by the participants (for example, an organization's personnel are listed as a strength or increasing market fragmentation is categorized as a threat). To guide decision making, however, these previously independent factors have to be examined in relation to one another—offering a more complete picture of the context (or system).

The author suggests a framework for examining the factors identified in a SWOT analysis, along the continuums of internal versus external organizational control as well as the degree to which each factor acts as inhibitor versus enhancer of performance. By adding these dimensions to the already useful SWOT analysis procedures, you can identify and create interventions that provide strategic direction, prioritize desired results, and relate potential performance interventions within the pragmatic context (strengths, weaknesses, opportunities, and threats) of the organization.

CHAPTER FIVE

SWOT Analysis

Doug Leigh

INTRODUCTION

Strengths, weaknesses, opportunities and threats are organizational influences known collectively as "SWOTs." At its best, SWOT analysis is a process by which a group of stakeholders (a) identify internal and external inhibitors and enhancers of performance, (b) analyze those factors based on estimates of their contributions to net value and approximations of their controllability, and (c) decide what future action to take with regard to those factors. Conventionally, however, organizations carry out only the first of these three tasks. To address this shortcoming, this chapter outlines a six-step process not only for identifying SWOTs, but also for meaningfully analyzing and synthesizing them to enable better organizational decision making. In this chapter I describe the history of SWOT analysis, its research base, applications, and its own strengths and weaknesses. The six-step process for conducting SWOT analysis is then described, followed by a discussion of factors critical for successful implementation.

DESCRIPTION

While the nomenclature of SWOT analysis is far from standardized, a paraphrasing of definitions suggested by Staffordshire University strategic management professor Claire Capon in her 2003 text on organizational context reflects their typical meaning:

- *Strength*: an internal enhancer of competence, valuable resource or attribute

- *Weakness*: an internal inhibitor of the competence, resources, or attributes necessary for success
- *Opportunity*: an external enhancer of performance that can be pursued or exploited to gain benefit
- *Threat*: an external inhibitor of performance that has the potential to reduce accomplishments

SWOTs are often arranged in a 2-by-2 table or matrix (see Figure 5.1), with internal enhancers of performance categorized as strengths and internal inhibitors as weaknesses. In turn, external enhancers are classified as opportunities with external inhibitors referred to as threats. Portraying SWOT factors in such a fashion aims to emphasize a holistic view of the four categories, though for practical purposes each may be broken out separately. This is true in part since, at least in traditional SWOT analysis, comparison-making between categories is not an explicit intent.

	Strengths a. b. c.	Weaknesses a. b. c.
Internal		
External	Opportunities a. b. c.	Threats a. b. c.
	Enhancer	**Inhibitor**

Figure 5.1 A Conventional SWOT Table.

As obvious as it may seem today, formally considering the internal and external factors that can help or hinder an organization's ability to reach its goals is a comparatively new development. Indeed, even the very concept of "strategic management" is a relative newcomer to the business world. Both notions emerged as recently as the 1950s, a time also known for advances in learning theory and social psychology, conceptual cousins of SWOT analysis.

Early History

MIT's Kurt Lewin is widely considered to be the father of social psychology, the study of how individuals and groups interact. Published in 1951, four years after his death, *Field Theory in Social Science* popularized several of his earlier theoretical papers. In the book Lewin advanced the notion that various forces can help or hinder the pursuit of goals within a given environment (which he called a "field"). Although he did not refer to it as such, this "force field analysis" has since become a ubiquitous tool within not only social psychology but also organizational development and change management.

On the heels of Lewin's work, the University of Connecticut's Julian Rotter published his groundbreaking work *Social Learning and Clinical Psychology* in 1954. In it, he argued that individuals tend to attribute successes and failures to reasons either internal or external to themselves. Those who attribute results internally tend to explain the performance they accomplish as being the product of their own abilities and efforts, while those who attribute externally see success or failure as being a matter of external circumstances such as fate, luck and the influence of powerful others.

Most likely due to independent development in psychology and business, the early history of SWOT analysis does not refer to the influence of Lewin's and Rotter's work. Nevertheless, in his classic 1957 text *Leadership in Administration*, Berkeley law and sociology professor Philip Selznick first offered that an organization's internal commitments as well as its external expectations can and should be assessed.

While this set the stage for SWOT analysis, not until Harvard Business School's Kenneth Andrews combined the internal/external dichotomy with the consideration of an organization's strengths and weaknesses did the technique start to become systematized. In a 2003 interview, Andrews explained that his writings sought to acknowledge a company's potential within the market, its particular strengths and weaknesses (termed core competencies), and the goals to which it aspired. This differentiation of an organization's internal strengths and weaknesses from its external opportunities and threats was picked up by Andrews' colleagues Bruce Scott and C. Roland (Chris) Christensen, who he claims developed "the idea of strategy."

Along with George Albert Smith, Jr., also of Harvard, the team further refined the practice through a series of modules within its Business Policy course, a cornerstone of the university's MBA program. SWOT analysis continued to garner attention throughout the 1960s, culminating in 1965's *Business Policy: Text and Cases*, which solidified its position within strategy development.

The heyday of SWOT analysis continued through the 1980s, which witnessed the publication of *Competitive Strategy* by Harvard's Michael Porter in 1980 and *Structure in Fives* by McGill University's Henry Mintzberg in 1983. Although Porter was much more a proponent of SWOT analysis than Mintzberg, both authors brought considerable recognition to the technique, whose application and refinement continues to this day.

Currently, SWOT analysis is most often used as a tool for scanning an organization's internal strengths and weakness as well as its external opportunities and threats. As described below, two approaches to SWOT analysis predominate today: market research and business strategy development.

Contemporary Applications

Within market research contexts, SWOT analysis tends to involve the identification of internal strengths and weaknesses and external opportunities and threats through "hard" extant data: information that is empirically obtained and independently verifiable. The general goal of such analyses is to provide an objective and impartial view of the organization's internal and external environment, although the ability to do so is tempered by the availability and accuracy of data collection and analysis. Leading firms providing such services include Research and Markets (researchandmarkets.com) and DataMonitor (datamonitor.com), whose reports range in price from hundreds to thousands of dollars.

In business strategy development, SWOT factors are generated by stakeholders and are typically led by one or more managers or consultants. These facilitators aim at soliciting "soft" perceptual data from participants who offer their opinions regarding the internal and external influences on organizational success. In this approach, the data obtained tends to reflect the collective memory and evaluations of the group.

Whether as market research or business strategy development, SWOT analysis serves to suggest the causes of results currently being achieved, with the intention of informing decision making regarding alternative means of accomplishing desired results. Beyond these few commonalities, the procedures for conducting a SWOT analysis are as varied as they are successful.

Characteristics and Potential Results

Milorad Novicevic and Michael Harvey, then both at the University of Mississippi, along with Chad Autry and Edward Bond III from Bradley University, advocate a "dual-perspective" SWOT analysis (presented in an adapted form within Table 5.1). In their 2004 article for *Marketing Intelligence & Planning,* they put forth that the method works best when it informs both back-end planning and front-end marketing. Back-end planning aims for a retrospective description of an organization's past by sorting factors among the four SWOT categories, a task they see as being a relatively objective one. Front-end marketing, on the other hand, seeks to provide a prospective evaluation of an organization's future by subjectively interpreting SWOT's potential within future markets in the light of competitive-intelligence.

To expand on this idea, when successfully applied, SWOT analysis is characterized by the candid attribution of the internal and external reasons for existing successes and failures. At the same time, the method should also be characterized by the creative consideration of the ways and means to capitalize on enhancers of performance and ameliorate performance inhibitors. Some organizations may see this sort of candor and imagination as utopian, thereby avoiding SWOT analysis if possible, or giving the method short shrift if not. Stakeholders

Table 5.1 Two Perspectives on SWOT Analysis

Perspective	back-end planning	front-end marketing
Outlook	retrospective/past	prospective/future
Goal	description of organizational control	prescription/evaluation of net value
Process	naming factors	interpreting meaning
Bias	objective	subjective
Logic	theoretical ("is")	normative ("ought")
Results	factors categorized	interrelationships analyzed
Requirement	honesty	creativity

may even falsify or withhold information out of self-preservation. Such actions are illustrative of the all-too-common tendency to use data for blaming rather than for learning. Be they in the context of SWOT analysis or otherwise, organizations with such cultures of distrust must address these tendencies before any meaningful discussion of their past, present and future can occur.

WHAT WE KNOW FROM RESEARCH

Like many interventions, empirical research *on* SWOT analysis is eclipsed by applications research *about* it. Nevertheless, various scholar-practitioners have investigated the efficacy of SWOT analysis as a decision-support tool. What is clear from this literature is that SWOT analysis, at least as it is commonly implemented, has limited utility for this purpose. However, several authors have suggested meaningful enhancements to the approach that address many of the complaints levied by its critics. I describe two of these advances within this section of the chapter, and then explain my own within the "Recommended Design, Development, and Implementation Process" section.

Terry Hill and Roy Westbrook, then both at the London Business School, do not equivocate in their 1997 article on SWOT analysis' efficacy. Their study audited twenty SWOT analyses conducted by fourteen different consulting firms within companies taking part in a UK-wide manufacturing planning and implementation initiative. The sponsor companies consisted of up to five hundred employees each, and more than one-third of the consulting firms were classified as "international," charging fees upwards from £750/day, with a high of £1,200/day.

Hill and Westbrook report that three general approaches were used in conducting these SWOT analyses:

- A single senior manager of the sponsor company conducted the SWOT analysis on his or her own, or the analysis was conducted alone by a consultant after discussion with senior managers;
- Several senior managers at the sponsor company conducted the SWOT analysis alone. These were then collated, after which a meeting might or might not have been held to develop a communal findings report; or
- A consultant or employee within the sponsor company held one or more meetings to develop the SWOT analysis.

General and vague terms were often used to describe factors, normally as phrases of no more than three or four words. Further, at no point within any of the twenty sessions was verification of any point undertaken. The SWOTs generated were assumed to apply universally to any product, function, or market. Perhaps most astonishingly, Hill and Westbrook report that "after the lists were produced, the consultants made their own lists, which differed significantly from those of company personnel. But there had been no onsite work by the consultant in the interim and no explanation of the differences between the lists was offered" (p. 48).

Half of the SWOT analyses generated forty or more factors across the four categories. On average, more weaknesses than strengths were identified, and more opportunities than threats. In nineteen of the twenty sessions, no prioritization, grouping, weighting, or sequencing of SWOTs was done. Numeric data was rarely used to make factors more explicit. Consultants almost never challenged or sought clarification regarding SWOTs that were offered, and if a factor was recorded under two or more categories, no reconciliation as to the apparent contradiction was ever undertaken. Consultants did not seek to increase the precision of SWOTs, nor did they consistently preserve the distinction between internal factors and external ones. Only three of the twenty analyses were used in subsequent work. In one other case, a consultant who could not find the SWOT analysis data explained that "it had only been used as a method of initiating discussion" (p. 50).

In what feels like a perfunctory discussion of positive findings from their study, Hill and Westbrook suggest that the analyses familiarized consultants with issues affecting the sponsoring company and initiated a discussion among some company personnel. This might have had value, they suggest, "if the process was followed up, lists were structured and prioritized, points were validated or investigated further" (p. 50). However, this did not occur in the vast majority of cases. Hill and Westbrook conclude their article – contemptuously subtitled "It's Time for a Product Recall" – by offering that the apparent intent of SWOT analyses within these implementations was "to raise a general debate, using general terms and without the need to link the analysis to application" (p. 50).

While Hill and Westbrook's study appears to be the only empirical investigations into SWOT analysis from a methodological point of view, others have proposed improvements aimed at increasing its precision and utility. What all share in common is a concern with bringing quantifiability to SWOT analysis for the sake of allowing "apples-to-apples" comparisons both *within* a category and *between* them.

In 2003 a group of forest management planning researchers led by Jyrki Kangas applied a process for group decision making in which incomplete, imprecise, and uncertain information can be structured, categorized, quantified, related to overall goals, and evaluated. Their particular application of multiple criteria decision-aiding "yields analytical priorities for the factors included in SWOT analysis and makes them commensurable. In addition, decision alternatives can be evaluated with respect to each SWOT factor" (p. 349).

Building on this work, a team of researchers led by Hidenori Shinno of the Tokyo Institute of Technology laid out an approach for determining the relative importance of one SWOT factor versus another in a 2006 article for the *Journal of Engineering Design*. Their approach allows for weighting and rating problems that involve complex decisions by informing the qualitative data that is generated within traditional SWOT analyses with quantitative measures of performance.

While both approaches permit marked improvements in determining the importance or intensity of SWOTs, the computational requirements of each renders them out of reach for most human performance technology (HPT) practitioners. At the same time, Kangas and Shinno's advances have important implications for next-generation approaches that portend the marrying of human-generated factors with real-time computer-supported polling, analysis, and graphical representations of findings.

WHEN TO APPLY

In my chapter on SWOT analysis for the 2006 edition of the *Handbook of Human Performance Technology*, I proposed that the method has application to at least four components of the HPT model:

- In *performance analysis* for identifying the degree to which internal practices and external environmental influences impact how results are currently being accomplished within an organization.

- In *cause analysis* for gauging what practices should be continued or expanded in the future, as well as those that should be discontinued or complemented by other methods and tools.

- In *strategic planning* and *needs assessment* for identifying the factors that contribute to or detract from organizational effectiveness.
- In *evaluation* for monitoring the internal and external environments of a program for change over time, for tracking new SWOTs as they emerge, and for documenting previously existing SWOTs as they become less influential on a program.

Beyond these general categories of HPT practice, SWOT analysis may also have applications within appreciative inquiry (for clarifying strengths and opportunities), benchmarking (for identifying opportunities and threats among best practices), industry analysis (for contextualizing market opportunities), situation analysis (for evaluating trends regarding customers, costs and competition), and scenario planning (for considering probable, possible, and preferred future scenarios).

STRENGTHS AND CRITICISMS

As can be seen from the "What We Know from Research" discussion, there are no shortage of criticisms concerning SWOT analysis. Ask people about the limitations of SWOT analysis and you'll likely hear gripes such as these:

- "There was no prioritization of the SWOTs once we identified them. Also, it didn't seem we could meaningfully compare the importance of one SWOT to another."
- "We identified the SWOTs, but I'm not so sure that the strengths and weaknesses were completely internal, or that the opportunities and threats were exclusively external."
- "What were listed as weaknesses and threats had upsides to them that went unacknowledged, just like the downsides of strengths and opportunities were ignored; still, the bucket we put them into is where they stayed."
- "There was no figuring of the costs and benefits of the SWOTS, or of different ways of using them to achieve our business objectives."

Scholars may be the biggest critics of SWOT analysis, as practitioners seem more willing to forgive and forget its shortcomings. A 2008 survey of business improvement and benchmarking by Massey University's Centre for Organisational Excellence Research included 450 practitioners from forty-four countries. The majority of responses came from Oceania, the UK, India, Germany and Canada. Manufacturing, services, government, education, healthcare, and finance were among the major business activities represented. Respondents from private organizations outnumbered those from public organizations two to one.

Asked to assess twenty popular interventions, participants ranked SWOT analysis as number 2 in familiarity and number 3 in use. While the technique ranked ninth in perceived effectiveness, it was still among the top three interventions likely to be used by respondents within the next three years. Clearly, despite having ebbed and flowed in popularity over the years, SWOT analysis is still very much alive, if not well.

Perhaps part of the disdain for SWOT analysis in the academic literature has to do with its inherent intuitiveness and ease of data collection. Across the literature, it seems that the most strident critics emphasize the problems with the method, typically without suggesting means for improving it. A backhanded compliment from Hill and Westbrook's "recall notice" is illustrative of this perspective: "SWOT survives, we suggest, because it is very straightforward and requires little preparation on anyone's part" (p. 51).

Setting aside zealous consultants and unconsciously uninformed practitioners, those who have the greatest hope for the practice tend to be those who see potential for improving the technique. For example, Novicevic and his team see the practice as existing "at the intersection between research and practice" (p. 85) and suggest that when successfully carried out, SWOT analysis can provide "valuable knowledge about both customer preferences and competitor intents" (p. 86).

As will be illustrated next, the myopia prevalent among traditional approaches to SWOT analysis can be remedied. Individual SWOTs can be examined in relation to one another according to estimates of their contribution to desired performance, along with approximations of the degree to which each factor is or is not within an organization's control.

RECOMMENDED DESIGN, DEVELOPMENT AND IMPLEMENTATION PROCESS

Myriad guidelines exist for conducting SWOT analyses. Just Google the phrase and you'll end up with hundreds of thousands of alternatives. This may seem somewhat surprising given its academic pedigree, but it is not inconsistent with the majority of other popular interventions discussed within this book. Since there is no "one way" to conduct a SWOT analysis, then, what follows is a synthesis of popular approaches that integrates an enhancement to the technique that I have refined over the past decade.

When applied to business strategy development, the use of focus groups within SWOT analysis can be a useful way to solicit the perspectives from performers and other stakeholders regarding the results achieved by their organization. A six-step approach to this involves recruiting stakeholders, convening the focus group, identifying and categorizing SWOTs, followed by systematically analyzing them, synthesizing them, interpreting the findings, and deliberating possible actions regarding the SWOTs.

Step 1: Recruiting Stakeholders

Various perspectives exist as to the most appropriate stakeholders to include with large group interventions, including SWOT analysis. In the 2008 edition of their *Exploring Corporate Strategy*, Gerry Johnson, Kevan Scholes, and Richard Whittington suggest mapping stakeholders according to their interest in a project and their power over its findings. A graphic representation of these alternatives appears in Figure 5.2.

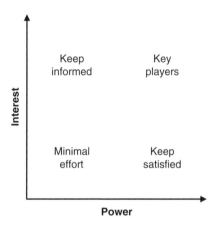

Figure 5.2 Power-Interest Matrix.

Beyond the issues of interest and power is that of expertise. While most stakeholders are able to provide a relatively accurate assessment of the degree of an organization's control over SWOTs, estimating the extent to which a factor is an enhancer or inhibitor of performance requires experiential knowledge of the organization. In support of this, Kangas and his colleagues offer that when working with non-experts as participants within a SWOT analysis, any involvement beyond naming SWOTs and ranking their importance might be unwieldy.

None of this is to say that there is not merit in having a variety of interest, power, and expertise participate in the focus group. However, the degree to which participants from opposite ends of these continua should intermingle depends on the importance of including a variety of perspectives versus having a consensus opinion, as well as the degree to which frank and productive conversations can be anticipated in mixed groups. Whatever the mix of stakeholders, focus groups should consist of eight to forty stakeholders to allow for a variety of opinions to be voiced and to more easily manage the data collection and analysis efforts.

Step 2: Convening the Focus Group

At its most basic level, the identification of factors within a SWOT analysis involves just two tasks: naming factors and deciding which category each belongs within. To convene a focus group for this purpose, facilitators must secure a location for the session, explain its purpose, describe the ground rules of the process, and clarify the scope of the undertaking.

Space. Conference rooms or work areas large enough to accommodate eight to forty stakeholders are appropriate for use as a venue for the analysis. While the stakeholders' first task is the identification of SWOTs, it is important to have considered the amount and type of structure to be provided. While one option is for participants to list SWOT factors on their own—with those being shared back to the larger group of stakeholders after a set period of time—collaborative focus group facilitation allows for greater interaction from the outset of the analysis. Five options for such an approach include:

1. All stakeholders take part in generating SWOTs, with the facilitator (or an assistant) recording them as they are called out by participants.

2. Four breakout groups are formed, each responsible for the generation of one of the four categories, followed by reporting back to the entire group.

3. As number 2, but groups are instructed to generate SWOTs related to each of the four categories in sequence according to a pre-set schedule.

4. Breakout groups are formed based on similarity or divergence in power, interest, and expertise. Each group is tasked with generating all four SWOT factors, followed by reporting back to the entire group.

5. As number 4, participants are rotated between breakout groups according to a pre-set schedule.

Purpose. One of the preliminary tasks involved in facilitating a SWOT analysis involves clarifying the intent of SWOT analysis as well as agreeing upon the definitions of each of the four categories of SWOTs. The "Introduction" and "Description" sections of this chapter provide definitions that I work from when conducting SWOT analyses, although it might help to flesh these out with examples such as those presented in Table 5.2. It is also useful for facilitators to emphasize that, since consensus of opinion is not the goal of the analysis, evaluations of organizational control and influence on performance not only can but should vary from stakeholder to stakeholder.

Table 5.2 Examples of SWOT Data Types

Internally Controlled		Externally Controlled	
capabilities, resources, culture, staffing practices, personal values, operating systems, etc.		suppliers, government policies, labor, economic conditions, competitors, market demand, etc.	
Strengths	*Weaknesses*	*Opportunities*	*Threats*
fidelity, precision, and alignment that make up an organization's competitive advantage	faults, defects and limitations that put an organization at a disadvantage relative to competition	favorable external trends that help an organization's ability to serve its clients and customers	unfavorable external trends that hinder an organization's ability to serve its clients and customers

Process. Facilitators should explain that organizations that successfully capitalize upon their internal strengths may in turn have them realized as external threats among their competition. Likewise, organizations that fail to curtail their internal weaknesses may in turn be creating opportunities for their competitors. The same, of course, holds true for an organization's competitors, any of which may themselves be seeking to act upon their own SWOTs.

These truths underscore the criticality of prudence in not overstating strengths, candor in acknowledging weakness, creativity in considering opportunities, and foresight in identifying threats. The potential of SWOT analysis depends first and foremost on the accuracy of the data that goes into it. The accuracy of the data is contingent on trust among stakeholders that information they share will not be used to punish (or, for that matter, to praise), only as input into the analysis.

Scope. A final task of this stage is determining what the focus of the SWOT analysis will be. The presenting issue in the analysis conducted by Kangas' team, for example, was the decision of whether a geographically disparate family should repair and rent out a remote and dilapidated cottage on their family property. The focus of the analysis conducted by Shinno and his colleagues, on the other hand, was more general: the machine tool industry in Japan. While such broad, generalized analyses can be useful within market research settings, a narrower focus concentrating on a specific organizational department, program, service, or situation provides a stronger basis for post-analysis decision making and action.

Step 3: Identifying and Categorizing SWOTs

After clarifying the definitions of SWOTs and organizing stakeholders into groups, a variety of approaches can be used to facilitate the generation of

SWOT factors. When I first began writing about quantifying SWOT analysis in 2000, I pointed out that conventional approaches to SWOT analysis models, explicitly or implicitly, operate from the basis of asking two binary questions about the factors influencing an organization: "Is this factor a benefit or cost?" and "Is this factor occurring within or outside this organization?" Responses to these questions are then normally categorized within a table, such as that illustrated earlier in Figure 5.1.

As suggested in Step 2, a common facilitation approach is to simply record SWOTs in whatever order they are offered by stakeholders. A more structured approach is for the facilitator to first solicit SWOTs by way of stakeholders' sense of organizational control over the SWOTs, and then to ask them to disaggregate these according to which act as enhancers versus inhibitors of desired performance. The rationale for this sequence is described well by Novicevic and his colleagues, who point out that, "The (inexperienced) analyst can readily categorize elements of SWOT by description as internal or external to the firm but does not have an experiential base by which to readily identify elements as desirable or undesirable" (p. 91). Beginning with the assessment of control, then, allows for the involvement of all stakeholders from the get-go, which may also provide a useful platform for learning, building rapport, and gaining momentum within the process.

Differentiating internal from external control. Facilitators should remind participants that having or seeking internal control over any or all SWOTs might neither be necessary nor advantageous. Also, just because opportunities and threats externally controlled does not mean they are "uncontrollable" or "out of control." Indeed, as Claremont Graduate University's Michael Scriven points out in his 1991 *Evaluation Thesaurus*, seeking control over all SWOTs may be indicative of unrealistic or unfounded ambitions.

A basic script for a facilitator to follow in seeking to identify and differentiate SWOTs by locus of organizational control begins as follows: "Today we're going to identify and categorize the internal and external factors that either help or hinder us from achieving the results we're setting out to accomplish with regard to [*insert scope determined in Step 2 here*]. First, consider what kinds of things impact our ability to get the results we're after, setting aside for the time being the matter of whether you see them as being assets or liabilities, and instead differentiating them only as being *within* or *outside* our organization's ability to control them."

In carrying out this task, participants may discover that new factors come to light and also that apparent contradictions may emerge regarding whether a particular SWOT is internally or externally controlled. These provide ripe opportunities to delineate and qualify SWOTs so that they operate most precisely within one category or another. For example, one parent-stakeholder in an analysis of the viability of an after-school mentoring program might offer that "transportation" is an externally controlled issue, only for another parent to counter that it's an internally controlled one. With a bit of delving, a skilled facilitator might uncover the reason for the apparent conflict of personal experience: the first uses public transportation to access the program, while the other commutes in a personal car. This might lead to differentiating "public transportation" as an externally controlled factor, while categorizing "private transportation" as an internal one.

Differentiating performance enhancers from inhibitors. Following this generation of SWOT factors, the facilitator then moves to distinguishing SWOTs that act as enhancers of performance from those that are inhibitors of it. Again, during this process it may be important for the facilitator to delineate and qualify contradictions as described above. Indeed, should the number of factors offered become cumbersome, facilitators may employ an intermediary step in which stakeholders collapse similar factors, or perhaps vote for the top ten factors within each category. In any case, a basic script for differentiating enhancers from inhibitors is as follows: "Now that we've sorted factors as being internally or externally controlled, we'll move on to distinguishing those that enhance our ability to achieve the goals of [*insert scope determined in Step 2 here*] from those that inhibit it. While at first it may seem that this involves making a value judgment about them being 'good' or 'bad,' the true intent is to help inform ways of establishing and maintaining and those things that help, and for improving those that hinder. We'll begin with the first SWOT identified, then go through both the internal and external lists until we reach the end."

An example. A case-in-point of the types of factors that can come from this step might provide some context. This one comes from my "How to Conduct Better SWOT Analyses," a 2005 article focusing on a construction company interested in reducing the amount of electrical conduit waste it generates. Since the material in Exhibit 5.1 will be used in subsequent pages, SWOTs are labeled using the first letter of their category followed by a subscript. The order of presentation of SWOTs is arbitrary; they are not rank-ordered in any fashion.

Step 4: Analyzing SWOTs

After having completed Steps 1 through 3, SWOTs will have been named, delineated, and qualified, sorted by internal versus external control, and disaggregated by their influence on inhibiting versus enhancing performance. But description alone is not analysis. In discussing the conclusions they reached from the audit of the analyses within their study, Hill and Westbrook offer that "it is arguable that this SWOT activity and its outputs do not constitute analysis at all, for they do not go beyond description, and description only in the most general terms" (p. 50). Analysis requires reduction of material to constituent parts, while synthesis involves identifying patterns and relationships among those parts. Steps 4 through 6 in the process involve quantitatively analyzing SWOTs, after which they may be synthesized through graphical representation for subsequent interpretation and deliberation.

Exhibit 5.1 SWOT Factors Identified Within a Construction Company

Strengths
- S_1) Frequent referrals
- S_2) Relatively low overhead costs
- S_3) Sizable storage space for inventory

Weaknesses
- W_1) High scrap production
- W_2) Purchases not coordinated across jobs
- W_3) No standards for returning surplus inventory

Opportunities
- O_1) Discounted pricing from vendors
- O_2) Waterfront revitalization project
- O_3) Tax incentives for waste management initiatives

Threats
- T_1) New competitors entering the market
- T_2) Disincentives for non-domestic goods
- T_3) Fines for improper waste disposal

The analytic aspect of SWOT analysis actually begins in the prior step through purposefully distinguishing SWOTs among the four categories. At its most basic level, this can be accomplished by asking stakeholders to rank-order SWOTs within each category with regard to a ranking variable, such as importance, urgency, stability over time, or some other matter. While rank-ordering SWOTs enhances the analytic process, it remains difficult however, to make apples-to-apples cross-factor comparisons both *among* and *between* strengths, weaknesses, opportunities, and threats. In addition, stakeholders are likely to rank-order SWOTs differently due to their own interpretations of the ranking variable. Gauging the relative net value added or subtracted of any single SWOT in relation to all other factors generated is not well served by conventional approaches to SWOT analysis.

In a process I refer to as IE^2 (internal/external, inhibitor/enhancer) analysis, stakeholders quantitatively evaluate SWOTs in relation to one another according to (1) estimates of the net value added or subtracted of each factor and (2) approximations of the degree to which an organization can exert control over those factors. From this, better informed decisions are available regarding what SWOTs to leverage or confront, which to exploit or avoid, or which simply require monitoring. Since stakeholders will have already identified factors and categorized each as a strength, weakness, opportunity or threat, IE^2 analysis (pronounced "IE-squared analysis") involves systematically asking and answering just two additional questions regarding SWOTs:

- To what degree is each SWOT factor internally or externally controlled?
- To what degree is each SWOT factor an enhancer or inhibitor of performance?

Answers to these questions add quantitative measures to what has hitherto been a purely qualitative undertaking and allow for an approach to SWOT analysis that meets the three aspects of the definition offered in the introduction of this chapter.

An IE^2 analysis proceeds as described in Steps 1 through 3 above. Instead of rank-ordering SWOTs, however, stakeholders rate the degree to which each factor is within or outside of the control of the organization, and then indicate the degree to which each SWOT acts as an enhancer or inhibitor of performance (see Figure 5.3).

Analyzing attribution of control and net value. Stakeholders are asked to rate the degree to which each factor is under the control of their organization (for strengths and weaknesses) or outside of it (for opportunities and threats) on a questionnaire developed for this purpose. To quantify these estimates, the strength and weakness sections of the questionnaire incorporate a scale that ranges from 0 (indicating the *absence* of control) to +5 (indicating complete *internal* control). For their part, the opportunities and threats sections of the questionnaire employ a scale that ranges from 0 (also indicating the *absence* of control) to −5 (indicating complete *external* control).

Alongside these evaluations, participants are asked to rate the degree to which each factor is an enhancer of performance (for strengths and opportunities) or an inhibitor of it (for weaknesses and threats). The strength and opportunity sections of the questionnaire use a scale that ranges from 0 (indicating a *negligible* impact on net value) to +5 (indicating the greatest possible *enhancer* of net value). The weakness and threat sections of the questionnaire make use of a scale that ranges from 0 (also indicating a *negligible* impact on net value) to −5 (indicating the greatest possible *inhibitor* of net value).

These scales are populated using the SWOTs generated in the Step 3 of the analysis. To continue the construction company example begun there, the questionnaire in Exhibit 5.2 was used to solicit the IE^2 ratings.

IE^2 questionnaires are completed individually and, depending on their intended implementation, may be distributed only to those that generated the SWOTs or may be sent to a larger group of stakeholders. In the prior case, a blank template can be prepared prior to the focus group, populated by the facilitator with the SWOTs generated in Step 3 during a break and either printed or

Exhibit 5.2 IE^2 Questionnaire

Instructions: For each factor listed below, indicate your sense of the degree to which each is **under** (+) or *outside* (−) of your organization's control. Also indicate the extent to which you believe each **enhances** (+) or *inhibits* (−) desired performance.

The Strength listed below . . .	. . . is **under** (+) our control:	. . . and **enhances** (+) performance:
S$_1$ Frequent referrals	0 1 2 3 4 5	0 1 2 3 4 5
S$_2$ Relatively low overhead costs	0 1 2 3 4 5	0 1 2 3 4 5
S$_3$ Sizable storage space for inventory	0 1 2 3 4 5	0 1 2 3 4 5
The Weakness listed below . . .	. . . is **under** (+) our control:	. . . and *inhibits* (−) performance:
W$_1$ High scrap production	0 1 2 3 4 5	0 1 2 3 4 5
W$_2$ Purchases not coordinated across jobs	0 1 2 3 4 5	0 1 2 3 4 5
W$_3$ No standards for returning surplus inventory	0 1 2 3 4 5	0 1 2 3 4 5
The Opportunity listed below . . .	. . . is *outside* (−) our control:	. . . and **enhances** (+) performance:
O$_1$ Discounted pricing from vendors	0 1 2 3 4 5	0 1 2 3 4 5
O$_2$ Waterfront revitalization project	0 1 2 3 4 5	0 1 2 3 4 5
O$_3$ Tax incentives for waste management initiatives	0 1 2 3 4 5	0 1 2 3 4 5
The Threat listed below . . .	. . . is *outside* (−) our control:	. . . and *inhibits* (−) performance:
T$_1$ New competitors entering the market	0 1 2 3 4 5	0 1 2 3 4 5
T$_2$ Disincentives for non-domestic goods	0 1 2 3 4 5	0 1 2 3 4 5
T$_3$ Fines for improper waste disposal	0 1 2 3 4 5	0 1 2 3 4 5

converted to an online survey for completion after the break. If sent to a larger group of stakeholders, the questionnaire can be prepared as just described, but mailed or emailed to a broader array of stakeholders than were present within the focus group. In any of these cases, participants can be asked to respond immediately based on their individual impressions, or instructed to ground and justify their evaluations in market or performance data. In many circumstances, both stakeholder input and financial data may inform this process.

Form of the IE^2 questionnaire. There are several aspects of the questionnaire worthy of mention. First, while a 0-to-5 Likert-type rating scale is used across all sections of the questionnaire, the meaning of the numbers within the scale differs. For this reason, the questionnaire employs various mnemonic devices: bold font and a plus sign to indicate internal control and enhancements to performance, and italic type and a minus sign to indicate external control and inhibitors to performance. Color codes can also be used to offset the four categories of SWOTs or to further reinforce the internal/external and inhibitor/enhancer distinctions. Second, the questionnaire allows stakeholders to provide side-by-side ratings for all SWOTs within a single space, better facilitating apples-to-apples assessments. For this reason, even though presenting all strengths, weaknesses, and opportunities on a single page may not be possible for lists much longer than that within Exhibit 25.2, effort should be taken to ensure that at least each of the four categories appears on a single page. Third, while it is true that from an evaluative perspective stakeholders' ratings are intended to be free of subjective value, from an affective perspective this tendency is difficult to temper. For this reason, the terms "enhancer" and "inhibitor" are assumed to be relatively less value-laden than those of "good" and "bad." Similarly, to make the concepts more concrete for stakeholders, the phrases "under our control" and "outside our control" replace the terms "internal" and "external." In short, the intent of the phrasing used is to keep participants focused on evaluating the internal/external distinction as the attribution of control, and the inhibitor/enhancer distinction as the net value added or subtracted.

Function of the IE^2 questionnaire. The questionnaire allows for bringing the individual's vote to a process that in Steps 1 through 3 had been a group undertaking. This permits those who may not have been as vocal in the identification and categorization of SWOTs to contribute their opinions to the process. It may be desirable to weight the responses of some stakeholder groups over others, perhaps on the basis of interest, power and expertise as introduced in Step 1. To enable this requires little more than a brief demographics cover page to the questionnaire for use in sorting responses by stakeholder group.

Consensus regarding the evaluation of SWOTs is rare, since this determination is obviously subject to participants' individual interpretations. Thus, it would make little sense to poll stakeholders for a "majority opinion" since there may be no clear majority, and even when there is, the approach ignores variation among opinions. As will be seen next, an advantage of IE^2 analysis is that it allows for the visual representation of SWOT data in a manner that recognizes both majority opinion as well as variation. It also provides more useful data for considering what actions, if any, to take with regard to SWOTs.

Step 5: Synthesizing SWOTs

Following the return of completed questionnaires, the facilitator compiles the data into a spreadsheet in preparation for synthesizing the findings and reporting the results of the IE^2 analysis back to the group. If the questionnaire was implemented within the focus group setting, this can be done by an assistant while the facilitator explains how this process will transpire. Obviously, for implementations of the questionnaire with geographically diverse audiences, "real time" analysis, synthesis, and reporting are not as plausible.

To continue with the construction example begun earlier, consider that the questionnaire was implemented within the focus group, resulting in twenty-eight completed surveys. After compiling the data within a spreadsheet, the summary statistics presented in Table 5.3 were calculated.

Treating these data as coordinates, they can be plotted within a two-dimensional graph—called an IE^2 Grid—such as that illustrated in Figure 5.3. This allows for the location and magnitude of each SWOT can be seen in relation to all others. Another alternative is to plot the ratings of multiple stakeholder groups separately (either on separate graphs or overlaid within the same graph) so their perspectives can be disaggregated by demographic.

Step 6: Interpreting Findings and Deliberating Action

Often, further deliberation pursues the potential vulnerabilities of ignoring threats and weaknesses, the means by which threats can be turned into opportunities, and alternative approaches for leveraging weaknesses into strengths. Such conversation commonly includes a consideration of how ambiguities regarding changing external environments can be best addressed. These deliberations may occur within the SWOT analysis session, at a follow-on focus group, or by independent work groups tasked with conducting formal inquiry into these matters.

Following the plotting of stakeholders' evaluations of strengths, weaknesses, opportunities, and threats within an IE^2 Grid, decision-makers are better able to determine which SWOTs to act on and how. This is supported by another feature of IE^2 analysis represented in Figure 5.3: decision guides. These thresholds, represented by the dotted lines in Figure 5.3, may be superimposed over the IE^2 Grid in order to facilitate decision making. The closer a SWOT factor is to one of these thresholds, the less definitive is the action that should be taken with regard to them. From left to right within the IE^2 Grid, these decision thresholds are described below.

Table 5.3 Summary of IE^2 Data

	Average Internal (+) or External (−) Rating	Average Enhancer (+) or Inhibitor (−) Rating
Strength		
S_1	+ 3.2	+ 2.1
S_2	+ 1.9	+ 3.2
S_3	+ 2.7	+ 1.0
Weakness		
W_1	+ 1.4	− 3.6
W_2	+ 4.8	− 2.1
W_3	+ 4.7	− 4.9
Opportunity		
O_1	− 3.2	+ 3.1
O_2	− 4.1	+ 1.3
O_3	− 4.5	+ 4.7
Threat		
T_1	− 4.1	− 3.1
T_2	− 4.7	− 0.9
T_3	− 0.1	− 1.2

(n = 28)

Monitor. In that they neither enhance nor inhibit performance substantially, those factors close to the horizontal axis of the grid are likely candidates for *monitoring*. This is more the case for those factors that are externally controlled (opportunities and threats), as the organization has less influence over them. Thus, these factors should be tracked over time for stability or change.

Mitigate Threats and Exploit Opportunities. While still externally controlled to some degree, the greater an opportunity acts as an enhancer to performance and the greater a threat acts as an inhibitor, direct action is warranted. Thus, *mitigating* threats that either subtract substantial value or are more within an organization's control is warranted. Likewise, opportunities that *either* add substantial value or are more within an organization's control deserve to be exploited.

Confront Weaknesses and Leverage Strengths. Factors under greater organization control are even more likely to benefit from direct action. Thus, strengths should be *leveraged* to support the accomplishment of desired results, all the

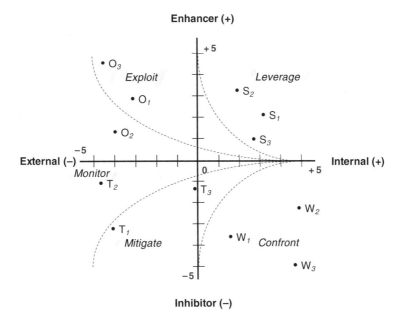

Figure 5.3 IE^2 Grid.

more so when they add substantial value to the organization. Similarly, weaknesses that are either under greater internal control or act as stronger inhibitors to desired performance should be *confronted*.

Although the thresholds of these decision guides are best established prior to the identification of SWOTs so as to preclude the manipulation of data to fit one action or another, it is also possible to adjust them on the basis of stakeholder input.

CRITICAL SUCCESS FACTORS

As many of the guidelines for conducting a successful SWOT analysis have been discussed earlier, there are only a few critical success factors to re-emphasize:

- It cannot be stressed enough that information shared by stakeholders within a SWOT analyses should never be used for blaming but only as a basis for continuous improvement.

- As a corollary, when it comes to weaknesses, a natural tendency (referred to by social psychologists Edward Jones and Richard Nisbett as the "actor-observer bias") is to blame others for faults emanating from their shortcomings, but to blame the situation for one's own deficiencies. Honest introspection, then, is essential.

- Depending on the resources and constraints that exist, SWOT analysis data can be collected simultaneously (live) or asynchronously (at participants' own pace), face-to-face or online, as well as individually or within groups.

- It may be useful to weight stakeholders' evaluations of SWOTs differentially, particularly within large-scale implementations across geographically diverse audiences. As explained earlier, weighting the perspective of experienced stakeholders over newcomers might be especially warranted, particularly regarding the evaluation of net value added or subtracted.

- Beware of analyzing and synthesizing SWOTS with intentions that are biased, whether from a positive or negative point of view. SWOT analyses concerned with back-end planning purposes may overemphasize specific, explicit, and operational descriptions of factors or, alternately, may be overly cursory and superficial. Similarly, SWOT analyses concerned with front-end marketing may err by being overly prescriptive or, conversely, overly suggestive.

SUMMARY

Although various descriptions and implementations of SWOT analysis exist, what they share in common is the consideration of the internal and external enhancers and inhibitors of organizational performance. However, most approaches forgo a true analysis of SWOTs to determine the controllability and net value of each in relation to all others. At best, this results in inaction; at worst, indiscriminate action.

To this end, my aim in this chapter was to describe the method, its research base, applications, and strengths and weaknesses, then to discuss IE^2 analysis as a process in which a group of stakeholders (1) identifies internal and external inhibitors and enhancers of performance, (2) analyzes those factors based on their net value and attribution of control, and (3) decides what future action to take with regard to those factors.

Notes

- While ubiquitous today, the practice of abbreviating and contracting phrases using their initial letters emerged around the time of World War II, not much more than a decade earlier, probably making "SWOT" among the first business acronyms.

- SWOT analysis also shares some similar characteristics with another 2 × 2 matrix, Ansoff's Product-Market Matrix, which suggests differential action based on whether a product and its market is either new or current. Other similar approaches, at least in form if not function, include the Growth-Share Matrix (which uses the graphical space of the matrix as a scatter plot), the 4P Marketing Mix (which facilitates thinking within and across key considerations), and PEST analysis (which, while not typically represented as a matrix, also examines an organization's business environment).

- For the complete worked example of an IE^2 analysis, my article "How to Conduct Better SWOT Analyses" provides additional detail.

- I have supervised two dissertations to date that have applied IE^2 analysis as their framework for data collection and analysis, both by graduates of Pepperdine University's Organizational Leadership doctoral concentration. One analysis, by Joannie Busillo-Aguayo, concerns families' experiences accessing supports for their special needs child between the ages of three and five. The other, by Anissa Jones-McNeil, uses IE^2 analysis to assess the capacity to provide free and appropriate education in the Santa Barbara school districts. Interested readers can download both dissertations through ProQuest "Dissertations & Theses" database.

References

Andrews, K. R. (2003). [Interview with Jeffrey Cruikshank]. *Kenneth Andrews audio.* Retrieved December 24, 2008, from http://www.hbs.edu/centennial/im/inquiry/sections/1/b/page28.html#navbar.

Capon, C. (2003). *Understanding organisational context: Inside and outside organisations* (2nd ed.). London: Financial Times/Prentice Hall.

Hill, T., & Westbrook, R. (1997). SWOT Analysis: It's time for a product recall. *Long Range Planning, 30*(1), 46–52.

Johnson, G., Scholes, K., & Whittington, R. (2008). *Exploring corporate strategy: Text and cases with companion website student access card* (8th ed.). Upper Saddle River, NJ: Prentice Hall.

Jones, E. E., & Nisbett, R. E. (1971). *The actor and the observer: Divergent perceptions of the causes of behavior.* Morristown, NJ: General Learning Press.

Kangas, J., Kurttilab, M., Kajanus, M., & Kangas, A. (2003). Evaluating the management strategies of a forestland estate: The S-O-S approach. *Journal of Environmental Management, 69*, 349–358.

Learned, E. P., Christensen, C. R., Andrews, K. R., & Guth, W. D. (1965). *Business policy: Text and cases.* Homewood, IL: Richard D. Irwin.

Leigh, D. (2000). Causal-utility decision analysis (CUDA): Quantifying SWOTs. In E. Biech (Ed.) *The 2000 annual, volume 2: Consulting* (pp. 251–265). San Francisco: Pfeiffer.

Leigh, D. (2005). How to conduct better SWOT analyses. In M. Silberman (Ed.), *The 2005 ASTD team & organization development sourcebook.* Princeton, NJ: Active Training/American Society for Training and Development.

Leigh, D. (2006). SWOT analysis. In J. Pershing (Ed.), *Handbook of human performance technology* (3rd ed.) (pp. 1089–1108) San Francisco: Pfeiffer.

Lewin, K. (1951). *Field theory in social science.* New York: Harper & Row.

Massey University's Centre for Organisational Excellence Research. (2008). *Global survey on business improvement and benchmarking* [online]. Palmerston North, New Zealand: Global Benchmarking Network. Retrieved January 14, 2009, from http://www.bpir.com/component/Itemid,143/option,com_mojo/p,12/.

Mintzberg, H. (1983). *Structure in fives: Designing effective organizations.* Englewood Cliffs, NJ: Prentice-Hall.

Novicevic, M. M., Harvey, M., Autry, C. W., & Bond, III, E. U. (2004). Dual-perspective SWOT: a synthesis of marketing intelligence and planning. *Marketing Intelligence & Planning, 22*(1), 84–94.

Porter, M. E. (1980). *Competitive strategy: Techniques for analyzing industries and competitors.* New York: Free Press.

Rotter, J. B. (1954). *Social learning and clinical psychology.* New York: Prentice-Hall.

Scriven, M. (1991). *Evaluation thesaurus* (4th ed.). Thousand Oaks, CA: Sage.

Selznick, P. (1957). *Leadership in administration: A sociological interpretation.* Evanston, IL: Row, Peterson.

Shinno, H., Yoshioka, H., Marpaung, S., & Hachiga, S. (2006). Quantitative SWOT analysis on global competitiveness of machine tool industry. *Journal of Engineering Design, 17*(3), 251–258.

Recommended Readings and Websites

1. Ansoff, I. (1965). *Corporate strategy.* New York: McGraw-Hill.

2. Lewin, K. (1943). Defining the "field at a given time." *Psychological Review, 50,* 292–310.

3. Lowy, A., & Hood, P. (2004). *The power of the 2 × 2 matrix: Using 2 × 2 thinking to solve business problems and make better decisions.* San Francisco: Jossey-Bass.

4. VisIt. A free visualization and graphical analysis tool that can be useful for preparing IE^2 Grids. Developed by the Lawrence Livermore National Laboratory, it may be downloaded at https://wci.llnl.gov/codes/visit/

 EDITORIAL CONNECTIONS

Improving performance takes place within the context of organizations. Future opportunities or potential threats that face your organization may, for instance, shift your choice of performance interventions. A SWOT analysis, for example, may identify that changes in the marketplace will require consolidation and centralization of your organization's financial units. This, in turn, might suggest that you may want to select performance interventions that are focused on improving team performance rather than individual performance. Further, by adding the dimensions of organizational control (internal versus external) and relationship to net value (inhibitors versus enhancers) to the traditional SWOT Analysis, the framework offered in Chapter Five becomes a valuable performance intervention for defining strategic direction—desired results—within your organizational context.

After all, since improving performance is synonymous with accomplishing desired results, you must be able to define your desired results in order to systematically achieve sustainable improvements. Thus, establishing strategic direction—through a Future Search, SWOT analysis, or other strategic planning exercises—is a critical first step in defining performance and what performance interventions will lead to significant accomplishments. These decisions form the foundation of any improvement effort, giving it both guidance and direction. By examining strengths and opportunities as well as weaknesses and threats, SWOT analysis adds valuable and varied perspectives on performance. These perspectives may complement or supplement perspective found through other activities.

Many times there are competing interests and diverse opinions regarding both what desired results should be accomplished as well as how they should be achieved. While the overarching objectives of the organization and its partners can guide decisions, the results of SWOT analyses help ensure that a balanced perspective is taken in making decisions. Carefully examine the challenges that are faced by your organization (weaknesses and threats), and this will provide you with valuable information for selecting performance interventions that have the capacity to address current limitations.

Expanding Your Options

Table top exercises—a focused practice activity that places the participants in a simulated situation requiring them to function in the capacity that would be expected of them in a real event.

Based on www.twlk.com/CEA/cea_tabletop.aspx definition (January 2009)

Analysis of the performance problems within your organization, however, is not in and of itself sufficient to improve results. As the SWOT analysis illustrates, you must also examine what is working (strengths and opportunities).This often goes against our instincts when we want to improve performance; we often focus solely on addressing performance problems or gaps in results. While identifying and addressing ''needs'' from this perspective is a vital step in improving performance, your approach should also augment those challenges with information on what is working well—in other words, what desired results are already being accomplished.

Often you will want to maintain or improve upon successful activities that achieve meaningful results. In addition, results from your analysis of the strengths and opportunities of your organization will inform your decisions about which performance interventions are most likely to accomplish desired results in the future, within the context of your organization. If you don't know what is working well now, it can be next to impossible to predict what will work well in the future.

Examining strengths and opportunities from a performance and results perspective is not, however, always within the culture of organization. Mother Teresa is credited with saying, "I was once asked why I don't participate in anti-war demonstrations. I said that I will never do that, but as soon as you have a pro-peace rally, I will be there." Similarly, performance improvement efforts often focus on battling performance problems without examining the positive side of the same coin: those efforts which are working.

WHAT'S COMING UP

To fashion a more complete picture of strategic direction and associated performance improvement opportunities, an appreciative inquiry approach can be used to complement a needs assessment in deriving strategic foundations. An appreciative inquiry-based analysis of performance can supplement the discrepancy focus of the needs assessment with valuable information on what is working well within the organization; identifying opportunities to expand on what is working in addition to addressing performance problems. Likewise, appreciative inquiry can be used as a valuable approach for establishing strategic direction that is both positive and forward looking.

Chapter Six offers practical guidance for how a positive and forward looking appreciative inquiry perspective can add value to your improvement efforts. From discovering the active ingredients that are leading to current success to defining concrete action steps for building upon current achievement, the appreciative inquiry approach described in the chapter puts theory into practice through systematic and productive processes. After all, appreciative inquiry is about more than just patting yourself on the back for a job well done: it is about learning analytically from past successes to accomplish significant results in the future.

Appreciative Inquiry

Marvin Faure
Jennifer Rosenzweig
Darlene Van Tiem

INTRODUCTION

Appreciative inquiry is a method for generating organizational change. At the same time it is also a valuable perspective—a *way of being*—that reflects a powerfully optimistic and constructive view of the world. Together, the perspective and methods of appreciative inquiry (AI) give us a useful tool for expanding our ability to introduce meaningful positive changes within an organization.

As a *method*, AI provides a practical process that encourages an entire system to come together to discuss "What is the best of what we do?" and "What kind of future can we imagine and pursue?" The result can be much greater levels of enthusiasm and commitment to the outcomes than generally obtained by other approaches to change.

As a *way of being*, AI rests on the belief that the way we perceive and experience the world depends on the way we talk about it. In other words, the more positive our conversations, the more positive the world we create for ourselves. To create a better future, therefore, we should focus on those factors that will accelerate us in the right direction. Paradoxically, the less attention we pay to the things that are slowing us down, the less important they become.

AI is often described in opposition to traditional change management. To highlight the differences, traditional change management is described as based on small groups of experts that identify the most pressing problems (deficits or gaps) and develop solutions that are then imposed on the organization. Almost everything in this description finds its opposite in the AI approach, which involves large groups of stakeholders in identifying what works best and agreeing all together on how to create more success.

The simplicity of this description sometimes leads to the impression that AI is no more than action research with a positive focus; this is however a fundamental misconception of AI. The central goal of AI is transformational change. The approach focuses directly on shifting people's points of view, in order to get them to embrace possibilities previously considered impossible or utopian. AI seeks to generate change through engaging the whole system—including all those affected (whether formally part of the central organization or not)—first in imagining how much better it could be, and then in bringing it about.

In most situations in which human and organizational performance needs to be improved, there are actually more things right than wrong. The risk of focusing solely on discrepancies is that of "throwing the baby out with the bath water" by creating needless disruption of things which are working well. Appreciative inquiry (AI) thus provides an effective counter-balance to the often negative perspective of solely discrepancy-focused methods.

For example, while a discrepancy-focused approach may effectively identify the root causes of slipping sales, the AI perspective can provide complementary information regarding the sales strategies, incentive programs, social networks, and knowledge sharing efforts that are effective. Together, both methods and perspectives are able to provide the most complete picture of individual and organizational performance, thus allowing improvements to be made where things are not working while at the same time championing the efforts that are successful.

DESCRIPTION

Appreciative inquiry (AI) was developed by David Cooperrider as part of his dissertation work with Suresh Srivastva examining generative change at a leading U.S. hospital (1987). The resulting methodology is usually described either by the "4-D Model," depicted in Figure 6.1, or the "5-I Model" described later in the chapter.

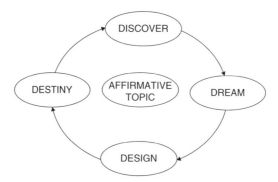

Figure 6.1 Appreciative Inquiry Cycle in 4-D.

In its simplest form, the starting point for an AI process is the decision by one or more leaders to mobilize a group of people for change. For robust results, it is important to identify an inspirational focus (referred to as an "affirmative topic choice") for the effort. It should be an area of importance to the organization's members and offer substantial potential for positive change. The focus should be framed using language that calls for something desirable rather than something to be avoided or eliminated. As an example, a theme might be "Exceptional Customer Relationships" rather than "Issues with Customer Service." See Table 6.1 for more examples of reframing common organizational issues as topics suitable for an AI approach.

Table 6.1 Organizational Issues Reframed as AI Topics

Organizational Issue	AI Topics
Unsatisfactory customer service	Delighting Our Customers
	Outstanding Customer Relationships
Increasing costs/decreasing margins	Operational Excellence
	Faster, Better, Cheaper
Lacking clear goals	Creating the Future We Want
	Taking Charge for Growth
Silos; poor inter-departmental teamwork	Winning Teamwork
	One for All, All for One
Management/labor conflict	Working Together; Partnership for Growth
Discrimination (age, gender, race)	Strength in Diversity
	Men and Women Working Together

Once the topic is determined, the participants are invited to come together and discuss the topic in depth. For best results the "whole system" should be represented in the room, including all departments and teams, as well as customers and members of the supply chain that may be affected. This diverse mix of voices gives the best chance for innovative and effective solutions to emerge.

The first "D" in the 4-D Model, *discover*, refers to a phase during which participants inquire into their most positive experiences relevant to the topic through a series of conversations, typically in interview format. These conversations serve to gather personal stories and insights about the topic. Sharing personal stories energizes the participants and provides a positive foundation from which change can occur.

The second "D," *dream*, then shifts attention to the future. It asks participants to imagine their organization at its very best, regardless of what the current state might suggest. Again, an emphasis is placed on strengths and assets, with no limits placed on possibilities. From there, a vision takes shape that will inspire and motivate the organization throughout the rest of the process.

Next, attention shifts to *design*, the third "D," in which practical ways for bringing the dream to life are identified. Participants split into small groups to work on specific projects and practical changes needed to reach the overall vision. Everyone is encouraged to play a role and take on responsibility for realizing the vision.

Finally, plans are implemented during the fourth "D," the *destiny* phase, and attention is given to consolidating the changes.

For well-defined topics and small groups, the first three "D's" in the process described above can be conducted in a single day. When the issues are complex and the group affected is large, the change process may stretch over many months.

Expanding Your Options

Values identification—systematic approach to discovering the principles, ideals, and standards that are inherent to the workforce and influence performance.

While the complete appreciative inquiry process represents a powerful approach for an organization to tackle substantial challenges, many components can become part of a practitioner's "toolkit." For example, the data collection phase of appreciative inquiry is based on a particular approach to question design that sparks positive emotions and seeks to uncover what's working well, rather than searching for gaps in performance. This technique can be applied in conjunction with other performance improvement methods when it would be helpful to avoid an excessive focus on the negative.

WHAT WE KNOW FROM RESEARCH

Appreciative inquiry was formed upon a solid theoretical foundation. Many different strands of research have provided a contribution, beginning with Social Constructionism. More recently, this has been influenced to a great extent with insights from two recent fields of social science: positive psychology and positive organization development.

Social Constructionism

With origins dating to early 20th century, social constructionism is anchored in the theory that we each experience a different version of reality, through the different ways in which we experience and interpret our dialogue and social interactions. By implication, the words we say, the stories we tell, and the nature of our interpersonal exchange with others all contribute to the ways that we interpret the world that surrounds us. Consequently, when we engage in organizational change, we need to pay careful attention not only to what we focus on, but also to how the experience takes place.

Kenneth Gergen, the Mustin professor of psychology at Swarthmore College, has studied and written about social constructionism extensively. His 1999 book *An Invitation to Social Construction* describes four assumptions that add substance to the concepts:

1. *Our understanding of the world can embrace many different "truths" rather than a single, empirical perspective.* If we interpret the world as we know it, then surely we can interpret it in any number of ways. Our past knowledge and experiences, the context we are in, the sensibilities that the other person brings, plus much more—all influence our reality.

2. *Relationships are a critical contributor to our understanding of reality.* Our relationships with the people around us shape what we know and believe in. Communities with which we are affiliated, our physical surroundings and the things with which we fill our lives all influence the way we perceive our reality.

3. *As the dialogue unfolds, the world around us is created.* Our world comes to life as we conduct conversations that reflect our unique view of the world. In other words, I make a statement of some sort, you respond in kind, and together we create a shared meaning. This conversation may be explicit, between two people, but can also be part of the implicit messaging we exchange inside groups or as members of society.

4. *Ongoing reflection adds substance and expands our meaning.* To create deeper meaning and consequential action, a simple exchange is not enough. We also need to reflect on the common understanding. And since the world is a dynamic place, the meaning can change if the dialogue changes or the relationships change (p. 49).

Social constructionist theory helps us understand that there are many different ways to look at the world; that our unique perspective is based on our unique experience and that our perspective can and often does change as we reflect upon and add meaning to new experiences.

In 2001, Watkins and Mohr summed this up when they said:

"Social Constructionism suggests that the social realities of our world (how people behave, the design or socio-technical architecture of organizations, the corporate culture, etc.) are neither fixed by iron laws of human behavior nor are they solely a function of past experiences and history. Neither are they social realities exclusively the result of contextual and environmental factors. Rather, social constructionists argue that our world is shaped by the many dialogues and discourse that we have with one another—conversations in which we both selectively make sense of our past and present experience and history and create shared images of what we anticipate in the future." (p. 28)

In simple terms, we see the world differently after a meaningful discussion with other people. AI makes full use of this to help people generate and see possibilities they would otherwise never have seen, thus mobilizing whole groups around new and energizing visions.

A typical example took place during an off-site event facilitated by one of this chapter's authors (Marvin Faure) for a pharmaceutical company in Switzerland. Prior to the event the organizational dialogue was predominantly negative, characterized by unfavorable comparisons with their own past history as well as with the competition. The exchange of personal stories of best experiences as well as hopes for the future during the discover phase were consolidated during the day into a series of energizing projects during the dream and design phases. By the end of the day, the participants had collectively developed a much more positive and optimistic view of their enterprise and were ready to make it come true.

Positive Psychology and Positive Organizational Development

Positive psychology was created in the late 1990s when members of the psychological community realized that their profession was almost entirely focused on illness. For instance, many therapeutic techniques focused exclusively on the diagnosis and treatment of psychological disorders; similar to the way in which many performance improvement efforts focus exclusively on the diagnosis and treatment of performance discrepancies. The champion of positive psychology, Martin Seligman of the University of Pennsylvania, lobbied for a greater awareness of the potential to support the development of optimum, vibrant states of mental health, and argued that mental health professionals had a responsibility to the much larger percentage of the population that, although not considered mentally ill, were not living lives as happy and fulfilled as they might be. In 2003 he and University of Michigan professor Christopher Peterson noted that "Scientific psychology has neglected the study of what can go right with people . . . positive psychology calls for as much focus on strength as on weakness, as much interest in building the best things in life as in repairing the worst, and as much attention to fulfilling the lives of healthy people as to healing the wounds of the distressed" (p. 15).

Just one example of contributions from this movement comes from the research of Barbara L. Fredrickson, at UNC Chapel Hill. Fredrickson has run a number of studies on the impact that positive emotions have on human behavior, and her "Broaden and Build" theory has been widely accepted. This theory suggests that people under the influence of positive emotions are able to broaden their ability to think and act in the moment, while those under the influence of negative emotions tend to narrow their focus to "fight or flight."

In one study focused on "experiences of pride" UNC Kenan Distinguished Professor of Psychology Barbara L. Fredrickson found that eliciting a strong sense of pride set the stage for two important outcomes. First, there was a boost to confidence and self-esteem for the persons feeling pride. More than that, it also encouraged them to envision an even brighter future with greater levels of achievement.

We see the application of this research during AI's discover and dream phases, during which individuals share stories of pride and achievement and thus set into motion the ability to imagine a vibrant future, free of today's constraints.

This focus on the positive applies equally well when organizational success is considered. Just as individuals benefit from focusing on positive emotions and personal success, so can organizations, thus leading to the evolution of the discipline of positive organizational development.

An example of the work emerging from this exciting new discipline comes from Jane Dutton, a professor at the University of Michigan (which is also the home of the Center for Positive Organizational Scholarship). Dutton's 2003 research interests included the study of "high-quality connections." When people connect in a way that is meaningful and effective, the relationship becomes life-giving (rather than life-depleting). Not only do these connections have the power to positively impact the individuals, but these relationships in turn create organizational energy. This energy is part of what propels an organization forward and provides resilience in times of stress.

AI projects range from those dealing with common business problems such as employee productivity and customer service to more expansive projects including work done by the United Nations, focused on bringing business and world leaders together to solve some of our planet's most pressing problems.

Case Study

One example where the monetary savings and business impact brought by AI were researched under controlled conditions was documented in 1998 by David A. Jones, of Wendy's International. In this study, a field experiment utilizing appreciative inquiry was conducted within ninety-four Wendy's fast-food restaurants in a major metropolitan area in the United States. The purpose of his study was to find out whether AI could be effective in reducing employee turnover. Jones discovered a 30 to 32 percent higher retention within the AI group than in two control groups. Subjects in the AI test group not only stayed with the company longer but also expressed an enhanced appreciation of working within the much-maligned fast-food industry itself.

The higher retention rate translated into $103,320 of savings in training dollars for a twelve-week period. Additional benefits include the savings in lost productivity, recruitment, costs, benefits, morale issues, and crew turnover caused by management turnover, crew turnover training costs, sales loss due to lost productivity, and legal costs associated with turnover.

The Five Principles of Appreciative Inquiry

Much of the underlying theory inherent in appreciative inquiry can be summed up in a series of five "principles" that serve as a conceptual foundation. The probable success of an AI process can be estimated by evaluating how well the principles are being woven into a given project.

Constructionist Principle. This refers to co-creating our world through dialogue. If we accept that there isn't any one "truth" and that each person experiences their own truth, then our dialogue becomes a way for us to generate a shared understanding.

Poetic Principle. Organizations and their individuals are rich with experience and opportunity. The prevailing dialogue may however prevent these riches from emerging. Changing the dialogue and exchanging personal stories of exceptional moments wakens the poet and the dreamer in people and opens the door to growth.

Simultaneity Principle. When we inquire into something with an open mind, the very act of inquiry causes our perceptions to shift and thus our view of the world to change. This means that change and inquiry are completely intertwined, and that the questions we ask are of utmost importance. If we ask questions about positives we will find positives; if we ask about negatives we will find them too.

Anticipatory Principle. Our image of the future affects our current actions. Change therefore doesn't need to be anchored in today's world, but can be fueled by imagination and possibilities.

Positive Principle. Strengths offer a powerful path for growth. Positive emotions also open up our thinking and enhance our creativity. Embracing the "positive" forges accelerated paths for organizations to flourish.

These five principles are at the heart of appreciative inquiry. Compromising on one or more of them might still lead to a successful intervention given the right circumstances, but it would not be appreciative inquiry. A well-designed process that incorporates all five principles stands the best chance of success.

WHEN TO APPLY

Appreciative inquiry is an appropriate intervention for creating positive change when the following conditions are present:

- The organization is ready to look forward, build, and grow.
- The situation is complex, and the best way forward is not obvious.
- The employees are likely to resist changes mandated in a "top-down" fashion.
- Management wants to engage part, or all, of the workforce in determining the way forward.

There is a broad spectrum of application for appreciative inquiry. An AI perspective can in fact be applied to almost any of the performance improvement activities described in this book. Examples of application include business strategy development, process redesign, expansions of customer service, employee engagement, retention strategies, and more.

Appreciative inquiry may not be the best intervention when:

- Management does not wish to use a participative approach;
- Management is not willing or able to be transparent on key aspects of the topic;
- Management is not sensitive to the fundamental differences between AI and whichever approach to change they have used in the past; and/or
- Ongoing downsizing or reorganization makes employees temporarily unwilling to engage in constructive dialogue.

How Appreciative Inquiry Is Applied in Relation to Other Human Performance Technology (HPT) Interventions

Since appreciative inquiry is as much a philosophy as a method, there are opportunities to use elements of AI in many if not most HPT interventions. Individual practitioners often cross-fertilize between the different approaches, adapting them as appropriate for a specific requirement. For example, AI principles may be incorporated in whole or in part in such interventions as change management (see Chapter Sixteen), leadership development programs, team building (see Chapter Twenty-Five), coaching (see Chapters Eleven and Twenty-Seven), and career counseling (see Chapter Twenty-Two). AI is thus tightly integrated and not a "stand alone" either/or solution. To demonstrate this view, the human performance technology model was updated, resulting in the *HPT Model: Appreciative Approach* shown in Figure 6.2.

The following are some highlights of how the model distinguishes itself from a more traditional "gap analysis" view:

- *Performance Analysis*: During the first stage of data collection, equal attention should be given to organizational strengths and "what's working well" as to the areas of weakness. This gives a more balanced view and provides a stronger foundation for initiating change.

- *"Distance" Analysis:* Rather than position the gap in performance as a deficit, the word "distance" was chosen to describe the difference between "where we are now" as compared to "where we want to be." By implication, the journey to our destination (desired state) may not be an extension of the current state, but rather a more desirable, inspirational view that represents a better future for all stakeholders.

The insights from these initial analyses set the stage for the selection of the specific interventions or activities, not only to remove problems but also to build on positive achievements already being accomplished within and by the organization. While the mix of interventions that might be chosen from are still those described within this book (mentoring, training, process redesign, communications, etc.), the specific choice may be influenced by the addition of the appreciative inquiry perspective.

Appreciative inquiry impacts all aspects of a systemic improvement process, including evaluation and change management. The measurement and assessment methods chosen should include the collection of "success factors" and a continued examination of strengths. In addition, it is important to recognize that change naturally begins when the first question is asked, due to the tension created between the current situation and the desired state implied by the question. This brings attention to the process of change management, which needs to be ongoing, and not just at the Intervention Implementation stage.

STRENGTHS AND CRITICISMS

There are various advantages to appreciative inquiry:

- A positive focus can lessen resistance to change; change becomes desirable rather than feared.

- By generating positive emotions such as enthusiasm, pride, and hope, AI most frequently appeals to the heart as well as the head, thus engaging the whole person.

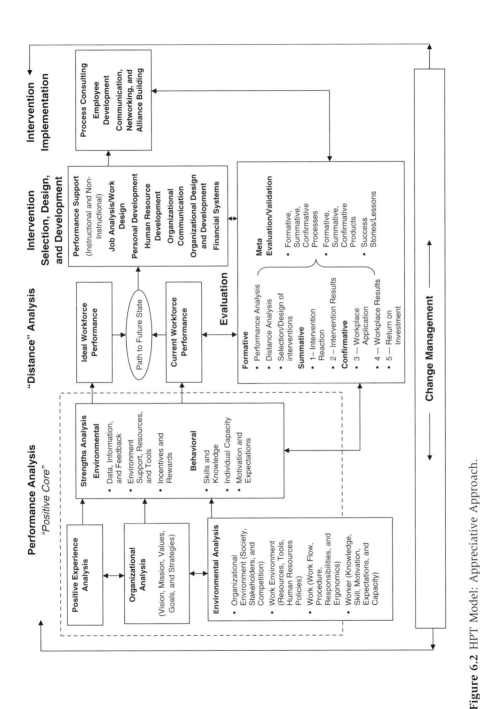

Figure 6.2 HPT Model: Appreciative Approach.

Source: Van Tiem and Rosenzweig, rev. 2-2007; based on http://www.ispi.org/services/whatshptmodel.pdf

- Inviting participation of the "whole system" (all those affected, including organization outsiders if appropriate) can lead to solutions that are both more innovative and more robust.

- It is less about incremental innovations around today's reality, and more about discontinuous leaps into the future.

- The change process generates energy rather than depleting energy at the individual, group, and organizational level.

- Positive change can enhance organizational pride.

- It tends to strengthen relationships across the organization through the conversations as well as the resulting collaborative activities.

- It is aligned with the younger generations' expectation of much greater participation in their organizations' decision-making processes.

- This combination of effort enhances the likelihood that the change effort will reach a successful conclusion.

These potentially huge advantages are balanced by a number of challenges for practitioners. One of these lies in the paradox of management highlighted by AI: if one truly wants a group to achieve, one's control over it must be *reduced*. Unfortunately, the rational strategy for individual senior managers concerned for their positions may often be the opposite. The strong executive decision-maker remains an enduring icon: those that succeed are widely trumpeted while the much greater number who fail are quickly forgotten.

Disadvantages of Appreciative Inquiry

As with the challenges of AI, many of the possible disadvantages of the approach have much to do with perceptions of a positive approach to inquiry:

- Appreciative inquiry can be viewed as "Pollyannaish" or New Age, as it runs counter to the accepted views on change as a function of gap or deficit analysis. Starting from strengths, rather than working directly with "what's wrong" does not feel like an obvious place to begin.

- The theories supporting AI can sound weak and counterintuitive to business-minded managers who are taught to be quantitatively driven.

- Any collaborative approach will take longer than a sole decision-maker strategy. As a consequence, an AI approach tends not to be appropriate to decide on emergency actions, although it can frequently be used to supplement such actions by providing longer-term inputs.

- In traditional "command-and-control" organizations, the apparent loss of control at certain stages of the process can be very threatening to insecure leaders.

- AI requires a higher level of social skills, more patience, and more understanding of human nature than "command-and-control."

RECOMMENDED DESIGN, DEVELOPMENT, AND IMPLEMENTATION PROCESS

There is no "one best way" to design and implement an appreciative inquiry process. Indeed, AI has often been compared to jazz, in which there is infinite variety around a central theme and structure. In AI, the structure is provided by the process model, and the theme is determined by the critical business issue the organization has decided to address.

Anyone wishing to use AI needs a solid understanding of the process and the ability to design the activities to best suit the culture and needs of the organization. It is not recommended to make fundamental changes in the process—such as re-ordering or omitting one of the phases—without a very good reason for doing so.

In Figure 6.3 we describe the process in five phases, using the 5-I model with the 4-D alongside for comparison purposes. For the majority of our business clients, the 5-I model language seems more apropos because the words used are customary business terminology. The 5-I model also provides more definition of readiness to begin an AI project. In reality, there is no substantial difference between the two models for the last four aspects of each. The two models side-by-side are illustrated in Table 6.2.

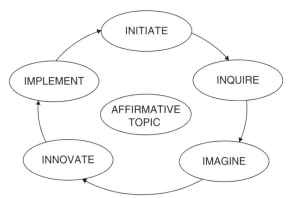

Figure 6.3 Appreciative Inquiry Cycle in 5-I.

Each of these phases is described below. Readers looking for a comprehensive "how-to" guide are referred to the book *The Appreciative Inquiry Summit: A Practitioner's Guide for Leading Large-Group Change* by James D. Ludema,

Table 6.2 Comparison of AI Implementation Models

"5-I" Model	⇔	*"4-D" Model*
Initiate	⇔	(pre-contracting)
Inquire	⇔	Discover
Imagine	⇔	Dream
Innovate	⇔	Design
Implement	⇔	Destiny

Diana Whitney, Bernard J. Mohr, and Thomas J. Griffin (2003). Readers interested in learning more about the origins of these different models are referred to *Appreciative Inquiry: Change at the Speed of Imagination*, by Jane Magruder Watkins and Bernard J. Mohr (2001).

1. Initiate (Pre-Contracting)

The objective of this initial phase is to set matters up for success. Typical activities include pre-contract research and discussions; agreement on the topic and objectives of the engagement; contracting; initial research; the creation and training of a core team; process design; and the development of interview questions adapted to the topic and the organization.

It is essential during this phase for the consultants to work closely with the organization's senior management, paying particular attention to the critical success factors for an AI engagement and taking care that the conditions are favorable. One of the most effective ways to do this is to hold a short AI session with the senior management team; their experiencing it for themselves is far more powerful than even the best presentation. The experience should lead to a frank discussion of the consequences of adopting a positive-focused, collaborative style. The managers must consider not only how they will react to and support the projects and proposals made by the participants, but also whether they are prepared to sustain this style of leadership in the future.

The session with senior management affords a good opportunity to finalize the topic. Centering the process on a critical business issue is one of the key success factors. If this is not the case, a great deal of time and effort will be expended, resulting, at best, in a temporary boost in motivation and, at worst, in demotivation and increased cynicism. As noted earlier, the topic of inquiry must be framed or reframed positively (see Table 6.1 for several examples).

Managers are sometimes concerned that the employee proposals resulting from an open, collaborative process will be unworkable or even irresponsible. This fear is generally misplaced, and the trust placed in employees is amply repaid. Given the chance, employees show a deep commitment to the success of their organization. If anything, the employees tend to be overambitious in their desire to change the organization for the better.

In larger projects it is highly recommended to create a core team of internal stakeholders. The core team may consist of volunteers or management nominees, but in either case they should be representative of each stakeholder group and all levels in the organization. Their role is two-fold:

1. Act as process champions, communicating the process objectives to their peers and creating interest, and

2. Assist in process design, helping the consultants learn the organization's culture and how to get things done effectively.

The core team is also trained by the consultants during the Initiate phase.

2. Inquire (Discover)

The objective of the Inquire or Discover phase is to bring to light the root causes of success. The fundamental question asked during this phase is: *"What works?"* In practical terms, this is done by means of "appreciative interviews," in which the widest possible cross-section of stakeholders is interviewed. The best of the stories and data gathered in the interviews is then shared in larger groups and ultimately across the whole organization. The creative tension thus set up between the stories of the organization at its best and the current reality becomes a very powerful driving force for change.

Let's look at this process step-by-step.

Step 2-1: Interview Design. The interviews must be carefully designed, not only to obtain the information needed but also to achieve the desired effect on the persons interviewed. One's state of mind—and more importantly one's ability to work constructively with other people—is quite different following a discussion focused on the positives than on the negatives. Imagine how different you might feel spending an hour talking about your greatest successes and your hopes for the future, compared with the same hour talking about failures, mistakes, problems, and what needs to change.

Prior research notes that high group potency correlates with team effectiveness as well as team cohesion, coordination, and team member development. This approach was explored in a 2006 study by Henry Peelle III, in which he compared cross-functional teams that were using either appreciative inquiry or creative problem solving to address organizational issues. The creative-problem-solving approach emphasized gap analysis and abstract brainstorming techniques, while the appreciative inquiry groups began with stories of personal success and identification of best practice experiences as a basis for completing their tasks. Peelle found that the AI groups measured higher in group potency and group identification. This suggests that the first stage of the AI interview process builds a foundation that contributes to team success.

Good practice is to structure the appreciative interviews in three sections:

1. General questions designed to create a positive, collaborative atmosphere ("Tell me about your best experience in this organization.")

2. Specific questions focused on the critical business issue or topic of the inquiry ("Tell me about your best experience in [e.g., customer service] in this organization.")

3. Forward-looking questions intended to elicit hopes and dreams for the future ("Imagine that in three years time this organization has become everything you dream it could be. What has changed?")

Step 2-2: Interview Process. It is important that the interviewers be well briefed on how to conduct the interview. A temptation for some interviewers will be to try to get through the interview quickly and summarize it into a series of bullet points; this temptation must be resisted. Their principal objective is to gather stories. The best stories will be told and retold, eventually acquire the status of myths, and continue to shape behavior at the organization long after their protagonists have departed.

The interviewers must therefore actively look for stories and, if necessary, patiently draw them out. They should adopt the attitude of a best friend or a sympathetic journalist who wants to hear all the details; using such questions as "Tell me what happened?" "Who did what?" "How did he do it?" "Why did that happen?" "What exactly did you do?" "What happened next?"

These interviews create a human connection between two people, as they begin to recognize that what they have in common is far greater than any eventual differences. For this reason it is advisable to create as much diversity as is possible in the interview pairs: people should not interview their closest colleagues, but rather a person in the organization who is as least like them as possible. It will generally be necessary for advance planning to pair off, for example, a junior sales person with the finance director or a production manager with a human resources specialist.

The benefit of these "improbable pairs" is that they create connections where none existed, and thus help to break down silos. The different functional viewpoints bring another potential benefit, stimulating cross-fertilization of ideas and thus innovation.

Step 2-3: Exploiting the Interviews. The interviews provide a goldmine of positive information about the organization. The best stories and quotes can be widely published, and the most telling interviews repeated on video to be placed on the intranet or used for such purposes as integrating new hires.

During an AI event, the interviews are debriefed in small groups, typically of six to ten people. Each person in turn repeats the highlights of the interview to the others in the group and asks the interviewee (if present) to repeat one of his or her stories. Each group is expected to select the most inspirational story and agree on the "root causes of success" illustrated by this and other stories from the group's members. Root causes of success mean the fundamental characteristics of the organization leading to the successes discussed.

The next step is to share the best stories from each small group with the large group in a plenary session. In this way everyone present hears the most inspirational stories. During this activity, the energy in the room is high: participants can feel the pride and excitement as people listen to each other's best experiences.

Step 2-4: Mapping the "Positive Core". The final activity in the discovery phase is called "mapping the positive core". The objective is to create a simple, meaningful image of the organization at its best. Asking a skilled graphics facilitator to create this "positive core map" in real time on a huge wall chart can be very effective; alternatives include creating a "mind map" or "concept map" in which the key points are grouped by themes branching out separately from the central topic (see Figure 6.2) or adding to an image that has relevance to the organization. For example, David Cooperrider and Diana Whitney describe in their 2005 book *Appreciative Inquiry: A Positive Revolution in Change* how they used the image of a delivery truck being loaded with the organization's strengths and hopes for the future during a series of AI summits with the delivery company Roadway Express.

New software suitable for collaboration in large groups is now available, providing another option to consider.

3. Imagine (Dream)

Step 3-1: Reviewing the "Positive Core". As people look at the wall chart, they tend to be struck by two things. The first is "Look at how good we are when we're at our best!" The second is "This is too good to be true . . . the picture has deliberately left out the negatives." It is important for the facilitator to acknowledge each of these sentiments. The facilitator might even point out that the group could just as well have created a picture of everything wrong with the organization, and ask the group to reflect on which approach would be the most constructive.

Taking specific examples, the facilitator can point out that the negatives can generally be reframed from the presence of something "bad" to the absence of something "good." This opens the door to a discussion of how to develop the desired positives through leveraging the organization's strengths.

Step 3-2: Break into Innovation Teams to Focus on Discrete Areas of Change. The objective of the imagine phase is to agree to a common, shared vision for what the organization should become. The facilitator's role is to guide the group in expressing their vision in specific, concrete terms, focused on the core topic of the inquiry. It is usually not helpful to call into question the organization's overall vision, but rather to define very precisely what it means in the area under focus. For example, organizational visions often contain a reference to customer satisfaction, but without going into detail. The vision related to customer satisfaction resulting from the imagine phase will describe in detail what this means.

Even in narrowly focused inquiries, it is typically necessary to work on different aspects of the organization's response to the challenge. For example, an inquiry focused on customer service may uncover the need to make changes in management processes and work assignments, in HR processes such as recruitment, selection, and training, and in service delivery processes and related systems.

In order to provide an appropriate level of focus on each of the major issues, the large group is invited to break up into "innovation teams." These teams are composed of volunteers with energy, passion, and expertise in the different areas associated with the next discussion.

An effective way to do this was first proposed by Harrison Owen and explained in detail in his 1997 book *Open Space Technology: A User's Guide.* Under the open space process, the entire group is first organized into a large circle (or two to three concentric circles if the group is very big), around an open space. Using the positive core map created during the inquire phase as the starting point, the facilitator asks the group for volunteers to lead small teams in developing key aspects of the picture. The volunteers stand up, move to the center of the space to declare their project, and then add their names and the details of the project to a pre-prepared roster of available meeting rooms and meeting times. Once all projects have been declared, all other participants are invited to sign up to work with the innovation team that interests them the most.

Participants are allowed—even encouraged—to move from one team to another if they feel they can add more value elsewhere. This can be an effective way to cross-pollinate ideas as well as to optimize the effectiveness of each team.

Step 3-3: Develop "Provocative Propositions". The first objective of the innovation teams is to create a clear vision for their chosen area of focus. This vision is usually expressed as a "provocative proposition," meaning a statement describing as precisely as possible the future desired state, in the present tense *as if it were already achieved.*

Taken together, the provocative propositions of each innovation team should provide a clear, coherent picture of how the organization wishes to be in the future. They will provide the target against which future actions should be planned, and they must ensure the alignment of the project with the organization's wider goals.

It is important that the provocative propositions result from the broadest possible consensus, and that all have the opportunity to comment on them. This is easily achieved during the meeting through presentations and feedback sessions. Input from the wider organization can be sought simultaneously, or at a later date, through appropriate collaboration software.

4. Innovate (Design)

Step 4-1: Develop Concrete Action Plans. These action plans should take the organization in the direction of the provocative propositions developed in the previous phase. The dynamic atmosphere and diverse mix of participants at an appreciative inquiry event provides excellent conditions for going beyond run-of-the-mill incremental changes to creating breakthrough innovations.

As in other steps, the facilitator's role is to provide the structure and process and then stand back to let the teams do the work. There are many different ways to structure such sessions, ranging from a simple brainstorming session with a couple of flip charts to the much more sophisticated innovation processes developed over the last few years. Whichever process is chosen will depend on the project's potential, the time allowed, and the available resources.

Step 4-2: Keep the Whole System Involved. In order to maintain overall coherence and to ensure that everybody remains engaged with each proposal, the innovation teams should regularly receive feedback from their peers in the large group. We often find that projects overlap or should be interfaced: it is far more efficient to build this within the open space environment rather than to have to rework two or more projects at the end of this planning process.

A useful technique can be to ask each innovation team to write key project milestones and resource requirements on cards or polystyrene ceiling tiles. These are then placed on a ''road map to the future,'' which is marked out in the form of a timeline on the conference room floor. This provides an easily grasped visual overview of the overall change initiative and highlights the need for careful resource allocation and coordination. Generally, each team wants to start its project at once and finish it within six months, resulting in a large pile-up of tiles at the beginning of the timeline. This visual effect is often sufficient to motivate the teams themselves to discuss priorities and improve the overall coherence; if not the facilitator should step in.

Step 4-3: Obtain Approval for the Action Plans. The final step of the innovate phase is for the innovation teams to present and obtain approval for their action plans. Different organizations prefer different approval processes: for some the majority approval of all those present will be necessary, while for others management approval will be necessary. Especially where the process is essentially hierarchical, it is important to recognize the sincerity and the efforts of the teams.

All approved projects then enter a project management process in the final phase, implement. Projects that are not approved may be given a second chance to meet the project approval criteria, or they may simply be dropped.

Step 4-4: Concluding the Meeting. It is generally at this point that the plenary meeting is brought to a close. Emotions are still running high, and there is often a mixture of fatigue and elation (*"Did we really do all this?"*). It is important to provide an appropriate closing ceremony before the participants split up to return home.

One approach that can work well is to form a large circle and ask people to, in turns, give their impressions of the day. If there are a lot of people, it can be helpful to ask for one word only. If enough time is available and the location is appropriate, the facilitator can ask participants before closing to take a fifteen-minute walk and come back with something symbolic to share with the group. The final word should generally be left for the senior person present, who should congratulate and thank all participants for their hard work and promise to support the agreed decisions.

5. Implement (Destiny)

The implement phase borrows much from standard project management techniques. It is important to bear in mind, however, the conditions under which these projects first came to life. They were not drawn up by a small project team of experts appointed by management, but came out of a highly collaborative process in which the whole organization may have participated. Management therefore needs to be sensitive about exercising its usual prerogatives and should think carefully before withdrawing support or mandating changes in any of the projects.

Step 5-1: Project Review Meetings. Project review meetings should be held in the appreciative spirit. Each meeting should therefore begin with a review of what has gone well. Challenges and unresolved difficulties should be addressed through a positive frame (*"Who has experience facing similar challenges in the past,"* or *"Who can tell us how they resolved them?"*).

Step 5-2: Develop and Execute a Robust Communication Strategy. As in any change management process, good communication is essential. Each organization will find its own most appropriate way to communicate progress; a communication strategy and clear responsibilities must be determined from the outset. People have invested a lot of energy and emotional commitment in the outcomes of the AI process and are hungry for information on progress of the various projects.

Case Study: "Take Charge for Growth"

This case study is a brief description of a one-day appreciative inquiry session for the European management team of a Silicon Valley high-tech company, referred to as "Hi-Tech EMEA," conducted by Marvin Faure. This company has been growing in excess of 50 percent per annum and wants to maintain this growth rate for the foreseeable future.

The selected topic was "Take Charge for Growth," with the top forty-five managers from the European region having been invited to take part in what was to be a strategic planning session. The objective of the day was to gain agreement on the critical changes they needed to make to maintain their growth rate. One full day was allocated to this (see Table 6.3 for the agenda).

After an introductory speech from the vice president of European Operations, the day began by each participant being interviewed and interviewing another person on his or her most successful experiences at the company, defined as those that created the most

Table 6.3 Agenda for Take Charge for Growth

	Time	Groups	Activity
INQUIRE	08.30 – 09.00	All together	Kick-off and Introduction Today's agenda
	09.00 – 09:10	Small Groups	Personal introductions
	09:10 – 10:10	Pairs	Appreciative interviews (one-on-one)
	10.10–10:25		***COFFEE BREAK***
	10:25 – 11:00	Small Groups	Discuss the interviews and share stories.
	11:00 – 11:45	All together	Small group report-out Wall chart of organizational strengths
	11.45 – 12.15	All together	Vote on key strengths to develop from innovation teams
IMAGINE	**12.15–13.15**		***LUNCH***
	13.15 – 14.15	Innovation Teams	Agree on the team's vision Prepare a creative presentation
	14.15 – 15.00	All together	Show Time!
INNOVATE	**15.00–15.15**		***COFFEE BREAK***
	15.15 – 16.00	Innovation Teams	Formulate 2008 goal(s) Agree action plans
	16.00 – 16.45	All together	Present action plans; discussion
	16.45 – 17.00	All together	Wrap-up and closing

growth. The best stories were then retold in small groups, who were tasked with identifying the "root causes of success." These were then reported out to the whole group, and the facilitator created a large wall chart in the form of a mind map (see Figure 6.4 for a simplified version).

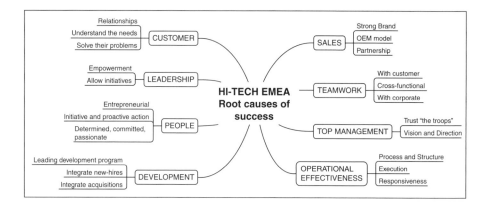

Figure 6.4 Hi-Tech EMEA Root Causes of Success.

The participants next used stickers to multi-vote for the themes on the mind map that they considered the most important for future success and then broke into volunteer teams to work on specific projects. The projects chosen were

- Empowerment
- Process and Structure
- Customer Satisfaction
- Passion
- Vision and Direction
- Branding
- Working with Partners

The teams worked on these projects during the afternoon. Light relief was provided by the humorous sketches each team put together to illustrate their vision, and by the end of the day each team's key objectives and initial project plan were approved by the whole group and validated by the vice president.

Reaction to the day was very positive, with many participant comments such as: "The day was not only highly productive but also great fun!" "I got to know and appreciate my colleagues much better," and "All meetings should be like this!"

Since the AI session, growth at Hi-Tech EMEA has if anything accelerated and they continue to set impressive sales records.

CRITICAL SUCCESS FACTORS

Building an AI initiative for success involves several important considerations:

- The objective must be compelling and clearly expressed in positive language.
- The leadership must be committed to the process and willing to relinquish some control.
- Maximize participation:
  - The more people involved, the more successful the outcomes.
  - This includes engaging people on the AI process design and facilitation team, which should include as many insiders as possible.
- Trust the process:
  - Positive questions and stories are essential.
  - Always begin with one-on-one appreciative interviews (nothing else is as effective in creating a positive effect and enthusiasm for the task).
  - Be flexible in language, while still true to the spirit of AI.
  - Do a small-scale change if skepticism persists.

Equally, there are various pitfalls to avoid:

- Forbidding the discussion of problems or other negatives can create intense frustration and/or total disengagement. Allow people to express what they don't want and then help them reframe to clarify what they do want.
- Be wary of the "flavor of the month" syndrome, where management seizes on AI as a "good idea" but has no strategy to follow through. Some managers try to use AI as a quick fix through a one-off event: the usual result is a short-term boost followed by a long-term slump and increase in cynicism.
- Situations in which AI may not be applicable include when the organization is in acute distress, requiring immediate and painful decisions. In these instances, AI may be viewed as irrelevant (even provocative) and not offering the needed short-term impact. AI can be an effective "next step" once the difficult decisions are made.

SUMMARY

Appreciative inquiry can be a very effective approach for organizational change, so long as the unique features and consequences of adopting this approach are well understood by senior management. Unlike a deficit approach, AI can bring energy and excitement to an organization and encourage visionary thinking that allows for a leap into the future. For managers who are willing to place faith in their employees and who can share the thinking and processes required for developing the organization's potential, the payoff can be substantial.

References

Cooperrider, D. L., & Srivastva, S. (1987). Appreciative inquiry in organizational life. In R. Woodman & W. Pasmore (Eds.), *Research in organizational change and development (Vol. 1)* (pp. 129–169). Greenwich, CT: JAI Press

Cooperrider, D. L., & Whitney, D. (2005). *Appreciative inquiry. A. positive revolution in change.* San Francisco: Berrett-Koehler.

Dutton, J. E. (2003). *Energize your workplace.* San Francisco: Jossey-Bass.

Dutton, J. E., & Heaphy, E. D. (2003). The power of high-quality connections. In K. S. Cameron, J. E. Dutton, & R. E. Quinn (Eds.), *Positive organizational scholarship: Foundations of a new discipline.* San Francisco: Berrett-Koehler.

Fredrickson, B. L. (2003). Positive emotions and upward spirals in organizations. In K. S. Cameron, J. E. Dutton, & R. E. Quinn (Eds.), *Positive organizational scholarship: Foundations of a new discipline,* San Francisco: Berrett-Koehler.

Gergen, K. (1999). *An invitation to social construction.* London: Sage.

Jones, D.A. (1998). A field experiment in appreciative inquiry. *OD Journal, 16*(4) 69–78.

Ludema, J. D., Whitney, D., Mohr, B. J., & Griffin, T. J. (2003). *The appreciative inquiry summit: A practitioner's guide for leading large-group change.* San Francisco: Berrett-Koehler.

Owen, H. (1997). *Open space technology: A user's guide.* San Francisco: Berrett-Koehler.

Peelle, H. E. III (2006). Appreciative inquiry and creative problem solving in cross-functional teams. *Journal of Applied Behavioral Science, 42,* 447–467.

Peterson, C. M., & Seligman, M. E. P. (2003). Positive organizational studies: Lessons from positive psychology. In K. S. Cameron, J. E. Dutton, & R. E. Quinn (Eds.), *Positive organizational scholarship: Foundations of a new discipline.* San Francisco: Berrett-Koehler.

Watkins, J. M., & Mohr, B. J. (2001). *Appreciative inquiry: Change at the speed of imagination.* San Francisco: Pfeiffer.

Recommended Readings and Websites

Brrett, F. J., & Cooperrider, D. L. (1990). Generative metaphor intervention: A new approach for working with systems divided by conflict and caught in defensive perception. *Journal of Applied Behavioral Science, 26,* 219–239.

Buckingham, M., & Coffman, C. (1999). *First, break all the rules: What the world's greatest managers do differently.* New York: Simon and Schuster.

Bunker, B. B., & Alban, B. T. (1997). *Large group interventions: Engaging the whole system for rapid change*. San Francisco: Jossey-Bass.

Bushe, G. R. (1998). Appreciative inquiry in teams. *Organizational Development Journal*, *16*, 41–50.

Bushe, G. R., & Kassam, A. F. (2005). When is AI transformational? A meta-case analysis. *Journal of Applied Behavioral Science*, *41*(2), 161–181.

Buzan, T. (1993). *The mindmap book*. London: BBC Books.

Cooperrider, D. L., & Whitney, D. (1999). *Appreciative inquiry*. San Francisco: Berrett-Koehler.

Faure, M. J. (2006). Problem solving was never this easy: Transformational change through appreciative inquiry. *Performance Improvement*, *45*(9), 22–31.

Fredrickson, B. L. (1998). What good are positive emotions? *Review of General Psychology*, *2*, 300–319.

Hammond, S. (1996). *The thin book of appreciative inquiry*. Bend, OR: Thin Book Publishing.

Katzenbach, J. R. (2003). *Why pride matters more than money: The power of the world's greatest motivational force*. New York: Random House.

Kelley, T. (2001). *The art of innovation: Lessons in creativity from IDEO, America's leading design firm*. New York: Doubleday.

Rosenthal, R., & Jacobson, L. (1968). *Pygmalion in the classroom: Teacher expectation and pupils' intellectual development*. New York: Rinehart and Winston.

Seligman. M. E. P. (1990). *Learned optimism: How to change your mind and your life*. New York: A.A. Knopf.

Weisbord, M., & Janoff, S. (2005). Faster, shorter, cheaper may be simple; it's never easy. *Journal of Applied Behavioral Science*, *41*(1), 70–82.

Whitney, D., & Trosten-Bloom, A. (2003). *The power of appreciative inquiry: A practical guide to positive change*. San Francisco: Berrett-Koehler

Whitney, D., Cooperrider, D. L., Trosten-Bloom, A., & Kaplin, B. S. (2002). *Encyclopedia of positive questions, volume 1: Using appreciative inquiry to bring out the best in your organization*. Euclid, OH: Lakeshore Communications.

Yaeger, T. F., & Sorensen, P. F. (2005). A seasoned perspective on appreciative inquiry: What we know, what we need to know. *Seasonings*, *1*(2). http://www.odnetwork .org/publications/seasonings/2005-vol1-no2/article_yaeger_sorensen.html (current February 1, 2006).

http://appreciativeinquiry.case.edu/. The Appreciative Inquiry Commons.

PART TWO

EDITORS'
DISCUSSION

Creating and aligning the strategic direction of your organization helps guide your selection of a useful set of performance interventions. Aligning the strategic direction of your organization will shape almost every decision you make. From the outside, the objectives of your clients, suppliers, and other external partners will help define what results you accomplish and why. Likewise, from within, the many performance objectives that already exist throughout your organization must be aligned to successfully avoid sub-optimization and to improve performance.

Building a solid foundation of strategic direction starts with the clear understanding of the results your organization wants to accomplish and how those results contribute to the success of your organization's partners. After all, your success and the success of your organization are inexorably tied to the success of others. Successful improvement efforts therefore recognize this essential alliance between the organization and its partners and systematically make decisions to achieve results that benefit all.

Similarly, successful improvement efforts build on the alignment of goals and objectives that cut across division, departments, units, and individuals. To improve performance, the relative value or worth of the many goals and objectives found within an organization must be assessed and prioritized in order to facilitate effective decision making. If a marketing department, for example, has competing goals with those of the sales department, then a dynamic assessment of those goals can help you make associated decisions when improving performance.

Expanding Your Options

Risk management—a structured approach to manage uncertainty related to a threat, a sequence of human activities including: risk assessment, strategies development to manage it, and mitigation of risk using managerial resources.

Based on wikipedia.org entry (January 2009)

While the desired results of some individuals or teams may seem divergent or even contradictory, by building alignment from the outside in, you should be able to link together what results must be accomplished for everyone to be successful. This allows performance improvement projects to align all that the organization uses, does, produces, and delivers to the desired outcomes of the organization, its partners, and society as a whole.

An aligned and unified strategic direction provides clear guidance as to what results should be accomplished at all levels of the organization. Individual employees can then rely on the strategic direction—as expressed in vision statements, annual goals, quarterly targets, performance objectives, and other messages—to guide their daily decisions. Also, teams and units within the organization can routinely consult the strategic plan to ensure that they are moving in the right direction and achieving necessary results.

Strategic direction provides the foundation for the selection of successful performance interventions. Without such direction, your performance improvement efforts are without a basis in the results to be accomplished. For that reason, the creation and alignment of strategic direction is the focus of Part Two of this handbook and is at the foundation of the Performance Pyramid described in Chapter Three. You should use the performance interventions described in Part Two of this handbook—Future Search, SWOT Analysis, and Appreciative Inquiry, and others—to generate, identify, analyze, and prioritize the strategic accomplishments that are to be achieved through your efforts to improve performance, going beyond the short-term results to align with the strategic objectives of your organization and its partners. Then use the strategic direction as the foundation for your decisions through the selection, design, development, implementation, and evaluation of all other performance interventions.

References and Resources from Editorial Contributions to Part Two

Kaufman, R. (2006). *30 seconds that can change your life: A decision-making guide for those who refuse to be mediocre.* Amherst, MA: HRD Press.

Kaufman, R. (2006). *Change, choices, and consequences: A guide to mega thinking and planning.* Amherst, MA: HRD Press.

Kaufman, R., Oakley-Brown, H., Watkins, R., & Leigh, D. (2003). *Strategic planning for success: Aligning people, performance, and payoffs.* San Francisco: Jossey-Bass.

Watkins, R. (2007). *Performance by design: The systematic selection, design, and development of performance technologies that produce useful results.* Amherst, MA: HRD Press.

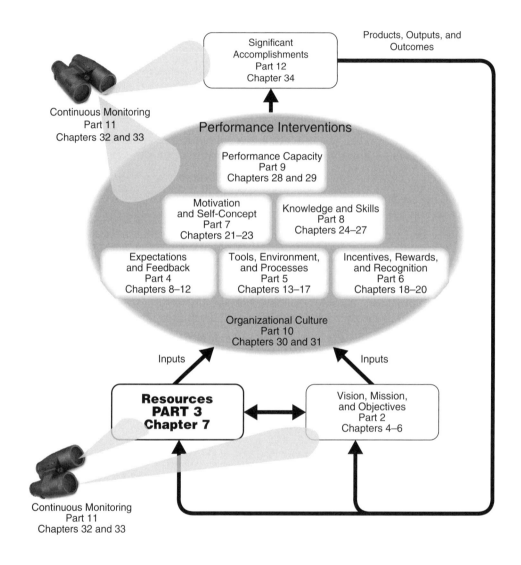

Continuous Monitoring
Part 11
Chapters 32 and 33

Significant
Accomplishments
Part 12
Chapter 34

Products, Outputs, and
Outcomes

Performance Interventions

Performance Capacity
Part 9
Chapters 28 and 29

Motivation
and Self-Concept
Part 7
Chapters 21–23

Knowledge and Skills
Part 8
Chapters 24–27

Expectations
and Feedback
Part 4
Chapters 8–12

Tools, Environment,
and Processes
Part 5
Chapters 13–17

Incentives, Rewards,
and Recognition
Part 6
Chapters 18–20

Organizational Culture
Part 10
Chapters 30 and 31

Inputs

Inputs

**Resources
PART 3
Chapter 7**

Vision, Mission,
and Objectives
Part 2
Chapters 4–6

Continuous Monitoring
Part 11
Chapters 32 and 33

PART THREE

RESOURCES

From inexpensive interventions that require just a little time and a few flip charts to the development of comprehensive improvement programs that require additional staff and annual expenditures, the range of resources required for improving performance can vary drastically. Consequently, the resources available for improving results, including financial, social, political, and human capital resources, will help shape decisions about which performance interventions you use. After all, the limitations of your resources will shape the boundaries of what interventions are feasible for your improvement effort. Resources are, therefore, an essential and foundational component for the Performance Pyramid model.

At the beginning of any effort to improve performance, it is important to ensure that adequate resources are available to accomplish desired results. Practically speaking, few improvement efforts have unlimited resources, and thus most projects have to carefully set priorities and make compromises when selecting performance interventions. While it would be nice to have ample resources when, for example, implementing a comprehensive performance coaching, a well-financed incentives systems, and an all-inclusive set of web-based performance support tools, the reality is that resource limitations (including budget, time, expertise, organizational support structures, and others) will play a crucial role in your selection of appropriate performance interventions.

Expanding Your Options

Supply chain management—a system of organizations, people, technology, activities, information and resources involved in moving a product or service from supplier to customer, encompassing manufacturing and procurement, and therefore involving multiple enterprises, including suppliers, manufacturers and retailers, working together to meet customer demand for a product or service.

Based on wikipedia.org definition (January 2009)

Candid conversations and plans related to resource requirements should therefore be part of your efforts to improve performance from day one. You can, of course, achieve significant accomplishments with limited resources; but how you go about accomplishing desired results differs widely depending on the resources available. Just as you can travel across the country in a large recreational vehicle or a small 1970s Volkswagen "Beetle," the routes you take, the equipment you pack, and the amount you will spend on gas will vary greatly depending on your choice of transportation. When striving to improve performance, you can be very successful with few resources, but its necessary to plan wisely—starting with your initial conversations.

Resources stretch beyond the financial to include the numerous components that go into the foundation of a successful improvement effort. While money is a common link among most resource considerations, it is also important to consider the other types of resources that will impact your ability to implement successful performance interventions. Political capital, for example, can play a substantial role in any performance improvement project. If you have the political capital (for instance, support from top managers or leaders in the organization or a history of leading effective improvement project yourself), then often you can utilize this capital to get things done. Alternatively, if you do not yet have sufficient political capital, your plans for implementing performance interventions will have to include "marketing" activities to build support for the effort.

Resources (including budgets, personnel, equipment, policies, and others) are classified, categorized, arranged, and accounted for through the structures of the organization. For example, your organization may rely solely on product lines to organize the distribution and management of resources. Alternatively, your organization may rely on functions to distribute and manage resources (for example, research, production, sales, or finance). Or you may work in a "matrix organization" in which resources are managed through a combination of functional and product-line structures at the same time. Whatever the case, the organizational structures in which the performance interventions will be implemented are critical for ensuring that adequate and appropriate resources are available for improving performance.

Expanding Your Options

Matrix management—an organizational or management structure that takes employees with similar skills and pools them around (typically two) functional tasks. For example, employees may have roles related to a specific product line, as well as roles related to a business process such as research, accounting, or sales that cut across multiple product lines.

Based on wikipedia.org definition (January 2009)

Organizational structures have influence both on how you go about implementing interventions to improve performance as well as on the accomplishment of desired results (that is, performance) outside of your improvement efforts. Traditionally hierarchical organizations, with their silo or stove-pipe structures, are influential in either supporting or challenging the improvement of performance, depending on the interventions you select and how you go about implementing your choices. These traditional structures may also present obstacles to how you expend the resources you do have for the improvement effort. For example, pulling resources from multiple departments may mean that you answer to "multiple bosses" for the improvement effort—each with his or her own perspective regarding the results to be accomplished. Even when this is not a problem, you do have to manage your improvement effort with this in mind.

Non-traditional organizations, with their flat or minimalist structures, can also support or present obstacles to the achievement of significant accomplishments. In these organizations, you can encounter situations in which you have sufficient resources for implementing a system of performance interventions but find the "political will" for meaningful change in performance is hard to come by. Without a clear top-down chain of command, it may be challenging to build across-the-board support for the numerous performance interventions required to accomplish desired results.

These implications derived from organizational structures also support or impede the accomplishment of desired performance in the workplace outside of your efforts to improve performance. Organizational structures may, for instance, dramatically slow procurement procedures to the point at which production is slowed or even stopped. Similarly, challenges presented by organizational structures can reduce communication, hinder knowledge sharing, create destructive competitions for resources, limit career development, and otherwise have an impact on almost all other aspects of performance.

Expanding Your Options

Cash flow analysis—the balance of the amounts of cash being received and paid by a business during a defined period of time, sometimes tied to a specific project. Measurement of cash flow can be used: (1) to evaluate the state or performance of a business or project; (2) to determine problems with liquidity (being profitable does not necessarily mean being liquid. A company can fail because of a shortage of cash, even while profitable); (3) to generate project rate of returns. Cash flow into and out of projects are used as input to financial models such as internal rate of return, and net present value.

Based on wikipedia.org definition (January 2009)

Because of their importance, The Performance Pyramid model includes resources (with organizational structures as a major component in the distribution and management of resources) as a foundation for accomplishing significant results. Resources are not only a factor in determining what results can be achieved, but also in how you go about improving the achievement of those same results. Therefore, improvement efforts will often include recommendations for organizational restructuring. Many times organizational structures are reshuffled or reorganized around the units and departments; but restructuring can also examine how finances are split among organizational structures or how social and political networks are used to cut across structures.

WHAT'S COMING UP

In Chapter Seven, Sally Lollie and Hillary Leigh explore the important roles of organizational structure in providing a foundation for improving human and organizational performance and how efforts to restructure organizations can be effectively implemented in order to improve performance. Within the context of

Expanding Your Options

Budget—generally refers to a list of all planned expenses and revenues. A budget is an important concept in microeconomics, which uses a budget line to illustrate the tradeoffs between two or more goods. In other terms, a budget is an organizational plan stated in monetary terms. In summary, the purpose of budgeting is to (1) provide a forecast of revenues and expenditures, that is, construct a model of how the business might perform financially speaking if certain strategies, events, and plans are carried out and (2) enable the actual financial operation of the business to be measured against the forecast.

Based on wikipedia.org definition (January 2009)

other resources, such as financial, political, and human capital, the foundations play a critical role in supporting the success of nearly any other performance intervention.

CHAPTER SEVEN

Organizational Restructuring

Sally Lollie
Hillary Leigh

INTRODUCTION

While the colloquial idea is that form follows function, we might also include something of the notion of circumstance. This is because, on an organizational level, the architecture of an organization is its response to the conditions in which it exists. More specifically, organizational structure can be equated with the configuration of its components and relationships among them. Sometimes these arrangements reflect the reporting relationships of individuals, teams, or departments within the organization, and at other times these structures illustrate the process relationships within a supply chain. This chapter frames organizations in the structural perspective and suggests a six-step process to align organizational structures with the achievement of meaningful results. We will explore concepts that support the analysis and design of effective organizational structures through a description of types of structure, issues for their management, and of factors for their variation. We also present a six-step process for design, development, and implementation. While this chapter predominately views organizational structuring and restructuring as proactive organizational design intervention, we will also emphasize its utility as a supportive strategy to managing any change initiative.

DESCRIPTION

There are multiple ways to conceive of an organization. Quite famously, Gareth Morgan argued that organizations could be viewed metaphorically (for example, as a machine, an organism, or a brain) and that each metaphor emphasized certain characteristics while minimizing others. In this spirit, Lee Bolman and Terrence Deal posit in their seminal work *Reframing Organizations* that multiple perspectives for thinking about organizations, stating that they can be framed in terms of their symbols, politics, human resources, and structures. The human resources approach may be the most intuitive to those in the field of human performance technology (HPT) as it "emphasizes dealing with issues by changing people (through training, rotation, promotion, or dismissal)," but the structural perspective "argues for putting people in the right roles and relationships" and therefore takes a dramatically different viewpoint on organizations (p. 47). They also propose that structuralism is based on the assumptions that:

1. Organizations exist in order to achieve a particular set of goals;

2. Goals are reached most efficiently when a balance is struck between the division of work, coordination of collective effort, and mitigation of individual agendas and extraneous issues by reason;

3. An organization's structures ought to fit its current circumstances; and

4. Deficiencies can be alleviated by the redesign these structures—that is, "restructuring"—can alleviate problems that occur as a result of structural deficiencies (p. 47).

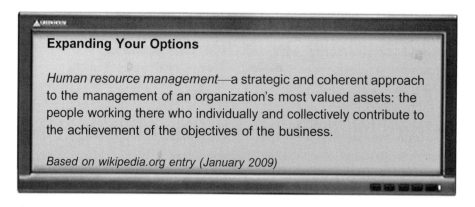

Expanding Your Options

Human resource management—a strategic and coherent approach to the management of an organization's most valued assets: the people working there who individually and collectively contribute to the achievement of the objectives of the business.

Based on wikipedia.org entry (January 2009)

At this point, we'd like to point out that readers who are already well-versed in the basis for the field in systems thinking and engineering ought to recognize striking parallels between these assumptions and the definition of a system as an ordered set of many components that are interrelated in their elements and their attributes and whose structures are determined by function. Additional characteristics include that a system is a complete whole unto itself, it is hierarchical in nature, and it may be open or closed, natural or artificial. Furthermore, as Rita Richey explains in her 1986 book on the topic of instructional design, a system is constrained by the environment and stabilized through feedback.

Taken together, these characteristics and the aforementioned structural assumptions about organizations suggest some of the key decisions involved in structuring an organization:

- Balancing the division and integration of work;
- How, where, and by whom decisions are made; and
- How information and power play a role in the organization.

While this chapter predominately discusses these decisions from the perspective of restructuring existing organizational components, the issues addressed may also be useful during the design of a new organization. Additionally, restructuring is distinct from interventions such as mergers, outsourcing, and budget cuts but application of the concepts and tools discussed here can enhance their success. That said, organizational structuring is closely related to budgetary and financial considerations within an organization. The relationship between organizational structures and financial practices is worthy of mention for the simple reason that most organizations measure financial results. By extension, accounting practices are heavily institutionalized and they can have an impact on structure, and vice versa.

Expanding Your Options

Outplacement services—efforts made by a downsizing company to help its redundant employees to help them re-orientate to the job market. This is frequently achieved through practical and psychological support either delivered through individual one-on-one sessions or in a group format. Common topics include career guidance, career evaluation, resume writing and interview preparation, developing networks, job search skills, and targeting the job market. Individuals may be offered other services such as the use of an office and online tools.

Based on wikipedia.org entry (January 2009)

WHAT WE KNOW FROM RESEARCH

On a very general level, organizational restructuring involves just two processes: analysis and synthesis. Drawing heavily from the work of Henry Mintzberg[1] at McGill University, this section refines this generalization through an explanation of structural components, types, and typologies of organizational structures, and closes with reasons why structural variations exist.

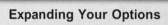

Expanding Your Options

Accounting—a system of recording, verifying, and reporting of the value of assets, liabilities, income, and expenses in the books of account (ledger) to which debit and credit entries (recognizing transactions) are chronologically posted to record changes in value. Such financial information is primarily used by leaders, managers, and other decision-makers to make resource allocation decisions between and within companies, organizations, and public agencies.

Based on wikipedia.org entry (January 2009)

Structural Components

In his classic 1980 work synthesizing the research on the design of organizations, "Structure in 5's," Mintzberg suggested that there are five basic components within an organization, the (1) operating core, (2) strategic apex, (3) middle line, (4) technostructure, and (5) support staff. The parts are defined in Table 7.1.

Table 7.1 Definitions of Organizational Parts

Organizational Part	Definition
Operating core	Those employees who are directly responsible for the operations of the organization (introducing its product or delivering the service it provides)
Strategic apex	Senior-level leaders who are responsible for the direction of the organization
Middle line	Those employees who are the authoritative liaisons between the strategic apex and the operating core
Technostructure	Those employees who do not fall within the strategic-operational line, but provide feedback to it (for example, internal consultants, analysts, accountants)
Support staff	Employees who are auxiliary to the strategic-operational line but whose work indirectly supports it (for example, benefits staff or community relations)

Based on Mintzberg's "Structure in 5's" (1980)

While this classification schema may seem somewhat classically oriented to a hierarchical perspective of the organization, Mintzberg's effort to distinguish between the central strategic-operational *line* and two types of auxiliary *staff* (technostructure and support staff) allows for the description of various types of organizational structures. More subtly, it suggests that an organization's structure is comprised of more than the names within the boxes on its organizational chart, but also includes those individuals' roles in basic operations and their relationships with one another.

This is a similar notion as that put forth is by Geary Rummler and Alan Brache in their 1995 book, *Improving Performance: How to Manage the White Space on the Organization Chart.* In 2006, Rummler proposed the anatomy of performance (AOP) model, which basically establishes a map of the relationships between the components within an organization, namely its individual employees, their jobs, work processes, functions/roles, and their management. Figure 7.1 illustrates this relationship map (including the traditional role of the HPT practitioner as a performance consultant that is external to the organization).

A relationship map such as this emphasizes both general organizational components and the individual workers' roles in the strategic-operational line. This is especially clear in the center of the diagram, where the roles and inter-relatedness of individual workers is illustrated within the organization's primary operational process. It is also evident as we look at the organization of these individuals into divisions (as indicated by boxes around them) and the reporting relationships (indicated by encompassing brackets) between them. An additional strength of the AOP relationship map is that it emphasizes the adaptability of an organization within the greater environment, including political, economical, and cultural factors as well as available resources, customers and competitors in its market, and its shareholders. This point relates to the issue of variability within organizational structures, because structures are formed as adaptations to these environmental factors and circumstances. The next section will discuss some of the ways in which an organization's structures may vary and describes specific types of organizational structures.

Variation in Organizational Configurations

An organization's structure exists as an adaptation to its specific circumstances. This reality might invite the simple conclusion that no organizations exist in exactly the same set of circumstances so there is no ideal structure for organizations and therefore that typologies of organizational structure provide little practical value. As an alternative position, we put forth that understanding the types of organizational structures exist is useful for two reasons: (1) since an organization's structure is entailed by its environmental circumstances, the ability to identify a particular type of organizational structure allows one the ability to understand the origins of a performance problem and the circumstances that led to it; and (2) once the decision has been made to implement a restructuring

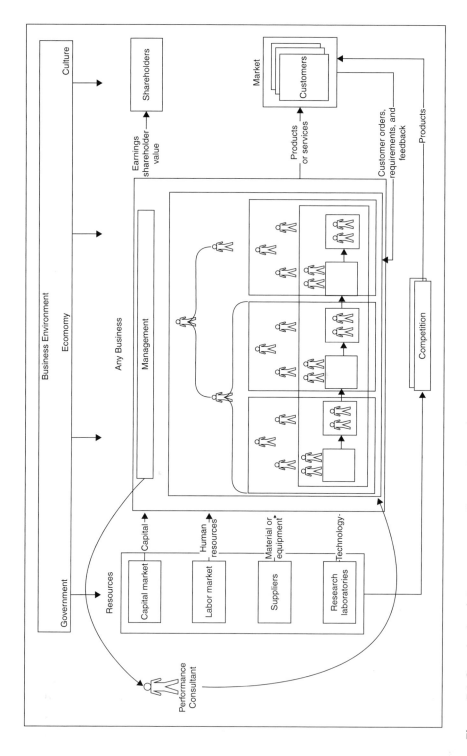

Figure 7.1 Organizational Components as Illustrated Through Rummler's Anatomy of Performance Model.

Source: G. Rummler. (2006). "The Anatomy of Performance." In J. Pershing (Ed.), *The Handbook of Human Performance Technology*

intervention, typologies aid in identifying critical structures that must be developed in order to support the current circumstances and adapt to circumstances that are likely to be the case in the future. Therefore, the next section reviews several organizational structure typologies.

Organic vs. Mechanistic. The most simplistic classification of organizational structures parallels the mechanistic and organic metaphors of organizations. This schema characterizes an organization's structure mostly based on complexity, formalization, and degree of centralization for decision making. The mechanistic and organic paradigms fall on opposite ends of the same spectrum (see Figure 7.2).

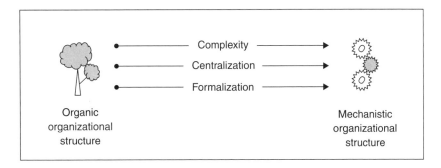

Figure 7.2 Features of Organic and Mechanistic Organizational Structures.

Differentiation Characterizations. A key consideration in the design of an organization's structures is how work is distributed across the organization and how workers' roles are distinguished from one another. There are basically four ways to divide work within an organization: by function, division, matrix, or network.

Functional structures group similar tasks together and each unit performs a different type of work. Since each unit is based on a unique body of knowledge and skills, functional structures lead to increased specialization of worker expertise. Figure 7.3 presents a simplified example of a functionally structured auto dealership where employees are organized into sales, service, marketing, and finance departments. While work may flow across these areas, it is primarily differentiated by employees' function within the organization.

In *divisional structures*, units may overlap in the types of work performed, but are hierarchically organized by product, customer, or region. While it might include characteristics of functional organization, it allows for the differentiation and tailoring of work based on characteristics relevant to the primary organizer. For example, an industrial organization might divide its core operations geographically by region, as shown in Figure 7.4. While it demonstrates

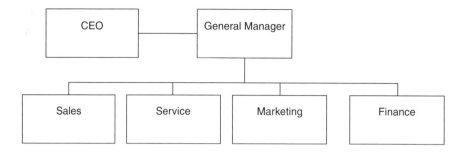

Figure 7.3 Functional Structure of an Auto Dealership.

only one part of an organization, Figure 7.4 shows that divisional structures are formalized and complex (the figure would be even larger if the entire organization were structured into divisions and mapped for our purposes). Additionally, specific functions may be duplicated in several divisions (as illustrated in redundant assembly, quality assurance, and shipping divisions).

In *matrix structures*, work is simultaneously organized by divisions and functions, thus it is a hybrid of the previous two structures. Matrix structures are process-oriented as work is distributed to cross-functional work groups. Figure 7.5 demonstrates a matrix structure for a health plan process for delivering physician performance reports.

Those employees who perform particular tasks and activities within this process are members of different functional units and simultaneously responsible to the work group itself.

According to Bruce Friesen's 2005 article for *Consulting to Management* journal, understanding of *network structures* is still emerging; an indication of this is that they are referred to in the literature in a variety of ways, including *lattice, cluster, and informal structures*. The themes that underlie all of these labels are that work and decision making are highly disaggregated and decentralized, information flows both through the chain of command and via informal network channels, and process differentiation plays an even larger role than in matrix networks. This final point is most evident in that work groups or teams are the primary organizer for work and this work is managed by a project champion instead of a traditional manager. A good example of a network structure is a virtual team that is widely dispersed geographically. The team is likely to be responsible to a project champion, they communicate freely with one another perhaps via informal channels such as email, instant messaging, or through collaborative document sharing. While work is somewhat oriented to process, it primarily leverages partnerships and alliances between members. Network structures are decentralized, or with many existing networks, they are what Bolman and Deal refer to as "multicentric" (p. 59).

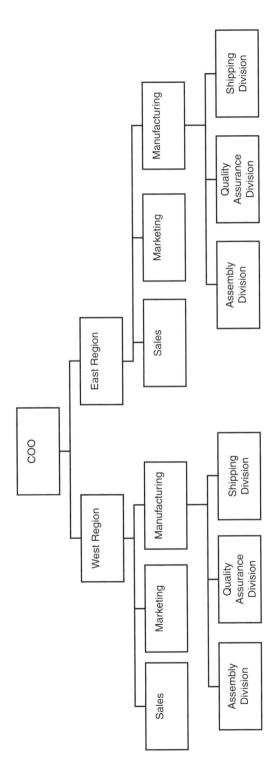

Figure 7.4 Divisional Structure in Core Operations (by Geography).

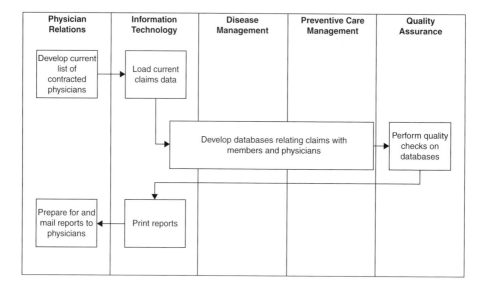

Figure 7.5 Matrix Structure Illustrating a Physician Performance Report Process.

Coordination Mechanisms. An equally important issue as differentiation involves how work will be integrated. Mintzberg (1980) said this coordination is achieved through mechanisms of supervision, standardization of work processes, outputs, and skills as well as *mutual adjustment* (self-regulation of work through informal communication with others). Through different degrees of emphasis on these mechanisms, organizational components exert force upon each other, resulting in varied structural configurations. For example, the structural apex tends to focus on the centralization of decision-making by emphasizing supervision as a mechanism for coordinating work. In this *simple structure* configuration, authority resides with only a small handful of leaders who oversee all of the operations. Another structure is derived in situations where those in the technostructure (consultants, accountants, analysts) push for standardization resulting in a *machine bureaucracy*, where the operational line is highly differentiated from other staff and those in the technostructure hold a great deal of informal authority. In a *professional bureaucracy*, the operational core resists authority of managers and technostructure staff (often through professionalization), and decisions are decentralized vertically and horizontally within the organization. In a limited form of decentralization, the middle managers derive power from the strategic apex and exert this authority over limited domains, resulting in a *divisional* structure. In the final type organizational structure suggested by Mintzberg, an *adhocracy*, support staff are able to self-regulate their work and communicate among themselves due to selective decentralization of authority.

Factors That Affect Organizational Structure

Bolman and Deal (2008) observed several relationships between organizational structures and existing circumstances:

1. As organizations grow larger and older, they become increasingly complex and formal.

2. The complexity of organizational structures parallel the complexity of its "core processes" (e.g. the structures of a university are more complicated than those of a fast food chain because teaching is a more complex process than food preparation).

3. Uncertain or turbulent environments require structures that are increasingly complex and flexible.

4. Both explicit and implicit strategies influence organizational structure.

5. Information technology decreases the levels of and centralization of authority structures while increasing their flexibility.

6. The changing characteristics of the workforce create new expectations (e.g. an increasingly professionalized workforce desires independence and autonomy) (pp. 62–68).

Similar themes run through much of the organizational structuring research, leading to the conclusion that effective organizations are well-suited to their circumstances. More particularly, reports Mintzberg in 1980, their structures are congruent with contingency factors such as age and size of the organization, technology systems, the nature of the environment, and power. Table 7.2 summarizes what structural effects can be expected in light of these factors.

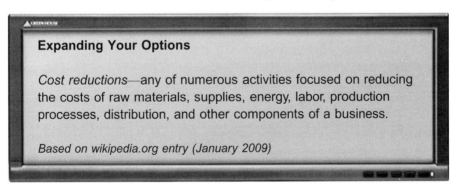

Expanding Your Options

Cost reductions—any of numerous activities focused on reducing the costs of raw materials, supplies, energy, labor, production processes, distribution, and other components of a business.

Based on wikipedia.org entry (January 2009)

WHEN TO APPLY

In a general way, the selection of a restructuring intervention is appropriate when the existing structure is outmoded to the circumstances (as may be indicated by the existence of a performance problem) and when it appears that these structures

Table 7.2 Factors and Their Effects on Organizational Structures.

Factor	Structural effects
↑organizational age	↑ formalization of behavior
↑organizational size	↑ formalization of behavior
	↑ size of an average unit
	↑ elaborate structures
	↑ specialization of tasks
	↑ differentiation of units
	↑ development of the administrative components of what Mintzberg calls *middle line* and *technostructure*
↑regulation of technology systems	↑formalized work by those who use the technology systems
	↑bureaucracy in the operational line
↑sophistication of technology systems	↑number of support staff
	↑professionalization of the support staff
	↓ centralization of technical decisions
	↑ usage of techniques for liaison across the organization
↑ automation of work by technology systems	↑ organic and adaptable structures
↑ change in the environment	↑ organic and adaptable structures
↑ complexity in the environment	↓ centralization
↑ hostility in the environment	↑ centralization (if only temporarily)
↑ disparities in the competitive environment	↑ differentiation between select structures
↑ market diversification	↑ differentiation by market base for grouping at an organization's upper levels
↑ externality of control	↑ centralization
	↑ formalization
↑ desire for power by CEO	↑ centralization
↑ popularity of a particular structure	↑usage of that particular structure (even when inappropriate)

* ↑ indicates an increase, and ↓ indicates a decrease.
Based on H. Mintzberg (1980). "Structure in 5's: A synthesis of the Research on Organizational Design." *Management Science* 26(3), 327–328.

are barriers to overcoming the performance problem. Michael Hammer and Steven Stanton argue in their 1995 article for *Government Executive* that it is important to distinguish restructuring from *reengineering*—which involves radical effort to redesign organizational processes on a large scale. While reengineering saw a great deal of growth during the mid-1990s, even its early proponents acknowledge that there are substantial challenges for their implementation and success (Champy in Bolman & Deal, 2008, p. 91). Moreover, there is growing evidence that large-scale restructuring efforts that are executed in response to performance problems may fall short of expected results (see, for example, Ronald Burke's 2001article "Hospital Restructuring and Downsizing").

As such, we advocate restructuring as more of a change management strategy to support the achievement of a desired change. This sort of restructuring approach may be appropriate when an organization has tried a technique to respond to a specific performance problem, but the intervention is failing or its results were short-lived. This sort of supportive restructuring is useful when, upon further examination, structures exist that preclude the intervention from achieving the desired results. Examples of this situation might involve an organization that:

- Reorganizes to a work group or team-based structure but continues to conduct performance evaluations at an individual level;
- Initiates cross-training, but still has its compensation systems based on individual job classifications;
- Advocates lean thinking but still has highly complex policies and procedures; and
- Executes training and development programs but never reviews the systems they have in place that punish the behaviors they target.

Alternatively, supportive restructuring may involve making incremental modifications to rules, policies, procedures, and systems that establish how organizations measure success. For example, if an organization implemented a measurement strategy involving evaluation of financial indicators by product line, but budgets and goals were organized by another component (for example, department, sales division, or customer groups), then that organization might want to examine how its structural components could be better aligned with the product lines.

STRENGTHS AND CRITICISMS

Strengths

- Organizational restructuring is derived from a dramatically different orientation than human resource–oriented interventions alone. Rather than focusing on changing people, Bolman and Deal point out, it targets their roles and responsibilities within the organization. Since it is framed from an alternative viewpoint, it may be especially well-suited to situations in which other perspectives and traditional HPT approaches have failed.

- A key issue in restructuring is the fit of the organization's structure to its purpose in its environment and the alignment of its internal components with this organizational goal. An extension of this logic is that, as people and their performance are synergized, value-subtracted work decreases[2] and the likelihood of the achievement of the organizational goals is increased.

Criticisms

- As a counterpoint to the first strength listed above, organizational restructuring changes roles and responsibilities, but not the *people* who function in them. "Pure" restructuring efforts that ignore the human elements of work—including structural effects on motivation—may face skepticism and resistance from the individuals that make up those new structures.

- Restructuring represents a dramatic change for the organization, and the interrelated and complex nature of organizational processes may make it difficult to execute large-scale structural change to support performance management process, payroll details, reporting structures in communication, and personnel processes. Moreover, the unintended consequences of such large-scale change may be detrimental to the organization.

- It is essential that the intervention is based on a sound and thorough analysis of the previous, current, and desired states. While this is true of many interventions, it is especially true of restructuring because organizational structures are contingent on a variety of contextual factors. To the extent that the rigor of the analysis may be outside the control of an external consultant, additional front-end work may be required.

RECOMMENDED DESIGN, DEVELOPMENT, AND IMPLEMENTATION PROCESS

The following six-step model is recommended.

1. Ensure that the strategic plan is aligned with the organization's societal purpose. The organization's high-level goals (as well as methods for measuring their attainment) ought to line up with this purpose. If such a

strategic plan does not already exist, refer to the first section of this handbook for considerations in establishing one. Because restructuring is useful when current structures do not fit with the present circumstances, pay special attention to orienting organizational strategy toward the future.

2. Fully analyze the current organizational structure by collecting data that allows you to answer the following questions:

    • What is/are the core operation(s) of the organization?

    • Who performs the work that contributes to this operation?

    • Who provides oversight or coordinates the operational workers?

    • For those that provide oversight, from whom do they receive direction?

    • Which processes, work outputs, and skills are standardized?

    • To what extent are these processes, work outputs, and skills standardized?

    • Where, by whom, and in what ways are decisions made?

    • How does information flow throughout the organization?

    • What is the nature of the organization's environment?

3. Based on the answers to these questions, develop a graphical representation of the structures. This chapter includes Rummler's Anatomy of Performance model as an example of this process, although other approaches may be more suitable to your needs.

4. Use this relationship map to isolate structures that impede the achievement of results. Keep in mind that structures can affect results at multiple levels in the organization, including lower-level results that are associated with other interventions in place in the organization.

5. When redesigning or modifying these structures, consider how these structures:

    • Fit with circumstantial factors such as age, size, technology systems, the nature of the environment, and issues of power (refer to Table 7.2 for a summary of how these factors relate to structure)

    • Ought to be coordinated through supervision, standardization of work processes, outputs, and skills, or self-regulation. Mintzberg (1980) offers more specific mechanisms for affecting differentiation and integration, including: (1) specialization of jobs, (2) formalization of behavior, (3) standardization of skills and knowledge through training, (4) grouping work units, (5) changing the span of control (or size) of work units, (6) planning and measurement systems, (7) communication devices, and (8) centralization of decision-making processes (pp. 325–326)

- May have unintended consequences on employee motivation and behavior

6. Prior to restructuring the organization, identify key messages that ought to be communicated to employees at all levels of the organization.

These steps are specifically relevant to a restructuring intervention, but their success can be aided by the generic processes of assessment, analysis, design, development, implementation, and evaluation that are inherent in HPT. In regard to evaluation, plan a strategy that both measures results and monitors progress toward them. This will allow the organization the flexibility to make small adjustments to its structure if desired results aren't immediately achieved.

When applied, this six-step process can lead to organizational structures that support organizational performance. As an example, it was used recently in consultation with a chemical company that had been using enterprise resource planning (ERP) and began integrating a maintenance process (MP) module from a highly recognized consulting firm. Historically, each unit managed its own maintenance and operational budget. This meant that structuring maintenance decisions at the company level (rather than the unit level) represented a fundamental structural change for the organization. Unfortunately, when the MP module was initially implemented, the company did not attend to modifying additional structures that related to the maintenance process, and the existing structure focusing on roles and process became dysfunctional, as evidenced by (1) delayed maintenance; (2) errors that resulted from faulty equipment; (3) increased operational complaints; (4) competition and distrust between the maintenance and operations functions; (5) failed attempts at accountability for utilizing the process and ostracizing of those who performed the process' gate-keeping function; and (6) inconsistency between performance incentives and expectations.

The consultant analyzed approximately eighteen months' worth of data, which led to a decision to recommend incremental changes to the structure of the company. The recommendations that resulted from the six-step process included:

- Delivering a message to the organization on how well the new maintenance process was achieving the anticipated results and the value that the people provided in following the new maintenance principles.

- Establishing a joint maintenance and operations taskforce to address all of the issues that people had identified, while not reducing the value principles of the process.

- Changing the reporting structure of the gatekeepers to the operations managers with a matrix reporting relationship to the operations director.

- Changing the performance metrics of the operations managers to be responsible for the entire operations budget, both operations and maintenance.

- Changing the performance metrics of the gatekeepers to be responsible for the entire organization budget and the unit-specific budgets.

- Establishing a continuous improvement maintenance and operations discussion monthly to foster dialogue between the entities.

- Establishing operational discussions between operations supervisors and gatekeepers to foster open communication about issues and education about decision making parameters.

CRITICAL SUCCESS FACTORS

The success of an effort to structure a new organization or restructure a failing one is dependent upon several key factors. The most important of these is that a set of clear organizational goals exists so that structures may be aligned with them. Moreover, if organizations do exist as a function of what they deliver to society, then it is arguable that these aims ought to also be socially important.

Once that relationship is established, then the next critical aspect of organizational structuring involves having a systemic perspective. This involves consideration of how each structural component affects other areas—both during the analysis of existing structures and in the synthesis of new structures.

In regard to these new structures, they must reflect an alignment with the current goals, environment, and capabilities, but must also be designed for flexibility and dynamic change that will continue in the future.

SUMMARY

Organizations fulfill a purpose in society, and the ways in which each is structured must be balanced with the circumstances of its existence and aligned to its purpose. The concepts and methods for restructuring organizations discussed here represent a philosophical alternative to human resource orientations to organizational performance improvement and as a supportive measure for managing change that develops out of other interventions. This chapter included:

- A review of seminal literature framing the structural perspective, structural analysis, types of organizational structures, and reasons for structural variation;

- General discussion of situations when examination of organizational structures is warranted and cursory analysis of strengths and criticisms of these efforts;
- A six-step process for the design, development, and implementation of restructuring interventions;
- A mini-case study of the applications of this process in practice; and
- A few factors that are critical to successfully restructuring.

Notes

1. Those familiar with Michael Hammer's advocacy of reengineering in the 1990s may be surprised that his work is not included in this review of the literature. But since reengineering involves a far more radical approach that is targeted at changing business processes rather than structures (Hammer & Stanton, 1995), his work is not heavily relied upon within this chapter.

2. For additional discussion of how performance and interventions can subtract value from an organization, refer to Dale Brethower and Karolyn Smalley's *Performance-Based Instruction: Linking Training to Business Results* from 1998.

References

Bolman, L. G., & Deal, T. E. (2008). *Reframing organizations: Artistry, choice, and leadership* (4th ed.) San Francisco: Jossey-Bass.

Burke, R. J. (2001). Hospital restructuring and downsizing: Taking stock: A symposium, part 1. *Journal of Health and Human Services Administration, 23*(4), 381–387.

Friesen, G. B. (2005). Organization design for the 21st century. *Consulting to Management, 16*(3), 32–51.

Hammer, M., & Stanton, S. A. (1995). The reengineering revolution. *Government Executive, 27*(9), 2A. Retrieved February 9, 2009, from ABI/INFORM Global database. (Document ID: 7719968).

Mintzberg, H. (1980). Structure in 5's: A synthesis of the research on organizational design. *Management Science, 26*(3), 322. Retrieved February 8, 2009, from ABI/INFORM Global database. (Document ID: 618221111).

Morgan, G. (1998). *Images of organization: The executive edition.* San Francisco and Thousand Oaks, CA: Berrett-Koehler and Sage.

Richey, R. C. (1986). *The theoretical and conceptual bases of instructional design.* London: Kogan Page.

Rummler, G. (2006). The anatomy of performance. In J. Pershing (Ed.), *Handbook of human performance technology* (3rd ed., pp. 986–1007). San Francisco: Pfeiffer.

Rummler, G. A., & Brache, A. B. (1995). *Improving performance: How to manage the white space on the organization chart* (2nd ed.). San Francisco: Jossey-Bass.

Recommended Readings

Bobic, M. P., & Davis, W. E. A kind word for theory X: Or why so many newfangled management techniques quickly fail. *Journal of Public Administration Research and Theory*, *13*(3), pp. 239–264.

Brickley, J., Smith, C., Zimmerman, J., & Willett, J. (2003). *Designing organizations to create value: From strategy to structure*. New York: McGraw-Hill.

Galbraith, J. (2002). *Designing organizations: An executive guide to strategy, structure, and process*. Hoboken, NJ: John Wiley & Sons.

Galbraith, J., Downey, D., & Kates, A. (2002). How networks undergird the lateral capability of an organization: Where the work gets done. *Journal of Organizational Excellence*, *21*(2), 67–78.

Hammer, M. (1997). *Beyond reengineering: How the process-centered organization is changing our work and our lives*. New York: HarperCollins.

Silvestro, R., & Westley, C. (2002). Challenging the paradigm of the process enterprise: A case-study analysis of BPR implementation. *Omega*, *30*(3), 215–225.

Thompson, A. A., & Strickland, A. J. (1995). *Strategic management: Concepts and cases* (6th ed.) Burr Ridge, IL: Richard D. Irwin.

PART THREE

EDITORS' DISCUSSION

U se organizational restructuring as an intervention to ensure that you have the right resources (money, time, expertise, etc.) in place to support the accomplishment of desired results. As you know, if adequate and appropriate resources are not available, then it is often impossible to achieve desired products, outputs, or outcomes. Likewise, use restructuring as a tool for supporting the implementation of performance interventions that will help improve performance. After all, without the availability and alignment of resources, you will not be able to design a mentoring program, develop training courses, offer meaningful incentives, or do most anything else within the organization to improve performance.

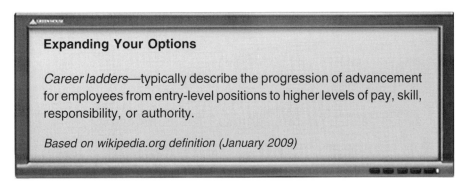

Expanding Your Options

Career ladders—typically describe the progression of advancement for employees from entry-level positions to higher levels of pay, skill, responsibility, or authority.

Based on wikipedia.org definition (January 2009)

Resources play a critical role in the whole system of improving performance. From culture and vision, to continuous monitoring and significant accomplishments, all components of the Performance Pyramid model are dependent in one way or another upon resources. Limiting your perspective of resources to solely financial capital will, therefore, limit your results. Take a broad perspective on resources—include elements of political, technology, social, and human capital—to ensure that you have all of the necessary resources to adequately design, develop, implement, and assess the results of your improvement effort.

Expanding Your Options

Career management—defined by Ball (1997) as (1) making career choices and decisions—the traditional focus of careers interventions. The changed nature of work means that individuals may have to revisit this process more frequently now and in the future than in the past, (2) managing one's organizational career—concerns the career management tasks of individuals within the workplace, such as decision-making, life-stage transitions, dealing with stress, and so forth, (3) managing "boundaryless" careers, which refers to skills needed by workers whose employment is beyond the boundaries of a single organization, a work style common among, for example, artists and designers, and (4) taking control of one's personal development—as employers take less responsibility, employees need to take control of their own development in order to maintain and enhance their employability.

Ball, B. (1997). *Career management competences: The individual perspective. Career Development International, 2*(2), 74–79

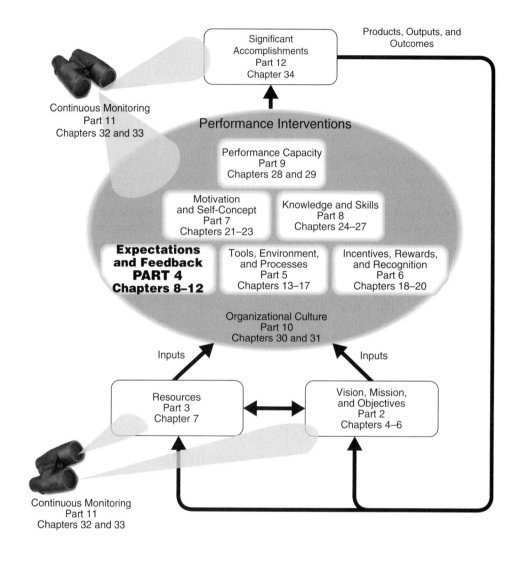

Products, Outputs, and
Outcomes

Significant
Accomplishments
Part 12
Chapter 34

Continuous Monitoring
Part 11
Chapters 32 and 33

Performance Interventions

Performance Capacity
Part 9
Chapters 28 and 29

Motivation
and Self-Concept
Part 7
Chapters 21–23

Knowledge and Skills
Part 8
Chapters 24–27

**Expectations
and Feedback
PART 4
Chapters 8–12**

Tools, Environment,
and Processes
Part 5
Chapters 13–17

Incentives, Rewards,
and Recognition
Part 6
Chapters 18–20

Organizational Culture
Part 10
Chapters 30 and 31

Inputs

Inputs

Resources
Part 3
Chapter 7

Vision, Mission,
and Objectives
Part 2
Chapters 4–6

Continuous Monitoring
Part 11
Chapters 32 and 33

PART FOUR

EXPECTATIONS
AND FEEDBACK

The accomplishment of significant results, whether at the individual, team, organizational, or society level, is much easier to achieve if everyone knows what results are to be accomplished. Regrettably, employees are often left guessing about what results are expected of them. Further, they are rarely given information on their current performance in relation to expectations—or even timely suggestions about how they can improve their performance. In most cases, managers, supervisors, colleagues, or even technology could provide this information, but due to a variety of issues employees are frequently left without knowledge of expectations or feedback on performance.

Expectations and feedback are often overlooked or forgotten. Managers all too commonly assume that employees know what results they should accomplish or that they can figure out how their performance stacks up against managerial expectations. At other times, those within an organization are so busy working (going to meetings, writing reports, sending emails, and so forth) that providing guidance and feedback on performance becomes a low priority.

However, the accomplishment of desired results requires clear performance expectations, as well as timely feedback on current achievements. From new employees to senior management, understanding expectations and receiving feedback are critical to accomplishing desired results. Expectations and feedback are as important to individual performance as they are to team and organizational performance. It is therefore essential that the strategic direction of the organization (the vision, mission, and objectives) be translated into understandable performance expectations for all.

WHAT'S COMING UP

Clear expectations and feedback do not have to wait until people have joined the organization. In Chapter Eight, Jim Breaugh, a professor of management and psychology at the University of Missouri, St. Louis, describes how realistic job previews can be a valuable intervention for improving performance in any organization. By offering job candidates an early glimpse of performance expectations, you can better match the interests and skills of applicants with performance expectations of the organization.

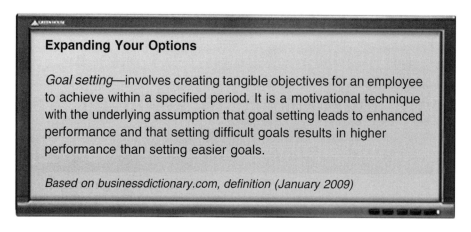

Expanding Your Options

Goal setting—involves creating tangible objectives for an employee to achieve within a specified period. It is a motivational technique with the underlying assumption that goal setting leads to enhanced performance and that setting difficult goals results in higher performance than setting easier goals.

Based on businessdictionary.com, definition (January 2009)

As a task that could potentially be delegated to a human resources department, matching the organization's and the prospective employee's expectations plays an important role in improving performance and accomplishing desired results. After completing a "realistic job preview," potential employees and their potential managers can determine whether the match is likely to lead to mutual success. Recruits want to enter organizations in which they can contribute results and grow professionally, and organizations want to be judicious in their selection of new employees because the costs associated with hiring, orienting, training, and managing new employees are significant. Realistic job previews may be an effective performance intervention that clarifies performance expectations at the earliest possible point to avoid mis-matching job and applicant—increasing the odds that new employees can contribute to the accomplishment of desired results.

CHAPTER EIGHT

Realistic Job Previews

Jim Breaugh

INTRODUCTION

Research has shown that job applicants frequently lack important information about positions for which they are applying. It has also been found that applicants often have inaccurate impressions concerning what these positions are like. Both of these conditions can result in applicants accepting job offers from employers for positions that are not a good fit in terms of the individuals' needs and/or abilities. This lack of fit can result in undesirable outcomes for both employers (employee turnover) and new employees (job dissatisfaction). The use of realistic job previews (RJP) has been shown to be an effective recruitment mechanism for increasing the accuracy of applicants' job and organizational expectations. Possessing accurate expectations, in turn, allows job candidates to make more informed job choice decisions. Discussions in this chapter include why a realistic job preview has beneficial effects, how to design an effective RJP, and situations in which an RJP works best.

DESCRIPTION

Unlike traditional recruitment practice, which involves an organization presenting an overly positive view of what working for it would be like, the use of a realistic job preview (RJP) involves an employer presenting both favorable and un-favorable position-related information (information about both the job and the organization) to job applicants. The relative balance of favorable to unfavorable information should be determined by the true nature of the position being filled. If designed and administered appropriately, an RJP should result in job candidates having a more accurate view of what a position entails than if no RJP were used.

In 2008, along with my colleagues Therese H. Macan and Dana M. Grambow, I noted that RJPs typically have been presented by means of a short booklet or video that is provided to a job applicant during an organization site visit. However, an organization can convey realistic information about a position by other means such as a tour of the work site, a work simulation, or a conversation with a prospective co-worker. Given that tradeoffs exist among the methods of presenting an RJP, a combination of RJP approaches generally is recommended for an organization that wants job applicants to truly understand what a job with it would involve. Stated differently, it is generally better for an employer to think of an RJP as a process of conveying job-related information rather than as a one-time intervention.

In terms of the likely results of providing recruits with realistic information, research (such as that reviewed in 2001 by industrial/organizational psychology experts Rodger Griffeth & Peter Hom in 2001) has shown RJPs to be associated with such important variables as new employee retention, performance and satisfaction. However, as will be discussed later in this chapter, the relative impact of an RJP on these outcomes is dependent upon a number of factors, such as when the RJP is received, the nature of the information the RJP provides, and whether RJP recipients see the information as credible. For example, with regard to timing, although a number of employers have provided RJPs late in the recruitment process (after a job offer has been received) or even after a person has accepted a job offer, RJPs are likely to have maximum effect when they are provided earlier in the recruitment process.[1]

In considering the use of an RJP, it is important for an employer to remember that an RJP is not a panacea; it can only do so much. For example, if a job opening has several negative attributes (for example, low pay, undesirable work hours), an RJP should convey such information. However, as management professors Robert Bretz and Timothy Judge pointed out in a 1998 article, the end result of doing so may be that a number of individuals will withdraw from job consideration. Although most experts believe such applicant withdrawal is preferable to hiring and training individuals who are likely to quit after a short period of time on the job due to job dissatisfaction, such applicant withdrawal is still not desirable. Thus, for an employer that intends to use an RJP, consideration should be given to whether undesirable job attributes might be improved (the job may be enriched or supervisors may receive training to improve their effectiveness).

WHAT WE KNOW FROM RESEARCH

RJPs have attracted considerable attention both in terms of theoretical development and empirical research. Prior to discussing empirical findings, it is useful to examine why RJPs have been hypothesized to influence voluntary turnover and other important work-related variables.

The Theoretical Rationale for RJP Effectiveness

To date, four explanations have been offered for RJP effectiveness: self-selection, met expectations, ability to cope with job demands, and commitment to job choice due to an employer being honest. The "self-selection" hypothesis is based on the assumption that RJP recipients who do not perceive a job opening as being a good fit in terms of their needs and/or abilities are likely to withdraw from job consideration. If the self-selection hypothesis is correct, in comparison to job applicants who do not receive an RJP, RJP recipients who accept job offers should be more satisfied with their new positions which, in turn, should make them less likely to quit. Furthermore, if RJP recipients have a good sense of their abilities, those who accept job offers should be better able to perform well in their new jobs than individuals who did not receive RJP information concerning what abilities a job requires.

A second explanation for why RJPs may improve job satisfaction and reduce voluntary turnover is the "met expectations" hypothesis. This hypothesis presumes that receiving an RJP results in recruits lowering their job expectations (research has found job expectations are generally inflated). This lowering of job expectations should result in new employees being more satisfied with their positions and hence less likely to choose to leave them.

The "ability to cope" hypothesis posits that RJPs reduce job dissatisfaction and turnover by improving a new employee's ability to cope with job demands (for example, rude customers). In this regard, research by Bernard L. Dugoni and Daniel R. Ilgen, who at the time were both with Purdue University, suggests that being aware of likely problems results in new employees being less disturbed by them since they are not caught off guard and/or such forewarning allows new hires to rehearse methods of handling these problems.

The final explanation for the effectiveness of RJPs is the "air of honesty" hypothesis. This hypothesis suggests that, in comparison to job applicants who did not receive an RJP, RJP recipients (having received candid information about a position under consideration from an employer) will feel greater commitment to their job choice decisions. Thus, even RJP recipients who accept job offers that are not seen as a good fit (a recruit may not have a more attractive job alternative) are likely to remain in their new jobs for a longer period of time than non-RJP applicants, given they made informed job choice decisions. The air of honesty hypothesis is based on the assumption that applicants who did not receive an RJP may feel misled by an employer if they are presented with an exaggerated view of what working there entails (which is frequently the case) and thus feel no hesitancy in quitting.

Figures 8.1, 8.2, and 8.3 present a simplified model of the RJP process.[2] Given the number of variables in this process, it has been broken into three sections to facilitate presentation of the various components of the model.

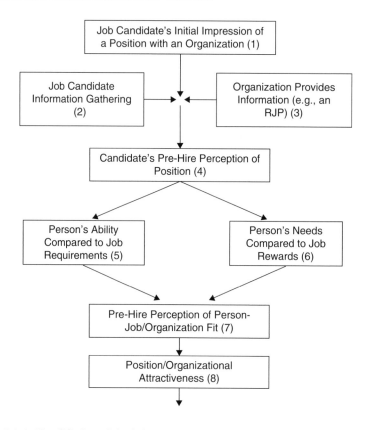

Figure 8.1 A Simplified Model of the RJP Process (Part 1).

Beginning at the top of Figure 8.1, one sees that job candidates are likely to have an initial impression of an organization before deciding to apply there (box 1). Based upon information a person gathers (box 2) and that supplied by an organization (box 3), job candidates develop a more complete picture of what working for that employer is like (box 4). The accuracy of this perception is a function of the information candidates attained on their own and that was provided by an organization (for example, was an RJP provided?). Having developed a pre-hire perception of a position, job candidates can assess how well their abilities meet the requirements of the job opening (box 5) and how well their needs will be met by what the position offers (box 6). These two comparisons result in a pre-hire perception of overall person-job/organizational fit (box 7). This perception should result in an overall assessment of how attractive a position with an organization is (box 8).

As portrayed in Figure 8.2, if a position is viewed as insufficiently attractive (box 8), job candidates (assuming other employment options exist for them) may remove themselves from job consideration (box 9). Alternatively, if a

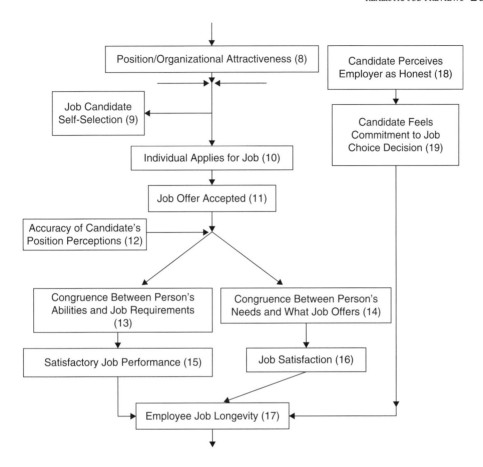

Figure 8.2 A Simplified Model of the RJP Process (Part 2).

position is viewed as attractive or a candidate has no other viable alternatives, he or she will likely apply for the job (box 10) and, if a job offer is forthcoming, it is likely to be accepted (box 11). Depending upon the accuracy of candidates' perceptions of a position (box 12), there should be a reasonable fit between their abilities and the job requirements (box 13).

As conveyed in Figure 8.2, when individuals' abilities match job requirements (box 13), satisfactory job performance should result (box 15). Such performance should result in job longevity (box 17) since a new employee who performs well is unlikely to be terminated and is more likely to enjoy the job and be rewarded for doing it well. Candidates who had an accurate perception of what a position entails (box 12) should also be more likely to end up in a job that fulfills his/her needs (box 14) which should result in job satisfaction (box 16). Such satisfaction should result in less likelihood of a new employee resigning (box 17).

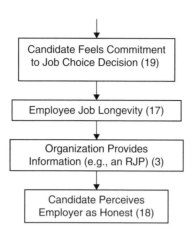

Figure 8.3 A Simplified Model of the RJP Process (Part 3).

With regard to the elements remaining within Figure 8.3, when organizations provide candid job information (box 3), candidates should perceive the employer as being honest (box 18). Thus, if hired, an individual should feel greater commitment to their job choice decision (box 19) which should result in the individual being less likely to resign from a new position (box 17).

Although the model portrayed in Figures 8.1 through 8.3 presents a simplified picture of the recruitment process (in our chapter within the 2008 *International Review of Industrial and Organizational Psychology*, Macan, Grambow, and I present a more complete treatment of the recruitment process), the relationships portrayed are logical and they have been supported by considerable empirical research. Some of this research will now be discussed.

The Results of a Comprehensive Meta-Analysis of RJP Research by Phillips

In terms of empirical support for the four explanations offered for why RJPs "work," a meta-analysis by Rutgers University's Jean M. Phillips' provides a good summary of much of the research on RJPs.[3] Following a review of her findings, I will examine in some detail three specific studies in order to provide a better sense of the type of research on RJPs that has been conducted.

Given that reducing voluntary turnover has been a major objective of many employers who have used RJPs, it is encouraging that Phillips found that RJPs reduced such turnover. In order to demonstrate the potential financial impact of RJP use, she presented an analysis that showed that "an organization experiencing an annual turnover rate of 50 percent using traditional recruitment methods would be able to make seventeen fewer hires per year per one hundred retained workers by adopting RJPs" (p. 687). Given that the cost of hiring a new employee has been estimated to be between one to two times a person's annual salary for many jobs (this estimate considers such matters as recruitment, selection, training, and separation costs), for workers making $30,000 per year, Phillips' estimated the savings from hiring seventeen fewer workers could be as much as $510,000. Readers interested in estimating the cost of turnover for a given job can find several "turnover cost calculators" on the web.

Expanding Your Options

Regular one-on-ones—regularly scheduled meetings between a manager and an employee. These meetings do not need to have an agenda and are meant to be rapport-building meetings that allow the team member to discuss whatever issues they may wish to.

Although RJPs have frequently been used to reduce voluntary turnover, they also have been found to have beneficial effects on other important variables. For example, Phillips found the use of RJPs to be linked to better employee performance, higher reported job satisfaction, and new employees perceiving that the organization hiring them was honest with them about what a new job involved. Although it is difficult to put a dollar value on such variables, clearly, improving job performance will have monetary value.

In summarizing her results, Phillips concluded that an RJP can have beneficial, but modest, effects on voluntary turnover, employee performance, job satisfaction, and perceptions of honesty. A limitation of drawing conclusions from the meta-analysis conducted by Phillips is that a sizable number of the studies included presented RJPs in circumstances that minimized their impact. Thus, her meta-analytic results may underestimate the potential value of using an RJP. In order to make this concern more concrete, consider the fact that in over one-half of the studies Phillips analyzed the RJP was provided after individuals had accepted job offers and begun working. Such timing does not allow candidates to self-select out of consideration for positions that are not a good fit. When RJP is provided after hiring, recipients also will be less likely to perceive an organization as being honest with them than if the RJP was provided early in the recruitment process (before they had turned down other job offers). In addition, RJP studies often have involved jobs that are quite visible to the public; thus, applicants are less likely to have unrealistic job expectations. Given these and other limitations of studies included in Phillips' meta-analysis, there is value in examining the effects reported in specific RJP studies more deeply.

An RJP Study by Suszko and Breaugh

A study I conducted with Mary Suszko provides a good example of the use of an RJP and the resulting benefits. This study was conducted at a firm that contracted with stores to take inventory. The firm was concerned about the high level of voluntary turnover it was experiencing for the inventory takers it hired. Such turnover was particularly costly given that the inventory taker position required considerable post-hire training. After familiarizing ourselves with the position and the type of people hired, Mary Suszko and I concluded that most job applicants would not have a good understanding of what the job of inventory taker involved. For example, in exit interviews departing inventory takers noted that as applicants they were unaware of such things as the amount of travel involved, the irregular work hours, and the dirty working conditions. Based upon what we knew of the inventory taker position, we thought it was an ideal situation for the introduction of an RJP.

In order to develop an effective RJP, we first conducted individual interviews with five current inventory takers. During these interviews, we investigated what the job of inventory taker involved and we probed what initial expectations they had of the job were inaccurate. Based upon the results of these interviews, we compiled a list of positive and negative job attributes. This list was examined by five additional inventory takers who were asked to edit the list (add new information if needed). Following this second step, we asked two managers to organize the information into what they saw as logical categories. Five categories resulted: (1) hours of work, (2) physical work environment, (3) duties and policies, (4) career opportunities, and (5) social relations with supervisors, co-workers, and clients.

To examine the benefits of providing the inventory taker RJP, we randomly assigned new job applicants to two groups. One group went through the traditional recruitment process and one group received a written RJP prior to the final selection interview (before receiving a job offer). Those in the RJP group also received an oral RJP as part of the training program they went through once hired (this oral RJP reiterated the information provided in the written RJP). The effects of the RJP were as hypothesized. In terms of withdrawal from job consideration, four of the fifteen individuals (27 percent) in the RJP condition rejected a job offer. In contrast, none of the thirteen individuals in the control group refused a job offer. In terms of the RJP effect on voluntary turnover, we found a strong effect. At the end of three months, of the eleven RJP recipients who accepted job offers, four inventory takers (36 percent) had quit. In contrast, eleven of the thirteen individuals (85 percent) in the control group who started work had resigned.

To better understand why the RJP had been effective in reducing turnover, we examined job satisfaction, ability to cope with job demands, and perceptions of organizational honesty after inventory takers had been on the job for six weeks. In comparison to those who did not receive the RJP, RJP recipients reported they were more satisfied, better able to cope with job demands, and they felt the inventory firm was more open and honest with them.

An RJP study by Griffeth and Hom

The study described above demonstrated the value of an RJP that was tied to a given job (inventory taker) in a given organization. However, RJPs can have value even when more generic in nature (not tied to a given position in a given firm). A 2001 study reported by Rodger Griffeth and Peter Hom serves as a useful example of such an approach. These researchers developed a "generic RJP brochure" for the job of auditor in public accounting firms (twenty-seven Arizona firms were involved in RJP development). In order to develop the content for their RJP, these authors went through a multi-step process that involved interviewing auditors, compiling a list of statements describing the job, having the statements rated for accuracy by another set of auditors, and selecting those statements that most experts agreed were descriptive of the job of auditor.

Griffeth and Hom compared the one-year turnover rate and the rate of resigning of newly hired auditors who had or had not received the RJP brochure. The one-year turnover rate for those receiving an RJP was 5 percent. This compares quite favorably to the rate of 17 percent for those in the control condition. With regard to resignation rate, Griffeth and Hom reported that RJP recipients resigned at a rate "that is 58 percent of that of the control group" (p. 53).

A Study by Buckley, Fedor, Veres, Wiese, and Carraher

As noted by person–organization fit researcher Jon Billsberry, one of the reasons that RJPs are thought to reduce voluntary turnover is because they lower the job expectations of recruits, which typically are inflated. Although most experts believe the best way to increase the accuracy of job expectations is by providing applicants with realistic information during the recruitment process, M. Ronald Buckley and colleagues noted that in some situations an organization may be unwilling or unable to provide an RJP (for example, an employer filling several different jobs may not have the resources to develop several different RJPs). Buckley and his team wondered whether in such a circumstance there may be value in trying to lower job expectations by instructing job candidates that they were likely to have exaggerated job expectations.

To test their idea, applicants were randomly assigned for manufacturing jobs to one of four groups. The first group received an RJP booklet. The second group attended an expectation-lowering procedure (ELP) workshop that emphasized the importance of having realistic job expectations, stressed the likelihood of applicants having unrealistic expectations, and discussed job dissatisfaction and turnover as likely outcomes of having unrealistic expectations. The third group received traditional recruitment information. The fourth group served as a control group and received no information.

Buckley and his colleagues found that those in the RJP group and those in the ELP group had much lower turnover than those in the other two groups. More specifically, the six-month turnover rates for the four groups were: RJP (6 percent), ELP (3 percent), traditional group (20 percent), and control group (22 percent). The value of offering an RJP or an ELP also held for job expectations being met (measured during the orientation period) and job satisfaction (measured at six months).

WHEN TO APPLY

The simple answer to this question is "always." Or to rephrase the question: "Why wouldn't an employer want to facilitate recruits having accurate job expectations?" Although I have never heard an organizational representative admit it, one can imagine that some employers intentionally mislead job applicants about the nature of a position so that they will accept job offers. I believe such a recruitment philosophy to be unethical.[4] Furthermore, given the likely benefits of providing an RJP, it is hard to make a persuasive case against offering an RJP.

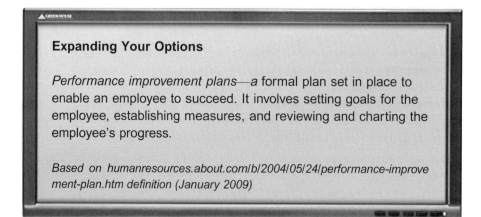

Expanding Your Options

Performance improvement plans—a formal plan set in place to enable an employee to succeed. It involves setting goals for the employee, establishing measures, and reviewing and charting the employee's progress.

Based on humanresources.about.com/b/2004/05/24/performance-improvement-plan.htm definition (January 2009)

Instead of addressing the question of "When to apply RJP?" it may be more instructive to address the question of "When is it best to apply an RJP?" From our review of the theory underlying the use of RJPs, three factors should immediately come to mind. First, RJPs are likely to be most beneficial for positions with which job applicants lack familiarity. Second, RJPs are likely to be most useful for positions with high turnover rates for new employees. Third, RJPs are likely to have the most impact when job applicants have other job options, such as when they can self-select out of job consideration if the position does not appear to be a good fit in terms of their needs or abilities. A final consideration is not driven by the theory underlying RJP effectiveness, but rather by political considerations. An RJP will be most effective when those in charge are committed to being open and honest during the recruitment process. Conversely, if decisions-makers will not allow certain types of factual but negative information to be presented in the RJP, it will be less effective.

STRENGTHS AND CRITICISMS

The use of a realistic job preview is a simple procedure to explain to managers, job incumbents, and recruits. Compared to many turnover-focused interventions (e.g., job enrichment, raising salaries), an RJP is inexpensive. An RJP can be developed and implemented quickly, and the practice has a demonstrated record of effectiveness.

At the same time, an RJP requires an employer to publicize negative aspects of a position. Some organizations will be unwilling to do this. In addition, the use of an RJP may result in desirable recruits dropping out as job candidates.

RECOMMENDED DESIGN, DEVELOPMENT, AND IMPLEMENTATION PROCESS

Here's how to undertake the RJP process.

1. Introduce the concept of an RJP to key decision-makers and people responsible for RJP implementation. Cite data on the turnover rate for new hires for the job for which the RJP is to be used. Cite examples of RJPs being used successfully to reduce such turnover. Note other benefits of using an RJP. Make sure that key individuals are aware that the use of an RJP may result in some job candidates withdrawing from the selection process. If available from exit interviews, cite examples of departing employees who had expressed unrealistic job expectations.

2. Emphasize the value of improving undesirable job attributes (when possible) prior to implementing an RJP.

3. Provide information on the dollar cost and other consequences of a new employee quitting after having completed the selection process, been trained, established relationships with customers, and so on.

4. Provide estimates of the dollar cost of developing the RJP, the number of hours needed to develop the RJP, and the dollar and labor costs of administering the RJP.

5. Generate commitment to the RJP process by having key individuals involved in RJP development.

6. Make a final decision concerning how to generate RJP content, such as through interviews with new employees and their supervisors, exit interviews with departing employees, surveys of former employees, or observations of new employees working. In determining how to gather information, heavy emphasis should be placed on the ultimate goal of providing information that job candidates see as (a) important or of personal relevance to them), (b) specific (tied to a given work group versus referring to work groups in general), and (c) broad in scope (the RJP not only focuses on job duties but also addresses such things as a specific supervisor's style, co-worker relations, work group politics, organizational values, how salary increases are determined, job security, and career development).

7. Gather information on job content using the means described in Step 6. Generally, the information-gathering step of RJP development will involve an iterative process in which initial content is developed, then edited by job experts. Following this, additional content that is seen as missing is added and the verbiage of the content is polished such that the language level is appropriate (for example, eliminating jargon that a recruit is not expected to know).

8. Finalize what information to convey in the RJP.

9. Decide how (website, booklet sent to applicants, tour of worksite, interview with recently hired employee) and when to provide RJP information. Generally, the use of a combination of RJP methods is most effective. For example, providing basic information (such as work hours, compensation level, and amount of travel) on a website or in a job description posted in the human resource department may be an initial RJP step. Following this, RJP information could be provided during a telephone interview. For job candidates who make it to the organizational site visit stage of the selection process, RJP information could be provided by means of a tour of the work site, an interview with one's prospective supervisor, and with one or more potential co-workers. Such interviews are particularly valuable because they allow applicants to ask questions about topics that are important to them but have not yet been addressed during the recruitment process. Furthermore, interactions with co-workers are valuable because recruits see co-workers as being a highly credible source of information in

comparison to corporate recruiters. Using such a multi-phase RJP process should reduce hiring costs such as travel and testing, since an employer should be able to eliminate some individuals from job consideration via applicant self-selection early in the recruitment process who otherwise might have progressed further into the selection process.

10. Pilot-test the RJP and evaluate its effectiveness. Although an RJP can be pilot-tested in various ways, I recommend having a panel of experts consisting of relatively newly hired employees and their supervisors go through the RJP process and comment on its effectiveness in conveying accurate information. An organization might also consider trying out a newly developed RJP with a small group of applicants and then interviewing them to discern whether they now have an accurate understanding of the position.

11. Implement the RJP as part of the recruitment process. In order to increase the likelihood that the RJP is implemented and continues to be used as intended, it is important to develop up-front commitment to its use by those charged with administering the RJP. Such commitment can be gained by involving these individuals in the RJP development process, such as in determining the content provided and the process used for conveying the information.

12. Once in use, evaluate the RJP periodically to investigate whether new employees believe they received realistic information concerning what a position with the organization involved. Where appropriate (such as due to changes in the job position), make modifications to the RJP.

CRITICAL SUCCESS FACTORS

From the contents of this chapter, it should be apparent that both theory and empirical results suggest RJPs should be widely used. However, there are some critical success factors that should be noted.

1. In order to develop an effective RJP, an employer must be committed to being honest with job candidates. That such commitment is critical should be obvious given that the idea of an RJP is based on the assumption that an employer wants recruits to have realistic job expectations. However, even a quick scan of corporate websites makes clear that many organizations present a very flattering view of what working there would be like. More surprisingly, I have seen examples of RJPs that failed to address important aspects of a position (such as the supervisor, the pay, and how decisions are made) about which job candidates are

likely to either lack information or have unrealistically positive expectations.

2. For an RJP to be effective, the RJP information must be seen as credible. In this regard, job applicants are more likely to believe the information presented if the source of the information is perceived as expert and trustworthy. Newly hired employees are viewed as a particularly credible source. Seeing things first-hand also enhances RJP credibility. For example, consider the case of an employer that is truly committed to having a diverse workforce and has made great strides in this area. Conceivably, the employer could convey its commitment by citing the diversity of its workforce in an RJP booklet. However, consider the difference in information credibility if a job candidate toured the work site and saw the diversity of the workforce.

3. In terms of allowing a job candidate to make an informed job choice decision, it is critical that an RJP provide information that is of personal relevance to the individual. Although certain job attributes such as starting salary and typical job duties are important to most applicants, some applicants have unique information needs. For example, a single father may be interested in whether a position allows for a flexible work schedule. Similarly, an unmarried job applicant who is considering whether to accept a job offer that requires moving to a new city may be interested in whether co-workers socialize after work. With traditional RJP approaches (booklets and videos), it is difficult for an organization to address a wide range of position attributes without the RJP overwhelming a recruit with information. The best way to address the unique information needs of a job applicant is to provide for one or more conversations with prospective co-workers. Such two-way interchanges allow a recruit to ask questions about job attributes that would be unlikely to be covered in an RJP booklet, video, or structured tour of a work site.[5]

4. In order to allow for job applicant self-selection, it is important that an RJP be provided prior to job offer acceptance. Ideally, some RJP information should be provided very early during the recruitment process. For example, if an employer's website states that a position will require considerable overtime and an irregular work schedule, some individuals may not even apply for a position, thus potentially saving an employer time and money.

5. An RJP has maximum impact when RJP recipients have insight with regard to their own abilities and needs. Without such insight, applicants may overestimate their ability to meet job requirements, and thus poor person-job fit may result. As an example, consider a case cited by Meryl

Louis in her article "Surprise and Sense Making: What Newcomers Experience in Entering Unfamiliar Organizational Settings." She described a newly hired individual who was told during the recruitment process that a job required considerable overtime. The individual believed that he would have no trouble handling the long work hours. However, after having worked long weeks for several months, fatigue and dissatisfaction with his job had set in. Similarly, several examples of individuals who lacked insight with regard to their needs are also discussed in Louis' article. For example, she discussed a job candidate who thought he wanted considerable job autonomy only to discover upon having such autonomy in a new job that it did not suit him. My chapter with Macan and Grambow discusses how, by targeting for recruitment individuals who have worked in similar jobs, an organization may be able to attract applicants with greater self-insight concerning their abilities and needs. A potentially useful way to help recruits assess whether they possess the ability needed to do a job is by having the individual participate in a work simulation. For example, in their 1978 article for the *Journal of Occupational Psychology*, Downs, Farr, and Colbeck provide an excellent example of how taking part in a sewing simulation resulted in less-skilled applicants withdrawing as job candidates.

SUMMARY

In this chapter, a strong case has been made for the use of realistic job previews. Both theory and empirical results were reviewed that suggest RJPs have value for reducing voluntary turnover and increasing new employee performance and job satisfaction. The benefit of providing an RJP in terms of individuals viewing an organization as being honest also was documented. In order to optimize RJP effects, specific guidance was provided on how to develop and implement an RJP. It was emphasized that an RJP should not be viewed as a one-time intervention, but rather as a process by which different RJP methods (a website, tour of the work site, an interview) have a cumulative effect on the accuracy of a recruit's job expectations. Although an RJP should not be viewed as a substitute for improving job attributes, since an RJP is inexpensive to develop and implement, its use should be of considerable benefit to most organizations.

Notes

1. Breaugh, Macan, and Grambow (2) have provided a detailed treatment of the importance of RJP timing.
2. The model in Figures 8.1, 8.2, and 8.3 only shows the RJP information as being presented at a single point in time when it may be provided in multiple places during the recruitment process.

3. In the ten years since Phillips' (1998) paper was published, research on RJPs has diminished.

4. Buckley, Fedor, Carraher, Frink, and Marvin (4) have discussed in detail why it is unethical to misrepresent what a job involves to job applicants.

5. Colarelli (6) has provided an excellent discussion of the value of two-way conversations for providing RJPs.

References

Billsberry, J. (2007). *Experiencing recruitment and selection*. London: John Wiley & Sons.

Breaugh, J. A., Macan, T. H., & Grambow, D. M. (2008). Employee recruitment: Current knowledge and directions for research. In G. P. Hodgkinson and J. K. Ford (Eds.), *International review of industrial and organizational psychology* (pp. 45–82). Hoboken, NJ: John Wiley & Sons.

Bretz, R. D., & Judge, T. A. (1998). Realistic job previews: A test of the adverse selection self-selection hypothesis. *Journal of Applied Psychology*, *83*(2), 330–337.

Buckley, M. R., Fedor, D. B., Carraher, S. M., Frink, D. D., & Marvin, D. (1997). The ethical imperative to provide recruits realistic job previews. *Journal of Managerial Issues*, *9*, 468–484.

Buckley, M. R., Fedor, D. B., Veres, J. G., Wiese, D. S., & Carraher. S. M. (1998). Investigating newcomer expectations and job-related outcomes. *Journal of Applied Psychology*, *83*, 452–461.

Colarelli, S. M. (1984). Methods of communication and mediating processes in realistic job previews. *Journal of Applied Psychology*, *69*, 633–642.

Downs, S., Farr, R. M., & Colbeck, L. (1978). Self-appraisal: A convergence of selection and guidance. *Journal of Occupational Psychology*, *51*, 271–278.

Dugoni, B. L., & Ilgen, D. R. (1981). Realistic job previews and the adjustment of new employees. *The Academy of Management Journal*, *24*, 579–591.

Griffeth, R. W., & Hom, P. W. (2001). *Retaining valued employees*. Thousand Oaks, CA: Sage.

Louis, M. R. (1980). Surprise and sense making: What newcomers experience in entering unfamiliar organizational settings. *Administrative Science Quarterly*, *25*, 226–251.

Phillips, J. M. (1998). Effects of realistic job previews on multiple organizational outcomes: A meta-analysis. *Academy of Management Journal*, *41*(6), 673–690.

Suszko, M. K., & Breaugh, J. A. (1986). The effects of realistic job previews on applicant self-selection and employee turnover, satisfaction, and coping ability. *Journal of Management*, *12*, 513–523.

Recommended Readings

Barber, A. E. (1998). *Recruiting employees*. Thousand Oaks, CA: Sage.

Breaugh, J. A., & Starke, M. (2000). Research on employee recruitment: So many studies, so many remaining questions. *Journal of Management*, *26*, 405–434.

Phillips, J. M. (1998). Effects of realistic job previews on multiple organizational outcomes: A meta-analysis. *Academy of Management Journal, 41*, 673–690.

Rynes, S. L., & Cable, D. M. (2003). Recruitment research in the twenty-first century. In W. C. Borman, D. R. Ilgen, & R. J. Klimoski (Eds.), *Handbook of psychology* (Vol. 12, pp. 55–76). Hoboken, NJ: John Wiley & Sons.

 # EDITORIAL CONNECTIONS

Grounded in research, realistic job previews offer value by setting appropriate and applicable expectations before a recruit formally joins your organization. By establishing performance expectations at this very early point, you can better ensure that an appropriate match is made during the hiring process for improving performance and accomplishing results. The introduction of realistic job previews as a performance intervention in most organizations will be closely tied to the role of the human resources (HR) department. Consequently, you will want to coordinate the design, development, and introduction of job previews with these partners within your organization. The success of the intervention is, after all, closely tied to the other hiring and performance improvement activities—such as recruitment plans, succession planning (see Chapter Twenty-Nine), and mentoring (see Chapter Twenty-Six)—that already may be undertaken by the HR unit.

While realistic job previews give candidates an opportunity to examine the performance expectations that would come with a position, it is equally important that when the appropriate candidate becomes a valued employee there is a supporting system of assessment and feedback. Feedback on performance is the second critical component of the expectations and feedback loop of the Performance Pyramid; while expectations establish clear objectives for what must be achieved, feedback on performance allows individuals and teams to systematically improve their processes in order to accomplish significant results.

Expanding Your Options

On-boarding—encompasses efforts to acquire, accommodate, assimilate and accelerate new team members, whether they come from outside or inside the organization.

Based on wikipedia.org definition (January 2009)

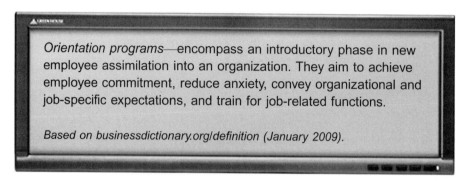

Orientation programs—encompass an introductory phase in new employee assimilation into an organization. They aim to achieve employee commitment, reduce anxiety, convey organizational and job-specific expectations, and train for job-related functions.

Based on businessdictionary.org/definition (January 2009).

From advice and pointers to corrective criticism, performance feedback should focus on the performance (results) rather than the performer. Therefore, assessing the interim achievements is an important element of performance improvement. When interim achievements are measured against desired accomplishments, only then can improvements to the processes, policies, tools, motivation, incentives, knowledge, skills, and other components of the performance system be made to support the accomplishment of desired results.

WHAT'S COMING UP

Systematic assessment and feedback programs are necessary to further clarify performance expectations, assess current performance, and ensure that people know how to improve results (as described in Chapter Nine, 360-Degree Feedback). However, candid assessment and feedback on performance is hard to come by in most organizations. Managers often fear conversations regarding employee performance, leading many to delay those conversations until an annual review period, and then they frequently struggle to differentiate performance levels across employees. Because organizations invest significant resources into employees performance—from recruitment and orientation to professional development and resource allocations—measuring and providing timely feedback on performance is an important duty of managers and a necessary step toward improving performance. Assessment and feedback systems must, then, be considered as an essential ingredient to success.

CHAPTER NINE

360-Degree Feedback

Eugene Kutcher
John Donovan
Steven J. Lorenzet

INTRODUCTION

This chapter provides a step-by-step tutorial for the development and implementation of a 360-degree assessment and feedback program that can be implemented in virtually any work setting in which key behaviors (for example, critical incidents) for successful performance can be identified and observed. Issues to consider when implementing this type of program within an organization are discussed, with special attention devoted to the strengths and weaknesses of various sources of assessment data (supervisors, peers, customers). Additional guidance is offered regarding methods for interpreting the data obtained from this type of program, as well as how to best use this data to give accurate and useful feedback to facilitate improvements in employee performance.

DESCRIPTION

Let us start with a basic principle: all employees require feedback—accurate and regular information about what they are doing correctly and what they could be doing differently. Ideally, this feedback is based on a comprehensive assessment of the individual's performance and is grounded in clearly communicated and specific behaviors. In this chapter, we present a three-stage performance improvement process that can work in almost any environment in which effective job relevant behaviors can be identified and the staff is committed to open and constructive feedback. In the first stage, a "critical incident technique" is used to define, in clear behavioral terms, what it means to be successful in the target job. In the second stage, a group of knowledgeable judges uses this model of job success to measure how well an individual employee performs the critical aspects of the job. Last, after these data have been collected and combined, this 360-degree feedback is then shared with the employee in a way that encourages commitment to better performance.

Phase 1: Defining Performance

The foundation of this approach, indeed of any human resource function or intervention, entails developing some model of effective performance of the target job. A specific method that is commonly advocated throughout research and practice is the critical incident technique. In this method, which was originally described by aviation psychologist John Flanagan in the 1950s, the job analyst (which may be the manager, a human resources professional, or a consultant) documents those behaviors that contribute strongly to either success or failure in the position. The output of this task is a list of job-relevant behaviors. These behaviors can be classified as "effective" (illustrative of employees who are skilled top performers) or "ineffective" (illustrative of the weakest performers). To add to the traditional critical incident technique, we also advocate listing "typical" or average behaviors (behaviors that are illustrative of a majority of satisfactory employees). This tends to make the list more representative of the range—and not only the extremes—of possible employee performance. For example, for a position of sales representative, critical incidents may include:

- Recalls a repeat customer's needs and preferences without asking or being told (effective);
- Asks questions to determine the needs and preferences of the customer (typical); and
- Tells the customer what he/she should want or feel (ineffective).

Note that these three critical incidents all happen to relate to the same overall performance dimension: customer service. A performance dimension is a category of behaviors that comprise some aspect of job performance. Other critical incidents in the sales representative's list will relate to other performance dimensions (for example, product knowledge or business development). Once a comprehensive list of critical incidents is created, the behaviors should be categorized into these performance dimensions. (A more detailed description of this process can be found later in the "Recommended Design, Development, and Implementation Process" section.) Then this output will guide the next phase of the process, "Phase 2: Assessing Performance."

Phase 2: Assessing Performance

We use the term "assessment" to refer to the process of measuring the skills and effectiveness of specific employees, with an aim of reinforcing their strengths and identifying areas in which development is needed. In our process, this activity is accomplished by having multiple witnesses to each employee's behavior complete an evaluation form, which we call a behavioral checklist. The three steps inherent in this phase are (a) development of the behavioral checklist, (b) selection of knowledgeable raters, and (c) raters' completion of the checklist.

Developing the Behavioral Checklist. The output from the first phase (Phase 1: Defining Performance through the identification of critical incidents) is a series of behavior lists. Depending on how complex the given job is, there may be several performance dimensions. Recall that in our example of the sales representative, there may be job dimensions of product knowledge, customer service orientation, business development, and others. Under each dimension, there will be effective, typical, and ineffective behavior statements. From this, the behavioral checklist can be built by simply placing a checkbox beside each behavior. An example of a behavioral checklist for the customer service dimension of a sales representative can be found in Exhibit 9.1.

Exhibit 9.1 Sample Behavioral Checklist (Dimension: Customer Service)

Name of Ratee:

Dimension: Customer service is an orientation toward maintaining or improving the satisfaction of internal and external customers.

Instructions: Several customer service–related behaviors are listed below. For each behavior, check the **Y column** if you have witnessed the individual demonstrate that behavior, the **N** column if you know that the individual has not demonstrated that behavior, or the **U** column if you have been unable to observe whether or not the individual has demonstrated that behavior.

Y	N	U	Behavior
√			Recalls a repeat customer's needs and preferences without asking or being told
			Behavior 2
			Behavior 3
			Behavior 4
			Behavior 5
			Behavior 6
			Behavior 7
			Behavior 8
			Behavior 9

Selecting knowledgeable raters. The object of this exercise is to obtain as complete and accurate an assessment of the individual's job performance as possible. To this end, care must be taken in recruiting the correct raters to evaluate each employee's performance. Traditionally, this has been considered a top-down endeavor, meaning that it is the job of the supervisor to assess and evaluate the employee's performance. In a 2005 review, management professors Frederick Morgeson, Troy Mumford, and Michael Campion summarized why this practice is flawed. Although "supervisors are valuable sources of information because they are typically familiar with the job," they write, "nevertheless these supervisors may observe only a small part of the performance of each subordinate" (p. 202). Instead, it is recommended that feedback be collected from a variety of different sources that each have unique exposure to the ratee's job performance. For example, perhaps a performer's co-workers can provide feedback about his or her level of cooperation and trustworthiness. The performer's customers would be best equipped to evaluate their service delivery, while the performer's subordinates may be best to describe their managerial style, trustworthiness, cooperation, and service delivery. Finally, the performer should be provided the opportunity to rate him- or herself in all categories.

It seems that any system that includes all of these observations into one evaluation would produce the most accurate and complete feedback. Any time performance feedback is being collected from more than one rater, this is known as multi-rater feedback. A specific type of multi-rater feedback is 360-degree feedback in which the ratee receives feedback from all directions. This feedback comes down from one's supervisor, up from one's subordinates, and across from one's co-workers. There may even be feedback coming in from one's clients. Multi-rater feedback, and 360-degree feedback specifically, have been supported as best practices for several important reasons. First, as suggested above, it is more likely to provide a complete picture of the employee's performance as it incorporates feedback from all relevant stakeholders. Second, when a performer can compare his or her own self-ratings with others' ratings, he or she can develop a greater self-awareness than would be otherwise possible. Third, the process places a premium on employee involvement and participation, which engenders not only compliance and acceptance, but also a culture of trust and engagement.

Completing the checklist. Once an appropriate cadre of raters is selected, the checklist should be distributed to them, along with instructions, a summary of how the data will be used, a contact for directing any questions, and a deadline for completion. To complete the task, the rater checks the behaviors that represent the ratee's performance for all behavioral categories, and returns the completed checklist. Exhibit 9.2 illustrates a completed checklist from a performer's subordinate. For each ratee, the data from all raters are combined and shared as developmental feedback in the third and final stage of the process.

Phase 3: Providing Feedback

Feedback is the delivery of evaluative reactions about another's behavior or performance. Inherent in this third phase are two main components: the feedback document and the feedback discussion. At this point in our process, feedback data have been collected from knowledgeable sources and combined in a succinct yet comprehensive summary. The document should outline who has contributed feedback, the instruments used to collect data, and the results themselves. Here, the performer wants to know not only "How am I doing?" but also "How does my supervisor think I'm doing?" and "How do my clients think I'm doing?" These data should be presented in a way that facilitates an identification of strengths and weaknesses and a detection of patterns across sources and categories. Furthermore, a performer should be able to compare

Exhibit 9.2 Sample Behavioral 360-Degree Feedback Report (Dimension: Customer Service)

This report focuses on the **Customer Service** performance dimension. **Customer Service** is an orientation toward maintaining or improving the satisfaction of internal and external customers. The behaviors included in this report exemplify excellent, typical, and poor levels of customer service related job performance.

Ratings: All raters were given a checklist of several job-related behaviors. For each behavior, the rater checked **Y** if (s)he witnessed demonstration of that behavior, **N** if (s)he knows that the behavior was not demonstrated, or **U** if (s)he was unable to observe.

Raters: In addition to your own self-assessment, feedback was collected from ten raters who are familiar with your job performance. This group consists of one supervisor, three peers, three direct reports, and three customers.

Behavioral Data: There are three tables below; the top table lists ineffective performance behaviors, the middle table lists typical behaviors, and the bottom table lists effective performance behaviors. For each behavior, you will be reminded of your own response (Y, N, or U), and you will see how many raters in each source category (e.g., supervisor, peers) replied with each response option.

Agreement: To help you understand how your self-assessment compares with the assessments from other raters, data cells are highlighted when there is either very high or very low agreement.

☐ More than 50 percent agreement on behavior

☐ More than 50 percent disagreement on behavior

(Continued)

INEFFECTIVE PERFORMANCE BEHAVIORS

	Self			Supervisor			Peers			Direct Reports			Customers			Behavior Total (-Self)		
	Y	N	U	Y	N	U	Y	N	U	Y	N	U	Y	N	U	Y	N	U
Behavior 1	1			1				3				3	1	1	1	2	4	4
Behavior 2		1				1		3		3			2		1	5	3	2
Behavior 3		1			1		3			3			2		1	8	1	1
Source Total	1	2	0	1	1	1	3	6	0	6	0	3	5	1	3	15	8	7

TYPICAL PERFORMANCE BEHAVIORS

	Self			Supervisor			Peers			Direct Reports			Customers			Behavior Total (-Self)		
	Y	N	U	Y	N	U	Y	N	U	Y	N	U	Y	N	U	Y	N	U
Behavior 1	1			1			3					3	1	1	1	5	1	4
Behavior 2	1					1	3				3		1	1	1	4	4	2
Behavior 3	1			1			3				3		1	1	1	5	4	1
Source Total	3	0	0	2	0	1	9	0	0	0	6	3	3	3	3	14	9	7

EFFECTIVE PERFORMANCE BEHAVIORS

	Self			Supervisor			Peers			Direct Reports			Customers			Behavior Total (-Self)		
	Y	N	U	Y	N	U	Y	N	U	Y	N	U	Y	N	U	Y	N	U
Behavior 1		1			1		1	2				3	1	1	1	2	4	4
Behavior 2	1					1	1	2			3			2	1	1	7	2
Behavior 3	1			1				3			3		1	2	1	1	8	1
Source Total	2	1	0	1	1	1	2	7	0	0	6	3	1	5	3	4	19	7

their self-assessment with ratings from other sources. This analysis—an application of gap analysis—is one of the key opportunities for growth that is built into this process. Not only does this give performers a clear idea of how different people see their strengths and weaknesses, but it trains them to be more empathetic and other-focused in their job activities. Exhibit 9.2 presents a model feedback summary document for one dimension (customer service) of an employee's job performance.

To fully realize the potential benefits from a 360-degree feedback exercise, the distribution of the summary document must be accompanied by a focused discussion with an appropriate advisor. While this advisor can be one of several people (one's supervisor, an executive coach, or external consultant), they should have knowledge of the full process and a commitment to the growth and development of the performer. Several agenda items should focus on this important discussion. *First*, the advisor should debrief the process itself, reinforcing how the component activities support the development purpose of the three-stage process. *Second*, the advisor should walk the performer through the ratings, clarifying any ambiguities over how they were calculated and what they represent. *Third*, the advisor and the individual should collaboratively interpret the results to identify key strengths and areas for needed development. During this portion of the discussion, it is critical to revisit the behavioral language in the original data collection instrument; the advantage of a behavioral checklist is that it maximizes the likelihood that the employee will repeat desired actions and modify undesired actions. *Fourth*, this past-focused, diagnostic evaluation should lead to a future-focused discussion. That is, the advisor will facilitate goal setting, where challenging and specific goals for future performance are established. *Finally*, the two parties should brainstorm and commit to action steps for attaining these performance goals.

The process outlined here can be an effective way to improve employee performance and encourage a culture of teamwork in an organization. It is a relatively straightforward system, based in a focus on behaviors and an appreciation of feedback from others. In the next section we summarize how these techniques not only have intuitive appeal, but are also well supported in the literature.

WHAT WE KNOW FROM RESEARCH

Behavioral approaches to assessment have been around for quite some time, and, as a result, a fair amount of research has been generated regarding the advantages of these techniques. In this section, we will outline the relevant research that pertains to the techniques advocated in this chapter. More specifically, we will discuss research that has been conducted on the use of the critical incidents technique and behavioral checklists for assessment purposes, as well as research on the effectiveness of 360-degree feedback systems.

The Critical Incidents Technique and Behavioral Checklists

Despite the fact that the concept of "critical incidents" in an evaluation context was first discussed in 1950 by John Flanagan (and later formalized by Flanagan in 1954), there has been relatively little empirical research examining how well critical incidents serve the assessment process. Instead, the vast majority of the work that has been done on the critical incidents technique has focused on providing the assessment community with an explanation of how this technique can be applied to different occupations or organizations and the specific issues that are likely to present themselves within the general process of generating critical incidents.

In one of the more informative works on the critical incidents technique, Rotam School of Management professor Gary Latham, along with his colleague Kenneth Wexley, identified several important issues that should be considered when gathering critical incidents from subject-matter experts (SMEs). First, employees should not be asked about their own performance so as to reduce the possibility of becoming defensive. Along the same lines, it is typically advisable to start the critical incident generation process by discussing effective behaviors. Jumping right into a discussion of ineffective behaviors may alarm the individuals generating these incidents and may lead them to conclude that the data generated is primarily going to be used in a negative manner (for example, to determine which individuals will lose their jobs). It may also be best to avoid using the term "critical incidents" entirely, given the negative connotation that may be given by the word "critical." Second, when generating critical incidents, SMEs should be told to focus on incidents that have occurred within the past six to twelve months. This reduces the likelihood that the job has changed substantially in the time since the critical incident was observed, while also lessening the cognitive distortions that may occur when asked to recall information that happened more than a year ago. Third, when generating critical incidents, it is important to ensure that the critical incidents being developed provide a specific description of the behavior itself, the outcome of this behavior, as well as the context of the behavior. SMEs may need to be prompted to provide the context for the behavior, or may need to be reminded to focus on observable behaviors (for example, "the performer missed an important deadline") rather than make inferences about the individual performing the behavior ("He's lazy").

Beyond this work by Latham and Wexley, work in the area of job analysis by University of South Florida psychology professor Michael Brannick and colleagues has made additional suggestions that may facilitate the generation of critical incidents. While the typical approach in generating critical incidents is to let the SMEs "free associate" and brainstorm, providing the SMEs with job performance dimensions (for example, "customer service") ahead of time has been found to actually generate a greater quantity of critical incidents, without a loss in quality. Additionally, if SMEs are having difficulty generating high-quality critical incidents, it may be helpful to have them think of a particularly successful individual that they have worked with and ask them to identify what behaviors made that person effective. Finally, when generating critical incidents, organizations must take great care to make sure that the incidents being generated always provide specific information regarding what the behavior was, why it was effective or ineffective, the organizational outcome of the behavior, and the context in which the behavior took place.

In contrast to the relative dearth of empirical research on the critical incidents technique, there has been much more research interest on the topic of using behavioral checklists as a means of assessment and evaluation in organization settings. In general, this research has focused on identifying the potential strengths and weaknesses of behavioral checklists, as well as an identification of situations in which this technique may best suit an organization's assessment efforts.

One of the more frequently discussed research studies on the use of behavioral checklists is a study by Stevens Institute of Technology management professor Richard Reilly and colleagues in 1990 that examined how these checklists may benefit organizations undergoing assessments of potential employees. In this study, the researchers compared the use of behavior checklists to the use of a more common rating format that required the evaluators to rate individuals on a scale from 1 to 5 in a number of areas.

The results of this study indicated that the use of behavioral checklists could be advantageous in several respects. First, the use of checklists may improve the quality of the ratings obtained by simplifying the assessment process for the rater, resulting in more objective and useful evaluations. It appears to be far easier for raters to complete a behavioral checklist as a means of assessing a performer than it is to fill out a scale requiring them to assign a numerical rating (1 to 5) to the individual. These sorts of numerical rating scales force these evaluators to (1) observe behavior, (2) recall that behavior, (3) categorize the behavior in to a relevant dimension, and (4) make a numerical evaluation of the behaviors as a whole. In contrast, the behavioral checklist is much more structured and thereby reduces the complexity of the rating process by removing the need to categorize behavior (step 3), since these checklists are already organized into explicit dimensions of performance. In addition, the behavioral checklist outlined in this chapter does not require raters to make any numerical evaluation whatsoever, eliminating this step (step 4) from the process.

Second, the checklist may also serve as a cue that stimulates the recall of behaviors or events that may have otherwise been omitted or forgotten from the evaluation process. Third, the behavioral checklist approach represents a relatively concise means of summarizing the observations of individuals during the assessment process. In doing so, it reduces the time required for interpreting these assessments while also making it easier to assess the level of agreement among those doing the evaluations. Finally, the behavioral checklist approach of assessment lends itself more readily to giving specific, behavioral feedback to the performers being evaluated. Simply being told that they received a score of 4 out of 5 on a work dimension does not tell a performer how he or she could improve. In contrast, the behavioral checklist revolves around specific behavioral examples (both effective and ineffective), thereby lending itself to the development process more readily.

In the time since the study by Reilly and colleagues, additional studies have provided evidence of the value of using behavioral checklists. For example, work by Lisa Donahue and colleagues in a special issue of the *Journal of Social Behavior and Personality* suggests that the use of behavioral checklists during the assessment process may result in more clearly defined and distinct ratings than other methods of evaluation such as the typical numerical scale used in the previous examples (for example, rating on a scale from 1 to 10). A study by Jo Hennessy and colleagues in 1998 also suggests that the use of behavioral checklists may reduce the variability in ratings that may be observed across different raters. Because variability in ratings across raters (rater disagreement) generally makes the assessment process more complex and time-consuming, the reduction in variability afforded by the behavioral checklist can have substantial benefits for organizations. More recent research by the University of Baltimore's Gunna Yun and colleagues in 2005 suggests that behavioral checklists may also have the added advantage of reducing one of the more common errors that is encountered in the assessment process: leniency error.

Leniency error refers to a situation in which the rater gives unrealistically positive ratings to all the individuals being assessed, resulting in a set of ratings that are restricted to the high end of the scale. To illustrate, if a rater were asked to observe and rate individuals on a scale from 1 to 10, leniency error would result in final ratings for most (if not all) of the individuals at the high end of this scale (8, 9, or 10). As mentioned before, leniency error is quite prevalent in organizations, with some sources suggesting that organizations are likely to encounter situations where 80 to 90 percent of their employees are rated as "above average." Obviously, this type of error creates enormous problems for organizations, as these types of ratings are typically used to assign merit raise increases, make decisions about promotions, training, or even employee termination. Within the context of employee assessment, the presence of leniency error results in raters failing to indicate the proper level of behavior or performance being displayed by a worker, which in turn means that the worker's assessment is inaccurate and therefore any developmental efforts that result from this assessment are likely to be misguided and ultimately ineffective. To put this in more practical terms, the occurrence of leniency error in an assessment context means that the rater is essentially failing to identify potential areas in which an employee can develop and grow to become a better worker. To the extent that these development opportunities are overlooked or omitted, this ultimately makes the employee development process less effective, thereby limiting its value to the organization. Given this background, the research by Yun and colleagues takes on more importance. The findings of this study suggest that, in situations where leniency error is likely to occur (a rater who is highly susceptible to leniency error), the use of behavioral checklists (rather than more traditional numerical ratings scales) reduces the likelihood of leniency error occurring. This indicates that behavioral checklists may represent a valuable tool in combating one of the more common errors that occurs during the assessment process.

360-Degree Feedback

The use of 360-degree feedback systems has increased substantially in recent years. To illustrate, recent surveys of Fortune 1000 firms indicate that over 90 percent of these firms report using some form of multi-source feedback as a part of their normal functioning. During this time, there has also been an accompanying surge in research on these systems, with over one hundred studies conducted on this topic since 1990. In this section, we will summarize what we consider to be the most important findings related to the use of 360-degree feedback systems in organizations as a means of assessment.

Perhaps the biggest question that must be answered about these types of feedback systems is, "Do they work?" In other words, does the implementation of 360-degree feedback systems improve the performance of individuals, teams, or the organization? Fortunately, there has been quite a bit of research on this topic, dating back to the mid-1970s. In a recent review of this research, Eli Broad Graduate School of Management's Fred Morgeson and his colleagues concluded that there is substantial research evidence suggesting that these systems lead to improvements in performance over time. However, beyond these general findings, their summary of the literature also suggested that these types of feedback systems are likely to be most effective with mid- to low-level performers. Initial high performers tended to show less of a positive response to these feedback systems, perhaps because they were already performing at high levels and therefore had little to no room for improvement. In addition, some of the largest improvements in performance in the research studies reviewed arose out of situations in which individuals initially gave themselves higher ratings than their subordinates gave them. This finding demonstrates perhaps one of the greatest advantages of these types of feedback systems: the ability to provide employees with a realistic sense of how others view them. In many cases, a lack of improvement on the part of employees may be due to the fact that they believe that they are already doing a great job and therefore do not need to change. This "reality check" provided by ratings from others seems to serve as a motivational force that stimulates individuals to make improvements, particularly in areas in which others indicate that they need development.

A 2005 review of the research conducted on 360-degree feedback systems by James Smither, associate dean of La Salle University's School of Business, and his colleagues also indicates that these types of feedback systems tend to result in performance improvements. It is worth noting that the results of their review also suggest that 360-degree feedback systems may hold more potential for improving performance beyond assessment systems that only rely on upward feedback from direct reports. One of the more interesting findings from this work by Smither, London, and Reilly is that organizations may see the greatest benefit from 360-degree feedback systems when they collect and distribute this feedback multiple times, rather than just once. While most of the performance gains observed in the research tend to come early on during this feedback process, the use of multiple feedback cycles may be useful in maintaining the performance improvement that is established by these programs over time.

The review of the research literature conducted by Smither and his colleagues also indicates that there are likely to be some situations that are more conducive to 360-degree feedback systems than others. First, these types of systems are likely to reap the greatest benefits when the feedback is presented to employees in a manner that reduces defensiveness. Individuals who become defensive when receiving this feedback tend to discard or ignore the feedback, thus ensuring that they will not use the feedback in a constructive manner to improve their performance. The goal of the organization in this sense is to couch all feedback in developmental terms that highlight both the individual's positive attributes and potential areas for development. Second, all feedback systems tend to be more effective when used with individuals who believe in the value of professional growth and development and believe that such development is under their personal control (that is, if they want to develop or grow, they have all the necessary personal or organizational resources to do so). In a separate five-year study, Alan Walker (of East Carolina University's Department of Psychology) and James Smither (1999) highlighted the best practice of integrating a formal feedback session as part of a multi-rater feedback process. Their findings showed that (1) managers who met with direct reports to discuss their upward feedback improved more than other managers and (2) managers improved more in years when they discussed the previous year's feedback with direct reports than in years when they did not discuss the previous year's feedback with direct reports.

Moving beyond answering the question of whether these programs are effective in improving performance, research suggests that 360-degree feedback systems are also likely to have additional benefits for organizations that choose to implement them. First, many studies suggest that, by gathering as many points of view during the assessment process, this increases the accuracy and utility of the information gathered, which ultimately allows the assessment process to function more effectively. Rather than relying on a single source of assessment data with the knowledge that all such sources of data have drawbacks or issues associated with them (self-ratings tend to be somewhat inflated relative to the ratings generated by others), this approach allows the organization to gather multiple data points, which provides them with a more comprehensive perspective on the individual being assessed. This gathering of multiple data points may also serve to enhance the legal defensibility of the assessment process if the need arises. Second, involving employees in the assessment process (particularly in their own assessment) tends to increase their commitment to the assessment and feedback system and enhances perceptions that this approach to assessment is fair and acceptable. For example, research by psychology professors Yochi Cohen-Charash of Baruch College and Paul Spector of the University of South Florida suggests that organizational practices (such as 360-degree feedback systems) that allow employees to voice their opinions and engage in open communications with the organization are associated with increased perceptions of fairness on the part of employees. These increased perceptions of fairness are likely to increase trust on the part of employees, which in turn may impact willingness and motivation to actively engage in the assessment and feedback process. All of these outcomes suggest that elements of 360-degree feedback systems can lead to more positive assessments of the organization by individuals involved in the assessment process, ultimately making the assessment and feedback program more effective.

WHEN TO APPLY

To this point, we have presented a three-part process for developing an assessment tool, collecting behavior-based data from a host of knowledgeable sources, and then delivering feedback in a way that facilitates improved performance. We have summarized some of the key research findings that support the components of this process. It is our assertion that such a process can be applied in a variety of work settings. As with the adoption of any intervention, it would be wise to first analyze the readiness of a specific work context given the nature of our assessment and feedback process. Some key considerations are summarized below.

A first consideration should be the intended purpose of assessing employees' performance. Is the goal to make administrative decisions about salary, promotion, or retention? Or is the goal to provide information to help employees improve performance? By now, it should be clear that the approach we propose is focused on an employee's professional development. Collecting feedback from all knowledgeable sources, including peers and subordinates, is useful in obtaining a complete view of the individual's performance. However, it may not lend itself as well to administrative decision making when there are political or relationship-oriented issues at play. As examples, if peers are competing for the same promotion, if a subordinate is retaliating against an unappreciated supervisor, or even if a co-worker is trying to help his friend by inflating his peer feedback, these could reduce the accuracy of the feedback and, ultimately, the administrative decision. So to realize the value of a 360-degree process, to safeguard from legal and fairness issues, and to neutralize any effects of competition or political maneuvering, our assessment and feedback process is intended to further employee development.

A second consideration involves the behavioral nature of the approach. We described the critical incident technique as a method for mapping out the important effective and ineffective behaviors, as well as the most typical behaviors displayed on the job. Thus, our approach will be most appropriate when there are specific behaviors that the organization feels are key to successful performance. If specific behaviors cannot be accurately identified, an alternative approach to defining and assessing performance may be optimal. For example, if results or outcomes are better indicators of effective perform-ance and if the behaviors required to reach those outcomes are more open to discretion and flexibility, then a results-based assessment mechanism may be preferred.

Assuming that a critical incident technique is followed, it should be noted that, once the catalog of job behaviors is developed, this list can be recycled as input for a host of other human resource functions. For example, job descrip-tions, selection systems, training needs analysis, and job evaluation efforts are all built upon an analysis of key job behaviors. Thus, if an organization would benefit from this kind of multi-purposing, the critical incident technique may be an even more worthy investment. Furthermore, as discussed, the outputs of the critical incident technique can serve as the content for the behavioral checklists. Checklists can be an especially useful rubric because they describe not only what successful performance looks like, but also what ineffective performance looks like as well. Because the checklist specifies actual behaviors, it facilitates sharing feedback with employees who want to learn what they are doing right and wrong. The behavioral checklist itself can be repurposed as a tool for the individual employee. As he or she is working toward his or her development goals, the checklist can be consulted as a resource of unambiguous desired behaviors to display, as well as a list of undesired behaviors to avoid.

360-degree feedback started as strictly a leadership development tool in-tended to assist managers in learning how their subordinates respond to their supervisory style. Over time, this practice has been extended to all employees. That is, receiving a report of one's strengths and weaknesses—as seen by the collective group of those who know his or her performance best—is not seen as valuable information to anyone wanting to perform to his or her potential. There are several characteristics that would make a particular work setting especially well suited for 360-degree feedback. First, consider a case in which there is no single party who would be sufficiently informed about the entirety of an individual's performance. Take, for example, the supervisor who manages up to ten different employees. She can only spend 10 percent of her time (at most—she has a job too, don't forget) observing a given employee as he does his job. What would be the odds that, in this brief observation time, the manager will have witnessed a true representation of what the employee accomplishes? In flatter organizations, where managers are accountable for more employees, or in team-based environments, where team-members are the most knowledgeable about an individual's effectiveness, 360-degree feedback makes good sense.

Consider a second case in which there are many aspects to someone's job, and each aspect involves different customers or co-workers. In order to get a more accurate appraisal of the incumbent's complete job performance, those different categories of customers and co-workers should provide input. Hence, the more multi-faceted a job is, the more sources would be involved and the more valuable 360-degree feedback becomes. A third case arises in situations in which an individual's job impacts different levels of the organization. Here, the performer is given a chance to see how his or her work is viewed by relevant others; if it is feasible that the witnesses to individuals' job behavior can be identified and relied on to provide meaningful and constructive feedback, then a 360-degree feedback system can be appropriate and effective.

A final, but crucial, consideration is the feedback culture of the organization (see Chapters Thirty and Thirty-One). Clearly, successful implementation of a 360-degree feedback process is based upon open and honest feedback. Organizations differ on how comfortable employees are with giving and receiving candid and balanced evaluations of each other's work. If this occurs regularly, then perhaps it is an environment that is ready for a 360-degree feedback system. If this does not occur regularly, introducing a 360-degree feedback system would best be couched within a broader cultural initiative (one that includes change management and training). A more in-depth discussion about a feedback culture is offered later in the "Critical Success Factors" section below.

STRENGTHS AND CRITICISMS

The research and considerations summarized above reveal that there are clear advantages and potential disadvantages to the components of the approach. The first step of the process employed the critical incident technique to fully define the job in question. Then, the critical incidents are translated into a behavioral checklist that guides data collection. The strengths of this approach are

- The model of job success is based on actual observed behaviors from the job. Hence, the validity of this process tends to be very high.
- When evaluation of employees is based on job-relevant behaviors and is therefore more valid, this translates into increased legal defensibility of the entire process.
- The critical incidents technique can yield a list of effective and ineffective demonstrations of performance.
- Employees are used to generate the critical incidents. This participation tends to engender acceptance with and commitment to the process and the results.

Weaknesses to this approach include:

- A general weakness of behavioral approaches to assessment is that there will always be some job-critical processes that are unobservable. For example, problem solving takes place cognitively and helps inform decision making. This processing—a behavior in itself—might not be well represented in a list of critical incidents.
- The critical incident technique can be time-consuming. If SMEs are observing the performance of the target job, this requires time removed from their own jobs. Furthermore, there may be some concern that the employees are behaving differently than they normally would simply because they are being observed (per the Hawthorne effect). Also, there is the danger that the sample of behavior would not be representative of the actual job.
- There may be some disagreement over what constitutes effective behavior. This process assumes that there is one correct way to complete a task, when in fact several behaviors could possibly lead to the same desired result.

The second step of the process involves distribution of the behavioral checklists to various sources to assess the performance of individual employees. Strengths of this approach are

- From the rater's perspective, a behavioral checklist is relatively easy to complete and requires no burdensome rater training. Whereas other rating approaches involve more interpretation and judgment, the fundamental activity of the behavioral checklist ("Did this behavior happen: yes or no?") is unambiguous and straightforward.

- Using a cadre of raters increases the possibility that the employee's true performance is being accurately captured.

- The combination of behavioral checklist and multi-rater feedback should be ultimately effective at addressing common rater errors. Because the rater only decides whether or not the performer has demonstrated the behavior and does not need to rate the quality of the behavior on a scale, there is a smaller chance for leniency effects to emerge. Also, any biases or rater errors should be tempered, as data are combined among many sources.

Weaknesses of this approach include:

- As a data collection instrument, a behavioral checklist may be overly simplistic. If the employee displays some effective behavior that is not included in the checklist, the rater needs to determine whether and how to include this performance data.

- By asking employees to provide feedback about other employees, there is the potential for unwanted influences to interfere. For example, political, self-protective, and interpersonal motives may compromise the validity of a performer's ratings. Again, this implies that multi-rater feedback is best used for developmental, and not administrative, purposes.

- Many people find it difficult to give negative feedback to others. As a result, they give only positive feedback, thereby reducing the validity of the activity. That said, this tends to be less of a problem in a checklist than it would be in other types of rating activities.

In the final step of the process, a summary document is shared with the individual, and an advisor discusses the feedback and a plan for improving performance. Strengths of this approach are

- Because of the behavior-based instrument, the feedback is given in behavioral terms. This provides unambiguous information about which behaviors should be continued, and which behaviors should be changed. In turn, this can facilitate the employee's ability to set goals, seek training opportunities, and monitor performance.

- The entire process builds the skills and mindset required of an open feedback culture. When completing a behavioral checklist for a co-worker or acting as an advisor to debrief the assessment results, one is developing his or her skills related to continuous learning and growth. On the organizational level, the process can help build teamwork, communication, and openness.

- The feedback process encourages ratees to more inclusively reflect upon their performance. By logging one's own self-assessment, the individual is given a voice in his or her own development; this can increase the perceived fairness and commitment to the process. Furthermore, analyzing the gaps between one's own ratings and the ratings of others helps respondents to identify previous blind spots, develop self-awareness, and become more empathetic to others' perspectives.

Weaknesses of this approach include:

- Because data are arriving from so many sources, it can be time-consuming to gather, calculate, and interpret the results.
- Similarly, there is the potential for data overload. That is, when performers are confronted with so much information, they are responsible for determining which data are most actionable and high-priority and which information is not. The simplicity of the feedback document and the role of the advisor are keys in overcoming this pitfall.
- When more raters are participating in the assessment process, there is the potential for conflicting evaluation information. While gaps across stakeholder ratings are expected, and in some ways are desirable, such discrepancies can lead to confusion and frustration.

RECOMMENDED DESIGN, DEVELOPMENT, AND IMPLEMENTATION PROCESS

Two guiding principles to consider when designing, developing, and implementing performance improvement tools are simplicity and specificity. In order to be accepted by both raters and ratees, the tool must be simple enough to be used with little to no confusion. At the same time, it must provide feedback with sufficient substance to be viewed as providing valuable information to the feedback recipient. The behavioral checklist shown in Exhibit 9.1 and the behavioral 360-degree feedback tool provided in Exhibit 9.2 meet both criteria. The behavioral checklist provides a simple framework for the rater to use ("yes," "no," or "unable to observe") and also provides specific behavioral examples of ineffective, typical, and effective performance. The examples are easy to understand and, because they were collected based on actual observations of individuals performing their jobs, they provide accurate and realistic examples of work behaviors associated with the job the person being rated performs. Further, the behavioral 360-degree feedback tool has the benefit of a simple design that provides specificity, through a comparison between the ratee and each category of rater (supervisor, boss, peer, direct report, and customer). As a result, the tool provides the ratee with specific information about how each category of rater evaluated his or her performance. Additionally, the shaded areas draw the feedback performer's attention to areas where there was substantial agreement or disagreement between their own ratings and those of the individuals who rated their performance.

Much of the design and development of the behavioral 360-degree feedback tool has already been discussed in previous sections; however, a brief review may be helpful. The three-step model we have proposed is based on: (1) defining performance, (2) assessing performance, and (3) providing feedback, as discussed in the following sections.

Phase 1: Defining Performance

Defining performance occurs first and consists of SMEs observing employees performing the job and recording examples of ineffective, typical, and effective performance (critical incidents). This process is known as job analysis. An important consideration at this point is to keep the focus on analyzing the job and not the individual. There will be a natural tendency to evaluate the individual being observed, but this tendency should be resisted. The goal at this point is not to make a determination as to whether the performer(s) being observed fall into the ineffective, typical, or effective category. Therefore, it is critical not to focus on the individuals being observed, but instead to focus on the behaviors involved in performing the job. If one could remove the person being observed from the equation, the job functions would still exist. The question to answer, then, is: "Regardless of who is performing the job, what types of behaviors are associated with doing the job?"

Remember that, whenever possible, multiple SMEs should be used. As previously stated, the use of multiple SMEs to record critical incidents is likely to lead to a fuller description of ineffective, typical, and effective behaviors associated with the job being analyzed. Additional sources that can be reviewed to aid in generating critical incidents include past performance appraisals of individuals in the job being observed, job descriptions, and prior job analysis data. Once the full range of critical incidents has been created, they may be classified into performance dimensions (for example, product knowledge, customer service orientation, business development, etc.). This will result in separate behavioral checklists (one for each performance dimension) and separate feedback reports (one for each dimension). Once the behavioral checklist has been created, the second step in the process is to assess the performance of the ratee(s) who are the subject of the 360-degree evaluation.

Phase 2: Assessing Performance

In order to assess performance, a behavioral checklist like the one depicted in Exhibit 9.1 is generated for each performance dimension. The checklist is then distributed to the raters who later evaluate the employee's performance. At this point, a copy of the checklist should also be given to the ratee, who should be asked to rate his or her own performance. As we have previously stated, care should be taken to ensure that appropriate raters are chosen. Raters should be chosen based on their experience with the employee being rated. In the example we have provided, the performers rate themselves and these self-ratings are supplemented with ratings from the supervisor, peers, direct reports, and customers. Whenever possible, it is desirable to have multiple peers, direct reports, and customers participate in the process. The reasons for this include getting the benefit of multiple viewpoints, but perhaps the most important reason of all is that it allows the data from these sources to be aggregated and ensures that the feedback cannot be traced back to an individual rater. This is important for all sources, but particularly for data from direct reports. If a supervisor's direct reports fear that the feedback they are providing will not remain confidential, they may be reluctant to provide honest feedback and, as a result, the data collected may be severely compromised.

Once the behavioral checklists have been distributed to all raters, collect and summarize the data. The data should be summarized separately for each performance dimension. A sample of how to present the summarized data, showing ratings across all data sources, as well as highlighting areas of significant agreement and disagreement between the ratee's self-ratings and the ratings of other categories of raters (supervisor, peers, direct reports, and customers), is provided in Exhibit 9.2

As can be seen in the exhibit, although the performer and the supervisor are often in agreement as to the ratee's performance, the ratee's peers, direct reports, and customers may tend to view the ratee's performance very differently than they see their own performance. Specifically, these raters report that, in their view, the employee is not performing some of the effective behaviors that they themselves checked off, is not performing some of the typical behaviors they themselves checked off, and is performing some of the ineffective behaviors they themselves did not consider to be displayed. There are also other forms of disagreement. For example, while the ratee believes he performs "Behavior 1" of the ineffective behaviors, all three peers disagree and do not feel that the employee performs this ineffective behavior. Despite this discrepancy, which would suggest the ratee's peers see him as being too tough on himself for this particular behavior, the general theme across peers, direct reports, and customers is that they view the ratee's performance less favorably than the ratee does. Such information that shows how multiple raters from varied perspectives see an individual's performance can be extremely valuable developmental feedback. In particular, the information in the shaded areas where substantial agreement and disagreement between raters and the ratee exist is especially valuable, as it provides the ratee with the otherwise unseen perspective of how he or she is viewed by others.

Phase 3: Providing Feedback

The behavioral 360-degree feedback report is a form of feedback in and of itself. Learning about one's behavior and how those behaviors are perceived by several different types of individuals is a valuable learning experience. However, one should remember that the full benefits of a 360-degree evaluation are not likely to be realized unless accompanied by a formal feedback session.

Considering the time and effort involved in conducting a thorough 360-degree feedback review, it makes good business sense to conclude the process with a feedback session. With effective coaching, it is the point at which ratees can internalize the feedback they receive and make appropriate changes in the behaviors that will make them more effective (see Chapter Twenty-Seven). In making the business case for the value of the feedback session, we suggest that it doesn't make sense to invest substantial time and effort into the 360-degree feedback process only to abandon it at the end—the point where a return on the time investment is most likely to occur.

In their 2006 review of the literature, Noe, Hollenbeck, Gerhart, and Wright identified several tactics to use when giving feedback. The tactics identified by Noe and his colleagues are presented below, augmented with additional tactics from the feedback literature and our own personal experience. The tactics can be integrated into the feedback session to increase the chances that 360-degree feedback will have a positive effect on the ratee's future job behavior. These tactics are recommended regardless of who is conducting the feedback session, be it the supervisor, consultant, or any other administrator. Tactics to integrate that are supported by the feedback literature include the following.

Separate strengths from areas for improvement. Make a conscious effort to avoid phrases like "You're doing a good job, but . . . " as the "but" in the middle of the feedback invalidates the praise just given. This is a simple tactic, but one that can have a big impact. Make a conscious effort to take note of how many times you make "but" statements throughout the course of your day. Instead of using the same statement to convey both positive and developmental feedback, separate the two types of feedback. Begin with highlighting areas on which the employee has genuinely received favorable ratings and, when appropriate, offer praise for the performer's good work. Then transition the conversation to areas on which the performer received less favorable ratings. This will create two distinct components: a component where positive results are discussed and a separate component where areas requiring improvement are discussed. Remember to keep the types of feedback separated from each other: starting a sentence with praise and ending with criticism, even constructive criticism, lessens the impact the praise was meant to have on performers.

Establish a context that is conducive to open and honest discussion. In order to do this, let the employee know the feedback session is an opportunity for both parties to develop: it's an opportunity for employees to learn about themselves and for you to learn about the employees too. One catch is that you have to mean it when you say it, and your actions must support your words. Going through the motions of creating a supportive context will ultimately fail. The supportive feedback context offered must be real; anything less will be perceived negatively by the ratee.

Allow the ratee to provide input during the feedback session. He or she has already had the opportunity to provide opinions about his or her performance when completing the self-rating. Now, the ratee should be given the opportunity to support these ratings with examples and explanations. He or she should also be able to discuss areas of agreement and disagreement between self-ratings and the ratings of the other raters, as well as areas that were particularly surprising or puzzling. If the goal of the feedback discussion is to have the performer committed to using the results to improve performance, then participation in the process will help facilitate the person committing to the conclusions reached as a result of the feedback session. Furthermore, if these individuals are allowed to express themselves throughout the process, they will likely perceive the organization as more fair and respectful of its employees.

Adopt a problem-solving focus. Identify the areas of weakness uncovered by the 360-degree review and, once those weaknesses are identified, don't dwell on them. Instead, transition the conversation to resolutions for the problems identified. It seems to be human nature to dwell on the negative, on problems. Once a problem is identified and agreed on, continuing to dwell on it is unproductive. Instead, use the feedback session to focus on solutions. The result will be a more productive feedback session and a greater chance that solutions to the areas identified as "needing improvement" will be discovered.

Keep the focus on the behavior, not the person. The message to be conveyed is that the behavior is deficient, not that the person is deficient. Focusing on behaviors should be easily accomplished, particularly considering the evaluation itself is based entirely on examples of ineffective, typical, and effective job behaviors. Even so, make sure the discussion centers on effective and ineffective behaviors for the job and does not stray to a lengthy discussion of what is "wrong" with the person. Such a strategy is likely to elicit defensiveness. In contrast, a strategy that emphasizes effective and ineffective behaviors can result in the performer having a better understanding of what behaviors to continue and which behaviors to change.

Give praise when it's appropriate. Acknowledging the strengths of ratees is a very important part of the process. It reinforces the positive behaviors they have demonstrated and also lets them know that their good work is valued. It is also important to not give false praise. At best, it will be perceived as disingenuous; at worst, it will lead to the employees' believing that negative aspects of their performance are acceptable or good when, in fact, they are problematic for the individual, for the team, and possibly for the entire organization.

Agree to goals and review dates. To close the feedback session and to ensure effective behaviors are repeated and ineffective behaviors are reduced, goals for future performance and review dates should be established. The goal setting theory, as set forth by R.H. Smith School of Business' Edwin Locke with Gary Latham in 1990 prescribes that goals should be specific (so as to focus performance) and difficult (so as to enhance the level of performance). Such goals have often been referred to as SMART goals: specific, measurable, action-oriented, realistic (challenging, but not out of reach), and time-bound. Goals that meet these aims are much more likely to lead to increased performance. When working with the ratee to create goals for future behavior and performance, our advice is to evaluate the goals using the SMART framework. If the goal is specific, can be measured, requires action on the part of the ratee, is realistic yet challenging, and has clear timelines, it is much more likely to have a positive effect on future behavior and future performance.

Create action plans that detail how the employee will change his or her behavior. Research by New York University's social, cognition, and perception professor Peter Gollwitzer, among others, has shown the value of creating action plans that address where, when, and how performance or behavior will be undertaken. The results of creating simple plans for goal attainment that include where the behavior will occur, when it will occur, and how it will be performed are dramatic. The implication for the feedback process is clear: in addition to setting specific and difficult goals, make sure an action plan for achieving the goals is also created. Effective action planning can turn a vague/general goal into a SMART goal.

Delivering feedback, especially developmental, can be a challenge for even the most seasoned managers. Using the above tactics can increase the chances that the 360-degree feedback will have a desirable effect on the ratee's future performance. One thing to keep in mind is that providing feedback is a skill and, as is the case with most skills, takes time to develop. It would be wise for organizations to invest in training their employees in best practices and techniques of giving and receiving effective feedback.

CRITICAL SUCCESS FACTORS

The assessment and feedback system presented within this chapter has the potential to boost individual performance and, ultimately, the performance and culture of one's organization. Before closing, this section will describe some of the situational and organizational factors that can facilitate or inhibit the success of such a program.

Purpose

First, it is important to be completely clear about the intended purpose of such an intervention. To reiterate, the process is meant to develop the skills and effectiveness of employees. It is not meant to replace a current performance appraisal process or to dictate decisions about compensation, promotion, or termination. That fact should be understood by all participants prior to implementation. That said, this feedback system will indirectly relate to an organization's performance appraisals. If this system works as it should, then employees will receive feedback that affects improved performance; this, in turn, should be reflected in performance evaluations. Because the critical incident technique reveals job-relevant behaviors, it would also make sense that the performance appraisal criteria and assessment and feedback criteria significantly overlap. In fact, organizations should be proactive in aligning the job criteria among sources like competency models, job descriptions, performance evaluation, and assessment and feedback systems.

Culture

As stated earlier, the effectiveness of an assessment and feedback system is built on a solid feedback culture in an organization. When there is a positive feedback culture, the human resources of the enterprise boast a collective skill set of giving and receiving regular feedback to each other. The following characteristics are symptoms of a strong feedback culture:

- Employees provide feedback to others, even when it is uncomfortable or inconvenient.
- Employees solicit feedback from others, even when they are not confident that they have done their best work.
- Employees receive training and coaching about how to deliver effective feedback and how to seek and receive feedback.
- There is an expectation for balanced feedback, so that it identifies positive and negative aspects of performance.
- Making mistakes is acceptable because it helps those within an organization to learn and raises concerns that could lead to a better result.
- There exists a trust between ratees and raters, and between the staff and the leadership.

Finally, it is important to note that the feedback system presented in this chapter is not intended to be the only feedback that takes place. Instead, informal feedback should be shared every day in the organization. It should be occurring by telephone, e-mail, and live conversations. It should be occurring at the conclusion of a project, directly after a meeting, or first thing in the morning. If feedback is part of the company's norms, then the system we advocate here will be only the formal and systematic component of a healthy feedback culture (also see Chapter Thirty).

Communication

Because the participation and involvement of all employees is so critical to the success of 360-degree feedback, a carefully constructed communication plan is paramount. A clear introductory message should be written that outlines some of the key elements of the program, and follow-up messages can clarify how successful implementation will take place. Some of the important elements of these messages include:

- The goal and rationale of the system.
- The major stages or activities in the process.
- The roles of the ratee and the raters, as well as any coach or SME.
- The format of the instruments (behavioral checklist, feedback sheet).
- The commitment to confidentiality: Although different employees will provide feedback to the ratee, only that individual and his or her coach or supervisor will have access to the results. The only individual-level data that will not be anonymous are the self-rating and the supervisor rating.
- Every effort should be made to make people feel safe in the knowledge that the ratings they provide will not be used to harm them; open and honest feedback is the only way that people can improve and become their best.

It is important that the leaders in the organization are the senders or clear supporters of these messages from the early implementation of the program. It is also important that there are human resources representatives or supervisors with knowledge and dedication to the program who can answer questions that arise. Finally, although the behavioral checklist was chosen for its simplicity, there may be some cases in which training needs to take place to ensure that all raters are comfortable with and capable of observing performance and completing the feedback instrument.

Pitfalls to Avoid

Technology. Many organizations have internal or external resources that can produce online surveys and advanced databases to collect and compile multi-rater feedback. Other organizations do not. The priority should be placed on the design and validity of the assessment instrument. The method by which raters submit their input or ratees are delivered their feedback is secondary. While technology-based solutions may be convenient and elegant, they should facilitate—not drive—the process.

Data Overload. Part of the rationale behind 360-degree feedback is that more information leads to more valid and accurate feedback. While more information can be better, there is likely a point at which too much data will compromise the value of the activity. Consider each stage of the process: if a job is very complex, the critical incident technique may yield several job dimensions, each with many behavioral statements. The more behavioral statements that appear on the behavioral checklist, the more effort will be required of raters. The more raters who are selected, the more information will need to be included in the feedback. The more information included, the more complex it becomes to reconcile any discrepancies and arrive at goals and action plans. It may be valuable for a given organization to set guidelines or limits around the amount of data it will manage.

Similarly, no one should feel like participation in the assessment and feedback process is a job in itself. It could be possible that one performer is a ratee and also recruited as a rater to several other ratees. Avoid creating situations in which there are constantly 360-degree feedback exercises in motion. The amount of data and time that employees spend participating in these initiatives will likely outweigh the potential gains that could be realized. One solution could be to establish a cycle wherein specific jobs go through a 360-degree feedback process every three years. That is, some jobs will receive 360-degree assessments in the first year and then again in the fourth year; other jobs will receive 360-degree feedback in the second and fifth year, and so on. With this strategy, the organization may always be in the middle of a 360-degree feedback cycle, but the amount of data collected and time required will be more manageable. Again, this is not to say that regular informal feedback will not occur: it absolutely should. Moreover, it allows for more time for each individual to develop his or her skills and adjust his or her behavior between assessment periods.

Focus on the Past. Finally, it should be reinforced that, while assessment is clearly a past-oriented activity, the feedback should inspire future-oriented planning. Highlighting those areas where development is required is not enough; that should be just the start of the conversation. From there, the supervisor or coach should collaborate with the employee in setting goals to drive performance improvement. Earlier in the chapter, we discussed the importance of SMART goals: those that are associated with commitment and follow-through. In fact, the coach or supervisor should decide how, exactly, the individual will accomplish his or her goals. What training, assignments, or other development opportunities will be completed to accomplish the goal in a given time period? This discussion will culminate in an action plan that explicates where, when and how the employee will change his or her behavior to reach his or her performance goals. When that occurs, the assessment and feedback process will have been successful.

SUMMARY

All employees have a need for feedback—accurate and regular information about what they are doing correctly and what they could be doing differently. This chapter presented an approach for assessing whether individuals are displaying the critical behaviors for the job and sharing this information to improve performance over time. The proposed techniques can be adopted by any organization in which job behaviors can be identified and employees are knowledgeable about each other's performance. Valuable by-products of the proposed system include individual-level self awareness, group-level participation in development, and an organization-wide healthy feedback culture.

References

Brannick, M. T., Levine, E. L., & Morgeson, F. P. (2007). *Job and work analysis* (2nd ed.). Thousand Oaks, CA: Sage.

Cohen-Charash, Y., & Spector, P. E. (2001). The role of justice in organizations: A meta-analysis. *Organizational Behavior and Human Decision Processes*, *86*, 278–321.

Donahue, L. M., Truxillo, D. M., Cornwell, J. M., & Gerrity, M. J. (1997). Assessment center construct validity and behavioral checklists: Some additional findings. *Journal of Social Behavior and Personality*, *12*(5), 85–108.

Flanagan, J. C. (1950). The critical requirements approach to educational objectives. *School and Society*, *71*, 321–324.

Flanagan, J. C. (1954). The critical incident technique. *Psychological Bulletin*, *51*, 327–358.

Gollwitzer, P. M. (1999). Implementation intentions: Strong effects of simple plans. *American Psychologist*, *54*, 493–50.

Hennessy, J., Mabey, B., & Warr, P. (1998). Assessment centre observation procedures: An experimental comparison of traditional, checklist, and coding methods. *International Journal of Selection and Assessment*, *6*(4), 222–231.

Latham, G. P., & Wexley, K. N. (1993). *Increasing productivity through performance appraisal* (2nd ed.). Reading, MA: Addison-Wesley.

Locke, E. A., & Latham, G. P. (1990). *A theory of goal-setting and task performance*. Englewood Cliffs, NJ: Prentice Hall.

Morgeson, F. P., Mumford, T. V., & Campion, M. A. (2005). Coming full circle: Using research and practice to address 27 questions about 360-degree feedback systems. *Consulting Psychology Journal: Practice and Research*, *57*, 196–209.

Noe, R., Hollenbeck, J. R., Gerhart, B., & Wright, P. (2006). *Human resource management: Gaining a competitive advantage*. Boston: McGraw-Hill/Irwin.

Reilly, R. R., Henry, S., & Smither, J. W. (1990). An examination of the effects of using behavior checklists on the construct validity of assessment center dimensions. *Personnel Psychology*, *43*(1), 71–84.

Smither, J. W., London, M., & Reilly, R. R. (2005). Does performance improve following multi-source feedback? A theoretical model, meta-analysis, and review of empirical findings. *Personnel Psychology*, *58*, 33–66.

Walker, A., & Smither, J. (1999). A five-year study of upward feedback: What managers do with their results matters. *Personnel Psychology*, *52*, 393–423.

Yun, G. J., Donahue, L. M., Dudley, N. M., & McFarland, L. A. (2005). Rater personality, rating format, and social context: Implications for performance appraisal ratings. *International Journal of Selection and Assessment*, *13*, 97–107.

Recommended Readings

Atwater, L.E., Brett, A.F., & Charles, A. C. (2007). Multi-source feedback: Lessons learned and implications for practice. *Human Resource Management*, *46*(2), 285–307.

Bracken, D., Timmreck, C., & Church, A. (2001). *The handbook of multi-source feedback*. San Francisco: Jossey-Bass.

Craig, S. B., & Hannum, K. (2006). Research update: 360 performance assessment. *Consulting Psychology Journal: Practice and Research*, *58*(2), 117–122.

Fletcher, C. (2001). Performance appraisal and management: The developing research agenda. *Journal of Occupational and Organizational Psychology*, *74*, 473–487.

International Society for Performance Improvement. (http://www.ispi.org/).

Lepsinger, R., & Lucia, A. D. (1997). *The art and science of 360-degree feedback*. San Francisco: Pfeiffer.

Levy, P. E., & Williams, J. R. (2004). The social context of performance appraisal: A review and framework for the future. *Journal of Management*, *30*(6), 881–905.

Noe, R. J., Hollenbeck, J. R., Gerhart, B., & Wright, P. M. (2006). *Human resource management: Gaining a competitive advantage* (5th ed.). New York: McGraw-Hill Irwin.

Seifert, C. F., Yukl, G., & McDonald, R. A. (2003). Effects of multi-source feedback and a feedback facilitator on the influence behavior of managers towards subordinates. *Journal of Applied Psychology*, *88*, 561–569.

Toegel, G., & Conger, J. A. (2003). 360-degree assessment: Time for reinvention. *Academy of Management Learning & Education*, *2*, 297–311.

Tornow, W. W., & London, M. *Maximizing the value of 360-degree feedback*. San Francisco: Jossey-Bass.

 EDITORIAL CONNECTIONS

Many might think of assessment and feedback systems as being limited to annual performance reviews or the subject of managerial meetings when an individual's performance drops. However, as Chapter Nine demonstrates, assessment and feedback can and should be integrated throughout any performance system. 360-degree feedback, specifically, is a valuable form of assessment and feedback because it integrates multiple perspectives on performance. Automated feedback systems to guide individual employee productivity or informal reviews and follow-up meetings with managers to discuss the results of current projects can complement 360-degree feedback by ensuring that individuals and teams receive timely and useful information on their current performance.

When improving performance, examine the system to determine whether employees are given clear expectations about what results are to be accomplished, routinely assessed to determine whether they are on the path toward success, and provided with useful feedback on how to improve. Breakdowns in these feedback loops are common, and small improvements here can lead to significant improvements in performance. For these reasons and the relatively low cost of associated interventions, assessment and feedback are often a good starting point for your improvement efforts. The systematic assessment of and feedback about performance are, after all, essential to the improvement of human and organizational performance.

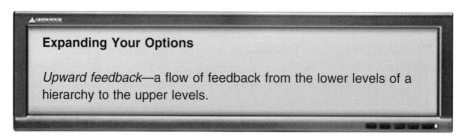

Expanding Your Options

Upward feedback—a flow of feedback from the lower levels of a hierarchy to the upper levels.

WHAT'S COMING UP

The importance and value of clear expectations and timely feedback is not, however, limited to the individual level. At the team and organizational level, performance measurement systems can provide timely data and information that inform decisions about how to improve results. Performance dashboards, as one example of a performance measurement system, help sort through the various performance data and information that are collected in organizations in order to provide valuable data on the essential variables that most directly impact performance. This information can then be used to make data-driven and justifiable decisions. As a pioneer in the application of performance measurement systems for systemic performance improvement, Ingrid Guerra-Lopez describes in Chapter Ten how effective performance measurement systems can become an integral part of your improvement efforts.

Performance Measurement and Management Systems

Ingrid Guerra-López

INTRODUCTION

What doesn't get measured doesn't get done . . . or at least it doesn't get done well. The group of scientists, engineers, and economists who comprise the MIT Commission on Industry Productivity specifically recommended that organizations must develop and use sound techniques for measuring and improving the efficiency and quality of their processes. Their 1989 landmark study, published in part as *Made in America: Regaining the Productive Edge,* further stated that it is necessary to identify opportunities for progressive improvements in their performance.

Without accurate and timely performance feedback—provided by ongoing measurement and tracking of performance indicators—it becomes nearly impossible to efficiently and effectively see progress toward desired ends. It becomes equally difficult to make intelligent decisions about what to change, how to change, what to leave alone, and what to abandon altogether. Performance feedback therefore provides a unique and crucial role in the improvement of human and organizational results.

Most performance improvement professionals would agree on the importance of establishing performance objectives that provide strategic direction efforts and resources. What often is forgotten is that without en-route timely measurement toward those objectives, organizations do not really know whether they are getting closer to or further away from them, whether they are using the most efficient way to get there, or whether they are taking unnecessary twists and turns. In this sense, performance measurement is the compass that keeps an organization on course toward a desired destination, while providing the intelligence to make day-to-day decisions about how to best get there. Performance measurement can, nevertheless, speak both to effectiveness (Was the target destination reached?) and efficiency (Was the destination reached in the most economical way—whether in terms of time, cost, and other resources?).

Since the popularization of total quality management in the 1980s, the subject of performance measurement has been generating ever-increasing interest among academics and practitioners alike. Meaningful advances have been made on establishing performance management and measurement systems that track performance beyond the traditional financial measures. However, many companies still rely on financial measures as their primary index of performance, thus limiting their decision-making to an incomplete—and often reactive—data set.

Without systemically measuring and tracking performance, an organization is not purposefully managing performance. In 1995, Geary Rummler and Alan Brache highlighted the central role of measurement in performance improvement and described the management function at the organizational and process levels as one that "involves obtaining regular [customer] feedback, tracking actual performance along the measurement dimensions established in the goals, feeding back performance information to relevant subsystems, taking corrective action if performance is off target, and resetting goals so that the organization is continually adapting to external and internal reality" (p. 21).

Performance measurement is not something done in addition to managing; rather, it is at the core of intelligent management. Measurement systems must be systemically linked to an organization's *value chain*, a term first proposed by strategy guru Michael Porter in 1985, in order to ensure purposeful measurement that feeds and supports management in obtaining top organizational performance. Moreover, performance measures must be set up such that they support coordinated performance improvement and management efforts. Managing any measure in isolation of the entire system could result in sub-optimization of the entire organization.

DESCRIPTION

Measurement Defined

Measurement—the estimation of an exact standard—serves to compare actual accomplishments to some predetermined standard of accomplishment. For example, an organization may want to compare actual sales volume to its sales goals for the month. Some measurement tools commonly used by performance improvement professionals include observations, extant data reviews, focus groups, and questionnaires. The focus or "object" of measurement refers to the matter that is to be under examination: a process, an intervention, a project, or an activity. The standard for performance should be stated in terms of measurable objectives that specify measurable criteria and conditions.

From a performance improvement process perspective, one measurement is typically conducted in the context of needs assessment, causal analysis, monitoring, formative evaluation, and summative evaluation. Performance measurement in the context of needs assessment allows for the determination of the gaps between current accomplishments and desired performance goals. In the context of summative evaluation, it enables the determination of whether these gaps have been reduced or eliminated through the performance solutions that were implemented.

Expanding Your Options

Benchmarking—a process in which organizations evaluate various aspects of their processes in relation to other organizations or to best practice, usually within their own sector. This allows for the development of a strategy for improvement or to adopt best practice, usually with the aim of increasing some aspect of performance.

Based on www.wikipedia.org definition (January 2009)

Further, overarching processes like strategic planning and management are part of a broader context for performance measurement. More directly, strategic planning identifies the cluster of long- and short-term goals and objectives an organization will commit to reaching based on its unique strengths, weaknesses, opportunities, and threats. It then provides a process for selecting the means that will best help the organization accomplish its goals. To make this series of decisions, relevant performance measures have to be identified: in order to establish the exact destination that is to be reached, where the organization is currently, how far you have to go, how to best get there, what adjustments have to be made along the way, and when. As a consequence, earch of these decisions rests on intelligence produced through well-designed and implemented measurement systems. Figure 10.1 illustrates this progression from decisions to data to intelligent action.

Regardless of the broader context in which measurement is taking place, perhaps the most important use of performance measurement is to stimulate or motivate behaviors targeted at demonstrably improving performance at all levels of the organization, rather than being used as an instrument for finger-pointing and punishment. Blaming people, after all, is rarely an effective way to achieve sustained improvements in performance.

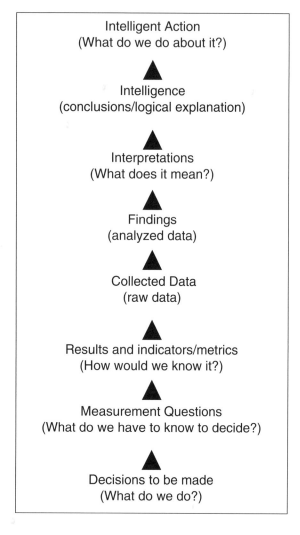

Figure 10.1 Progressions from Decisions to Data to Intelligent Action.

Goals, Objectives, and Performance Indicators

Similar to any performance improvement effort, the starting point of creating a performance measurement and management system is identifying or verifying the ultimate ends the organization wishes to accomplish. These ends are results, accomplishments, products, outputs, outcomes, or consequences (rather than the processes, activities, or resources to be implemented and used).

While "ends" are what the organization exists to accomplish and deliver, "means" are *how* it goes about doing that. Means include processes, programs, projects, activities, resources, and a host of others things that the organization uses and does to accomplish the desired ends. To expand upon our example above, one potential means to increasing sales might be introducing a new sales incentive plan for the sales force, another might be a new quoting and sales process, another still might be a new promotional program for customers.

One useful framework for portraying this means and ends distinction is the organizational elements model (OEM), introduced by Florida State University's Roger Kaufman in the 1960s. The OEM consists of five overarching elements in two major categories: ends and means. This is a useful conceptual framework for beginning to think about the relationships among different levels of results and between these results and the means used to accomplish them. According to Kaufman, the three levels of results are

1. *Strategic:* Long-term organizational results that ultimately benefit clients and society, often stated in terms of a consistent vision. James Collins, the leader of a management research center, and Jerry Porras, Professor Emeritus from Stanford, provide an excellent discussion of an organizational vision and define it as the organization's reason for being and the foundation for strategic planning and execution. Their recommended timeline for the achievement of strategic aims tends to be at least a decade.

2. *Tactical:* Shorter-term organizational results that help operationally define the vision, usually stated in terms of an organizational mission. The timeline for the achievement of such accomplishments tends to be set on an annual basis. It is not so much that the types of results sought change every year, but rather that there are concrete annual targets to reach.

3. *Operational:* The building-block objectives—perhaps at the department, unit, team or individual level—that contribute to the accomplishment of the organization's mission. In settings such as the military, *operations* are used to describe not only the building-block results, but also the processes used to produce them.

All levels of results must be aligned and identified in the context of strategic planning and alignment. Desired results drive both the processes we employ and how we carry them out. *Processes* and *inputs* may be important to achieving results; however, performance goals and objectives exclusively concern results, not how they are achieved.

Identifying Indicators and Metrics

Performance indicators, also referred to as *measures*, are specific and concrete gauges of a result, process, or activity that allows us to make complex systems palpable and manageable. Much as the gauges on your car's dashboard provide a synopsis of its performance, performance indicators provide organizations with the essential information for making decisions. These indicators become the data points tracked both now and into the future (in fact, continuously), and are used to make decisions regarding specific actions for improvement. British management professors Andy Neely, Chris Adams, and Mike Kennerley make a distinction between a performance *measure*, a parameter used to quantify a result, and a performance *metric*, the definition of the scope, content, and component pars of a broader performance measure. Similarly, a result can, and usually will, have multiple performance indicators. For the purposes of this chapter, the broad accomplishments will be referred to as performance *results*, with specific measureable indicators of those results being referred to as performance *indicators* or *measures*. For example, customer satisfaction is a performance result that can be measured through various performance indicators such as referrals, repeat business, account activity, returns, and customer opinion, to name a few possibilities.

Expanding Your Options

Accountability—the acknowledgment and assumption of responsibility for actions, products, decisions, and policies including the administration, governance and implementation within the scope of the role or employment position and encompassing the obligation to report, explain and be answerable for resulting consequences.

Based on www.wikipedia.org definition (January, 2009)

A comprehensive set of indicators for each desired result should be developed. Depending on what measures are picked to measure a result, different pictures of what is actually going on within an organization could emerge. For example, customer satisfaction might be measured through a traditional customer survey, with 100 percent of those surveyed responding that they strongly agree with the statement "overall, I am satisfied with company ABC"). This might be interpreted as evidence that, since customers are satisfied, then we should continue to do whatever we are currently doing. However, a closer look at other indicators, such as repeat business, could reveal that fewer than 20 percent of customers ever come back. A complete and relevant set of indicators must be referred to simultaneously before making interpretations and drawing conclusions. Different vantage points lead to different interpretations, conclusions, decisions, and actions.

Interrelationships between and among measures should be considered across the entire organization. Doing so avoids fragmenting or isolating data from other important organizational measures. For instance, an organization's production line may focus solely on the results and indicators related to production, while the product returns department focuses on warranty issues, with the sales department measuring only sales. Each of these departments may reach its internal measures but negatively impact other areas. The production line might be measuring success by how many widgets they produce each cycle, while the returns department might be measuring success by how many defective widgets were sent back by customers (which speaks to quality and, in turn, cost). For their part, the sales department might be measuring success solely through meeting or exceeding sales goals, while at the same time contributing to the high volume of returns due to pushing widgets that don't meet the needs (gaps in results) of their customers. By communicating with one another, departments manage for top organizational performance, thus enhancing their efficiency and effectiveness—matters rarely achieved when departments manage only for operational results within their silos.

Sources of performance indicators. One fundamental source for deriving relevant results indicators to track is first and foremost the decisions that stakeholders, particularly management and other data users, will have to make with the measurement data collected. Naturally, different stakeholder groups will require timely access to different measures, particularly those that are relevant to their own areas of influence and responsibility. Thus, a primary step in setting up any performance measurement and management system is to identify all stakeholder groups and have each well represented in the process. Without a sound understanding of the needs and requirements of stakeholders, setting up such a system could become an exercise in futility.

Another source for identifying appropriate measures is the set of performance objectives that the organization as a whole, as well as its functions, teams, and individuals, find relevant to performance management and improvement. Ideally, these performance objectives should have been the product of a strategic planning process in which organizational results at various levels of the organization (strategic, tactical, and operational) were identified. Additionally, these objectives are also the foundation for the sorts of decisions management must make.

According to Bob Mager, performance objectives should address:

1. *Who or what entity* is to be responsible for the accomplishment.
2. The actual *accomplishment* to be observed.
3. What *measurable criteria* would be used to determine whether or not the result was accomplished satisfactorily (measureable targets or

standards that then allow us to make comparison to the current state and, in turn, allow us to identify performance gaps).

4. The *conditions* under which this result would be acceptable.

For example, one organizational objective might be: ABC Financial will attain 50 percent or better of the mortgage market share in the Midwest within two years without sacrificing current quality of services ratings and profit margin. One performance indicator, then, is actual market share. The measurable criteria or standard is 50 percent or better; thus we want to know what our current market share is and track our progress toward that 50 percent threshold by the end of the second year. Tracking quality of service indicators as well as the profit margin are both relevant, since both are required conditions for obtaining that 50 percent market share. Neither results nor indicators are stagnant, and it is possible that a new target might be set before those two years are up, in light of our current accomplishments, strengths, challenges, and so forth. Equally, it is also possible that market and technology changes make it necessary to track additional performance indicators.

WHAT WE KNOW FROM RESEARCH

Popular Measurement and Management Frameworks

Over the last decades, many frameworks for measuring performance have been proposed. These range principally from more commercial and somewhat generic frameworks offered from vendors who may know little about perform- ance improvement to more rigorous measurement frameworks that have been proposed by credible experts with demonstrated competence in business, management, measurement, and performance improvement. Some of these latter examples include:

- Kaplan and Norton's "balanced scorecard," which focuses on financial, customer, learning and growth, and internal business processes mea- surement dimensions;

- Lynch and Cross's "performance pyramid," which focuses on quality, delivery, cycle time, and waste as the foundation for their measurement system;

- Fitzgerald, Johnston, Brignall, and Sivestro's results and determinants framework, which focuses generally on results of interest and the determinants that impact those specific results; and

- Neely, Adams, and Kennerley's "performance prism," which focuses on stakeholder satisfaction, strategies, processes, capabilities, and contri- bution dimensions.

Moreover, while Geary Rummler's anatomy of performance (AOP) model is perhaps more commonly known as a performance improvement model rather than a performance measurement model, he has argued that these are intimately related functions necessary for performance management and improvement. Thus, it lends itself well for use as a measurement framework. The dimensions stressed by the AOP are the business view, the organization system views, the performer view, and the management view.

Any of the models or frameworks mentioned above can guide in the identification and tracking of key performance indicators in the long term. However, as with most tools, they must be customized to fit the requirements of a given situation. It is unlikely that any one framework will meet all measurement and management requirements of each and every organization. While their categories, dimensions, and sample measures will likely be helpful in generating custom sets of relevant measures, avoid borrowing irrelevant measures that will ultimately not help in managing your organization's performance efficiently and effectively.

The most well-known performance measurement framework is the balanced scorecard. It was developed by David Norton, CEO of the Nolan Norton Institute, a research organization of KPMG, and Robert Kaplan of the Harvard Business School in response the belief that performance measurement approaches primarily relying on financial accounting measures were becoming obsolete. Their aim was to provide a more responsive management system to enable management to make better decisions. The four basic performance measurement areas are financial, customer, learning and growth, and internal business processes. However, even this framework has met its critics, and Neely, Adams, and Kennerley, for example, cite their shortfalls in addressing the perspectives of end-users, employees, suppliers, regulators, and local communities.

If there is no particular measurement framework that can best help identify a collection of key performance indicators for your organization, you may want to create your own measurement framework, using a sound performance improvement model as an overarching framework (for example, Kaufman's OEM or Rummler's AOP). If you create your own framework, it is critical to have input from the various stakeholder groups, particularly those that will use it to manage performance. This will better ensure it is responsive to their needs and will increase the likelihood of consistent and effective use. It is also important to focus on the key measures that are directly related to the performance that must be managed. Collections of unrelated measures become obstacles to, rather than drivers of, managing performance. One key consideration here is that all stakeholders clearly see that the measurement framework is only a tool—albeit a critical one—for management. Building a measurement system in isolation of a performance system and the performance management system will lead to fragmented decisions and actions.

Maskell and other authors propose that important considerations for selecting performance indicators are that they relate specifically to strategic objectives (whether directly, or through some other mediating objective); the understanding that these measures will vary from organization to organization; and that these will change over time.

Automated Performance Measurement Tools: Performance Dashboards

A performance measurement and management system is essentially the collective set of measures or metrics used to gauge performance and in turn manage and improve it. Thus, automated performance measurement and management systems, also known as performance dashboards, are computerized, often web-based, instruments that can support objective and proactive decision making for improving performance. The concept of a dashboard was adopted from automobile dashboards, which provide drivers with critical data that helps them drive and maintain the automobile safely, efficiently, and effectively.

From a global perspective, this system is a multi-criteria instrument for informing decision-makers about a variety of different things. For example, it can track current level of performance, the set of factors for poor or good performance, and the criteria required for improvement in an efficient and timely manner. Berrah, Mauris, and Montmain write in a 2008 article that a responsive performance tracking and management system can also track the resources consumed for an observed performance, in order to determine the net value of the performance.

Performance dashboards can provide multiple views to multiple levels of users so that each group has access to information that is related to that group's responsibilities. What they are able to see are usually graphical representations of quantitative data that enable them to detect gaps between optimal and current levels of performance. In my book *Performance Evaluation*, I pointed out that, depending on the design of the system, root causes can be linked to such indicators, although the complexity of organizations represent a challenge in tracking all possible factors impacting the indicators.

Performance dashboard views can also provide aggregate information, summarize, reports, context, and highlight exceptions. Some dashboards provide strata for various levels of concerns (for example, high risk, moderate risk, low risk), that can be defined with specific criteria by stakeholders. This also enables users to detect trends more easily, without the use of more sophisticated analysis techniques. Some performance dashboards are configured to offer various plausible courses of action, in part related to potential causes, and the level of risk. Both Beer in 1979 and Blenkinsop in 1993 write about the benefits of using performance measurement to support strategic objectives and to pinpoint and monitor improvements in performance. Independent studies by

Neely (1991) and Grady (1991), as well a joint study by Eccles and Pyburn the following year have noted the links between performance measures and strategic goals and/or critical success factors at the organizational level.

Issues with Performance Measurement and Management Systems

If measurement systems are to really facilitate the continual improvement process through monitoring and sound decision making, some issues must be addressed. A 2002 article by Santos, Belton, and Howick point to two key issues that inhibit performance measurement and management systems from reaching their full potential: (1) problems in their design and implementation and (2) problems with the analysis and use of the information produced by the measurements.

Poorly designed measurement systems can compromise their implementation and, in turn, their effectiveness. As previously presented, one important factor for organizations to consider is the selection of an appropriate measurement framework. Some strides have been made to design procedures to identify and group performance measures in a way that makes interpretation more straightforward. However, both a 1999 article by Neely and one from 2000 by Biticci and colleagues recognize that much still has to be done by way of identifying relationships between measures. While some may recognize the importance of understanding relationships between the various performance measures tracked, organizations continue to design performance measurement systems without formally accounting for the interdependencies between the measures, which could ultimately undermine the validity and utility of the information produced by the system.

To address the identification of relationships, in 2000 Suwignjo, Biticci, and Carrie developed quantitative models for performance measurement systems (QMPMS) using cognitive maps, cause-and-effect diagrams, tree diagrams, and the analytic hierarchy process. They describe a technique used to identify factors impacting performance and their relationships, structure them hierarchically, quantify the effect of the factors on performance, and express them quantitatively. Meanwhile, Kaplan and Norton's balanced scorecard advocates the use of strategy maps (essentially the connection between a strategy paper and an operative implementation plan) as a tool for linking strategy to the balanced scorecard. While both of these approaches are useful in beginning to address the importance of establishing interdependencies, further research and application is warranted. Santos, Belton, and Howick's 2002 article recommends the use of both qualitative and quantitative modeling to enrich analysis and produce a more insightful design of performance measurement systems.

In addition to design considerations, organizations that are interested in using performance measurement systems must also consider a thoughtful implementation. Poor implementation is a common reason that new organizational initiatives fail. Effective implementation requires careful planning and management of the desired change. Leadership must play an active role in establishing expectations and appropriate consequences, modeling desired behaviors, and motivating those affected. A performance measurement and management system must be seen as one component within an entire performance management system, not as an addition seemingly unrelated to work and management responsibilities.

Improving Performance

Another set of challenges facing these systems is related to the proper analysis of the data and the use of the information to improve performance. A rigorous analysis must take into account the context of the performance data observed. This includes the many other factors that are actually impacting performance. With the obvious limitations of the human mind and the performance measurement system in accounting for every performance factor, the task is not straightforward. For instance, one may have to account for the fact that the gains in one performance indicator come at the expense of another performance indicator. If one studies the latter independent of the former, they might draw wrong conclusions, which could lead to poor and costly decisions. Performance improvement professionals often face this situation in conducting needs assessment and analyses, where they limit their search to symptoms and stop before they identify actual performance gaps and root causes.

Santos, Belton, and Howick point out that many authors have argued that the organizations cannot succeed in every single performance indicator and that explicit decisions about tradeoffs must be defined. Once again, further work and observations in performance measurements systems are warranted.

According to a 2008 article by Berrah, Mauris, and Montmain, decision making can be simplified if you view overall performance as merely the sum of independent, elementary performances. However, the authors warn: ''In the current context of transverse interactions between criteria, it has become more difficult for decision-makers to identify the performance criteria causing a poor overall performance, or presenting a high-priority need of improvement'' (p. 341).

Performance monitoring or measurement systems are instrumental in supporting decision making by serving as an overarching framework for timely intelligence gathering. Both Eisenhardt (1998) and Nutt (2007) write that, while fundamental to responsible decision making, the most neglected aspect of decision making in the literature is intelligence gathering. Decision making begins when stakeholders see a triggering trend (for example, declining revenues or sales) or event (for example, a threat to unionize) as significant, prompting steps to obtain intelligence. Decision-makers are often inundated with signals from customers, employees, shareholders, attorneys, competitors, regulators, and suppliers. Finding which trends or events are worthy of priority attention can be an overwhelmingly challenging proposition.

In the past thirty years, several researchers, from William F. Pounds in 1969, to D.A. Cowan in 1990 and Paul Nutt in 2007, have suggested that signals should be decoded as performance gaps and that the gap will be considered significant when an important performance indicator, such as market share or revenue, falls below a preset criteria. Conversely, the signal would be ignored if performance equals or exceeds the expected performance criteria. Cowan's 1990 article states that, when a performance gap is detected, it also reveals the magnitude of the concern to be overcome. This magnitude can be one major consideration in prioritizing performance problems for resolution. Decision making is then undertaken to find ways to deal with closing the performance gap and reduce or eliminate the concern.

In 2007, Nutt pointed to another problem with decision making, one that comes form social motivation research. He notes that in the social motivation view, decision-makers' actions are prompted by dissonance (which can be thought of as perception of incompatibility between two ways of thinking about something), resulting in their beliefs, motivations, and drives enticing them to look for information that supports these personal beliefs, motivations, and drives. In other words, decision-makers look for information that reinforces their initial position. Decision-makers, perhaps unconsciously at times, form the impression that their conclusions are well founded and unbiased by making their interpretations seem fair to all concerned. Nutt further points out that these decision-makers likely look for information about a diversion to avoid making sense of signals that could render their preferred interpretation as invalid. The consequence would be that only some kinds of performance gaps would be recognized and others ignored, leaving these gaps to grow larger with time.

These are some of the critical issues to keep in mind when considering performance measurement and management systems and how decision-makers actually make decisions about what performance to improve and how. Now we turn our attention to considerations for implementation.

WHEN TO APPLY

Performance measurement and management systems are particularly useful if organizational leaders are committed to integrating them into their management practices and decisions. These systems are particularly helpful in supporting the processes of clarifying and deploying organizational objectives and plans, tracking the status and relative effectiveness of various organizational initiatives, and making timely decisions about what to change, what to keep, and what to modify and how. For example, if a top-level executive wants to ensure that everyone within the organization clearly understands what the strategy over the next three years is and wants sound and justifiable leadership decisions that are well aligned with this strategy, she may call for the implementation and use of a performance dashboard as a tool. However, if those intended users are not "on board" with the idea of using the performance dashboards or they do not receive support on the proper use of the dashboard (for example, the performance indicators that are most relevant to their area of responsibility and management, how to interpret data, how to "translate" data into useful information and recommendations, etc.), the dashboards will likely not be used either consistently or appropriately—or at all.

In most organizations, timing plays an important role in the effectiveness of performance dashboards. Having timely and, in some cases, real-time performance data can save time, costs, and other precious resources that can be lost as a result of waiting for end-of-cycle reports (such as monthly, quarterly, or annual reports). Performance dashboards simplify the process and time required to have access to and use these data.

Performance measurement and management systems will not be helpful if the wrong measures are being tracked, that is, if irrelevant or generic measures are being tracked independent of important management decisions. They also will not help if intended users do not actually use the information from the systems to support their decision making. Finally, cost is an important consideration. While a useful system will require resources, it is also important to weight the costs with the potential benefits. The system does not have to be the most expensive and sophisticated for it to work well; it just has to enhance the management function, particularly as it relates to decision making. To accomplish this while not spending exorbitant amounts of resources on a system, you may want to limit the measures and system functions to the most critical.

STRENGTHS AND CRITICISMS

Some strengths and criticisms of performance management systems are listed below.

Strengths

- If properly designed, performance measurement systems allow users to appreciate, manage, and improve the entire performance system, not just incomplete or fragmented parts.
- They can also dramatically and measurably improve every function in an organization when well designed.

- Positive impact is measured and documented by default.
- Negative or lack of impact is also measured, documented, and used for learning and proactive improvements.
- Performance measurement can increase efficiency and effectiveness of information and communication.
- Performance measurement increases efficiency and effectiveness of management. It promotes the use of relevant data for decisions making (which reduces poor decisions based on hunches, intuition, and hearsay).

Criticisms

- If the wrong indicators are being tracked, the performance measurement systems will not help improve performance.
- If poorly implemented, they can do more harm than good.
- Performance measurement systems are not helpful if people do not use them or do not interpret the data appropriately.
- Performance measurement systems have limited scope and view.
- If poorly designed, overabundance of information may hinder decision making.
- Visualizations and graphical representations present within performance dashboards can be deceiving to the untrained eye.
- Performance measurement systems can be misused to punish people rather than used and aligned with incentives for cooperation and finding systemic solutions to problems.

RECOMMENDED DESIGN, DEVELOPMENT, AND IMPLEMENTATION PROCESS

Assessment, Analysis, Design, and Development

The process requires the following steps:

1. Gain leadership commitment and support for the long-term success of the performance measurement and management system because, without commitment and resources, you cannot proceed. Agree on the scope and ultimate purpose of the performance measurement and management system.

2. Identify the best people for the following roles: lead for launching the project, lead for design, lead for implementation, and lead for sustaining

the measurement and management system. While you want to have continuity among the various system teams, it is also important to realize the strengths and limitations of each team and leader. Some may be better suited to lead the design of the system, but not be well suited to lead an effective and efficient implementation.

3. Identify strategic and tactical objectives (perhaps from a current strategic plan, specifically organizational vision and mission) from those responsible for setting organizational direction. After all, the performance measurement system is supposed to help organizational members accomplish organizational objectives. Not starting with organizational objectives could misalign a system, which will ultimately not deliver on its intended benefits.

4. Identify performance indicators and metrics that must be managed in order to impact organizational objectives and their relationships to one another. Recall that it is imperative that the right measures be tracked. Building a system that houses a seemingly unrelated and trivial list of measures could be overwhelming, demoralizing, and could affect the adoption of the performance measurement system as a legitimate management tool.

5. Identify who is responsible for the various sets of indicators, and confirm intended system users and their roles. This will be critical for the design, implementation, and ultimate use of the system. No one knows the measures of a given area of responsibility better than the person responsible for it. Consult with them and this will create buy-in from the start, as well as a more useful and responsive system.

6. As a follow-up to the previous point, consider what questions related to the various set of indicators must be asked and answered to effectively manage them. Each of the performance measures will have specific decision points, so be sure you understand what decisions have to be made and what questions have to be answered so that the system is designed to provide support for making these decisions.

7. Find out where to get these answers (data sources). Knowing where to locate the data is just as important as the data itself. For example, when it's important to track complaints of feedback, some examples of data sources might include daily or weekly sales reports, human resource records, or customers.

8. Set standards or target levels for each indicator to be tracked. In order to determine whether there is a performance gap, you have to have two data points. First, what is the ideal or desired level of performance for that indicator that is identified through consensus building of the relevant

stakeholders, industry standards, and the like. Second, we require the actual level of performance of the indicator, which is essentially what we seek to track on a timely basis with the performance measurement system. The difference between these two levels provides us with the performance gaps to be addressed.

9. Determine how to analyze and display these answers. This has to be addressed in the front end, when the system is being designed. Consult with people who are well versed in data analysis to set up system functions that allow users to easily view the data in multiple ways with the push of a button. The simpler it is, the more it will be used.

10. Design and develop a customized schedule for finding these answers (some might be minute-to-minute, some hourly, daily, weekly, monthly, quarterly, or annually). Again, consult with those responsible for the different areas of measures to inform you on the frequency with which the various measures have to be measured and tracked.

11. Partner with information technology (IT) to secure the specific technology appropriate for your organization (you may not want to purchase large software and service packages, but rather create your own customized dashboard).

12. Integrate systems into the overall organizational performance management system. Measurement will be useful to the extent that measurement data is used to manage and improve performance.

13. Design and develop a change creation and management plan that will ensure smooth transition toward using this tool effectively. Just because the system is available, it doesn't mean that people will automatically accept it and begin using it as intended. Careful thought about how to manage the integration of this change has to be given at the beginning.

14. The system design should be flexible and continually updated to reflect any relevant changes that will impact results and objectives to be pursued and tracked.

Implementation

1. Implement a change management plan by:
   - Aligning usage requirements with clear and appropriate consequences and
   - Ensuring all relevant players have access to the data.

2. Track how well users are adapting to systems. You might want to set coaching and feedback sessions with users so that they can bring up any glitches they may have encountered with the usage as well as the

technology. This will give the project leaders (or those responsible for coaching and support) the opportunity to help users be more comfortable with the system.

3. Adapt systems based on reliable and feasible feedback.

4. Beware of inconsistent data, analysis, and interpretation, and use mechanisms to identify and resolve inconsistencies.

5. Be sure that implementation is going according to plan; if it is not, ensure your current approach will get you to your desired ends more efficiently and effectively.

6. Keep in mind the limited perspective of performance measurement systems, and take all necessarily steps to find and use data from others sources when required.

Evaluation and Continual Improvement

1. Continually evaluate to determine whether measures being tracked are still appropriate, up-to-date, and sufficient.

2. Track the usage of system for its effectiveness. You may want to compare current usage (frequency, in what ways is it being used, what impact usage is having) to expected usage. If you see meaningful gaps, explore the reasons for these gaps so that you come up with plausible alternatives. While the idea is for usage to be up to standards, it may be that current usage is actually more appropriate than what you had initially planned, given what you knew at the time.

3. Track feedback from users as to how to improve the system for their requirements.

4. Track progress toward desired results.

5. Continually update required indicators so that the information used to make decisions is always current, relevant, and reliable.

6. Revise as required. It may be necessary for you to revise the design of the system, or you may have to adjust the way in which it is being used. Stay open to revisions that would enhance the utility and positive impact of the system.

CRITICAL SUCCESS FACTORS

Use a Systemic Perspective

As with everything in an organization, these measurement and management systems must be understood and used from a systemic perspective. Simply implementing this kind of system without aligning it to organizational strategy and management will not render the potential benefits. Consider external factors (social, geopolitical, cultural, economic, legal, etc.) that impact the organization as well as what impact the organization has or could potentially have on these external factors. What impact could your performance measurement and management system have on these factors? How could these factors impact the design, use, and value added of the performance measurement and management system?

Align Expectations with Appropriate Consequences

It is also important to think about the entire performance system and how well the measurement and management systems are aligned to continually deliver desired results that contribute to an efficient and effective organization. One critical element is proper linkage between performance expectations, measures, and consequences or incentives. Effective use of the measurement and management system will in great part depend on the positive consequences—for individual users, teams, and the organization—associated with its use. If well aligned and organized, the measurement and management systems will support continual improvement.

Stakeholder Buy-In

Begin by asking for and obtaining answers about the benefits and threats to each stakeholder group. If you cannot count on having the resources and authority to integrate your system within the organization, no amount of desire to do it will be enough. You must gain the buy-in of not only the leadership, but other stakeholders who could either impact or be impacted by the system. Be sure that all those affected by the system or who have influence over the system (note that any organizational member has the capacity to influence the system and the organization, not just top leadership) are well informed of the intent, process, benefits, and challenges of implementing the performance measurement and management system.

Proper Design

It's worth noting once again that the success of the performance measurement and management hinges on tracking the appropriate sets of indicators, at the appropriate times, for the appropriate reason: managing and improving performance. If the system is not thoughtfully designed with this end in mind, the effort and technology spent on designing the system will be wasted. Again, the system cannot stand on its own. Proper design means aligning the performance measurement and management system with other performance improvement activities—such as coaching, training, and reward systems. In turn, the data from those activities feed back into the measurement system.

Consistent and Appropriate Usage

Just having a system will not automatically result in better management decisions. The system must be consistently and appropriately used if it is going to be helpful. Integrate usage as part of a broader performance management system, especially by clarifying expectations and consequences for usage and non-usage. Also, it will be necessary to train users and other stakeholders on what proper usage is (for example, reviewing the facts, trends, and likely causes before selecting performance improvement solutions), what proper usage is not (for example, singling anyone out to chastise him or her for sub-par performance).

Balance of Costs and Benefits

Last, it is important to weigh costs against potential benefits. While performance measurement and management systems have the promise of many benefits such as eliminating redundancies, reducing costly mistakes and wasted resources, and the early detection of and response to performance problems, it is important not to lose sight of potential costs. Collecting and organization data can be time-consuming and costly, even with the help of technology. Be sure to focus on functions and activities that will have an acceptable amount of positive return.

SUMMARY

Performance measurement and management systems are integral tools for continually improving performance. If well designed, implemented, and used, they provide timely and relevant feedback that can be used for proactive performance improvement actions. They must be based on a systemic perspective and be part of a comprehensive performance management system, in which desired goals are aligned with desirable consequences for performers. For performance and management systems to meet their full potential, a culture of *measurement for motivation and improvement* rather than *measurement for finger-pointing and punishment* must be designed, modeled, and sustained.

References

Beer, S, (1979). *The heart of enterprise*. Hoboken, NJ: John Wiley & Sons.

Berrah, L., Mauris, G., & Montmain, J. (2008). Monitoring the improvement of an overall industrial performance based on a Choquet integral aggregation. Special issue on multiple criteria decision making for engineering. *Omega, 36*(3), 340–351.

Bititci, U. (1995). Modeling of performance measurement systems in manufacturing enterprises, *International Journal of Production Economics, 42*, 137–147.

Bititci, U. S., Turner, T., & Begemann, C. (2000). Dynamics of performance measurement systems. *International Journal of Operations & Production Management, 20*(6), 692–704.

Blenkinsop, S. A. (1993). Organizational aspects of information processing systems. Doctoral Thesis, University of Loughborough.

Collins, J., & Porras J. (1996, September/October). Building your company's vision. *Harvard Business Review*, pp. 1–14.

Cowan, D.A. (1990). Developing a classification structure of organizational problems: an empirical investigation. *Academy of Management Journal, 33*(2), 366–390.

Dertouzos, M. L., Lester, R. K., Solow, R. M., & the MIT Commission on Industrial Productivity. (1989). *Made in America: Regaining the productive edge.* Cambridge, MA: MIT Press.

Eccles.R. G., & Pyburn, P. J. (1992). Creating a comprehensive system to measure performance. *Management Accounting*, pp. 41–44.

Eckerson, W. (2007). *Performance dashboards: Measuring, monitoring, and managing your business.* Hoboken, NJ: John Wiley & Sons.

Eisenhardt, K. (1998). Decision making and all that jazz. In V. Papadakis & P. Barwise (Eds.), *Strategic decisions.* Boston, MA: Kluwer.

Fitzgerald, L., Johnston, R., Brignall, S., Silvestro, R., & Voss, C. (1991). *Performance measurement in service businesses.* London: CIMA Publishing.

Grady, M. W. (1991). Performance measurement, implementing strategy. *Management Accounting*, pp. 49–53.

Guerra-López, I. (2007). *Evaluating impact: Evaluation and continual improvement for performance improvement practitioners.* Amherst, MA: HRD Press.

Guerra-López, I. (2008). *Performance evaluation: Proven approaches for improving program and organizational performance.* San Francisco: Jossey-Bass.

Kaplan, R. S., & Norton, D. P. (1992). The balanced scorecard: Measures that drive performance. *Harvard Business Review*, pp. 71–79.

Kaplan, R. S., & Norton, D. P. (2001). *The strategy-focused organization: How balanced scorecard companies thrive in the new business environment.* Boston: Harvard Business School Press.

Kaufman, R. (2000). *Mega planning.* Thousand Oaks, CA: Sage.

Lynch, R. L., & Cross, K. F. (1991). *Measure up! How to measure corporate performance.* Oxford, UK: Blackwell.

Mager, R. (1984). *Preparing instructional objectives* (2nd rev. ed.). Belmont CA: Lake Publishing.

Maskell, B. (1992). *Performance measurement for world class manufacturing: A model for American companies.* Cambridge, MA: Productivity Press.

Neely, A. D. (1991). Production management: A two-dimensional function? *International Journal of Operations and Production Management, 11*(7), 49–54.

Neely, A. D. (1999). The performance measurement revolution: Why now and what next? *International Journal of Operations & Production Management, 19*(2), 205–228.

Neely, A. D., Adams, C., & Kennerley, M. P. (2002). *The performance prism: The scorecard for measuring and managing business success.* London: FT Prentice-Hall.

Neely, A. D., Mills, J., Plats, K., Gregory, M., & Richards, A. (1991). Realizing strategy. *Management Accounting,* pp. 49–53.

Niven, P. R. (2002). *Balanced scorecard step by step: Maximizing performance and maintaining results.* Hoboken, NJ: John Wiley & Sons.

Nutt, P. (1979). Calling out and calling off the dogs: managerial diagnoses in organizations. *Academy of Management Review, 4*(2), 203–14.

Nutt, P. (2007). Intelligence gathering for decision making. *Omega,* (35), 604–622.

Pounds, W. (1969 fall). The process of problem finding. *Industrial Management Review,* pp. 1–19.

Porter, M. E. (1985). *Competitive advantage.* New York: The Free Press.

Rummler, G. (2004). *Serious performance consulting: According to Rummler.* Silver Spring, MD: International Society for Performance Improvement.

Rummler, G. A., & Brache, A. P. (1995). *Improving performance: How to manage the white space on the organization chart* (2nd ed.). San Francisco: Jossey-Bass.

Santos, S., Belton, V., & Howick, S. (2002). Adding value to performance measurement by using system dynamics and multi-criteria analysis. *International Journal of Operations & Production Management, 22*(1), 1246–1272.

Suwignjo, P., Bititci, U. S., & Carrie, A. S. (2000). Quantitative models for performance measurement system. *International Journal of Production Economics, 64,* 231–41.

Recommended Readings

Beer, S. (1966). *Decision and control: The meaning of operational research and management cybernetics.* Hoboken, NJ: John Wiley & Sons.

Berman, E. (2002, June). How useful is performance measurement. *Public Performance & Management Review, 25*(4).

Frigo, M. (2002, May). Strategy, business execution and performance measures. *Strategic Finance, 83*(11).

Guerra-López, I. (2007). Planning a responsive evaluation: Establishing solid partnerships by clarifying expectations and purpose. *Performance Improvement Journal, 46*(8).

Guerra-López, I. (2007). The impact evaluation process: Building a case for demonstrating the worth of performance improvement Interventions. *Performance Improvement Journal, 46*(7).

Guerra, I. (2005). Outcome-based vocational rehabilitation: Measuring valuable results. *Performance Improvement Quarterly, 18*(3), 65–75.

Guerra, I. (2003). Asking and answering the right questions: Collecting relevant and useful data. *Performance Improvement Journal, 42*(10), 24–28.

Lingle, J., & Schiemann, W. (1996, March). From balanced scorecard to strategic gauges: Is measurement worth it? *Management Review 85*(3).

Neely, A. (Ed.). (2002). *Business performance measurement: Theory and practice.* Cambridge, MA: Cambridge University Press.

 # EDITORIAL CONNECTIONS

Technology such as electronic monitoring systems, online survey tools, and even e-mail has both promoted and hindered the use of performance data within organizations. While technological tools have increased both the collection of performance data and the dissemination of that data, the sheer volume of data and information that people now have to guide their decisions leads to very little of it ever being used—information overload. The Internet is one practical example of a technology that routinely provides more data and information than you can realistically use to guide decisions. Who, after all, hasn't had the daunting experience of making a simple keyword search only to be faced with deciding which web pages contain potentially useful information among the thousands of alternatives?

As illustrated in Chapter Ten, you can use performance measurement systems to distill essential performance data, and present useful information to decision-makers. Such systems provide a useful starting place for sifting through available data to isolate those variables that should be routinely reviewed to monitor and improve performance. Collecting and disseminating essential performance data by itself is not sufficient for accomplishing significant results; rather, data must be used to inform decisions if desired results are going to be achieved.

Expanding Your Options

Delegation models—a framework for the process by which sharing or transfer of authority and the associated responsibility occur within an organization, from an employer or superior to an employee or subordinate. There are three types of situations in which delegation takes place: backup of roles, decentralization of authority, and collaboration of work.

Based on jrpit.acs.org.au/jrpit/JRPITVolumes/JRPIT38/JRPIT38.1.3.pdf and businessdictionary.com definitions (January 2009)

WHAT'S COMING UP

Within organizations, improving performance frequently requires the ability to identify, analyze, and apply only the most useful information for making decisions. Supporting this application of performance data in decision making, managerial coaching has become a strategic investment within many organizations. With a deliberate focus on improving performance, it can assist decision-makers in improving individual, team, and organizational performance. In Chapter Eleven, Andrea Ellinger and her colleagues describe the important role that managerial coaching can have in the improvement of performance.

Achieving Improved Performance Through Managerial Coaching

Andrea D. Ellinger
Alexander E. Ellinger
Robert G. Hamlin
Rona S. Beattie

INTRODUCTION

In recent years, coaching has emerged as a powerful developmental and performance improvement intervention that organizations are considerably investing in. It is currently estimated that upward of $1 billion to $2 billion worldwide are spent by organizations to provide coaches for their employees, and that there are over forty thousand coaches operating throughout the world. Organizations are increasingly using external coaches, executive or career coaches, and professional business coaches. At the same time, coaching by line managers within organizations is also growing, as human resource development and management responsibilities become further devolved to front-line supervisors, managers, managerial leaders, and organizational leaders.

Consequently, managerial coaching has become a very popular topic in the practitioner-oriented and scholarly literatures. Although empirical research on managerial coaching is still relatively limited and in its infancy, scholars suggest that the benefits of this developmental intervention are enormous. For example, coaching has been associated with producing long-lasting learning, contributing to higher levels of motivation, improving employee performance, enhancing working relationships, job satisfaction and organizational commitment.

DESCRIPTION

Coaching is not a new phenomenon. According to a 2005 *Human Resource Development Quarterly* article by Texas A & M University's Gary McLean and his colleagues, various fields such as sports behavior and psychology, youth and adult education, counseling, clinical psychology, family therapy, industrial and organizational psychology, and management have discussed this concept. While a general base of literature exists from a sports and athletic perspective, Roger Evered and James Selman purport in a 1989 article that coaching in the context of management emerged in the 1950s as a master-apprentice type of relationship. It evolved into managerial contexts in the 1970s, with the application of athletic and sports coaching. Whether translating and using the sports analogy of coaching is sufficient for business settings has been questioned, despite Evered and Selman's contention that coaching is the heart of management and that creating a coaching context is an important managerial activity. As a consequence, coaching has gained considerable popularity in general, as evidenced by the escalating number of practitioner-oriented books and articles on the topic. Yet in 2005, David Peterson and Bobbie Little of the firm Personnel Decisions International pointed out that limited empirical research exists on coaching in general—and managerial coaching in particular—that is aimed at helping practicing managers to coach their employees better. The purpose of this chapter is to define and contextualize the concept of managerial coaching, as well as to synthesize the empirical research on the topic, so that scholars and practitioners can become better informed about the use of this potentially powerful intervention for improving individual and team performance.

Given confusion with the terminology that is often used interchangeably with coaching and managerial coaching, it is important to distinguish among coaching, mentoring, and counseling, all of which are distinct concepts. *Coaching* is often conceived as a day-to-day, hands-on process of helping employees recognize opportunities to improve their performance and capabilities. It is a way to guide, encourage, empower, and support learners by creating conducive relationships. *Counseling*, however, generally addresses the employee's emotional state and/or the causes of personal crises and problems, and involves interventions designed to remedy such problems that interfere with the employee's job performance. In contrast, Catherine Hansman of Cleveland State University suggests that *mentoring* typically describes a longer-term process that is developmental, career focused, and covers all life structures.

A recent review of the literature by Hamlin, Ellinger, and Beattie in *Human Resource Development International* journal revealed at least thirty-six definitions of coaching and its variants, executive coaching, business coaching, and life coaching. The results of this review and comparative analysis have suggested that there is a high degree of commonality among all of the definitions of

Expanding Your Options

Upward, 360, or peer evaluations—occur when performance appraisal data is collected from all around an employee—his or her peers, subordinates, supervisors, and sometimes, internal and external customers. Its main aim is to assess training and development needs and to provide competence-related information for succession planning, rather than for promotion or salary decision making.

Based on businessdictionary.com definition (January 2009)

coaching in general and the three variants indicated above. Providing help to individuals and organizations through some form of facilitation activity, with intent to improve their performance in various domains, and to enhance their personal effectiveness, development, and growth, were held in common.

Coaching has historically been conceived as an approach to remedy poor performance. However, more contemporary conceptualizations have suggested that coaching is synonymous with facilitating learning and that providing relevant learning opportunities can yield improved performance as a by-product of learning. Coaching can be provided by external consultants (executive coaches) and other coaching professionals (professional business coaches, career coaches, and life coaches, for example). However, managerial coaching is conceptualized as a form of coaching that is provided by a supervisor or manager serving as a facilitator of learning. The manager or supervisor enacts specific behaviors that enable the employee (coachee) to learn and develop, and thereby improve performance.

WHAT WE KNOW FROM RESEARCH

Research on managerial coaching is limited but growing, and can be categorized into several domains: the managerial coaching mindset, catalysts for managerial coaching, managerial coaching skills and behaviors, and the effectiveness and ineffectiveness associated with managerial coaching. The following sections provide an overview of research within each of these domains.

The Managerial Coaching Mindset

Within the sports and athletics coaching literature, the concept of coaching efficacy has been considered to be a powerful variable in coaching effectiveness. Deborah Feltz and her colleagues at Michigan State University suggest in a 1999 article that coaching efficacy in this context refers to "the extent to which coaches believe they have the capacity to affect the learning and performance of their athletes" (pp. 765–766). Feltz and colleagues' concept of coaching efficacy is comprised of four dimensions: *game strategy* ("the confidence coaches have in their ability to coach during competition"); *motivation efficacy* ("the confidence coaches have in their ability to affect the psychological skills and states of their athletes"); *technique efficacy* ("the belief coaches have in their instructional and diagnostic skills"); and *character building efficacy* ("the confidence that coaches have in their ability to influence personal development and positive attitude toward sport in their athletes"). They also contend that these coaching efficacy dimensions are influenced by the coaches' past experience, coaching preparation, and performance and suggest that such influences are sources of efficacy information. Their research has indicated that coaching efficacy is important in coaching effectiveness and athletic performance. Subsequent studies have offered support for these concepts and extended the sources of coaching efficacy.

Within the context of work organizations, a limited amount of empirical research has explored the mindsets and beliefs associated with managerial coaches. However, stories and practical experiences have been made available in some books published on the topic of managerial coaching. Based on their work with business professionals serving as coaches in an assessment center at Babson College, James Hunt and Joseph Weintraub have acknowledged in their 2002 book *The Coaching Manager* that, for managers who have become coaching managers, a common set of attitudes and beliefs exist that they call the "coaching mind-set" (p. 33). They summarize the commonalities by referring to the concept of an attitude of helpfulness. According to Hunt and Weintraub, coaching managers have less of a need for control. Instead, they tend to believe that most people do want to learn. Coaching managers are empathic and are open to feedback and coaching from their employees. The attitudes and beliefs held in common and articulated in their book have been supported by empirical research published by Andrea Ellinger and Robert Bostrom in 2002. This study has provided some preliminary insights with regard to managerial coaching beliefs.

Ellinger and Bostrom's qualitative study of exemplary managerial coaches identified five clusters of beliefs that emerged from the data that were place into the following three categories:

1. Beliefs about roles and beliefs about capabilities;

2. Beliefs about the learning process and beliefs about learning; and,

3. Beliefs about learners.

For these coaching managers, facilitating employees' learning and development was considered their role and responsibility. These managers also distinguished between coaching and managing and acknowledged that management often involved telling subordinate employees what to do, whereas coaching comprised helping people grow and develop. In considering their capabilities, coaching managers believed they possessed skills and process capabilities to coach effectively, had experiences that they could apply, and also cared enough about their employees to want to help them. Further, establishing trust and building relationships was deemed critical. In terms of the learning process and learning, these coaching managers felt that feedback was critical, that learning and work should be integrated, and that individuals should be encouraged to learn for themselves. Learning was considered important, ongoing, and shared. Coaching managers acknowledged their beliefs that learners are capable, must be willing to learn, desire a solid foundation, and desire to understand the "whys." While these beliefs have not been operationalized for further testing, they do suggest that beliefs influence the coaching behaviors of managers.

Catalysts for Managerial Coaching

Drawing upon informal workplace learning and management development research, best-selling author Alan Mumford acknowledged in his 1993 book *How Managers Can Develop Managers* that any managerial activity contains the potential for learning. Mumford has identified several catalysts for learning, which include: a new assignment, a new challenge, a new project, a shock or crisis, problem solving within a group, different standards of performance, or an unsuccessful project. Other research exploring the catalysts or triggers specifically associated with managerial coaching interventions similarly have produced results that support Mumford's findings. Although coaching has typically been perceived as a remedy for poor performance, any opportunity for learning can be a catalyst for managerial coaching. In a qualitative study published by Ellinger in a 2003 issue of *Performance Improvement Quarterly*, gaps and deficiencies of existing employees' skills were reported to be the predominant catalysts for managerial coaching. However, political and developmental issues that served as triggers for coaching interventions were also identified. Examples included high-consequence issues catalyzing the need for managerial coaching, along with assignments, projects, and employee transitions that stimulated the need for coaching in which managers actively looked for ways to develop their employees' skills and capabilities.

Managerial Coaching Skills and Behaviors

The conceptual literature has often described the requisite skills associated with managerial coaching as including listening, analytical and interviewing skills, as well as effective questioning and observation techniques. Coaching behaviors have been similarly described and typically include giving and receiving performance feedback, communicating and setting clear expectations, and creating a supportive environment conducive to coaching.

Expanding Your Options

Performance appraisals—a process in which a supervisor or consultant evaluates an employee's work by comparing it with pre-set standards, documents the results, and utilizes them to provide feedback about where improvement is needed and why. Performance appraisals are used to determine whether training is needed and what kind, as well as to make decisions about promotion, retention, and dismissal.

Based on businessdictionary.com definition (January 2009)

In terms of managerial coaching skills, Gary McLean and his colleagues' recent research has yielded a self-assessment of coaching skills based upon a four-dimension coaching model. This model suggests that the "manager as coach" reflects four aspects of managerial behavior. The manager as coach should:

1. Communicate openly with others,
2. Take a team approach instead of an individual approach with tasks,
3. Tend toward valuing people over tasks, and
4. Accept the ambiguous nature of the working environment.

Their findings suggest that managerial coaching is a multidimensional construct that supports their four-dimension coaching model. In responding to this work, Peterson and Little questioned in 2005 whether the team approach is a primary component of effective coaching since coaching is often considered a one-on-one managerial intervention. Further, they have noted that other factors associated with coaching skills as reported in the literature should be considered, such as developing a partnership, effective listening skills, providing feedback, as well as the capabilities for facilitating development. In a subsequent study designed to revise and extend the original instrument, McLean and his colleagues added a component related to facilitating employees' development and reported the psychometric properties of the revised instrument.

While having the requisite skills associated with managerial coaching is important, being able to translate such skills into practice by enacting specific coaching behaviors is paramount to being an effective coach. With regard to managerial coaching behavior, a base of empirical research has been growing that explores the behaviors enacted and engaged by managerial coaches. Within the sales management context, in 1994 Steven Graham led a team of researchers in examining the specific behaviors that employees associate with managers who possess effective coaching skills. Incorporating eight behaviors associated with successful sales managers, Graham and his colleagues interviewed account representatives and obtained their ratings of their respective managers' coaching capabilities prior to the implementation of a manager coaching skills training program. The findings supported the existing literature on coaching concerning the importance of providing feedback, setting clear expectations, and creating a climate for coaching that involves a positive trusting relationship.

Ellinger's (1997) and Ellinger and Bostrom's (1999) research identified a taxonomy of thirteen managerial coaching behaviors that were grouped into facilitating and empowering clusters. The empowering cluster consisted of the following behaviors:

- Question framing to encourage employees to think through issues;
- Being a resource—removing obstacles;
- Transferring ownership to employees; and
- Holding back—not providing the answers.

The facilitating cluster consisted of the following behaviors:

- Providing feedback to employees;
- Soliciting feedback from employees;
- Working it out together—talking it through;
- Creating and promoting a learning environment;
- Setting and communicating expectations;
- Stepping into other roles to shift perspectives;
- Broadening employees' perspectives—getting them to see things differently;
- Using analogies, scenarios, and examples; and
- Engaging others to facilitate learning.

Rona Beattie of Glasgow Caledonian University conducted research on managerial coaching in the context of social service organizations in 2002. Her findings revealed twenty-two discrete effective facilitative behaviors that were then classified and allocated into one of nine identified behavioral categories consisting of:

- Thinking—reflective or prospective thinking;
- Informing—sharing knowledge;

- Empowering—delegation, trust;
- Assessing—feedback and recognition, identifying developmental needs;
- Advising—instruction, coaching, guidance, counseling;
- Being professional—role model, standard setting, planning and preparation;
- Caring—support, encouragement, approachable, reassurance, commitment/involvement, empathy;
- Developing others; and
- Challenging employees to stretch themselves.

Considerable similarity between the managerial coaching behaviors identified by Ellinger, Ellinger and Bostrom's work and that of Beattie has been found in subsequent analyses. Comparisons with Bob Hamlin's 2004 generic model of managerial and leadership effectiveness has suggested that managerial coaching is at the heart of managerial effectiveness. In addition, other recent studies have been conducted that have revealed managerial coaching behaviors that are strikingly similar to those previously identified here.

The Effectiveness of Managerial Coaching

A growing body of research has recently emerged in the academic literature that empirically examines the influence of the manager-as-coach concept in business and industrial contexts. Collectively, these studies suggest that managerial coaching has a significant positive influence on a variety of affective and behavioral work-related outcome variables. Table 11.1 presents a summary of the key empirical studies that have variously assessed the effectiveness of managerial coaching.

Accordingly, the overall implication for practice from the collective findings of these studies is that that managerial coaching appears to be a very valuable and appropriate tool for creating performance-related value.

Ineffective Managerial Coaching Behaviors

At present, much of the research on managerial coaching suggests that there are many beneficial outcomes associated with this intervention when it is effectively applied. A limited base of research exists that has explored the ineffective practices associated with managerial coaching. In Ellinger's 1997 dissertation into exemplary managerial coaches, four ineffective behavior sets were subsequently analyzed when managers had acknowledged that they had not been as effective as they had intended to be. These included:

- Being too authoritarian and directive;
- Being too intense and emotional;

- Being an ineffective communicator; and
- Employing inappropriate approaches and/or behaviors.

Table 11.1 Recent Empirical Studies on Managerial Coaching

Findings	Sample and Method	Study
Supervisory coaching behavior positively influences warehouse employee job satisfaction and job-related performance.	438 front-line employees and sixty-seven supervisors in eighteen U.S. distribution centers (survey)	Ellinger, Ellinger, & Keller (2003)
Workplace coaching is a viable means for improving individual and organizational performance.	Forty-five on-train customer service employees in the U. K. rail industry (case study)	Hannah (2004)
Managerial coaching intensity consistently influences the performance of subordinates.	328 salespeople reporting to114 middle managers, and ninety-three middle managers reporting to thirty-two executive managers in multi-national manufacturing company (survey)	Agarwal, Angst, & Magni (2006)
In some situations, more managerial coaching may not always yield the most beneficial outcomes.	307 customer contact personnel in the U.S. third-party logistics industry (survey)	Ellinger, Elmadag, & Ellinger (2007)
Managerial coaching skills positively influence employees' learning, organizational commitment, and turnover intentions.	187 U.S. employees in global technology organization (survey)	Park, McLean, & Yang (2008)
Managerial coaching has a stronger positive influence on front-line service employee commitment to service quality than formal customer service training or rewarding.	268 front-line service employee/line manager dyads (survey)	Elmadag, Ellinger, & Franke (2008)

(Continued)

Table 11.1 (*Continued*)

Findings	Sample and Method	Study
Managerial coaching moderates the links between market orientation and organizational and employee performance.	123 logistics service provider organizations (survey)	Ellinger, Ketchen, Hult, Elmadag, & Richey (2008)
Managerial coaching moderates the relationships between organizational investments in social capital and a variety of attitudinal and behavioral work-related outcome measures.	408 working adults in southeastern U.S. (survey)	Ellinger, Elmadag, Ellinger, Wang, & Bachrach (2008)

Eight categories of inhibitory behaviors were also identified in Beattie's 2002 study and included:

- Not giving time;
- Being dogmatic;
- Controlling;
- Not thinking;
- Being task-oriented;
- Being unassertive;
- Withholding information; and
- Not assessing.

Five negative behavioral categories were identified in Hamlin's 2004 study of managerial effectiveness and included:

- Shows lack of consideration or concern for staff, or ineffective autocratic or dictatorial style of management;
- Uncaring, self-serving management, undermining, depriving, and intimidating behavior;
- Tolerance of poor performance and low standards, ignoring and avoidance;
- Abdicating roles and responsibilities; and
- Resistance to new ideas and change, or a negative approach.

Ellinger, Hamlin, and Beattie conducted a comparative analysis of their respective findings in 2008, revealing considerable overlap in ineffective managerial behavior. The predominant ineffective behavior held in common among all three studies was an autocratic, directive, controlling, dictatorial managerial style. This is often associated with a "traditional bureaucratic management paradigm," characterized by command, control, compliance, and coercive styles of management. This is not considered appropriate for promoting a "coaching management paradigm" that encourages empowerment, inclusion, and participation.

Another commonality revolved around ineffective communication and dissemination of information. A further ineffective behavioral theme was the use of inappropriate behaviors and approaches, including, among others, not spending enough time with employees. There were only a few behaviors for which overlap, congruency, and similarity did not become readily apparent. These included Ellinger's "being too intense and emotional" behavior set, Hamlin's "tolerance of poor performance and low standards, ignoring and avoidance," "resistant to new ideas and change, and negative approach," and Beattie's "being task-oriented" behavior set. Despite the few exceptions noted, overall the degree of alignment, overlap, similarity, and congruence of meaning between the categories and criteria of the three models and frameworks was very high and provides some insight into the managerial behaviors that are associated with ineffective managerial coaching.

WHEN TO APPLY

Managerial coaching is a viable intervention that can be used by supervisors, managers, managerial leaders, and organizational leaders to facilitate employees' learning and enhance their performance. However, it is not the only intervention that can be used to promote professional development and improve performance. There may be circumstances in which coaching is not deemed appropriate given the needs of the employee, the skill sets and capabilities of the manager, and the culture and context of the organization.

As the research literature has indicated, managerial coaching may be an intervention that can be applied when managers believe that coaching employees is a role and responsibility that is valued and encouraged within the organization. Not only must managers possess a managerial coaching mindset, but they must also have the requisite skills and capabilities to effectively coach their respective employees. As a result, coaching interventions are often most successful when they are part of systemic initiatives that include other interventions such as assessment-feedback (see Chapter Nine), incentive systems (see Chapters Eighteen and Nineteen), career counseling, or knowledge management (see Chapter 15).

Paramount in the process is the nature of the relationship that exists between the coaching manager and employee. A mutually developed relationship that embeds trust is critical in this process, along with the manager's ability to recognize opportunities to intervene as a coach. Furthermore, coaching is predicated on the existence of a two-way relationship. Unless there is receptivity to coaching on the part of the employee (coachee), often managers cannot coach effectively.

STRENGTHS AND CRITICISMS

The efficacy of managerial coaching has been reported in both academic and practitioner literatures. Both strengths and criticisms are outlined below.

Strengths

The strengths of effective managerial coaching as an intervention to help individual staff members improve performance are as follows:

- Empirical evidence demonstrates that effective managerial coaching has been linked to enhanced job satisfaction, job-related performance, learning, organizational commitment, and turnover intentions for employees.
- Managerial coaching may be informally applied and integrated with work when a coaching opportunity presents itself.
- Managerial coaching can be flexibly applied when specific coaching behaviors are engaged based upon the coaching opportunity.

However, it is not always appropriate or effective to promote and support managerial coaching within organizations, particularly if the managers and employees are not open or receptive to coaching interventions and are unwilling or insufficiently skilled to develop healthy and productive coaching relationships.

Criticisms

Managerial coaching may be inappropriate in certain contexts. Such circumstances can arise if:

- Managers do not believe that developing and facilitating their respective employees' learning is a core activity of an effective manager in the workplace.
- Managers have not been sufficiently prepared and supported to assume coaching roles.
- Managers lack the self-efficacy, skills, capabilities, and reservoir of experiences to draw upon that effective coaching entails.

- Employees are resistant to receiving coaching.
- Managerial coaching interventions are overly used with highly empowered employees, which may actually lead to counterproductive results.

RECOMMENDED DESIGN, DEVELOPMENT, AND IMPLEMENTATION PROCESS

In their seminal 2005 text, *Organization Development and Change,* Thomas Cummings and Christopher Worley suggest that the coaching process often includes six steps:

1. Establish the principles of the relationship;
2. Conduct an assessment;
3. Debrief the results;
4. Develop an action plan;
5. Implement the action plan; and
6. Assess the results.

However, these six steps tend to reflect the coaching process as practiced by an external coach who has been contracted to work with an organizational client. While this may be the case for some readers, most frequently, managerial coaching efforts rely on managers within the organization who adopt roles as coaches. In contrast, because managerial coaching leverages and builds upon relationships between managers and their respective employees, the process may be less formal and step-wise, and may be dependent upon the situation in which coaching is determined to be the most appropriate option. Given the limited empirical research on the optimal process of managerial coaching, this chapter offers adaptations to the developmental coaching model Hunt and Weintraub propose in their 2002 book.

Hunt and Weintraub suggest in *The Coaching Manager: Developing Top Talent in Business* that, within a coaching-friendly environment, it is important that managers possess a coaching mindset and that employees are open to the possibilities of learning through coaching. Rather than devise a complex model, Hunt and Weintraub advocate that managerial coaching should be "slipped into their [managers'] daily routine" (p. 18). They suggest that a coaching dialogue should be created that enables the managers and employees to look for opportunities for learning and to use questions that encourage the employees to think critically about their own learning needs. Next, it is important to observe what is occurring, a process that they conceptualize as the coaching mirror, which is used to provide balanced and helpful feedback. They suggest that the manager and employee (coachee) work together to understand what needs to change and to mutually set goals for change and follow-up.

Given the empirical research that has been conducted to date, coupled with Hunt and Weintraub's developmental approach, a modified approach is suggested in this chapter. A managerial coaching mindset is critical for managerial coaching to occur. Therefore, if managers would like to become managerial coaches, or are being encouraged to adopt such developmental roles within their organizations, they will likely need to:

1. Engage in some critical self-reflection and examine their own beliefs and mental models about coaching. What developmental responsibilities do managers believe they are required to perform? What types of past experiences, skills, and capabilities do managers possess that may influence their self-efficacy beliefs about their ability to be effective at coaching? What beliefs do managers hold about learners? Do they believe their employees (coachees) are capable of learning, growing, and developing a sense of self-direction and empowerment when provided with appropriate guidance? What do managers believe about the process of learning? Do they believe that learning is a two-way process that may involve some trial and error, discovery, and is being used to promote and enhance the employee's decision-making capability?

2. Consider developmental needs necessary to be skillful at managerial coaching. If effective coaches need to possess communication, analytical, and observation skills and techniques, is training pertinent to developing these a necessary pre-requisite?

3. Consider what may constitute "coachable moments" when an employee and a manager may have the opportunity to engage in a coaching intervention. As the literature has reported, gaps, deficiencies, and poor performance are typically associated with the need for coaching. However, new assignments, jobs, challenges, crises, problems within a work team, and so forth may also be among the catalysts that encourage the coaching dialogue that Hunt and Weintraub advocate. Managers should be knowledgeable about these potential coaching opportunities as some may need to be initiated by the manager, while others may be initiated by an employee seeking the manager's guidance through coaching.

4. Determine the most appropriate behavior or sets of behaviors to engage as a managerial coach. For example, in some instances, employees may need to be given clear expectations and feedback, while in other circumstances encouraging employee reflection through, say, question-framing techniques, may be optimal. In yet other situations, it might be more appropriate to share an example, or draw upon an analogy from the

manager's experience that may be beneficial in promoting the employee's learning. It might be that some degree of role modeling is required. The research literature has identified several behaviors associated with effective managerial coaching that may be enacted separately or may be combined with each other to promote the type of learning that is required during the coachable moment.

5. Examine outcomes corresponding to the coaching to determine whether learning has occurred as a consequence of the coaching, or if additional coaching or perhaps some other intervention is required.

CRITICAL SUCCESS FACTORS

Many of the benefits of managerial coaching have been established in the growing base of empirical research. However, scholars have acknowledged that managerial coaches are often rare in organizations because the culture of the organization does not promote, support, or reward coaching. As Hunt and Weintraub report in their 2002 *Journal of Organizational Excellence* article—and as still others have acknowledged—managers are often ill-prepared, lack the requisite skills and capabilities, and have no time. Furthermore, they may believe that developing employees is not a core managerial role, but one that should be undertaken by human resource professionals. Although research examining the contextual factors associated with influencing managerial coaching is limited, Rona Beattie's study provides some insight into the importance of environmental and organizational factors that influence this form of coaching. The environmental factors identified include:

- Political
- Economic
- Societal
- Technological

These factors influenced the management framework and learning needs within the two organizations Beattie studied. With regard to organizational influences, she acknowledged that organizational factors included:

- History
- Mission
- Strategy
- Structure
- Culture

Specifically in the organizations that she studied, the aspirations to become learning organizations contributed to line managers' roles as coaches and people developers. In terms of human resource development strategy, the provision of training for managers to assume developmental roles as coaches by supporting their learning needs was also considered a critical influence.

SUMMARY

The body of research discussed in this chapter adds considerable credence to the many conceptual and normative articles that have long advocated the beneficial outcomes associated with managerial coaching. In today's highly competitive and increasingly service-oriented industrial markets, firms' efforts to build superior performance depend on leveraging the most potent developmental practices and deciding how to allocate scarce resources for maximum impact. Performance payoffs can be considerable for those organizations that can create a climate conducive to coaching and who support and reward managers for assuming the role of a coach. Similarly, there can be considerable performance payoffs for managerial coaches who possess the mindset and capabilities to coach effectively. However, it is critical for managers to be well prepared to serve in this capacity.

Notes

- Distinctions between coaching, mentoring, and counseling have been articulated by King and Eaton (1999); Minter and Thomas (2000).

- Coaching as a form of learning has been described by Mink, Owen, and Mink (1993), who viewed this form of coaching from an empowerment paradigm.

- Coaching skills and behaviors have been further described by Graham, Wedman, and Garvin-Kester (1993) and (1994); King and Eaton (1999); Marsh (1992); Orth, Wilkinson, and Benfari (1987); Phillips (1994) and (1995); and Zemke (1996).

- Empirical research examining facilitative learning behaviors, managerial coaching behaviors, and facilitative leadership behaviors have been conducted following the Ellinger and Ellinger et. al studies and Beattie's research by the following researchers: Amy (2005); Longenecker and Neubert (2005); Noer (2005); Noer, Leupold, and Valle (2007); Powell and Doran (2003); Shaw and Knights (2005). The findings from these studies have been strikingly similar to previous research by Ellinger, Ellinger, and Bostrom, and Beattie and support their findings. Furthermore, comparative analyses of the Ellinger, Ellinger et al. and Beattie findings have been done with Hamlin's (2004) "Generic Model of Managerial and Leadership Effectiveness" which suggests that managerial coaching is indeed at the heart of managerial effectiveness (Hamlin, Ellinger, & Beattie, 2006). The efficacy of the Hamlin (2004) model has been examined relative to Bergmann, Hurson, and Russ-Eft (1999) and Russ-Eft, Berry, Hurson, and Brennan (1996).

References

Agarwal, R., Angst, C. M., & Magni, M. (2006). The performance effects of coaching: A multi-level analysis using hierarchical linear modeling. Working Paper No. RHS-06-031, University of Maryland, Robert H. Smith School of Business.

Amy, A. H. (2005). Leaders as facilitators of organizational learning. Unpublished doctoral dissertation. Regent University, Virginia Beach, Virginia, USA.

Beattie, R. S. (2002). Line managers as facilitators of learning: Empirical evidence from voluntary sector. *Proceedings of Human Resource Development Research and Practice Across Europe Conference*. Edinburgh, Scotland: Napier University.

Beattie, R. S. (2006). HRD in the public sector: The case of health and social care. In S. Sambrook & J. Stewart (Eds.), *Human resource development in the health and social care context*. London: Routledge.

Bergmann, H., Hurson, K., & Russ-Eft, D. (1999). *Everyone a leader: A grass roots model for the new workplace*. Hoboken, NJ: John Wiley & Sons.

Cummings, T. G., & Worley, C. G. (2005). *Organization development and change* (8th ed.). Cincinnati, OH: Thomson Southwestern.

Ellinger, A. D. (1997). Managers as facilitators of learning in learning organizations. Unpublished doctoral dissertation, University of Georgia.

Ellinger, A. D. (2003). Antecedents and consequences of coaching behavior. *Performance Improvement Quarterly*, *16*(1), 5–28.

Ellinger, A. D., & Bostrom, R. P. (1999). Managerial coaching behaviors in learning organizations. *Journal of Management Development*, *18*(9), 752–771.

Ellinger, A. D., & Bostrom, R. P. (2002). An examination of managers' belief about their roles as facilitators of learning. *Management Learning*, *33*(2), 147–179.

Ellinger, A. D., Ellinger, A. E., & Keller, S. B. (2003). Supervisory coaching behavior, employee satisfaction, and warehouse employee performance: A dyadic perspective in the distribution industry. *Human Resource Development Quarterly*, *14*(4), 435–458.

Ellinger, A. D., Hamlin, R. G., & Beattie, R. S. (2008). Behavioural indicators of ineffective managerial coaching: A cross-national study. *Journal of European Industrial Training*, *32*(4), 240–257.

Ellinger, A. E., Elmadag, A. B., & Ellinger, A. D. (2007). An examination of organization's frontline service employee development practices. *Human Resource Development Quarterly*, *18*(3), 293–314.

Ellinger, A. E., Elmadag, A. B., Ellinger, A. D., Wang, Y., & Bachrach, D. G. (2008). Measurement of organizational investments in social capital: The service employee perspective. Working paper.

Ellinger, A. E., Ketchen, D. J., Hult, G. T., Elmadag, A. B., & Richey, R. G., Jr. (2008). Market-orientation, employee development practices and performance. *Industrial Marketing Management*, *37*(4), 353–366.

Elmadag, A. B., Ellinger, A. E., & Franke, G. R. (2008). Antecedents and consequences of frontline service employee commitment to service quality. *Journal of Marketing Theory and Practice*, *16*(2), 95–110.

Evered, R. D., & Selman, J. C. (1989). Coaching and the art of management. *Organizational Dynamics*, *18*, 16–32.

Feltz, D. L., Chase, M. A., Moritz, S. E., & Sullivan, P. J. (1999). A conceptual model of coaching efficacy: preliminary investigation and instrument development. *Journal of Educational Psychology*, *91*(4), 765–776.

Graham, S. W., Wedman, J. F., & Garvin-Kester, B. (1993). Manager coaching skills: Development and application. *Performance Improvement Quarterly*, *6*(1), 2–13.

Graham, S. W., Wedman, J. F., & Garvin-Kester, B. (1994). Manager coaching skills: What makes a good coach? *Performance Improvement Quarterly*, *7*(2), 81–94.

Hamlin, R. G. (2004). In support of universalistic models of managerial and leadership effectiveness: implications for HRD research and practice. *Human Resource Development Quarterly*, *15*(2), 189–215.

Hamlin, R. G. (2005). Toward universalistic models of managerial effectiveness: a comparative study of recent British and American derived models of leadership. *Human Resource Development International*, *8*(1), 5–25.

Hamlin, R. G., Ellinger, A. D., & Beattie, R. S. (2006). Coaching at the heart of managerial effectiveness: A cross-cultural study of managerial behaviors. *Human Resource Development International*,.

Hamlin, R. G., Ellinger, A. D., & Beattie, R. S. (2008). The emergent coaching industry: A wake-up call for HRD professionals. *Human Resource Development International*, *11*(3), 287–305.

Hannah, C. (2004). Improving intermediate skills through workplace coaching: A case study within the UK rail industry. *International Journal of Evidence Based Coaching and Mentoring*, *2*(1), 17–45.

Hansman, C. (2002) (Ed.). *Critical perspectives on mentoring: Trends and issues*. Columbus, OH: ERIC Clearinghouse on Adult, Career, and Vocational Education.

Hunt, J. M., & Weintraub, J. R. (2002a). How coaching can enhance your brand as a manager. *Journal of Organizational Excellence*, *21*(2), 39–44.

Hunt, J. M., & Weintraub, J. R. (2002b). *The coaching manager: Developing top talent in business*. Thousand Oaks, CA: Sage.

King, P., & Eaton, J. (1999). Coaching for results. *Industrial and Commercial Training*, *31*(4), 145–148.

Longenecker, C. O., & Neubert, M. J. (2005). The practices of effective managerial coaches. *Business Horizons*, *48*, 493–500.

Marsh, L. (1992). Good manager: Good coach? What is needed for effective coaching? *Industrial and Commercial Training*, *24*(9), 3–8.

McLean, G. N.Yang, B., Kuo, M. C., Tolbert, A. S., & Larkin, C. (2005). Development and initial validation of an instrument measuring managerial coaching skill. *Human Resource Development Quarterly*, *16*(2), 157–178.

Mink, O. G., Owen, K. Q., & Mink, B. P. (1993). *Developing high-performance people: The art of coaching*. Reading, MA: Addison-Wesley.

Minter, R. L., & Thomas, E. G. (2000). Employee development through coaching, mentoring and counseling: A multidimensional approach. *Review of Business*, *21*(1/2), 43–47.

Mumford, A. (1993). *How managers can develop managers* (2nd ed.). Aldershot, UK: Gower.

Noer, D. (2005). Behaviorally based coaching: A cross-cultural case study. *International Journal of Coaching in Organizations*, *3*, 14–23.

Noer, D. M., Leupold, C. R., & Valle, M. (2007). An analysis of Saudi Arabian and U.S. managerial coaching behaviors. *Journal of Managerial Issues*, *19*(2), 271–287.

Orth, C. D., Wilkinson, H. E., & Benfari, R. C. (1987). The manager's role as coach and mentor. *Organizational Dynamics*, *15*(4), 66–74.

Park, S., McLean, G. N., Yang, B. (2008). Revision and validation of an instrument measuring managerial coaching skills in organizations. In T. J. Chermack, J. Storberg-Walker, & C. M. Graham (Eds.), *Proceedings of The Academy of Human Resource Development* (CD-ROM). Panama City Beach, Florida.

Peterson, D. B., & Little, B. (2005). Invited reaction: Development and initial validation of an instrument measuring managerial coaching skill. *Human Resource Development Quarterly*, *16*(2), 179–183.

Phillips, R. (1994). Coaching for higher performance. *Management Development Review*, *7*(5), 19–22.

Phillips, R. (1995). Coaching for higher performance. *Executive Development*, *8*(7), 5.

Powell, T., & Doran, M. (2003). Managers' perceptions of their role in facilitating employee learning. *Proceedings of 2003 International Academy of Human Resource Development conference*.

Russ-Eft, D, Berry, C., Hurson, K., & Brennan, K. (1996). Updating the meaning of leadership: A grass roots model for the new workplace. *An essay from Zenger Miller, M2021 V.2.0(10/50)*San Jose, CA: Zenger Miller.

Shaw, S., & Knights, J. (2005). Coaching in an SME: An investigation into the impact of a managerial coaching style on employees within a small firm. *Proceedings of the Sixth International Conference on HRD Research and Practice Across Europe*.

Zemke, R. (1996). The corporate coach. *Training*, *33*(12), 24–28.

Recommended Readings and Websites

Bianco-Mathis, V. E., Nabors, L. K., & Roman, C. H. (2002). *Leading from the inside out: A coaching model*. Thousand Oaks, CA: Sage.

Flaherty, J. (1999). *Coaching: Evoking excellence in others* Burlington, MA: Butterworth-Heinemann.

Hargrove, R. (1995). *Masterful coaching.* San Francisco: Pfeiffer.

Hunt, J. M., & Weintraub, J. R. (2002). *The coaching manager: Developing top talent in business.* Thousand Oaks, CA: Sage.

Hunt, J. M., & Weintraub, J. R. (2007). *The coaching organization: A strategy for developing leaders.* Thousand Oaks, CA: Sage.

European Mentoring and Coaching Council: http://www.emccouncil.org/

International Federation of Coaching: http://www.coachfederation.org/ICF/

International Journal of Evidence Based Coaching and Mentoring: http://www.business.brookes.ac.uk/research/areas/coaching&mentoring/

Other Published Resources

Anonymous. (2001). Mentoring and coaching help employees grow. *HR Focus, 78*(9), 1–6.

Antonioni, D. (2000, September/October). Leading, managing and coaching. *Industrial Management*, pp. 27–33.

Armentrout, B. W. (1995). Making coaching your management metaphor. *HR Focus, 72*(6), 3.

Bartlett, C. A., & Goshal, S. (1997). The myth of the generic managers: New personal competencies for new management roles. *California Management Review, 40*(1), 92–116.

Burdett, J. O. (1998). Forty things every manager should know about coaching. *Journal of Management Development, 17*(2), 142–152.

Chase, M. A., Feltz, D. L., Hayashi, S. W., & Hepler, T. J. (2005). Sources of coaching efficacy: the coaches' perspective. *International Journal of Sport and Exercise Psychology, 3*(1), 27–40.

Cseh, M. (1998). *Managerial learning in the transition to a free market economy in Romanian private companies.* Unpublished doctoral dissertation. University of Georgia.

Dechant, K. (1989). *Managing change in the workplace: Learning strategies of managers.* Unpublished doctoral dissertation. Columbia University Teachers College.

de Jong, J. A., Leenders, F. J., & Thisjssen, J. G.I. (1999). HRD tasks of first-level managers. *Journal of Workplace Learning, 11*(5), 176–183.

Fournies, F. F. (1987). *Coaching for improved work performance.* Kingston, Jamaica. Liberty Hall Press.

Gilley, J. W. (2000). Manager as learning champion. *Performance Improvement Quarterly, 13*(4), 106–121.

Goleman, D. (2000, March/April). Leadership that gets results. *Harvard Business Review*, pp. 78–90.

Grant, A. M. (2003). Executive and life coaching, UKCLC Professional Development Workshop. London, Royal Society of Medicine. [Unpublished Presentation].

Grant, T., & Cavanagh, M. (2004). Toward a profession of coaching: Sixty-five years of progress and challenges for the future. *International Journal of Evidence Based Coaching and Mentoring, 2*(1), 7–21.

Grant, T., & Zackon, R. (2004). Executive, workplace and life coaching: Findings from a large-scale survey of international coach federation members. *International Journal of Evidence Based Coaching and Mentoring, 2*(2), 1–15.

Hall, L., & Torrington, D. (1998). Letting go or holding on: The devolution of operational personnel activities. *Human Resource Management Journal, 8*(1), 41–55.

Hankins, C., & Kleiner, B. H. (1995). New developments in supervisor training. *Industrial and Commercial Training, 27*(1), 26–32.

Honey, P. (1995, September). Everyday experiences are opportunities for learning. *People Management*, p. 55.

Hyman J., & Cunningham, I. (1998). Managers as developers: Some reflections on the contribution of empowerment in Britain. *International Journal of Training and Development, 2*(2), 91–107.

Kampa-Kokesch, S., & Anderson, M. Z. (2001) Executive coaching: A comprehensive review of the literature. *Consulting Psychology Journal, 53*(4), 205–228.

Kilburg, R. R.(Ed.). (1996). Executive coaching [Special issue]. *Consulting Psychology Journal: Practice and Research, 48*(2), 203–267.

Kirk, J., Howard, S., Ketting, I., & Little, C. (1999). Type c workplace interventions. *Journal of Workplace Learning, 11*(3), 105–114.

Kraines, G. A. (2001). Are you L.E.A.D.ing your troops. *Strategy and Leadership, 29*(2), 29–34.

Larsen, H. H. (1997). Do high-flyer programmes facilitate organizational learning? *Journal of Managerial Psychology, 12*(1), 48–59.

McGill, M. E., & Slocum, Jr., J. W., (1998). A *little* leadership please? *Organizational Dynamics*, pp. 39–49.

McGovern, P., Gratton, L., Hope-Hailey, V., Stiles, P., & Truss, C. (1997). Human resource management on the line? *Human Resource Management Journal, 7*(4), 12–29.

McLean, G. N., & Kuo, M. (2000). Coaching in organizations: Self-assessment of competence. In K. P. Kuchinke (Ed.), *Proceedings of The Academy of Human Resource Development Conference* (pp. 638–645). Raleigh-Durham, NC.

McNutt, R., & Wright, P. C. (1995). Coaching your employees: Applying sports analogies to business. *Executive Development, 8*(1), 27–32.

Mills, J. (1986). Subordinate perceptions of managerial coaching practices. *Academy of Management Proceedings*, pp. 113–116.

Mindell, N. (1995). Devolving training and development to line managers. *Management Development Review, 8*(2), 16–21.

Mobley, S. A. (1999). Judge not: How coaches create healthy organizations. *The Journal for Quality and Participation*, *22*(4), 57–60.

Morgeson, F. P. (2005). The external leadership of self-managing teams: Intervening in the context of novel and disruptive events. *Journal of Applied Psychology*, *90*(3), 497–508.

Piasecka, A. (2000). Not leadership but leadership. *Industrial and Commercial Training*, *32*(7), 253–255.

Popper, M., & Lipshitz, R. (1992). Coaching on leadership. *Leadership & Organization Development Journal*, *13*(7), 15–18.

Ragsdale, S. (2000). Finding a high speed button: New management paradigm. *Triangle Business Journal, (Raleigh, NC)*, *16*(7), 23.

Redshaw, B. (2000). Do we really understand coaching? How can we make it work better? *Industrial and Commercial Training*, *32*(3), 106–108.

Slater, S. F., & Narver, J. C. (1994). Market orientation, customer value, and superior performance. *Business Horizons*, *37*(2), 22–28.

Slater, S. F., & Narver, J. C. (1995). Market orientation and the learning organization. *Journal of Marketing*, *59*, 63–74.

Schuler, R. S. (1990). Repositioning the human resource function: Transformation or demise? *Academy of Management Executive*, *4*(3), 49–60.

Talarico, M. (2002). Manager as coach in a pharmacy benefit management organization: A critical incidents analysis. Unpublished doctoral dissertation, University of Minnesota.

Thornhill, A., & Saunders, M. N. K. (1998). What if line managers don't realize they're responsible for HR? Lessons from an organization experiencing rapid change. *Personnel Review*, *27*(6), 460–476.

Yarnall, J. (1998). Line managers as career developers: Rhetoric or reality? *Personnel Review*, *27*(5), 378–395.

Yukl, G. (1994). *Leadership in organizations* (3rd ed.) Upper Saddle River, NJ: Prentice Hall.

 EDITORIAL CONNECTIONS

Managerial coaching, with its deliberate focus on improving performance of one group through the application of HPT principles by another, can be a very effective intervention in many situations. Whether performance issues are at the individual, team, or systemic-organizational level, managerial coaching opens a critical dialogue that expands discussion of performance issues beyond the boundaries of the annual performance reviews of individual employees. Effective coaching begins with the establishment of clearly communicated principles of the relationship. This is an essential characteristic of managerial coaching, as this brings forth significant results.

While many other forms and focal points can drive coaching relationships, the focus on improving the achievement of measurable and beneficial results distinguishes managerial coaching. Consequently, coaching can become a pragmatic component of your improvement effort, assisting in the creation of feedback loops that use measures of performance as the starting place for collegial discussions on how to improve.

Expanding Your Options

Reference manuals for processes and procedures—provide information about standard methods of conducting tasks or activities within the organization.

In addition to their unique capabilities as individual performance interventions, each of the performance interventions described in the preceding chapters (realistic job previews, assessment and feedback systems, performance measurement systems, and managerial coaching) can also be useful components of a comprehensive performance management system. When coordinated with other performance measurement and feedback systems (such as production statistics, customer service feedback, project management data, team-based evaluations, employee development progress, competency development, and employee performance appraisals), an inclusive performance management system can be created to guide and improve performance.

Expanding Your Options

Quality assurance programs—activities specifically designed to ensure that products (goods and/or services) consistently satisfy customer requirements. QA programs ensure that the products are suitable for the purpose they are intended to serve, and that production mistakes are eliminated or minimized.

Based on wikipedia.org definition (January 2009).

WHAT'S COMING UP

Performance management systems, as described David Gliddon in Chapter Twelve, are broad systems that use numerous measures of performance to inform cyclical feedback loops that strive to improve the accomplishment of results. By integrating numerous performance interventions into a holistic system, you can use performance management to develop and guide decisions at all levels of your organization. From individual and team performance issues (such as productivity, timeliness, accuracy, readiness, outputs, efficiency, and relationships) to organizational and societal performance issues (such as return on investment, client satisfaction, supply-chain breakdowns, quality of life, safety and well-being, and sustainability), your performance management system should systemically unite multiple expectation and feedback interventions to improve performance at all levels of organizational impact.

CHAPTER TWELVE

Performance Management Systems

David G. Gliddon

INTRODUCTION

A performance management system combines and coordinates an organization's efforts to grow or become more efficient by motivating employees through evaluation, development, reward, and promotion. A 1999 article by David Otley of Lancaster University's Management School defines performance management as a practical framework that improves both employee skills and operational activities to increase organizational efficiency. For an organization, a performance management system provides a structured and legally defensible approach to cascading goals, objectives, and expectations to employees. By integrating these tasks using technology, the organization creates an interdependent dialogue among senior leaders, managers, employees, and its human resource function. Establishing performance as the basis for this dialogue creates a positive framework for the holistic evaluation of an employee's contribution to the profit and growth of an organization.

DESCRIPTION

Inherent in this systems-based approach is a multi-faceted strategy for measurement of human performance that encourages excellence in each process in the organization's workflow system. Performance data should be gathered and aggregated using an exhaustive variety of resources including, but not limited to: financial metrics, production statistics, customer service feedback, project management data, team-based evaluations, employee development progress, competency development, and employee performance appraisals. The responsibility of the non-technology aspects of administering an organization's performance management system typically rests with the human resource function. A 1996 Academy of Management article by Delaney and Huselid reports that HR professionals typically lead these efforts in the areas of compensation, benefits, training, development, and employee relations. Key stakeholders in each team provide their skills and efforts to ensure that the processes, policies, and workflow in the system are aligned to an employee-focused, service-driven perspective. An ethical performance management system should demonstrate an organization's commitment to the mutual growth of the employees who comprise it.

A performance management system requires senior leaders of organizations to communicate in their mission and vision statements that they commit to the understanding that a shareholder's and owner's profit and success are fundamentally based on the performance and growth of its employees; this is the foundation of success in a capitalist economy. When providing input into the design of a performance management system, senior leaders should leverage their power to demonstrate this commitment by encouraging the use of goal-setting theory and crafting SMART (specific, measurable, attainable, realistic, and timely) objectives emphasized by Mertins, Krause, and Schallock in their 1999 book *Global Production Management*. When adopted at all levels in the organization, the performance dialogue that exists between managers and employees shifts to a forward-thinking, positive, and improvement-based form of feedback through coaching, mentoring, and applied leadership.

Performance management systems have emerged in organizations as a combination of many theoretical perspectives. Research in 1993 by Jeffrey S. Yalowitz and his colleagues supports W. Edwards Deming's 1981 findings that in the frame of total quality management theory, performance management systems apply the standard of total quality to the employee and the organization to encourage a long-term focus on performance improvement. As I reported in my own dissertation work, which supports Konovsky and Fogel's 1988 work, among others, innovation leadership theory encourages employee creativity and their ability to create and diffuse innovations to drive an organization's overall performance and competitiveness. Performance management systems that are competency-based support employee development and promotion by encouraging organizational learning activities to increase employee performance; this is supported by Rothwell, Hohne, and King's 2007 research. According to Warren Bennis' landmark 1969 book *Organization Development*, the practice of organization development provides change management support and interventions that can be applied to organizations with performance or motivation challenges. Performance management systems simplify and streamline many common HR duties to create a more efficient and accurate means of servicing employees' needs. For example, Becker and Gerhart's research shows that performance management systems provide a multi-disciplinary approach to promotion for succession planning.

WHAT WE KNOW FROM RESEARCH

A 1999 article by J. S. Bowman for *Public Personnel Management* journal reports that many common forms of employee evaluation are more subjective than objective in nature, differentiating in the degree of subjectivity likely in the judgments made. Thus, both the employee and the organization are responsible for an employee's performance, motivation, and fair evaluation of performance to strive for a less subjective, more objective measurement of performance. The organization's responsibility is to provide or improve a performance management system that motivates employee and encourages organizational growth. To answer the question, "What motivates my employees?" is to discover an employee's and organization's needs by completing a gap or needs analysis that includes both statistical measures and employee feedback. Ang and colleagues, in a 2006 article entitled "The Cross-Section of Volatility and Expected Returns," describe understanding how employees are motivated as understanding what outcomes they value, how much of the outcome they expect to receive based on their performance, and the amount of effort they will put forth to achieve the outcome.

Fairness Theory

The organizational culture within this adaptive environment must maintain, as a fundamental principle, fairness with all employees. A 1998 article by Judge, Locke, Durham, and Kluger describes the basis of fairness theory as justice within an organization that encourages employee accountability. Unless fairness theory is applied effectively in an organization's culture, political forces may arise to create a culture that is demotivating, breaking down an employee's commitment and accountability. Greenberg and Colquitt also address this in their 2005 *Handbook of Organizational Justice*. Fairness theory combines two perspectives that create a fair playing field for all employees. The first perspective, equity theory, focuses on maintaining a careful balance between performance and reward to ensure legal defensibility and job satisfaction. The second perspective, procedural justice, focuses on the process of how employees are rewarded for performance. Procedural justice is necessary to ensure that HR processes are applied reliably to each employee. When creating or redesigning a compensation strategy and process or performance appraisal tool, the same strategy, process, and appraisal should be applied to each employee or relevant employee group. This provides additional support to the legal defensibility of a performance management system. Siegel, Schraeder, and Morrison's 2008 article, "A Taxonomy of Equity Factors," further emphasizes these issues.

When the organizational culture reflects an application of fairness theory, it can begin to design or redesign its form of employee evaluation. The most common form of employee evaluation is a performance appraisal. In a 2008 article for *Industrial and Organizational Psychology* journal, Harris, Ispas, and Schmidt outline the performance appraisal as consisting of two components: the performance evaluation criteria to be appraised and the discussion that takes place with the appraiser or appraisers. If an organization uses only a single appraiser, bias can occur because there are fewer sources of data to review to determine the employee's performance contribution holistically. Likewise, differences in personality type, values, attitude, mood, perceived power, or social influence of a single appraiser can skew the feedback given in an interdependent performance dialogue. Daly and Geyer report in a 1994 article concerning fairness and change that this can cause the performance appraisal to become a less-meaningful event to employees, can demotivate them, and lower their performance.

To avoid these pitfalls, performance appraisals should instead use multiple appraisers to increase the quality of the employee evaluation and performance discussion. A common form of using multiple appraisers is the 360-degree feedback evaluation. Kein's 1999 article "Searching 360 Degrees for Employee Evaluation" describes a 360-degree evaluation as including an appraisal from an employee's internal and external contacts in addition to internal and external performance data. This begins a more interdependent performance discussion that applies multiple points of view on the employee's level of performance (see Chapter Nine). Aggregating the quantitative measures with qualitative feedback, say Harris and colleagues in a 2008 article for *Industrial and Organizational Psychology*, is critical to ensuring a clear understanding of the employee's level of performance. When closing a performance discussion, David Cooperrider and colleagues explain in their 2003 *Appreciative Inquiry Handbook* that an appreciative inquiry approach can be used to provide detailed and specific praise for the employees' strengths and, more importantly, their efforts to develop strengths from their weaknesses (see Chapter Six).

Competency Theory

The basis for the discovery of employee strengths and weaknesses in a performance management system is established with applied competency theory. Competencies are the foundation of the modern organization's human resource function and are typically expressed as a competency model. Rothwell, Hohne, and King explain in *Human Performance Improvement* that competency models provide a description of the (1) knowledge, (2) skills, (3) capabilities, and (4) behaviors required to perform a job or function, or to sustain the desired organizational culture. Competency models can be created for each position within an organization and can be multi-dimensionally used as a tool for measuring employee development. Gresh and colleagues assert in a 2007 article concerning supply chain optimization that a performance appraisal built on the foundation of employee development aids in increasing employee motivation and inspiration through leadership, and it provides the ability for detailed statistical analysis of employee development data for workforce planning needs. Tailored to the organization's compensation strategy, a competency-based system of performance encourages higher levels of performance while also providing an increase in the growth and performance of the organization as employees apply their increased competence to their work.

Goal-Setting Theory

Goal-setting theory provides the basis for the vision statement of an organization and defines its next steps in growth. This desire to grow is inherently driven in a capitalist economy, Hirshleifer asserted in 1994. Henry Mintzberg, in *The Rise and Fall of Strategic Planning*, points out that goals should be lofty in terms, defining the future state of the organization in five to ten years to ensure they incorporate future market opportunities and focused strategic planning efforts. Likewise, goals help an organization to focus on long-term survival and encourage its ability to generate societal-level innovations. When broken down into SMART (specific, measurable, attainable, realistic, and timely) objectives, goals define the basis for an organization's project management system. According to Meredith and Mantel's *Project Management: A Managerial Approach*, project management tools can provide organized cascading of objectives and strong evaluation data for an individual's, team's, or department's appraisal of performance. Combined with external market performance data, an organization may evaluate its progress toward its goals.

Goal setting, when applied to an individual employee, should focus primarily on the employee's career goals within the organization. Career goals provide a basis to encourage employees to seek developmental opportunities, improve their capacity to complete objectives, and take on responsibilities until they have the competencies to be promoted or included in succession planning efforts. This matter is discussed further by Greenhaus and Parasuraman in their 1993 article for *Organizational Behavior and Human Decision Processes*. When the employees reach their career goals, they may then choose to pursue others. In their seminal 2002 article for *American Psychologist*, Edwin A. Locke and Gary P. Latham report that individual employee goals are also impacted by social factors such as a supervisor's management style, leadership approach, or personality-type. Managers who adopt the role of a mentor, coach, or leader demonstrate a focus on employee development in their interactive performance discussions. In a performance management system, mentoring, coaching, and leading provide inspiration and motivation to encourage an employee's long-term pursuit of their career goals.

Innovation Leadership Theory

In my 2006 dissertation at Pennsylvania State University, I define innovation leadership as a collection of practical evolution strategies that organizations can implement to create a culture of innovation, develop innovation leaders, increase performance, and become more innovative. According to innovation leadership theory, success in the adoption of innovations is increased when leaders collaboratively interact with their employees and support high levels of teamwork, providing opportunities to share innovations. There is a vast body of literature exploring innovation leadership theory concepts. Some of these include Damanpour's "Organizational Complexity and Innovation," Gifford's "Innovation, Firm Size, and Growth in a Centralized Organization," Martinsons' "Strategic Innovation," "Factors Affecting a Firm's Commitment to Innovation," by Schoenecker, Daellenbach, and McCarthy, and Prather and Turrell's "Involve Everyone in the Innovation Process." Curious readers are also advised to examine works by Gruber (1972), Lee (1995), Lewis (1993), Meyer (1988), Ripley and Ripley (1992), Roffe (1999), Russel (1990), and Tannenbaum and colleagues (1994), all listed within the references section at the end of this chapter

In a 2000 qualitative study, Jones reviewed leadership programs that promoted innovation in organizations. Results suggested that, in order to lead others in an innovation, leaders should be trained to promote (1) imagination, (2) community, and (3) the application of the innovation in the workplace. Rogers in 1995 explains that once an innovation has been shared, employees should be empowered to then adopt the innovation if it is useful. Employees can then support the innovation leader by initially adopting the innovation and encourage the diffusion of the innovation throughout the organization's social system. In his research published in 2003, Peter Bingham links innovation to the economic growth of existing enterprises and development of new enterprises. As new products, services, technologies, and enterprises are created, new opportunities for employment arise. Pagano and Verdin note in their 1997 text *The External Environment of Business* that innovation can support the creation of new jobs in an economy.

Approaches to Employee Evaluation

Traditionally, performance evaluations are an annual, semi-annual, or quarterly event that at times can be seen by employees as routine and trivial. In order to fend off this negative stereotype, Woodford and Maes suggest in their 2002 article "Employee Performance Evaluations" that an organization should support a valid set of employee evaluation criteria that measures performance as the basis for compensation and brings meaningfulness and motivation in the interdependent performance dialogue. A foundation for evaluation criteria of the interdependent performance dialogue is found in Kirkpatrick's four levels of learning evaluation. At Level 1, an initial reaction is expressed about the performance dialogue. At Level 2, the participants in the performance dialogue reflect upon their leaning experiences. At Level 3, employees transfer information learned in the performance dialogue to their daily work activities. At Level 4, an employee's performance data is reviewed for increased employee effectiveness.

Performance management systems are developed using a specific approach to employee evaluation depending on the areas for improvement or coordination of performance management system components discovered in the needs or gap analysis. The approaches can be grouped as trait-based, behavior-based, or results-based systems. Likewise, elements of each approach can be combined together to produce a hybrid-system tailored specifically to an organization focusing on its relevance to the values instilled in its culture. Each approach provides the fundamental basis and reasoning for specific employee evaluation criteria included in a performance appraisal.

Banner and Blasingame describe in their 1988 article regarding a developmental paradigm of leadership that a trait-based system is one that evaluates an employee based on the degree to which the employees demonstrate characteristics deemed important to the organization or to their positions. Appraisal tools such as personality profiles, tests, and measurements are commonly used to discover employees' personality types to more clearly understand their work behaviors. Although personality testing is useful in the establishment of or analysis of an organizational culture or as part of organization development interventions, Bowman, in his 1999 article "Performance Appraisal," notes that it lacks reliability and validity as a measure of performance. Furthermore, it should not be used to establish an employee's compensation because a trait-based system has poor legal defensibility. However, trait-based systems are more useful than other approaches for employee self-discovery within an organization's social system. Trait-based measurements are beneficial in development planning to discover an employee's learning style and approach to group dynamics. This knowledge can increase performance within the context of employee development.

A behavior-based evaluation system reviews an employee's job activities and rewards an employee based on work effort. Behavior-based evaluation, using competency theory as its foundation, rates employees on how well they demonstrate the competencies defined in the competency model for their positions when compared to their actual work behavior. This activity is central to the employees' development as it clearly outlines their areas of improvement. According to Edvardsson and Roos' 2001 article of the same name, the "Critical Incident Technique" can also be used in behavior-based evaluation in situations in which the employee's work has high visibility in the organization or is necessary for the successful completion of an important objective. Critical incidents can be evaluated using data from personal interviews, focus groups, and employee observations. Halinen and Tornoos describe in 2004 how this data is used to create a case of the activities and approach of the team or employee completing the objective during the critical incidence.

Results-based evaluation systems attempt to discern an employee's contribution to the success of the organization. Using goal-setting theory as a foundation, Banner and Blasingame argue that this common form of employee evaluation establishes an organization's objectives from its goals and delegates this work in a cascading fashion to appropriate work groups, managers, and employees. Dreyer noted in 1988 that the challenge in this form of employee evaluation is to ensure the alignment of each organizational objective with each employee. In this, the employee and manager, as part of the performance discussion, talk about the relevance of the objective to the employee's career goal. The disadvantages of this form of evaluation, as described by Mahoney and Sanchez in 2004, include: measurements are more focused on business or financial outcome, rather than the level of performance or effort that is put forth to achieve the outcome; conflicting cascading objectives at the manager or employee level; focus on short-term results, rather than long-term market growth; discouragement of team building; and employee preoccupation with objectives.

Organizations may create performance management systems that employ a hybrid approach to employee evaluation, using the most reliable and valid appraisal tools from among the previous three traditional approaches. This is summarized in my 2004 article for *Performance Improvement* journal and discussed at some length in my 2006 dissertation, as well as in Edwards' 1990 article "An Alternative to Traditional Appraisal Systems." The foundational theory behind this type of employee evaluation is innovation leadership theory. It suggests that the interdependent dialogue that is critical to employee evaluation should be based on a perspective of leader-follower interactions, rather than solely on a management-by-objectives approach, which is supported by Kuczmarski's 1996 article "What Is Innovation? The Art of Welcoming Risk." A clear difference exists between the role of a leader and the role of a manager in a performance management system. A manager is tasked with the efficient delegation of work and distribution of resources, whereas a leader is tasked to provide inspiration to employees. Employees with supervisory responsibilities take on both of these roles but, as is noted in two 1995 articles by McNerney and by Houston, they should leverage their leadership skills to encourage motivation through praise, while also providing inspiration through leadership. This approach to employee evaluation provides a fundamentally stronger level of motivation built into a performance management system. Yoon argues in 2002 that this is because innovation leadership theory places value on creativity and the generation of innovations as a critical aspect of employee motivation.

The advantages of performance management systems are numerous. In a 2000 article, Panktrantz asserts that performance management systems encourage motivation through collaboration and encourage active manager and employee participation in appraisal of performance. Likewise, the interdependent dialogue that is necessary as the basis for a performance management system is supported as evaluations become more peer-based, providing increased reliability through the use of multiple raters. As early as 1982, Bricker contended that ratings in the form of comments on an employee's work, based in praise, create motivation, encourage the employee to generate innovations in his or her work, and allow those innovations to be diffused and adopted more effectively in an organization. In performance management systems, performance can be appraised in real time, providing a quicker and more employee-relevant feedback loop. During an annual performance review process to determine compensation, additional multi-faceted qualitative data is available to make reward decisions, and data can be analyzed in a more systematic manner.

Performance management systems address many of the weaknesses associated with current methods of employee evaluation. Martinez's 1995 article and Merit's in 1999 suggest that these can include being seen as a trivial routine annual event, rating errors, inconsistencies, cost, turnover, emotional impact on employees, conflict, increased fear, short-term focus, reduced motivation and productivity, increased job-related stress, reduced employee privacy, lawsuits trigged by demotion, failure to promote, layoff, and dismissal. Considering ongoing feedback and coaching, performance management systems increase the quantity and quality of employee feedback by framing the performance discussion positively, and embracing emergent technologies that can increase the volume of employee, peer, and manager participation in the evaluation process. The emotional impact of some current methods of employee evaluation can demotivate an employee by focusing only on short-term results. Within a 1981 article for *Academy of Management Journal*, DeNisi and Stevens argue that this causes a limiting of the employee's long-term planning abilities, increasing employee fear, increasing employee rivalry, undermining teamwork, and causing political conflict. In the same year, Buschardt and Schnake observed that an employee's attitude toward his or her manager can often skew the results of performance appraisal. These rating biases are addressed in performance management systems by encouraging active multi-rater appraisal.

Legal Considerations

Performance appraisals are a key source of evidence when employees are suing former employers for wrongful termination or discrimination. A legally defensible performance appraisal process evaluates employees based on their merit. If merit is evaluated by only a few limited, rudimentary measures, the legal defensibility of a performance appraisal process is reduced. Eyres in 1989 categorized four types of actions that may typically trigger a lawsuit: demotion, failure to promote, layoff, and dismissal arising from an employee's view of unfairness, inconsistency, and illegality. High court costs, attorney fees, and lost management time, disruption of employee performance, low motivation, and public relations challenges characterize the obstacles that are created to an organization's profit and growth because of employment lawsuits. In cases in which the organization has developed an ineffective performance management system that does not allow for employee feedback, Belanger in 1991 observed that the organization will be less likely to have strong evidence to support its employment decision. Likewise, organizations are increasingly using performance evaluation tools that may invade employees' privacy and reduce their level of autonomy, such as screening employee telephone calls, reading their e-mails, and monitoring work on video displays without their knowledge. Per Clement, this type of evaluation can reduce employees' motivation by increasing their stress and thus provides a bias because employees' knowledge of observation does not allow for a true assessment of their performance.

According to a 1991 article by North Carolina State University's Dennis M. Daley, many modern compensation systems attempt to fit performance ratings on a bell curve to distribute employee rewards. This form of distribution can be statistically valid; however, Grensing notes in a 1985 article for *Manage* magazine that a majority of employees typically fall within the average category of ratings. This label is subjective from the organization's point of view and does not provide an objective view of a single employee or team. As most employees view themselves as above average, lower ratings than expected can demotivate employees, alienate strong performers, and discourage weak performers. In their 1995 article "Implicit Stress Theory," Fernandez and Perrewe assert that this may be attributed to the bell curve that is used to rank employees to a standardized descriptive statistic, rather than a mutually exclusive objective evaluation of their individual contributions to the organization, suggesting a need for a more complex compensation algorithm. Likewise, employee behaviors and outcomes are substantially affected by systemic factors that are outside of the organization's control, which may not be accounted for adequately in a performance appraisal. Therefore, Carson and colleagues' 1993 article expressed their belief that a well-crafted performance appraisal should attempt to correct for the influence of these factors on an employee's performance patterns and avoid strategies that use employee comparison to evaluate performance.

WHEN TO APPLY

A performance management system should be applied when an organization is large enough to require an effective means of evaluating its employees. A needs or gap analysis should be conducted to discover areas for improvement or coordination of performance management system components (see Chapter Thirty-Two). Also, if an organization has implemented the components of a performance management system but has not yet integrated these components, a performance management system can coordinate and streamline these efforts throughout the organization. If the organization implements emergent technologies as part of its IT infrastructure, then a performance management system can leverage these resources to create an interdependent performance dialogue and multi-rater approach to employee evaluation using improved web-based evaluation, reporting, communication, or e-learning tools.

If an organization uses a pay for performance strategy of compensation (see Chapter Twenty), an effective performance management system is necessary to gather data for employee rewards. Performance management systems integrate both quantitative measures of employee performance for statistical measures and qualitative evaluations that holistically encourage employee motivation as a fundamental design element of an employee evaluation system. If an organization has recently gone through a radical change such as a merger or acquisition, a performance management system can support the organizational integration of employee evaluation and increase the level and quality of employee communication.

The unique aspect of a performance management system is that it is tailored to the specific needs of the organization and adaptable to change. With this approach, members of an organization and performance management experts complete the necessary in-depth analysis to fully uncover an organization's employee evaluation needs and create specific, scalable processes that coordinate the efforts of employees to accurately measure performance while ensuring that its customized performance management system creates motivation. Once the performance management system is in place, performance management experts, HR professionals, and senior leaders can evaluate the implementation of the system and adapt it as the organization grows or changes. Change management techniques such as organization development can be applied to ease in its implementation, and attention should be paid to its typically positive effects on an organization's culture (see Chapter Thirty).

STRENGTHS AND CRITICISMS

Performance management systems have made a significant impact on employees work responsibilities. The strengths in a performance management system are the coordination and refinement of many mutually exclusive processes that, when combined, improve the organization's overall efficiency. In the same way, the interdependent performance dialogue creates a culture that values and motivates employees while providing an accurate evaluation of their efforts. The weaknesses in a performance management system arise primarily because the performance management system is poorly designed or training on the performance management system has not transferred into the organization to support its utilization.

Strengths

- Performance management systems have a high rate of effectiveness.
- They streamline HR functions for managers and employees and improve processes.
- Evaluations are legally defensible in employment-related lawsuits.
- They provide an accurate measurement of performance.
- They encourage employee development, succession planning, and promotion.
- They strengthen links between performance and compensation.
- They support fair, equitable, ethical, and valid multiple-rater evaluations.
- They clarify organizational goals and demonstrate employee expectations.
- They encourage constructive feedback, coaching, and mentoring.

Criticisms

- Can be seen by employees as a trivial routine annual event;
- Rating errors, inconsistencies in administration;
- Costly annual process, implementation, and design;
- Can lead to turnover if not designed carefully;
- Can have emotional impact on employee, create conflict, and increase fear;
- Can lead to short-term focus on employee objectives;
- Can reduce motivation and productivity if poorly managed;
- Can increase job-related stress and reduce employee privacy; and
- Can trigger lawsuits from demotion, failure to promote, layoff, and dismissal.

RECOMMENDED DESIGN, DEVELOPMENT, AND IMPLEMENTATION PROCESS

The design, development, and implementation of a performance management system can be driven by an organization's current project management system.

In the design process, the organization should take into account its current and future workforce planning needs to ensure that the performance management system is scalable. As the performance management system is developed, documentation should be created for policy and training needs. Careful attention should be paid to communicate the benefits of the performance management system to employees when it is introduced to counter any resistance to change.

1. Identify the key stakeholders in the development of a performance management system.

2. Create a cross-functional team, including employees, managers, HR functions, senior leaders, IT, and performance management experts.

3. Complete a needs analysis and/or gap analysis to discover the areas for improvement or coordination of performance management system components.

4. Design the performance management system and its components:

   • Seek buy-in, input, agreement, and approval from key stakeholders on designing the performance management system.

   • Redesign each component of the performance management system.

   • Link performance management components and compensation strategies.

   • Map new processes, including involvement of each stakeholder.

   • Identify roles for each participant in the performance management system.

   • Develop policy to ensure that employees understand how and why a performance management system is used.

   • Create timelines for the administration of the performance management system.

   • Create a name or acronym for the performance management system.

   • Develop, create, or purchase products to manage and coordinate information technologies and reports for the performance management system.

5. Appoint a member of the cross-functional performance management system design team as the ''advocate'' on the system. Appoint an incumbent employee as the internal employee service contact for questions about the performance management system.

6. Develop training materials, classes, webcasts, and just-in-time e-learning simulations describing the performance management system's techniques, purpose, use, and timing.

7. Complete beta testing of information technologies used in the perform-ance management system and related e-learning tools.

8. Appoint a respected senior leader to announce the new performance management system to the organization, providing an honest and posi-tive description to employees. Host training sessions, distribute all train-ing materials.

9. Go live. Continue to provide training materials and frequently highlight tips on performance management in company communications and on the company intranet.

10. Keeping the cross functional performance management system design team permanently intact, periodically review its effectiveness, imple-ment changes as needed, and provide updates to key stakeholders.

CRITICAL SUCCESS FACTORS

These critical success factors represent how many of the pitfalls in designing, developing, and implementing a performance management system can be avoided. Members of the cross-functional performance management systems team and key stakeholders should take time during planning to discuss how they will approach and respond to each factor. A change in a performance management system requires the careful analysis of an organization's processes to ensure that efficiency is maintained or raised in that process. If the organiza-tion finds barriers to its success, it may be helpful to seek out performance management consultants to guide the efforts:

- Identifying, coordinating, and seeking buy-in from key stakeholders;
- Framing the implementation of or changes to a performance management system as a project using project management tactics;
- Completing a thorough needs and/or gap analysis to identify the key areas of improvement;
- Designing the system to motivate employee performance and avoiding strategies that are demotivating or will create employee inequality;
- Creating employee evaluations that are fair, valid, accurate, reliable, non-discriminatory, and legally defensible;
- Ensuring that information technologies are more efficient, quicker, and easier for employees to use than in previous evaluation systems;
- Using competency-based initiatives to streamline performance manage-ment in all HR functions;

- Linking performance results directly with employee compensation plans, succession planning, and promotion;
- Creating management training programs that highlight the importance of and effective use of all components of the performance management system;
- Providing adequate just-in-time e-learning programs for use during performance management activities;
- Providing adequate HR internal customer service for the performance management system; and
- Ensuring that employees believe the performance management system to be credible, motivational, and more relevant than other forms of evaluation.

SUMMARY

Performance management systems provide organizations with a multi-rater approach to employee evaluation that fundamentally encourages employee performance through motivation, enriches and increases the interdependent performance discussion through collaboration, and ensures that both qualitative and quantitative appraisals are used. It streamlines and coordinates the administration of the performance management system, links organizational goal setting with employee objectives and expectations, focuses on employee development, and is based on an organization's economic need for profit and growth. Furthermore, it effectively applies a legally defensible form of employee evaluation and encourages positive perspectives of employees' merit.

References

Ang, A., Hodrick, R. J., Xing, Y., & Zhang, X. (2006). The cross-section of volatility and expected returns. *Journal of Finance*, *61*(1), 259–299.

Banner, D. K., & Blasingame, J. W. (1988). Toward a developmental paradigm of leadership. *Leadership and Organization Development Journal*, *9*(4), 7–11.

Becker, B., & Gerhart, B. (1996). The impact of human resource management on organizational performance: Progress and prospects. *The Academy of Management Journal*, *39*(4), 779–801.

Belanger, K. (1991). Intelligent software for performance evaluations can be legal protection. *Employment Relations Today*, *18*(1), 27–29.

Bennis, W. G. (1969). *Organization development: Its nature, origins, and prospects*. Reading, MA: Addison-Wesley.

Bingham, P. (2003). Pursuing innovation in a big organization. *Research Technology Management*, *46*(4), 52–55.

Bowman, J. S. (1999) Performance appraisal: Verisimilitude trumps veracity. *Public Personnel Management*, *28*(4), 557–577.

Bricker, G. A. (1992). Hiring and training: Performance agreements: The key to increasing motivation. *Sales and Marketing Management 144*(2), 69–76.

Buschardt, S. C., & Schnake, M. E., (1981). Employee evaluation: Measure performance, not attitude. *Management World*, *10*(2), 41–48.

Carson, K. P., Cardy, R. L., & Dobbins, G. H. (1993). Upgrade the employee evaluation process. *Survey of Business*, *29*(1), 29–34.

Clement, R. W. (1987). Performance appraisal: Nonverbal influences on the rating process. *Review of Public Personnel Administration*, *7*(2), 14–28.

Cooperrider, D. L., Whitney, D., Stavros, J. M.., & Fry, R. (2003). *Appreciative inquiry handbook*. San Francisco: Berrett-Koehler.

Daley, D. M. (1991). Great expectations, or a tale of two systems: Employee attitudes toward graphic rating scales and MBO-based performance appraisal. *Public Administration Quarterly*, *15*(2), 188–200.

Daly, J. P., & Geyer, P. D. (1994). The role of fairness in implementing large-scale change: Employee evaluations of process and outcome in seven facility relocations. *Journal of Organizational Behavior*, *15*(7), 623–639.

Delaney, J. T., & Huselid M. A. (1996). The impact of human resource management practices on perceptions of organizational performance. *The Academy of Management Journal*, *39*(4), 949–969.

Damanpour, F. (1996). Organizational complexity and innovation: Developing and testing multiple contingency models. *Management Science*, *42*(5), 693–717.

Deming, W. E. (1981). Improvement of quality and productivity through action by management. *National Productivity Review*, *1*(1), 12–22.

DeNisi, A. S., & Stevens, G. E. (1981). Profiles of performance, performance evaluations, and personnel decisions. *Academy of Management Journal*, *24*(3), 592–613.

Dreyer, R. S. (1997). Why employee evaluations fail. *SuperVision*, *58*(7), 19–21.

Edvardsson, B., & Roos, I. (2001). Critical incident techniques: Toward a framework for analyzing the criticality of critical incidents. *International Journal of Service Industry Management*, *12*(3), 251–260.

Edwards, M. R. (1990). An alternative to traditional appraisal systems. *Supervisory Management*, *35*(6), 3.

Eyres, P. S. (1989). Legally defensible performance appraisal systems. *Personnel Journal*, *68*(7), 58–62.

Fernandez, D. R., & Perrewe, P. L. (1995). Implicit stress theory: An experimental examination of subjective performance information on employee evaluations. *Journal of Organizational Behavior*, *16*(4), 353–363.

Gifford, S. (1992). Innovation, firm size and growth in a centralized organization. *The Rand Journal of Economics*, *23*(2), 284–299.

Gliddon, D. G. (2004). Effective performance management systems. *Performance Improvement*, *43*(9), 27–34.

Gliddon, D. G. (2006). Forecasting a competency model for innovation leaders using a modified Delphi technique. Retrieved on July 30, 2008, from http://etda.libraries. psu.edu/theses/approved/WorldWideFiles/ETD-1273/Dissertation-Gliddon_Final .pdf.

Greenberg, J., & Colquitt, J. (2005). *Handbook of organizational justice*. New York: Routledge.

Greenhaus, J. H., & Parasuraman, S. (1993). Job performance attributions and career development prospects: An examination of gender and race effects. *Organizational Behavior and Human Decision Processes*, *55*(2), 273–297.

Grensing, L. (1985). How to avoid "rating errors" in employee evaluations. *Manage*, *37*(4), 6–8.

Gresh, D. L., Connors, D. P., Fasano, J. P., & Wittrock, R. J. (2007). Applying supply chain optimization techniques to workforce planning problems. *Business Optimization*, *51*(3). Retrieved July 30, 2008, from https://www.research.ibm.com/ journal/rd/513/gresh.html,.

Gruber, W. H. (1972). Pup innovation in the organizational structure. *California Management Review*, *14*(4), 29–36.

Halinen, A., & Tornoos, J. (2005). Using case methods in the study of contemporary business networks. *Journal of Business Research*, *58*(9), 1285–1297.

Harris, M. M., Ispas, D., & Schmidt, G. F. (2008). Inaccurate performance ratings are a reflection of larger organizational issues. *Industrial and Organizational Psychology*, *1*(2), 190–193.

Hirshleifer, J., Jensen, M. C., Hall, R. E., Shleifer, A., & Meckling, W. H. (1994). Economics and organizational innovation. *Contemporary Economic Policy*, *12*(2), 1–21.

Houston, R. (1995). Integrating CQI into performance appraisals. *Nursing Management*, *26*(3), 48–50.

Jones, M. E., Simonetti, J. L., & Vielhaber-Hermon.M. (2000). Building a stronger organization through leadership development at Parke-Davis Research. *Industrial and Commercial Training*, *32*(2), 44–49.

Judge, T. A., Locke, E. A., Durham, C. C., & Kluger, A. N. (1998). Dispositional effects on job and life satisfaction: The role of core evaluations. *Journal of Applied Psychology*, *83*(1) 17–34.

Kein, K. (1996). Searching 360 degrees for employee evaluation. *Incentive*, *170*(10), 40–42.

Kirkpatrick, D. L. (1998). *Evaluating training programs*. San Francisco: Berrett-Koehler.

Konovsky, M. A., & Fogel, D. S. (1988). Innovation in employee evaluation and compensation. *The Personnel Administrator, 33*(12), 92–96.

Kuczmarski, T. D. (1996). What is innovation? The art of welcoming risk. *The Journal of Consumer Marketing, 13*(5), 7–10.

Lee, Z. (1995). Bridging the gap between technology and business strategy: A pilot study on the innovation process. *Management Decision, 33*(8), 13–22.

Lewis, L. K., & Seibold, D. R. (1993). Innovation modification during intra-organizational adoption. *The Academy of Management Review, 18*(2), 322–355.

Locke, E. A., & Latham, G. P. (2002). Building a practically useful theory of goal setting and task motivation: A 35-year odyssey. *American Psychologist, 57*(9), 705–717.

Mahoney, J. T., & Sanchez, R. (2004). Evaluation process get mediocre grades. *HRMagazine, 40*(5), 14–15.

Martinez, M. N. (1995). Evaluation process gets mediocre grades. *HRMagazine, 40*(5), 14–15.

Martinsons, M. G. (1993). Strategic innovation: A lifeboat for planning in turbulent waters. *Management Decision, 31*(8), 4–12.

McNerney, D. J. (1995). Improved performance appraisals: Process of elimination. *HR Focus, 72*(7), 1–4.

Meredith, J. R., & Mantel, S. J. (2002). *Project management: A managerial approach.* Hoboken, NJ: John Wiley & Sons.

Merit, D. (1999). Evaluate performance evaluations. *American Printer, 224*(1), 164–165.

Mertins, K., Krause, O., & Schallock, B. (1999). *Global production management.* Berlin: Springer,

Meyer, A. D., & Goes, J. B. (1988). Organizational assimilation of innovations: A multilevel company. *Academy of Management Journal, 31*(4), 897–924.

Mintzberg, H. (1994). *The rise and fall of strategic planning.* Upper Saddle River, NJ: Pearson Prentice Hall.

Otley, D. (1999). Performance management: A framework. *Management Accounting Research, 10*(4), 363–382.

Pagano, A. M., & Verdin, J. (1997). *The external environment of business: Political, economic, social and regulatory.* Champaign, IL: Stipes.

Pankratz, W. (2000). Employee evaluations are a valuable tool. *Facilities and Design Management, 72*(2), 52–54.

Prather, C. W., & Turrell, M. C. (2002). Involve everyone in the innovation process. *Research Technology Management, 45*(5), 13–17.

Ripley, R. E., & Ripley, M. J. (1992). The innovation organization and behavioral technology for the 1990s. *Advanced Management Journal, 57*(4), 30–37.

Rogers, E. M. (1995). *Diffusion of innovations.* New York: The Free Press.

Roffe, I. (1999). Innovation and creativity in organisations: A review of the implications for training and development. *Journal of European Industrial Training*, *23*(4), 224–232.

Rothwell, W. J., Hohne, C. K., & King, S. B, (2007). *Human performance improvement*. Vancouver, BC: Butterworth-Heinemann.

Russel, R. D. (1990). Innovation in organizations: Toward an integrated model. *Review of Business*, *12*(2), 19–28.

Schoenecker, T. S., Daellenbach, U. S., & McCarthy, A. M. (1995). Factors affecting a firm's commitment to innovation. *Academy of Management Journal*, *38*, 52–57.

Siegel, P. H., Schraeder, M., & Morrison, R. (2008). A taxonomy of equity factors. *Journal of Applied Social Psychology*, *38*(1), 61–75.

Tannenbaum, S. I., Dupuree, B., & Group, L. M. (1994). The relationship between organizational and environmental factors and the use of innovation human resource practices. *Organization Management*, *19*(2), 171–203.

Woodford, K., & Maes, J. D. (2002). Employee performance evaluations: Administering and writing them correctly in the multi-national setting. *Equal Opportunities International*, *21*(7), 1–9.

Yalowitz, J. S., Schroer, B. J., & Ziemke, M. C. (1993). Application of Deming's principles to evaluating professional staff members in R&D services companies. *Engineering Management Journal*, *5*(1), 27–32.

Yoon, L. (2002). Employee evaluations that extend beyond the end-of-year "to-do" list improve performance. Retrieved December 18, 2002, from http://www.cfo.com.

Recommended Readings

Anonymous. (1989). Should managers be evaluated by those they manage? *Sales and Marketing Management*, *141*(9), 10–15.

Anonymous. (1991). Evaluating an employee's performance. *SuperVision*, *52*(4), 17–20.

Anonymous. (2000). Employee evaluation system can make agency more productive. *National Underwriter*, *104*(46), 8–10.

Beckert, J., & Walsh, K. (1991). Development plans replace performance reviews at Harvey Hotels. *Cornell Hotel and Restaurant Administration Quarterly*, *32*(4), 72–81.

Blanchard, K. (1994). Performance appraisals. *Executive Excellence*, *11*(10), 15–17.

Daley, D. M. (1985). An examination of the MBO/performance standards approach to employee evaluation: Attitudes toward performance appraisal in Iowa. *Review of Public Personnel Administration*, *6*(1), 11–29.

Derven, M. G. (1990). The paradox of performance appraisals. *Personnel Journal*, *69*(2), 107–110.

Flynn, G. (1995). Employee evaluations get so-so grades. *Personnel Journal*, *74*(6), 21–24.

Galin, A., & Benoliel, B. (1990). Does the way you dress affect your performance rating? *Personnel*, *67*(8), 49–53.

Hoehns, S. (1982). Why is effective employee evaluation critical? *Journal of Systems Management*, *33*(4), 25–29.

Nichols, D. (1987). Monitoring employees: When measurement goes too far. *Incentive Marketing*, *161*(12), 27–32.

Rigg, M. (1992). Reasons for removing employee evaluations from management's. *Industrial Engineering*, *24*(8), 17–18.

Ramsey, D. R. (1998). How to write better employee evaluations. *SuperVision*, *59*(6), 5–8.

Treese, M. A. (1982). Supervision by objectives: A workable approach. *SuperVision*, *44*(8), 12–16.

Webster, G. D. (1988). The law of employee evaluations. *Association Management*, *40*(5), 118–120.

PART FOUR

EDITORS' DISCUSSION

As you can see from variety of performance interventions described in this part of the book, addressing issues of Expectations and Feedback is as complex as it is critical to improving performance. From establishing realistic performance expectations among employees, supervisors, managers, and others to providing timely and specific feedback on individual, team, and organization performance, the varied performance interventions that can be used to improve this indispensable component of a complete performance system are impressive. While systemic performance management systems work to link this together in order to achieve significant results, it is also important to align your efforts related to expectations and feedback to the remaining elements of Wedman's Performance Pyramid model (for example, Capacity, Motivation, Vision, Mission and Objectives, and Culture).

As with all of the performance interventions described in this handbook, those related to expectations and feedback, while potentially effective on their own to resolve some performance issues, are most valuable when introduced as part of a comprehensive improvement system that integrates the various components of the Performance Pyramid. Through comprehensive efforts to link together interventions, such as performance measurement systems and managerial coaching, with effective interventions for addressing elements of motivation, culture, knowledge and skill, and other components of the Pyramid,

319

you can create a performance improvement system that is capable of achieving improvements at multiple levels of performance (results). As a holistic system, they can accomplish significant results—linking together individual and team products, organizational outputs, and societal outcomes within Kaufman's Organizational Element Model.

It is easy, nevertheless, to lose focus on the systemic nature of improving human and organizational performance. This is especially true when you are examining the strengths, criticisms, and processes for implementing specific performance interventions. You can easily begin to see any one intervention (whether it be realistic job previews as discussed in Chapter Eight, for example, or knowledge management as discussed in Chapter Fifteen) as *the* solution for the performance issues found in your organization. Even for experienced professionals, the appeal of individual performance interventions that they have used successfully in the past can be challenging to overcome (whether it is Incentive Systems or Outsourcing, as discussed in Chapters Eighteen and Twenty-Eight, respectively).

In response to this known risk, start by examining the complete performance system (the whole Performance Pyramid) to identify and prioritize the critical components to be addressed through specific performance interventions. Then examine the various performance interventions described in the associated parts of this handbook to determine which comprehensive set of actions can be taken to best improve performance within your organization. Analyze the role of expectations and feedback in achieving current results and desired accomplishments; then examine the many performance interventions that can be used to improve the setting of expectation and the communication of feedback in order to select which will lead to desired improvements. Likewise, systematically examine your options for each component of the Performance Pyramid. By doing this, you are effectively and systemically improving performance and building the capacity to accomplish significant results.

Reference from Editorial Contributions to Part Four

Kaufman, R., Oakley-Brown, H., Watkins, R., & Leigh, D. (2003). *Strategic planning for success: Aligning people, performance, and payoffs.* San Francisco: Jossey-Bass.

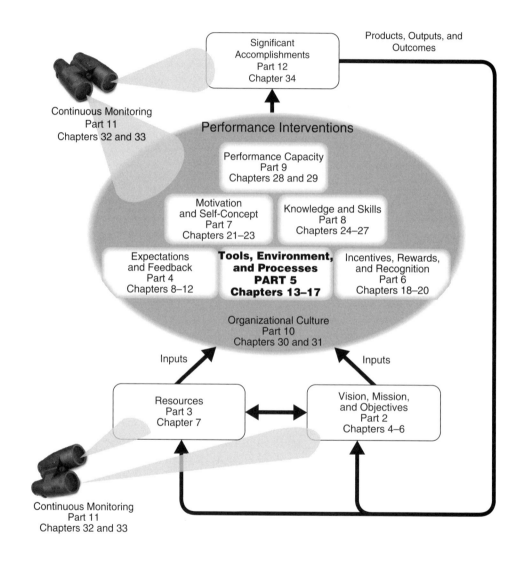

Significant
Accomplishments
Part 12
Chapter 34

Products, Outputs, and
Outcomes

Continuous Monitoring
Part 11
Chapters 32 and 33

Performance Interventions

Performance Capacity
Part 9
Chapters 28 and 29

Motivation
and Self-Concept
Part 7
Chapters 21–23

Knowledge and Skills
Part 8
Chapters 24–27

Expectations
and Feedback
Part 4
Chapters 8–12

**Tools, Environment,
and Processes
PART 5
Chapters 13–17**

Incentives, Rewards,
and Recognition
Part 6
Chapters 18–20

Organizational Culture
Part 10
Chapters 30 and 31

Inputs

Inputs

Resources
Part 3
Chapter 7

Vision, Mission,
and Objectives
Part 2
Chapters 4–6

Continuous Monitoring
Part 11
Chapters 32 and 33

PART FIVE

TOOLS, ENVIRONMENT, AND PROCESSES

Improving human and organizational performance involves the recognition that individual and team performance—a cornerstone for accomplishing significant results—happens within unique organizational contexts. From large global corporations to small family-owned businesses, every organization provides a unique context in which individuals and teams strive to accomplish valuable results. Each is a unique combination of available tools (computers, software systems, cell phones, and production equipment), support environments (managerial culture, attitudes toward change, and organizational flexibility), and applicable performance processes (rules, policies, procedures, traditions, and guiding principles).

The accomplishment of significant results is dependent on systems that integrate, and improve when necessary, the tools, environment, and processes that provide context to human and organizational performance. You would not, for instance, want to develop an incentive system (see Part Six of this handbook) around the use of new procurement software only to later learn that the software will not be available until next fiscal year or that the incentives conflict with current organizational policies.

In many situations, the root cause of performance problems lies with the lack of appropriate tools, environments that do not encourage the achievement of desired results, or processes that impede the achievement of results rather than support accomplishment. In many organizations you can find examples of performance issues related to these elements of the performance system. From human resource policies that encourage managers to give low performers satisfactory evaluations in order to prevent lawsuits, to sales teams that do not have technology access to client information when traveling, the improvement of performance is dependent on the performance interventions that comprise the tools, environment, and processes block of the Performance Pyramid.

WHAT'S COMING UP

In Chapter Thirteen, Frank Nguyen introduces electronic performance support systems (EPSS) as a powerful tool for achieving sustainable improvements in performance. An EPSS provides real-time access to resources, tools, templates, simulations, and information supporting performance, using various electronic media such as the Internet, cell phones, PDAs, DVDs, iPods, and so forth. EPSS systems offer flexible and dynamic support tools that you can use to accomplish a variety of desired results.

CHAPTER THIRTEEN

Electronic Performance Support Systems

Frank Nguyen

INTRODUCTION

The frequency with which we are unable to find the right information in a timely fashion can cause such occurrences to become viewed as commonplace, expected, and even accepted in most organizations. Electronic performance support systems (EPSS) serve as a performance improvement intervention to address this inefficiency. EPSS have been used to provide on-the-job support to automotive mechanics through the use of easily accessible technical bulletins. They have guided insurance agents in dealing with customer claims. They have been used by taxpayers to simplify the process of filing a tax return. By providing performers with tools and information when and where they are required, EPSS have been documented to enhance user performance. This chapter discusses examples from the literature illustrating how performance support has been implemented in a variety of organizations, a recommended process to implement EPSS, evidence-based guidelines, and critical success factors.

DESCRIPTION

A doctor informs a concerned parent that there is hope for his son, but he will require extensive surgery and care to fight the rare condition he has contracted. Faced with mounting medical bills, the parent pores through reams of documentation provided by his insurance carrier, searches through the company's website, and navigates through a maze of phone prompts on the carrier's 1-800 help line. He caves in frustration and contacts a customer service representative to help him understand how much financial support he can expect from his family's health insurance policy.

The insurance representative retrieves the customer's information in the account database. He then launches a separate application to locate detailed policy information. Unable to find any specifics to address the customer's question, the representative searches through a help desk knowledge base, the company intranet, and eventually asks a more senior representative for his help in locating the relevant information.

Gloria Gery, an HPT consultant, felt that this inefficiency was unnecessary; senior staff should not have to be involved in finding information that should be at the fingertips of all call center representatives. As a training manager at Aetna in the late 1980s, Gery observed that training interventions were often used to teach workarounds that could have been avoided with carefully designed work interfaces and the introduction of support to assist employees when and where they needed it. As Gery argued in her 1991 eponymous book, rather than training employees beforehand to cope with inadequate tools and processes, it would be better for performance technologists to provide the workers with "individualized online access to the full range of . . . systems to permit job performance." Gery called these performance interventions *electronic performance support systems* (EPSS).

Based on her initial work, Gery proposed three categories of performance support systems in a 1995 article (see Table 13.1). These three types differ in the level of integration between the support system and the users' work interface. For instance, *external* systems have minimal integration and therefore require the learners to stop what they are doing, find information in the EPSS, learn it, and then return to the task at hand. Meanwhile, *intrinsic* systems are so integrated into the work interface itself that users do not have to interrupt their workflow to learn. Gery described this as "They simply feel that they are just doing the work."

While Gery originally targeted EPSS as an intervention to address the alignment of software and associated procedures, a number of authors have since expanded the scope and potential application of performance support. Barry Raybould, for example, contended in a 2000 article for *Performance Improvement* that performance support is a continuum that includes constructs ranging from those embedded in the work itself, such as menus, dialogs, and on-screen instructions, to those that are separate from the work, including tutorials, computer-based training, peer support, and help desks.

In 2006's *Handbook of Human Performance Technology*, Steve Villachica and his colleagues proposed a broader definition of performance support to include "an optimized body of integrated online and off-line methods and resources

Table 13.1 Types of Electronic Performance Support Systems

Type	Definition	Examples
External	Performance support that is not integrated into the users' workspace that "requires a worker to break the work context entirely."	• Help Desk • Job Aids • Manuals • Search Engines
Extrinsic	"Performance support that is integrated with the system, but is not in the primary workspace."	• Context-Sensitive Help • Online Help
Intrinsic	"Performance support that is inherent to the system itself. It's so well integrated that, to workers, it's part of system."	• Human Factors Engineering • User Centered Design • Wizards

Source: Adapted from Gery, 1995, p. 51

providing what performers need, when they need it, in the form they need it in" (p. 540). This expanded the scope of performance support to include electronic resources such as those identified in Raybould's article, but also printed resources such as manuals, handbooks, and job aids (see Chapter Fourteen). They acknowledged the range of definitions and terminology (electronic performance support systems, performance support, EPSS, PSS, PST), but Villachica and his colleagues argued that the goal of performance support is universal: "expert-like performance from day one with little or no training" (p. 540).

Also in 2006, Allison Rossett and Lisa Schafer offered an even more expansive view of performance support to not only include tools that support performers at the moment of need, but also ones before or after the moment of performance. Conventional notions of EPSS focus on support during the work, also known as *sidekicks*. Other systems, called *planners*, support when performers are preparing to act or reflecting on a completed action.

WHAT WE KNOW FROM RESEARCH

Since its introduction more than twenty years ago, research studies have validated the notion that implementing performance support can significantly improve user performance and attitudes. In 1985 Charles Duncan published his meta-analysis of research on the application of job aids—a paper-based form of performance support—to train military personnel. Results indicated that user performance improved in twenty of the twenty-two military job aid studies conducted from 1958 through 1972. He concluded that "job aids produce more accurate performance, usually in a faster period" (p. 4).

Similarly, Dereck L. Hunt and his colleagues at McMaster University in Ontario conducted a meta-analysis in 1999 regarding performance support systems within the medical field, also known as clinical decision support systems (CDSS). They reviewed a total of sixty-eight studies in their analysis. The systems ranged in application from drug dosing and patient diagnoses to preventive care. The results indicated that user performance improved in forty-two of the studies reviewed, was not significantly changed in nineteen cases, and decreased in only seven instances. While studies on performance support systems for diagnoses and certain types of dosing were inconsistent, the researchers noted that systems for other areas such as preventive care demonstrate positive results for these systems in ambulances, clinics, and hospitals.

Moving into the assessment of electronic performance support tools, in 2004 Abbas Darabi implemented a performance support system that guided students through human performance analysis tasks. Although his study involved a very small sample size, results indicated that the participants' attitudes toward performing a successful analysis improved significantly after using the EPSS. Darabi reported a 10 percent increase in students' confidence that they could conduct a human performance analysis and 21 percent increase in confidence that they could conduct organizational and environmental analyses. By continuing to illustrate similar results as their paper-based predecessors—job aids—the research on the effectiveness of EPSS is promising.

Expanding Your Options

Social networking—the grouping of individuals into specific clusters (for example, a specific line of employment). Although social networking is possible in person, especially in schools or in the workplace, it is most popular online.

Based on whatissocialnetworking.com definition (January 2009)

I partnered with Jim Klein and Howard Sullivan in 2005 to examine the most effective types of performance support systems by testing three different types that aligned with Gloria Gery's intrinsic, extrinsic, and external EPSS categories. We provided performers different types of performance support systems (or none at all) and asked them to complete a software procedure. Our results, published in *Performance Improvement Quarterly*, indicated that performers provided with more integrated performance support such as extrinsic and intrinsic systems performed significantly better on a task compared to a control group with no EPSS. In addition, all of the performers provided with an EPSS had significantly more positive attitudes than the control group.

Research from the human factors engineering field also validates some of these results. Bailey, for instance, conducted a meta-analysis, which found that linking to support content, as one would do in an intrinsic or extrinsic performance support system, tends to be more effective than searching, as one would in an external system. To confound the difficulties with search-type external EPSS, Jakob Spool disseminated the results of his usability studies in 2001, reporting that "the more times performers searched, the less likely they were to find what they wanted" (p. 1). In fact, he observed that performers were successful in finding the correct support information 55 percent of the time on the first try. On the second search attempt, only 38 percent were successful, and none were successful on the third attempt. The same year that Spool's findings were released, Jakob Nielsen reported similar results in another study in which 51 percent were successful on the first search attempt, 32 percent on the second, and 18 percent on the third attempt.

A 1983 study by John Morrison and Bob Witmer suggests that there is no significant difference between the types of media used for external performance support systems. They examined the effectiveness of print-based and computer-based job aids for Army tank procedures. They provided one treatment group with instructions for tank gunner procedures in a printed manual, while the other received the same content in a computer program. Results indicated that there was no significant difference between the two groups in the number of errors committed by the performers or in the time it took to complete the task. This finding aligns with results from research comparing various media used for instruction. After reviewing almost seventy years' of research, the University of Southern California's Richard Clark concluded in 1983, much as Morrison and Witmer did, that there are no significant advantages between different media or technologies used for learning.

Case studies have demonstrated that performance technologists can apply EPSS to a wide range of settings and performance problems. Performance support systems have been used in educational settings. In 1993, Indiana University's Thomas Brush and his colleagues developed a performance support system to improve collaboration among teachers in rural communities. Cindy McCabe and Chet Leighton created an EPSS to help master's students with analysis and instructional design. As mentioned earlier, Abbas Darabi explained how a similar system was used to help graduate students with performance analysis.

Performance support systems have also been widely used, documented, and studied in a variety of industries. Both Dorsey, Goodrum, and Schwen's

1993 article for *Educational Technology* and Cole, Fischer, and Saltzman's 1997 article for *Communications of the ACM* applied performance support systems to support sales employees. In 1999, Huber, Lippincott, McMahon, and Witt provided three examples of how intrinsic, extrinsic, and external EPSS were applied to automobile manufacturing, insurance, and civil engineering. The following year, Kasvi and Vartiainen demonstrated four different ways EPSS were employed for use in factories. Then, in 2003, Gloria Gery cited examples of how performance support systems have been used in investment and financial planning, real estate, travel, and government applications. More recently, a survey conducted by Paul McManus and Allison Rossett in 2006 showed that performance technologists have applied EPSS to problems ranging from vessel tracking in the United States Coast Guard to coaching restaurant managers.

In addition to the performance support systems that have been developed in the past, in 2005 I published a study which examined the types of EPSS that performers may want in the future. In it, I conducted a needs assessment among employees and performance technologists in Fortune 100 companies. Results of the assessment indicated that the types of performance support systems corporate employees find useful tend to be extrinsic or external in nature. In particular, the most highly rated performance support systems were those that are aware of a user's job role or location in a software system and are then able to deliver appropriate information. External performance support systems that rely on visuals to navigate to support content, such as equipment diagrams or business processes, were also rated highly.

In summary, performance technologists can rely on the fact that performance support systems have been empirically tested to improve user performance and attitudes. Research has also demonstrated that EPSS can be applied to many different settings, and the performance support systems that are integrated and linked to work interfaces tend to be better than those that require the user to search for information.

WHEN TO APPLY

The literature illustrates how performance technologists have applied EPSS as an intervention to address many different types of performance problems in many different settings. When considering Gery's original software specific view, performance support would be an ideal intervention for:

- Performance problems that include poorly designed work interfaces or business processes;
- Performance problems that include tasks that are performed infrequently;

- When task performance makes it necessary to have access to a vast amount of information; or
- When the support information is volatile and changes frequently.

In thinking of the broader definitions of EPSS that have been proposed more recently, the potential applications for performance support expand. EPSS can be a viable intervention to help performers make decisions. For example, decision support systems (DSS) such as SelectSmart analyze users' preferences and select the right type of character, computer, dog, food, or hobby that suits their needs. Performance support can also automate complex or labor-intensive tasks. For instance, tools like Intuit's popular TurboTax software simplifies the complex task of preparing personal income taxes.

How to Apply

When choosing to use EPSS as an intervention, there are several guidelines performance technologists should follow to ensure maximum success from both a performance and cost perspective.

Combine EPSS and training as complementary information interventions. Practitioners and researchers have both reported that the implementation of performance support alongside training interventions has led to equal or improved user performance and attitudes. Consequently, performance technologists should not eliminate training entirely in favor of EPSS solutions. Performance problems that include tasks that are performed frequently, or where there are serious consequences for incorrect task performance, are best delivered through up-front training. In addition, to support adoption of EPSS once performers return to the job, performance technologists should consider ways to incorporate the use of the EPSS into training programs. For example, learners could complete practice activities using the tools that may be available to them in the workplace including performance support. Curious readers are encouraged to review published works by Bastiaens and his colleagues (1997), Chase (1998), Mao & Brown (2005), and Nguyen & Klein (2008).

Vary the volume of performance support and associated training interventions as performers gain expertise. As performers master their jobs through training or experience, they develop mental models of the tasks and information used in their work. As their mastery grows, their requirements and motivation to take time away from their jobs and attend formal training events diminish. At the same time, their ability to search for and locate the information they need to address issues in their content domain increases. Figure 13.1, which I adapted in 2006 based on a *Performance Improvement Quarterly* article by Gloria Gery, illustrates the notion that up-front training should comprise a more significant portion of the information interventions provided to novice performers. Meanwhile, the quantity of performance support systems can be increased to provide

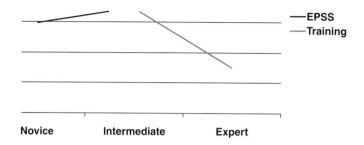

Figure 13.1 Expertise Reversal Applied to EPSS and Training Interventions.
Source: Nguyen, 2006, p. 10

more advanced performers access to larger databases as they increase the scope and complexity of their work.

Integrate performance support into the work. That performance support content should be embedded as deeply into the work as possible has been argued by many authors, for instance, Bailey (2003), Carroll and Rosson (1987), Gery (1995), Nguyen, Klein, and Sullivan (2005), and Raybould (2000). By doing so, the amount of work required for the performer to find the right information to perform a task is reduced. At the same time, the likelihood that the performer will locate the correct information increases, and the disruption to the performer's workflow is reduced or eliminated. Higher use of more integrated forms of EPSS—as compared to those that required the performer to search for information—was also reported within my 2005 article with Jim Klein and Howard Sullivan.

Vary the type of electronic performance support systems offered to performers based on their level of expertise. This notion has been consistently supported across the 2001 studies by Nielsen and Spool, as well as Bailey's 2003 study. When novice learners are presented with a non-integrated performance support system, such as a search engine, they often do not know where to start and struggle to find the correct support information. As performers gain expertise and their mental models for their job domains grow, their ability to find information and cope with the demands of such non-integrated systems also increases. While such advanced performers may still benefit from more integrated EPSS, the extra cost involved with such systems may not be justified. As a result, performance technologists should vary the type of EPSS offered to homogenous groups of novice or advanced performers. For mixed audiences, it is wise to provide EPSS that is integrated into the workflow.

Stress electronic performance support systems as first-level support during on-the-job training. As performers are introduced to the workplace or to a new task in an existing work setting, provide them with immediate access to an intuitive and integrated EPSS to help them learn how to perform while on the job. While other common OJT support interventions should continue to exist, such as coaches and mentors (see Chapters Eleven and Twenty-Six), encourage performers to use the EPSS as their first resource for support. By doing so, performers will learn to rely on the EPSS longer term after the additional support has been removed.

Provide performers with access to a broad range of content and resources through EPSS. Performers do not care about where support information comes from; they are simply concerned with quickly finding the most relevant content to address their immediate needs. So look to leverage content from knowledge management systems, publish job aids online for immediate access, and locate any relevant information in eLearning courses. Doing so will bring the support that the performer needs closer to the work and eliminate content redundancies that may occur between the different interventions.

STRENGTHS AND CRITICISMS

There are a number of documented benefits for implementing EPSS including:

- Increased performance;
- Improved user attitudes; and
- Reduction in monetary costs.

Less tangible advantages include the ability to:

- Provide performers with memory support particularly for infrequent tasks;
- Rapidly provide a broad group of performers with the updated information; and
- Expose performers to a broader spectrum of support content that is not possible or practical to provide during training.

However, performance support is not without its share of disadvantages:

- Since very few vendors specialized in performance support until recently, early adopters were often forced to develop custom systems, which led to expensive implementation and sustaining costs.
- Electronic performance support systems are often one of a number of training and support-related systems within a larger organization's infrastructure. Content developed in an EPSS is typically isolated from the other enterprise systems, often forcing the development of redundant content.

- Some have also criticized the fact that performers are not forced to learn or master the content delivered by an EPSS. In a sense, rather than growing their knowledge and expertise, performers can become dependent on real-time support tools.

RECOMMENDED DESIGN, DEVELOPMENT, AND IMPLEMENTATION PROCESS

Figure 13.2 illustrates a process that performance technologists can use to design, develop, and implement EPSS. Phases 1 and 2 of the process focus on the steps involved in performance analysis and needs assessment once EPSS has been identified and selected as an intervention. Because these steps are documented elsewhere within this book, the remainder of this chapter will focus on Phases 3 through 5 of the EPSS process.

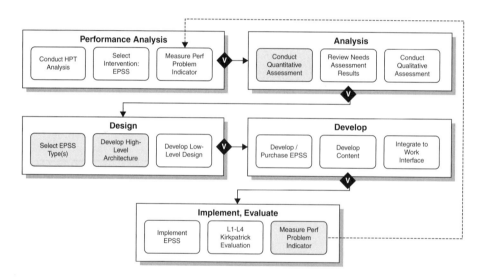

Figure 13.2 A Practitioner's Model for Designing EPSS.

Source: Nguyen and Woll, 2006, p. 38

Phase 3: EPSS Design

Step 3.1: Select EPSS Type. After collecting the requisite analysis information, the next phase in the performance support design process is to use this data to inform the design of the EPSS. Arguably the most important yet most often neglected step in the EPSS design process is the careful and deliberate selection of the appropriate type of performance support system. As mentioned earlier, a performance technologist should generally strive to integrate performance support into the workflow depending on the performers' level of expertise.

It is also important to note that, under certain circumstances, performance technologists may choose to implement more than one type of system. Integrated performance support solutions may not be possible in all circumstances or may prove too costly to build. For example, the root cause of your customer's performance problem may be related to an off-the-shelf software application. Because the software was purchased from a vendor, the interface may be compiled in a way that prevents modifications required by integrated EPSS. In addition, certain workers, such as those in factories, warehouses, or repair centers, perform tasks that are not primarily computer-based. In fact, they may not have immediate access to computers, making it inconvenient or impossible to use electronic forms of performance support. As Raybould noted in 2000, "When a particular [EPSS] proves infeasible, practitioners may need to look at less-embedded support systems" (p. 35).

Step 3.2: Develop High-Level Architecture. Once the type (or types) of performance support systems have been selected, the next step in the process is to develop a high-level architecture. In an article I wrote with Craig Woll in 2006 for *Performance Improvement* journal, we identified the basic components that should to be considered when designing an EPSS: the performance problem, the end-user, the type of electronic device (if any) that can be used to access the performance support system while on the job, the EPSS or work interface that will be used to access the support content, and the databases or content repositories that can be accessed from the EPSS. Figure 13.3 illustrates

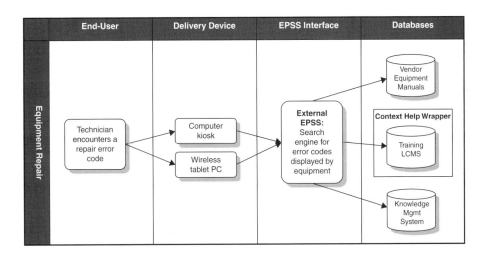

Figure 13.3 EPSS Architecture Example.

Source: Nguyen and Woll, 2006, p. 43

an example of the architecture of an EPSS. Findings from the analysis phase will affect this high-level architecture. For example, you may uncover during the environmental analysis that performers all have access to notebook computers or iPods, which can be candidates for the EPSS delivery device. Alternatively, they may not have access to any electronic device at all. You may also find that performers commonly use a company intranet site. You can take advantage of this existing adoption and integrate a performance support system.

Upon completing an initial version of the architecture, it is not unusual to change the selected performance support systems. For example, the needs assessment data may suggest that users require access to more content repositories than the work interface can realistically support. To accommodate this, a practitioner may choose to integrate certain content into the work interface. The remaining content may be accessed externally through an FAQ or search engine.

Step 3.3: Develop Low-Level Design. The next step in the process is to define in more detail the design of the performance support system. The goal of this activity is to develop a design of sufficient detail so that an EPSS that will address the identified performance problem can be built or purchased.

Phase 4: EPSS Development

Step 4.1: Develop/Purchase EPSS. Once the design for the EPSS has been completed, the next phase in the performance support process is to use the design to build a system, purchase an off-the-shelf EPSS tool that meets the design requirements, or adapt an existing system to the current performance problem.

Where possible, it may be more cost-effective to purchase vendor-developed software packages to support your performance support system design. A comprehensive list of EPSS tools is available from the EPSS Central website (whose URL is located at the end of this chapter).

It is quite common for an EPSS design to require a system that does not currently exist or that cannot be met by off-the-shelf software. Such circumstances are particularly likely for highly integrated performance support such as intrinsic systems. In these instances, organizations are forced to pursue a custom-developed performance support system.

Step 4.2: Develop Content. It may also be necessary to develop new content to support users on the job and store in a database or repository. For example, if your EPSS is designed to assist performers in using a new software application, you will likely need to develop procedures to support the performers' use of the system. To optimize project timing and resources, this step could be done in parallel with the preceding EPSS development step. In addition, materials developed for the purposes of performance support could be leveraged for training interventions or vice versa. Content delivered during training can also be repurposed in an EPSS and redelivered to performers on the job.

Step 4.3: Integrate to Work Interface. For integrated EPSS designs, it is necessary to integrate support directly into the work interface. It is sometimes helpful to consult with a usability expert, human factors engineer, or industrial engineer. By doing so, the human performance technologist can determine potential problem areas, opportunities for interface redesign, and other strategic locations in the work interface to integrate performance support content. Even in external performance support designs, it may be helpful to provide a link in the users' work interface to the EPSS. This is often seen in software applications that provide a "Help" button that launches an external search engine, "frequently asked questions" page, or help index.

Phase 5: EPSS Implementation and Evaluation

The implementation and evaluation of the EPSS occurs following the development. In reality, the foundation for both implementation and evaluation are laid long before the end of the project. During the analysis phase, the metrics that will be referenced in the evaluation should be created and validated by stakeholders. The population that would use the EPSS as an intervention should be identified, and an assessment of their needs should be performed. A sample from that audience should be carefully selected to represent the population. This same sample or a small audience of choice was likely used during functional testing of the EPSS. During implementation, emphasis must be placed on communication, training, change management, support, and marketing of the system. Each component plays an important role in the adoption of the performance support system by employees.

During evaluation, baseline data collected during the analysis phase should be compared with data collected during implementation and at predefined intervals for some time after implementation. Success and/or failure of the system to meet the predetermined success criteria should be reported out to the key stakeholders. This will not only help guide continuous improvement of the system, but it will also act as a reference point for future performance analyses to determine if EPSS is the right intervention.

CRITICAL SUCCESS FACTORS

In following the recommended EPSS process, there are several factors a performance technologist must consider to ensure maximum success and adoption of performance support as an intervention.

Social. In addition to implementing the system, a performance technologist should consider the people who will use it. Performance support is only effective when it provides timely, relevant, and current content. Even if performers are able to quickly locate the information they require for task performance, if that information is not correct, they will likely be unable to perform the task correctly. Performance technologists should provide tools and processes whereby performers can identify information that is not correct, report it for prompt revision, or even edit the content on their own as one would with Web 2.0 tools such as blogs, podcasts, and wikis. If such mechanisms are not provided, the performer will be less likely to use the EPSS for future support needs and may tell co-workers about unpleasant experiences in the use of the EPSS. No single factor will drive down adoption of the intervention sooner than poor perception of the EPSS among performers.

Political. With a robust EPSS and process in place to sustain the support content, a performance technologist's task of driving adoption among performers should be relatively easy. It is still generally a good idea to develop and execute a transition change management (TCM) plan to make performers aware of the system, benefits to them, and how to use it.

However, the change management strategy should not only target performers but others as well: performance technologists, trainers, information technology (IT) managers, software developers, and any others who are involved in providing tools or information to aid performers. For example, both performance technologists and trainers are critical to the selection of EPSS to address performance problems as well as integration of EPSS into training curricula and TCM plans. Information technology managers and the developers that create the organization's software must be also be educated on the potential benefits of integrating performance support into work interfaces, including improved worker performance, decreased training time, and decreased IT support costs.

Economic. The most obvious costs to selecting EPSS as an intervention are the hardware and software expenses involved with the system itself. Performance support systems require servers to host software that can either be purchased or developed as a custom effort. Such costs should be calculated and funded to provide baseline success. There are other longer-term costs that should also be considered. The time or money involved with ongoing revision and maintenance of support content must be allocated. In addition, if your EPSS design calls for integration into work interfaces, funding for developers to modify new existing software to build links to the relevant support content must be secured. Hassan Altalib's 2002 article provides a comprehensive approach to calculate the cost and return on investment for EPSS.

Legal. The currency of support content is not only a social and economic factor but in some cases a legal requirement. The advent of the Sarbanes-Oxley Act (SOx) of 2002 has placed compliance with government mandates around data quality, intellectual property, and integration at the forefront of many organizations. Depending on the type of content stored in the EPSS, it may be subject to SOx or other legal controls and regulations. In addition, any performance support systems provided by federal agencies are subject to the Rehabilitation Act of 1998.

More commonly known as Section 508, this act legally requires electronic and information technology, including EPSS, to be made accessible to those with disabilities.

Technical. Electronic performance support in its strictest interpretation implies that performers should receive on-the-job support using some form of electronic device. Gloria Gery's original focus on software procedures made this requirement trivial: performers are already in front of computers. However, when performance technologists extend EPSS to other settings—such as supporting technicians repairing equipment in a factory, warehouse employees driving forklifts, or military mechanics servicing aircraft—one cannot assume that performers will have such access. In these instances, performance technologists must select, procure, and deploy electronic devices. Such candidates include computer workstations placed strategically throughout a factory, laptop computers issued to sales representatives in the field, or even mobile devices such as Smartphones, personal digital assistants, portable game devices, and MP3 players.

SUMMARY

A doctor uses a support system to match his patient's symptoms with a broad database of common and rare medical conditions. In a short period of time, she is able to identify the illness and treatment options. The tool also links the doctor to recent research and practitioner reports on the success of various treatments.

The doctor informs a concerned parent about the situation and provides him with access to the same information so that he can educate himself. Faced with mounting medical bills, the parent accesses his insurance carrier's online help system to determine the amount of financial support he can expect. The system identifies the diagnosed illness, common treatments, and policy coverage for each treatment. It also recommends other related websites and support groups for those afflicted with the same condition.

While scenarios such as this may be more often fantasy than reality, electronic performance support systems have the ability to transform otherwise frustrating and time-consuming experiences into timely and efficient performance. By providing support at the moment of need, performance technologists can rely on EPSS to be a powerful intervention to address a broad range of performance problems.

References

Altalib, H. (2002). ROI calculations for electronic performance support systems. *Performance Improvement, 41*(10), 12–22.

Bailey, B. (2003). Linking vs. searching: guidelines for use [Electronic version]. Retrieved January 17, 2006, from http://www.webusability.com/article_linking_vs_searching_2_2003.htm.

Bastiaens, T. J., Nijhof, W. J., Streumer, J. N, & Abma, H. J. (1997). Working and learning with electronic performance support systems: an effectiveness study. *International Journal of Training and Development, 1*(1), 72–78.

Brush, T., Knapczyk, D., & Hubbard, L. (1993). Developing a collaborative performance support system for practicing teachers. *Educational Technology, 33*(11), 39–45.

Carroll, J. M., & Rosson, M. B. (1987). Paradox of the active user. In J. M. Carroll (Ed.), *Interfacing thought: Cognitive aspects of human-computer interaction* (pp. 80–11), Boston: Bradford Books/MIT Press.

Chase, N. (1998). Electronic support cuts training time [Electronic version]. *Quality Magazine*. Retrieved January 12, 2005, from http://openacademy.mindef.gov.sg/OpenAcademy/Learning Resources/EPSS/c16.htm.

Clark, R. E. (1983). Reconsidering research on learning from media. *Review of Educational Research, 53*(4), 445–459.

Cole, K., Fischer, O., & Saltzman, P. (1997). Just-in-time knowledge delivery. *Communications of the ACM, 40*(7), 49–53.

Cross, J. (2007). Whatever happened to performance support [Electronic version]. Retrieved December 26, 2007, from http://www.internettimegroup.com.

Darabi, A. (2004). Contributions of an electronic performance support system to learning a complex cognitive skill. In K. Morgan & M. J. Spector (Eds.), *The internet society: Advances in learning, commerce, and security* (pp. 215–225). Billerica, MA: WIT Press.

Dorsey, L. T., Goodrum, D. A., & Schwen, T.M. (1993). Just-in-time knowledge performance support: A test of concept. *Educational Technology, 33*(11), 21–29.

Duncan, C. S. (1985). Job aids really can work: A study of the military application of job aid technology. *Performance & Instruction, 24*(4), 1–4.

Gery, G. (1991). *Electronic performance support systems*. Tolland, MA: Gery Associates.

Gery, G. (1995). Attributes and behaviors of performance-centered systems. *Performance Improvement Quarterly, 8*(1), 47–93.

Gery, G. (2003). Ten years later: A new introduction to attributes and behaviors and the state of performance-centered systems. In G. J. Dickelman (Ed.), *EPSS revisited: A lifecycle for developing performance-centered systems* (pp. 1–3). Silver Spring, MD: ISPI.

Huber, B., Lippincott, J., McMahon, C., & Witt, C. (1999). Teaming up for performance support: A model of roles, skills and competencies. *Performance Improvement Quarterly, 38*(1), 10–14.

Hunt, D. L., Haynes, R. B., Hanna, S. E., & Smith, K. (1999). Effects of computer-based clinical decision support systems on physician performance and patient outcomes: A systematic review. *Journal of the American Medical Association, 280*(15), 1360–1361.

Kasvi, J. J., & Vartiainen, M. (2000). Performance support on the shop floor. *Performance Improvement, 39*(6), 40–46.

Mao, J., & Brown, B. (2005). The effectiveness of online task support versus instructor-led training. *Journal of Organizational and End User Computing, 17*(3), 27–46.

McCabe, C., & Leighton, C. (2002). Developing best practices for knowledge work: ISD plus KM, supported by software [Electronic version]. *The eLearning Developers Journal*. Retrieved August 13, 2002, from http://www.elearningguild.com.

McManus, P., & Rossett, A. (2006). Performance support tools delivering value when and where it is needed. *Performance Improvement*, *45*(2), 8–16.

Morrison, J. E., & Witmer, B. G. (1983). A comparative evaluation of computer-based and print-based job performance aids. *Journal of Computer-Based Instruction*, *10*(3), 73–75.

Nguyen, F. (2005). Oops, I. forgot how to do that: A needs assessment of electronic performance support systems. *Performance Improvement*, *44*(9), 33–39.

Nguyen, F. (2006). What you already know does matter: Expertise and electronic performance support systems. *Performance Improvement*, *45*(4), 9–12.

Nguyen, F., & Hanzel, M. (2007). Linking vs. searching: a case study of performance support use. *Performance Improvement*, *46*(10), 40–44.

Nguyen, F. & Klein, J.D. (2008). The effect of performance support and training as performance interventions. *Performance Improvement Quarterly*.

Nguyen, F., Klein, J. D., & Sullivan, H. (2005). A comparative study of electronic performance support systems. *Performance Improvement Quarterly*, *18*(4), 71–86.

Nguyen, F., & Woll, C. (2006). A practitioner's guide for designing performance support systems. *Performance Improvement*, *45*(9), 37–45.

Nielsen, J. (2001). Search: Visible and simple [Electronic version]. *Alertbox*. Retrieved March 19, 2006, from http://www.useit.com/alertbox/20010513.html.

Raybould, B. (2000). Building performance-centered web-based systems, information systems, and knowledge management systems in the 21st century. *Performance Improvement*, *39*(6), 69–79.

Rossett, A., & Schafer, L. (2006). *Job aids and performance support*. San Francisco: Pfeiffer.

Spool, J. M. (2001). Performers don't learn to search better [Electronic version]. Retrieved April 3, 2005, from http://www.uie.com/articles/learn_to_search.

Villachica, S. W., Stone, D. L., & Endicott, J. E. (2006). Performance support systems. In J. Pershing (Ed.), *Handbook of human performance technology: Improving individual and organizational performance worldwide* (3rd ed.) (pp. 539–566). San Francisco: Pfeiffer.

Recommended Readings and Websites

Dickelman, G. J. (2003). *EPSS revisited: A lifecycle for developing performance-centered systems*. Silver Spring, MD: ISPI.

Gery, G. (1991). *Electronic performance support systems*. Tolland, MA: Gery Associates.

Gery, G. (1995). Attributes and behaviors of performance-centered systems. *Performance Improvement Quarterly*, *8*(1), 47–93.

EPSS Central @ http://www.epsscentral.info

EPSS Central Awards & Samples @ http://www.epsscentral.info/knowledgebase/
awardssamples/

PCD Innovations @ http://www.pcd-innovations.com

Select Smart DSS @ http://www.selectsmart.com

 # EDITORIAL CONNECTIONS

Supporting desired performance by providing beneficial resources and information at the time of individual or team performance is not a new idea. Databases, blueprints, checklists, and job aids of many varieties have been used to support performance for years (see Chapter Fourteen). What *is* new is that electronic performance support systems (EPSS) make performance support tools available in a variety of flexible and dynamic media that people can use at the time and location of performance. Sometimes this might be a video on how to perform a task; at other times it might be an electronic checklist that registers the completion of each sub-task along the way. At yet other times, the EPSS may include simulations that employees can use to determine the likely consequences of their decisions before they make decisions. As you can see, the optional resources and information that can be included make EPSS a very dynamic performance intervention.

Expanding Your Options

Communication models—existing frameworks for the exchange of information within an organization.

While an EPSS can support performance in the workplace through the use of new and emerging technologies, many improvement efforts can benefit from lower-cost solutions such as job aids that also support the achievement of desired results. These often low-tech tools represent a very effective, yet often overlooked, performance intervention that can accomplish significant results with relatively few resources. From simple process flowcharts or checklists to more complex decision algorithms, job aids can capture information in useful formats that can be used.

WHAT'S COMING UP

Job aids, or "performance aids" as Miki Lane reconstitutes them in Chapter Fourteen, range from signs and checklists to price matrices and drawings on the floor. Each of these represents low-tech performance interventions that can significantly improve results by providing people with reminders and on-the-job learning tools. Performance aids can, and should, be considered whenever you are improving performance due both to both their low costs and their tremendous performance potential.

CHAPTER FOURTEEN

Performance Aids

Miki Lane

INTRODUCTION

Job aids are dead! Job aids are dead! Long live performance aids!

Now for all of you who have used or still use job aids, please don't burn this chapter. While the title may be provocative, I postulate that the term "job aids" has become genericised, much like the term Kleenex. "Job aid" has become a term used when describing most any performance aid, even if it has nothing to do with on-the-job performance. While job aids have focused on providing the worker with specific knowledge and skills to complete the immediately required job task, performance aids are any one of a number of different interventions specifically designed to remove barriers to, as well as facilitate performance. So I suggest that we call them performance aids to more accurately reflect the all-encompassing usage they now enjoy.

Those of you who are not familiar with performance aids may have wondered how a busy and harried waitress with over thirty customers remembers to not only bring your decaf coffee but also remembers to refill your cup with decaf? When you are on board a flight between New York and Los Angeles, have you wondered how the pilot remembers the hundreds of required pre-flight checks that ensure the safety of all the passengers? The simple answer to these questions is *performance aids*. While you may think that performance aids are relatively new to our environment, it can be argued that prehistoric cave drawings were a form of job aid that helped new learners visualize hunting strategies and locations.

In this chapter we will look at the history, current usage, and development of performance aids. We will also examine the learning multiplying effect of combining performance aids with other performance interventions listed in this book.

DESCRIPTION

We all have favorite performance aid stories, and mine comes from two different dry cleaners in my neighborhood. When I went to the first cleaner, a new employee was evidently learning the job. There was one person in front of me in the process of dropping off his cleaning. The new employee was trying to calculate the ticket, which included some pants to be cleaned, shirts to launder, and a suit that had a wine stain. He looked at the bill book, wrote some numbers down, and gave an outrageous price to the customer. The customer complained and the owner of the establishment came over to rectify the situation. He said to the employee; "You have this all wrong . . . remember when we learned the pricing yesterday . . . the pants are . . . ." He then proceeded to review the pricing structure on the spot. This was repeated when it was my turn. Two weeks later I went to a different cleaner with an armful of a variety of items for both dry cleaning and laundering and my ticket was calculated, accurately, within a couple of seconds. I asked the employee how long she had been working there and she said that she doesn't work there; she was just filling in for a friend for the day. When I said that I was surprised at how efficient she was, she pointed to a chart on the wall that I hadn't noticed. It was a matrix that listed all of the calculations for single or multiple pieces of clothing for both cleaning and laundering. All she had to do was to count up my items, look at the list and complete the bill. The matrix even listed special situations like stains, alterations, silk, and leather. I remembered the previous cleaner and saw that this was a wonderful example of instant performance without training.

It may have surprised you earlier that cave drawings can be construed as early performance aids, but man has been leaving messages to decode since he could make a permanent mark in his environment. When the message to be decoded has task performance implications, it can be defined as a performance aid. We have all been exposed to and have used these "mind mnemonics" for as long as we can remember. It is part of our shared cultural and genetic heritage.

> **Expanding Your Options**
>
> *Labeling and color-coding*—simple, yet often overlooked, the labeling or color-coding of the tools, equipment, document, folders, and other resources used by employees can significantly improve performance at little cost.

Let's take the example of a trail in the woods. Originally trails were marked (blazed) to show a path from one location to another. Perhaps the initial marking was made just to ensure that the marker or "trailblazer" would not travel in circles and could get to a new place or back to his original location. Different trailblazers used different markings and a subsequent traveler needed to learn to follow whatever marking was used on that trail. Eventually, travelers learned to look for any markings in the woods that would lead them to the desired destination. What was learned was not to follow a specific marking, but to follow the concept of marking whether it was a cut in a tree, a wooden disk, a painted stripe or a sign that said "Bridge Out."

Similar to the notion of trail markings, it is not what specific job aid is used, it is the concept of performance aids that is important. The critical part of trail marking in relation to performance aids is that it is much better to follow a trail of red painted dots on trees than to remember: "Oh, you want to get to the next town . . . well you walk into the woods for 100 yards, turn right at the fourth poplar tree, then head east for a mile until you come to a stream. Cross the stream, turn left at the big rock and head north . . . you can't miss it!" Well, of course, you miss it unless you have a phenomenal memory and can visualize the directions from the description. That is why performance aids are so important: they are external tools that help you accomplish a task or procedure.

Harold Stolovitch and Erica Keeps define performance aids in 2006's *Beyond Training Ain't Performance Fieldbook* as "anything that improves job performance by guiding, facilitating, or reminding performers what to do in accomplishing job tasks." They further state that performance aids are one category in a group of non-learning interventions which are

> "Actions or events designed to change conditions that facilitate attainment of performance (for example, eliminates an inefficient procedure, removes a physical obstacle to facilitate the flow of goods, or reduces a level of supervision that hampers rapid decision making) or adds a facilitative element to the performance system (for example, provides more efficient, safer tools; introduces a new procedure that speeds up order processing; or adds speed bumps to reduce accidents) qualifies as a non-learning intervention."

Many of the other categories of non-learning interventions are discussed in other chapters of this book.

Currently, there are two opposing viewpoints of the efficacy of performance aids. In 1979, Gagné and Briggs defined learning as acquiring knowledge and skills to change behavior. It can be argued that providing a pilot a safety checklist before a flight ensures correct performance of the safety check without having the pilot learn anything new that changes his or her behavior. But it can be equally argued that the constant, required use of the performance aid causes the pilot to think in a safety-focused process that will change the way he or she reacts in emergency situations. In this case the performance aid can work as a prompt or scaffolding to effect a change in the pilot's behavior. Going back to the trailblazer analogy, following a particular performance aid (trail marking) can lead the performer to learn to look for markings (whatever they might be) whenever they head out on a trail.

Some, however, argue that the constant use of performance aids in completing tasks might have just the opposite effect and cause the performer to always rely on the performance aid to perform the task. Like an automaton, the performer would then never use the experience to acquire new knowledge and skills that would eventually lead to a change in the performer's behavior. Indeed, Doug Leigh, editor and contributing author of this book, provides a personal experience he and his wife have had in using a global positioning satellite (GPS) system in their automobile: "We certainly get from point A to B (and often many interesting waypoints along the route), but we have the growing sense that that we are not learning the gestalt of the map . . . a matter which impairs not only our driving, but our development of familiarity with our surroundings."

Both of these viewpoints are valid and dependent on the specific situation. To explore this point and see the relationship to theories of human performance improvement, let's now look at performance aids in greater detail.

Like anything that has had a long life, performance aids have evolved considerably over the years. Technology has changed the scope, design, development, and implementation of performance aids. Today performance aids are also categorized with both electronic performance support systems (EPSSs) and performance support tools (PSTs). As Marci Paino and Allison Rossett note in their 2008 *Performance Improvement* journal article, "EPSSs and PSTs are terms used more or less interchangeably to describe technological tools that help people make decisions, plan for activities, and perform tasks." They are a natural extension of performance aids based on the capability of technology to advance the field. Performance aids, PSTs, and EPSSs are all external to the performer and provide information and instructions for completing tasks that do not have to be memorized (see Chapter Thirteen).

Since other chapters in this book will look at EPSSs and PSTs in much more detail, this chapter focuses on their antecedent, but still relevant, performance helper: performance aids. Performance aids in relation to improving performance at work are anything that helps the performer succeed in achieving the required results. This help can take the form of facilitating the task, guiding the accomplishment of the task, or simply reminding the performer what to do. Let's look at finalizing the definition of performance aids that we will use in the rest of the chapter.

Performance aids have "critical attributes" and "variable attributes." In their 1992 book *Teaching Concepts*, M. David Merrill and his colleagues described a critical attribute as a characteristic of the concept that must be present in all examples of the concept, while variable attributes can be useful for distinguishing one performance aid from another. The critical attributes of performance aids are

- The performer must use the performance aid during performance of the task;
- The performer must already have all of the knowledge and skills required to use the performance aid;
- The performer must have all of the skills and knowledge necessary for accomplishing the task solely using the performance aid;
- The performance aid must either contain the instructions for using the performance aid or be self-evident; and
- The performer must be able to use the performance aid without external instruction.

Often, the sum of the critical attributes translates into a good definition of the concept. So in this case we can define a performance aid as:

A performance tool that provides information during the performance of a task that the performer needs to complete the task. In order to use it effectively the performer must already have the knowledge and skills to both use the performance aid and complete the task. The performance aid must be able to be used without external instruction.

Variable attributes that are useful for differentiating related concepts and approaches can relate to:

- Content (work procedures, safety requirements, organizational tasks, etc.);
- Size (three to four lines of text, one page, several pages, etc.);
- Design (color, pictures, drawings, graphic elements); and
- Family (checklists, tables, etc.).

While all of the variables are important, the family that the performance aid belongs to ultimately determines how the end-user will employ it. To the designer of the performance aid, the family choice is usually made after a thorough user and task analysis. Different performance aid families can include:

- Flowcharts or algorithms;
- Examples or models of the completed task;
- Text-based procedures;
- Tables;
- Text or picture lists; or
- Checklists.

To provide a clearer idea of the performance aid families, let's look at each one and discuss how they are used, how they can be constructed and what an example might look like.

Flowcharts or Algorithms

The terms flowchart and algorithm can be used interchangeably. Most people are familiar with what one looks like. It usually depicts, in a graphical format, a procedure for accomplishing a task. There is a language of flowcharts, complete with representational symbols that let the user know when to start, when to input something, when to process something, when a decision has to be made, when to move to another part of the procedure, and when to end.

Novices or experts typically use flowcharts or algorithms equally well. They do, however, lend themselves more to procedures that have multiple actions and multiple decisions that lead the performer to a wide range of results. As such they tend to be used extensively by expert performers. Imagine that you are an expert in a particular procedure. You have all of the prerequisite knowledge and skills to accomplish any task related to that procedure. To accomplish any task that you have not committed to memory, all you would need is a flowchart on that specific procedure. If you were not an expert, you would need more information than the flowchart could provide. That additional information could include: definitional issues regarding what appears in the flowchart, the conceptual issues that the terms presented refer to, the "language" of the symbols of the flowchart, and any other information required by the flowchart novice. So the greater the expertise of your performers, the more likely it is that their preferred performance aids would be flowcharts or algorithms.

Flowcharts and algorithms have been used from everything from simple tasks, like setting a personal video recorder, to highly complex ones like shutting down a nuclear reactor. Construction of a flowchart or algorithm is similar in design and development to that of all the families of performance aids. The example in Figure 14.1 demonstrates a job aid for a company-wide performance improvement process.

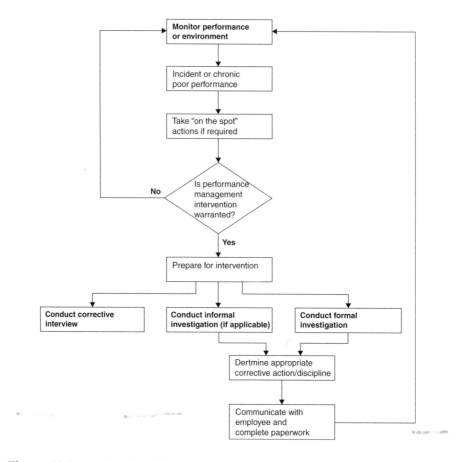

Figure 14.1 Sample Job Aid for a Company-Wide Performance Improvement Process.

Examples or Models of the Completed Task

Have you ever tried to put together a 1,000-piece jigsaw puzzle? What is it that helps you with the process? It is the picture on the box cover of the completed puzzle. Can you imagine the difficulty you would have in constructing the puzzle just by listening to someone describing the scene you were to reproduce? It would be close to impossible.

The picture serves as a model or example of the finished task. It is used to help the novice performer achieve the required task performance without intervention. Models or examples can be specific to the task, exact replicas of the finished product, or more general in nature. They provide the form and parts of the finished product or task, within which the performer replaces the general content with the task-specific content. Application forms, sample proposals, do-it-yourself legal forms, all are examples of this family of perform-ance aids. In using them, the performer either fills in the blanks or replaces the example content with his or her own content. The end result is a completed task or product that meets specified criteria.

Models can also be graphical representations of ideas and concepts, such as the International Society for Performance Improvement's the Human Performance Technology Model. While models may sometimes look like flowcharts or algorithms, they differ in that they are not the procedure outlining how to complete the final task, but are examples of what the final task might look like. Using a model or example leaves accomplishing the final task to the previously attained skills and knowledge of the performer.

Table 14.1 presents an example of a model that is a worksheet template for developing competencies. This completed worksheet shows one example of an

Table 14.1 Worksheet Example of Commitment to Action

Competency to develop:	Delegate and empower staff
Developmental goals:	• Be able to delegate easily and effectively • Be able to empower direct reports to reduce their dependency on me for routine tasks

Developmental Actions

Developmental Strategy	Actions I Will Take	Resources I Will Use	Target Dates
Self-study	Read up on delegating	Articles and blogs on the Internet; order self-help books from amazon.com	Immediate and ongoing
Training	Attend the next series of in-house supervisory workshops	HR to register and my manager for okay	Last two weeks of May
Learn on the job	Practice delegating with a direct report and assess the results	Delegate the stats report to Sam Brown	Over the next two weeks
Coaching	Ask other supervisors to show me how they delegate and get feedback on how I do	Jim Hawes and Betty Lewis in production	As soon as they are able

action in each type of strategy. In your own plan, you may have several actions in one or two strategies, and none in others. It will depend on the competency to be developed and the resources that you have available to you.

Text-Based Procedures

How to use your new digital camera, how to make your grandmother's lasagna, and how to troubleshoot a computer problem: all are examples of text-based procedures. Any situation that calls for performers to carry out without error a task or procedure that they do not often perform is a candidate for this family of performance aids.

What makes text-based procedures useful is that they prevent errors of omission. If you are following the instructions of an expert in completing a task, the expert may take a step in the procedure for granted and inadvertently leave it out or modify it. Documenting the process in a text-based procedure may not help prevent that problem from occurring, but it will make the revision process easier and more accurate.

A text-based procedure is a list of the steps required to reach the desired outcome. It outlines both the way to do it (required behaviors) and what the results (accomplishments) should be. If the desired results are not achieved, then it is likely that either a step was missed in writing the procedure, a step was done incorrectly, or a fault occurred in the equipment. Table 14.2 illustrates a text-based procedure.

What makes constructing this performance aid different from other families of performance aids is the total reliance on the expert performer or—in the case of pre-existing documentation—the certification of that documentation by the expert performer.

Decision Tables

If there are rules to be followed in completing a task and the performer has to make decisions on how to follow those rules, then a decision table is the performance aid family to use. We are most familiar with them in "if/then" situations. Take, for example, choosing a color scheme for a room. *If* the room is small, and you want it to appear to be larger, *then* use a neutral, monochromatic color scheme. You would set this up in a table format that would provide options for making decisions about complimentary, analogous, and monochromatic color schemes. Table 14.3 an example of a decision table that helped participants learn and use the appropriate Union Collective Agreement Provisions.

Tables help the user to make decisions about fairly complex issues that might have multiple aspects to the ultimate decision. They allow the user to make accurate decisions as long as the issues to be determined remain within the parameters of the criteria in the table.

Table 14.2 A Text-Based Procedure for Conducting Successful Meetings

Strategies	*Description*
Start the meeting and welcome participants	• Greet participants as they arrive. Introduce participants who don't know each other.
State the purpose of the meeting	• Remind participants of the desired outcome of the meeting. This will help keep the participants focused.
Give background information	• Ensure all participants are up-to-date on activities or issues previously discussed.
Review "topics"	• Review the topics to be discussed and make any additions or changes. This is especially important if adjustments are required to the list of topics that you communicated at the time the meeting was called. • Be prepared to deal with participant suggestions for topics. Either accept or reject with reference to topic compatibility with purpose of the meeting.
State times for topics, presentations, discussions	• Allocate appropriate time to each meeting topic, presentation, or discussion. Do this by importance or complexity, keeping in mind the overall duration of the meeting and the meeting goal.
Communicate ground rules	• State the ground rules when people are meeting for the first time, when new people are participating, or when people seem to have forgotten what the rules are.

Text or Picture Lists

Look around you. If you are sitting at a desk reading this, you probably have any number of text or picture lists in front of you. You might have a list of phone numbers for extensions within your company. You also might have a phone list for people outside of the company whom you may call, but have not committed their numbers to memory. You might have instructions for what to do in case an alarm goes off. If you are like me, you also have a calendar on your desk or wall.

Small text lists can be relevant to matters like how to make a conference call, and large text lists can take forms such as phone books and dictionaries. Picture lists usually provide directions or instructions in pictorial format. Road maps, subway maps, bus routes, airline safety cards, cooking instructions, medical care instructions, the trail markers we talked about earlier, are all examples of

Table 14.3 Informal Investigation: Collective Agreement Provisions Sample

	Collective Agreements			
	3.1, 3.5	**4.1, 4.2, 4.3**	**6.2, 6.3**	**3.1**
Informal process	No	Yes	No	Yes
Maximum discipline	10 demerits, but cannot result in discharge from accumulation	5 demerits, but cannot result in discharge from accumulation	10 demerits, but cannot result in discharge from accumulation	15 demerits, but cannot result in discharge from accumulation
Discipline record limitation	Employee must have less than 40 demerits	Employee must have less than 40 demerits	Employee must have less than 35 demerits	Employee must have less than 25 demerits
Representation	No	Yes	No	Yes
Decision made within	20 days of meeting	15 days of meeting	20 days of meeting	10 days of meeting
Time for employee to respond to decision	72 hours to request formal investigation; 15 days to grieve level of discipline	15 days to request formal investigation; 30 days to grieve level of discipline	72 hours to request formal investigation; 20 days to grieve level of discipline	15 days to request formal investigation; 15 days to grieve level of discipline
Training	N/A	Company must train union reps and supervisors	N/A	Company must train union reps and supervisors

picture lists or displays. Figure 14.2 presents a partial example of a picture list on how to tie a bow line knot.

Checklists

Checklists occupy a unique niche in human performance technology. They can be used as a performance aid, a training tool, or an on-the-job evaluation

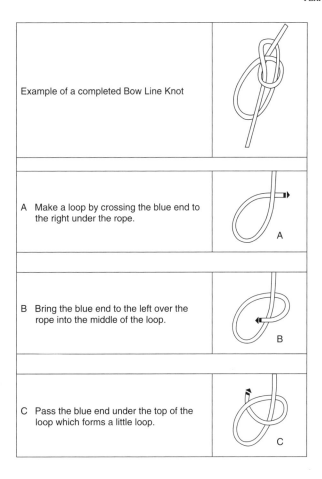

Example of a completed Bow Line Knot

A Make a loop by crossing the blue end to
   the right under the rope.

B Bring the blue end to the left over the
   rope into the middle of the loop.

C Pass the blue end under the top of the
   loop which forms a little loop.

Figure 14.2 Tying a Bow Line Knot (Partial Sample).

instrument. As a matter of fact, the same checklist can be used for all three purposes. In training, the learner uses the checklist to ensure that he or she is practicing the required behavior correctly. At the end of the training, the checklist can be used by an observer to record whether or not the behavioral procedures have been followed accurately. On the job, performers can use the same performance aid to ensure that they are following correct procedures.

A checklist can be a simple three-to-five item "to do" list that you check off after accomplishing each item on the list. Alternatively, it can be a set of complicated procedures that the achievement or recognition of each step or item builds to the completion of the next one. The pilot's safety checklist used before each flight is a good example of this type of performance aid. Checklists can also have examples of what the desired behavior looks like embedded in each item on the checklist. A behaviorally anchored rating scale is an example of this type of checklist. Checklists can also be used to ensure that a product meets specified quality criteria. Aside from noting whether or not the required performance step has been completed, a quality rating scale can measure how well the step was accomplished. Exhibits 14.1 and 14.2 present two examples of checklists.

Exhibit 14.1 Checklist for Proposal/Contract.

Content: The proposal/contract includes the following components:	1, 2, 3	Comments
Description in the info/context and objectives that demonstrates an understanding of the client's needs		
Work plan appropriately detailed for the scope of the project		
Clear statement of potential benefits for the client that does not overstate what can be achieved		
Cost breakdown detailing professional fees and other expenses		
Final budget appropriate to the scope of project		
Description of the project deliverables		
Description of the project schedule including milestones		
Roles and responsibilities of all stakeholders		
Description of past work that demonstrates expertise required in proposed project		
Relevant information about the external consultant and his or her capabilities		
Terms of payment that are in accordance with the policy of the bank or approved by the managing partner or vice president		
Accurate information about the client and client needs in the contract section		

Note: 1 = Poor; 2 = Needs some improvement; 3 = Meets expectations

Exhibit 14.2: On-the-Job Coaching Evaluation Checklist.

Did the coach:	Give specific examples of what the coach did well or suggest improvements

• Prepare the coachee by:
  • Providing a rationale?
  • Stating the objective(s)?
  • Providing an overview of what will happen?
  • Confirming the coachee's level of knowledge and skill?	

• Explain the skill by:
  • Being logical?
  • Explaining the 'why'?
  • Being clear and precise?
  • Checking for understanding?	

• Demonstrate the skill by:
  • Presenting in stages?
  • Being visible?
  • Previewing what the coachee will see?
  • Supporting with an explanation?	

• Observe practice by:
  • Having the coachee verbally walk through steps?
  • Having the coachee demonstrate?	

• Give feedback by:
  • Having the coachee self-assess?
  • Telling the coachee how he or she did?
  • Recognizing what the coachee did well or correctly?
  • Providing information to correct errors or poor techniques?	

• Wrap up by:
  • Reviewing the learning objective
  • Discussing development actions	

WHAT WE KNOW FROM RESEARCH

Performance aids, despite being such a critical instructional and performance tool, have not been the subject of extensive research over the years. A likely reason for this is simply that they work, and they work quite well. That is not to say that performance aids always do what they are supposed to do or that sometimes they interfere with achieving the accomplishments they were meant to achieve. However, if the need for the performance aid was well analyzed and the performance aid was designed, produced, and tested effectively, the performance aid usually achieves its purpose. It is difficult to argue with something so elegantly simple and effective. Performance aids have a proven track record and they can substantially reduce the training time required for many tasks. To measure their success would be redundant.

Nevertheless, there has been some interesting research into the efficacy of performance aids. Under the auspices of the United States Government, study grants were provided to examine ways to help increase drug compliance in third world patients. A landmark study done by Wendy N. Edson and her colleagues in 2002 looked at the role of research in developing performance aids for pneumonia treatment in Niger. The researchers knew going into the study that there would be reluctance on the part of caregivers to use the medications in the dosages and regimens required. This was caused by barriers in communications, traditional versus modern medicine, attitudes toward health care systems, and perceptions of severity of the illness. To combat these barriers, the team conducted qualitative research that enabled them to design and produce effective performance aids. Through focus groups, interviews, home visits, and clinic observations, they analyzed current knowledge and practices of health care workers and patient caregivers. They then determined with subject-matter experts the desired behaviors of these two groups. The subsequent design and development of the performance aids were based on the information gathered in the qualitative research. These performance aids, posters, and counseling cards for health care workers and medication packets with pictorial messages for caregivers were then tested and revised. The qualitative research provided the information to develop performance aids that overcame the previously mentioned barriers.

For the performance improvement specialist, the critical outcome of this study was not that performance aids significantly helped in achieving drug compliance, but that the front-end analysis done before the performance aids were designed and produced contributed to the adoption and use of the performance aids.

In most of the books and materials on developing performance aids written by performance improvement specialists, the authors clearly state that the job aid should be developed in consideration of both the needs of the learners as well as what will achieve the desired results. Interviewing the performer, subject-matter experts, and sometimes representatives of the management of the organization can accomplish this. The focus of these interviews should be on what behaviors the performer uses to realize the desired goals. What Edson and her colleagues point out is that there can be many barriers to the effective use of the job aid, not the least of which is the culture of the organization and circumstances in which the performance aid is used.

In Edson and her colleagues' study, the front-end analysis pointed out that the culture of the caregivers caused a reluctance to use modern medicine and only turned to it when traditional medicines didn't work. When we look at developing performance aids for our clients, what are the hidden messages and cultural issues that could interfere with the efficacy of the job aid?

Learning from the Research and Experience

Historically, performance aids have been designed and developed by people using them or those helping them to perform the task more effectively or efficiently. The focus has always been on the task and the performer.

When we look at what performance aid to use for certain tasks or content, the decision should be based on how it will support the performance required. This may mean that multiple performance aids might be required depending on the complexity of the task(s). As an example, to help ensure drug compliance in Africa, performance aids were produced as posters, reference cards, medication envelopes, checklists for healthcare professionals, and materials for caregivers. This multiple approach led to the desired results. Frank Nguyen's contribution, Chapter Thirteen in this volume of the handbook, summarizes the additional recent research in this area.

The research that Edson et al. and others have conducted on performance aids points to another focus for the future of performance aids. They stressed the need for analysis as a way of providing information not only about the user of the performance aid, but also the environment or context the performance aid was used in.

Humans have used performance aids since they were first curious about improving the way things were done. While they have had a long history in improving performance, they still are viable in today's environment. As long as we need ways to provide guidance, information, how to's and confidence to performers in a just-in-time manner, performance aids will be there.

RECOMMENDED DESIGN, DEVELOPMENT, AND IMPLEMENTATION PROCESS

Flowcharts or Algorithms

These are the common developmental processes for all families of performance aids, along with a few flowchart-specific ones:

- Decide what end result you want your performance aid to achieve.
- Look for tasks that require total accuracy and include a number of action and decision steps.
- Have an expert both perform and explain the task to you.
- If it is not an observable task, have the expert talk you through the covert (hidden) parts of the procedure.
- Be sure to obtain the rationale from the expert for why he or she is making the decisions.
- Construct a prototype of the performance aid and review it with your expert.
- Try to accomplish the task yourself using the performance aid prototype.
- Have the expert watch you as you talk through the steps of the procedure.
- Revise as necessary and re-test with a new performer.

Examples or Models

While there are similarities to the methods used in developing other families of performance aids, what differs with examples and models is that design involves the following steps:

- Gather as many examples or models that you think might be relevant to the one you want to produce. If none are available, ask experts to design them.
- Make a first cut, with your experts, to make the number more manageable.
- Create a set of instructions to use with the models or samples.
- Test them out with inexperienced performers and revise as necessary.

Text-Based Procedures

The steps to developing text-based procedures include:

- Observe and document the steps performed by an expert performer in all stages of completing the task or product.
- Ask the expert questions to be sure your observations are correct (separate true on-target behaviors from those that might be superstitious or idiosyncratic behaviors).

- Ensure that the text is both appropriate for the level of the performer and graphically laid out in a manner that helps rather than hinders task achievement.

- Test and revise as necessary.

Decision Tables

To construct a decision table:

- Identify experts in the decision-making process. This is especially true if there are any legal or health and safety issues.

- Test each one of the if/then decision steps with an expert.

- Build and test scenarios to ensure accuracy of the entire decision-making process.

- Verify the table with members of the target audience and revise, if necessary, with the help of the experts.

Text or Picture Lists

In order to design and develop text or picture lists:

- Determine what content needs to be in the performance aid.

- Determine the best format or formats to display the content (remember that with this family of performance aids, the easier it is for the performer to access the information in the performance aid, the better).

- Test a variety of formats with appropriate target population members.

- Revise as necessary.

Checklists

In order to create an effective checklist:

- Work with a subject-matter expert to ensure accuracy of required behaviors/procedures.

- Ensure that the items in the checklist follow a logical sequence (checked by an expert).

- Test the checklist with target population performers and revise as required.

CRITICAL SUCCESS FACTORS

As stated earlier in the chapter, there are a number of critical steps, required information, and points to look out for in order to ensure the success of performance aids. In summation these are

- The performer must use the performance aid during performance of the task.
- The performer must have all of the skills and knowledge necessary for accomplishing the task solely using the performance aid.
- The performance aid must either contain the instructions for using the performance aid or be self-evident.
- The performer must be able to use the performance aid without external instruction.
- Look for tasks that require total accuracy and include a number of action and decision steps.
- Have an expert both perform and explain the task to the performer.
- If it is not an observable task, have the expert explain the covert (hidden) parts of the procedure.
- Be sure to obtain a rationale from the expert for why he or she is making the decisions he or she makes.
- Construct a prototype of the performance aid and review with your expert.
- Try to accomplish the task yourself using the performance aid prototype.
- Have the expert watch you as you talk through the steps of the procedure.

CRITICAL SUCCESS FACTORS

Models or Examples

- Gather as many examples or models that you think might be relevant to the one you want to produce. If none are available, ask experts to design them.
- Make a first cut, with your experts, to make the number more manageable.
- Create a set of instructions to use with the models or samples.

Text-Based Procedures

- Observe and document the steps performed by an expert performer in all stages of completing the task or product.
- Ask the expert questions to be sure your observations are correct (separate true on-target behaviors from those that might be superstitious or idiosyncratic behaviors).
- Ensure that the text is both appropriate for the level of the performer and graphically laid out in a manner that helps rather than hinders task achievement.

Decision Tables

- Identify experts in the decision-making process. This is especially true if there are any legal or health and safety issues.
- Test each one of the if/then decision steps with an expert.
- Build and test scenarios to ensure accuracy of the entire decision-making process.
- Verify tables with members of the target audience and revise, if necessary, with the help of the experts.

Text or Picture Lists

- Determine the best format or formats to display the content (remember that with this family of performance aids, the easier it is for the performer to access the information in the performance aid the better).

Checklists

- Ensure that the items in the checklist follow a logical sequence (checked by an expert).
- Test them out with inexperienced performers and revise as necessary.

References

Clark, R. C. (2007). *Leveraging multimedia for learning. Adobe Systems Inc. White Paper.* San Jose, CA: Adobe.

Clark, R. C., Nguyen, F., & Sweller, J. (2006). *Efficiency in learning.* San Francisco: Pfeiffer.

Edson, W., Koniz-Booher, P., Boucar, M., Djbrina, S., & Mahamane, I. (2002). The role of research in developing job aids for pneumonia treatment in Niger. *International Journal for Quality in Health Care, 14*(1), 35–45.

Gagné, R. M., & Briggs, L. J. (1979) *Principles of instructional design* (2nd ed.) (p. 43). New York: Holt, Rinehart and Winston.

Harless, J. H. (1986). *Guiding performance with job aids. In Introduction to performance technology* (pp. 106–124). Silver Spring, MD: International Society for Performance Improvement.

Merrill, D. M., Tennyson, R. D., & Posey, L. O. (1992). *Teaching concepts. An instructional design guide.* Englewood Cliffs, NJ: Educational Technology Publications.

Nguyen, F., Klein, J. D., & Sullivan, H. (2005). A comparative study of electronic performance support systems. *Performance Improvement Quarterly, 18*(4), 71–86.

Paino, M., & Rossett, A. (2008, January). Performance support that adds value to everyday lives. *Performance Improvement, 47*(1), 37–44.

Rossett, A., & Gautier-Downs, J. (1991). *A handbook for job aids.* San Francisco: Pfeiffer.

Stolovitch, H., & Keeps, E. (2006). *Beyond training ain't performance fieldbook*. Alexandria, VA: American Society for Training and Development.

  EDITORIAL CONNECTIONS

Performance aids (job aids) have been a mainstay of performance improvement efforts for decades. From quick-reference pilots' manuals to diagrams used by grocery store baggers, performance aids can provide valuable support at the time of performance. Nevertheless, these low-tech performance interventions are frequently overlooked as more complex or high-tech solutions are considered. Be creative and consider your options when improving performance, and in many cases you will find performance aids to be a low-tech, low-cost option that make a substantial contribution to improving performance in your organization.

Both EPSS and performance aids, as described in the previous chapters, provide critical information and just-in-time support for the accomplishment of significant results. As a consequence, both are valuable performance interventions that provide useful tools to the individual and teams that are in the process of achieving desired results. In the next chapter, knowledge management is presented as an intervention that is designed to ensure that important information is available to individuals and teams. Knowledge management, both as a tool and as a process, offers organizations practical solutions for what would otherwise be an almost continuous loss of data, information, and knowledge.

Expanding Your Options

Ergonomics—the scientific discipline concerned with designing according to human needs, and the profession that applies theory, principles, data, and methods to design in order to optimize human well-being and overall system performance. Ergonomics is concerned with the 'fit' between people and their work and takes account of the workers' capabilities and limitations in seeking to ensure that tasks, equipment, information, and the environment suit each worker. Workstation design, workspace planning, and safety planning are just some of the many performance interventions you can use in relation to ergonomics.

Based on wikipedia.org definition (January 2009)

WHAT'S COMING UP

Within organizations knowledge management is often discussed solely in relation to the tools (especially software systems) that are used to facilitate the gathering, storing, and later dissemination of information. While this represents a valuable component of knowledge management, as you will see in Chapter Fifteen, knowledge management has much broader and more wide-ranging applications within organizational improvement efforts. From developing an organizational culture that promotes the sharing of information to building individual capacity for converting information into knowledge, this performance intervention is routinely intertwined with numerous other activities to improve human and organizational performance.

CHAPTER FIFTEEN

Knowledge Management

Debra Haney
James T. Driggers

INTRODUCTION

Knowledge management (KM) has come to mean many different things to different professions in the private and public sectors. KM has the potential to increase productivity, decrease costs, and raise the skills and competencies of employees. It can be applied at the individual, team, department, and organizational levels. Likewise, it is a support tool for distance learning, electronic performance support systems, virtual teaming, and succession planning, among others (see Chapters Thirteen, Twenty-Four, Twenty-Five, and Twenty-Nine for more information on these topics).

With its wide applications, knowledge management is recognized as a critical part of leveraging human and organizational performance. Whatever the maturity stage or degree of information technology in an organization, knowledge management can support performance improvement. This flexibility is especially pertinent to the training and development community, which is often challenged to improve knowledge and skills with limited resources. Nevertheless, KM is neither a Band-Aid solution nor a quick fix. Gaining the potential benefits of quality knowledge management requires a systematic and systemic effort that involves stakeholders throughout the organization.

DESCRIPTION

Knowledge management is, simply, controlling the process of identifying, organizing, storing, disseminating, using, and maintaining knowledge in order to support strategic goals. Those strategic goals can be at the individual, team, department, and organizational level. Mats Alvesson, a leading knowledge management researcher, states in a 1993 article that KM is used in one form or another in thousands of private corporations, public institutions, and government offices around the world. The number and type of industries that use and benefit from KM is diverse: British Petroleum, Chrysler, Electricité de France, Harley-Davidson, IBM, Merck, Nissan, Royal Bank of Canada, Sears, and the U.S. Navy, to name a few. This diversity gives an indication of the wide range of KM applications that can be used to support a variety of organizational performance goals, and provides a glimpse at the challenges of limiting knowledge management down to a single initiative or time limited project.

This variety with KM includes many performance improvement (PI) and training applications, from supporting electronic performance support systems to strategic linkages to e-learning content to intranet information, templates, and expert resource lists. KM can be used effectively in organizations with limited information technology, with dispersed and diverse workforces, and in knowledge worker organizations, as well as in more traditional settings. Knowledge management, however, is not and cannot be all things to all people; but it is a tool with many applications not bounded by synchronous timing or specific technologies, approaches, or geographical locations.

These boundaries and definitions are important, since practitioners' perspectives on KM will shape their responses to and effective use of knowledge management. The diversity of applications means that KM frequently can be misunderstood and then misapplied in an organization. It can be difficult to implement, and even harder to maintain. KM's success increases with the degree of alignment between the organization's goals and employees' support of those goals. It increases with greater understanding of what is necessary for implementation, and especially for what is necessary for usage and maintenance. It increases with the explicit understanding that an organization's knowledge requirements are shaped by the business context in which that organization operates.

Because of the IT component, KM initiatives typically have drivers from outside of the organization more frequently than many other types of performance tools. These external drivers include vendors and external consultants who often appeal to the IT-based easy solution: purchase and install, and your performance problem is solved. When it turns out that the problem is not solved, KM can be judged to be a failure when it actually is the faulty implementation or misapplication that has failed, and not the knowledge management system. After all, KM is not simply an IT system. Rather, KM is an organizational process for efficiently and effectively managing information and knowledge.

These external drivers are contrasted by the internal drivers for knowledge management: employees' desire to work smarter and management's support of that desire. The implementation of KM should be unique to each organization, as each organization is different, with a unique profile of strengths, weaknesses, opportunities, threats, and goals. Implementation is based on the unique combination of economic, cultural, and technological factors, among others, found in each organization. These internal factors or aspects are the most important components of successful implementation, usage, and maintenance.

Different organizational aspects are commonly referred to as either *hard* (for example, IT, measurement, and organizational structures such as roles and responsibilities) or *soft* (for example, personnel, culture, leadership, and processes). Identifying and understanding these aspects is the basis for the design, development, implementation, and maintenance of a knowledge management system, as they are for other performance improvement initiatives. Capitalizing on these unique aspects of the organization is a critical success factor to any KM system.

WHAT WE KNOW FROM RESEARCH

Knowledge management, as a term, is a relatively new expression for something that has been formally researched in organizational studies since the 1940s by Friedrich Hayek. It is still referred to by other terms as well. In their 1991 article "Organizational Memory" for the *Academy of Management Review*, James Walsh and Gerardo Ungson call it organizational decision making and organizational cognition.

In the past fifteen years, the importance of KM to organizational performance has been emphasized by leading business authors, such as in Peter Drucker's "Knowledge-Worker Productivity" article, Thomas Stewart's book *Intellectual Capital*, and Michael Porter's *The Competitive Advantage of Nations*. More recently still, and within our performance improvement community, it has been identified as a legitimate performance improvement tool in the preface to Harold Stolovitch and Erica Keeps' *Handbook of Human Performance Technology*. In 2006, one of us (Deb Haney) discussed knowledge management in the performance improvement field as follows:

> "In the early 1970s, nobody was talking about knowledge management. In 2025, perhaps nobody will be talking about it, except for historians. However, the challenge in managing effective and purposeful communication of what individuals in organizations know will remain (Drucker, 1993). The actions involved in KM, even if they are termed organizational development actions, or another type of HPT intervention, will be an ongoing part of organizational success. HPT has a role in those actions, whatever they are called, and HPT professionals have a stake in that success." (p. 619)

Since the 1940s, knowledge management has evolved from a concept in management and organizational studies to a valuable addition to the performance improvement toolkit. As a new area of practice in performance improvement, it is building a research base of initiatives and results: what was tried, how it was tried, and how well it worked. This research base will inform both the research and the practical, applied areas of our field.

This chapter is practitioner-focused. In it we will discuss some of the major research findings that support better decision making about KM implementation, usage, and maintenance. At the end of the chapter is a resources section that gives information on useful books, articles, and online sources. We encourage you to make use of these resources to support your practice.

Data, Information, and Knowledge

Data, information, and knowledge are different points on a continuum of usefulness, organization, and context. In a 1994 article for the *Harvard Business Review*, Stan Davis and Jim Botkin describe the relationship of data, information, and knowledge. They define *data* as unorganized, unanalyzed facts and figures, and *information* as data that has been organized, analyzed, and made meaningful. *Knowledge* is the next logical step in this continuum because it is the most contextualized, organized, and useful (see Table 15.1).

Tacit and Explicit Knowledge

Knowledge can be either tacit or explicit—or some point in between. Ikojiro Nonaka and Hirotaka Takeuchi write in their 1995 book *The Knowledge-*

Table 15.1 The Data-Information-Knowledge Continuum

Least Useful, Organized, and Contextualized		*Most Useful, Organized, and Contextualized*
Data	Information	Knowledge
Raw, unorganized facts that must be interpreted to be meaningful	Organized, meaningful facts	Organized, meaningful facts set in a context, productive skills, and cognition. Supports decision making.
Example: 1,000 widgets were made last year at the Chicago plant.	Example: Last year's 1,000 widgets produced was an increase of 25 percent over the previous year's for the Chicago plant.	Example: Last year's widget production met its target (and therefore management will not shut down the Chicago plant).

Creating Company that tacit knowledge is based in individuals, not groups, and is difficult to explain or write down for others. An example of this is an expert who consistently produces high-quality reports on international marketing, but who cannot tell you exactly how he does it. This is unconscious competence, the term Ruth Clark uses in her 1999 *Developing Technical Training* to describe internalized, tacit expertise.

Explicit knowledge, according to Annie Brooking's 1996 *Intellectual Capital*, "Can readily be written down. It is well-organized in the mind of the individual and may also be written down in books, manuals, procedures, and so forth" (p. 51). An example of this is a standard operating procedure (SOP) for producing high-quality computer components.

Thus, the question becomes how does tacit knowledge become explicit knowledge? Different authors give different interpretations of this process, but most are variations or subsets of Nonaka's and Takeuchi's four-step model for this conversion (See Figure 15.1).

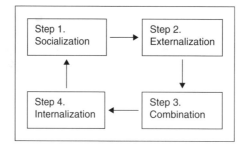

Figure 15.1 Nonaka and Takeuchi Model.

Based on Nonaka and Takeuchi, 1995

- Step 1. *Socialization*: The organization creates a culture that allows employees to share understandings and perceptions (mental models). This yields sympathized knowledge such as technical skills.
- Step 2. *Externalization*: Employees discuss how they perform work, often using metaphors that help them articulate tacit knowledge. This yields conceptual knowledge.
- Step 3. *Combination*: Newly created knowledge and existing knowledge are combined by employee teams into a single new product, service, or work process. This yields systemic knowledge.
- Step 4. *Internalization*: The employees learn by doing; this internalizes the new knowledge within the employees. This yields operational knowledge.

Notice that the conversion is dependent on a culture of communication and sharing. Communities of practice, with their basis in shared understanding and communication, are important to the socialization, externalization, and combination steps. Management must support this culture and the community or they will not thrive. For a more in-depth discussion of organizational culture, see Chapter Thirty.

Organizational Levels

Organizational knowledge exists on different levels: individual and collective. Individual knowledge is that which resides in an individual. This individual knowledge can be supported through a variety of human resource functions within organizations (for example, recruiting, retention, training, succession planning, and promotion). Collective knowledge is more frequently the focus of KM activities. Common collective levels of knowledge within organizations are team, department, division, organization, and inter-organizational (for instance, in which a company, its suppliers, and its customers share knowledge) levels. These organizational levels are important to knowledge management because different types of knowledge are found at different levels, and different approaches for managing those knowledge types must be developed by both the individual users and the organization. The type of knowledge that a company president finds useful, for example, is different from the type an accounts receivable clerk finds useful. Managing knowledge at the organizational level is different from managing it at a team or department level. At the organizational level, the best approach may be using reports or databases; at the team or departmental level, it may be face-to-face discussions.

Getting the right knowledge to the right people at the right time in the most useable form is an ongoing organizational challenge. Performance improvement professionals can support their organizations in this because of their skill sets in organizational culture and experience in dealing with different levels in an organization.

Knowledge Repositories

Different types of knowledge exist on different organizational levels and therefore require a variety of repositories (see Table 15.2). Tacit knowledge only resides in individuals. Individuals also know explicit knowledge, but collective organizational levels cannot know tacit knowledge. Collective, explicit knowledge resides in databases and paper archives and also within organizational processes. As knowledge is created and recognized, it then can be used on different levels in the organization. As a consequence, it must be stored in a repository or be lost. The more thoughtfully and formally the repositories are created and used, then the more the organization can benefit from that knowledge, because neither organizations nor individuals can use what they cannot find. Knowledge is dynamic, not static, and is always changing because what is useful to know continually evolves.

Table 15.2 Organizational Levels, Knowledge Types, and Repositories

Organizational Level	Type of Knowledge	Knowledge Repository
Individual	Tacit	Individuals
Collective: • Team • Department • Organization	Explicit	Collective: • Databases • Paper documents • Processes

Return on Investment

Return on investment (ROI) is an appealing concept that presents a deceptively simple equation: (benefits–cost)/cost. However, how to actually calculate ROI, especially over a period of time, is a complex decision that inspires much debate. American Productivity and Quality Center's *Knowledge Management Practices Book*, published in 1998, has compiled evidence of KM's positive and substantial ROI in a variety of industries across the world: steel manufacturing, petroleum refining, aerospace and defense industries, energy, hotels, communications, banking, and investment management, among others. The financial scale of KM's potential ROI is impressive. In their 2004 article for the *Journal of Knowledge Management Practice*, Eugene Yelden and James Albers discuss a study of five hundred firms that averaged 6 percent annual revenue lost because of missed knowledge opportunities. This translates into many billions of dollars per year. Nevertheless, and unfortunately, data on the actual returns from KM investments have not been collected from these diverse industries.

ROI can be derived from either increasing profits (increasing effectiveness) or minimizing losses (increasing efficiencies). Both are important, as they give an organization competitive advantage, although increasing profits is the aspect most often discussed (see Chapter Thirty-Four). In any organization, the opportunity to minimize losses exists in most functions and processes.

A brief example of KM's effect on ROI is found in succession planning. Every year, thousands of employees who have critical knowledge retire or leave for another organization, taking that knowledge with them. Hamilton Beazley, Jeremiah Boenisch, and David Harden state in their 2002 *Continuity Management* book that the typical cost in terms of productivity is approximately 85 percent of the employee's base pay. This is due to lost knowledge, lost skills, and the ramp-up time for the replacement employee to become proficient. Multiply the salary of every employee who leaves your organization each year by 85 percent to get an appreciation of the impact that a KM intervention can have on the performance of your organization. Knowledge management, especially in partnership with succession planning efforts (see Chapter Twenty-Nine) can help minimize that loss by capturing that departing knowledge.

Knowledge Management Systems: Information Technology Versus Communities of Practice

As we presented briefly before, knowledge management is often associated with information technology, but it is not the same. Data warehouses and computers are a means of storing and communicating knowledge but, by themselves, they cannot comprise a KM system. A KM system relies on people. It is made up of the same organizational factors or components as other organizational development initiatives. *California Management Review* articles by Rudy Ruggles (1998) and Andrew Inkpen (1996), as well as a 1998 article for *Sloan Management Review* by Tom Davenport, David De Long, and Michael Beers, all offer that the most important KM factors are people, culture, leadership, processes, structure, technology, and measurement.

These seven factors can be thought of as either *hard* or *soft*, depending on how overt or obvious they are. The hard factors, structure, technology, and measurement, are the overt ones, and they are relatively easy to plan, purchase, install, implement, and evaluate (see Table 15.3). They are politically neutral in many organizations. They frequently are not the most important factors in KM success, although often the focus of the lion's share of the attention in the planning process. That success or failure, Rudy Ruggles determined in a study of over one hundred KM initiatives in different companies, industries, and continents, is based largely in the soft factors: people, culture, leadership, and processes. Paradoxically, the most important factors are those that are the most difficult to implement. Each of these factors is discussed in a chapter in this book, which provides you with a guide to developing a systemic approach to KM in your organization.

Table 15.3 Knowledge Management Factors

Factors	Soft Factors	Hard Factors
	1. People	5. Technology
	2. Culture	6. Measurement
	3. Leadership	7. Structure
	4. Processes	
Importance	Primary	Secondary
Ease of Implementation	Difficult	Relatively Easy

Organizational factors either support KM as enablers, or limit it as constraints. Further, a single factor can act as either an enabler or constraint, based on the situation. Each factor therefore must be assessed and planned for while implementing a KM system. Ruggles' study listed all four soft factors as acting as constraints in many organizations. The top problems were people not sharing knowledge (51 percent) and organizational culture that did not encourage sharing (54 percent). This reluctance to share, endemic in many organizations, may be remedied by an organization formally supporting communities of practice, in addition to disincentivizing knowledge hoarding and incentivizing knowledge sharing in performance evaluations.

A community of practice (CoP) is a group of people with a single common interest, shared understanding and assumptions, and collective knowledge. This collective knowledge is frequently of strategic importance to the organization. It is often embedded in work processes. A CoP contains all the soft factors (people, culture, leadership, and processes), and because of this, is often the focus of KM initiatives in companies.

For example, many of us in the performance improvement business also are involved in training communities, and thus we belong to both professional communities—perhaps formally through membership in professional societies or informally through e-mail listservs. At the same time, we also belong to a CoP at work, typically within a department or division. If we also are involved in information technology, we may belong to that community as well. Thus, most people belong to multiple communities of practice at the same time.

Knowledge management is a performance improvement tool that has multiple applications. Because of this, KM has linkages to other performance improvement tools and initiatives. Some of these linkages are obvious, such as that to e-learning, discussed below. Some linkages may be new to you, and not so obvious, such as the linkages to lean six sigma, succession planning, coaching, mentoring, or outsourcing (see Chapters Eleven, Twenty-Six, Twenty-Eight and Twenty-Nine). As a result, a knowledge management initiative could link you to several new communities of practice within your organization or through other professional groups.

Knowledge Management, Electronic Performance Support Systems, and e-Learning

KM, electronic performance support systems (EPSS), and e-learning share important goals and components, even though they arrived as performance improvement tools from different organizational routes. Figure 15.2 shows the relationship between KM, EPSS, e-learning, and training. Electronic performance support systems, according to Steve Villachica, Deborah Stone, and Jon Endicott's (2006) chapter for the *Handbook of Human Performance Technology*, offer the ability to improve performance by supporting workers in being able to

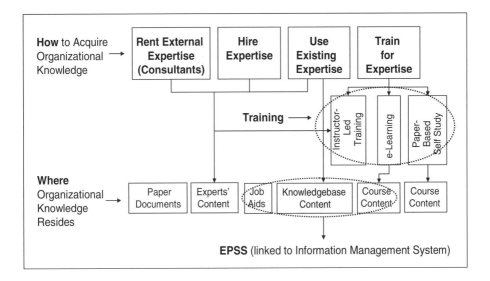

Figure 15.2 Knowledge Management, EPSS, e-Learning, and Training.

© 2002 Deb Haney. Reprinted with permission.

"learn, use, and reference necessary information within a single context and without breaks in the natural flow of performing their jobs" (p. 540). The emphasis is on supporting the immediate, on-the-job, performance of employees through computer-based information. Learning, using, and being able to find what is needed to perform are mainstream KM activities. For a more in-depth discussion of EPSS, see Chapter Thirteen.

e-Learning, in contrast to EPSS, is focused more on supporting future performance by increasing employee skills. Ryan Watkins presents a fuller discussion of e-learning in Chapter Twenty-Four in this book. Briefly, e-learning may be described as using computers as a delivery medium of training and educational content; thus it is focused on the knowledge and skills block of the Performance Pyramid developed by John Wedman (Chapter Three further elaborates on his framework). This content may come from internally developed materials that reside in the organization's databases and knowledge bases. It may have been originally identified or created by employees in the course of performing their jobs.

Knowledge Management and Virtual Teaming

Because the content residing in a knowledgebase is always available to an employee when needed, KM supports performance continually. Because the content is available to employees wherever they work, KM supports performance wherever it takes place. This ability to support employee performance, both individually and collectively, wherever and whenever the employees need it, is evidence of KM's support of virtual teams, because it reduces the team member's dependence on face-to-face meetings to share information. The knowledge stored in a KM system therefore can be used as a job aid (see Chapter Fourteen) in many instances.

Knowledge Management and Lean Six Sigma

Knowledge management has much in common with a current focus of both practitioners and researchers: lean six sigma (LSS). Lean six sigma thinking has been incorporated in many organizations representing a variety of industries. It has been implemented both on the shop floor and in the office. LSS is a continuous improvement system.

One component of LSS is *Lean*, focusing on eliminating all process steps that do not directly contribute to the final product. The other component of LSS is the *six sigma*, which is the statistical measurement and control of the work processes and outputs. Six sigma refers to the goal of increasing defect-free products to six standard deviations from the mean, or no more than 3.4 defects per one million units of production. Previously, only management and supervisors had access to this information, not the workers who actually did the work and were the closest to the processes and outputs. The goal of KM and LSS is the same for this: get the information to the employees who can most use it to improve the process and outputs. This benefits the workers, the process, the outputs, the organization, and the customers, too.

In their 2003 book *Lean 101*, Joachim Knuf, Deb Haney, and Mark Lauer did not use the term "knowledge management" in discussing LSS's continuous improvement aspect, but there is much similarity when they discuss continuous improvement efforts as being based in observation and sharing. They write that "lean" focuses on both current performance and future capabilities, which KM also supports. Another convergence of KM and LSS is the emphasis on management sharing information with employees and including the employees in discussions on how to improve work processes. It should be no surprise that both KM and LSS have deep roots in Japanese organizational development and production engineering and are linked to initiatives such as total quality management.

Knowledge Management and Succession Planning

As the baby boomer generation ages and retires, gaps of expertise and knowledge in the organization often are created. Wayne Grossman's 2007 article "Intra-Industry Executive Succession, Competitive Dynamics, and Firm Performance" discusses the need to include knowledge management strategies at both ends of succession planning: first, capturing what the exiting person knows, and then specifically making the desired knowledge one of the recruiting goals for the successor. The successor may be recruited from inside the company or outside it, so having a clear understanding of the knowledge the successor needs to bring with him or her is critical.

How to go about it? Mark Evans' 2007 article for *New Zealand Management* presents KM as supporting succession planning (see Chapter Twenty-Nine) as a two-step process that begins by identifying those employees who are important repositories of organizational knowledge. This is followed by capturing what they know through formal documentation procedures, perhaps by assigning someone as an understudy. Wayne Grossman points out that recruiting a successor presents an opportunity to not only replace what the outgoing employee knows, but also to identify what other, additional knowledge the incoming person should possess that the outgoing person did not.

Knowledge Management Practices: Future and Developmental Focus

Knowledge management is evolving as organizations and the performance improvement field evolve. Although we cannot predict the future, there are some indications of the directions KM programs are going. Several of these directions are of interest to us in performance improvement, especially e-learning and organizationally supported innovation. KM's technology component supporting computing, content repositories, searching, and communication will likely continue to evolve rapidly. As it does so, it will expand the capabilities of KM in new directions.

WHEN TO APPLY

Knowledge management can support many organizational goals and functions, but it is not a solution to every problem. The goal of KM is to control the processes of identifying, organizing, storing, disseminating, using, and maintaining knowledge. It is most effective when it is directed to specific goals linked to those processes. Symptoms of problems that KM may be useful in solving exist on different organizational levels. Many symptoms will exist on multiple levels at the same time, because organizational structures, processes, and culture affect all employees.

At the organizational and department level, symptoms of a KM problem include:

- Not using learning to support core business competencies;
- Not investing in employees' expertise;
- Not evaluating or rewarding employees for their contributions to organizational knowledge;

- Innovation not being valued;
- Information technology for communication and collaboration not user-friendly; and
- No processes for collecting, documenting, and disseminating best practices and lesson learned.

At the individual employee level, symptoms of a need for KM include:

- Employees re-creating the same thing;
- Employees hoarding what they know and not sharing;
- The same correctable problems occurring time and time again;
- Employees not taking responsibility for their own learning; and
- Employees unable to access the information they need to do their jobs.

These are just some of the symptoms that knowledge management may be of benefit to an organization. Determining whether KM may be beneficial starts with assessing the readiness of the organization before committing resources to a KM system or solution. Suggestions for designing, developing, and implementing are given below, and they start with identifying, analyzing, and assessing your organization's current situation and goals.

STRENGTHS AND CRITICISMS

Strengths

- Knowledge management gives ways to make use of corporate knowledge, not just archive it;
- KM can lead to increases in productivity;
- KM has both organizational and individual benefits (see previous discussion);
- Knowledge is an organizational asset with monetary value;
- KM reduces redundancies and reinventing the wheel; and
- Increases inter-organizational and inter-departmental cooperation.

Criticisms

- Information technology is often used as substitute for knowledge management;
- KM projects that address all critical success factors can be expensive;
- KM is not effectively used in many organizations that have implemented KM programs;

- People do not want to share; after all, the belief that "knowledge is power" remains part of many organizations' cultures;
- KM is not intuitive and can be difficult to do right; and
- Management is often willing to fund implementation but not maintenance.

RECOMMENDED DESIGN, DEVELOPMENT, AND IMPLEMENTATION PROCESS

While the long-term management of a KM system is an ongoing process, the design, development, and implementation of a KM system is a project that you can manage like other organizational projects. The project nature of the implementation means that project management orientation and actions will result in a smoother project: fewer resources required, less time spent, and better results.

To fully discuss project management here is beyond the scope of this chapter or book, but we do wish to present a few concepts from the Project Management Institute (PMI), which certifies project management professionals, and maintains the project management "bible," *A Guide to the Project Management Body of Knowledge* (see the resources list at the end of this chapter for more information on PMI). Most of these concepts are also endorsed by Vivien Martin, whose 2006 *Managing Projects in Human Resources, Training and Development* focuses on project management of training projects. In our project management experience as well, all these following aspects, actions, and phases have proven necessary.

Project Management Phases

Project management, according to PMI, consists of four phases:

1. Initiate (start)
2. Plan
3. Implement
4. Close out

Deciding on whether or not to actually launch a KM system is the first step. Deb Haney and Noriko Hara's 2000 manuscript for *Selected Papers of the 38th ISPI International Conference* suggests that assessing organizational readiness for KM and e-learning are similar; we have previously seen that the two performance improvement tools are linked. A guide for assessing your organization's readiness is listed in the resource section at the end of this chapter.

Most of the total project time is spent in planning, which consists of the design, development, and prototype phases. If you don't spend most of your time on planning, you will spend even more of it on correcting problems due to poor planning. The project phases listed below are adapted from the ADDIE model (analyze, design, develop, implement, evaluate), which is familiar to us in the training community. ADDIE, as a generic process, contains most of the formal project management phases that are supported by the project management literature.

In the discussion below, evaluation is included in each phase as a quality check; prototyping is included with the design and develop phases. The last phase is formative evaluation, not summative evaluation, because evaluating the success of the implementation will depend on how well the KM system is used and maintained. These further activity phases do not have end-points as you would in summative evaluation, since KM, once started, is an ongoing initiative to continually capture and share new knowledge within the organization. As long as the KM system is up and running, all evaluations should be formative, with the goal of continuous improvement. Table 15.4 presents a comparison of the project phases: the expanded project phases given in this chapter to guide you, phases from ADDIE, and phases from project management.

Table 15.4 Comparison of Project Phase Models

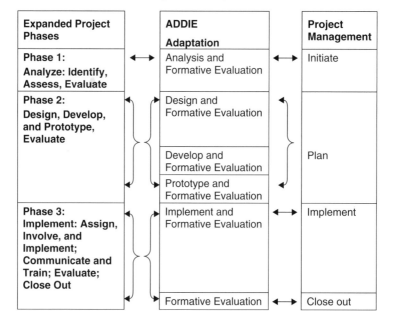

Expanded Project Phases	ADDIE Adaptation	Project Management
Phase 1: Analyze: Identify, Assess, Evaluate	Analysis and Formative Evaluation	Initiate
Phase 2: Design, Develop, and Prototype, Evaluate	Design and Formative Evaluation	
	Develop and Formative Evaluation	Plan
	Prototype and Formative Evaluation	
Phase 3: Implement: Assign, Involve, and Implement; Communicate and Train; Evaluate; Close Out	Implement and Formative Evaluation	Implement
	Formative Evaluation	Close out

Project Management Aspects

Project management has nine aspects that must be addressed throughout the project: *integration* (this is the overall management, and includes documentation of decisions), *scope, time, cost, quality, human resources, communications, risk*, and *procurement*. Different aspects will take more attention at different times in your project, but time, communications, and risk are the ones that require much attention throughout your project. Assuring that these aspects are addressed throughout the process will greatly support success. Also, be sure to note the overlap between these project management aspects and the critical success factors for launching and maintaining a KM system given below.

Project Phases

Phase One: Analyze.

Team. Performance Improvement (PI), IT, Finance (Executive Management approves)

Goal. An *informed decision* on whether to implement a specific type of KM system for a specified cost. This decision addresses project scope, time, cost, and quality.

Actions

1. Identify
   - Identify goal of knowledge management system: what exactly is it supposed to result in?
   - Identify key enablers, constraints, and deficiencies. The constraints and deficiencies will likely evolve into a list of risks and problems, so document and track them.
   - Identify and talk to key internal and external stakeholders to define their needs, desires, and concerns.
   - Identify communities of practice and current process for creating and sharing knowledge.
   - Define what knowledge is necessary for each community or department.
   - Identify skills and resources needed.
2. Assess
   - Conduct needs assessment and identify gaps: what skills do you need that you do not have for the KM system?

- Assess high-impact communities for involvement (think low-hanging fruit).
- Assess current competencies and training regarding knowledge use and sharing.
- Assess culture for acceptance of sharing and using others' knowledge.
- Compare organization's results to a benchmark group.
- Assess current knowledge management process, if any.
- Assess commitment from internal client in terms of personnel's availability to participate in knowledge management activities.
- Assess whether a KM system is going to be useful, practical, and possible to implement and maintain. If you determine that it is not, cancel or postpone further actions.

3. Evaluate
- Revise as necessary; this is an iterative process. If the KM project team is not sure about any of these items, repeat them until you are confident. Formative evaluation serves to improve performance.

Phase Two: Design, Develop, and Prototype.

Team. PI, IT, Representative End-Users (Executive Management and Finance approves)

Goal. A *functional, replicable prototype* of the KM system that will be supported by the stakeholders and sponsors.

Actions

1. Design
- Design tactics incorporating all KM factors.
- Engage end-users in design.
- Design workshops to create buy-in among internal client's personnel. These workshops should be different for different audiences, similar to the targeted communication plans. The workshops should address the entire KM system, and not just the IT component.
- Design communication plans to gain employees' support both during the KM implementation and maintenance phases. Tell people what to expect, when to expect it, and how it will affect them. Remind them of the benefits of the KM system to the organization and to them. Remind them that their support is necessary for KM success. Create a sense of positive anticipation. Different messages should go to different targeted audiences: end-users, those employees who will be affected indirectly by the KM system, stakeholders, etc.

- Design new roles, responsibilities, networks, performance standards, and incentives. This should include not just the launching of the KM system, but the ongoing usage and maintenance, too. For example, a team meeting quarterly to re-assess the system, determining if changes are needed or more training conducted.
- Design meetings, both formal and informal, for knowledge sharing.
- Design *corporate yellow pages* as a directory of sources for information and knowledge, including people who are subject matter experts.
- Design your risk management program. This can be as simple as a list of risks, and who is responsible for monitoring, evaluating, and dealing with them.
- Design a prototype process of limited scope and high impact.

2. Develop
   - Develop measurement criteria for success.
   - Develop roles and responsibilities, networks, performance standards, and incentives.
   - Involve key stakeholders and end-users in development.
   - Develop communication plans to gain employees' support both during the KM implementation and maintenance phases.
   - Develop workshops to create buy-in among internal client's personnel.
   - Develop meetings, both formal and informal, for knowledge sharing (for example, brown bag lunches).
   - Develop corporate yellow pages.
   - Develop your risk management strategy.

3. Prototype
   - Involve key people and end users in all prototyping activities.
   - Advertise: marketing and communication of the KM engagement to set expectations.
   - Pilot workshops on the KM system for education and commitment.
   - Pilot initial process, technology, yellow pages, meetings, metrics, etc.

4. Evaluate
   - Revise as necessary; this is an iterative process. Compare your prototype with your original conception of the KM system. Be ruthless: keep the identified and agreed-on main goal the main goal. Beware of scope creep.
   - Risk management: revisit list of risks and problems: pay attention to your identified risks and your strategies for dealing with them.

Phase Three: Implement.

Team. PI, IT, Representative End Users (Executive Management and Finance approves)

Goal. A *successful, functional KM system* that is supported by the stakeholders and sponsors.

Actions

1. Assign, Involve, and Implement
   - Assign staffing for change management processes and permanent roles.
   - Involve key people and end-users by assigning specific tasks.
   - Implement the system: processes, structures, technology, metrics, personnel, and all other aspects needed.

2. Communicate and Train
   - Advertise: communication of all KM activities to personnel who will be involved or affected. This is the expanded execution of the previous work of designing, developing, and prototyping advertisement and communications.
   - Train on new roles, responsibilities, networks, performance standards, and incentives. This is the expanded execution of the previous work of designing, developing, and prototyping roles and responsibilities, etc.

3. Evaluate (Formative Evaluation in Order to Improve)
   - Verify that all personnel who have ongoing KM roles are performing to standards.
   - Revise as necessary; this is an iterative process.

4. Close Out the Project
   - After the implementation is running smoothly, wrap up the project implementation actions.
   - Ensure smooth transition to the maintenance tasks, roles responsibilities, performance standards, and metrics to the employees who will be responsible or accountable for these actions.
   - Close out the risk management list: verify all risks have been adequately addressed.
   - Discuss and document lessons learned: both the aspects that went well and those that did not.
   - Verify all vendor and supplier deliverables, accounts, and payments are complete and correct.

- Present results to executive leadership, key stakeholders, and sponsors.
- Communicate status and success of KM system to end-users and other employees.
- Celebrate your success.
- Return project team members to their home departments.

CRITICAL SUCCESS FACTORS

The following critical success factors are composed of both hard and soft components, although, as previously noted, many of the critical components of a successful KM system are the soft factors (people, culture, leadership, and processes), which are more difficult to manage. You must be dynamic and flexible in how you address all the critical success factors.

Personnel—how employees view learning and sharing, and their comfort level with technology. Survey and interview employees from different personnel levels to identify knowledge gaps, their perspectives on organizational knowledge, and how they think KM should be institutionalized in their organization. Are people eager to learn more in order to do their jobs better? To what extent do they ask questions and challenge the standard operating procedure?

Culture and politics—the extent to which an organization's culture supports sharing and helping. Assess these aspects in your organization so you can plan for them in your KM project. Do employees view each other as colleagues or competitors? Is knowledge power and therefore a career commodity? Does the organization encourage sharing through public recognition? Is making mistakes acceptable? Are employees comfortable in communicating work problems to their supervisors?

Processes— the extent to which KM is part of organizational processes, linkage to performance evaluations, and decisions in regard to what extent each employee is responsible. Examine training, informal brown bags, job aids, and EPSSs from a KM perspective: how do these support KM? Coordinate with HR for identification of desired KM competencies, pools of potential employees who possess them, and linkage of job descriptions, responsibilities, performance evaluation, and incentives. Are attention and resources given to finding out what the organization (or department or team) does not know?

Sponsorship—leading through financial support as well as encouraging KM is incorporated into employee daily activities. Assess sponsorship aspects so you can incorporate them into your design. Does senior leadership lead by public example? Do they link KM initiatives to organizational strategy? How often do they promote knowledge management, sharing, and using others' ideas?

Financial—initial investment commitment and ongoing maintenance costs. Consider technology, training, and personnel costs in terms of recruitment and retention, as well as key employee succession costs. How much should be invested in new employee orientation and training on the KM system? How much should be invested in ongoing, refresher training for all employees?

Technology—user-friendliness and extent of accessibility. Assess how easy the technology is for employees to access and use. Which existing technologies can be used for knowledge sharing (for example: e-mail)? Do all employees have access to computers? Does the technology support virtual teams and collaboration?

Measurement—contributions, usages, and results as well as costs and resources used. Both inputs and outputs should be monitored. Track both war stories and victory stories. Track recruitment and retention of valuable, highly skilled employees and the number of employee certifications, college degrees, continuing professional education credits (CPEs) held. Evaluate training at Kirkpatrick's Levels 2 (learning) and 3 (on-the-job transfer). Compute ROI on different organizational levels, especially team and department levels, where ROI can affect budget decisions.

Common sense—last but not least, this may be the most important CSF of them all. It is necessary to fully understand and use the other CSFs. Does some part of your plan seem unrealistic or overly optimistic? Is the timeline too ambitious? Are you tempted to forecast too much ROI and too little expense? Will all that legacy technology really work together?

SUMMARY

Knowledge management is a performance improvement tool that can be applied in situations involving a need for identifying, saving, locating, and using contextualized knowledge, skills, and expertise. It is linked to many other performance improvement tools, especially e-learning, traditional training, electronic performance support systems, virtual teaming, and succession planning. As such, KM can be a useful tool for filling the gaps between the blocks of Wedman's Performance Pyramid. KM can be used, for example, when performance problems related to knowledge and skills are paired with minimal performance feedback and insufficient capacity to perform within the organization. Knowledge management can provide linkages between initiatives to ensure that a systemic, integrated solution is implemented that addresses all of the performance challenges.

KM can be useful on individual, department, and organizational levels. It is comprised of the same components that many other initiatives share: personnel, culture, leadership, processes, structures, information technology, and measurement. Successful implementation and maintenance of a KM system are based in honest assessment, thoughtful planning, thorough implementation, and rigorous monitoring and measurement. It requires sufficient funding and public executive sponsorship. Although KM will not solve all organizational problems, it supports many organizational performance goals and will benefit many organizations, either as a stand-alone initiative or in conjunction with other initiatives. It is a powerful tool for the performance improvement community.

References

Alvesson, M. (1993). Organizations as rhetoric: Knowledge-intensive firms and the struggle with ambiguity. *Journal of Management Studies, 30*(6), 997–1015.

American Productivity and Quality Center. (1998). *Knowledge management practices book*. Houston, TX: American Productivity and Quality Center.

Beazley, H., Boenisch, J., & Harden, D. G. (2002). *Continuity management: Preserving corporate knowledge and productivity when employees leave*. Hoboken, NJ: John Wiley & Sons.

Brooking, A. (1996). *Intellectual capital*. London: International Thomson Business.

Clark, R. C. (1999). *Developing technical training: A structured approach for developing classroom and computer-based instructional materials*. Silver Spring, MD: International Society for Performance Improvement.

Davenport, T. H., De Long, D. W., & Beers, M. C. (1998). Successful knowledge management projects. *Sloan Management Review, 39*(2), 43–57.

Davis, S., & Botkin, J. (1994). The coming of knowledge-based business. *Harvard Business Review, 72*(5), 165–170.

Drucker, P. (1999). Knowledge-worker productivity: The biggest challenge. *California Management Review, 41*(2), 79–94.

Evans, M. (2007, March). TECHWISE: Walkouts & wikis. *New Zealand Management*, pp. 70–74.

Grossman, W. (2007). Intra-industry executive succession, competitive dynamics, and firm performance: Through the knowledge transfer lens. *Journal of Managerial Issues, 18*(3), 340–361.

Haney, D. S. (2006). Knowledge Management, Organizational Performance, and Human Performance Technology. In J. A. Pershing (Ed.), *Handbook of Human Performance Technology: a Comprehensive Guide for Analyzing and Solving Performance Problems in Organizations* (3rd ed., pp. 619–639). San Francisco: Jossey-Bass.

Haney, D. S. (2003). Assessing organizational readiness for e-learning: 70 questions to ask. In J. Strayer (Ed.), *ISD revisited* (pp. 214–220). Silver Spring, MD: International Society for Performance Improvement.

Haney, D. S., & Hara, N. (2000). Assessing organizational readiness for knowledge management (pp. 3–8). *Selected papers of the 38th ISPI International Conference, Cincinnati, Ohio.*

Hayek, F. A. (1945). The use of knowledge in society. *American Economic Review, 35*(4), 519–530.

Inkpen, A. C. (1996). Creating knowledge through collaboration. *California Management Review, 39*(1), 123–140.

Knuf, J., Haney, D. S., & Lauer, M. (2003). *Lean 101: Lean manufacturing foundations for work teams.* Bloomington, IN: Performance Knowledge.

Martin, V. (2006). *Managing projects in human resources, training and development.* Philadelphia, PA: Kogan.

Nonaka, I., & Takeuchi, H. (1995). *The knowledge-creating company: How the Japanese companies create the dynamics of innovation.* New York: Oxford University Press.

Overfield, K. (1998). *Developing and managing organizational learning: A guide to effective training project management.* Alexandria VA: American Society for Training and Development.

Porter, M. E. (1990). *The competitive advantage of nations.* New York: The Free Press.

Ruggles, R. (1998). The state of the notion: Knowledge management in practice. *California Management Review, 40*(3): 80–89.

Stewart, T. (1997). *Intellectual capital: The new wealth of organizations.* New York: Doubleday/Currency.

Stolovitch, H. D., & Keeps, E. J. (1996). Preface. In H. D. Stolovitch & E. J. Keeps (Eds.), *Handbook of human performance technology: A comprehensive guide for analyzing and solving performance problems in organizations* (2nd ed., pp. xix–xxv.). San Francisco: Jossey-Bass.

Villachica, S. W., Stone, D. L., & Endicott, J. (2006). Performance support systems. In J. A. Pershing (Ed.), *Handbook of human performance technology: Principles, practices, potential* (3rd ed., pp. 539–566). San Francisco: Pfeiffer.

Walsh, J. P., & Ungson, G. R. (1991). Organizational memory. *Academy of Management Review, 16*(1), 57–91.

Yelden, E. F., & Albers, J. A. (2004, August). The business case for knowledge management. *Journal of Knowledge Management Practice.*

Additional Readings and Websites

We have found the following useful as both practitioners and researchers.

The Classic KM Library (Also See References Above)

Alvesson, M. (1995). *Management of knowledge-intensive companies.* Berlin: Walter de Gruyter.

Brown, J. S., & Duguid, P. (1998). Organizing knowledge. *California Management Review, 40*(3), 90–111.

Edvinsson, L., & Malone, M. (1997). *Intellectual capital: Realizing your company's true value by finding its hidden roots*. New York: HarperCollins.

Leonard-Barton, D. (1992, Fall). The factory as a learning laboratory. *Sloan Management Review*, pp. 23–38.

Sveiby, K. E. (1997). *The new organizational wealth: Managing and measuring knowledge-based assets*. San Francisco: Berrett-Koehler.

Wiig, K. M. (1995). *Knowledge management methods: Practical approaches to managing knowledge* (Vol.3). Arlington, TX: SCHEMA Press.

www.brint.com. Delightful, thoughtful observations and research findings written in plain English

www.cio.com. An IT-based perspective, but useful and updated regularly

www.ejkm.com. Electronic *Journal of Knowledge Management*: for easily accessible, current research in organizational settings

www.pmi.org/Pages/default.aspx. Homepage for Project Management Institute

Subscription Research Services

Delphi Group: www.delphigroup.com

Gartner Group: www.gartner.com

Publications

Special topic issues of mainstream management journals for knowledge management:

California Management Journal, 1998, *40*(3)

Long Range Planning, 1997, *30*(3)

Organization Science, 1996, *7*(5)

Strategic Management Journal, 1996, *17* (Winter Special Issue)

 # EDITORIAL CONNECTIONS

As suggested in Chapter Fifteen, the successful introduction of knowledge management (or other performance interventions for that matter) is dependent on the ability of the organization to adopt new practices within its culture, as well as to adapt many traditional practices in order to support performance within the emerging culture (see Chapters Thirty and Thirty-One). This development of an organizational culture that supports—rather than hinders—performance is a challenge that must be addressed within any improvement effort. The traditions, values, and often-unspoken policies of an organization must be aligned with the accomplishment of desired results. For knowledge management to be successful, your organization's culture must value the sharing of information, the creation of knowledge from data, and the long-term benefits of using knowledge to accomplish significant products, outputs, and outcomes.

Changing an organizational culture is rarely easy. Nevertheless, all performance interventions introduce something new into current organizational systems—thus change is a component of any effort to improve performance. Whether it is new feedback procedures, a new training course, a new reward for performance, or a new policy for recruiting job candidates, the introduction of new systems into the current system will bring about change—change for individuals, teams, and the organization, as well as change for the clients and society in which the organization operates. In some cases, changes begin even in anticipation of "the new;" in others, they persist long after it has been carried out. For some, the change will be subtle, for others it could be quite traumatic. In response, you must plan for and manage the changes you are creating.

Expanding Your Options

Team co-location—occurs when all members of a project team are physically located in the same office vicinity.

When introducing knowledge management into an organization, for example, it is critical to recognize the change implications of this performance intervention. As Debra Haney and James Driggers discuss in the previous chapter, building an organizational culture that encourages—through formal and informal processes—the sharing of knowledge is an essential element of any successful knowledge management intervention. Likewise, the introduction of performance assessment and feedback systems (see Chapter Ten) also changes both individual behavior and an organization's culture—as do most other performance interventions. Consequently, to support the implementation of performance interventions, integrate your approach to equally include creating change within your organization and then managing those changes.

WHAT'S COMING UP

When change is created but not managed, it is generally difficult for sustainable and significant results to be accomplished. Short-term benefits may be realized in a few cases, but most often these do not lead to the long-term results that organizations desire. In response, plan for both the creation and management of change in your improvement efforts. As Dale Lick and Roger Kaufman have pointed out, the first principle of change is that "learning must precede change." Learning, in this instance, stretches far beyond building knowledge and skills through training to include a variety of capacity-building activities to ensure that individuals and teams within the organization are ready for pending changes.

In Chapter Sixteen, change readiness is discussed in practical terms, providing a useful matrix for assessing your organization's readiness for intended changes and laying the groundwork for improvements in performance.

The Change Readiness Rubric

Bea Griffith-Cooper
Karyl King

INTRODUCTION

Projects drive change and change is an inherent result of a project. Successful projects require change readiness to demonstrate sustainable outcomes. However, documented success rates for project change initiatives are low. Coupling the strengths of project management (PM) methods with change leadership (CL) strategies can increase the likelihood of project success. Change management (leadership) refers to a set of principles, techniques, or activities applied to the human aspects (behaviors) of executing change in order to influence individuals' intrinsic acceptance while reducing their resistance to change. Project management, according to the Project Management Institute's 2004 PMBOK® Guide, refers to the application of knowledge, skills, tools, and techniques to project activities to meet the project requirements. Adequately determining the overall project change scope can lead to a more accurate assessment of readiness and organizational capacity for sustained project success. The change readiness rubric is a tool that leverages the strengths of CL and PM methods to inform project scope, readiness, and capacity.

Organizational Change Management

Change management is a set of principles, techniques, and prescriptions applied to the human aspects of executing major change initiatives in organizational settings, according to the author of *Managing at the Speed of Change*, Daryl

Conner. In his foreword to Anderson and Anderson's 2001 book *The Change Leader's Roadmap*, Conner further expands the idea that change management is a focus on how to orchestrate the human infrastructure that surrounds key projects.

In their 2001 book, *Beyond Change Management*, Anderson and Anderson categorize change in organizations as developmental, transitional, and transformational. The authors repeat these key points again in their book, *The Change Leader's Roadmap*, also published in 2001. In summary, what the authors refer to as developmental change is an improvement on an existing way of operating— like increased sales or improvement of a business process. Transitional change requires design and implementation of something different by dismantling the current way of operating such as installation of new computer system. Importantly, as William Bridges explains in his 1980 classic *Managing Transitions*, transitional change includes a loss, accompanied by the grieving process that may begin a rollercoaster ride of emotion from sadness, anger, to depression for all those individuals impacted by the transitional change. Finally, "Transformational change occurs when the organization recognizes that its old way of operating," offer Anderson and Anderson in 2001. "Even if it were to be improved, it cannot achieve the business strategies required to succeed in its radically different business environment." So transformational change represents a new future that is fundamentally different from the current culture, behaviors, mindset, and business practices of the organization.

Projects and Change Readiness

Organizational change readiness is a method to determine the level of preparedness of individuals within an organization about to embark on a project that will result in change. Time and resources to assess change readiness should be reflected in the overall project plan and readiness assessed early in the project lifecycle.

In a 1995 homage to Kurt Lewin, Edgar Schein reminds us that it was Lewin who in 1952 first identified three stages of change (unfreezing, transition, and refreezing) that are foundational to change models today. Lewin used the word "unfreeze" to mean getting people from an unready state to a ready state so that they may take the first step toward change. Building on Lewin's ideas, Schein expresses a version of readiness to change as "survival anxiety." He said, "It is my belief that all forms of learning and change start with some form of dissatisfaction or frustration generated by data that disconfirm our expectations or hopes." But, according to Schein, disconfirmation is not enough because we may simply deny it. "The disconfirmation," Schein continues, "must arouse what we can call 'survival anxiety' or the feeling that if we do not change we will fail to meet our needs or fail to achieve some goals or ideals that we have set for ourselves."

Armenakis, Harris, and Mossholder state in a 1993 article for *Human Relations* that "readiness is the cognitive precursor to the behaviors of either resistance to, or support for, a change effort." Furthermore, the authors describe readiness in terms of the organizational members' beliefs, attitudes, and intent.

DESCRIPTION

When beginning a project that will require behavioral change by those involved in the project and those receiving the project deliverables, there are at least three very important questions that we need to ask. The answers to each of these three questions will inform the level of readiness of those individuals who will complete the project and those who will receive the project outcomes. For example, a project team must bring together all the stakeholders who will be impacted by the implementation of a new computer system. This collaborative inclusion of stakeholders may be a new way of working for the team. Then the impacted stakeholders who will receive the new computer system will likely have to change their work processes as a result of the new system. Further, their attitudes toward the new system will have to include a willingness to learn how to use it.

The first of the three questions will address the scope of change resulting from the project. The traditional project management definition of scope is a statement of "what is included" and "what is not included" in a project. The Project Management Institute's 2004 PMBOK Guide refers to it as the sum total of all of a project's products and their requirements or features.

We are proposing an enhancement to the traditional project scope definition. When defining scope, it is critical to think of the scope of change as well as more traditional matters. The cultural change levels described by Anderson and Anderson's 2001 model provide a conceptual framework for thinking about change. The simplest change in terms of scope, referred to as developmental change, falls on the lowest end of the change continuum and places the least demand on behavioral change as depicted in Figure 16.1.

Developmental changes as defined by Anderson and Anderson as an improvement in current operating procedures, considered the smallest, least disruptive changes to processes or procedures. A moderate change in terms of scope is transitional change, which drives a redesign of what currently exists. Transitional change builds on developmental change, but adds an element of loss (and grieving) that can be more disruptive to productivity of impacted individuals within the organization. At the high end of the continuum, transformational change represents the most complex level of change in terms of scope. Transformational change, building upon the developmental and transformational change, represents the most organizationally disruptive and

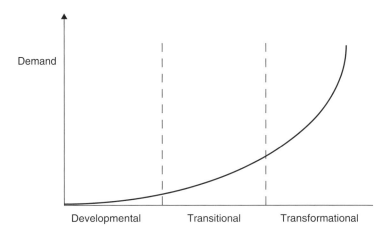

Figure 16.1 Demand on Behavioral Change in Relation to Levels of Organizational Change.

time-consuming level of change because it requires cultural and behavioral changes that the others do not. It places the most demand on individuals impacted by the change.

In order to illustrate the differences in the levels of change we have described, consider three students: Sam, Susan, and Brian. Sam is going to college while living at home. His parents helped him purchase his first car and he is now commuting to college—no more rides with mom and dad to school. This is a simple example of developmental change or process change because Sam's mode of transportation to school has changed but little or nothing else in his life is impacted. Our second student, Susan, is also planning to attend college in the fall, but in another state. She is making arrangements for housing, buying furniture, and saying goodbye to friends and family. This is an example of transitional change, where there will be more adjustment time required. Susan will likely experience a sense of loss as she leaves family and friends behind and embarks on traveling to and finding her way in a new town. Our third student, Brian, is planning to study abroad in Germany. He has a passport, visa, and is making current his immunizations. He has been studying German, which he will have to speak in most of his classes. He is also saying goodbye to family and friends, whom he may not see for at least one year. He is going to be living with a family he has not met (except virtually) and will be working while in school to help defray costs. This is transformational change, a much more complex change requiring adaptation to a new family culture, living within the German culture, and a loss of familiar surroundings, family, and friends.

Determining the scope of change is not a simple process but may be determined by exploring key questions later in the chapter using a change leadership tool we call the "change readiness rubric" and a project management tool we call a "scope document." This assessment can help identify the change scope and the project scope. Understanding both aspects of scope and addressing both provide a higher probability of project success. Schein's 2002 article for the Society for Organizational Learning's *Reflections* magazine reminds us that it is important to analyze and decipher the state of the system before embarking on an intervention.

The second question addresses the degree to which the organization is ready to adopt and support the inherent changes that will be required. Assessing readiness for change is not a new idea. There are many researchers and change leaders who warn of the dangers of launching change initiatives without a good understanding of the readiness or organizational climate for change. For example, when an organization is not ready to adopt change, then a great deal of time, frustration, and money will likely be expended later in the project lifecycle managing resistance to the change. It is possible that the resistance can be so great that the project's progress stalls because the constraints are too great to overcome. Therefore, conducting a cultural audit of the organization project and resulting change help us see the organization's current state and level of readiness. "Assessing organizational attitudes before starting a project is critical to success," said Columbia University's W. Warner Burke in 2003.

Readiness assessment starts at the leadership level with leaders who have a clear vision for the end game or the project outcome. Leaders model the new behaviors. In his 1989 article for *California Management Review* Charles O'Reilly stated, "Norms are the unwritten and socially transmitted guides to behavior. Norms that promote change include risk taking, openness, shared vision, respect and trust, high expectation for action and a focus on quality." Cultural audits, staff satisfaction, and internal surveys are ways in which we can get an early measure of readiness on paper. Behavioral demonstration of readiness is also an important validation of readiness.

Such a behavioral demonstration of leadership readiness would be a well-documented business case for change. Burke advised that we determine whether a case exists for the change that top executives want. This case, developed cooperatively by key leaders, includes a clear strategic vision articulated through tactical communication plans. If leaders author the case for change, their ownership and continued support is more likely to remain constant.

When leadership has imparted the case for change, then behavioral readiness of managers and staff can be determined. Executive consultant David Miller reminds us in his 2002 article for the *Journal of Change Management* that

"Strong leadership is central to successful major change." The successful leader is aware that his or her own behavior is critical. How managers interpret the vision and disseminate the message is one example of their readiness. The importance they place on the change message is reflected in the quality or amount of time they spend interpreting and discussing the topic with staff. A staff member may (or may not) be influenced by the manager's interpretation of the change message. A staff person's willingness to take steps toward changing is an intrinsically personal decision. People may decide to express resistive behaviors or may decide to adopt new processes, attend necessary training, and exhibit the new behaviors that need to be adopted in the new culture. When modeled by leadership, all employees (leaders, managers, and staff) in the organization will be expected to let go of the old way of doing business in order to adopt the new way of doing business.

Kurt Lewin believed that in order to move the organization toward change one must move the forces that maintain the status quo or equilibrium through unfreezing individual behavior and driving toward desired behavior. Therefore, Alicia Kritsonis points out in her 2005 "Comparison of Change Theories," Lewin suggested that we assess the driving forces and restraining forces that maintain the status quo. Lewin's model illustrates the effects of forces that either promote or inhibit change. Specifically, driving forces promote change, while restraining forces oppose change. While some of the restraining forces that stop movement toward change may be too challenging to solve, identification and clarification of the restraining forces allow for development of actionable plans to address them. Rather than delaying or canceling the project, leadership may need to slow the project in order to take action to support the identified barriers or increase the driving forces.

Consider Brian, our college student who is going abroad. If Brian is unprepared to travel with a current passport—a requirement for admittance into Germany—then his choice may result in his being denied admittance through customs. This restraining force might delay his admittance into the country and therefore into school. With proper planning, a current passport would remove a potential restraining force.

Finally, determine the extent to which the necessary resource capacity exists in the organization to complete the work. Resource capacity is the ability (or potential) to accommodate or accomplish goals or deliver outputs. Resource capacity includes people, materials, equipment, and money necessary to complete the project. Answering the question of resource capacity is equally important because it helps determine whether the project team and organization can deliver the expected outputs (for example, new product, service, and associated behavior). In the most fundamental steps of project planning, the project manager builds an overall plan that defines the project scope. As a part of that plan, the project manager creates a resource plan to determine capacity.

The project manager defines (with help from knowledgeable team members) all the tasks to be accomplished, resources, and skill sets required to perform the tasks. Based on all of this information, the project manager estimates the amount of time required. Identification of gaps in capacity early, while there is still time to redefine the project scope and related change scope or increase the capacity, will also support project success by ensuring the project is appropriately resourced. Reluctance or failure to align resources with the scope of the project or scope of the change initiative are likely to put the project and related change initiative at risk.

The Change Readiness Rubric

The purpose and intent of the change readiness rubric is to identify the organization's readiness to proceed with the project, to guide investigation into the project elements, and to provide clarity and stakeholder inclusion, which are critical to a successful project/business outcome. The rubric breaks down the complexity and the interconnectedness of each element into manageable parts. Each of the project elements are composed of building blocks that examine the interrelationships among the project elements.

It is important to note that this is *not a one-time effort*, and to consider revisiting the rubric throughout the lifecycle of the project, especially if there are changes to the scope of the project.

For the benefit of the reader, we will investigate each project element, the readiness indicators, and questions to consider as you complete the change readiness rubric.

The basic outline for the Change Readiness Rubric appears in Exhibit 16.1. As you build the rubric, you will:

1. Start with the each project element and answer Yes/No/Don't Know to each of the corresponding indicators.
2. Based on your answers, choose the column definition that most closely describes your project's level of readiness (Low, Medium, High).
3. In the Readiness/Action column put an L, M, or H (Low to High) to reflect the readiness of the project element.
4. In the corresponding action column, determine possible action(s) that will move the project element to a higher level of readiness.

Project Element 1: Project Objectives

In this element you are focusing on the alignment with the organizational strategy and obtaining agreement on how to measure success. The risk of not considering this element is that you will have a lack of a shared vision or understanding of the business opportunity to uncover.

Exhibit 16.1 The Basic Change Readiness Rubric

	Readiness Indicator			
Project Element	High Readiness	Medium Readiness	Low Readiness	Readiness/ Action(s)
Y/N/DK				L/M/H
Insert Project Elements from below				

Readiness Indicators to Consider

1. The project sponsor has described the purpose of the project and how it aligns with the business vision.
2. The project's benefits have been articulated or documented.
3. There is a common definition of success for the project.
4. The proposed project outcome supports the ongoing organizational strategy.
5. The opportunities are surfaced and understood and could be documented.

The next section of the rubric asks you to determine your readiness based on how you answered the readiness indicators. If you have *high readiness*, project objectives, benefits, success measures, organizational alignment, and opportunities to be solved are reasonable and clearly defined. If you have *medium readiness*, project objectives, benefits, success measures, organizational alignment, and opportunities to be solved are subjectively described. If you have *low readiness,* project objectives, benefits, success measures, organizational alignment, and opportunities to be solved are unreasonable and descriptions are ambiguous or may not exist in any form.

Now that you have assessed your readiness, define action(s) to move the project element to a higher level of readiness.

Project Element 2: Sponsorship

In this element you need a fully committed project sponsor who will help drive the project forward. You will determine the key decision maker and the process for making decisions; remember, your stakeholders should have a voice, but not everyone gets a vote. The risk of not considering this element is that you may have an absent or uncommitted sponsor who increases the likelihood of project failure. Without a key decision-maker, you have no single authority to make tough decisions.

Readiness Indicators to Consider

1. The project sponsor can define project success.

2. The project sponsor is committed to the success of the project.

3. The sponsor's approach and attitude to decision-making is clear.

The next section of the rubric asks you to determine your readiness based on how you answered the readiness indicators. If you have *high readiness*, the sponsor identified fully understands the project, supports it, and is willing to lead it. If you have *medium readiness*, the sponsor identified may have only partial understanding and commitment to the project. If you have *low readiness*, the sponsor identified lacks understanding and/or enthusiasm and may not support the project.

Now that you have assessed your readiness, define action(s) to move the project element to a higher level of readiness.

Project Element 3: Stakeholders

In this element you need to include the right stakeholders (anyone impacted by the outcome of the project) and allow them to provide input to the solution that answers the business opportunity. The risk of not considering this element is that you can easily leave out key stakeholders, which may damage relationships and unnecessarily increase resistance. This may result in an incomplete picture for stakeholders impacted by the project change and, in turn, may cause the project manager and sponsor to redefine the project scope. The project may be larger than was initially conceptualized.

Readiness Indicators to Consider

1. We can list all stakeholders impacted by this project or implementation.

2. The key stakeholders understand the product or service outcome (what you are trying to accomplish through the project).

3. The key stakeholders can define the benefits of the project as articulated or documented.

The next section of the rubric asks you to determine your readiness based on how you answered the readiness indicators. If you have *high readiness*, all stakeholder groups impacted have been identified and have been involved in the project planning process from the project's initiation. If you have *medium readiness*, some stakeholder groups impacted have been identified and some have been involved in the project planning process. If you have *low readiness*, very few to no stakeholder groups impacted have been identified and very few to no stakeholders have been involved in the project planning process.

Now that you have assessed your readiness, define action(s) to move the project element to a higher level of readiness.

Project Element 4: Organizational Infrastructure and Process

In this element you need to define the oversight or governance for the project. Who will oversee the portfolio of work, prioritize and address issues, and head off or remove barriers? The risk of not considering this element is that there will be no clear line to leadership authority and decision making, a difficulty that will be continually revisited.

Readiness Indicators to Consider

1. We have defined oversight for the project (approval bodies, steering committees, etc.).
2. The process for decision making is clear to all involved (voice versus vote).
3. We understand the impact of the project on business processes.
4. We know the change will impact a unit, multiple departments, or the whole system/organization.
5. There are other initiatives going on in the organization tied to this project.
6. There are other initiatives going on that take priority to this project.

The next section of the rubric asks you to determine your readiness based on how you answered the readiness indicators. If you have *high readiness*, the project has a defined oversight structure and has assessed the impact on the organization. If you have *medium readiness*, the project may have started to define the oversight structure and may have begun assessing the impact on the organization. If you have *low readiness*, very little or no oversight structure has been defined, and there is no assessment of the impact on the organization.

Now that you have assessed your readiness, define action(s) to move the project element to a higher level of readiness.

Project Element 5: Resource Availability/Work Effort

In this element you need to ensure that all resources needed are available and possess the right skill sets to accomplish the tasks defined. The risk of not considering this element is that you will not have the resources at your disposal to get the work done or that they may lack the right skill sets to accomplish the tasks defined.

Readiness Indicators to Consider

1. We know what people, equipment, or materials are available for the project.
2. There are resources that are off-limits.
3. The equipment/materials we need are available and possess the right skill sets required to complete the work.
4. There are budget dollars available if additional resources are required.
5. The skill set of the resources will impact my timeline.
6. We know what internal and external resources are required.
7. There are constraints for external resources.

The next section of the rubric asks you to determine your readiness based on how you answered the readiness indicators. If you have *high readiness*, resources (people, equipment, or materials) are available and have the necessary skills to complete the work, and your budgets support resource requirements. If you have *medium readiness*, resources (people, equipment, or materials) may not be available or have the necessary skills to complete the work, and budgets may not be available to support resource requirements. If you have *low readiness*, very few or no resources (people, equipment, or materials) will be available to complete the work, and there is no budget to support resource requirements.

Now that you have assessed your readiness, define action(s) to move the project element to a higher level of readiness.

Project Element 6: Innovation

In this element you need to understand and protect your intellectual property (concept, idea, discovery, invention, improvement, trade secret, or technology development) as you develop the project. The risk of not considering this element is that you may give away your intellectual property and lose the opportunity to protect it. Also innovative products and services may create unknowable risks—a change that is new or unforeseen providing a new dimension of performance that results in financial or other organizational stress.

Readiness Indicators to Consider

1. Our culture has an appetite for discovery and inherent risks.
2. Adopting innovative products and services poses unknown risks to budget and planning.
3. The project sponsor is an advocate for innovative risk. If yes, is there a process in place to support the required communication and dialogue with the sponsor?
4. We are going to use new materials, processes, or equipment that are untried in our industry.

The next section of the rubric asks you to determine your readiness based on how you answered the readiness indicators. If you have *high readiness*, the sponsor and organization understands, supports, and advocates for innovative risk. If you have *medium readiness*, the sponsor and organization may not understand, support, or advocate for innovative risk. If you have *low readiness*, there is very little or no understanding from the sponsor and the organization in supporting or advocating for innovative risk.

Now that you have assessed your readiness, define action(s) to move the project element to a higher level of readiness.

Project Element 7: Organizational Sustainability

In this element you need to plan and define the project and organization infrastructure to support the new product or service to sustain it for the future. The risk of not considering this element is that long-term considerations for the new product or service you have implemented may not be sustainable during the product or service lifecycle.

Readiness Indicators to Consider

1. We can define what the ongoing support will look like.
2. We can identify resources involved in the support model.
3. We know how much work effort will be required to sustain the project into the future.

The next section of the rubric asks you to determine your readiness based on how you answered the readiness indicators. If you have *high readiness*, the organization has defined and can support the long-term monitoring and maintenance of the project. If you have *medium readiness*, the organization may not have defined and may not support the long-term monitoring and maintenance of the project. If you have *low readiness* very little to no understanding of necessary work to support long-term monitoring and maintenance of the project exists within the organization.

Now that you have assessed your readiness, define action(s) that will move the project element to a higher level of readiness.

Project Element 8: Implementation Risks and Readiness

In this element you need to plan and anticipate what events may stop or impede the project's progress. The risk of not considering this element is that, by ignoring potential risk, you may be setting the project up for failure.

Readiness Indicators to Consider

1. We can identify the risks that might push the project off its strategic course.

2. We have a risk plan.

3. We have identified the project's biggest hurdle.

4. The project due date or timelines for delivery are realistic.

5. Education budget and resources will be included in the project plans.

6. A product or service test plan will be established.

The next section of the rubric asks you to determine your readiness based on how you answered the readiness indicators. If you have *high readiness*, the organization has defined and supported the risk, test, and education plans. If you have *medium readiness*, the organization may not have defined and supported the risk, test, and education plans. If you have *low readiness*, very little or no planning has been done to support the risk, test, or education plans.

Now that you have assessed your readiness, define action(s) to move the project element to a higher level of readiness.

Project Element 9: Budget

In this element you need to define a budget that provides transparency to the organization and a clear path for approval and decision making. The risk of not considering this element is that, without budget transparency and a clear path for approval and decision making, you may overspend and jeopardize the project's success.

Readiness Indicators to Consider

1. There is a budget allocated for this project.

2. We know at what point we need approval to exceed the budget.

3. A process has been defined to update and communicate the budget status.

The next section of the rubric asks you to determine your readiness based on how you answered the readiness indicators. If you have *high readiness*, the organization has defined and can support a transparent budgeting process with established protocols for decision making. If you have *medium readiness*, the organization may not have defined and can support a transparent budgeting process and may not have a clear path for decision-making protocols. If you have *low readiness*, very little to no transparency on the budgeting process exists and few to no protocols for decision making exist.

Now that you have assessed your readiness, define action(s) to move the project element to a higher level of readiness.

Project Element 10: Change Leadership

In this element of the rubric you need to define the scope of change (developmental, transitional, or transformational) and how the impact of change will affect the organization. The risk of not considering this element is that you may underestimate the breadth of change required, and potentially impact the success of the project.

Readiness Indicators to Consider

1. We have performed a cultural readiness assessment.
2. There is a loss (for example, loss of team members, ownership of work associated with the change).
3. We understand the extent of the change impact on a team or unit, multiple departments, or the whole system or organization.
4. This initiative will require a significant shift in behaviors, processes, or mindsets in order to be adopted fully within the culture.
5. We will need new policies, procedures, and training to support the change.
6. We can identify the formal and informal leaders and early adopters or champions who may influence perceptions of the project.
7. We have a strategy to deal with the natural resistance to this project.

The next section of the rubric asks you to determine your readiness based on how you answered the readiness indicators. If you have *high readiness*, the organization understands the impact of change, has completed an assessment, and has defined strategy and tactics to address the change. If you have *medium readiness*, the organization may not understand the impact of change and may not have completed an assessment with a strategy and tactics to address the change. If you have *low readiness*, very little or no work has been done to understand the impact of change, and no readiness assessments have been completed.

Now that you have assessed your readiness, define action(s) to move the project element to a higher level of readiness.

WHAT WE KNOW FROM RESEARCH

Challenges to implement projects that require changes in strategy, structure, process, and culture exist in many organizations. The results of successful, sustainable change in organizations are disappointing.

Two-thirds of total quality management (TQM) programs fail, reports Peter Senge in 1999's *The Dance of Change*, and reengineering initiatives fail 70 percent of the time. Senge goes on to describe the difficulty organizations face in sustaining change over time, even when they have early success. He believes organizations have complex, well-developed immune systems aimed at preserving the status quo.

David Miller's 2002 article offers that change initiatives crucial to organizational success fail 70 percent of the time. In his article, Miller explores the question: What makes a good change leader? According to Miller, the good leader builds high levels of commitment and resolve, which is important, but ultimate success depends on discipline and the right implementation framework.

Of one hundred companies that attempted to make fundamental changes in the way they did business, reports Harvard Business School professor John P. Kotter in 1995, only a few were very successful. Examining close to one hundred cases, Kotter found that most people in organizations did not handle large-scale change well. They made predictable mistakes because they did not have access to examples of successful transformations. In his 1996 book *Leading Change,* Kotter exposes some successful examples of change initiatives by implementing his eight-step process.

Methods of Assessing/Building Readiness

Assessing organizational attitudes before starting a project is critical to success, says W. Warner Burke, especially if the project will require significant changes to the way people work. Through his work with large organizations like NASA, Burke has guided organizations to consider the culture as they drive change through their organizations. He suggests a particular forty-two-question survey, the results of which will help predict the likelihood of project success.

Evidence provided in a 1984 article for the *Journal of Applied Behavioral Science* by North Carolina State University's Samuel B. Pond and his colleagues as well as evidence within a 1988 article by a team led by David G. Fox of the Institute for Behavioral Research in Creativity indicate that readiness can be assessed through survey research methodology. This can include the use of questionnaires, interviews, and observation. Decisions about implementing readiness programs should be guided by the urgency of the change and the extent to which employees are ready for the needed change. These authors suggest that culture and climate be measured before a change initiative is begun.

Anderson and Anderson's online newsletter *Being First* offers a free, online assessment that will immediately generate a report of your change effort's key strengths and potential challenges. The assessment tool results show where your potential problem areas are. The assessment questions, similar to those in the readiness rubric, ask questions to clarify scope, strategy, resources, change processes, conditions for success, and communication strategies and to evaluative feedback for course correction. Their focus is on how to orchestrate the infrastructure so that individuals affected by the change are prepared to accept it.

In their 1995 article for *Public Productivity and Management Review*, David McNabb and Thomas Sepic used a qualitative and quantitative data-gathering method. They suggest that, if an organization's culture and climate refuse to accept change, initiatives will fail regardless of management desires and plans to move to some future desired state.

According to a 1993 *Human Relations* article by Armenakis, Harris, and Mossholder, "The primary mechanism for creating readiness for change among members of an organization is the message for change. In general, the readiness message should incorporate two issues: (a) the need for change, that is, the discrepancy between the desired end-state (which must be appropriate for the organization) and the present state; and (b) the individual and collective efficacy (i.e., the perceived ability to change) of parties affected by the change effort."

In a comprehensive study of twelve large companies in which top management was attempting to revitalize the corporation, a team led by Harvard Business School's Michael Beer reported in 1990 that change efforts that successfully produce sustained change focus on the work itself—referred to as "task alignment"—reorganizing employee roles, responsibilities, and relationship to solve specific business problems. They found that "companies need a particular mind-set for managing change; one that emphasizes process over specific content, recognizes organization change as a unit-by-unit learning process rather than a series of programs, and acknowledges the payoffs that result from persistence over a long period of time as opposed to quick fixes."

This overview of research affirms the importance of adopting a method to determine readiness and build readiness for change early in the project lifecycle. The research further substantiates the need for clarifying specific project elements that further clarify project scope such as strategy, resources, change processes, conditions for success, and communication strategies. Finally, the literature suggests the benefits of persistence, learning, and measuring to help sustain the change brought about in project implementation.

WHEN TO APPLY

The Change Readiness Rubric, when used as an intervention tool, fits in the upstream early stage of a project to determine the capacity, help define project and change scope, and build strategy. The iterative nature of the inquiry process that the rubric provides will drive to an increasingly detailed picture and therefore more accurate understanding of the project. According to Schein, while change is a perpetual process, we may also think of change in terms of phases like those of Lewin's unfreezing, changing, and refreezing phases. A conscious process design that integrates content with the "people" changes is depicted in Figure 16.2 as a simple upstream, midstream, and downstream process that reflects the components of Anderson and Anderson's 2001 change process model. Early in the project lifecycle or upstream in the change process model, there are specific activities that should happen as the organization prepares to change. For example, the change team can be identified and their specific roles defined. In the midstream phase of the change activities, the desired future state should be designed, but this cannot happen until the current state is determined, which will likely happen in the upstream phase.

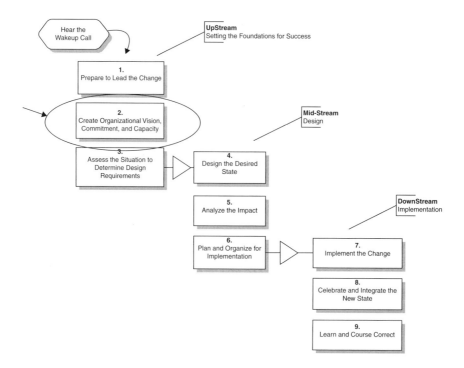

Figure 16.2 Change Process Model.

Source: Adapted from Griffith-Cooper and King, 2007

Early in the project lifecycle, determining the scope and complexity of a project will drive the required change leadership activities. Based on what we learn, the rubric then acts as a guide into our initial inquiry of project readiness. Anderson and Anderson's model of change suggests that not all change is the same. Change may range from developmental to transitional or even to complex transformational initiatives. Therefore, strategic and tactical planning should match the scope of the predicted change efforts. The level or complexity of a project and predicted change (the scope) will dictate the type of resources, the amount of time and budget needed to develop the strategy, and implementation tactics for a successful project with sustained change.

It is common practice of many project managers to address project readiness just prior to the implementation phase of a project. Because the traditional implementation phase is late in the project lifecycle, this "go-no-go" decision point leaves little margin for adjustment in terms of the scope of the change. Assessment of readiness, while best if addressed early, is an iterative process. If the project is not in the appropriate state of readiness, the project plan should allow space in the schedule for course correction.

In Figure 16.2, a comparison of the project lifecycle with the change process model (originally published by Griffith-Cooper & King in a 2007 issue of *Performance Improvement*) depicts timing of the rubric tool. The rubric, while implemented early in the initiating phase of the project should be revisited throughout the lifecycle of the project to leverage ongoing opportunities for improvement as they emerge.

How to Apply the Readiness
Rubric/Implementation Process

Determining organizational readiness before initiating a change project is a critical step on the road to success. Researchers of organizational readiness remind us that culture and climate, at the least, be analyzed before making a decision to embark on a change project. Further, the research shows that survey, interview, and observation techniques help gather analysis data that inform the "go-no-go" decision points that happen throughout the project lifecycle. Indicators in the readiness rubric (such as cultural audits and risk plans) can be implemented from day one of a project to determine a systemic perspective on readiness that builds upon assessment of cultural readiness. The rubric, like most assessment tools, assesses the following to some degree: well-defined scope, resources and capacity, budget, change processes and strategy, conditions or environment, communication strategies, support mechanisms, and stakeholder awareness and involvement.

A systemic approach to change considers several key indicators of readiness that orchestrate the organizational infrastructure. A systemic approach considers the context for the change or the environment in which it occurs and is driven by a roadmap or change process model like the adapted Anderson and Anderson model. Finally, a systemic approach considers and involves the impacted stakeholders. These stakeholders fill critical roles with related responsibilities that can drive change or generate resistance. While it would be difficult to prescribe one step-by-step method to determine whether the rubric project elements are in place, an inquiry into these elements is essential.

So who is responsible for driving the inquiry to readiness? A role-based stakeholder approach like in Table 16.1 provides an examination of the responsibilities and behaviors that contribute to and provide evidence of readiness.

In Table 16.1 the project elements from the readiness rubric are aligned with the primary project roles and the corresponding responsibility or observable behavior. These roles work interdependently to move the project and maintain its momentum. Assessing the degree to which these roles are assigned and responsibilities are being carried out can provide a comprehensive picture of the organizational degree of readiness.

Achieving optimal success requires a high degree of readiness, clearly defined roles, and responsibilities fulfilled. When disconnects occur between the project elements in the rubric and the role and responsibilities table then action plans need to be put in place to close the gap. The project sponsor and project manager roles are closely aligned and require an ongoing discourse of open, healthy dialogue.

Successful Application

What can come from a successful application of the rubric's tool and techniques proposed in this chapter? First and foremost, the rubric application will result in an informed project scope and change scope that will more effectively lead to the defined business objective. Second, the culture and climate readiness assessment will be complete and data available for interpretation and action. Third, the capacity for the organization to meet the demands of the project is clear. Further, supporting characteristics for successful application are key stakeholders that feel included and have a clear understanding of the project benefits. Project roles and responsibilities are defined and communicated so that individuals are clear about the parts they play in project and change success. Further, the behaviors of the key stakeholders are clear and there is willingness to adopt them. Finally, a shared vision of what the project/change will accomplish and a way to support and sustain it is considered and implemented.

Potential Impact of Omissions

Failing to assess your organization's readiness for change is planning to fail. A good readiness plan provides foresight into the organization's ability to adapt and accept the change by providing a viable foundation for project success. If you choose not to use the Change Readiness Rubric, you may not have a sustainable, successful outcome and may experience the following: (1) a lack of clear project vision or goals, (2) a lack of resources able to complete the tasks required due to key skills, (3) a lack of clear authority in decision making, (4) a lack

Table 16.1 Rubric Elements and Roles/Responsibilities Matrix

Project Element	Role	Responsibility
Project Objectives	Sponsor	Communicates corporate strategy down through the organization; Measures business results and ensures alignment with business strategy and other ongoing initiatives
	Project Manager	Engages with key stakeholders to develop project objectives
	Stakeholders/Project Team	Reviews and aligns project objectives
Sponsorship	Executive Sponsor/Project Manager	Determines timing for project reviews, plans, and decisions needed at gates
Stakeholders	Project Manager	Identifies market/customers
	All areas affected by the project outcome/Change Leader	Engages stakeholders in reviewing and aligning around the project scope; Defines communication plan to keep all stakeholders informed and engaged through the project
Organizational Infrastructure and Process	Project Sponsor/Project Manager	Defines and approves organizational/team structure; Defines and approves project governance; Defines and approves organizational responsibility matrix; Defines reporting structure and meeting schedule
	Project Manager/Change Leader and Project Team	Determines how each project element will affect the project organization, processes, plans, activities, and team; Team development and training
Resource Availability and Work Effort	Project Manager	Break scope into detailed work packages and activities; Determine what resources (people, equipment, materials, etc.) are required to complete the project; Define major phases, gates, and milestones

(*Continued*)

Table 16.1 (*Continued*)

Project Element	Role	Responsibility
Innovation	Project Sponsor	Determine the organization appetite for risk
	Project Manager	Define innovation risk in the project risk assessment
Organizational Sustainability	Project Manager/Customer accepting the end product/ service	Determine the ongoing support model; Identify role/responsibilities to support the project sustainability
Implementation Risk and Readiness	Project Sponsor	Determine the level of autonomy, project monitoring, and contingency plans needed based on the project scope and complexity
	Project Manager/Change Leader/Project Team	Estimate uncertainty in initial requirements and maintain as project progresses; Define education plan; Define testing plan
Budget	Project Sponsor/Project Manager	Define and approve the project budget; Determine approval process to exceed project budget
Change Leadership	Project Sponsor/Project Manager/Change Leader	Define a cultural readiness assessment; Determine the organizational impact on the extent of change and where there may be potential risk

of communication strategy and tactics to carry a consistent message to the organization, (5) minimal or a lack of clear understanding of the scope and potential impact of change and the education required to sustain the change initiative long-term, and (6) a lack of defined measurements for success.

CRITICAL SUCCESS FACTORS

There is not a single perfect solution to project change leadership. The rubric is not a silver bullet nor is it a static document, but a guide that should be revisited as the project and changes to the organization evolve.

The rubric is advantageous because it summarizes the project's readiness at the time the data is gathered, but that snapshot in time should not give us a false sense of security. Changes occur in projects that create risks to be managed— sometimes unknowable risks. Raising risk awareness protects the organization, and risk should be assessed continually throughout the project's lifecycle. The rubric's elemental detail allows us to pinpoint or break down readiness and address low or moderate levels of readiness.

A potential disadvantage in uncovering the readiness risks can be used against the project by political enemies to stall the project, and there is danger when the dialogue does not occur with the appropriate leaders who have decision-making authority. Also, while the rubric may provide opportunity for the right discussions with key stakeholders and leaders, the tool alone will not guarantee buy-in, support, and long-term sustainable success.

SUMMARY

The combined power of project management methodologies and change leadership strategies offers an integrated approach to managing the human aspects of change while driving projects forward. The rubric, combined with careful consideration of project roles and responsibilities, can serve as a dynamic, iterative approach to early readiness assessment that prepares the organization for change and identifies potential risks. These tools and techniques used in the earliest, initiating phases of a project begin by informing and refining the project scope and the resulting change scope. At first blush, they guide targeted planning and implementation of tactical activities and deliverables. If used skillfully, they can be important strategic tools for leadership to deal with the cultural issues. During the life of the project, revisiting the rubric may further refine planning and illuminate emergent risks. The resulting information from the rubric sets up project managers, sponsors, and stakeholders to manage those identified risks.

Randall L. Englund & Ralf Müller offer in their 2004 article for *Projects & Profits* that leading change "involves assessment, identification, skill-building, planning, and application. It also involves knowing the potential of project management and the willingness to apply a disciplined process to a web of simultaneous projects across the organization." The tools and techniques outlined in this chapter are dynamic guidelines that have arisen from practical, organizational application and experience. This shared learning is an embodiment of collective application of project management and change leadership—a powerful partnership. Therefore, further research and study will enable future development and evolution of these tools and techniques to improve organizations' odds of success.

References

Anderson, L. A., & Anderson, D. (2001). *The change leader's roadmap: How to navigate your organization's transformation.* San Francisco: Pfeiffer.

Anderson, L. A., & Anderson, D. (2001). *Beyond change management: Advanced strategies for today's transformational leaders.* San Francisco: Pfeiffer

Anderson, L. A., & Anderson, D. (2006, January). Ensuring your organization's capacity to change. *Results from Change* e-Newsletter.

Armenakis, A. A., Harris, S. G., & Mossholder, K. W. (1993, June). Creating readiness for organizational change. *Human Relations, 46*(6), 681–704.

Bridges, W. (1980). *Managing transitions: Making sense of life's changes.* Reading, MA: Addison-Wesley.

Beer, M., Eisenstat, R. A., & Spector, B. (1990). Why change programs don't produce change. *Harvard Business Review, 68*(6), 158–166.

Burke, W. W. (2003, May). Workplace culture and project readiness. *Baseline.* Ziff Davis Media Inc.

Conner, D. (1993). *Managing at the speed of change.* New York: Villard.

Englund, R. L., & Müller, R. (2004, November). Leading change toward enterprise project management. *Projects & Profits.*

Fox, D. G., Ellison, R. L., & Keith, K. L. (1988). Human resource management: An index and its relationship to readiness for change. *Public Personnel Management, 17*(3), 297–302.

Griffith-Cooper, B., & King, K. (2007, January). The partnership between project management and organizational change: Integrating change management with change leadership. *Performance Improvement, 46*(1), p. 14–20.

Kotter, J. P. (1995, March/April) Leading change: why transformation efforts fail. *Harvard Business Review, 73*(2), 59–67.

Kotter, J. P. (1996). *Leading change.* Cambridge, MA: Harvard Business School Press.

Kritsonis, A. (2005) Comparison of change theories. *International Journal of Scholarly Academic Intellectual Diversity, 8*(1), 2.

Lewin, K. (1952). Group decisions and social change. In G. E. Swanson, T. N. Newcomb, & E. L. Hartley (Eds.), *Readings in social psychology* (rev. ed.) New York: Holt.

Miller, D. (2002). Successful change leaders: what makes them? What do they do that is different? *Journal of Change Management, 2*(4), 359–368.

McNabb, D. E., & Sepic, F. T. (1995). Culture, climate, and total quality management: Measuring readiness for change. *Public Productivity and Management Review, 18*(4), 369–385.

O'Reilly, C. (1989). Corporations, culture and commitment: Motivation and social control in organizations. *California Management Review, 31*(3), 9–25.

Pond, S. B., Armenakis, A. A., and Green, S. B. (1984). The importance of employee expectations in organizational diagnosis. *Journal of Applied Behavioral Science, 20,* 167–180.

Project Management Institute. (2004). *A guide to the project management body of knowledge* (PMBOK Guide 3rd ed.). Newtown Square, PA: PMI Publications.

Senge, P. (1999). *The dance of change.* New York: Currency Doubleday.

Schein, E. H. (1995). Kurt Lewin's change theory in the field and in the classroom: Notes toward a model of managed learning. From www.sol-ne.org/res/wp/10006.html and from www.a2zpsychology.com/articles/kurt_lewin's_change_theory.htm.

Schein, E. (2002). Models and tools for stability and change in human systems. *Reflections* 4(2) 34–46.

Recommended Readings

Englund, R. (2006). *Project sponsorship: Achieving management commitment for project success.* San Francisco: Jossey-Bass.

Yin, R. K. (1978). *Changing urban bureaucracies: How new practices become routinized.* Santa Monica, CA: The Rand Corporation.

 # EDITORIAL CONNECTIONS

As illustrated in Chapter Sixteen, effectively creating and managing change plays a significant role in the improvement of human and organizational performance. Performance interventions of all varieties induce change within organizations; as a consequence, unless intentionally created and managed, the systemic impacts of change can often go unchecked within your improvement effort.

Unfortunately, the latter is very common in most organizations. With good intentions managers may, for example, introduce a new incentive system without adequately managing the repercussions of that change. From human resource policies to compensation and from motivation to performance evaluations, the introduction of a new performance intervention must be from a systems perspective—noting that changes in one system will typically lead to changes in all of the associated systems.

Similarly, when the information technology (IT) department introduces new software solutions that are supposed to improve individual productivity, they can routinely fail to adequately plan for the training of staff, training of trainers, ongoing performance support, stress of learning new software systems, or other implications of their decision. In such cases, the introduction performance interventions without adequate attention to change creation and management can drive down the impact of your improvement efforts—or even lead to new performance problems.

While all performance interventions will lead to change in your organization, process improvements are performance interventions that directly and intentionally change the processes, procedures, guideline, rules, and other controls that lead to the development results. Process improvement efforts characteristically lead to significant changes—changes that often impact on many subsystems within the organization. Whether it is reworking procurement or purchasing procedures or changing the lines of production within a factory, process improvements can lead to significant improvement in the efficiency and effectiveness of individuals and teams within almost any organization.

Expanding Your Options

Process reengineering—described by Hammer and Champy as "the fundamental reconsideration and the radical redesign of organizational processes, in order to achieve drastic improvement of current performance in cost, services and speed." Rather than organizing a firm into functional specialties (such as production, accounting, marketing, and so forth) and to look at the tasks that each function performs, Hammer and Champy recommend considering complete processes, from materials acquisition to production to marketing and distribution.

Based on www.12manage.com/methods_bpr.html definition (January 2009)

Evolution, rather than design, leads to the development of the processes and procedures used in most organizations. What starts out as a few simple steps can quickly evolve into a complex maze of rules, policies, and guidelines. Many of these might be in place for good reason and many should stay, but the order, duration, prioritization, relevance, and other characteristics of each step should be regularly re-examined to ensure that what remains are necessary and add value. Michael Hammer, author of *The Reengineering Revolution*, suggests that you ask and answer the question: If everything were gone tomorrow, would we rebuild it the same way?

WHAT'S COMING UP

In Chapter Seventeen, Marcey Uday-Riley and Ingrid Guerra-López provide practical guidance on how to use process improvement to accomplish significant results. Taking lessons and principles from quality management and six sigma, the authors discuss steps for making measurable improvements to the processes that create results within your organization.

Process Improvement

Marcey Uday-Riley
Ingrid Guerra-López

INTRODUCTION

Process improvement has taken on meaning and significance in many areas of business over the last half-century. It has been equated with a wide variety of business movements from total quality management to lean six sigma. When an organization is looking for ways to become more competitive, to reduce costs or time, it often looks to improve its processes.

One of the challenges that has been evident in many organizations that have embraced process improvement is that the value of process improvement is not as much in the improvement of the processes as it is in aligning the desired outcomes with some measurable requirement that has been identified and validated as adding value to an internal or external customer. For this reason, a thorough look at what process improvement is and is not, including where it came from and where it might go, is a valuable task for performance improvement professionals who are concerned with measurable outcomes.

DESCRIPTION

In seeking to understand what process improvement is and how to use it to help achieve organizational goals, we must first clarify what is meant by the term "process." The *American Heritage Dictionary* defines process as "a series of actions, changes, or functions bringing about a result," for example: the process of getting payroll checks out on time converts timesheets or pay-plan schedules along with tax information to paychecks going into the mail or into pre-arranged direct deposit employee accounts.

Processes are the way work gets done. If nothing ever changed with work, processes would never require improvement. But life has a way of changing things. And because of this, when anything changes in an organization, there is a high probability that the processes that are associated with the change will also require change to ensure that they are still adding the greatest amount of value possible.

The Certified Quality Process Analyst Handbook (2007) reports the American Society for Quality (ASQ) definition for process improvement as "the act of changing a process to reduce variability and cycle time and make the process more effective, efficient and productive" (p. 355). In other words, processes change, either by happenstance or intention, but an improvement must make something about the process better. Moreover, relates the ASQ, "Continuous improvement is an ongoing effort to improve products, services, or processes. These efforts can seek 'incremental' improvement over time or 'breakthrough' improvement all at once."

Process improvement is not the same as problem solving or decision making; however, problem-solving and decision-making tools are used to support process improvement.

When thinking of processes in terms of organizations or businesses we must also think in terms of what goes into a process (inputs); what the value of the results of the process are (outputs); and who determines the value of the outputs (customers). Processes in organizations exist for the benefit of their customers, and customers can be internal or external to the organization. The next person who receives the outputs of the process is the customer.

Typical *inputs* to a business process include people, time, equipment, money, or material. Typical *outputs* include documentation, data, information, decisions, or some tangible item such as a product. However intangible outputs, such as morale or enthusiasm—although these could be certainly be quantified in tangible terms—are often included in the common lists of outputs. What makes a process important is that the outputs, or deliverables, are more valuable to the customer than a non-processed combination of the inputs.

Organizations strive for process improvement because they must become adept at doing more with less, achieving more in less time, accomplishing more with fewer resources. All this and more can be accomplished with carefully thought-out and well-implemented process improvement applications.

History

Many practitioners don't know the interesting history of "quality" in the Western world. The Guilds of medieval Europe in the late 13th century started paying attention to what it took to keep their customers happy. Their approach to what we now call "customer satisfaction" persisted until Great Britain started the factory system with an emphasis on a new way to keep customers happy, "product inspection." This focus continued throughout the Industrial Revolution and into the early 20th century.

The real demand for quality as we know it in the United States emerged during WWII, when it became apparent that the bullets manufactured in one state had to fit the rifles manufactured in another state. This challenge initially led the military to engage in 100 percent inspection, but that soon became too burdensome. They then created and published military-specification standards and sampling techniques for inspection. This new approach was then elaborated by Walter Shewhart, a physics academic who worked with Western Electric and who introduced training in statistical process control techniques.

Then-President Eisenhower asked Joseph M. Juran and W. Edwards Deming to help rebuild the failed economy of Japan. Rather than focus on inspection, Deming and Juran focused on improving all organizational processes through the people who used them. Thus was born the first big quality fad, with total quality management (TQM) and process improvement becoming inexorably linked to one quality methodology after another.

WHAT WE KNOW FROM RESEARCH

Several quality methodologies embrace the philosophy reflected through process improvement. Some of these titles and the mixed successes they have brought to their users have been documented over time though a multitude of research studies, far too many to document here. Many of the methodologies listed below at one time were considered common organizational practices. Some pertinent research is also listed for each of these methodologies, although the research literature on the proven effectiveness of each of these methods is either scarce or mixed. What is abundant is practitioner literature that either describes what these methods are and how to implement them or case studies, some of which speak to the effectiveness of the method, in one inherently limited scenario.

Total Quality Management (TQM). TQM means engaging all members of an organization to participate in improving processes, products, and services within the culture of an organization. Its success depends on full commitment by management, since there are a lot of elements to be managed. Small companies, reports Steven C. Jones in his 2005 *Quality Management Journal* article, have difficulty adopting TQM principles because full commitment requires compliance in up to twelve areas; thus these managers avoid TQM due to resistance to change, fear of risk, or the belief that current practices are appropriate.

Malcolm Baldrige National Quality Award. Applying seven criteria around everyday business operations determines eligibility for this prestigious quality award. Several other national awards have been patterned after this model; some of which are specific to an industry. For example, the Magnet Award is for healthcare organizations that demonstrate adherence to a specific set of quality criteria in nursing and patient care. Between 1987, when it was first passed into law, and 2005, there have been sixty-eight recipients of the Malcolm Baldrige Award, reports the National Institute of Standards and Technology. While some researchers believe that earning this award is quite prestigious, others, reports Vicki Smith-Daniels in 2003, question the cost, value, and persistence of giving the award. One thing cited by critics is the superficiality of top-down programs, along with the stress and inability of top management to lead and manage sustainable change.

ISO 9000 and Other Standards. These use specific internationally agreed-on standards to achieve the base level of quality management or a quality system to address the needs of specific industries. In a 2003 study, Rajendran and Anantharaman found that certified ISO 9000 firms did not necessarily have a higher return on quality (ROQ).

Six Sigma. Six sigma uses a specific statistical philosophy to drive customer satisfaction and bottom-line results by reducing variation and waste. The research literature on the effectiveness of six sigma is scarce. The typical six sigma goal, as reported by University of Leicester professor Tony Bendell in a 2006 article for *TQM Magazine*, is to reach a return on investment of 3:1. In his 2002 book *Lean Six Sigma*, Michael George claims that the gaps between customer and supplier are reduced with six sigma, and that profit increases.

Kaizen. *Kaizen* uses the power of participation to make slow, incremental, and positive ongoing/continuous change based on the 6Ss and common sense. According to William Feld's 2000 book *Lean Manufacturing*, Kaizen projects can realize organizational benefits of 30 to 90 percent reduction in work-in-process, 25 to 75 percent reduction in processing steps; 20 to 90 percent reduction in manufacturing lead time; up to a 30 percent increase in cellular productivity; 25 to 50 percent reduction in non-value-added activities; 10 to 50 percent reduction in space utilization; 15 to 75 percent reduction in die changeover time; and 30 to 80 percent reduction in travel distance.

Lean Manufacturing. With lean manufacturing, focus is placed on elimination of waste, reductions in costs, improvements of process flow, identification of value streams and standardization of work. In her 2002 dissertation study of over 270 firms, the University of Minnesota's Rachna Shah observed various traits among "lean" organizations that non-lean organizations did not possess. Among these, it was observed that lean firms had higher rates of change, they were more likey to be more responsive in terms of business strategy, their costs and volume flexibility were significantly different, they were more aware of customer requirements due to more contact, and these firms made it a priority to be involved with customers, vendors, and within their own organizations. Similarly, Robert Paden reports in his 2003 dissertation that lean manufacturing improves productiviy by 10 to 30 percent, increases quality by 85 percent, reduces rework by 90 percent, decreases space utilization by 50 percent, and reduces lead time for products by 90 percent.

Popular Process Improvement Tool Sets

Most of the quality methodologies above share the use of common tools. Many of these tools are used to help a team or individuals make a decision or to solve a problem. In and of themselves, they are not process improvement tools but support a process improvement methodology. Some of the most popular and successful quality tool sets as identified by ASQ include:

- *Cause Analysis Tools*—Tools for the first step to improvement: identifying the cause of a problem or situation.

- *Evaluation and Decision-Making Tools*—Tools to support making informed decisions and choosing the best options with a simple, objective rating system and determining the success of a project.

- *Process Analysis Tools*—Tools to identify and eliminate unnecessary process steps to increase efficiency, reduce timelines, and cut costs.

- *Data Collection and Analysis Tools*—Tools to collect the data you require and help make sense of them once they're collected.

- *Idea Creation Tools*—Tools to stimulate group creativity and organize the ideas that come from it.

- *Project Planning and Implementing Tools*—Tools to track a project's status and look for improvement opportunities in the project.

Technology Tool Sets

Additionally, there are also technology-enabled process improvement tools that help enhance the non-technology-enabled tools, as well as the basic design, redesign, and maintenance of a process. Because process improvement activities are performed by various people in the organization, transparency becomes particularly important in order to properly align these activities. Automated process improvement systems are particularly valuable to accomplish this. Web portals have been used to support organizational processes at every stage, and with interfaces for both employees and customers. We see examples of this every time we check our bank balances online, order a book, or purchase and download music for our MP3 players. Whereas these processes used to require face-to-face interaction, web-supported processes enable business to be conducted from anywhere by anyone.

Automated workflow systems are another technology available for improving processes. These systems are particularly useful in reducing the amount of time a particular task is in queue to be processed. Often, wasted time can be found in the interface between one stage of a process and the next. For example, a customer care center might depend on two different agents to complete a sales process: one describing the product and taking the order and another for obtaining payment information and completing the purchase. Once she has completed her stage of the sales process, the first agent sends the call to the next station, but if that second agent is still tending to the previous customer, then the entire flow of the process is halted until the second agent is available. An automated workflow system would automatically route the call to the next available agent, with minimal wait time for the customer.

Electronic technology and digitalization has also contributed to the efficiency of many processes, allowing convenient storage and access to all sorts of documents. Invoices can be created, delivered, received, and paid immediately in electronic form. Likewise, contracts, reports, and other documents can be created, exchanged, edited, and signed in little time. Employees, clients, vendors, and other stakeholder groups dispersed all over the globe can all come together in a meeting at little or no cost with virtual conferencing systems.

There are myriad other technology tools that organizations can use to improve their processes. What the best technology is depends on the fit between the technology and the process and the organization. When streamlining a process, it is useful to carefully consider whether technology can contribute to the efficiency and effectiveness of that process, and to the organization as a whole. This last caveat is important because of the systemic nature of organizations. Sometimes a particular technology can indeed improve a process, but may be more costly than the savings it is producing, or it may create problems in other parts of the organization.

It is also important to consider whether the organization and its affected members are ready to use this type of technology. If those affected have never used the technology selected, or anything close to it, the technology may be more of a hindrance—at least at first—than a process enhancer. The key is to provide the necessary resources and support to enable those involved to successfully use the technology so that the targeted process can indeed be improved.

The most important thing here is that the desired process goals and organizational context drive the technology, rather than the other way around.

Linking Improvement to Organizational Goals and Objectives

It is important to make a distinction between ends and means. Ends are results, as communicated by organizational goals and objectives. Means are how we accomplish ends. Processes are always means, and we seek to improve them in order to improve results, and ultimately results are defined by customer needs and expectations. It is important to reiterate that these customers are both internal and external.

If process improvement is taking inputs and transforming them to outputs that meet or exceed customer expectations, then continuous process improvement is doing this on an ongoing business to meet the ever-changing customer expectations. This is reflected by the organization's changing objectives.

Process Goals

Some goals connect directly to external customers (for example, sales) and others (for example, purchasing) link only to internal customers. Either way, process goals should always be driven by customer requirements. One common mistake is for organizations to only track primary processes that connect to the external customer and neglect to also track and improve those supporting processes that, while not connected directly to external customers, make it possible for the primary processes to satisfactorily meet customer requirements.

While every step in a process must add value to the next, Geary Rummler and Alan Brache indicate in their 1995 classic *Improving Performance* that processes must be assessed not only for the value they add, but also for the number of inputs (for example, capital, people, time, equipment, and material) they require to produce that value. Moreover, the authors state that each process "exists to make a contribution to one or more organizational goals. Therefore, each process should be measured against process goals that reflect the contribution that the process is expected to make to one or more organizational goals" (p. 47).

Identifying Measurable Indicators (Metrics)

Indicators or metrics are concrete measures of some result or process that allows us to make complex systems manageable. These indicators become the data points we seek to track, and in turn use, to make decisions and take specific actions for improvement (see Chapter Ten for a more in-depth discussion of performance indicators).

One of the most well-known organizational measurement frameworks is Robert Kaplan and David Norton's balanced scorecard. Originally created to help managers look beyond financial measures, this framework includes four basic areas of measurement: customers; finances; internal business processes; and knowledge, education and growth. The business process category impacts all the others; in fact, they all impact each other in some way. Thus highly effective organization not only track, manage, and improve processes, but they do so in the context of—and in coordination with—other organizational measures.

Time, Quality, and Cost Measures

The traditional dimensions of internal value are *time, quality, and cost.* Each of these dimensions can and should be measured in order to ensure that each is meeting or surpassing its objectives and standards. Time is important because it can easily translate into money, for instance, usually the longer it takes to deliver goods and services, the greater the cost. Time measures are important because they are describing the cycle within which the process is taking place, and cycle time is one indication of efficiency. Quality measures are obviously important to improvement, particularly if the measures are proactive, rather than reactive. Cost is important because it is reflective of everything from the cost of materials to the cost of manpower, and it directly impacts customer satisfaction and perception of value.

Table 17.1 illustrates some common indicators of time, quality, and cost.

WHEN TO APPLY

Process improvement begins when employees or managers in a department, function, or other work area determine that the way they are doing their work is not providing results that are meeting the needs of their customers. With this initial recognition comes the need to establish a working group or team. The people who do the work in the process are identified and recruited to become the heart of the process improvement activity and are dedicated to the improvement of the identified process. It is essential that the group is either skilled in the use of process improvement tools and methodologies or can retain the services of a facilitator who can guide them. Process improvement is a serious process that requires serious work and focused attention.

How to Apply

The team begins by clarifying specifically the expectations of its customers (as previously stated, internal customer expectations are just as important as

Table 17.1 Indicators of Time, Quality, and Cost

Category	Indicator
Time	On-time delivery receipt
	Order cycle time
	Order cycle time variability
	Response time
	Forecasting/planning cycle time
	Planning cycle time variability
Quality	Overall customer satisfaction
	Processing accuracy
	Perfect order fulfillment
	In-time delivery
	Complete order
	Accurate product selection
	Damage-free
	Accurate invoice
	Forecast accuracy
	Planning accuracy
	Schedule adherence
	Profit and profit over time
	Meeting of corporate social responsibility requirements.
	Safety
Cost	Cost of manpower
	Cost of raw goods
	Cost of transportation
	Cost of inventory
	Cost of energy
	Cost of downtime
	Cost of rework

Adapted from Guerra-López, I. (2008) *Performance Evaluation: Proven Approaches for Improving Program and Organizational Performance.*

external customer expectations). The expectations must be clearly identified and agreed to as being not only appropriate but as adding significant value to the desired results of the process and to organization goals. This list of customer expectations identifies the goals for the process and the process improvement activity.

Next, the boundaries for the process to be improved are identified. Identifying and reaching agreement on the boundaries of the process can be the difference between success and failure for any process improvement activity. When we refer to boundaries, we are referring to the points at which the process improvement activities will begin and end. For example, if an organization wants to improve its hiring process, it has to decide how extensive or contracted the process improvement activity will be. The hiring process can arbitrarily be considered to begin when the organization recognizes it wants to bring someone into its ranks, or it can arbitrarily be considered to begin with recruiting or when candidate applications are received. There is no right or wrong place to begin or end a process for the purposes of improving it. Most important is the recognition that, the bigger the process, the greater the probability of requiring more people and time to make realistic and measureable improvements. The smaller the process, the fewer people will most likely have to be involved and the more likely the process will impact and be impacted by other processes. In many organizations, small processes are considered sub-processes and take on a life of their own. Wherever the process is considered to begin and to end, perhaps the most important consideration is that of the organization's systems, as there is an endless interdependence between and among organizational subsystems. Defining a process too narrowly and outside of its context could lead to a process that is perhaps more efficient, but ultimately ineffective in the context of helping the organization reach its goals.

Any rules, laws, or guidelines that regulate or dictate the way the process works are collected. Inputs and suppliers of the inputs are identified. Then the people who do the work describe what happens now, what is done by whom, in what sequence at the task level, what decisions are made now and by whom, using what criteria, and when are they made as they impact any task. For each task and each decision, all inputs and suppliers are identified and a process map or flowchart is created to reflect the workflow to make it visible and more easily understood as how the process is at this time.

By returning to the goals of the process improvement activity (customer needs and expectations), the employees can begin making decisions about what metrics are associated with the various steps or decisions in the as-is and, in turn, what data will have to be collected and how. The process improvement team will use cause analysis tools to get to the root cause of why a step or series of steps is not adding the value required by the customers and, in turn, determine solution criteria. The team will use decision-making tools to identify alternatives and choose the most appropriate ones for achieving desired results. The team may want to use idea creation tools to think outside the proverbial box to identify alternatives that meet the required criteria. And when the process is re-created in a graphic format it will become the to-be version of the way work is done. A good business case for all changes has to be created, with the expectation that all suggestions and recommendations for change to any step or decision in the as-is process will be appropriately challenged.

Once a thorough business case for any and all process changes has been created, representative customers and stakeholders (people who are not direct customers but have a stake in the process and how it works) should be invited for preliminary review and analysis of the potential to-be process. A well-defined review conducted by the process team that did the work will reduce the pushback and resistance that often accompanies process change. At this point, the thoughtful application of specific project planning and implementation tools will also reduce pushback and resistance.

Examples

Below are several examples of process improvement applications. The first example describes a situation in which a marketplace or a key customer changed requirements and the organization had to respond efficiently. The second example is a situation in which two organizations merged and redundant processes were made obsolete. The last example describes a situation in which inconsistencies in carrying out the same job function caused employee and workplace confusion.

- *Example 1.* A healthcare organization was struggling with getting patients checked out by noon the day of their scheduled checkout in order to make the room ready for a new patient and thereby increasing the utilization of bed space. Clearly the health and safety, the quality of the healthcare services for the patients, and the impact on the patients' family was the number one priority, but also important was ensuring all the "paperwork" was correctly completed to guarantee payments would be forthcoming. The institution created a "FastTrack" team that included representatives of each of the types of individuals who participated in the checkout process. This team met over a compressed period of time and was given a clear charge, well-defined boundaries, and requirements from all parties who might be impacted. Decisions were made after all risks were analyzed and evaluated. People who would approve any recommendations were required to stay within contact distance and time during this team's activities. Approvals were made real-time, and "noon checkout" was created and implemented with success.

- *Example 2.* Two large banks merged. Small teams were set up in work-shop-like settings with representatives from each institution from around the country. They were trained to map core business processes and determine which were redundant and then make recommendations on how best to merge or eliminate them as appropriate. The employees who participated were quite excited about what they were learning and what they were doing. Unfortunately, two large constituencies were left out. The employees who were in the workshops were supposed to share with all others from their geographic area what they were doing and why decisions were being made as they were. However, no one taught them how or gave them tools to do so. It was assumed this was something they all knew how to do. But even more importantly, no one ever asked the customers of these two banks which set of processes that impacted them were most user-friendly and most appreciated. When the dust settled from the merger, enough customers had left the new merged organization that once again it was a target for a merger.

- *Example 3.* As a result of rapid growth in a mid-sized financial institution, recruiting was taking on increasing importance, and many training and development resources were diverted to that activity. On-boarding activities and skill training for the new recruits to perform their jobs were not assessed to ensure accuracy and bottom-line value. It was assumed that the existing training that had served so well for the past four years would do the job. It was not understood that the on-boarding training and supportive activities were incomplete and had many details filled in during the first few weeks of work by the immediate supervisor and co-workers. It was also assumed that the skill training taught in the first month was teaching the skills required to do the various jobs to meet the metrics against which the employees were being measured. It was not understood that many of the work processes done by the job categories being filled by the recruits had changed and that existing employees had created individual workarounds that may or may not have been con-sistent with what management really wanted; but as long as the employees were making their numbers, the supervisors didn't know about the workarounds until the new recruits started doing their jobs. New employees were seen very often asking co-workers how to *really* do what was taught in the skill training sessions and were given multiple different messages by incumbent employees, creating confusion and demoralizing new recruits who had once been enthusiastic about their new employment.

STRENGTHS AND CRITICISMS

Continuous process improvement can be just as easily met with enthusiasm as with skepticism, depending on the experiences that those involved have had in the past. The following strengths and criticisms represent some of the most-cited observations and should be considered when an organization considers entering into a process improvement activity:

Strengths of continuous process improvement include:

- It can dramatically and measurably improve every process in an organization if done with a systemic perspective.
- It can provide significant positive impact if the work and its outputs are well aligned and measured; it can provide a roadmap for continuous improvement.
- It can become a training guide for new employees or for transferred employees at all levels in the organization.
- It can provide a foundation for functional and cross-functional team development.
- It clearly describes the suppliers and customers for all work.
- It identifies internal and external customer requirements that can be measured for maintenance and improvement.
- It can increase the efficiency and effectiveness of information.
- It is a powerful performance management tool.

Criticisms of continuous process improvement include:

- There is the potential danger of improving things that are either already at peak performance or are obsolete.
- There is also the danger of fixing one component of a process while seriously damaging another.
- If it is poorly implemented, it can do more harm than good.
- It is not helpful if people do not adhere to the improved process.
- If not carefully done, it can misalign key metrics and significantly damage the process.
- Process visualizations can be deceiving because different people see and interpret them differently.

RECOMMENDED DESIGN, DEVELOPMENT, AND IMPLEMENTATION PROCESS

The following is a list of thought starters for each step of a typical process improvement initiative.

1. *Confirm that this is the best solution for the business issues at hand.* Ask questions of the highest-ranking leader or the champion of the initiative to ensure that other options have been considered. Is this a problem to be solved, that is, is the issue to be addressed a deviation from what is expected and therefore doing some type of root-cause analysis will be a better solution? Is this reflecting a tough decision that someone doesn't want to make and may be looking for "justification"? If so, the politics that may influence the activity could get in the way of real process improvement.

2. *Determine what other performance improvement interventions are in place and how it might impact them.* Are there other teams or task forces already working on other processes elsewhere in the organization? One must remember that an organization is really a connected system of processes that may or may not be visibly interrelated. Almost like stubbing your toe and walking with a limp for a while to protect it can cause a back ache, so can making a short-term fix or unanalyzed change cause severe pain to an organization.

3. *Choose the methodology or technology that will be supporting the process improvement activity.* In a previous section of this chapter, we listed several tools, methodologies, and technologies that can support a process improvement initiative. It is too easy to use the one or two that are the most familiar or comfortable to a team or its leader. We recommend that the urge be resisted. Carefully review the options to ensure that the best solution is selected. One way of doing this is to create a decision matrix. Establish the criteria for choosing the best tools or methodologies based on what the tool or methodology must do and what would be helpful if it did it. Evaluate each option against the criteria matrix.

4. *Select and gather the individuals who are best suited to map, measure, and improve the process.* The best people are not always the ones who are available, willing, or accessible. It may be foolish to launch a project without having access to the people who can really describe the as-is and can use their most creative thinking in considering and discussing the what-ifs that could create the most rewarding improvements. Sometimes, but not always, the people who are closest to the process, although good at describing the as-is, may be the most stuck in the way it

is done now. It is also critical to identify and enlist the people who can provide or collect the data to establish a baseline of the metrics and to measure the real improvements once changes have been properly implemented.

5. *Identify the boundaries for the process to be improved.* The boundaries will define the scope of the process improvement project. This is where the rubber meets the road and defines what the real process is that is going to be improved. Is it the size of a bread box or the kitchen? Remember that the smaller the process is, the easier it will be to improve, but a small process increases the likelihood of hidden implications and impacts lurking in the background. Bigger processes are by nature more complex, more integrated into other processes and systems, and typically have more conflict around what is being done now (the as-is) and the way to do it in the future (the to-be.)

6. *Identify all external and internal customers of the process and their requirements.* It is too easy to assume that the team that is improving the process really knows what the customers (either internal or external) are saying and will want; after all, don't they already tell you? Please resist the temptation to go with what you think you know. Use a valid methodology to ask the customers of this process what they must have and why, what they would like to have and why, and what they would be hurt by and how if and when the process changes.

7. *Use the method or tool to make the process visible as it is presently being followed (the "as-is").* For people who are always in a hurry or who are working to save time or money, it is tempting to jump to the to-be, in other words, to describe what they would like to see once the process is changed. Although there are ways of making this almost work, there are also risks. By going right to the future state, you may lose the details of the existing process that are most functional and may be better to keep or those that are the most dysfunctional and therefore must be changed. You may also lose the ability to create real as-is metrics from the various steps in order to determine the real value of any changes. There is also the risk of not getting the buy-in up-front from the people who are presently doing the work and must be invested in making and supporting any changes. The list of risks can continue, but most importantly, we believe you should not skip this step if at all possible.

8. *Identify in the as-is model specific points at which the process does not meet customer expectations or is followed inconsistently.* Clearly this step cannot be done if the *as-is* version is not being mapped. The importance of this step is to once again align the requirement for change with desired

and measurable goals and in turn set up the process improvement initiative for optimal success, as required by the needs of its customers.

9. *Identify methods or processes to determine the measurable impact of process deviation or variation.* Many technology solutions can create what-if scenarios that can provide reasonable assumptions around metrics. Don't overlook this step!

10. *Collect data on the proposed process performance using the technology options for a given period of time.* Reach agreement on the amount of time and the conditions under which the data collected will be considered valid from the perspective of the customer as well as from the perspective of management.

11. *Analyze the data to determine what requires change.* Analyze the data from the perspective of the customers, because they are the reason that the changes have been made. Once again, resist the temptation to assume that you know what your customers will say. Ask them!

12. *Prioritize changes to be made and create the changed process map ("to-be").* Recognize that, even though there may be a dozen value-added changes, making them all at one time may add more chaos into the system than it can absorb. This decision has to be made carefully, as there may be divergent positions. Some people want to pull a Band-Aid slowly, letting the pain settle down before pulling the next little bit; others want to yank it off all at once. Regardless of the method chosen, do a mini-risk analysis. Ask: What could go wrong? What is the probability that it will? What can we do to prevent it from happening? What can we do to reduce the negative impact if it does happen? Make the choice with good information rather than because "that is the way we always do it."

13. *Validate the "to-be" with all stakeholders.* They are your customers. Even after you hear their perspectives and believe you are responding to them, things have a way of changing in a process improvement activity. Changes need to be validated before they become a reality that you are stuck with.

14. *Create and implement a communication strategy.* Determine target populations that will be affected in any way by the changes in the process. Determine how best to communicate with each and what each needs to know by when. Create communication methods and vehicles. Deploy communication methods and vehicles, and measure the effectiveness of all communications and adjust as needed.

15. *Create and implement a robust change management strategy.* Determine what jobs or tasks will be changing. Determine how other performance improvement interventions may be impacted. Identify specific

employees who will be directly and indirectly impacted by the changes. Determine whether training, coaching, or job aids will be required to support process compliance. Ensure that performance management system reflects changes in the process. Ensure managers and other workforce leaders understand how to coach performance in the new process.

16. *Evaluate for continuous improvement opportunities.* Track progress toward desired results. Continually revise the process as internal/external influences or customer requirement change.

Equally important is the ability of the process improvement team to recognize and acknowledge that this project is, in fact, a project and therefore must adhere to the best practices of project management. Table 17.2 shows eight key considerations for managing projects effectively.

CRITICAL SUCCESS FACTORS

The process improvement project must be based on a systemic perspective and must be created with input from those closest to the process. Buy-in from all key stakeholders and stakeholder groups is required, and their input must be framed with the right metrics and customer requirements. Because changing a process changes the way work is done, the changes in the work must be reflected and integrated into the performance management system. Appropriate support and activities must be provided when required to assure employee success. Last, changes in all work must take into consideration other key factors for success. These can include social, political, economic, legal, intercultural, and technical considerations.

Integrating these critical success factors will increase the probability of process improvement success in your organization.

SUMMARY

Process improvement as described in this chapter uses many tools and methodologies in order to achieve measurable business objectives. One of the biggest challenges in process improvement is keeping all associated activities aligned with and focused on using metrics as indicators of success. Successful process improvement activities begin with well-defined customer needs (internal or external) that can be measured and therefore can be measured again during and after a process is improved to ensure adequate value has been added. They also include clear boundaries so that the focus of the activity is able to stay within its designated scope. They include the right people, not just people who are available or who are convenient, and they use technology as an enabler, not

Table 17.2 Key Considerations for Project Management

Project Management Process Element	Rationale	Key Questions
Project Definition	Gets agreement and keeps everyone focused on the same goal, the same scope, the same metrics and customer requirements	What are we trying to accomplish and why?
Team/ Stakeholder Identification	The correct functions, stakeholders are involved for the right reasons	Who is required for long term as well as project success?
Plans, Schedule, and Budgets	All involved must be totally clear on their roles and how they will be evaluated	What needs to happen by when and by whom?
Hand Off Management	There are customer/supplier relationships on and off the team, including the hidden ones	Who needs what from whom to make this work?
Measurement	What is measured is what gets managed	How will we know that customer requirements will be or are being met?
Communication	Everyone involved directly and indirectly can and will influence project outcomes	How will we assure that everyone receives accurate, timely information?
Risk Management	Removing problems before they occur saves time, money, and good will	What could go wrong and what are the early warning signs?
Team Performance Management	Good performance can be facilitated and reinforced	Are the criteria for team success being met?

Adapted from David Po-Chedley (2007), *Systems Approach to Project Management*.

as a driver. Process improvement should not be confused with problem solving or decision making, nor should it be overlooked as something trendy or too complex. When a proven process improvement methodology is followed and metrics are integrated into the process, it will help an organization achieve its business and customer objectives.

References

Bendell, T. (2006). A review and comparison of six sigma and the lean organizations. *TQM Magazine, 18*(3), 255–262.

Feld, W. (2000). *Lean manufacturing: Tools, techniques, and how to use them.* Boca Raton, FL: CRC Press.

George, M. (2002). *Lean six sigma: Combining six sigma quality with lean speed.* New York: McGraw-Hill.

Jones, S. C. (2005). Selected quality practices of small manufacturers. *Quality Management Journal, 12*(1), 41–53.

Paden, R. (2003). ISO 9000 impelentation in the chemical indsutry. Doctoral Dissertation, North Central University, Arizona.

Rajendran, C., &. Anantharaman, R. (2003). Do quality certifications improve software industry's opeational performance? Retrieved November 25, 2008, from http://www.asq.org/pub/sqp/past/vol6_issue1/issac.pdf.

Rummler, G., & Brache, A. (1995). *Improving performance: How to manage the white space on the organization chart* (2nd ed.). San Francisco: Jossey-Bass.

Shah, R. (2002). *A configurational view of lean manufacturing and its theoretical implications.* Published Doctoral Dissertation, Ohio State University.

Smith-Daniels, V. (2003). Why total quality management programs do not persist: The role of management quality and implications for leading TQM tranformation. *Decision Science Journal.*

Technology Institute of Standards and Technology (2005, Febrruary 25). Year of the 1,000 applicants. Retrieved December 3, 2008, from National Institute of Standards and Technology: htttp://www.quality.nist.gov/Improvement_Act.htm.

Recommended Readings

American Society for Quality. (n.d.). Continuous improvement. Retrieved from http://www.asq.org/learn-about-quality/continuousimprovement/overview/overview.html.

Andersen, B. (2007). *Business process improvement toolbox* (2nd ed.). Milwaukee, WI: ASQ Quality Press.

Becker, J., Kugeler, M., & Rosemann, M. (2003). *Process management by Jörg Becker, Martin Kugeler, and Michael Rosemann.* Berlin: Springer-Verlag.

Born, G. (1994). *Process management to quality improvement: The way to design, document and re-engineer business systems.* West Sussex, UK: John Wiley & Sons.

Christensen, E. H., Coombes-Betz, K. M., & Stein, M. S. (2007). *The certified quality process analyst handbook.* Milwaukee: ASQ Quality Press.

Covey, D. (2003). *Mind your Ps & Qs: How to achieve quality through process improvement: A handbook for humans.* Lincoln, NE: iUniverse Inc.

Fryman, M. (2001). *Quality and process improvement*. Albany, NY: Delmar Cengage Learning.

George, S., & Thomas, C. (2006). *Process improvement and quality management in the retail industry*. Hoboken, NJ: John Wiley & Sons.

Graham, B. (2004). *Detail process charting: Speaking the language of process*. Hoboken, NJ: John Wiley & Sons.

Harrington, H. (1991). *Business process improvement: The breakthrough strategy for total quality, productivity, and competitiveness*. New York: McGraw Hill.

Harrington, H., Esseling, K., & Nimwegen, V. (1997). *Business process improvement workbook: Documentation, analysis, design, and management of business process improvement*. New York: McGraw-Hill.

Jeston, J., & Nelis, J. (2008). *Business process management: Practical guidelines to successful implementations* (2nd ed.). Burlington, VT: Butterworth-Heinemann.

Kerzner, H. (2006). *A systems approach to project management*. Hoboken, NJ: John Wiley & Sons.

Madison, D. (2005). *Process mapping, process improvement and process management*. Houston, TX: Payton Press.

Persse, J. (2006). *Process improvement essentials: CMMI, six sigma, and ISO 9001*. Sebastopol, CA: O'Reilly Media.

PART FIVE

EDITORS'
DISCUSSION

This part of the handbook has provided a variety of performance interventions focused on how tools, environment, and processes can be leveraged to improve the accomplishment of results. As with other interventions, process improvement comes in a variety of shapes and sizes. Some improvement projects may involve merely adding (or removing) a signoff from a manager to improve quality or process efficiencies, while other projects may include the complete redesign of accounting practices within the organization. Regardless of the size or scope of your improvement efforts, it is worth the time and energy to examine (or re-examine) the processes, procedures, rules, and policies that currently guide performance to see whether changes could be of value.

Together, the interventions described throughout this part of the book provide a key component in the systemic improvement of performance. Without adequate tools, a supportive environment, and a set of processes that works, the accomplishment of desired results is typically stymied. Hence, it is essential that your improvement efforts analyze the current availability and quality of these three elements—tools, environment, and processes—to determine whether they are capable of supporting the achievement of your desired results. Then implement appropriate performance interventions to address any gaps that may be present in the current system.

Reference from Editors' Contributions to Part Five

Lick, D., & Kaufman, R. (2009). Applying change creation to improve online learning. In P. L. Rogers, G. A., Berg, J. V., Boettcher, C. Howard, C., L. Justice, & K. Schenk (Eds.), *Encyclopedia of distance learning* (2nd ed.) Hershey, PA: Information Science Reference.

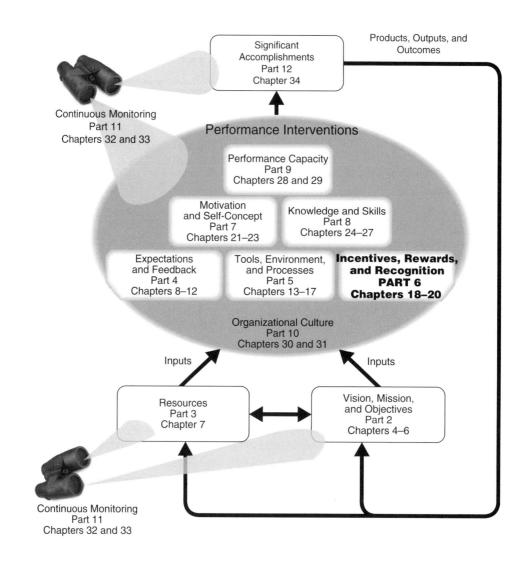

Products, Outputs, and Outcomes

Significant
Accomplishments
Part 12
Chapter 34

Continuous Monitoring
Part 11
Chapters 32 and 33

Performance Interventions

Performance Capacity
Part 9
Chapters 28 and 29

Motivation
and Self-Concept
Part 7
Chapters 21–23

Knowledge and Skills
Part 8
Chapters 24–27

Expectations
and Feedback
Part 4
Chapters 8–12

Tools, Environment,
and Processes
Part 5
Chapters 13–17

**Incentives, Rewards,
and Recognition
PART 6
Chapters 18–20**

Organizational Culture
Part 10
Chapters 30 and 31

Inputs

Inputs

Resources
Part 3
Chapter 7

Vision, Mission,
and Objectives
Part 2
Chapters 4–6

Continuous Monitoring
Part 11
Chapters 32 and 33

PART SIX

INCENTIVES, REWARDS, AND RECOGNITION

With few exceptions, improvements in organizational performance are contingent on improvements in individual or team performance. In other words, the accomplishment of desired organizational results is in most instances dependent on the achievement of desired results by individuals and teams both inside and outside of the organization. As a consequence, successful improvement efforts frequently include one or more performance interventions that address results at the individual, team, and organizational levels; achieving desired results at each of these levels creates an effective performance improvement system.

In the same manner, partners external to your organization (such as clients, suppliers, community groups, and society) rely on the achievement of results by your organization, its teams, and its individual employees, as well as the results from other organizations to create an effective performance system. These relationships are the hallmark of systems theory as it applies to performance, and is discussed by Thomas Gilbert in his book *Human Competence: Engineering Worthy Performance*. When performance systems within your organization are effective and contribute to performance systems outside of your organization, then significant accomplishments can be achieved.

Improving performance is therefore not synonymous with simply changing individual or team behaviors. After all, changing how individuals or teams perform may or may not lead to improvements in performance (or desired results). For example, just because an improvement effort increases the number of calls taken by customer service representatives doesn't necessarily mean that customer satisfaction will also increase.

Thus, just changing how people work within your organization does not guarantee that they will achieve desired results, nor does it guarantee that those results will contribute to the accomplishment of organizational results. Just as changing your route to work doesn't necessarily get you there any faster; as buying a new computer doesn't necessarily improve your writing; and as adding more spices doesn't necessarily improve your cooking—performing is not the equivalent of performance.

The relationship between performance and performing is frequently over-looked, but is the foundation of improving performance. You must look beyond what people do, what procedures they follow, and what tools they use; you must examine the results they are currently accomplishing and compare those against expectations. Focusing on results, first and foremost, is the only way to identify, select, and implement performance interventions that accomplish significant and sustainable results.

Expanding Your Options

Bonus systems—a type of employee motivation plan in which employees are rewarded for achieving high productivity or other such worthwhile objectives.

Based on businessdictionary.com definition (January 2009)

When building a system for improving performance, you will therefore want to examine the incentives, rewards, and recognition related to performance. Incentives, rewards, and recognition interventions achieve desired results when they focus on performance rather than performing, providing incentives for individuals and teams to achieve desired results and then recognizing or rewarding those accomplishments.

Unfortunately and too frequently, informal systems tend to move away from the desired focus on performance, focusing solely on perform*ing*. An example is incentive programs that focus on the number of training courses taken rather than the results achieved by learners. When people are rewarded or recognized for behaviors that do not lead to desired results, it can inhibit the organization from being successful.

Every organization has examples of these misguided incentives, rewards, and recognitions. From cigarette smokers getting extra breaks throughout the day to CEOs who take large bonuses as their companies file for bankruptcy protection, these inverted management systems add to the complexity of any performance improvement project. In response, your improvement effort should include interventions that focus on incentives, rewards, and recognition for accomplishment of desired results.

Incentives can offer a valuable tool for shaping performance. By managing incentives, you can focus people on the achievement of desired results; encouraging them to accomplish goals that are aligned with the goals and objectives of your organization and its partners. You can also use incentives to connect people to other performance interventions you are implementing. For example, if you are introducing a new managerial coaching program (see Chapter Eleven) as part of your improvement efforts, then you may want to examine incentives as a tool for encouraging employees to participate in this new program. Incentives are an especially valuable intervention when they are used to encourage the achievement of desired results or link to other performance interventions.

WHAT'S COMING UP

In Chapter Eighteen, Steven Condly examines the diverse and valuable applications of incentive systems as a performance improvement intervention. As an intervention directly tied to the accomplishment of desired results or a technique for engaging people in other performance interventions, the use of incentives will find multiple applications in any improvement effort.

Incentive Systems

Steven J. Condly

INTRODUCTION

Incentive systems are motivation-focused structures designed to maximize improvements in employee behavior and/or decision making to the benefit of the organization. They are specifically associated with particular goals or outcomes and thus are distinguished from the more general compensation systems. Although governed by different circumstances, all incentive systems include common elements: goals, stakeholders, incentives, time frames, implementation and data collection procedures, and support structures. The system can be a success to the degree that management and targeted employees negotiate the details of the incentive system, institute and trust fair and reliable procedures, and incorporate system goals within the larger goals of the organization. As with any system, potential pitfalls abound, such as offering unacceptable incentives, not communicating the existence of the program, or changing rules or criteria midway through without consultation. However, evidence is abundant that properly designed systems have positive effects that are reliable, replicable, and measurable.

DESCRIPTION

An incentive system is not a tool or a technique; rather, it is a self-contained, but organizationally nested, collection of goals or desired outcomes, objects (for example, money), people (managers and incented employees), procedures, rules, strictures, and measurable outcomes. A well-designed and implemented incentive system can realize increases or improvements in both targeted thinking and behavior. Specifically, one can expect employees to *choose* to do what they were avoiding in the past, to *persist* more in the performance of their tasks (to spend more time doing what they're doing), and to exert greater amounts of *effort*, both mental and physical, in the performance of their jobs. In motivational terms, such a system increases employee self-efficacy, builds higher levels of task value, and improves employee mood and emotion vis á vis the task. These motivational improvements can reasonably be expected to lead to *more* and/or *better* work products.

Expanding Your Options

Commission systems—payment of a fixed fee accruing to an agent, broker, or salesperson for facilitating, initiating, and/or executing a commercial transaction.

Based on businessdictionary.com definition (January 2009)

In his chapter for the 1999 edition of the *Handbook of Human Performance Technology*, Florida State University's John Keller asserts that performance improvement systems deal with three primary entities: ability or knowledge, motivation, and opportunity or environment. Incentive systems do not directly affect the first or third; they have their main influence on employee motivation. The implementation and use of an incentive system is appropriate only to the degree that one can verify that employees are suffering motivational deficits with regard to specified improvement goals. Before any incentive system is adopted, designed, borrowed, or utilized, it is incumbent upon management to ensure that employee productivity is at less than desired levels for reasons of poor motivation. If employees either *can't* perform their tasks because they do not know how to do them, or if they are *being prevented* from performing their tasks due to an inefficient bureaucratic structure, red tape, mutually contradictory rules, and the like, then training (in the case of the former) or organizational restructuring (in the case of the latter) is in order.

In *Analyzing Performance Problems*, Robert Mager and Peter Pipe (1997) discuss quick and easy, but functional, methods for diagnosing and solving performance problems. Essential to the entire process is the core method of gathering data on which to base one's conclusions and take action(s): questioning and observation. By asking questions of employees (this does not have to be live; survey results are "past tense" but still may contain useful input for diagnosis and decision making) and by observing what people actually do in situations, evidence not only amasses, it clusters. Mager and Pipe suggest that, when employees are punished for engaging in desired performance, rewarded for engaging in undesired performance, or receive no consequences for action or inaction, the use of an incentive system is appropriate.

The primary, and most general, characteristic of the successful application of an incentive system is improvement, measured qualitatively or quantitatively. More directly, however, motivation is improved in three fundamental ways: One, employees *value* their task engagement more; that is, they perceive their engagement in the incentivized work activities to be worth their while and their interest in task participation grows. Two, they become more *efficacious* or convinced of their ability to accomplish their goals as they start to garner the rewards associated with their improved performance. And three, their *mood* at work shifts to the positive as they enjoy success, achievement, and reward. These motivational improvements are indicated by the aforementioned improvements in *choice*, *persistence*, and *effort*. Finally, these motivational improvements, which influence behavior, result in more and better work outcomes, which are measurable and quantifiable outcomes that serve as the ultimate form of feedback to both managers and employees regarding the merits of the incentive system.

Before more is said on the subject, it is important to distinguish incentive systems from other related phenomena discussed within the three chapters that comprise this section of this handbook. An incentive system is one element in the larger sphere of employee motivation, which includes theories and perspectives such as Frederick Herzberg's 1966 motivation hygiene theory, Abraham Maslow's 1954 hierarchy of needs, and David McClelland's 1961 achievement motivation theory. Likewise, incentive systems, as described in this chapter, are not the same as employee compensation systems in that, while employee compensation is a necessary part of the work experience, incentive systems are not. This chapter restricts the description and use of incentive systems to those instances in which management identifies a motivationally based performance deficit, designs or adopts a system of "rewards" and rules and procedures for obtaining those rewards, and limits the system to a particular facet of the job. In other words, incentive systems are more specific than are employee compensation and motivation. Employees must always be compensated and should always be motivated; incentive systems are restricted to particular issues and goals.

WHAT WE KNOW FROM RESEARCH

Everything from everyday experiences at home ("Eat your veggies and you can have dessert!") to those in school (five-point bonus question on the physics final) and at work (a cash award for meeting a sales goal) informs us that incentives seem to work. However, what matters is not our intuition, suspicions, or even our own experiences, but research. For every reason one person can cite explaining why incentives work, another person can counter with an equally reasonable explanation for why they don't. There are stories of both success and failure with regard to incentives and improved performance; thus, one can prove one's point by simply referencing the "right" story. Fortunately, there is enough research in the business, psychology, and education literature to allow us to understand whether and to what degree incentives might be effective. It is to this we now turn.

General Findings

Harold Stolovich, Dick Clark, and I produced a very large report in 2001 examining and summarizing research related to incentives and their use in the workplace, designing an incentive systems model, and conducting a national survey to determine the present state of affairs. We meta-analyzed available research and reported our findings in a 2003 article for *Performance Improvement Quarterly* titled "The Effects of Incentives on Workplace Performance." The meta-analysis confirmed and extended the 1998 findings of G. Douglas Jenkins and his team of researchers.

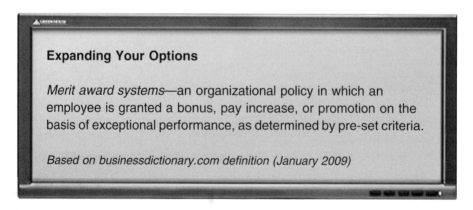

Expanding Your Options

Merit award systems—an organizational policy in which an employee is granted a bonus, pay increase, or promotion on the basis of exceptional performance, as determined by pre-set criteria.

Based on businessdictionary.com definition (January 2009)

Our 2003 article revealed that incentives realized an overall improvement of 22 percent over baseline performance (that is, performance that was not incentivized). There were also many important findings regarding particular aspects of incentives and incentive systems. For example, we found no statistically significant difference between those studies conducted at businesses from those conducted at schools; additionally, the kind of study (work simulation, laboratory experiment, or worksite field study) also revealed no significant differences. These two findings allow the reader to "breathe a sigh of relief" and trust that the research literature that reports results of studies on incentives and their use are trustworthy, believable, and transferable. They also help put to rest the objection that neither school-based studies nor laboratory experimental work can relate to the "real" world of work and, therefore, should be ignored. If incentives only improved performance in schools (in improved test scores or attendance), and showed no positive effects on employee performance at worksites, then decision-makers would have reason to treat claims of the benefits of incentive systems with suspicion. However, in accordance with general scientific convention, when findings (such as the positive effects of incentives) are shown to be demonstrated in a variety of situations, with different kinds of individuals, doing different kinds of tasks, one can safely conclude that the finding is reliable and applicable to his or her own situation.

Other results from the Condly, Clark, and Stolovitch study include the following:

- Monetary incentives had twice the positive effect on performance as did non-monetary tangible incentives (27 percent vs. 13 percent). This implies that there is something inherently more powerful in monetary incentives. In our 2001 study (for which Stolovich served as lead author), we hypothesized that monetary incentives have a greater utility value than do other incentives. For example, management could incentivize employees to increase their number of sales per month by offering them $1,000 cash or a vacation package worth $1,000. Both are attractive, but the cash can be used for a wide variety of things (including paying for necessities), whereas the vacation package might be to a location the employee does not prefer or it might be limited to times that are inconvenient.

- Long-term incentive systems (greater than six months) realized a 44 percent performance improvement; intermediate-term systems (between one and six months) realized a 29 percent performance improvement; and short-term systems (less than one month) realized the smallest performance gain (20 percent). The longer the term of the incentive program, the more time employees have to learn of it, "buy in," and experience its positive effects; also, management has more time to publicize the program and troubleshoot any deficiencies.

- Incentivized teams greatly outgained incentivized individuals (48 percent vs. 19 percent). This demonstrates that incentives can counter the phenomenon Karau and Williams refer to as "social loafing" in their 1995 article of the same name. In team settings, it is often tempting to limit one's efforts if one believes that others on the team can make up for one's own lack of effort. However, in incentive conditions, since extra effort is normally required, slacking off can cost not only the individual the incentive, but cost the entire team. Social pressure, real and perceived, can keep one working so as not to cost everyone the reward. Additionally, within a team, each member has access to the assistance of others, and all of the individual members can serve their own interests by assisting underperforming members.

- Finally, and interestingly, we found no significant differences between the effects of incentives on quantity or quality improvements (that is, between producing more or performing better) or between improvements in persistence or effort. All were positive. The upshot of this is that incentives do not work better for one kind of improvement over the other. In essence, then, whether management wishes to get *more* or *better* production, either through increased *effort* or *persistence*, targeted incentives lead to these desired improvements.

Incentive System Formats

Individuals who wish to implement an incentive system can rest assured that, all things being equal, its presence will improve employee performance. The problem, of course, is in the details. A 2000 review led by the University of Southern California's Sarah Bonner for the *Journal of Management Accounting Research* analyzed incentive systems and classified them into four groups:

- *Quota:* an incentive is paid an employee for meeting or exceeding a specified goal;
- *Piece rate:* the employee is incentivized on a "per unit of productivity" basis;
- *Tournament:* individuals qualify by meeting certain performance standards, and then are given the opportunity to receive incentives on a (presumably unbiased) chance basis; and
- *Fixed rate:* the employee is incentivized by receiving an ongoing high salary or other remunerative benefit.

The system types mentioned above are listed in descending order of effectiveness. In the review of the literature by Sarah Bonner and her team, quota systems are identified as the most effective of all and are significantly more effective than piece rate systems, which themselves are significantly more effective than both tournament and fixed rate. Interestingly, tournament systems were rated as slightly more effective than fixed rate systems, but not by a statistically significant amount. This implies that, in terms of motivating improved performance, neither tournament nor fixed rate systems is likely to offer much in return for what management would have to invest.

Stolovich, Clark, and I put forward an explanation for these findings with reference to both Albert Bandura's 1997 conceptualization of self-efficacy and that of goal theory (Lee, Locke, & Phan, 1997; Locke, 1968, 1996; Locke & Latham, 1990). An incentive system is implemented because management has determined that there is some undesirable outcome that is reflective of inadequate performance. To get employees to work harder and/or smarter, management offers an incentive. If employees see a clear and reliable link between their extra efforts and the incentive, they are likely to improve their performance. Employees also hypothesize about, and seek evidence to determine, the amount of control they have within the system; perceptions that they can't really do well enough to secure the incentive diminish effort. Additionally, somewhat counter-intuitively, goals that are assigned tend to produce higher levels of commitment, effort, and ultimately performance than do goals that are self-set. Quota systems, then, are the best among the four because they increase perceptions of utility and control and have goals that are assigned. Piece rate systems increase perceptions of utility and control, but have self-set goals. Tournaments increase perceptions of utility, but not those of control, and often do not have assigned goals. Finally, fixed rate systems tend not to have any effect on increasing perceptions of utility and control (the remuneration amount is set), and there are no specified assigned goals (beyond what is normally expected).

The Main Reason for System Failure

Given the above, it may seem as though it might be difficult *not* to have an incentive system work, especially if it is a quota system. In fact, Stolovitch, Clark, and I found quite the opposite. In our survey of individuals whose organizations use incentive systems, 57 percent of respondents indicated that their organization's incentive system met or exceeded its objectives, and fully 92 percent indicated that it at least partially met objectives. Additionally, 99 percent of respondents stated they would use the same or a similar incentive system again. However, nearly 100 percent of the suggestions for change referred to *how* the system was run; complaints focused on lack of support, perceived fairness and clarity, the subjectivity of assessment, unreliability, and poor communication. Anecdotes spanned the range from complaints about not getting what they thought they deserved to having no idea why they were receiving a bonus check at all (but they were happy enough to cash it quickly!).

Even the best intentioned of incentive systems—one offering highly attractive rewards—will fail if individuals perceive the system to be unreliable or unfair. After all, there is no sense in doing *more* or *better* work (assuming one's job is secure) if one is not convinced that one's efforts actually secure the desired reward. It is especially damaging to employee morale if there is evidence of demonstrable bias; in all likelihood not only will the incentive system fail, but other aspects of work might begin to suffer as well. Above all, Stolovitch, Clark, and I argue in our 2001 article, recipients desire "clarity of objectives, clarity and reliability of process, fairness, support, clear communication and reasonable, reliable metrics" (p. A197).

The Effect on Interest and Internal Motivation

A common, and reasonable, objection to using an incentive system is that you're paying extra for what you'd normally get without it. The research cited earlier in this chapter belies that assertion; it is quite clear that incentives do indeed improve performance over baseline. But this does not stop the objections. A related plaintive assertion, however, is that incentives decrease internal motivation or task interest, that is, engaging in an activity or a task for its own sake, because of the enjoyment it brings, without reference to any external benefit, command, or dictate. This presumes that students and employees ought to be studying and working for reasons of pure interest and not for any external reward (or in response to an external threat), and that lower levels of internal motivation ultimately lead to poorer performance (for further discussion, see Edward Deci and Richard Ryan's 1985 text, as well as Alfie Kohn's 1993 book *Punished by Rewards*).

Virtually all of the authors who object to the use of incentives cite the research of Stanford University's Mark Lepper and David Greene (1975, 1978; Lepper, Green, & Nisbett, 1973). They found that students who were offered incentives for engaging in activities of their own choice exhibited less of the behavior when the incentives were no longer offered. They also found that children's reasons for engaging in activities were different depending on whether they were being watched by adults. When unwatched, they reported that they were doing their activities because they liked them (internal motivation), whereas when they were being watched, they stated that they were trying to earn adult approval (external motivation). These studies led them to conclude that incentives and other forms of external motivation were deleterious to both internal motivation and performance.

Robert Eisenberger and Judith Cameron (1998; Eisenberger, Rhoades, & Cameron, 1999) assert, based on their review of the literature, that this is not the case: external rewards often have no negative effects on internal motivation at all and very often improve performance. In turn, Edward Deci, Richard Koestner, and Richard Ryan counter that this is untrue, and in 1999 published their own meta-analysis that demonstrates the harmful effects incentives can have on internal motivation and performance. This kind of "back and forth" can leave practitioners with something of a headache, as they have to decide whether to use incentive systems or not.

There are two things to keep in mind with regard to the ongoing debate on the merits of incentives and their effects on motivation and performance. One, it is important to understand the nature of interest itself. Interest, say Suzanne Hidi and K. Ann Renninger in their 2006 *Educational Psychologist* article, is a single concept with two dimensions: value and knowledge. Almost everyone is quick to agree that, by definition, one has high value for an activity if one is interested in it. But, according to researchers in the field, one can only be said to be interested in a subject or activity if one also possesses a sufficiently high knowledge base. If one knows very little about something, but has high value for it, one is *attracted*, not *interested*. This difference is more than mere semantics; it has a direct effect on the efficacy of any incentive system in that a properly designed incentive system cannot only improve performance, but it can improve interest. The means are described next.

The second thing to keep in mind is the idea that incentives should only be offered *when appropriate*. It is true that when one offers cookies to children for making crayon drawings, they'll switch their reason from "I like drawing" to "I want the cookies." But if the children are already making drawings, why would it be necessary to offer them an incentive? This is not a subtle point. Incentives are offered to employees only when they are *not* producing well or enough. A well-designed incentive system encourages an employee to start doing things differently. Additionally, if the incentive is sufficiently attractive, employees begin learning more about their tasks and how to perform them in order to secure the incentive; in other words, their knowledge base improves. This has the effect of actually *increasing* interest, as Stolovitch, Clark, and I reported in 2001. In short, managers should steer clear of the moral imperatives associated with calls to shelve incentive systems "because employees ought to be doing these things anyway." Maybe they should, but if they're not, then managers have a real problem to solve. The point of an incentive system is that it gives employees an immediate reason to persist and exert effort in ways that previously they have not. Interest in doing their work in new and better ways can develop because the incentive offers employees a reason to learn (to improve their knowledge base).

Ultimately, the tension between the "pro-incentive" and "anti-incentive" camps can be resolved by a closer examination of Eisenberger and Cameron's 1998 findings and those of Edward Deci and his colleagues from the following year. In a very real sense, they argue past each other. The evidence is fairly clear that incentives do improve performance. There is also evidence that the offer of incentives can have a depressing effect on internal motivation. However, what is frequently conveniently ignored is, this depressing effect is short-lived. The relatively rare follow-up research that is conducted indicates that interest levels rebound after the end of the incentive program. Most research only examines the immediate effect of incentives on interest. Suffice to say that, in the long run, incentives have positive effects on both performance and on employee motivation.

When to End It

A final objection to the use of incentive systems is that employees will come to expect the incentives always to be there; that, in essence, it's simply part of salary. Stolovitch, Clark, and I give evidence that, as long as employees are aware of the lifespan of the particular program and have participated in its design and development, such objections are infrequent. Again, it must be emphasized that incentive systems target particular deficits in performance. Great amounts of effort might be expended in order to secure a large cash bonus, but it would be unreasonable either for management to expect employees to maintain such performance levels in the absence of incentives or for employees to expect management to offer large bonuses on a continual basis. At the end of the day, people tend to be fairly reasonable and willing to negotiate; thus, there is no reason to reject the use of an incentive system for fear that it will never end.

WHEN TO APPLY

The implementation of an incentive system is appropriate when the motivation necessary to sustain the levels of persistence and effort required to reach performance goals above and beyond the norm for the organization is itself inadequate. Incentive systems are not suitable to address deficits in knowledge or for organizational procedures that interfere with job performance (see Dick Clark and Fred Estes' 2002 book *Turning Research into Results*).

When performance is inadequate for reasons of lack of skills, knowledge, or ability, training is a solution. When performance is inadequate for organizational reasons, a restructuring is in order. Incentive systems are in the "motivation" category; they have direct influence upon employee perceptions of task value and self-efficacy. Note, however, that incentive systems can be used to influence knowledge or organizational deficits if there is evidence that motivation is a component. For example, employees who lack adequate knowledge to raise their performance levels could probably benefit from task-specific training. If, however, these employees are reluctant to engage in the training, an incentive system can serve to motivate them to participate in the training, gain the necessary knowledge, and thereby improve their performance. Generally speaking, if employees are reluctant to put in the time or effort necessary to improve their performance to reach established goals, an incentive system, properly designed, can serve to increase their motivation to persist or exert the required effort.

STRENGTHS AND CRITICISMS

Incentive systems differ from other employee motivation techniques in that they are specific to a particular task and constrained by time and rules. Employee stock ownership, profit sharing, company picnics, and the like are all reasonable ways of improving employee motivation, but each is somewhat more general in its focus and more difficult for an individual directly to influence him- or herself. Honoring employees on their birthdays is probably an enjoyable experience for one and all, likely to engender positive feelings in those who participate and serve to get employees' minds off everyday irritants, but this is not likely to affect either performance or the organization's bottom line. It is simply a myth that a happy employee is a productive employee.

Strengths and Advantages

1. Even inexpensive incentives can have a markedly positive effect on employee motivation and performance.

2. The designing of an incentive system can "force" management and employees to communicate with each other, thereby often bringing facts to light that might otherwise have remained hidden.

3. The earning of incentives can increase employees' perceptions of control and autonomy which, at least for North Americans, is a valued commodity.

4. Well-designed systems have built-in safeguards, rules, and procedures; these can help all parties understand what is required to meet performance objectives and earn incentives.

5. For team-targeted incentives, collegiality generally improves as employees sink or swim together; the incentives provide a rationale for assisting others in their job performance.

Criticisms and Disadvantages

1. They can be "too effective." For example, in offering highly attractive incentives to technical support staff to field more service phone calls, quality may suffer as the staff spends only minimal amounts of time with each client so as to increase the number of calls they field.

2. An incentive can be chosen by management that is actually not an incentive at all. For example, management might be able to obtain frozen turkeys that they could then offer as an incentive for improvements in employee performance around Thanksgiving but, if the majority of employees are vegetarian, the incentive has not only no value, but will probably be perceived as an insult.

3. Incentive systems can be selected to improve performance when really what's called for is either training (to build employee knowledge and skills) or organizational restructuring (to streamline procedures and build support).

4. Incentives can be thought to be a routine part of compensation, and thus come to be as expected as salary.

5. Changing circumstances in the general business climate may necessitate changes to the structure of the incentive system that may not be well-received by incentivized employees.

6. It is widely believed that incentives are a waste of resources, as it is simply "paying people extra to do what they should be doing anyway." In fact, the issue isn't whether people *should* be doing something; if they are *not* doing it, then there's usually some sort of motivational deficit.

7. Incentives destroy interest or intrinsic motivation (which is thought always to be preferred state). In fact, of Eisenberger and Cameron's 1998 study, as well as Eisenberger, Rhoades, and Cameron's 1999 research, demonstrates quite clearly that not only do incentives typically have no long-term deleterious effects on intrinsic motivation, but incentives can actually improve task interest.

RECOMMENDED DESIGN, DEVELOPMENT, AND IMPLEMENTATION PROCESS

This section will assume, as per Mager and Pipe's 1997 performance analysis framework, that there is in fact a performance discrepancy, that baseline performance is undesirable, and that the discrepancy fix is worth pursuing. Based on these, the following steps are recommended for the design and implementation of an incentive system.

1. *It's necessary.* Conclude for certain, based on observations and questions, that there not only is a performance gap, but that the root of the performance gap is motivational in nature, not organizational or knowledge-based. After you receive answers and observe behaviors, you know that you have a motivation basis for the performance discrepancy when you determine that employees *won't* perform as desired. Higher levels of prior performance would indicate that employees *can* perform as desired. An examination of the organization's physical plant, processes, and procedures might indicate that employees are not *being prevented* from performing as desired. If evidence accumulates that

employees either are unable to perform or are being prevented from performing as desired, then an incentive system is unwarranted.

2. *It's appropriate.* Part of the diagnosis process described in Step 1 involves identifying those individuals who are responsible for the performance gap (or, to put it another way, those who are performing in an undesirable way). These are the individuals who are "targeted" by an incentive system; they are the ones to be incentivized. Bring targeted employees into the design process (don't just assume they'll accept anything). Negotiate the type of incentive (cash, restaurant coupons, vacation days, "employee of the month" plaque), the format of the system (whether individuals or teams will be targeted; whether it's competitive or based on criteria), the length of time the system will be in place, and what merits earning the incentive. Although management normally assigns the goals, make sure employees are brought into this aspect of the design process as well.

3. *It's worth it.* Question employees to determine whether they perceive the required extra work or persistence to be worth their while and whether they have an interest in earning the incentive under the conditions specified in the system. This kind of questioning must convey two sentiments. One, the organization is serious about improving performance. Two, the organization needs to know what employees think about closing the performance gap, in spite of however attractive the incentive might be. General indications that the changes in performance are too difficult to reach, sustain, or that other tasks will suffer warrant a reexamination of the structure of the incentive system and its goal (improved performance to a stated level).

4. *I/We can do it.* Once work begins in earnest, check employee efficacy or confidence (self- or team-based, depending on the details of the incentive system) by having line supervisors ask employees whether they believe the work is doable or sustainable, and then have the line supervisors report their impressions to upper management. Provide corrective feedback that is performance-related, not personal in nature. Assist middle managers and supervisors in dealing with over- and under-confident employees. Over-confident employees exert reduced effort because they believe so strongly in their ability to do the work that they don't need to work any harder. When their performance fails to meet expectations, they refuse to accept responsibility and accuse others or the organization. Under-confident employees (who may be in the minority and thus may not have spoken out against the institution of the system at first) also exert reduced effort because they do not believe that they are capable of reaching the desired level of performance. In both

cases, supervisors and managers can talk with these employees to ascertain whether their perceptions of their abilities are realistic, given their present level of performance and the levels of performance of their colleagues. Assistance can be offered, so long as others do not view this assistance as an unfair boost.

5. *It'll work.* Check the reliability and fairness of the system not only by talking with incentivized employees, but also by comparing the stated details of the system with actual practice. For example, severe delays in the receipt of incentive checks might lead employees to conclude either that the program was never real in the first place or that it somehow has been cancelled. In either case, employee effort or persistence is likely to suffer as a result. Ascertain that employee perceptions of the system are correct and warranted. Publicize organizational support for employees to meet goals. Make adjustments to the system as employee (mis)perceptions warrant.

6. *It feels good enough.* By communicating with employees, observing behavior, and by keeping one's finger on the pulse of the organization, check to see that emotions regarding the incentive system are positive rather than negative (the four main negative emotions being fear, disgust, anger, and sadness). Negative emotions, no matter their kind, have the singular effect of driving people to escape the unpleasant situation. They can do this either by fight (directing action and thought away from work tasks toward settling the unfairness issue, "getting what's rightfully theirs," actively sabotaging the system), or flight (leaving the system or refusing to engage). Either reaction is detrimental to the success of the system and is a hallmark call for managerial attention.

7. *I'm/We're working better.* Verify that employees are, compared to pre-incentive conditions or baseline, starting tasks they have avoided in the past, continuing tasks and overcoming obstacles, and being more mindful of their work. Additionally, managers and supervisors need to ensure that other work tasks are not being ignored in favor of those that can earn the incentive. Ideally, this last point would have been mentioned, if not stressed, when the details of the incentive system were being negotiated. However, the incentive system might prove to be overpoweringly attractive and employees may end up avoiding certain tasks just to concentrate on those that can earn the incentive.

8. *ROI.* The organization has to monitor progress toward goals and perform a cost/benefit analysis to determine the effectiveness and feasibility of the system as it is running. A well-designed system anticipates potential pitfalls such as spending too much on incentives to

solve a minor performance problem, but even the best designed systems require ongoing and end-of-life reviews. Assuming the system is not suffering a catastrophic loss of organizational resources, even a relatively poor ROI need not be interpreted to mean that the incentive system was ill-advised. Reviews could reveal problems (such as communication) that are not expensive to solve at the time and might prevent major failures of the system if attended to in a timely manner.

CRITICAL SUCCESS FACTORS

An incentive system might look good on paper but, since it involves people, time, and circumstances, it needs to be made with certain considerations in mind. Some are more important than others, but problems in even one of these areas might be enough to derail the whole enterprise.

Social

- An incentive system is a human system at its core; the incentives are incentives only in the sense that they resonate with human perceptions, needs, and desires. It is thus crucial that all affected parties be brought into the design of the incentive system.

- Culturally, people have very different perceptions of their job responsibilities, what constitutes adequate performance, how much they should contribute to decision making, and what makes an attractive incentive. Again, it is vital that employees be brought into the process of the design of the system so as best to avoid potential conflicts and misunderstandings.

Political

- Pay careful attention to those aspects of the job that are *not* subject to the incentive system. It's possible that employees might ignore some work requirements in order to concentrate on those that could earn them bonuses and rewards.

- Maintain squeaky-clean adherence to the rules established for the system, lest cries of bias or prejudice be raised. To the degree that there are any differences at all, either between individuals or among groups, it is important for management to demonstrate that superior rewards were earned for superior performance. It might also be wise to make supervisorial support more visible and readily available.

- Avoid unintended perverse incentives such as punishing performers by severely cutting their benefits when they meet minimal standards, thus making it more attractive *not to perform*.

Economic

- Extremely generous incentive systems might very well improve employee performance to stratospheric levels, but be cost-prohibitive (one doesn't offer $1,000 to realize $100 in performance improvement). Make sure the money is available, and don't promise what can't be delivered.

- Analyze ROI. There's no sense in maintaining a popular incentive system that rewards employees for performance, but doesn't actually contribute to the bottom line.

Legal

- A variety of laws govern work hours and loads (such as the number of hours firefighters and pilots can work without rest, what constitutes overtime, and prohibitions on intentional or unintentional bias that might result if one group of employees is targeted in an incentive program and that group is predominantly of one sex or a particular ethnicity). Incentive systems obviously cannot run afoul of these. Ensure that labor laws are obeyed, especially when overtime is involved.

Technical

- Don't set performance criteria too high or too low. The prior can alienate everyone and probably precipitate a backlash, while the latter can cost the organization too much relative to any gains in productivity.

- Avoid making any changes to the system mid-stream without employee consultation. If changes have to be made, make sure the changes benefit both the employees and the organization.

- Institute procedures and record-keeping that are easily understood and readily available.

SUMMARY

Incentive systems are often attractive to employees, even when they don't have demonstrable effects on the organizational bottom line, simply because an opportunity to get something for (possibly) little extra effort or time is not to be dismissed. However, when employees have no say in the design of the system, there is often something that offends and hence greatly mitigates any improvements that might have been realized. Properly designed, incentive systems have a demonstrated ability to improve employee motivation to meet or exceed specified goals, provided employees are capable and are supported by the organization.

References

Bandura, A. (1997). *Self-efficacy: The exercise of control*. New York: W. H. Freeman.

Bonner, S. E., Hastie, R., Sprinkle, G. B., & Young, S. M. (2000). A review of the effects of financial incentives on performance in laboratory tasks: Implications for management accounting. *Journal of Management Accounting Research, 12*, 9–64.

Clark, R. E., & Estes, F. (2002). *Turning research into results: A guide to selecting the right performance solutions*. Atlanta, GA: CEP Press.

Condly, S. J., Clark, R. E., & Stolovitch, H. D. (2003). The effects of incentives on workplace performance: A meta-analytic review of research studies. *Performance Improvement Quarterly, 16*(3), 46–63.

Deci, E. L., Koestner, R., & Ryan, R. M. (1999). A meta-analytic review of experiments examining the effects of extrinsic rewards on intrinsic motivation. *Psychological Bulletin, 125*, 627–668.

Deci, E. L., & Ryan, R. M. (1985). *Intrinsic motivation and self-determination in human behavior*. New York: Plenum.

Eisenberger, R., & Cameron, J. (1998). Reward, intrinsic interest and creativity: New findings. *American Psychologist, 53*(6), 676–679.

Eisenberger, R., Rhoades, L, & Cameron, J. (1999). Does pay for performance increase or decrease perceived self-determination and intrinsic motivation? *Journal of Personality and Social Psychology, 77*(5), 1026–1040.

Herzberg, F. (1966). *Work and the nature of man*. Cleveland, OH: World Publishing.

Hidi, S., & Renninger, K. A. (2006). The four-phase model of interest development. *Educational Psychologist, 41*(2), 111–127.

Jenkins, G. D., Mitra, A., Gupta, N., & Shaw, J. D. (1998). Are financial incentives related to performance? A meta-analytic review of empirical research. *Journal of Applied Psychology, 83*(5), 777–787.

Karau, S. J., & Williams, K. D. (1995) Social loafing: Research findings, implications, and future directions. *Current Directions in Psychological Science, 4*(5), 134–140.

Keller, J. M. (1999). Motivational systems. In H. D. Stolovitch & E. J. Keeps (Eds.), *Handbook of human performance technology* (2nd ed.) (pp. 373–394). San Francisco: Pfeiffer.

Kohn, A. (1993). *Punished by rewards: The trouble with gold stars, incentive plans, A's, praise, and other bribes*. Boston: Houghton Mifflin.

Lee, T. W., Locke, E. A., & Phan, S. H. (1997). Explaining the assigned goal-incentive interaction: The role of self-efficacy and personal goals. *Journal of Management, 23*(4), 541–559.

Lepper, M. R., & Greene, D. (1975). Turning play into work: Effects of adult surveillance and extrinsic motivation. *Journal of Personality and Social Psychology, 31*, 479–486.

Lepper, M. R., & Greene, D. (1978). *The hidden costs of reward: New perspectives on the psychology of human motivation*. Mahwah, NJ: Lawrence Erlbaum Associates.

Lepper, M. R., Greene, D., & Nisbett, R. E. (1973). Undermining children's intrinsic interest with extrinsic rewards: A test of the overjustification hypothesis. *Journal of Personality and Social Psychology, 28,* 129–137.

Locke, E. A. (1968). Toward a theory of task motivation and incentives. *Organizational Behavior and Human Performance, 3,* 157–189.

Locke, E. A. (1990). Motivation through conscious goal setting. *Applied and Preventive Psychology, 5,* 117–124.

Locke, E. A., & Latham, G. P. (1990). *A theory of goal setting and task performance.* Englewood Cliffs, NJ: Prentice-Hall.

Mager, R. F., & Pipe, P. (1997). *Analyzing performance problems* (3rd ed.). Atlanta, GA: CEP Press.

Maslow, A. (1954). *Motivation and personality.* New York: Harper.

McClelland, D. C. (1961). *The achieving society.* Princeton, NJ: Van Nostrand.

Stolovitch, H. D., Clark, R. E., & Condly, S. J. (2001). *Incentives, motivation, and workplace performance: Research and best practices.* Silver Spring, MD: International Society for Performance Improvement.

Recommended Readings

Bonner, S. E., & Sprinkle, G. B. (2002). The effects of monetary incentives on effort and task performance: Theories, evidence, and a framework for research. *Accounting, Organizations and Society, 27,* 303–345.

Cameron, J., & Pierce, W. D. (2002). Rewards and intrinsic motivation: *Resolving the controversy.* Westport, CT: Bergin and Garvey.

Campbell, D. E. (2006). *Incentives: Motivation and the economics of information* (2nd ed.). New York: Cambridge University Press.

Clark, R. E., & Estes, F. (2002). *Turning research into results: A guide to selecting the right performance solutions.* Atlanta, GA: CEP Press.

 # EDITORIAL CONNECTIONS

Incentives are a proactive performance intervention that can be used to bring focus to the achievement of desired results. The effective use of incentives has been a hallmark of successful sales teams for many years. And while incentives can play an important role in accomplishing desired results, unmanaged or mismanaged incentives can also hinder your efforts to improve performance.

Without much effort, you can probably identify several performance problems within your organization that are currently the result of mismanaged incentives. For example, are there incentives within your organization that encourage employees to spend their remaining budget by the end of the fiscal year—even if those expenditures are not on necessary items. Or maybe the incentives of the annual performance reviews in your organization encourage people to take on only the safest and least-risky tasks. In these, and thousands of other examples of mismanaged incentives, the impact on performance is significant. Incentives are, after all, a core component of any organization's culture; if they not aligned with achievement of desired results, then they might just be fighting against improvements in human and organizational performance.

Well managed incentives can, on the other hand, be a valuable tool for engaging people in other performance technologies about which they may otherwise be skeptical. For example, you can use incentives to encourage people to mentor other employees, attend a motivation workshop, participate in a process redesign project, or complete an e-learning training course. Therefore you may want to include incentives as a component of overarching performance improvement efforts, as well as tools for ensuring the success of the other performance interventions also included in the performance system.

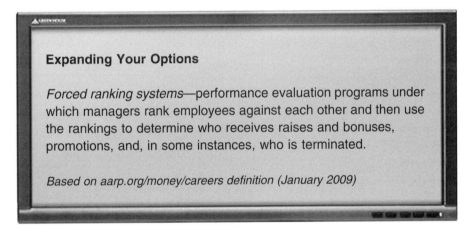

Expanding Your Options

Forced ranking systems—performance evaluation programs under which managers rank employees against each other and then use the rankings to determine who receives raises and bonuses, promotions, and, in some instances, who is terminated.

Based on aarp.org/money/careers definition (January 2009)

While incentives are a precursor to performance, managing what happens after desired results are achieved is equally important. When desired results are accomplished, use rewards and recognitions to emphasize the value of these achievements and to encourage future performance.

WHAT'S COMING UP

Developing and managing successful rewards and recognition programs is challenging. Without deliberate design and coordination with other performance improvement efforts, you can easily find that well-meaning programs are rewarding behaviors that are not producing desired performance and/or punishing desired behaviors. Likewise, you could mistakenly bring recognition to individuals or teams that achieve short-term success at the expense of long-term performance. So it is important that you diligently design rewards and recognitions interventions in alignment with all other components of your performance systems, including incentives, strategic direction, motivation, knowledge and skills, expectations and feedback, as well as the related performance interventions from each block of the Performance Pyramid (see Chapter Three).

Given the importance of their alignment, the benefits and challenges of adequately managing the implementation of successful rewards, recognition, and incentive systems are also explored in Chapter Nineteen. The chapter illustrates the importance of thinking systemically about how related performance interventions interact and contribute to the achievement of results, while providing practical guidance for how you can successfully implement these interventions within your organization.

CHAPTER NINETEEN

Rewards, Positive Reinforcement, and Incentive Systems

Jessica Jean Frumkin

INTRODUCTION

It seems that whenever the topic of motivation in the workplace is mentioned, people get excited and want to tell me stories of their own workplaces. Some tell me about how much they love their workplaces and how they feel valued at work. Others tell me horror stories about their places of work, describing how they have to drag their lifeless bodies through the front door of their offices every morning. However, there are countless more people who fall in between these extremes; these are people who would like to see changes in their work environments so that they feel better about their jobs.

There is a consistency throughout the research on workplace motivation that boils down to this: *people want to feel valued*. The only problem is that most people, including managers, CEOs, and even the employees themselves, don't know how to design a workplace in which everyone feels valued. Therefore, they end up with haphazard displays of appreciation, such as a pizza party or holiday bonuses, which typically backfire in the end; unmotivated by such action, the positive impacts may have a short half-life, and employees may even feel offended. In response to these typical challenges, this chapter will help you make the right decisions when designing a workplace that makes each employee feel valued, therefore creating a work environment that is full of motivated, productive people.

The topics of rewards, positive reinforcement, and incentives spark heated discussions, often resulting in high-pitched arguments over what works and what does not. For instance, in his book *Punished by Rewards*, Alfie Kohn argues that, while interest in rewards, incentives, and positive reinforcement have been ubiquitous since the early 1900s, to this day well-informed scholars disagree on their efficacy. The purpose of this chapter, then, is not to extol one theory over another, but rather to define and differentiate rewards, positive reinforcement, and incentives and to suggest how each can benefit you and your organization.

DESCRIPTION

The field of performance improvement borrows from many disciplines, including psychology, human resources, education, and business. Our field seeks to extract the best parts of each discipline in order to improve the whole. We must, however, take care to avoid confusing concepts with terminology that lacks standardization. In their 2006 book, Stanford University professors Jeffery Pfeffer and Robert Sutton point out that the terms "rewards," "positive reinforcement," and "incentives" are not used the same way throughout every discipline. Thus, each of us may bring a different definition or perception when we encounter each of these terms.

Ambiguous use of terms can, after all, lead to ill-formed conclusions. If, for example, one wants to speak of incentives but ends up speaking of rewards, misleading conclusions may occur.

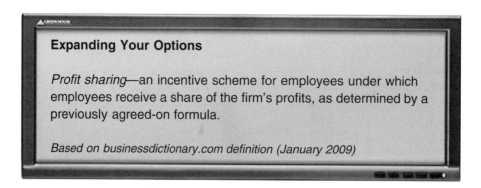

Expanding Your Options

Profit sharing—an incentive scheme for employees under which employees receive a share of the firm's profits, as determined by a previously agreed-on formula.

Based on businessdictionary.com definition (January 2009)

As performance improvement practitioners, it is our job to know how to differentiate rewards from incentives and positive reinforcement, so that we know how to best communicate with subject-matter experts, how to implement each, and what results we can expect. Many, such as Marcy Driscoll and Alfie

Kohn, believe that it is natural and appropriate to use the psychological definitions within the theory and practice of performance improvement.

Rewards

"Rewards" are often used as a catch-all term for incentives and positive reinforcement; however, "rewards" have their own specific definition. Widener University psychology professor Edward Rozycki defines a "reward" as a gift contingent upon behavior that may or may not result in the desired performance. Kohn suggests that contingency-based gifts are those based upon the "do this and you will get that" mentality of exchange. In such an arrangement, a gift is promised in return for the proper execution of a behavior and, if a behavior is performed properly, the gift will be presented.

While punishment is not always the flip side of reward, rewards can have unintended complications and implications. Consider an example of a reward implemented at a common suburban department store. The department store makes the majority of its money not from selling merchandise, but from the interest made on in-store credit cards. As a consequence, the department store strongly encourages each employee to "sell" in-store credit cards to every customer. If an employee successfully opens an in-store credit card with a customer, he or she is entered into a raffle with every other successful employee of that day, with the winner receiving, say, a full-size candy bar at the end of the day.

Some problems with the candy bar as a reward may be:

- Some employees may be allergic to the candy bar;
- Some employees may not like the candy bar;
- Some employees may be on a diet or be diabetic; and
- The size of the reward does not match the size of the importance of "selling" an in-store credit card.

Rewards don't always work the way they are intended, and, as Kohn's 2000 *Punished by Rewards* and Rozycki's 1973 missive for *Ethics* both point out, therefore cannot guarantee to produce the desired results. The notion of *the carrot or the stick* nicely illustrates the closely knit relationship that can exist between rewards and punishment. Problems may also exist for those who do pursue rewards, as the "do this and you will get that" approach works equally for reward and for punishment in that strengthening of a behavior is usually complemented with an attempt to eliminate another behavior. In the department store example, if employees do not get customers to open in-store credit cards, they are subsequently "punished" by their supervisor. Supervisors threaten to fire the employees and harass the employees until the behavior changes. In effect, "do this and you will get that" can translate into "do this or else," warns Kohn. In order to get the effects of rewards but have a better guarantee of results, positive reinforcement is usually a better choice.

Positive Reinforcement

Positive reinforcement was popularized by B. F. Skinner, and is a particular topic of study within the field of behavioral psychology. Positive reinforcement is the presentation of something that the participant needs or wants (called a "positive reinforcer") contingent upon behavior. In turn, this is followed by an increase in a desired performance. Positive reinforcement is very similar to rewards, except that the needs and desires of the participant are taken into account when choosing what stimulus to present to the participant, thus allowing positive reinforcements to be more specifically tailored for the audience.

In order to establish another's needs or desires, the individual must participate in the identification of what sort of items, resources, or changes in the workplace would act as a motivator for increased production. Then, in accordance with schedules of reinforcement, the chosen motivator would be distributed on a variable interval schedule.

Positive reinforcements require maintenance to ensure that the provided motivator does not become an anticipated part of the employee's salary or benefits. Schedules of reinforcement and even increases in motivators may be necessary. Positive reinforcement has been shown to work well for short periods of time; however, according to Kohn as well as Lepper and Greene, there is not sufficient evidence to substantiate its effect on sustaining performance over a long period of time.

Incentives

There has been much research conducted on incentives; however there is no standardized definition of "incentives" within the literature of performance improvement or psychology. Therefore, it is assumed that they can be given either after a desired performance has been completed (contingent) or regardless of performance (non-contingent). Incentives can be positive (providing a promised reward) or negative (removing a perceived punishment). A positive incentive adds something to the workplace in order to strengthen a particular behavior, such as providing child day care for employees with a perfect attendance record. A negative incentive removes something from the workplace in order to strengthen a behavior, such as allowing employees with perfect attendance to avoid the hassle of logging in and out of the office for lunch. Note that both approaches may well have the same aims: improving morale and reducing tardiness.

Incentive Systems

Incentive systems incorporate the necessary characteristics of a motivational intervention, while aligning the goal of the employee with that of the entire organization (see Chapter Eighteen). An incentive system is systemic, far-sighted, designed to give the participants what they need and want, non-contingent, and incorporates a tracking and feedback procedure. Incentive systems improve employee motivation while sustaining an organization. Incentive systems seek long-term effects that are beneficial to all who engage in desired performance. The details of an incentive system and how to design one will be described in detail later in this chapter.

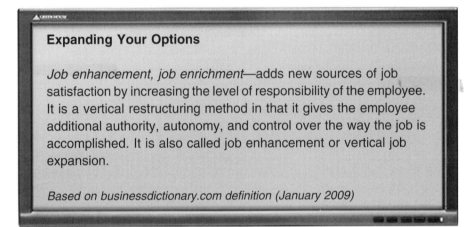

Expanding Your Options

Job enhancement, job enrichment—adds new sources of job satisfaction by increasing the level of responsibility of the employee. It is a vertical restructuring method in that it gives the employee additional authority, autonomy, and control over the way the job is accomplished. It is also called job enhancement or vertical job expansion.

Based on businessdictionary.com definition (January 2009)

WHAT WE KNOW FROM RESEARCH

While there may be disagreements in the field of performance improvement over how to implement motivational interventions, research tends to illustrate that incentive systems are among the most effective and efficient motivational interventions within the workplace.

Every year, when the *Fortune* 500 is published, it is accompanied by the "100 Best Companies to Work For," a list Fortune co-develops with the Great Place to Work Institute. According to *Fortune*'s Robert Levering and Milton Moskowitz, it is the largest corporate survey in America, one which seeks to find out what employees think about their organizations. From these surveys, indicators of a good workplace are developed. Fortune (2008a) reports some of these indicators to be:

- Job turnover
- Diversity
- Number of hours of training

- Paid sabbaticals
- Heath care coverage
- Onsite child care
- Flexible work/life
- Salary

None of these indicators is contingent upon behavior; rather these programs are non-contingent, that is, available to each employee as soon as he or she joins the company. Such programs are positive reinforcers and, when implemented correctly, they can benefit the organization and the individual alike.

An organization doesn't have to spend any money to properly develop some incentive systems. According to Daniel Goleman and Richard Boyatzis' 2008 article "Social Intelligence and the Biology of Leadership," one of the biggest drivers in organizational motivation, and thus performance, is how the workers are treated. By encouraging a positive atmosphere that includes laughter, positive attitudes, and social intelligence, organizations have lower turnover and superior performance.

In 1968, while heading the department of psychology at Case Western Reserve University, Frederick Herzberg published the results of his research on employee motivation within *Harvard Business Review*. He found leading causes of job dissatisfaction to be company policy and administration, supervision, relationship with supervisor, and work conditions. Such issues are not those that can be easily addressed by financial rewards. In order to resolve these ills in the workplace, systemic solutions must be utilized and incentive systems should then be developed to address specific concerns and gaps.

In order to redesign incentive systems, we must throw away our old ideas of what works when evidence proves them wrong. Organizations often mistakenly choose to give out financial rewards in lieu of properly designed incentive systems. While it is true that paying an employee what he or she is worth shows an employee value (indeed, salary is one of *Fortune*'s indicators of a good workplace), using a contingent motivator such as a financial bonus does not necessarily have the same positive effect. Pfeffer and Sutton warn that "financial incentives can undermine motivation and performance."

Florida State University professor emeritus Roger Kaufman (2004, 2006) agrees with Geary Rummler and Alan Brache that, in order to have a fully effective and efficient work environment, the goals of the organization must be aligned top to bottom, from worker to the overall goal of the organization (which is also aligned to the good of society). The goal of the organization should, after all, direct every action—big and small—within the organization. Therefore, how the organization wants to benefit society should direct how it does its business, everything from motivational interventions to customer service. An organization is a system, and each division is a subsystem of the greater whole. All changes within the organization should support the larger systems, and therefore reinforce the overall goal of the organization.

If, however, a non-systemic method is used, then new products or procedures may have nothing to do with the goals of the larger system, thus causing misalignments and likely disasters. As Jamshid Gharajedaghi describes it in his book *Systems Thinking*, the system may reject the new and foreign objects, as one's body seeks to do when introduced to a virus. Ensuring sustainable results that align with your organization's system, it is necessary to remain mindful of your organizational goals, sub-systems, and how interventions are designed, developed, and implemented.

The Capabilities of a System

Recognizing the capabilities of a system and its subsystems is important not only for delegating tasks and promoting efficiency within an organization, but also for motivational issues related to incentive systems. For instance, part of the problem with candy bars in the earlier example is the ease of short-circuiting the contingent functioning of the reward: employees who value candy bars can purchase them on their own, and some may find it easier to obtain them on their own rather than complying with the store's objectives.

Of course, there are many potential incentives or rewards that employees cannot provide for themselves—health care, paid leave, onsite child care, training, and diversity—which may make for a more sustainable motivation program. It is the purview of the larger system, the organization, to provide those services for the employees because it is within the capacity of the organization. If the organization is in financial straits and does not have the capacity to provide such services, then it can help the employees find a way to gain access to those services. It is the organization's role to take care of its employees, its clients, and the shared society; with this capacity comes great responsibility.

Case Study: Google

Google has been ranked by *Fortune* as the number one place to work in 2007 and 2008. *Fortune* studied Google in order to find out why people are so happy there and why they just don't seem to want to leave the company. What they found was some great basic benefits, and a whole bunch of perks that help make Google's work life famous.

In addition to the stellar ratings gathered by *Fortune*, here are some of the perks you will find at Google:

- Eighteen weeks of paid maternity leave for new mothers and seven weeks of paid paternity leave for new fathers;

(Continued)

- Green-friendly solutions in corporate buildings, including solar panels, recycled materials, public transportation between buildings, and "green" air filtration systems;
- Free-plus-one movie theater that shows movies before they hit the theater;
- Support for minorities and their affiliations, including The Black Googler Network, Google Women Engineers, and the GLBTG (Gay, Lesbian, Bisexual and Transgender Googlers); and
- Gourmet food available at all times (they even have a rule that food can never be more than one hundred feet away from workers).

These are just some of the initiatives that have made Google one of the most desirable places to work in the United States. Combine these perks with competitive salaries and comprehensive health care packages and it is obvious why the ratio between applicants and new jobs created in 2008 was 250:1.

Google uses an incentive system to create a motivating environment for its employees. It is classified as an incentive system because:

- *It is systemic.* All of *their goods and services are aligned to Google's goal of "Don't Be Evil." This also works into mega, as all of their actions are about not just doing something right, but about doing the right thing. This is evident in their care of the environment.*
- *It is far-sighted.* These services are a part of the corporate culture and are meant to have long-lasting effects on the employees.
- *It is designed to give the participants what they need and want.* Not only does Google freely supply its employees with what they can easily gain on their own (food, movie tickets), but it also owns up to its responsibility to take care of the services employees cannot take care of within their own capacity (maternity and paternity leave, support for minorities).
- *It is non-contingent.* The goods and services are available to the employees regardless of performance.
- *There is a feedback and tracking procedure.* Googlers have their own version of the popular social network, Facebook, where they can talk about whatever is on their minds. There is a constant exchange of ideas within the organization, and the CEOs are on the floor, not in ivory towers.

As with all properly designed and implemented incentive programs, the services provided by Google benefit the company as much as they do the individual employees. An example of this is the gourmet meals provided free of charge to all Google employees. This benefits Google employees because it saves them money and time; plus the employees enjoy food that is good for them, which in turn, promotes healthy living.

Google benefits from this practice in that the employees are more likely to eat in-house and are therefore less likely to take lunch breaks that run over their allotted time. During their lunch breaks, employees are eating with their fellow employees, building relationships and eventual foundations for teamwork. Conversations with fellow employees are likely to turn toward the topic of work and may even lead toward brainstorming. All of this makes lunch time productive work time for Google employees.

Google pays for health care for its employees. If Googlers eat healthy food, they are more likely to be healthy people and lessen overall health care costs for Google. While free gourmet food may seem altruistic, it is not without its corporate benefits. This is a perfect marriage of employee and stakeholder responsibility.

Case Study Comparison

Another corporation tried to provide employees with free meals by supplying them with McDonald's and Taco Bell gift cards. However, this corporation missed the Google boat by not providing nutritious meals for their employees; fast food will only increase healthcare costs for the corporation in the long run. A short-term result is sluggish employees who have less energy after lunch.

It should be noted that Google is very profitable. While it is only listed as number 241 on the *Fortune* 500, it does not yet have the retirees to support that many of the older companies do. It also has a high profit margin of 29 percent, which surpasses that of most organizations. However, less-profitable organizations can develop many of the same incentive systems, just with a smaller budget. Of course, the question does have to be asked: Is Google able to provide these incentive systems because it is so profitable, or is it so profitable because it provides its employees with such great incentive systems?

WHEN TO APPLY

A common response to performance problems within the workplace is often to blame individual motivation rather than look at the motivation systems within the organization. It is easier to say, "John is lazy" than it is to conduct an assessment to find out what barriers exist to John's optimal performance and how organizational motivation programs may be affecting performance. The options of either *the carrot* or *the stick* may not include the right answer; maybe the cart is simply missing a wheel.

It should be noted that this chapter does not address *the stick* (punishments) as a legitimate motivational intervention. Punishment can result in negative feelings that do not easily dissipate. While accountability is important, it must never be reinforced through punishment. If there are employees who do not respond to the best incentive systems, and the organization has done everything within its power to ensure a barrier-free work environment, it is possible that the employee does not agree with the particular brand identity or goals of the organization. In this situation, it is appropriate to remove employees from their positions or help them find other roles in the organization that are better suited for their interests.

Because incentive systems are not contingent upon performance, they are not implemented in response to employee performance. Rather, incentive systems, like those outlined in the case of Google, should be implemented within an organization regardless of employee performance. If an organization's perform-ance is acceptable, incentive systems provide an opportunity to improve employee performance. Motivational interventions are not dependent upon a problem in order for them to be executed appropriately within an organization.

The Importance of Assessment

A solution will only work if it addresses the right problem. Finding out whether motivation is a root problem or a symptom of a larger problem is a critical first step when deciding whether or not to apply an incentive system. For instance, a problem that exists in most organizations (and usually sparks conversations whenever the scenario is proposed) is employee tardiness. Managers and human resource personnel might report in some instances that tardiness exists out of laziness and lack of respect—usually when they are not the ones late for work. As a consequence, the solution most often given is punishment in order to enforce personal accountability. Some examples of punishment include exclud-ing tardy employees from meetings or docking tardy employees of pay. If a positive motivational intervention is proposed, it may take the form of a "token economy" wherein an employee earns a token for being on time for work. When an employee receives ten tokens, he or she is able to exchange the token for a prize or reward.

Kohn has studied token economies, examining research from the 1970s to present. Kohn found that there is typically an initial spike in the behavior the organization desires to increase. However, as time progresses, employees will steadily abandon the reward. After some time has passed, the token economy has lost its hold on the employee and the motivational value of the reward will abate.

If we were to apply Kohn's research to the tardiness example, we would find that, in the beginning, employees would show up to work on time. However, if an employee would slip up and be late, he would loose out on getting that token. Once the cycle is broken, the reward's effect starts to decline. This is especially true if the employee needs to be on time to work every day of the week in order to receive a token. If you are late on Monday, there is no reason to show up on time for the rest of the week—you are not going to earn that week's token anyway.

If the organization conducts an assessment and finds the true cause of tardiness, it is much more likely to find a sustainable set of solutions that solves the problem. Possible causes of tardiness could include:

- *Unhappiness at work:* It could be that it takes every fiber of the employee's being to drag his or her body through the front door. No token economy can fix this problem. Only a true systemic solution can tackle this problem. Incentive systems can help address it, but it may not be the only solution. An assessment must be done to find what is causing the unhappiness.

- *Childcare issues:* Dropping children off at childcare can take up a big chunk of the day. It can also demand that the employee leave at a specific time every day. However, by having in-house childcare, these issues can be addressed. In-house childcare can also help mothers go back to work earlier, and nursing mothers can breastfeed their young ones during lunch time.

STRENGTHS AND CRITICISMS

As expressed within the definition section, each intervention (rewards, positive reinforcement, and incentive systems) has its strengths and weaknesses. It is necessary to choose the intervention that best suits the requirements of your performance improvement program. Table 19.1 summarizes the strengths and criticisms of each intervention in order to make your selection process easier.

RECOMMENDED DESIGN, DEVELOPMENT, AND IMPLEMENTATION PROCESS

The following process can be followed to implement rewards, positive reinforcement, and incentive systems.

1. Conduct an assessment in order to determine whether or not poor motivation is the root cause of the performance problem or a symptom of something else. Too often motivation is pointed to as the culprit when there are other issues such as an inefficient environment, insufficient resources, or a lagging economy. Without a properly conducted assessment, the true cause of the performance problem will never be found, and therefore a proper solution cannot be implemented.

2. Perform an analysis on your workers and workplace. It is essential to know for whom you are designing the intervention. Each population has a different need or desire, and being able to best suit those needs and desires will make for a better incentive system. A work population that is primarily male, eighteen to twenty-five, and computer-savvy, for example, will have different needs and desires than a work population that is primarily forty-five to sixty, female, and conservative and religious. What each population considers to be a comfortable work environment may differ completely; go-carts may be completely applicable in one workplace and religious artifacts in another, but these items may be offensive if put in the wrong workplace. Knowing the population is extremely important.

3. Create an incentive system that supports your participants and is fiscally responsible. It is important to have happy workers, but the bottom line is success of the business. If an incentive system is not fiscally responsible and can actually drive a company out of business, it goes against its own interest.

4. Align short-term incentives with long-term incentives for the company in order to ensure that all incentives support the goal of the organization. Systemic design is the only way to guarantee that the organization stays on message with all outputs, including incentive systems.

5. Have a change-creation plan that is presented to the employees at the beginning of the change process and is consistent throughout the entire progression. Be prepared for any sort of push-back when change happens, even when the change is for the benefit of the company and its employees. Instead of getting angry or upset with unhappy employees (which will only worsen a tense situation), encourage employees to take part in the change process. By using their suggestions in your design and implementation process, the employees will feel a sense of ownership over the change, and resistance can lessen.

6. Track progress and record feedback to ensure that incentive systems are performing as desired. Adjustments may be necessary in order to achieve and maintain desired results. Perfection is not always achieved on the first try; a hole in one is not the goal, but rather a really good start toward an evidence-based, systematic process toward continuous improvement.

CRITICAL SUCCESS FACTORS

Some of the critical success factors follow:

- Conduct an assessment to find out whether motivation is a root cause or rather just a symptom of something greater.
- Conduct proper analysis to know what drives your participants.
- Design and develop systemic solutions that are aligned—all the way from the needs of the employee to that of society.
- Make sure that all interventions are evidence-based. There is no need to base decisions upon trial and error or anecdotal evidence.
- Ensure that all interventions are non-contingent; banish the carrot and the stick.

Table 19.1 Strengths and Criticisms of Rewards, Positive Reinforcement, and Incentive Systems

Rewards

Strengths	Criticisms
Easy to design and implement	Piecemeal solution
Inexpensive	Short-sighted
	Does not address the needs or desires of the participants
	Contingent upon performance
	Does not incorporate a tracking and feedback procedure
	Not guaranteed to work

Positive Reinforcement

Strengths	Criticisms
Addresses the needs and *desires of the participants*	Piecemeal solution
Guaranteed to produce desired results	Short-sighted
	Contingent upon performance
	Does not incorporate a tracking and feedback procedure
	No evidence of sustainable effects.

Incentive Systems

Strengths	Criticisms
Systemic design	Expensive*
Far-sighted	Time-consuming*
Addresses the needs and desires of the participants	
Not contingent upon performance	
Incorporates a tracking and feedback procedure	

*Note: It is true that incentive systems are not fast and cheap solutions. However, picking an intervention for a business is like picking a caretaker for a child. You need to take your time and make sure that you pick the very best for the one you care about. You would not pick a random stranger off the street to care for a child; hastily choosing a business intervention can be just as risky.

SUMMARY

Everybody wants to work in a place that is full of happy, motivated people. However, developing that environment takes time and effort. Some traditional solutions have plagued the workplace by being implanted over and over again, regardless of fit or results. In order to ensure that we create the best organizations possible (financially, socially, morally), we need to look to evidence. Evidence states that we should motivate our employees with non-contingent incentive systems that provide for employees what they cannot provide for themselves. And if we take care of our employees, our employees will take care of us.

Notes

- For a cheeky but scholarly look at how leadership can affect motivation, readers are encouraged to refer to Robert Sutton's *The No Asshole Rule*.

- To read about how laughter and social intelligence can affect motivation, see: Social Intelligence and the Biology of Leadership. *Harvard Business Review*, by Daniel Goleman and Richard Boyatzis

- To read more about Frederick Herzberg's study, see: Herzberg, F. One More Time: How Do You Motivate Employees? *Harvard Business Review.*

- For a differing viewpoint on incentives, see Chapter Eighteen.

References

Burton, J. K., & Merrill, P. F. (1991). Needs assessment: Goals, needs, and priorities. In L. J. Briggs, K. L. Gustafson, & M. H. Tillman (Eds.), *Instructional design principles and applications* (2nd ed.). Englewood Cliffs, NJ: Educational Technology Publications.

Cameron, J., & Pierce, W. D. (1994). Reinforcement, reward, and intrinsic motivation: A meta-analysis. *Review of Educational Research, 64*(3), 363–423.

Csikszentmihalyi, M. (2003). *Good business: Leadership, flow, and the making of meaning.* New York: Penguin Books.

Driscoll, M. P. (2004). *Psychology of learning for instruction.* Boston: Allyn & Bacon.

Fortune. (2008a). 100 best companies to work for 2008. Retrieved May 02, 2008, from http://money.cnn.com/magazines/fortune/bestcompanies/2008/full_list/index.html.

Fortune. (2008b). 100 best companies to work for 2008: Google snapshot. Retrieved May 02, 2008, from http://money.cnn.com/magazines/fortune/bestcompanies/2008/snapshots/1.html

Gharajedaghi, J. (2006). *Systems thinking.* Boston: Butterworth-Heinemann.

Goleman, D., & Boyatzis, R. (2008). Social intelligence and the biology of leadership. *Harvard Business Review, 86*(9), 74–81.

Herzberg, F. (1987). One more time: How to do you motivate employees? *Harvard Business Review*, *65*(5), 109–120.

Kaufman, R. (2004). Mega as the basis for useful planning and thinking. *Performance Improvement*, *43*(9), 35–39.

Kaufman, R. (2006). *Change, choices, and consequences*. Amherst, MA: HRD Press.

Kohn, A. (1999). *Punished by rewards: The trouble with gold stars, incentive plans, a's, praise, and other bribes*. New York: Houghton Mifflin.

Lefrancois, G. R. (2000). *Theories of human learning: What the old man said*. Belmont, CA: Wadsworth.

Lepper, M. R., & Greene, D. (Eds.). (1978). *The hidden costs of rewards: New perspectives on the psychology of human motivation*. Hoboken, NJ: John Wiley & Sons.

Lepper, M. R., Keavney, M., & Drake, M. (1996). Intrinsic motivation and extrinsic rewards: A commentary on Cameron and Pierce's meta-analysis. *Review of Educational Research*, *66*(1), 5–32.

Levering, R., & Moskowitz, M. (2008). *Fortune*: Best companies to work for. Retrieved May 02, 2008, from http://money.cnn.com/.element/ssi/sections/mag/fortune/bestcompanies/2008/box_how.popup.html.

Pfeffer, J., & Sutton, R. (2006). *Hard facts, dangerous half-truths, and total nonsense*. Cambridge, MA: Harvard Business School Press.

Rozycki, E. G. (1973). Rewards, reinforcers, and voluntary behavior. *Ethics*, *84*(1).

Rummler, G. A., & Brache, A. P. (1995). *Improving performance: How to manage the white space on the organization chart*. San Francisco: Jossey Bass.

Skinner, B. F. (1971). *Beyond freedom and dignity*. Indianapolis, IN: Hackett Publishing Company.

Skinner, B. F. (1974). *About behaviorism*. New York: Random House.

Stewart III, G. B., Appelbaum, E., Beer, M., Lebby, A. M., & Kohn, A. (1993). Rethinking rewards. *Harvard Business Review*, *71*(6), 37–49.

Recommended Readings and Websites

Buckingham, M., & Coffman, C. (1999). *First, break all the rules: What the world's greatest managers do differently*. New York: Simon and Schuster.

Harvard Business Review (2003). Harvard Business Review on motivating people. Boston: Harvard Business School Press.

Pfeffer, J. (1994). *Competitive advantage through people: Unleashing the power of the work force*. Boston: Harvard Business School Press.

Roger Kaufman and Associates: www.megaplanning.com.

Sutton, R. I. (2007). *The no asshole rule: Building a civilized workplace and surviving one that isn't*. New York: Business Plus.

EDITORIAL CONNECTIONS

The integrated application of incentives, rewards, and recognitions as performance interventions can bring a coordinated focus on the achievement of desired results to nearly any performance improvement effort. From incentives that motivate to rewards and recognitions that illustrate the value of achieving results, use all three of these interventions to accomplish desired results. This may include, for example, the deliberate design of a recognition system that supports other performance interventions you are including in your improvement system; such as a quarterly breakfast to recognize those in your organization who have been successful performance coaches for others, or certificates denoting those units that have implemented employee retention programs that achieved desired results.

By integrating incentives, rewards, and recognitions into multiple aspects of your improvement effort, you can better ensure the sustainable accomplishment of desired results. But no discussion of these performance interventions would be complete without a focus on employee compensation. Compensation is a key motivator of most employees, and as such, compensation is a performance intervention that can—and should—be examined in any effort to improve individual and organizational performance.

Compensation can be directly tied to individual and organizational performance, as it frequently is for sales staff working on commission or firms in which a significant part of employee compensation comes through annual bonuses based on company performance. Often closely linked to incentives or rewards, compensation systems can be an important intervention to the success of any improvement effort. If, for instance, employee compensation is tied to annual financial returns, then your efforts to improve performance should recognize the importance of compensation and adjust activities to ensure that changes brought about in order to improve performance do not conflict with the established compensation system.

Expanding Your Options

Peer recognition systems—a systematic procedure set in place by an organization that enables its employees to recognize and appreciate the extraordinary efforts or achievements of their colleagues.

Based on becker.wustl.edu/libdept/peer/ definition (January 2009)

Likewise, if your organization uses fixed compensation, this may have implications for other performance interventions you are planning to use to improve performance, including, but not limited to, incentives, rewards, and other motivation-related interventions. Sometimes you may recommend changes in compensation in order to support improvement in performance, while at other times you may have to work your performance interventions around the constraints of the current compensation plan. In all cases, compensation plays such a critical role in performance that it should not be overlooked.

WHAT'S COMING UP

In Chapter Twenty, employee and executive compensation is examined as a viable tool for improving individual and organizational performance. While the chapter focuses on compensation at the executive level, the lessons are pragmatic and can easily be applied to compensation systems at any level of an organization. Compensation is, after all, a vital component of any improvement effort, at any level or within any organization.

CHAPTER TWENTY

Employee and Executive Compensation

Tahir M. Nisar

INTRODUCTION

Employee compensation has attracted much attention recently. Academic studies and media have published accounts of the high level of pay awarded to chief executive officers (CEOs) and top executives, raising questions about the rationale and validity of current compensation packages. In explaining these pay awards, extant research, such as Lucian Bebchuk and Jessie Fried's 2004 book *Pay Without Performance,* has pointed to the exercise of managerial power in contravention of the general standards of corporate governance. This, coupled with deficiencies in executive pay contracts, makes it evident that high-level executives' pursuance of their own personal gains has in certain cases resulted in substantial deviations from shareholders' interests. It is therefore of great interest to investigate how and on what basis companies incentivize and reward their executives.

Modern incentive schemes are designed to align the interests of employees with those of the company through their effect on the pay-performance relationship. The use of performance measures tied to the vesting of equity and equity-like instruments such as stock options and restricted stock is one example. However, research, including a 1988 study by Baker, Jensen, and Murphy published in the *Journal of Finance,* has shown that difficulty is often encountered in linking managerial incentives to exact performance metrics. The problem is more pronounced in incentive schemes such as discretionary bonuses whereby payments are mostly contingent on employees meeting a set of performance targets designed to reflect various dimensions of performance. The challenge of creating an effective compensation package thus centers on linking incentives to performance measurement.

The present chapter aims to explore various components to employee (and especially executive) compensation in relation to incentives and human performance interventions. Our discussion of these performance interventions focuses on how performance measures are linked to pay-performance structures in various sets of incentive plans. The first section provides a brief description of compensation packages that include base salaries, bonuses, stock options, and deferred compensation plans. The next section is devoted to literature survey. The goal of this section is to outline various existing perspectives on compensation and performance management. The section also develops ideas on how performance measures can be specified at two levels of aggregation: specific performance measures and aggregate performance measures. Using this taxonomy, the next section examines the application of various incentive schemes. Strengths and criticisms of these schemes are then considered, followed by a recommended design and implementation process. After discussing critical success factors in the design of compensation packages, the final section concludes the study with an overview of the major areas of concern.

DESCRIPTION

Compensation packages are mostly designed to attract, motivate, and retain able employees. An organization can work with several elements of the compensation package, but in the present chapter, we will focus on base salaries, bonuses, stock options, and deferred compensation plans. We will consider how salaries are set, how different types of bonus pay plans are structured, and how stock options are awarded and valued. University of Southern California Professor of Business and Law Kevin Murphy writes in 1999's *Handbook of Labor Economics* that, in recent years, a major portion of executive pay has come from bonuses and stock options and not from base salaries, partly because a base salary is based on organization membership and not job performance. Executives also receive non-financial incentives and may value intrinsic factors of job, promotion, organizational culture, and the like as much.

Base Salaries

Most executives are paid monthly or annual salaries that are based on the amount of time spent on an activity. A base salary is independent of output or performance considerations, as it may be costly to measure individual output or performance. Determining base salaries is thus in large part a process of discovering the "going" market rate. Companies will try to find out roughly what others are paying and then set base salaries that approximate the competitive rate. The steps toward "benchmarking" the base salaries involve general industry salary surveys and, where appropriate, the use of selected industry or market peers analyses. In some industrial sectors, compensation system information is not easily accessible between firms, and so the amount to pay employees may be unknown in the market. In a hypothetical, perfectly competitive market, it is possible to see this information, but in reality it may be difficult because of fears of companies losing their employees to competitors. Depending on the extent to which this is the case, an external market comparison may become inadequate for base salary decisions. Moreover, those who have been with the organization for a long time tend to acquire firm-specific skills, which are more valuable inside the organization than outside. In such situations, job evaluations will enable the organization to size up each job and identify and compare them with similar roles internally and, whenever possible, externally.

Several characteristic features of base salaries pertain to executive compensation contracts. Goal-driven incentives such as bonuses and stock options are measured relative to base salary levels, which means that each dollar increase in base salary has a positive effect on these incentives. Risk-averse executives may be particularly responsive to the fixed component feature of base salaries, and thus any increase in base salary will be preferable to an increase in "target" bonus. Often, this is the subject matter of employment contract negotiation, as base salaries are usually determined at the entry level.

Bonus Pay Schemes

A bonus is a goal-driven incentive payment. Bonus pay can be an effective motivational tool because it enables an employee's effort and good performance to translate into recognition and a reward. Bonuses thus help to align the interests of the employee with that of the firm, thereby creating an incentive for the employee to perform efficiently and to a high standard. An annual bonus scheme covering company executives and paid annually based on a single year's performance is a common industry practice, but bonus plans that link pay to a specific areas of company business strategy, such as employee recruitment and retention, quality and customer service, have now gained the attention of company management (IDS, 2007). The practice of tying bonuses to multiple business goals can take many different forms. For instance, it is possible to operate several bonus schemes providing appropriate incentives for different employee groups, while also operating corporate level (or business unit level) schemes to reward all staff for the overall performance of the company. This is based on the conjecture that both personal and corporate-level factors are important when devising optimal incentives in new industrial environments. Thus, targets can be set for specific jobs, teams, or departments, alongside company-wide elements. The outcome of these schemes critically depends on a combination of factors, including performance measurement methodologies and the structure of the pay-performance relation.

> ### Expanding Your Options
>
> *Job sharing*—alternative schedule of work in which two employees voluntarily share the responsibilities of one full-time job and receive salary and benefits of a pro-rata basis. Job sharing creates regular part time (half-days, alternative days, alternative weeks, etc.) where there was one full-time position, and thus avoids a total loss of employment in a layoff.
>
> *Based on businessdictionary.com definition (January 2009)*

Stock Option Plans

Stock option plans are used to increase the equity stake of CEOs and top executives so their interests match those of the shareholders. The underlying assumption is that when executives own stock it will motivate them to take actions that improve the firm's market value. A stock option is given to a CEO at a specific exercise or strike price (C), which is typically the market price of the stock when the option is granted. The CEO is then in the possession of a contract that entitles him to purchase shares at the option's fixed exercise price (C) rather than at the market price (P). Since the value of the option increases with the rise in the market price of the company's stock, it also increases the value of CEO's holdings. The option is "in-the-money" when the current market price of the stock exceeds the exercise price of the option.

$$P - C = \text{(Reward) (Total number of options granted)}$$

The options normally require three to five years of service to vest. If the executive leaves before this period is over, he or she is generally asked to surrender the granted options to the firm. If the executive remains with the firm past the vesting period, he or she can then proceed to exercise the options, either immediately or at any point up to a specified contractual period (that is, the life of the option, which is usually ten years) by obtaining the stock shares in exchange for the strike price. He can then sell these shares at the market price and pocket the difference. Firms use this vesting period to encourage executives to remain with the firm to receive the full value of their stock option plans. Thus, stock option plans with service-based vesting conditions can influence executive retention. However, for upper-level executives such as CEOs, performance or market based conditions on vesting are more common.

Stock options are valued at the firm's cost of making the grant. The Black-Scholes (1973) formula, a widely used method, calculates the firm's cost of granting an executive stock option as the opportunity cost forgone by not selling the option in the open market. However, stock option plans will need to address valuation issues because of the difference of the cost to the company of granting the option and the value to an executive from receiving the option. Because the outside investor can freely trade or sell the firm stock and is well diversified, the amount he would pay for the stock is different from that of an executive who is unable to act in this way. Consequently, firm executives' valuation of the options is much lower than the value placed on them by the outside investors. Murphy's 1999 chapter suggests that options should only be granted if the "incentive effect" (that is, the increased performance created by improved stock-based incentives) exceeds the difference between the firm's cost and the executive's value.

Other Forms of Compensation

Companies offer a great variety of broad-based executive benefit plans, including "restricted" stock plans under which shares are forfeited to take advantage of favorable tax and accounting treatment of these stocks, and "long-term incentive plans" (LTIPs) that are based on rolling-average three- or five-year cumulative performance and are tied to specific targets such as earnings growth and return on invested capital. Top executives also receive special benefits, such as life insurance and supplemental executive retirement plans (SERPs). SERPs are available in addition to company-wide retirement programs. With the adoption of IRC (Internal Revenue Code) Section 409A in 2004, the scope of a deferred compensation plan has been strengthened in both its design and implementation. It is important to note that the Section was enacted by the American Jobs Creation Act of 2004 to prevent perceived abuses by executives and corporations of deferred compensation amounts. Such plans pay supplemental income to key executives in the future and permit them to defer their own income. Under the plan, an employee can exercise more control and diversification as performance targets for the deferred amounts are set in collaboration with the employee. A company-funded deferred compensation account can be set up in many different ways, providing flexibility in payout methods and timing. The payout method can use a wide variety of performance measures such as output, revenue, profits, and so forth, a marked improvement on stock option plans that rely solely on the stock value.

WHAT WE KNOW FROM RESEARCH

One can identify three distinctive strands of incentives and compensation literature. The first, which involves the principal-agent model, seeks to align the interest of a principal (shareholder) with an agent (CEO/manager). As early as 1932, Berle and Means defined modern corporations as being characterized by a separation of ownership and control, which, as Bebchuk and Fried noted in a 2003 article for the *Journal of Economic Perspectives*, gives an opportunity to managers to pursue their own personal interests. Employment contracts, representing the mutual interests of both principals and agents, are intended to minimize the divergence of interests and motivate the CEO and other executives to maximize company value. Contracts can also specify how incentives and performance measures are selected based on the total information conveyed by them on the actions of managers.

Bebchuk and Fried's book (2004) also points out an alternative view to the principal-agent framework, which suggests that CEOs set pay in collusion with corporate board and compensation committee members. Excessive pay practices, commonly seen in many sectors of the economy, can then be explained by how managers exercise power at the cost of the firm. This managerial power explanation of executive compensation thus argues that companies' boards of directors and compensation committees are held captive by powerful executives, and even when there are huge drops in earnings and losses in shareholder value, company CEOs and top executives still manage to vote themselves major pay raises. Another example is stock ownership by management that leads to a reduced level of oversight by directors and shareholders.

Finally, William Ouchi's organization control theory of 1979 sheds light on how incentives and performance measurement are related to the specific jobs employees perform and attempts to establish better linkages between them. Using a two-step approach, the theory first delineates those actions through which an employee contributes toward the achievement of the organization's goals. The offer of a financial reward for each such action will then induce the employee to increase the rate of performance of these actions. This approach thus deals with specific purpose incentive plans. It is less useful in explaining the practice of executive compensation but can be helpful in designing incentives that are closely linked to executive jobs. In relation to the design of executive compensation packages, these approaches emphasize the following sets of pay-performance linkages.

> **Expanding Your Options**
>
> *Flex hours*—non-traditional schedule of work that allows full-time employees to choose their individual starting and leaving times.
>
> *Based on businessdictionary.com definition (January 2009)*

Informativeness: The incentive design is about making available all necessary information about managerial actions during the course of performance measurement. Fama and Jensen describe in their 1983 article "Agency Problems and Residual Claims" that the economic rationale for this observation is rooted in the traditional agency-theory framework, which suggests that the choice of performance measures should be a function of the informativeness of each measure that reveals the agent's action. Specifically, as MIT economics professor Bengt Holmstrom described in his 1979 manuscript "Moral Hazard and Observability," the relative use (weight) of particular performance metrics should be a decreasing function of the measure's noise and an increasing function of the measure's sensitivity to agent effort or decision. Financial or quantitative performance measures such as profits and costs fit the bill, as they provide incremental information on the actions of agents that the principal can use to elicit optimum effort, thus creating congruence between the goals of the principal and the agent. Healy asserts in a 1985 article for the *Journal of Accounting and Economics* that they are also likely to be used for the purpose of reducing gamesmanship and cheating, such as earnings management.

Stakeholder interest: Contrary to the normative predictions of agency theory, the managerial power approach forwarded in Ittner and Larcker's 2002 article for the *Journal of Labor Economics* argues that incentives and performance measures are selected under the influence of various competing stakeholder groups. Organizations are sometimes seen as "political arenas" in which stakeholders of different hues mobilize their resources to set performance criteria that serve their particular interests, per Daniel B. Waggoner, Andy D. Neely, and Mike P. Kennerley in a 1999 article for the *International Journal of Production Economics*. For example, operational efficiency in many organizational settings is a very wide term. It has different and often subjective connotations for various groups that have an interest in the performance of the organization, such as investors, management, customers, staff, government, and the local community in the area of operation, including non-customers. Eunmi and Hahn's 2006 article in *Personnel Review,* among other compensation literature, has widely documented that top executives tend to have more favorable compensation contracts than lower-level employees. However, as noted by Heery's 2000 chapter in *Reward Management*, other powerful groups such as unions may also be able to affect the design and implementation of incentive plans.

Specific performance measurement objectives: Ouchi's organizational control theory is concerned with the quality of the relationships between employees and their supervisors, with a particular emphasis on how such relationships affect organizational outcomes. Performance measurement systems are designed with a view to generating specific information about the decision-making process. For example, employee participation in shop floor decision making requires substantial amounts of qualitative information. Evaluating success in these environments entails much more specific information (information about monitoring, evaluating, and rewarding an employee's performance) than implementing financial controls, detailed in Simons' book *Performance Measurement and Control Systems for Implementing Strategy* from 2000. However, the way this subjective information is produced and how it is utilized for incentive purposes pose important questions about the efficacy of adopting such measurement tools. The fact that distortion in the performance measure used may also drive down incentive strength may limit the utility of such measures. For example, some noisy performance measures (that is, when events other than the worker's efforts influence the measure, such as pieces produced in a machine shop) may feature heavily in an incentive scheme, while others (keystrokes made by a typist) may receive low weight. It is likely that in the latter case employees will take actions that increase the performance measure without simultaneously increasing organizational value.

Aggregate vs. Specific Performance Measures

As Kevin Murphy emphasizes in his 2000 article "Performance Standards in Incentive Contracts," it is very important to choose the appropriate performance measures in executive compensation plans. A suitable performance measure creates an alignment between company goals and executive interest through its effect on the pay-performance relation. In general, as Holmstrom's 1979 article notes, performance measures vary in terms of their effect and ability to provide accurate, informative, and timely indications of the individual's contribution to company goals. For example, although the quantitative performance measures or bi-variate financial ratios (such as return on investment) mostly used in extant research are simpler to conceptualize and easier to calculate, not all aspects of employee performance can be measured by these methods. Jobs invariably involve some elements of discretion that are difficult to observe and appropriately assign for rewards.

The emphasis of the incentives research with the principle of informativeness has meant that this line of research has focused mainly on the design and implementation of aggregate performance measurement classifications (such as net income or return on assets), while largely disregarding the specifics of base level performance measurement choices (such as quality and customer service). On the other hand, although management and organizational control literature deals in depth with the question of how valid inferences can be drawn from the use of non-financial or specific performance measures, it takes little effort to establish the link between aggregate and specific performance measures. As we show below, it will be instructive to examine both these aspects of performance so as to explicate all relevant influences on executive performance.

"Aggregate" performance measures are used when (some) information is needed about "all" actions, and this can be usefully contrasted with "specific" performance measures that provide (some) information about a subset of actions (see Table 20.1 for a comparison of aggregate and specific performance measures). For example, employee performance at the firm level may be measured using metrics that aggregate information such as profit or output. For evaluating the impact of individual actions, one need not look at the aggregate measures but at specific performance metrics such as the number of pages typed by a secretary. With aggregate performance measures, company management can freely make tradeoffs among all available activities. In particular, management can promote desirable actions by tying them to pay via performance measures associated with the actions. Booth School of Business's Canice Prendergast sums this up in his 2002 article "The Tenuous Trade-Off Between Risk and Incentives," stating that aggregate performance measures not only provide discretion to employees as they possess the relevant information and skill, but they also enable the management to limit the misuse of such discretionary powers.

Furthermore, since, as Ittner and Larcker's article suggests, it is sometimes difficult to have performance measures for each type of activity. Aggregate

Table 20.1 Aggregate vs. Specific Performance Measures

	Aggregate Performance Measures	Specific Performance Measures
Desirable Consequences	Forward looking; Easy to measure; Aggregate decentralized information; Difficult to "game"	Good "line of sight"; Tell employees what to do; Controllable
Undesirable Consequences	Noisy; Impose risk; Uncontrollable	Limited availability of actions; Easy to "game"; Measurement errors

performance measures such as those suggested by Holmstrom and Milgrom in 1987 can be used when broadening the scope of activities. Anil Arya and his colleagues argue in a 2004 article that such types of measures may also allow the company to economize on bounded measures (a notion offered years earlier in Williamson's *The Economic Institutions of Capitalism*). As summary financial measures reflect the consequences of all decisions, they can be considered the most aggregate performance measures. However, empirical studies, such as those conducted by Wruck and Jensen in 1994, suggest that financial measures provide weak direction to managers and make it difficult to communicate how employee actions affect performance goals. Within the context of modern organizations that operate in highly complex environments, Ohio State University Management and Human Resources professor Robert L. Heneman and his colleagues put a premium on the measures' controllability and show that measures that provide a strong ''line of sight'' are more effective than the aggregate financial or objective metrics. There are cases of non-financial performance measures that will to an extent aggregate information about an employee's action, including, for example, defects rates that provide information about quality improvement activities or market share that provides information about customer service. The problem with the use of these measures is that they only capture a partial decision-making outcome, such as the costs of gaining market share. Their overall value is also limited, as they are associated with a very limited range of decisions including quality or customer service. Defined in this way, qualitative or non-financial measures are ''specific'' performance measures, designed to provide information about a specific subset of employee actions. In addition to Wruck and Jensen's 1994 article for the *Journal of Accounting and Economics*, Ittner and Larcker elaborate on these matters in their 1998 article ''Innovations in Performance Measurement.''

WHEN TO APPLY

The use of bonuses and stock options rather than other forms of incentives may seem justified, as investors and company management are seen as being able to exercise greater control over rewards and they are linked to performance. But where there is a misalignment of goals and rewards, there is also a strong incentive for an individual to engage in earnings management (for example, pile up excess inventory with customers) or distort achievement indices (for example, use of selective performance data). For example, a 1975 *Academy of Management Journal* article by Kerr describes ''tunnel vision''—whereby employees only focus on what gets rewarded to the neglect of other important performance tasks—as a common outcome of poorly designed bonus schemes. Another difficulty is that it is often impracticable to separate out the specific contribution of employees to improvements in company performance. This suggests that reward schemes should be offered in a way that carefully establishes appropriate links between incentives and performance. We discuss below the application of various executive reward schemes in relation to the use of different sets of performance measures.

Incentive Plans Using Aggregate Performance Measures

The principal-agent model ascertains congruence between goals of shareholders and managers to offset a tendency among managers to focus on the short-term and ignore the long-run implications of their actions. This is because the time horizons of managers differ from those of investors. Lazear's *Personnel Economics for Managers* and Kaplan and Norton's (2001) article in *Accounting Horizons* attest to this. Because the stock price of the company reflects the capitalized value of future profits, an action that increases future profits makes the company more valuable to investors, who can enjoy the higher profits through future dividends or unanticipated capital gains. Shareholders therefore want managers to take actions that increase the long-term value of the company. But a manager may be more concerned about securing short-term financial return; for example, managers may not replace existing technologies because of fear of losing power. One solution to this problem is to provide equity stakes to the executive through a stock options plan. Such incentives are normally linked to aggregate performance measures such as stock market appreciation of the firm so as to motivate the executives to make decisions that improve the firm's overall value. However, there might be a need to mitigate executives' excessively short-term focus by additionally evaluating their performance on specific measures. Without such measures, executives will be inclined to commit to those actions that appreciate a firm's current market price, but that do not benefit the firm's long-term future, as various instances of earnings management suggest (such as manipulation of firm stock performance).

Aggregate performance measures may also be limited in their capacity to isolate the impact of noise factors (uncontrollable variables). For instance, industries face a turbulent economic climate from time to time due to substantial macroeconomic events, resulting in events beyond the control of economic agents. A bank's loan executive may receive a negative return from the bank's investment despite conducting thorough research before agreeing to a loan. As Eisenhardt puts it in 1985's "Control: Organizational and Economic Approaches," "good outcomes can occur despite poor efforts and poor outcomes can occur despite good efforts." Understandably, executives will be reluctant to have their pay contingent on a change in the external environment over which they have no control. To the extent that companies are willing to account for uncontrollables, thereby reducing the "noise" element in incentive pay plans, incentives such as stock options will be a useful motivational tool. However, this requires that specific performance measures are also used in a way that eliminates the negative effects of changes that are outside the control of executives. In this respect, supervisors can use their own judgment about the likely impact of external factors on individual employee performance.

Incentive Plans Using Specific Performance Measures

Incentives such as bonuses are used when goal-based performance is encouraged, with specific performance measures indicating the degree of accomplishment. Bonuses can be an effective incentive tool for executives as long as they are set correctly, but often when a narrowly defined performance criterion is utilized there can be less than optimal outcomes. For example, output-based pay is normally associated with performing a single-dimensional task (for example, sale of unit products), resulting in an incentive to exert effort in that dimension only. Hence, remuneration tied to piece rate induces workers to exert effort in the quantity dimension of produced output, whereas the quality of the output is neglected. One reason is that employees have insufficient incentive to allocate their effort to both sets of dimensions under the piece rate system. In their 1991 article "Multitask Principal-Agent Analyses," Holmstrom and Milgrom, argue that this issue illustrates a deeper problem in the design of incentive programs, that is, how to balance incentives for employees. Setting up incentives for quantity works well when quality can be directly observed (or when two tasks are complementary). But in many situations both effort and quality are unobservable, thus creating an incentive design problem. By way of analogy, if teachers' performance is measured by the achievements of students in standardized tests, they are likely to teach students only those subjects in the tests and neglect other important but untested knowledge. For some teachers there may even be an incentive to cheat: that is, give the answers to the students. Likewise, if bank managers are rated on bank revenue, it may result in them losing focus on other important areas such as customer satisfaction. Similarly, in business situations sometimes bonuses are paid only if the current year's earnings are up, for example, 10 percent from that of the past year. Harvard's Michael C. Jensen states in his 2001 article "Corporate Budgeting Is Broken—Let's Fit It," that in such situations it is likely that employees will generate earnings growth of exactly 10 percent, even if more is possible.

These examples show that when jobs involve both qualitative and quantitative performance dimensions, it becomes necessary to provide balanced incentives for both. That is, when two equally important activities must be performed, but one of them cannot be easily measured, then the company will need to make a tradeoff between strength and balance of incentives. It may then be desirable to choose a low-powered incentive scheme (such as paying a flat salary). As University of California Berkeley's Oliver E. Williamson notes in his 1985 text *The Economic Institutions of Capitalism*, low-powered incentives are a common occurrence in organizational environments. However, when low-powered incentives are used, aggregate measures will be necessary to improve performance outcomes. In the teacher example, if knowledge that cannot be tested is to be taught, perhaps performance measures such as a teacher's overall work performance can be used.

When multiple tasks are performed, incentives used may also have some unintended and negative consequences. Kerr's "rewarding A while hoping for B" problem from 1975's *Academy of Management Journal* calls for supervisors to take steps that moderate unintended negative effects of the sort discussed in Mager and Pipe's *Analyzing Performance Problems*, originally published in 1970. Companies may use bonuses to promote specific behaviors such as risk, which may have the effect of attracting and retaining executives who like pursuing risky ventures. The consequence is that the type of high-level executives—not only their behavior—will change. Similarly, bonus targets are often set to direct effort in a certain direction to the exclusion of others. For example, a company might want to channel executives' discretionary effort in the direction of superior customer service by using a targeted bonus scheme. However, if the bonus was paid based entirely on customer satisfaction, executives might achieve this by giving too many inducements to customers, at the company's expense. Such pay-performance non-linearities are often the reason that companies seek to apply multiple performance indicators—combining in various proportions both quantity and quality measures—that tie pay more closely to performance. For instance, it may be more appropriate to link bonuses with customer satisfaction and fix norms (indicators) of customer satisfaction to make it more practical. Each type of indicator employed can tap different aspects of performance. None of them is a perfect indicator and all of them have noise and distortions. However, much like the use of multiple test items, when the various indices of performance are taken together, it is hoped that the noise and distortions will average out to produce a more comprehensive and more reliable index of performance.

This solution to the problem of distortions in the use of specific performance measures is based on how performance measurement is conducted in relation to other relevant organizational and personnel policies. There is now substantial evidence suggesting that incentives work best when they are combined with companies' organizational practices. As Kandel and Lazear argue in their 1992 article "Peer Pressure and Partnerships," for example, bonus incentives increase pay satisfaction when bonuses coalesce around organizational systems. The underlying assumption, as explained in Milgrom and Roberts' 1995 article "Complementarities and Fit," is that a set of mutually interdependent practices is likely to increase the benefits and reduce the costs of managerial actions. This means that companies will need to examine how different performance measures support each other or if there is any complementarity between them.

For example, according to Amazon.com, the company focuses on the profit earned on each customer visit for a range of products sold under the Amazon brand, rather than profit per book sold (one of many product lines served by Amazon)—a standard practice for other booksellers. Amazon will utilize profit per book sold as one performance indicator, but its performance measurement system also takes into account employee drive and initiative in selling other kinds of Amazon products. Thus, measuring sales performance per customer visit, instead of products sold in separate product categories, closely aligns company strategy with what Amazon employees actually do in their jobs. Books, music, and video sales now account for less than 50 percent of Amazon revenue; the rest comes from sales of hundreds of other kinds of products.

Similarly, bonuses for quality output produce positive outcomes only if the company's operational procedures are geared toward minimizing defective items. The provision of training opportunities in customer service when customer satisfaction is important for the company enhances the effectiveness of bonuses targeted at customer service. Likewise, paying for communication skills bonuses when jobs merely involve moving things from one platform to another does not make sense. However, when selling requires an understanding of a product's complex features and the ability to explain them, this is something that incentives can target. Similar reasoning can be applied when deciding between the competing priorities of performance indicators to ensure complementary relations, that is, how performance measures reinforce each other's impact.

New trends in the organization of work have also made it possible to specify more accurate performance goals—a factor especially responsible for the payment of large bonuses in the financial services industry over the last few years. The increased emphasis on controls and processes means that credit and risk professionals are now seen as equally important as the front-end specialists. With the recent increase in trading volumes plus the growth of new and more structured and technical products, opportunities in risk management have increased, with the result that the nature and scope of the job of a risk manager are now more clearly outlined and enumerated. The risk professional enjoys recognition at par with the front-office employees and is no longer relegated to a mere auxiliary role. Consequently, a better definition of job activities has led risk management executives to claim that their bonuses should be tied to the front office, as a reflection of their input into the organization. Similar trends resulting from more structured products and services can be observed in other job categories.

STRENGTHS AND CRITICISMS

According to the compensation consultant benchmarking firm Equilar, for two hundred companies that filed their proxies by March 28, 2008, and had revenues of at least $6.5 billion, average compensation for CEOs in 2007 who had held the job at least two years was $11.2 million, up 5 percent from 2006. This figure rises to $11.7 million if new CEOs are counted. One contributory factor to this increase in CEO compensation was the expansion in bonus payouts. Average total bonus payout increased 1.1 percent in 2007, to $2.8 million for CEOs who had held their jobs for two years. The past data show that CEO pay is not completely insulated from the changes in the economy. As Figure 20.1 shows, median CEO pay at the largest 350 publicly held companies fell 13 percent from 2001 to 2002. It took a while for it to recover from this dip, reflecting to an extent the burst of the Internet bubble and its aftermath.

Bonuses are particularly useful when their impact can be measured in terms of specific performance achievement goals. Then a percentage can be set so that individuals will be motivated to increase their performance as much as possible to achieve a higher bonus. As an individual-based bonus pay plan, it is more useful for senior executive positions or people in sales, because performance can be measured. Although such bonus incentives can make employees very driven, they can also have negative consequences, especially if the bonus scheme has not been designed properly. To start with, the bonus has to be large enough to matter. Then there is concern over lack of team cooperation.

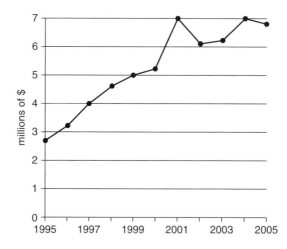

Figure 20.1 Median CEO Pay, 1995–2005.

The more employees are motivated toward achieving higher bonuses, the less they cooperate with each other, especially if payouts are tied to individual performance. Reduced cooperation can have negative effects if important information is not shared. A strongly competitive culture in an organization is not always healthy and can cause conflict when one employee receives greater financial compensation than another.

When performance cannot be so easily measured and teamwork is important, a group-based bonus system can be used. The overall performance of the company can be measured, and then a set amount can be handed out to executives in each job category. While this may mean that there is less individual motivation, it is more likely that the employees will want to work together to get the company performing well in order to receive as much of a bonus as possible. On a company-wide scale, this is known as gain sharing or profit sharing. This can be particularly helpful when there is interdependence between team members or business units, therefore fostering cooperation and providing everyone with a common goal.

Reliance on specific or subjective performance measures in bonus schemes means that bonus payouts will be determined by senior managers or supervisors, since they will be in a position to exploit any additional relevant information that arises during the measurement period. However, there may be frequent problems of bias and favoritism. In their 1996 article ''Discretion and Bias in Performance Evaluation,'' Prendergast and Topel argue that superiors in organizations are often not the residual claimants of subordinates' outputs and therefore have no incentive to renege but rather attempt to bias the performance evaluation. This claim has largely been borne out by research, such as Yariv's ''Mum Effect'' article from a 2006 issue of *Journal of Managerial Psychology,* which suggests that superiors give more lenient performance ratings when these are used for incentive purposes. The ensuing rating compression is problematic because it not only distorts employee incentives but may also negatively influence promotion or job-assignment decisions. For example, a common occurrence is the case when ''all'' employees seem to be above-average performers, making it difficult to select the ''right'' subordinate for the ''right'' job. Employee motivation and morale also suffer, as they become disenchanted with the biased assessments they receive.

The problems of bonus incentives can to some extent be reduced by stock option plans. A stock options plan is a method for a company to positively impact executive attitude and behavior, as it aligns the executive interest with that of the company. If the executive works harder and more efficiently, thereby increasing the performance of the company, it will be reflected in the company's share price; the higher the share price, the greater the reward for the executive. These perspectives led regulators and shareholders in the 1990s to encourage the use of stock option plans to make pay more sensitive to performance. Consequently, equity-based compensation became a staple executive incentive for the top S&P 500 companies. According to Perry and Zenner's 2001 article for the *Journal of Financial Economics*, as a percentage of total compensation, options increased from 21.8 percent of total compensation in 1992 to 37.65 percent in 1998. Over the same period, salary as a component of total compensation declined from 35.53 percent to 20.89 percent.

2007 saw a big increase in stock options grants and shares with performance-based vesting criteria. According to Equilar, stock options and shares awarded to executives jumped to 14.7 percent in the fourth quarter of 2007 from 8.2 percent in the fourth quarter of 2006. The traditional non-qualified stock option plans have been used by companies as a cashless incentive package with vesting restrictions. Executives also benefit, as they receive substantial payouts if the company has performed well but, more importantly, since they typically have several years to determine when to exercise options once they have been vested, it gives them the opportunity to time taxation of payouts. However, there are now new tax and accounting requirements of these plans, limiting their scope and incentive effect. For example, discounted stock options are now treated as deferred compensation. This means that an entirely new governance regime is needed for managing such stock option plans, involving the design and management of payout accounts. A more stringent requirement for the company is to expense the stock options at the date of their grant. This departure from the old practice, when the company was able to book the liability only if and when the option was exercised, means that the company now records the liability for a stock option much earlier. Given the fact that there are difficulties in evaluating the true value of the granted stock options until they are exercised, companies will be understandably reluctant to assume a liability that they are not sure about.

RECOMMENDED DESIGN, DEVELOPMENT, AND IMPLEMENTATION PROCESS

The following are some notes about designing, developing, and implementing the plans discussed above:

1. A bonus incentive plan can take many forms, such as a project completion bonus or a lump-sum annual bonus. In each case, the purpose will be to encourage employee attention to specific dimensions of performance. In this respect, companies can use a wide range of factors or specific performance measures to cover a broader set of business objectives, including quality, customer service, safety,

teamwork, and various other HR-related measures. The key will be to specify performance metrics in relation to the performance goals of the bonus plan.

2. Payouts from a bonus scheme are usually made when a target or a performance hurdle has been crossed, and these can induce company executives to go the extra mile if they know their rewards will be greater for that extra push. This works especially well with increasing bonuses, implying that the pay-performance structure is linear. One particular example of a non-linear bonus is earnings-based bonus award, where payouts are made only when earnings exceed a specified threshold or "hurdle rate." When companies cap bonuses in this way, managers may also defer income when that cap is reached. This suggests that managers can maximize the value of their bonus awards by increasing (or decreasing) reported earnings. Therefore, incentive plans should ideally avoid non-linearities in pay-performance structures, such as the 15 or 20 percent targeted earnings growth bonus scheme.

3. Bonuses should be offered that use performance standards or targets that encompass the interactions among different job dimensions. Because jobs normally involve multiple dimensions, it will be important to provide incentives that encourage employee attention to all relevant dimensions of performance. Performance measurement should reflect interdependencies present in employee jobs, both in how different performance measures are used and in how supervisors take into account the subjective elements of performance. In instances such as quality-related or customer-service related bonuses, company's operational procedures should be in line with these goals.

4. Multiple performance metrics are best used when they include some offsetting drivers that mitigate the ability to manipulate accounting measures or drive poor business decisions to reach goals. For example, if revenue growth is a desired performance target, it should be accompanied by a profitability or margin measure to ensure that the "incentive" is not to increase revenue at any cost. It is likely that when the various indices of performance are taken together, the noise and distortions will average out to produce a more reliable index of performance.

5. As bonuses are usually paid when certain performance thresholds are realized, the benefits derived from such incentives may be restricted if performance targets cannot be linked closely to work. In these situations, it would be more suitable to use low-powered incentives such as a flat wage.

6. Stock options are generally based on aggregate performance measures such as a firm's stock market performance and, hence, these should be used as a general incentive for executives to put forth optimum effort throughout the plan period. Instead of receiving cash in hand, employees are awarded company shares that can be cashed in a few years. However, it is important that options be set at a worthwhile value; lacking this, employees will not be encouraged to increase their work efforts. They should also be vested in a reasonably short period of time, such as three to five years. Over longer periods employees will forget about them and they are at more risk to lose value.

7. Stock option plans involve issues such as vesting (and "accelerated vesting") of stock options and how stock options align the holder's interest with those of the company's shareholders. Primarily, how long should the share options last? There needs to be an adequate length of time to keep the employee motivated. Stock options could be a benefit if used well because they can lead to long-term attachment, which is especially useful for a growth company. Also, what price should the strike price be set as? It needs to be a value that minimizes the tradeoff between cost to firm and performance of employee. More important, the stock option plan should filter out stock price rises that are due to general market trends. This can be achieved by giving more weight to executives' own performance, as measured by senior managers or immediate supervisors.

CRITICAL SUCCESS FACTORS

Incentives are linked closely to motivation and therefore it is important that incentive schemes be used to get the best out of company executives. When setting bonuses, stock options schemes, or deferred compensation plans, such objectives should be taken into account as incentives, cost, legal compliance, and fairness. This suggests that an effective incentive plan will ideally need to meet a specific set of social, political, and economic conditions.

Social

- Stock options remain a better way to improve the executive effort over time, but for individual tasks, bonuses may be preferable because of the ease with which the impact of the incentive can be measured using specific performance metrics. However, the extent to which bonuses are successful depends on the culture of the company and the willingness of the workforce. Therefore, setting the right type of bonus in the right setting is crucial. If it is set too high, employees could become demotivated and work effort may decrease because of a belief that there is no reason to work since they would not be rewarded for it. If it is set too low, it could be costly to employers who have to bear the expense for every worker who has achieved target. Also, once employees reach the target, they may no longer be motivated to continue working productively.

- As stock options are exercised when the company's stocks appreciate in a set time frame, executives' attitudes will be linked to the future performance of the company in alliance with its corporate strategy. Executives are likely to perform in a way that will also take into account the impact of their actions on other members of the organization. They would be willing to help others if this improves the company's performance. Companies thus use a stock option scheme so that employees feel like owners, thereby creating the atmosphere of a team working toward attainment of common goals.

Political

- Bonus targets are meant to direct executive effort in a certain direction to the exclusion of others. However, in their 1995 article for the *Journal of Accounting and Economics* Gaver and Austin argue that the strategy has been found to cause too much neglect of many vital company actions and outcomes. Bonus schemes targeted at company goals such as customer service often fail because managers can easily manipulate the performance measure. Current bonus payout practices reflect companies' desire to avoid the potentially distorting effects of focusing too much on a single performance measure. Therefore, a wide range of factors may be introduced to cover a broader set of business objectives. This is based on the assumption that bonuses linked to other components of wages and employee benefits and tied into the culture of the organization are far more effective than those which are not.

- In their 2005 article "Accounting for Stock Options," Bulow and Shoven find that CEOs and top executives may obtain substantial option pay without giving up corresponding amounts of their cash compensation. Executives may also be able to capture much larger gains than more cost-effective and efficient option plans would provide. This is because the options executives receive do not link pay tightly to the executives' own performance. Consequently, executives are able to reap windfalls from that part of the stock price increase that is due solely to market trends beyond their control.

Economic

- Incentive pay critically depends on the type of performance measures used. There are various organizational and strategic settings in which stock option plans will usefully utilize aggregate performance measures to capture executive actions. However, specific performance measures and the resultant subjectivity in performance measurement have the capacity to better signal the executives' activities as, for example, when there is a need to isolate the contribution of individual executives or activities or when it is important to provide better executive control over work.

- Concerns about the effective design and implementation of incentives are to some extent related to the critical role of subjectivity in incentive pay plans. The need to mitigate noise in stock option plans and the wide prevalence of discretion in bonus payouts—an outcome of linking bonuses to the company's business goals—have inevitably increased the significance of subjectivity in performance evaluation. Supervisors use subjective assessments to eliminate problems arising from unobservability or when bonus plans use a multitude of business goals as performance measures. Supervisors can exploit any additional relevant information that arises during the measurement period, as bonuses are usually a reward for achievement paid retrospectively.

- Companies may find that subjectivity of performance criterion is problematic in certain situations. Under a discretionary incentive system, executives may be rewarded based on their qualitative performance, especially when factors such as customer service, investment in intangibles, or quality improvements are important. In these cases, forming fair and accurate assessment is likely to be a managerial concern. Companies can use two mechanisms for ameliorating such problems of subjective performance measurement. First, better alignment of incentive pay with company organization is likely to overcome potential distortions in the use of specific performance measures. Second, recent trends in organizational design allow companies to develop specific performance measures more accurately, thus reducing the likelihood of distorted presentation of one's performance.

SUMMARY

This chapter provides a brief introduction to major components to compensation packages and how executive incentive schemes can be designed more effectively. The following elements are specifically considered: (1) base wage and salaries and how various internal and external factors influence the magnitude of base wage; (2) different types of bonus schemes (for example, annual bonuses, business goal-linked bonuses) and their determinants and methods of payouts; and (3) stock options and long-term incentive plans (including deferred compensation plans). An important difference between executive compensation and average worker pay is that executive pay is more risky and strongly underscores pay-performance linkages. Stock options and restricted stock may take years to vest and are often tied to performance targets. If the firm's stock falls, these options lose their value. Similarly, as payouts from bonus schemes are usually based on employees meeting specific performance targets, it underlines the desirability of linking pay closely to performance.

In conclusion, stock option plans are a beneficial way of aligning incentives with that of the firm, but they must be thoughtfully designed to ensure that executive payouts are not tied too closely to external factors beyond their control. Bonus schemes can also help company executives improve their performance and behavior; however, the scheme should match the structure and culture of the company and consider employees' propensity to reach targets. The benefits and negative effects to the employee need to be balanced such that the employee works in cooperation with others, while at the same time ensuring the best possible individual performance. A good use of incentive schemes, which draw on work-related interdependencies, will lead to executives having this "sense of ownership," leading to improved abilities and performance.

Notes

- Literature on pay for performance covers compensation systems for different sets of employee groups. For an executive compensation focus, see J. Core, W. Guay, and R. Thomas (2004). Is S&P 500 CEO compensation inefficient pay without performance? A review of pay without performance: The unfulfilled promise of executive compensation. Vanderbilt Law and Economics Research Paper No. 05–05; U of Penn, Inst for Law & Econ Research Paper 05-13. http://ssrn.com/abstract_648648_.

- Paul Healy (1985). The effect of bonus schemes on accounting decisions, *Journal of Accounting and Economics*, *7*, 85–107 is a classical article on earnings management. See also E. Bartov & P. Mohhanram (2004). Private information, earnings manipulations and executive stock option exercises, in *The Accounting Review*, *79*, 889–920.

- The managerial power approach argues that compensation committee member incentives align with CEOs and top executives, rather than shareholders. However, empirical research does not find much support for this observation, as executive pay is no greater if compensation committees contain affiliated directors. See R. Anderson and J. Bizjak (2003). An empirical examination of the role of the CEO and the compensation committee in structuring executive pay. *Journal of Banking and Finance*, *27*(7): 1323–1348.

- Data on executive compensation are compiled and produced by various compensation consultants, including Equilar (www.equilar.com) and Mercer Human Resource Consulting (www.mercerhr.com). "ExecuComp" database of Standard and Poor's includes proxy statement data for top executives in the S&P 500, S&P Mid-Cap 400, S&P Small-Cap 600, and other supplemental S&P indices.

References

Amazon.com (2008). Investor relations. http://phx.corporate-ir.net/phoenix.zhtml? p = irol-irhome&c = 97664, accessed 8 August 2008.

Arya, A., Glover, J., & Liang, P. (2004). Intertemporal aggregation and incentives. *European Accounting Review, 13*, 643–657.

Baker, G. P., Jensen, M. C., & Murphy, K. J. (1988). Compensation and incentives: Practice vs. theory. *Journal of Finance, 43*, 593–617.

Bebchuk, L., & Fried, J. (2003). Executive compensation as an agency problem. *Journal of Economic Perspectives, 17*(3), 71–92.

Bebchuk, L., & Fried, J. (2004). *Pay without performance: The unfulfilled promise of executive compensation.* Cambridge, MA: Harvard University Press.

Berle, A. A., & Means, G. C. (1932) *The modern corporation and private property.* New York: Macmillan.

Black, F., & Scholes, M. (1973). The pricing of options and corporate liabilities. *Journal of Political Economy, 8*, 637–659.

Bulow, J., & Shoven, J. (2005). Accounting for stock options. *The Journal of Economic Perspectives, 19*, 115–135.

Eisenhardt, K. (1985). Control: Organizational and economic approaches. *Management Science, 31*, 134–149.

Eunmi, C., & Hahn, J. (2006). Does pay-for-performance enhance perceived distributive justice for collectivistic employees? *Personnel Review, 35*, 397–412.

Fama, E. F., & Jensen, M. C. (1983). Agency problems and residual claims. *Journal of Law and Economics, 26*, 327–349.

Gaver, K., & Austin, J. (1995). Additional evidence on bonus plans and income management. *Journal of Accounting and Economics, 19*, 3–28.

Healy, P. (1985). The effect of bonus schemes on accounting decisions. *Journal of Accounting and Economics, 7*, 85–107.

Heery, E. (2000). Trade unions and the management of reward. In G. White & J. Drucker (Eds.), *Reward management: Critical perspectives.* London: Routledge & Kogan Paul.

Heneman, R., Ledford, G., & Gresham, M. (1999). *The effects of changes in the nature of work on compensation. Working Paper.* Columbus: Ohio State University.

Holmstrom, B. (1979). Moral hazard and observability. *Bell Journal of Economics, 10*, 74–92.

Holmstrom, B., & Milgrom, P. (1987). Aggregation and linearity in the provision of intertemporal incentives. *Econometrica*, *55*, 303–328.

Holmstrom, B., & Milgrom, P. (1991). Multitask principal-agent analyses: Incentive contracts, asset ownership, and job design. *Journal of Law, Economics and Organization*, *7*, 24–52.

IDS (2007). Bonus schemes, incomes, data stream. *HR Study 843*. London: IDS.

Ittner, C., & Larcker, D. F. (1998). Innovations in performance measurement: Trends and research implications. *Journal of Management Accounting Research*, *10*, 205–238.

Ittner, C., & Larcker, D. F. (2002). Determinants of performance measure choices in worker incentive plans. *Journal of Labor Economics*, *20*, 58–90.

Jensen, M. C. (2001). Corporate budgeting is broken—Let's fix it. *Harvard Business Review*, *79*, 94–101.

Kandel, E., & Lazear, E. (1992). Peer pressure and partnerships. *Journal of Political Economy*, *100*, 801–817.

Kaplan, R. S., & Norton, D. P. (2001). Transforming the balanced scorecard from performance measurement to strategic management, part 1. *Accounting Horizons*, *15*, 87–104.

Kerr, S. (1975). On the folly of rewarding A, while hoping for B. *Academy of Management Journal*, *18*, 769–783.

Lazear, E. (1998). *Personnel economics for managers*. Hoboken, NJ: John Wiley & Sons.

Mager, R. F., & Pipe, P. (1997) Analyzing performance problems. Atlanta, GA: The Center for Effective Performance.

Milgrom, P., & Roberts, J. (1995). Complementarities and fit: Strategy, structure, and organizational change in manufacturing. *Journal of Accounting and Economics*, *19*, 179–208.

Murphy, K. (1999). Executive compensation, in O. Ashenfelter & D. Card (Eds.), *Handbook of labor economics* (Vol. *3*) New York: Elsevier.

Murphy, K. J. (2000). Performance standards in incentive contracts. *Journal of Accounting and Economics*, *30*, 245–278.

Ouchi, W. (1979). A conceptual framework for the design of organization control mechanisms. *Management Science*, *25*, 833–848.

Perry, T., & Zenner, M. (2001). Pay for performance? Government regulations and the structure of compensation contracts. *Journal of Financial Economics*, *62*, 453–488.

Prendergast, C. (2002). The tenuous trade-off between risk and incentives. *Journal of Political Economy*, *110*, 1071–1102.

Prendergast, C., & Topel, R. (1996). Discretion and bias in performance evaluation. *European Economic Review*, *37*, 355–365.

Simons, R. (2000). *Performance measurement and control systems for implementing strategy: Text and cases*. Englewood Cliffs, NJ: Prentice-Hall.

Shorter, G., & Labonte, M. (2007). The economics of corporate executive pay. CRS Report for Congress. May 18, 2009, at http://opencrs.com/document/RL33935/.

Waggoner, D. B., Neely, A. D., & Kennerley, M. P. (1999). The forces that shape organizational performance measurement systems: An interdisciplinary review. *International journal of Production Economics*, *60–61*, 53–60.

Williamson, O. E. (1975). Markets and hierarchies: Analysis and antitrust implications. New York: The Free Press.

Williamson, O. E. (1985). *The economic institutions of capitalism: Firms, markets, relational contracting*. New York: The Free Press.

Wruck, K. H., & Jensen, M. C. (1994). Science, specific knowledge and total quality management. *Journal of Accounting and Economics*, *18*, 247–287.

Yariv, E. (2006). ''Mum effect'': Principals' reluctance to submit negative feedback. *Journal of Managerial Psychology*, *21*, 533–546.

PART SIX

EDITORS' DISCUSSION

The value and importance of incentives, rewards, and recognitions as performance interventions should not be underestimated. By complementing other motivating factors, each of these tools can be effectively used to bring individual and organizational focus to the accomplishment of desired results. From achieving quarterly sales targets to completing a software installation on time and within budget, performance interventions that reward, recognize, or provide incentives offer an opportunity for you to creatively engage others in the accomplishment of desired results. Differing combinations of these three performance interventions can be applied throughout your improvement efforts to find creative solutions to complex performance challenges.

Expanding Your Options

Telecommuting—involves the substations of telecommunication for transportation in a decentralized and flexible work arrangement, which allows employees to work from home, using a computer attached to the employer's data network.

Based on businessdictionary.com definition (January 2009)

As with all components of the Performance Pyramid model, incentives, rewards, and recognition (as a block of the pyramid) play a central role in the successful achievement of results. Use, create, or manage incentive systems within your organization as an antecedent to future performance. To acknowledge the successful accomplishment of desired results, rewards and recognition systems should be crafted and applied within your organization. These precursors to performance and follow-on acknowledgement of desired performance can become a valuable component of any improvement system.

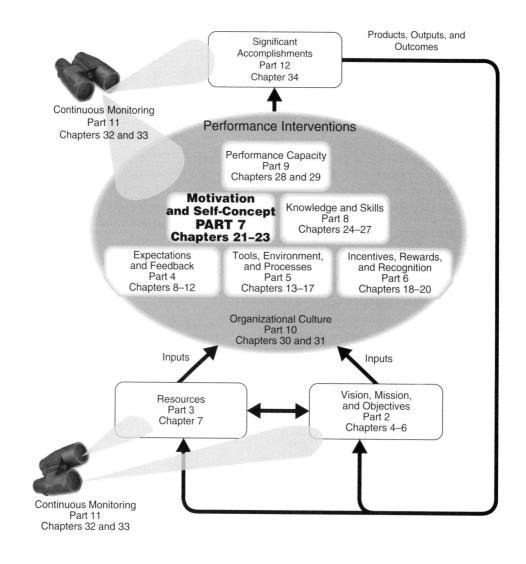

Continuous Monitoring
Part 11
Chapters 32 and 33

Products, Outputs, and
Outcomes

Significant
Accomplishments
Part 12
Chapter 34

Performance Interventions

Performance Capacity
Part 9
Chapters 28 and 29

**Motivation
and Self-Concept
PART 7
Chapters 21–23**

Knowledge and Skills
Part 8
Chapters 24–27

Expectations
and Feedback
Part 4
Chapters 8–12

Tools, Environment,
and Processes
Part 5
Chapters 13–17

Incentives, Rewards,
and Recognition
Part 6
Chapters 18–20

Organizational Culture
Part 10
Chapters 30 and 31

Inputs

Inputs

Resources
Part 3
Chapter 7

Vision, Mission,
and Objectives
Part 2
Chapters 4–6

Continuous Monitoring
Part 11
Chapters 32 and 33

MOTIVATION AND SELF-CONCEPT

In most work situations, people are more likely to achieve significant results when they want to perform and believe that they can accomplish results valued by the organization. While incentives, rewards, and recognition interventions (see Part Six of this handbook) provide valuable tools to help people focus on accomplishing desired results, these interventions are most effective when people are also motivated to perform and believe that they can perform successfully. In addition, other performance interventions described throughout this handbook are also dependent on employees' motivation and positive self-concept to be effective. Your organization can create, for example, a state-of-art electronic performance support system (see Chapter Thirteen) or develop cohesive performance feedback systems (see Chapter Nine), but without adequate employee motivation and positive self-concept any improvements in results will likely be minimal or short-lived.

Motivation, as discussed in the chapters of this part of the book, is a foundation of any performance improvement system. As a form of motivation, the desire to achieve results that have meaning is often what brings employees to work each day, engages staff in projects that keep them at the office late into the night, brings exciting discussions to the office, and challenges individuals, teams, and organizations. While incentives may help employees to focus on specific achievements, it is the motivation to be successful that drives performance. Also, while knowledge and skills are fundamental elements of performance, motivation to achieve results lead people to apply what they have learned.

Success may be defined by the individual, although it is often shaped by the organization, peers within the organization, and the society in which the organization and individual employees strive to achieve success. But both human and organizational performance come down to motivated individuals performing tasks, making decisions, and achieving results. Motivation, however, is not a one-size-fits-all component of a performance improvement system but rather is a very complex and enormously important element of your efforts to improve performance.

Expanding Your Options

Alignment of desires and work—a state in which personal career goals are fulfilled under current employment conditions.

As discussed in the chapters within Part Two of this handbook, the alignment of personal goals and ambitions with those of the organization and its clients is a critical component of motivation. Research in the 1980s by Israel researchers Vardi, Weiner, and Popper illustrated that alignment of people's values with an organization's vision and mission statements was essential to employee commitment. By aligning organizational objectives with the values of the external clients and the society they serve, you can take the first step toward making people's work experiences more meaningful. Whether we consider it as value or worth, *meaning* is, after all, what most employees are looking for in their work and careers . . . a source of motivation. By linking individual and team results to the achievements of the organization as a whole, you make the first connection. Next, align the achievements of the organization with the desired results of external partners, clients, communities, and society as a whole; this makes clear the value of individual performance.

Self-concept, a counterpart to motivation, plays an important role in performance because people must believe that they can accomplish desired results. Self-concept includes the important internal functions of self-esteem, confidence, positive thinking, physical and mental well-being, as well as other dimensions of the individual that are often forgotten in the workplace. Much like the performance of world-class athletes, employee performance is as much about these internal dimensions (within the motivation and self-concept block of the Performance Pyramid) as it is about tools, resources, training, and other external factors, although traditionally these other factors, especially training and resources, have garnered most of the attention.

WHAT'S COMING UP

One practical first step in improving employee motivation is recognizing the importance that communications—whether they be e-mails, newsletters, reports, or presentations—play in establishing and maintaining positive motivation. To this end, in Chapter Twenty-One, Lya Visser examines the significant role of motivational communications in improving human and organizational performance.

Motivational Communication

Lya Visser

INTRODUCTION

Motivational interventions have been shown to effectively and efficiently increase the motivational levels of individuals, leading to improved commitment to tasks and significant increases in performance. Working with motivated people is necessary for organizations to be successful. Often, however, organizations may underestimate the importance of stopping actions that decrease the motivation of their workers and are often slow at taking actions that will motivate them. This chapter discusses motivational interventions in the human performance area that have been shown to effectively and efficiently increase the motivational levels of people.

DESCRIPTION

This chapter is written for decision-makers in organizations, human resource managers, learners, trainers, instructors, and others who are actively involved in improving human performance. The human performance interventions discussed in this chapter focus on adjusting and attending to the motivational needs of people so as to optimize human and organizational performance. Specific attention is given to the potential use of the *motivational message*. Motivational messages are communications transmitted in the form of an e-mail, a letter, a postcard, a text message, or another form of written or oral communication that

515

516 HANDBOOK OF IMPROVING PERFORMANCE IN THE WORKPLACE

aims at increasing the motivation of the receiver through systematic motivational strategies. A motivation message has the following characteristics:

- It targets the perceived or identified motivational requirements of the receiver;

- It is preferably designed in such a way that it gets the immediate attention of the receiver;

- It is short, to the point, and aims at increasing or sustaining the motivation of the receiver;

- It may be developed in such way that it can, just like a Christmas or birthday card, be used to remind the receiver of the personal or personalized care that is shown in the message;

- Its impact is enhanced if the message is a real attention-getter and aims at one or more of the four main motivational components that contribute to the interest and effort people put in carrying out a task; and

- It should not be seen as a one-way information tool but as an effective and affective process recognizing that the effective process leads to the desired result, while the affective element influences how the message is perceived and received.

Motivational messages can work very well under many different circumstances. A motivational message that targets instilling confidence to be able to effectively carry out a challenging task is often effective, as are messages that emphasize that assisting in a training course will ultimately be very satisfying. It is important, however, to make sure that the content of a motivational message is realistic. It is useless, for example, to send a motivational message to someone who enrolls in a course to learn Spanish expressing confidence that she will speak Spanish fluently in four weeks, or to send a message to someone who will have to work overtime every night expressing that he will find it a very satisfying experience. Motivational messages have been shown to effectively impact motivation and performance in studies of education and training in a variety of contexts and international settings (by researchers including myself, Jan Visser, Damith Wickramanayake, and Charles Schlosser).

Motivational messages are designed along the lines of John Keller's ARCS model (1983) of motivational analysis and incorporate the three behaviors of effective communication outlined by Carl Rogers in his seminal work for *Harvard Educational Review*, 1962's "The Interpersonal Relationship."

Influences on Performance

Many factors influence human and organizational performance. According to John Keller, a leading researcher in motivational theory, motivation is one of the three general influences on performance; the other two factors are capability

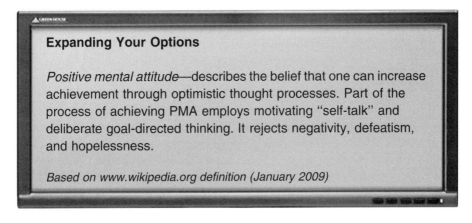

Expanding Your Options

Positive mental attitude—describes the belief that one can increase achievement through optimistic thought processes. Part of the process of achieving PMA employs motivating "self-talk" and deliberate goal-directed thinking. It rejects negativity, defeatism, and hopelessness.

Based on www.wikipedia.org definition (January 2009)

and opportunity. Elements of all three, wrote Keller in 1998, should be present in order to have a positive level of performance. Motivation can be described as the process that energizes our knowledge and that encourages us to use our skills effectively so that we achieve our goals. In addition, motivation encourages people to take on challenges, to be creative, and to increase not only the quantity of work, but the quality as well. Motivated people generally feel satisfied with what they are doing.

A person's motivation fluctuates, but there can be stable and predictable aspects of motivation. It is thus important to develop and apply motivational interventions that enhance motivation where and when necessary, so as to ensure success and satisfaction.

The root of human motivation is in important ways determined by the beliefs and the expectations that one can be successful. People have a tendency to attribute their failures and successes to internal and/or external causes. Following success, confidence rises, but after failure or perceived failure, confidence drops. Strategies that target confidence and other motivational areas such as feelings of belonging and trust are thus important.

Human motivation is also impacted by external factors such as expectations of performance, reward structures, organizational ethos, and the capacity of organizations to identify the needs of their employees and to interact efficiently and effectively with them. How to determine which needs can be addressed with motivational interventions and when and how to apply motivational strategies is crucial to effective interventions. This will now be discussed.

WHAT WE KNOW FROM RESEARCH

Motivation: Theory and Research

The study of motivation has been described by Graham and Weiner in their 1996 chapter for the *Handbook of Educational Psychology* as the study of why people think and behave as they do. Motivation does not look at what a person *can* do, but at what a person *will* do. According to Florida State University's John Keller (1983, 1987), motivation refers to choices people make as to what experiences or goals they will approach and the degree of effort they will exert in that respect. Unfortunately, there are scores of people in the workforce who are not, or are hardly, motivated to perform certain tasks. In 1995 when studying work attitudes in the USA, Dean Spitzer found that more than 50 percent of the workers admitted that they only did the minimum so as to prevent being fired, while 80 percent admitted that they could work much harder. Therefore, as the University of Southern California's Richard Clark suggested in 2003, significant performance increase is possible when adequate motivational strategies are used.

Overcoming motivational challenges is, however, not always easy because human motivation is complex. Graham and Weiner therefore emphasize that it is important to increase success expectancies and to alter the perception of ability, so that ability is seen as a varying condition instead of a static one.

In their research carried out in the 1970s, Covington and Omelich (1979) showed that there is a close match between aspiration or goals and the expectancy that these goals can be met. Expectancy plays an important role in how someone will react to a task. Hoska's chapter within 1993's *Interactive Instruction and Feedback* emphasizes the importance of believing that it is possible to realize a goal and that the current situation can be an important motivational factor. Turner and Paris, for example, worked with six motivational tools in encouraging people to use their motivation in effective ways. Their six C's, reported in a 1995 article for *The Reading Teacher*, are choice, challenge, control, collaboration, constructive comprehension, and consequences. In related research, Malone and Lepper focused in 1987's ''Making Learning Fun'' on increasing motivation for learning through computer games. They concentrated on factors like fantasy, curiosity, and control. The resulting motivational effect was attributed to empowerment and self-determination.

Two main distinctions are frequently made in the general concept of motivation: intrinsic motivation and extrinsic motivation. Intrinsic motivation refers to the internal desire to perform a task because it gives pleasure, helps to develop certain skills, is useful, and/or is morally the right thing to do. Extrinsic motivation, on the other hand, is related to factors external to the individual and unrelated to the task to be performed; examples include money, good grades, and a promotion. Over the years a number of motivational inducement sources have been developed so as to energize and sustain behavior in an organization. Richard Clark, for instance, offers examples including financial rewards, increased responsibility, job enrichment such as delegating management tasks, and increased status like recognition by co-workers and managers.

The main sources of intrinsic and extrinsic motivation are presented in Table 21.1.

Table 21.1 Sources of Intrinsic and Extrinsic Motivation

Sources of Intrinsic Motivation	Sources of Extrinsic Motivation
Enjoyment, curiosity, fantasy	Pay, promotion, recognition
(Job) enrichment	Increased status
Accomplishment	Need for power

Models of Motivation

Most models of motivation have been derived from the main motivational theories. Using a model or framework makes it easier to enhance motivation in a systematic way and helps to effectively identify and address barriers to performance. Three models are discussed.

Wlodkowski's Time Continuum Model of Motivation. This model is based on approaches from linguistics, cognitive psychology, and research in motivation. It has many similarities with John Keller's ARCS model of motivational analysis, yet the focus of the time continuum model is on the role motivation plays in the different stages of the learning process. The continuum of the learning process has, according to Raymond Wlodkowski of Antioch University in Seattle and The Fielding Institute in Santa Barbara, three critical stages/factors: the beginning of the learning process with emphasis on attitudes and needs; the actual learning process with emphasis on stimulation and affect; and the ending of the learning process when competence and reinforcement play an important role. Wlodkowski asserts in 1993's *Enhancing Adult Motivation to Learn* that the process of instruction and motivational strategies must be thoroughly planned for each of these three factors. This classifies the model as a prescriptive model.

Moshinskie's Model of Motivation. A recent motivational model that has gained some recognition is the Moshinskie model. Jim Moshinskie argues that there are two different types of people: those with an active attitude toward life and those with a passive attitude. The former are mostly intrinsically motivated and largely do things without external inducement. The latter, however, lack intrinsic motivation and build more on extrinsic motivation. Moshinskie thinks along Wlodkowski's lines and offers a model to improve extrinsic motivation before, during, and after training or instruction. The focus of the model, as expressed in a 2001 article for *Performance Improvement* journal, is mostly on creating and explaining extrinsic motivational techniques that may complement the intrinsic needs of learners. Table 21.2 provides a summary of these techniques.

Table 21.2 Extrinsic Motivational Techniques

Before the Course or Training	During	After
Know the learner (audience analysis)	Create conducive environment	Celebrate successes
Know the work environment	Chunk information	Provide support when trainee returns to workplace
Match values and motives	Build on existing knowledge	Reinforce the learning
Prepare/motivate the work environment	Vary the stimulus	View learning as a process not as an event
Apply push and pull strategies	Give "solid" feedback	Investigate the meta-cognitive strategies used by the trainees/learners
Include non-instructional strategies	Provide a human touch	
Offer a learning portal	Offer a social context	
	Build opportunities for fun	
	Stimulate curiosity	

Source: Moshinskie, 2001

Moshinkie asserts that a collaborative approach makes learning and training effective. Trainers, students, and others who can provide substantive input in the motivational state of people should be seen and recognized as contributors to increasing employee success rates.

Keller's ARCS Model of Motivational Analysis. Keller's 1987 ARCS model of motivational analysis, which is based on the main concepts and theories of human motivation, assumes that people's motivation can be influenced, that motivation in relation to performance is a means and not an end, and presupposes that systematic design of learning and training materials can predictably influence motivation. An important strength of the model is that it is usable in many different circumstances and contexts and that it, unlike Wlodkowski's model, is not prescriptive. The four components of the ARCS acronym are briefly discussed below.

> *Attention*—Refers to sensation-seeking needs and to the knowledge-seeking curiosity and interest. Curiosity is, according to Malone and Lepper, an important ingredient in motivation.

Relevance—In early work, John Keller refers to relevance as "value." He distinguishes personal value, instrumental value, and cultural value. Relevance is thereby, according to Moshinkie, closely related to goal orientation and is ideally intrinsic.

Confidence—Most people want to do well and to be in control of what they are doing. Confident people rely on their own actions to reach their goals. How success and failure are explained is closely related to confidence. Keller argues that instruction and training should help people to attribute their learning outcomes to what is controllable and not to good luck.

Satisfaction—Satisfaction is the result of an action that has been a positive experience. Financial rewards often lead to satisfaction (extrinsic motivation), but as Turner and Paris point out, other people's recognition is fortunately also a strong satisfaction tactic. A condition to be satisfied is that one should feel that the amount of work required was appropriate and that the task was doable.

A person's motivational level is not stable; it can unexpectedly increase or decrease. The perception of ability, for instance, is a varying condition. There are, however, also stable and predictable aspects of motivation, such as the individual's need for satisfaction. Although an outsider cannot directly change the motivational disposition of someone else, a good manager or human performance specialist will aim at creating conditions and environments that have a positive influence on the motivational levels of people. These approaches should allow an honest and direct communication process that is not top-down but participative. Regular feedback on performance also helps ensure that enhanced performance is recognized and rewarded.

The Science of Communication: Effective Communication, and Affective Comprehension

In training and learning, communication—as a science—has only received the attention it deserves in the last seventy years. Strongly influenced by the exciting possibilities offered by audiovisual instruction, David Berlo, a well-known communication specialist, added in 1963 to the identified skills of speaking and writing (encoding) and listening and reading (decoding) a crucial fifth skill that relates to both: thought and reasoning. How we think, what we think about, and how we express our thinking is determined by our ability to use language effectively. How we see the world and how and what we think are affected by the codes we use and by how skillfully we use these codes. Berlo claimed that as a "communication man," he must argue strongly that it is the communication process that is central and that the media, though important, are secondary. These days it is generally agreed that effective communication is not enough; it has to be supplemented by affective (emphatic) comprehension.

Carl Rogers posited that communication processes are related to building relationships and that relationships in turn are vehicles for growth. He identified three behaviors that are essential to effective and affective communication: (1) open disclosure, meaning that the relationship is mutual and based on more than the minimum information to work together; (2) warm affirmation, being the extent to which communicators feel at ease with each other; and (3) empathic comprehension, meaning that it is the capacity of the "other" to place him- or herself in the position of the opposite party and to be partial and understanding to the other's position. Rogers' conceptualization of empathy aims at dissolving alienation and at creating positive outcomes.

Motivational Strategies

Although many of the theories and models of motivation have been around for decades, organizations are still struggling with how to incorporate them in their training activities and in the daily running of their organization. Organizations are looking for a kind of "universal motivator"—a strategy or tool that helps to increase work motivation and encourages people to increase their dedication and persistence. While such a panacea may never be found, factors that may impact negatively on motivation such as bureaucracy, dishonesty, negative feedback, and top-down leadership should be disabled.

Effective motivational strategies should include at least some of the main elements of the ARCS model, as well as Rogers' concept of empathy. Strategies should aim in general at increasing the daily level of relevance of the work that one is doing, raising self-confidence, augmenting the level of satisfaction (fulfillment), and including communication processes that are effective but also affective. Effective motivational strategies have impact on the performance of the organization and on its qualitative and quantitative output. Motivational strategies can, nevertheless, only be effective if the leadership style that is adopted involves employees in decision making, teamwork, and tackling problems.

Before continuing, it is important to emphasize once more that motivation is unstable in nature, but as Keller points out in his chapter for the 1998 *Handbook of Human Performance Technology*, it can be influenced by, among other approaches, the use of motivational strategies. Furthermore, motivational strategies cannot in themselves solve behavioral problems such as emotional immaturity or severe anti-social behavior. These challenges belong to the area of psychological counseling and/or related disciplines. Motivational strategies can lead to improved motivational states and traits, especially when aimed at improving the work environment and the preparedness to learn and to perform well. Motivation is difficult to measure and, as a consequence, the influence of motivational strategies is equally difficult to measure. One can, however, measure both confidence and the intensity of effort as forms of self-improvement. The role of the human performance specialist is a challenging one, as it involves determining under which conditions a motivational strategy will increase work motivation and lead to improved results. Motivational strategies used should be cost-effective and ethically sound, and should occur within an organizational environment that is supportive and conducive to performing well.

In summary, it has been seen that, when looking at motivational strategies and following somewhat loosely the ARCS model discussed earlier, the areas of attention or curiosity aim at work goals that should be concrete, varied, challenging, and clearly indicate the quality of performance that is expected and when it is expected. Reflecting on the "relevance" category in the ARCS model, it is important that what one is expected to do should be perceived as being useful, of value, and concrete. These expectations are related to Maslow's seven major categories of self-realization. People who want to achieve like clearly defined goals and chances for taking personal responsibility and initiative.

Most people want to be in control of what they are doing. As I put forth in my 1998 dissertation work, the third area in the ARCS model—confidence—may be the most important. Although competition is often seen as a motivating experience, the first goal is to make sure that people have a high level of personal confidence in their ability to achieve the performance goals set. Being convinced that one has the skills to be successful may be more important than the quality and quantity of mental effort that are invested in the work. If, on the other hand, people have the adequate knowledge and skills but continue to make mistakes and cannot correct these, Clark's 2003 *Performance Improvement* journal article argues that they are most likely either under- or over-confident. For example, offering opportunities to work in teams—provided that they have a shared interest—may be an adequate motivational strategy to achieve certain tasks. Regular feedback, which is embedded in the resource management strategies of the organization, is another important strategy.

It is generally true that people like to feel good about themselves, their environment, and the tasks they are doing, have done, or have to do. Personal feedback that conveys appreciation is another important motivational strategy to express satisfaction, in addition to more costly but often appropriate financial systems. People generally react most strongly when presented with positive recognition for their hard work and accomplishments. A variety of symbolic rewards exist, such as being recognized as employee of the month, getting a special parking spot, or receiving a personal note showing appreciation. All these strategies can make a person feel a valued contributor to the goals of the organization.

Motivational Strategies in the Area of Communication

How you communicate influences the motivational levels of the workers. There are many examples of de-motivational communication. Executive orders, bureaucratic announcements, and annual reviews that tell workers what they did wrong and why they will not receive a salary raise are all examples. In addition, threatening conversations (such as, "If you do not get this done by the end of the month I do not know what to tell the president, especially now that he is looking for ways to decrease the cost of personnel") and impersonal notes, such as "cold" letters or e-mails, are also examples of communications that cannot be considered as tools for effective collaboration.

Michael Schrage of MIT's Media Lab suggests in his 1990 book *Shared Minds* that to motivate, communications—including letters, e-mails, text messages, conversations, etc.—should serve to create *a shared experience* and *not an experience that is shared.* Following the ARCS model, here are some suggestions on how to design motivational communications.

In the area of attention:

- Get the attention of the addressee in a non-threatening way through, for instance, a provoking question or a sharp joke;
- Increase the feeling of being a valued person in the organization by communicating new and relevant information, such as technology availability, in a personalized way;
- Make sure that the addressee is approached with the correct name and, if appropriate, job title;
- Invite people to participate in possible new developments of the organization; and
- Employ strategies that increase the feeling of belonging of the addressee by showing care and empathy.

Relevance strategies could include:

- Building a match between the motives and values of people, and the job conditions and culture of the organization;
- Capitalizing on the need for achievement;
- Stating well-defined goals and personal responsibility; and
- Communicating that someone did well in the organization in the previous period, that what has been done is of value for the future of the organization and for the person him- or herself.

Fear of failure is widespread. Many people struggle with confidence problems. Confidence strategies that can be used include:

- Communicating often with employees to help them understand the criteria for successful performance;
- Giving credit (a short call or a quick e-mail) for even a minor improvement, as this will increase the awareness that performance is related to effort;

- Offering opportunities to make decisions and encourage the workers to see that personal effort and ability contribute to greater confidence;
- Encouraging, where appropriate, the possibility to participate in a course or seminar;
- Sharing work with others during an event or a wider meeting; and
- Collaborating with others on relevant tasks or being part of a work group in the organization.

The area of satisfaction also offers many opportunities to increase the motivational levels by:

- Encouraging workers to identify and use opportunities to learn new skills (intrinsic motivation);
- Giving positive feedback (if appropriate);
- Offering opportunities for personal growth;
- Praising good work, preferably in writing so the receiver can reread the message;
- Ensuring that excellent work is seen not only by colleagues but also by superiors;
- Recognizing good work, for instance, with a bonus check, an additional vacation day, or a nice letter; and
- Praising intensive efforts, even if they are relatively low in results.

The Synergy of Motivation and Communication: Motivational Communication

Various strategies can be used to increase the motivation of people. Motivational communication first and foremost is based on more than the minimum information to carry out a task, but is built on creating understanding and the wish to share. It is a form of open disclosure. Motivational communication expresses that the relationship is one of feeling at ease with each other. It shows that there is a mutual relationship. It is not top-down in the sense of giving orders but aims at sharing a concern, developing a relationship that aims at development, at getting the input and ideas of the other and trying to avoid stagnation. It aims at warm affirmation. Motivational communication also expresses the capacity to place oneself in the situation of the other party and to be understanding of the other's position. A human performance specialist should aim at dissolving alienation and creating positive relationships and a form of empathic comprehension.

Motivational communication goes beyond the traditional dry information bulletin, memo, e-mail, or fax. It requires that one see communication not as a one-way information tool but as an effective and affective process. The effective process leads to the defined result, while the affective element influences how the message is perceived.

Open disclosure results in communication that is frank, honest, and clear. As mentioned before, the leadership style is crucial. Participative management involves employees in decision making and thus fosters two-way communication. Discussing what can reasonably be expected work-wise, argues Keller in his 1998 manuscript "Motivational Systems," increases the sense of relevance to organizational goals and achievements. Open disclosure also means that there is more than the minimum information—that there are communication processes that involve making oneself "known" to the other and vice versa. When Rogers writes about "warm affirmation," he touches upon the need to show understanding for the challenges of the other. Motivational feedback that aims at helping people make use of opportunities for reinforcement of knowledge and skills (for example, retraining and upgrading) is important, but it should be linked to expressing confidence in the other's capacities and capabilities. confidence building, and practical advice. Specific and concrete help and an empathic attitude and approach are the core motivational strategies.

Motivational Communication: The Motivational Message

In summary, a motivational message can be defined as a form of communication that, through its content, positively targets the identified or assumed motivational needs of the receiver and causes the receiver to feel personally addressed by the message, resulting in appropriate motivational alignment.

Motivational communications among participants attending training in instructional design, for example, have been researched by Jan Visser. The majority of the participants were not overly interested in being trained, as they were troubled by the daily horrors and the hardship of trying to survive in a country where food, medication, utilities, and other essentials had all but disappeared. The researcher used motivational messages based on the ARCS model of motivational analysis and a detailed motivational needs assessment to attend to the motivational needs of the participants. These messages were regularly distributed before a training session began, but also at other opportunities, for example, when feedback on tests was given, when leaving for the weekend, and sometimes delivered at a student's house when he or she had missed a class. Students indicated that the messages had positively influenced their motivational state. Two participant observers documented the observations and comments made during the training, coffee breaks, and after sessions. All but one student finished the four-month training course successfully. The motivational messages had been effective.

The same type of message was subsequently used in an international context in a pilot study and a multiple case study I conducted ten years later.

Conducted at the University of London, the multiple case study involved four facilitators and seventy-eight students within a master's program that was offered at a distance. In this research, the participants of three courses received motivational messages while those in a fourth course served as the control group. Two types of motivational messages were used: the *personal* message, attending to the identified motivational need of a person, and the *personalized* message, a general message with, if deemed effective, a personal note on the message. The latter were based on perceived or assumed motivational needs, the former on specific identified motivational needs of the individual. The completion rates in the three courses more than doubled when compared to completion rates over the preceding three years. The main findings were that:

- The use of motivational communications had been effective;
- The messages increased the confidence of the students; and
- The personal messages were *not* more effective than the personalized messages;
- The learners greatly appreciated the messages and, without having been informed about the goal of the study, spontaneously mentioned that their motivation had been positively influenced.

In a 2006 study by Wickramanayake & Schlosser, motivational messages were used within a course in a school of computing and information technology in Jamaica. In this case the motivational messages were either delivered on mobile phones by text message or by e-mail. The latter was used to deliver messages that had a length of more than 160 characters. The ARCS model guided the content of the messages. The researchers used a personalized motivational message system and a group motivational message system, with the goal of determining whether the effectiveness of personalized motivational messages was greater than that of group messages. The researchers concluded that there was no significant difference.

STRENGTHS AND CRITICISMS

Strengths

The use of motivational messages resulted in higher completion rates in training and instruction in two of the three studies discussed. In the third study the goal was not to look at completion rates, but at the effectiveness of a group versus personal message system. The motivational message as communication tool provides motivational support where needed and conveys the message that the receiver is important to the sender.

Designing a motivational message is not difficult. It requires the manager or colleague to be aware of how the "other" functions in the daily work situation. In instructional design terms, it means knowing the audience. It requires attention for the motivational situation/level of the "other."

Using a motivation message may initially have important implications for the sender, as it may require a change of attitude. Co-workers can no longer be neglected, the sender must be aware of the factors that enable and/or hinder effective performance, and he or she must feel and show empathy. Change is not easy, and the effectiveness of the messages depends on the extent to which the sender and the organization are prepared to learn and to change or adapt established ways of working. This often includes recognizing the effort of those who effectively use these messages in the context of the organization. An experienced human resource manager could even have pre-prepared messages ready that only require a personal note. The content may be related to what are seen as universal motivators, such as openness, trust, confidence in work skills, humor, and respect.

A challenge is to avoid the expression of empathy or affection that is fake. Sending a motivational message by e-mail is not difficult and can be very effective. As we have seen, most motivational problems fall into the four factors of the ARCS model of motivational analysis. A motivational communication is thus likely to address one or more of these factors.

Criticisms

It is likely that the main challenge lies in getting started: in changing attitudes and in beginning to show real empathy and caring. When discussing motivation in class, one of my students brought up the yearly Christmas letter she received from the human resource director of her organization. She was disappointed that it was a standard letter and that there was nothing about her performance or her role in the organization in the letter. In fact, she said she would have preferred not to have received this letter. This led to a discussion, as most of her classmates shared her feelings. It turned out that there were recognizable sentence chunks in all these end-of-year communications. You could almost say that they were standardized not only within the organization but also across organizations. Not one of the fifteen students had received a letter with a personal note on it. This example illustrates how poor organizational understanding of basic motivation principles and of Rogers' empathy concept is. So how should motivational communication be used?

Helping people become more motivated for the tasks they have to carry out and for their roles in the organization should not be based on empty inspirational and motivational quotations. Persuading or telling someone to be motivated is, predictably, not very effective. Instead, apply the motivational strategies discussed in earlier sections of this chapter as well as within other chapters in this section of the handbook.

A motivational message can greatly influence the attitudes of people, but do not expect miracles. The motivational communications will work best if they are part of an overall motivational process and should thus not be looked upon in isolation.

RECOMMENDED DESIGN, DEVELOPMENT, AND IMPLEMENTATION PROCESS

To discuss how to use motivational messages let's first summarize the characteristics of a motivational message.

- A motivational message is a simple form of communication that supports someone in staying or becoming motivated.
- A motivational message is based on identified or assumed motivational needs of the targeted person.
- A motivational message works best if the content is based on one or more components of the ARCS model (as this model includes the principal elements of motivation).
- A motivational message includes more than the minimum information/message to contact someone.
- A motivational message shows real (not fake) affection and understanding of the other's position.
- A motivational message may be personal, but research (as discussed earlier in this chapter) showed that a general message with a personal note can be very effective as well.

The above characteristics already imply design requirements. First, the messages should only be used in appropriate circumstances: an identified motivational need. A very confident person should not receive a message that aims at strengthening confidence. A motivational need can be identified via an audience analysis, but also and possibly more often by careful observation and putting oneself in the position of "the other." The worker who complained that every Christmas the same standard letter was sent to her thanking her for her work in the organization rightly felt that her motivational needs were not attended to, and the trainee who mentioned that the opening letter in a course was impersonal and showing "fake care" realized that affection was missing. Motivational needs should be carefully identified and be addressed along the lines of one or more of the main "pillars" of the ARCS model. It may be that the opening letter sent to new students in a course should address the confidence and satisfaction area, while an employee receiving a "thank you" letter at the end of the year may have needs in the areas of relevance and satisfaction. The message should be designed in such way that it shows real care and interest. Most people prefer oral communication to written communication. It allows for the joy of hearing words that have inherent timbre, passion, care, and interest, but also can transmit worry, anger, or lack of passion. It is also true that, given lack of time and improved technology, many communications will be written. At the same time, such written messages offer the advantage of rereading what has been said and enjoying the attention given to a person several times over.

In what form the message is presented is not very important; if at all possible humor should be part of it, but make sure it is culturally appropriate. The message may be in the form of a text message or an e-mail, a personal message, or a general message with a personal note. I have recently seen that a snail-mail message is currently very much appreciated, as it has a surprise effect and people apparently still like to receive "real" communications in their postboxes.

The motivational message used in the research of Jan Visser (1990) and within my own in 1998 is a short written message, the content of which is reinforced by a drawing and offered in the form of a wish card. The format used was a white A4 sheet, folded in four with graphics and a verbal attention-getter on the outside and a short written message, based on one or more components of the ARCS model, on the inside. Drawing and message should reinforce each other.

Jan Visser emphasized the surprise effect of the messages. He also discussed the possibility that these messages offered to make suggestions for improvement. An example in his research was getting people to start class on time. The message, with a drawing of a clock (attention) and text that suggested that everyone would benefit from starting on time, was rated in an evaluation as highly successful. A very simple message sent a few weeks before the end of a course, containing a drawing of a runner very close to the finish line but looking rather exhausted and a text telling participants that they were "almost there" and needed just a last push, was also considered highly motivating by the participants. They liked the drawing, but considered the message strong, as it was their reality and showed that the instructor understood their situation. As said before, the messages can come in various forms but it is most important that they be sent when necessary. This asks the sender to be aware of the situation of the receiver, to be part of a motivational system that does not end with the distribution of motivational messages. My own work emphasized the advantages of using messages that were pre-designed, yet personalized.

The following steps contribute greatly to affective and effective motivational communication:

- Know your audience—not only as staff but as people with different cultural and social backgrounds;
- Try to place yourself in their positions;

- Identify the performance or relationship you want to improve, emphasize, or praise;
- Select the medium for the communication, taking into consideration that a paper-based message will stick longer than a text message;
- Decide on which elements of the ARCS model (attention, relevance, confidence, or satisfaction) you want to target;
- Think carefully about how you could design the message so that it is on target, for instance, a surprise effect in the opening sentence, a relevant and sharp cartoon, or an appropriate photo;
- Read the communication carefully and evaluate how you would react to such a message; and
- Try the message out with a few people; if you send to large groups, for instance, an "end of the year message" or an organizational result communication.

CRITICAL SUCCESS FACTORS

Human resource managers and trainers who want to use motivational communication should have a basic understanding of the importance of both motivation and communication in the workplace and their role in realizing optimal performance. Trainers, managers, instructors, and the organization in general should be willing to invest some time in getting to know the motivational needs of their employees or trainees. Critical success factors include:

- A thorough critical and analytical look at how communication processes in the work environment take place;
- An understanding that communication processes cannot be seen as independent of the existing management and leadership strategies that are used;
- The recognition that a top-down leadership style is not conducive to motivational communication;
- The importance of investing time in monitoring the motivational level and needs of the worker (this may take some time in the beginning, but it is time well spent);
- Awareness that motivational communication cannot be seen as being separate from the environment and from the approach to training and learning, but is an essential part of the organization's vision and mission;
- The knowledge that, if motivational communication is used, the user should be able to creatively attend to the motivational needs of the "other" and deal seriously with these needs in the daily work circumstances;

- A design of motivational communication that aims at a personalized approach, avoiding all kinds of "fake" interest and/or boring buzzwords; and

- Distributing a message that would please and motivate the sender if it were sent to him or her.

SUMMARY

In summary, the value of a tool like a motivational message lies in its simplicity, its directness, and its proven effectiveness. The manager, trainer, or human resource person can use this easy way to give personal attention to a group member and thus strengthen the feelings of belonging that are often crucial in performance improvement.

References

Berlo, D. K. (1963). You are in the communication business. *Audiovisual Instruction, 8*, 372–381.

Berlyne, D. E. (1965). Motivational problems raised by exploratory and epistemic behavior. In S. Koch (Ed.), *Psychology: A study of a science*. New York: McGraw-Hill.

Böhlin, R. M. (1987). Motivation in instructional design: Comparison of an American and a Soviet model. *Journal of Instructional Development, 10*(2), 11–13.

Clark, R. E. (2003). Fostering the work motivation of individuals and teams. *Performance Improvement, 42*(3), 21–29.

Covington, M., & Omelich, C. (1979). It's best to be able and virtuous too: Student and teachers evaluative responses to successful effort. *Journal of Educational Psychology, 71*, 688–700.

Graham, S. W., & Weiner, B. (1996). Theories and principles of motivation. In D.C. Berliner & R. C. Calfee (Eds.), *Handbook of educational psychology* (pp. 63–85). New York: Macmillan.

Hoska, D. M. (1993). Motivating learners through CBI feedback: Developing a positive learner perspective. In J. V. Dempsey & G. C. Sales (Eds.), *Interactive instruction and feedback*. (pp. 105–132). Englewood Cliffs, NJ: Educational Technology.

Keller, J. M. (1983). Motivational design of instruction. In C. M. Reigeluth (Ed.), *Instructional design: Theories and models. An overview of their current status* (pp. 386–431). Mahwah, NJ: Lawrence Erlbaum Associates.

Keller, J. M. (1987). The systematic process of motivational design. *Performance & Instruction, 26*(9), 1–8.

Keller, J. M. (1998). Motivational systems. In H. Stolovitch & E. Keeps (Eds.), *Handbook of human performance technology* (2nd ed.). San Francisco. Pfeiffer.

Malone, T. W. (1981). What makes computer games fun? *Byte, 6*, 258–277.

Malone, T. W., & Lepper, M. R. (1987). Making learning fun: A taxonomy of intrinsic motivation for learning (pp. 223–253). In R. E. Snow & M. J. Farr (Eds.), *Aptitude, learning and instruction. Vol. 3. Cognitive and affective process analysis*. Mahwah, NJ: Lawrence Erlbaum Associates.

Maslow, A. H. (1954). *Motivation and personality*. New York: Harper & Row.

Moshinskie, J. (2001). How to keep e-learners from e-scaping. *Performance Improvement, 40*(6).

Rogers, C. (1962). The interpersonal relationship: The core of guidance. *Harvard Educational Review, 32*(4), 416–429.

Rowntree, D. (1992). *Exploring open and distance learning*. London: Kogan Page.

Schrage, M. (1990). *Shared minds: The new technologies of collaboration*. New York: Random House.

Spitzer, D. (1995). *SuperMotivation*. New York: AMACOM.

Turner, J., & Paris, S. G. (1995). How literacy tasks influence children's motivation for literacy. *The Reading Teacher, 48*(8), 662–673.

Visser, J. (1989). Enhancing learner motivation in an instructor-facilitated learning context. Tallahassee, FL. Florida State University (unpublished dissertation).

Visser, L. (1998). The development of motivational communication in distance education support. Enschede, University of Twente (unpublished dissertation).

Wickramanayake, D., & Schlosser, C., (2006). A comparison of group and individualized motivational messages sent by SMS and e-mail to improve student achievement. Paper presented at the Third International Conference on e-Learning for a Knowledge-Based Society. Bangkok, Thailand.

Wlodkowski, R. J. (1993). *Enhancing adult motivation to learn: A guide to improving instruction and increasing learner achievement*. San Francisco: Jossey-Bass.

Zuckerman, M. (1971). Dimensions of sensation seeking. *Journal of Consulting and Clinical Psychology, 36*, 45–52.

Zvacek, S. M. (1991). Effective affective design for distance education. *TechTrends, 36*(1), 40–43.

 EDITORIAL CONNECTIONS

Motivation plays a central role in the success of any performance improvement effort; just as it is an essential ingredient to the successful implementation of most—if not all—performance interventions. From building intrinsic motivation to identifying extrinsic motivators, intentional planning and actions are routinely required in the design of performance improvement projects to ensure that employees are motivated to accomplish desired results. Use motivational communication techniques throughout your improvement effort to engage your partners (both those that are internal and external to the organization), building their motivation to achieve results.

When creating project documents or presentations, sending out internal memos related to your improvement project, or even writing e-mails to team members, reflect on the motivational aspects of your messages to ensure that all messages are constructing the positive motivational environment that will lead to the success of the improvement effort. Our messages have a powerful influence on individual and team motivation—sometimes unintentionally. Therefore, only finalize and send out those messages that will continue to engage and motivate your partners.

Expanding Your Options

Self esteem—respect for or a favorable opinion of oneself.

Based on thefreedictionary.com definition (January 2009)

Also consider motivational communications as a performance intervention to improve the results being achieved by others. By linking motivational communications to elements of e-learning (see Chapter Twenty-Four), mentoring (see Chapter Twenty-Two), or change management (see Chapter Sixteen), you can begin to integrate motivation communications into the culture of your organization (see Chapter Thirty). Motivational communication is not concerned with one-time activities or workshops, but is an integral part of how your organization accomplishes significant results.

Communications are, nevertheless, not on their own enough to motivate and adequately support the accomplishment of desirable results (performance). Frequently, individuals benefit from additional attention and time to guide them in achieving both the objectives of the improvement effort and their personal goals. Mentoring is therefore among the most valued of the performance interventions to achieve results. Mentoring provides the one-on-one relationships that frequently build motivation and self-concept—leading to the accomplishment of desired results at the individual/team, organizational, and societal levels.

WHAT'S COMING UP

Christine Hegstad, in Chapter Twenty-Two, focuses attention on one particularly valuable format of mentoring: career mentoring. Career mentoring, while similar in name to other mentoring or coaching performance interventions (see, for example, Chapter Twenty-Six), can provide organizations with an indispensable tool for building self-esteem, confidence, positive attitudes, institutional camaraderie, employee retention, knowledge sharing, as well as commitment to the organization and its performance objectives. As a consequence, career mentoring interventions are frequently a component of systemic performance improvement programs. When reviewing Chapter Twenty-Two, reflect on how career mentoring can achieve at least some of these diverse results within your organization.

Career Mentoring

Christine D. Hegstad

INTRODUCTION

Although an age-old phenomenon, formal mentoring has only relatively recently claimed recognition as a powerful training and career development intervention in the workplace. Formal mentoring programs offer a cost-effective method for employee development—utilizing internal sources—with substantial benefits to participants as well as the overall organization. The implementation of formal mentoring programs has thus been on the rise for the past two decades, with increasingly positive results. When coupled with career counseling, specifically the development of personal growth plans, the value of each intervention is profound. Thorough research, clearly outlined program objectives, and carefully considered design and development all play important roles in ensuring the success of career mentoring programs.

DESCRIPTION

Businesses conduct mentoring in a variety of ways, including hierarchical mentorships, peer or lateral mentoring, group mentoring, cross-team mentoring, and even self-guided mentoring. In their 1992 article comparing formal and informal mentorships, Georgia Chao and her colleagues offer a widely accepted definition of formal mentoring programs, which includes those sanctioned and managed by the organization, typically utilizing a systematic selection and matching process for participants. In such programs, the mentor is usually a knowledgeable and experienced member of the organization who is committed to the development of a less experienced employee, also called the protégé. The mentor and protégé develop a professional relationship—or mentorship—through which they meet regularly to discuss career goals, strategize action plans, and further their growth and development within the organization. The mentor thus serves as an advisor, offering guidance in vocational, psychosocial, and role-modeling capacities.

Formal career mentoring may be confused with other forms of mentoring and, more recently, developmental coaching; however, distinct differences exist. Informal mentorships develop spontaneously, are not managed by the organization, and pursue their relationship in whatever direction they deem most appropriate. In group programs, mentoring functions emerge from the group as a whole rather than from one distinct partner as in a dyadic relationship. As its name suggests, peer—or lateral—mentoring occurs when two individuals of comparable pay, job level, or status enter into a mentorship.

Expanding Your Options

Self-efficacy—a person's belief about his or her ability and capacity to accomplish a task or to deal with the challenges of life.

Based on businessdictionary.com definition (January 2009)

While coaching functions similarly to career mentoring and with comparable outcomes, the relationships are markedly different; namely, mentors are employees within the same organization, can offer experience-based guidance, and typically focus on the protégé's growth within the organization. Coaches, on the other hand, usually come from outside the organization and, rather than focusing on employer- or job-specific development, they provide an objective perspective. While mentors often give advice based on their experiences in the organization, a coach's role is more probing and questioning in nature, encouraging the client to find the answers within himself or herself. Just as managers may incorporate mentoring techniques into their supervisory roles, mentors might use coaching techniques with their protégés; each of the three developmental positions—mentors, coaches, and managers—is distinct, however (see Chapters Eleven and Twenty-Seven for more information on coaching interventions).

Formal mentoring programs can be found within all types of organizations— public and private, for-profit and nonprofit, large and small. Likewise, organizations implement mentoring programs for a variety of reasons, from increasing employee retention to developing stronger leaders. Other motivators with proven results include enhancing diversity initiatives (see Chapter Thirty-One), assisting with new employee socialization, facilitating knowledge and skill transfer, and helping employees adapt to organizational change.

Underlying all of these rationales is the expectation that mentoring serves to enhance individual career development. When combined with career counseling initiatives, such as creating personal mission statements or individual growth plans, mentors serve as powerful reinforcements and internal guides to the goals protégés have identified. Minimally, career mentoring enhances the likelihood for career success; ideally, mentors will help protégés move from what they may consider "just a job" toward a sense of meaning, purpose, and contribution within their work. Mentors can smooth the path toward what Kevin and Kay Marie Brennfleck call "vocational integration," in which a person's work is essentially an expression of himself or herself. Additionally, career counseling techniques coupled with mentoring help an employee see his or her role and value within the larger structure of the organization, increasing a sense of loyalty and purpose.

While often rolled out as a stand-alone initiative, mentoring is typically best suited to support other performance interventions. If an organization creates a leadership development program, for example, mentoring could serve as a critical component for that objective, most likely in addition to training, performance feedback, and external group involvement (participation in professional associations). If the primary goal is transfer of knowledge, again mentoring will serve as a useful strategy, perhaps in addition to the development of manuals and resources, online knowledge management systems, and career journaling. Mentoring can achieve strategic goals on its own but can also support many performance and development interventions.

WHAT WE KNOW FROM RESEARCH

Since the seminal reports by Boston University's Kathy Kram on mentoring effectiveness in 1985, research in the area has flourished and addresses all aspects of the development of and processes involved in formal mentoring programs. Following a similar research and awareness timeframe is career counseling theory, specifically the constructivist approaches most applicable to the mentoring relationship. Theory, outcomes, and applications of career mentoring programs are briefly summarized here.

Mentoring Theory

While mentoring has been in practice throughout the ages and recognized within businesses for many years, only in the last two decades has the application of theory—particularly driven from the social and behavioral sciences—been used to interpret and predict mentoring behaviors and outcomes. Since the early 1990s mentoring has been linked to adult development theory, social networking, and the development of learning organizations. Perhaps the most viable theoretical application for mentoring is that of social exchange theory. This theory, which is grounded in economics and deeply explored by the University at Buffalo's Peter P. Ekeh in 1974, examines mentoring relationships in terms of perceived costs and benefits based on issues of reciprocity, social scarcity, equity, and social cost. Rather than the typical exchange of money for goods and services, mentors and protégés expect fairly even exchanges of resources of a different nature.

On a micro level, mentors and protégés attempt to maintain a balance of give-and-take within their relationships. Protégés may expect assistance from mentors in working through barriers with their career development plans, for example, while mentors may expect protégés to put forth considerable effort toward their organizational goals and thus reflect positively on them. Social exchange theory also suggests that mentors will prefer protégés whom they perceive as demonstrating valuable and promising competencies. Tammy Allen, one of the most widely published researchers in the mentoring field, identifies such competencies as ability, potential, and willingness to learn as examples.

On a macro level, social exchange theory can be applied in terms of mentorship continuity: protégés may wish to reciprocate their mentors' guidance and actions by serving as mentors themselves or by repaying the organization in terms of loyalty, commitment, and productivity.

Barbara Seels and Zita Glasgow's instructional design structure proves to be a valuable framework when designing a career mentoring program. When the five stages of the process—needs analysis, design, development, implementation, and evaluation (ADDIE)—are applied to the creation of mentoring programs, their likelihood for success increases. While the stages are addressed more thoroughly in other chapters throughout this book, some components unique to mentoring are worth addressing. For example, organizations create mentoring programs to address a variety of career development needs. In her examination of the mentoring program at the Federal Deposit Insurance Corporation (FDIC), Barbara Suddarth discusses management's concern that lower-level employees did not have access to developmental opportunities like their higher-level colleagues did, thus prompting the development of their mentoring program. Other programs have emerged out of employee needs such as gaining access to internal resources, enhancing difficult-to-train skills like political savvy, and providing support in nontraditional careers. Both psychosocial and vocational needs can be attended to through effective mentoring.

In the design phase, careful consideration of mentor and protégé criteria will also help ensure a smooth program. In her 2005 article, "Making a Commitment to Mentoring,'' Nedra Klee Hartzell describes successful mentors as those who are dedicated to career development, have strong communication skills, and show a commitment to the mentoring process. Furthermore, in a review of NASA's human resource guidebook, criteria for a successful mentor include characteristics such as being respectful and people-oriented, a strong motivator, and secure in (and proud of) one's position. Similarly, protégés will demonstrate a positive attitude, an eagerness to learn, a willing stance toward risk, and a desire to be a team player.

Career Counseling Theory: The Constructivist Approach

As career counseling evolves with the changing nature of work, so do the strategies and approaches used to bring employees closer to their individual goals, plans, and ideals. Many traditional career counseling theories were created when employees were expected to stay in one career, with one employer, often for one purpose—money—over the course of their working lives. Constructivist theory and assessment, a viable and holistic approach to career counseling, addressing current issues and changes in career development, has emerged in the field over the past several decades.

In the past, career counselors were primarily known to offer standardized personality and skills testing to clients. Counselors would then provide career "fits" based on the individual's scores in various areas. Constructivist (or postmodern) approaches move employees away from a "test me then tell me what to do" mentality into a more active role in which they review life roles, expectations, and personal history in order to uncover deeper meaning and patterns within their work lives. In her 2004 article for the *Journal of Career Development* discussing constructivism within career counseling, Pamelia Brott succinctly summarizes this approach, writing, "The holistic and integrative picture drawn from both quantitative and qualitative methods of career assessment . . . reflects a shift from finding a job to finding oneself."

Mentoring blends seamlessly within the framework of constructivist career counseling. With this approach, a wide variety of assessments are used to uncover career growth patterns: life roles circles, biographies, conceptual/goal mapping, and journaling, to name a few. By exploring one's career journey over the course of one's lifetime, themes and influences emerge that can broaden the scope of future possibilities. Mentors can partner and guide this effort, encouraging protégés to discover their vocations and increase a sense of meaning, passion, and purpose within their careers.

This qualitative approach to career counseling stands to reap many benefits. First and foremost, the relationship between counselor (or mentor) and participant becomes much more collaborative and active. These methods also lend themselves well to diverse populations, as they are more flexible and adaptable than standardized personality and career-type testing. Some of the methods, such as the development of "occupational trees" (called genograms) and life career rainbows, may prove especially helpful with visual and tactile learning preferences as well. Conversely, such methods can prove quite time-consuming and more labor-intensive than traditional counseling approaches, with the open-ended or subjective tools also bringing concerns regarding validity and reliability. When used in conjunction with formal mentoring, however, opportunities for holistic, directed growth and learning have ripe opportunities to emerge.

Mentoring Outcomes

The results of formal mentoring have been studied extensively and are abundant within performance improvement and career development literature. While both positive and negative outcomes appear, the benefits generally seem to outweigh the costs. An overview of typical findings is shown in Table 22.1.

Organizations benefit from career mentoring in a variety of ways, such as increased employee motivation, commitment, retention, and leadership. Mentoring also provides a form of on-the-job training that is often more cost-effective than traditional classroom training, potentially decreasing the need for additional (and more costly) development initiatives for participants. On the other hand, organizations may experience setbacks due to workday interference and job disruption necessitated by participants devoting time to mentoring. If mentorships are poorly matched or program objectives are not clearly communicated, interpersonal conflict may also arise.

Individual participants can experience numerous benefits from their mentorship involvement as well. In addition to the career development benefits cited earlier, protégés often enjoy increased pay, job satisfaction, and promotion opportunities as a result of their mentoring experience. Conversely, their careers may suffer if they have been ineffectively mentored; they may also develop a dependence upon the mentor, thus causing them difficulty in reaching career goals when the mentorship dissolves. Mentors benefit from increased visibility, professional identity, and career rejuvenation—especially if they have begun feeling stuck in their careers. Alternately, mentors may be negatively affected by the time and energy mentoring requires—especially if it does not fall within their job responsibilities or they gain little reward for their commitment.

Mentoring as a Career Development Strategy

By definition, career development includes the processes and factors that affect how an employee shapes and performs his or her work. Mentoring serves many important career development strategies for both mentors and protégés: building interpersonal relationships, expanding professional networks, and honing specific career-related skills. When the parties come to the relationship with written career development plans, completed individually or with the assistance of a career counselor, they are able to focus their efforts on developing

Table 22.1 Mentoring Outcomes for Organizations, Mentors, and Protégés

	Positive Outcomes	*Negative Outcomes*
Organizations	Increased employee motivation	Workday interruption
	Enhanced productivity	Tension if perceived unfairness
	Increased retention	Challenges between mentor, protégé, and supervisor
	Leadership development	Difficulty terminating mentorship agreeably
	On-the-job training	
	Identification of talent	
	Improved performance	
Mentors	Increased visibility	Time commitment
	Greater professional identity	Envy protégés' fresh opportunities
	Improved performance	Potential for disappointment
	Career rejuvenation	Resentment if feeling "stuck"
	Self-satisfaction	Increased responsibility with little incentive/reward
	Enhanced focus	Poor protégé performance reflecting negatively on mentor
	Increased power and respect	
	Success of protégé reflects positively on mentor	
Protégés	Increased pay	Disillusionment
	Improved job satisfaction	High dependence on mentor stunts independent growth
	Higher organizational commitment	Jealousy among co-workers
	Increased promotion opportunities	Ineffective mentor costs time, reflects poorly on protégé
	Broadened career guidance	Mentor taking credit for protégé's work
	Greater resource power and access	
	Friendship, acceptance	
	Enhanced interpersonal skills	
	Increased visibility	

professionally and reaching their career objectives. In some cases, protégés may create their career development plans with the help of their mentors as part of their mentoring relationship.

While the nature of work continues to evolve over time, so must our methods for developing and retaining quality, satisfied employees. Career counselors recognize that employees make career decisions at various developmental stages throughout life; no longer are the stages marked simply by life events such as graduation, new jobs, and retirement. As a result, career counselors must adapt to these changing needs by providing experiences that prompt broadened exploration among employees. It is in this vein that David Duys and his colleagues emphasize in their 2008 article for *The Career Development Quarterly* how having a variety of empowering development tools and methods available helps employees create more intentional careers and make decisions more purposefully. Developing formal mentoring programs is a valuable, cost-effective method with which to do this.

Ensuring a formal mentoring program's likelihood for success requires much consideration, summarized in my Mentoring Process Model (see Figure 22.1). Prior to implementation, the model describes several organizational antecedents that should be in place: visible top management support for the program, a supportive and open work culture, and a history of open communication and trust, for example. Individual participant considerations include demographic attributes (race and gender, for instance), previous mentoring experience, and career stage or organizational level. Likewise, several factors inherent in the

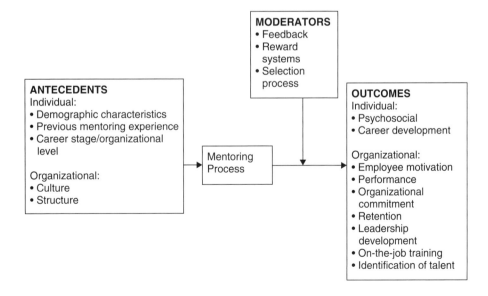

Figure 22.1 Mentoring Process Model.

mentoring program will play a role in moderating its outcomes including the frequency and level of feedback/communication occurring in the mentorships, whether or not participation is linked to corporate rewards or incentives, and the process by which mentors and protégés are matched.

Summary

Research in the areas of career development and mentoring has flourished over the past two decades, often pointing to the many outcomes evident with the implementation of formal mentoring programs. Mentoring serves as a feasible tool within the constructivist approach to career development, supporting employees in creating and fulfilling holistic career goals and recognizing patterns in their work histories. When viewed within the framework of social exchange theory and created with the ADDIE principles, career mentoring can result in benefits such as improved productivity and motivation, career rejuvenation, and enhanced satisfaction and morale, to name a few.

WHEN TO APPLY

Mentoring can be implemented in conjunction with other performance improvement interventions or as a stand-alone program, depending upon the goals and objectives of the program. For example, many companies implement mentoring programs as part of a greater diversity initiative to encourage understanding and appreciation of the many differences within today's workforce. The corporate diversity director of a Fortune 500 pharmaceuticals company explained, as an example, that the company's mentoring program helped new employees build relationships that may otherwise not emerge. Enhancing diversity not only addresses gender and racial differences but also broadens diversity of thought—especially within a global marketplace. When implemented systematically, mentoring can also help retain quality employees and assist employers in identifying talent from within the organization, a strategy that aids in leadership development and succession planning (see Chapter Twenty-Nine). Other appropriate purposes for mentoring programs include enhancing communication throughout departments and hierarchical layers, improving corporate culture, and hastening acclimation of new employees. Successful mentoring initiatives also serve as helpful recruitment and attraction tools.

While the benefits of mentoring abound, it does not serve as a cure-all for career development and organizational deficiencies. In fact, if inappropriately implemented, a mentoring program can prove detrimental to an organization. A period of extreme turbulence, such as downsizing or restructuring, may not be an appropriate time to implement mentoring, as trust levels and uncertainties fluctuate significantly during such times. Also, if potential protégés far outnumber available mentors, many protégés may not be selected to participate, which can result in disappointment and resentment. If mentors obtain multiple protégés in order to involve all hopeful participants, however, they will struggle with appropriating enough time and energy to each in addition to their regular work responsibilities. This may result in disappointment and ineffective mentoring. To counter this, the purpose of the program needs to be stated clearly and aligned with the overall mission and vision in order to reap the greatest possible benefits. If the organization is not in a position to devote adequate resources to design a solid, well-planned program, it may prove safer to wait for a more appropriate time than risk implementing a deficient program.

If the environment is conducive to supporting a mentoring program and clear goals and objectives have been outlined, then mentoring may serve as a viable initiative for performance improvement and career development. In the same way, if related initiatives (for example, executive coaching or performance training programs) have been implemented with success and employees are receptive to new opportunities, chances for effectiveness will increase. Organizations with multiple locations bring unique challenges to the mentoring process; however, with open communication and built-in flexibility, such challenges can be addressed through the design and development phases.

STRENGTHS AND CRITICISMS

The strengths of mentoring are many, and include:

- Mentoring offers an opportunity for internal transfer of learning, including areas that are difficult to address (organizational politics or work culture specifics, for instance) through traditional training and development methods.

- One-on-one mentoring relationships can encourage, reinforce, and solidify individual career development plans on an ongoing basis.

- Mentoring provides a unique, organizationally approved opportunity to build relationships and enhance communication, especially across teams, throughout hierarchical levels, and among employees who may not otherwise develop such relationships.

- All parties—mentors, protégés, and the organization as a whole—can benefit from effective mentoring.

- Since in-house talent is utilized, mentoring is a cost-effective strategy that can continue year after year with few maintenance expenses.

Criticisms of mentoring are also relevant to consider and include:

- Mentoring relationships require regular time and energy from both parties, which can be challenging to find without affecting other areas of work.

- A mentoring program that does not clearly support the organization's mission or purpose can spur frustration and distrust among participants.

- Mentoring may be viewed as a "soft skill" and, if measurable outcomes are not in place, the value may be unseen or misinterpreted.

- Necessary up-front costs—monetary as well as time and research—to develop a solid, effective mentoring program may be inhibiting.

- An ineffective matching system may hinder relationships and frustrate participants, counteracting the intent of the program.

RECOMMENDED DESIGN, DEVELOPMENT, AND IMPLEMENTATION PROCESS

Careful planning and preparation can improve a career mentoring program's effectiveness. Steps to consider include:

1. Conduct a thorough needs analysis in order to determine how a mentoring program will accomplish your organization's desired results or whether a different intervention may work more effectively.

2. Clearly define the purpose of the mentoring program and ensure that it aligns with your organization's mission. Your purpose—for example, to enhance diversity appreciation or identify and build internal talent—will also determine your target participants.

3. Secure upper-level support prior to implementing the mentoring program, and make this support visible throughout the program's existence. If employees see that organizational leaders are taking time away from their work to devote to mentoring processes, they will believe in its value and importance more readily. Leaders can demonstrate visible support by offering feedback during the design and development, participating in orientation and training events, encouraging participation through memos and meetings, and serving as mentors themselves.

4. Devote adequate time and resources for thorough program design, using a variety of internal and external resources. Options may include hiring external design consultants, utilizing internal career development specialists, benchmarking best practices (especially of organizations similar in industry, size, and/or type to yours), and appointing a coordinator or team to oversee the program. Specific mentoring program design needs must be met whether the program is stand-alone or part of a greater performance improvement initiative.

5. In accordance with your program's purpose and goals, determine an appropriate participant selection process. Considerations include whether

participation in the program is voluntary or mandatory, how site locations of participants may bring up special needs and how those needs will be addressed, ensuring an adequate number of mentors for the protégé pool, and what criteria (if any) mentors and protégés need to meet prior to participation in the mentoring program.

6. Once you have determined how participants will be selected, you'll need to decide how to match partners in order to reach your program's goals. Again, a number of options exist: the mentoring coordinator or team might pair up participants, mentors might select whom they desire as their protégés, or protégés might offer a short list of requested mentors. Potential issues arise with each of these methods; for example, mentors will often choose protégés who are "like them" or remind them of themselves at an earlier time, thus resulting in a proliferation of same-gender or same-race mentorships. While such a relationship may increase interpersonal comfort levels between pairs, it may hinder the overall program goals. Similarly, protégé-driven matching might result in choosing a mentor who will give them the most visibility as opposed to the greatest career development benefit and expertise.

7. Regardless of the selection and matching processes you select, enrollment applications (ideally based on individual growth plans) and other tools will ease the process and clarify individual goals for participants. Applications might address a variety of personal and professional areas such as work experience, demographic data, career development goals and expertise, personal interests and values, and geographic location. Applications can also help align mentor strengths with protégé needs. Black, Suarez, and Medina suggest self-assessments among participants as well, covering four specific areas: personal qualities (perceived strengths and weaknesses); factual knowledge about mentoring; expectations for the mentorship; and goals to achieve through mentoring. This ensures that participants are clear on what the mentoring relationship can and cannot provide and promotes active participation in the process rather than assuming that mentoring is something that happens "to" them.

8. Develop clear guidelines for participants, some of which partners may then adapt to meet their needs. Program guidelines might include a suggested mentorship length (typically one year) and frequency of meetings, such as once per month. Other guidelines might include expectations, topics for discussion (using career development plans as a guide), and agreeing on certain details at the start of the mentorship. Marilyn Maze emphasizes the importance of this up-front agreement on goals and expectations, stating that it provides not only a clear direction for the relationship but also a way to assess progress. Supporting materials with

guidelines outlined for participants will ensure consistent messages among participants and coordinators.

9. Pilot the program on a small scale, such as with career counseling recipients or within a particular department, before widespread implementation. Even with rigorous design and development procedures, unexpected issues will arise once the program is in place. Offering the program on a small scale first allows you to address these concerns with minimal disruption and create an environment with greater likelihood for success once the program is rolled out on a larger scale or company-wide.

10. Offer appropriate training for the goals of your mentoring program, as well as an orientation program to address questions, dispel myths and rumors, and make the purpose of the program clear. Training efforts might focus on a variety of interpersonal skills such as effective listening and feedback; career development skills such as goal setting and creating action plans; and personal development skills, including time management and prioritizing. In addition, career counseling can play an important role in the program's success. Encourage participants to meet with a career counselor to define individual goals and growth plans prior to engaging in the mentoring relationship.

11. Evaluate the program at regular intervals using quantifiable and anecdotal measures. Again, the program's purpose and goals need to be clearly defined in order for this step to occur. If one of your goals for the mentoring program is to decrease turnover, for example, gather your organization's retention data as a baseline prior to implementing the program. You can then compare this to future retention rates to help determine whether the mentoring program is meeting this objective. As with any performance improvement initiative, an extended period of time may need to pass before results are consistently seen. Data obtained throughout will clue you in to necessary adjustments and enhancements.

CRITICAL SUCCESS FACTORS

Although unexpected challenges may appear while implementing a new development initiative, a conducive environment can increase a mentoring program's effectiveness. Factors to address include:

Social

- If open communication—including that between teams and throughout structural hierarchies—is not currently a part of your organizational

environment, consider focusing on enhancing this area prior to implementing a formal mentoring program. A commitment to respectful idea
exchanges and the opportunity to discuss issues openly will ease the
promotion and implementation of the mentoring program.

- Mentoring relationships take time in order to develop—time to prepare for
  meetings, create growth plans, work toward goals, participate in training
  and other mentoring activities, and meet regularly. To encourage a
  successful program, allow participants the time to build their relationships
  and work toward their goals. Inform them of the win-win benefits, making
  the program enlightening and entertaining whenever possible, so that
  mentoring is viewed as an enjoyable, developmental process rather than a
  burdensome responsibility.

Political

- When a new career development initiative is rolled out, visible top
  management support and involvement are crucial. This is especially true
  of initiatives like mentoring, where the benefits may not reveal themselves
  for a period of time. Organizational leaders need to take an active stance in
  promoting and endorsing the mentoring program from the onset. One of
  the best ways to demonstrate support is for leaders to be involved in the
  program themselves, serving as mentors, or protégés, and/or to be on the
  development team.

- Some employees may perceive mentoring as favoritism or special
  treatment, a "teacher's pet" phenomenon, especially if participants can
  choose their partners. To avoid rumors and uncooperative behavior,
  share the purpose and expectations of the program as clearly and
  frequently as possible. Again, open communication among leadership,
  mentoring program coordinators, career counselors, and participants is
  crucial.

Economic

- While mentoring is a cost-effective form of development compared to
  many other initiatives, it does require funding (up-front, especially) in
  order to ensure proper design and development. Gather estimates from
  outside consultants and consider expenses associated with materials,
  support, promotion, and training for the program. Secure adequate
  funding in advance and ensure the mentoring program has future support
  earmarked in the development budget.

- Participation in mentoring will require participants to step away from their
  desks and regular work in order to engage in developmental meetings and
  activities. Notifying participants that their time spent in mentorship is

respected by allowing it to occur during normal work hours, while providing expectations of how much time partners might devote to relationship building, will place importance on the program without disrupting the work week significantly.

Legal

- Confidentiality and privacy during mentorship meetings is critical for a true developmental relationship to grow. Mentors and protégés need to know that they can express opinions and values without the risk of their statements being shared with others or being used against them. Rules and expectations of confidentiality can be covered during training sessions and should be clearly outlined in the mentoring materials as well.

- In order to avoid claims of favoritism, blocked opportunities, or other dissatisfactions, legal counsel should be involved in the design and development phases of the program. Legal review of all mentoring activities and materials should also take place prior to implementation.

Intercultural

- If participants are allowed to self-select their partners, a "similar to me" phenomenon has a greater likelihood of appearing in which individuals will tend to choose someone like themselves. Team- or coordinator-appointed partnerships will help alleviate this concern.

- Awareness of and appreciation for cultural differences in communication, goal setting, and prioritizing increases the value of mentorship meetings. Diversity training (see Chapter Thirty-One) and multiple opportunities for connection outside of mentoring will instill greater understanding and interpersonal comfort between employees with varying racial, gender, economic, and cultural backgrounds.

Technical

- Organizations with multiple sites, where mentors and protégés are housed at different locations, will require technological support for mentoring programs. Videoconferencing, instant messaging, and meetings via tele-conference can help promote communication between the two parties when regular face-to-face meetings are not a viable option.

SUMMARY

When faced with an ever-changing global marketplace and climate, employers need specific, proven methods to enhance individual development as well as organizational productivity and outcomes. Career mentoring programs offer a unique, person-focused framework from which to simultaneously develop protégés, mentors, and overall organizations. By clearly outlining program objectives, thoroughly addressing design and development challenges, and creating an environment conducive to developmental learning, career mentoring can serve as a cost-effective means of internal growth with potentially significant results for all parties.

Notes

- For more on mentoring in its various forms, see Dansky (1996), Geiger-DuMond and Boyle (1995), Hardy (1998), Kram and Isabella (1985), and Pellegrini and Scandura (2005).

- Further exploration of the theoretical aspects of mentoring can be found in Caldwell and Carter (1993), Dansky (1996), and Higgins and Kram (2001).

- A thorough review of mentoring outcomes identified in the literature can be found in Hegstad (1999).

- For overviews of human resource development and, more specifically, career development, see Herr (2001) and Pace, Smith, and Mills (1991).

- More on interpersonal comfort and the "similar to me" phenomenon can be found in Allen, Day, and Lentz (2005) as well as Kanter's classic book, *Men and Women of the Corporation*.

References

Allen, T. D. (2004). Protégé selection by mentors: Contributing individual and organizational factors. *Journal of Vocational Behavior, 65*, 469–483.

Allen, T. D., Day, R., & Lentz, E. (2005). The role of interpersonal comfort in mentoring relationships. *Journal of Career Development, 31*, 155–167.

Allen, T. D., & Eby, L. T. (2004). Factors related to mentor reports of mentoring functions provided: Gender and relational characteristics. *Sex Roles, 50*, 129–139.

Allen, T. D., Poteet, M. L., Eby, L. T., & Lima, L. (2004). Career benefits associated with mentoring for protégés: A meta-analysis. *Journal of Applied Psychology, 89*, 127–126.

Black, L. L., Suarez, E. C., & Medina, S. (2004). Helping students help themselves: Strategies for successful mentoring relationships. *Counselor Education and Supervision, 44*, 44–56.

Brennfleck, K., & Brennfleck, K.M. (2005). *Live your calling*. San Francisco: Jossey-Bass.

Brewer, E. W. (2001). Vocational sojourn paradigm: A model of adult development to express spiritual wellness as *meaning, being,* and *doing* in work and life. *Counseling and Values, 45,* 83–93.

Brott, P. E. (2004). Constructivist assessment in career counseling. *Journal of Career Development, 30,* 189–200.

Burke, R. J., & McKeen, C. A. (1989). Developing formal mentoring programs in organizations. *Business Quarterly, 53,* 69–76.

Caldwell, B. J., & Carter, E. M. A. (1993). Transforming the workplace. In B. J. Caldwell & E. M. A. Carter (Eds.), *The return of the mentor: Strategies for workplace learning* (pp. 205–220). London: The Falmer Press.

Chao, G. T., Walz, P. M., & Gardner, P. D. (1992). Formal and informal mentorships: A comparison on mentoring functions and contrast with nonmentored counterparts. *Personnel Psychology, 45,* 619–636.

Coley, D. B. (1996). Mentoring two-by-two. *Training & Development, 50,* 46–48.

Dansky, K. H. (1996). The effect of group mentoring on career outcomes. *Group and Organizational Management, 21,* 5–1.

Duys, D. K., Ward, J. E., Maxwell, J. A., & Eaton-Comerford, L. (2008). Career counseling in a volatile job market: Tiedeman's perspective revisited. *The Career Development Quarterly, 56,* 232–241.

Eby, L. T. (1997). Alternative forms of mentoring in changing organizational environments: A conceptual extension of the mentoring literature. *Journal of Vocational Behavior, 51,* 125–144.

Ekeh, P. P. (1974). *Social exchange theory: The two traditions.* Cambridge, MA: Harvard University Press.

Fagenson-Eland, E. A., Marks, M. A., & Amendola, K. L. (1997). Perceptions of mentoring relationships. *Journal of Vocational Behavior, 45,* 55–78.

Geiger, A. H. (1992). Measures for mentors. *Training & Development, 46,* 65–67.

Geiger-DuMond, A. H., & Boyle, S. K. (1995). Mentoring: A practitioner's guide. *Training & Development, 49,* 51–54.

Guindon, M. H., & Richmond, L. J. (2005). Practice and research in career counseling and development–2004. *The Career Development Quarterly, 54,* 90–137.

Hardy, L. C. (1998). Mentoring: A long-term approach to diversity. *HR Focus, 75,* S11.

Harris, J. I., Winskowski, A. M., & Engdahl, B. E. (2007). Types of workplace social support in the prediction of job satisfaction. *The Career Development Quarterly, 56,* 150–156.

Hartzell, N. K. (2005). Making a commitment to mentoring. Retrieved April 12, 2008, from http://www.ncda.org.

Hegstad, C. D. (1999). Formal mentoring as a strategy for human resource development: A review of research. *Human Resource Development Quarterly, 10,* 383–390.

Herr, E. L. (2001). Career development and its practice: A historical perspective. *The Career Development Quarterly, 49,* 196–211.

Higgins, M. C., & Kram, K. E. (2001). Reconceptualizing mentoring at work: A developmental network perspective. *The Academy of Management Review, 26,* 264–288.

Kanter, R. M. (1977). *Men and women of the corporation.* New York: Basic Books.

Kirchmeyer, C. (2005). The effect of mentoring on academic careers over time: Testing performance and political perspectives. *Human Relations, 58,* 637–660.

Kram, K. E. (1985). *Mentoring at work: Developmental relationships in organizational life.* Glenview, IL: Scott-Foresman.

Kram, K. E., & Isabella, L. (1985). Mentoring alternatives: The role of peer relationships in career development. *Academy of Management Journal, 28,* 110–132.

Maze, M. (2006). The impact of the NCDA mentoring program. Retrieved April 16, 2008, from http://www.ncda.org.

Menttium. (2001). Corporate advantages to organized mentoring programs. Retrieved January 10, 2002, from http://www.menttium.com.

Molm, L. D. (1994). Dependence and risk: Transforming the structure of social exchange. *Social Psychology Quarterly, 57,* 163–176.

Okocha, A. G. (1998). Using qualitative appraisal strategies in career counseling. *Journal of Employment Counseling, 35,* 151–159.

Ostroff, C., & Kozlowski, S. W. (1993). The role of mentoring in information gathering processes of newcomers during early organizational socialization. *Journal of Vocational Behavior, 42,* 170–183.

Pace, R. W., Smith, P. C., & Mills, G. E. (1991). *Human resource development: The field.* Upper Saddle River, NJ: Prentice Hall.

Pellegrini, E. K., & Scandura, T. A. (2005). Construct equivalence across groups: An unexplored issue in mentoring research. *Educational and Psychological Measurement, 65,* 323–335.

Perrewe, P. L., & Nelson, D. L. (2004). Gender and career success: The facilitative role of political skill. *Organizational Dynamics, 33,* 366–378.

Quimby, J. L., & DeSantis, A. M. (2006). The influence of role models on women's career choices. *The Career Development Quarterly, 54,* 297–306.

Seels, B., & Glasgow, Z. (1998). *Making instructional design decisions* (2nd ed.). Upper Saddle River, NJ: Prentice Hall.

Suddarth, B. (2005). Making mentoring an organizational value: A look at the FDIC's mentoring program. Retrieved April 16, 2008, from http://www.ncda.org.

Whitmarsh, L., Brown, D., Cooper, J., Hawkins-Rodgers, Y., & Wentworth, D. K. (2007). Choices and challenges: A qualitative exploration of professional women's career patterns. *The Career Development Quarterly, 55,* 225–236.

Wilson, J. A., & Elman, N. S. (1996). Organizational benefits of mentoring. In G. R. Ferris & M. R. Buckley (Eds.), *Human resources management: Perspectives, context, functions and outcomes* (pp. 217–233). Upper Saddle River, NJ: Prentice Hall.

Recommended Readings and Websites

Bloch, D. P., & Richmond, L. J. (Eds.) (1997). *Connections between spirit and work in career development.* Palo Alto, CA: Davies-Black.

International Mentoring Association. (http://www.mentoring-association.org)

Murray, M. (1991). *Beyond the myths and magic of mentoring.* San Francisco: Jossey-Bass.

National Career Development Association. (http://www.ncda.org)

Wellington, S. (2001). *Be your own mentor.* New York: Random House.

 # EDITORIAL CONNECTIONS

Career mentoring can create a valuable link between the people who make up the organization, their individual aspirations and career ambitions, and the strategic performance objectives that define success for the organization and its partners. When complemented by other mentoring programs—such as performance mentoring, upward mentoring, or informal mentoring—and other performance interventions in your improvement system, these tools become central to the achievement of desired results. Creating such positive relationships within the organization, however, does not in and of itself build motivation and enhance self-concept. Instead, creative programs such as job crafting (see Chapter Twenty-Three) can also be used to develop individual self-concept and confidence within an organization.

> **Expanding Your Options**
>
> *Alignment of desires and work*—a state in which personal career goals are fulfilled under current employment conditions.

WHAT'S COMING UP

As estimated by the American Institute of Stress, nearly one million Americans are absent from work every day due to stress. Consequently, they estimate that the total health and productivity cost of worker stress to American business is from $50 to $150 billion annually. In Chapter Twenty-Three, Michelle French examines the role of job crafting as a performance intervention for promoting emotional well-being in the workplace. As illustrated in the chapter, job crafting can be an effective performance intervention for reducing stress, improving workplace relationships, and overcoming cognitive boundaries to performance.

Job Crafting

Michelle French

INTRODUCTION

Research has found that many workers are looking for—but not finding—emotional well-being in their work. Research also shows that individuals and organizations alike suffer when people do not experience emotional well-being in their work. Kieran Mathieson and Cynthia Miree's 2003 manuscript "Illuminating the Invisible," for example, points out that employers who ignore the issue will frequently be faced with increasing absenteeism and turnover. Yet this does not have to be the case, because we can use interventions such as job crafting to support the emotional well-being of employees in the workplace.

Employees engage in job crafting when they actively create what their job is physically, socially, and psychologically. While not well-known, job crafting has been shown to be a means for effectively improving emotional well-being in organizations. In order to help employees achieve emotional well-being in the workplace and the positive outcomes that go along with it (such as increased organizational commitment, organizational citizenship behaviors, and improved performance), it is important to craft jobs so that employees can use their greatest strengths. Job crafting has been shown to increase productivity, quality, and efficiency while decreasing turnover and absenteeism. This chapter examines the benefits of job crafting, how to design the job crafting intervention, and factors critical to job crafting success.

DESCRIPTION

The job crafting intervention (JCI) introduced in this chapter consists of assessing employees' strengths, communicating both strengths and performance goals to employees, and supporting employees in re-crafting their jobs within the boundaries of the employer's desired performance outcomes. This extends beyond the view that job crafting is a process in which employees engage without a manager's involvement. Since all employees are prone to engage in job crafting— formally or informally— it is wise for managers within organizations to understand how job crafting works. Further, it is important for employees' job crafting activities to be aligned with the organization's performance measures and goals. Managers can create the conditions that foster the alignment of employee job crafting with organizational goals.

What is job crafting exactly? The concept of job crafting was introduced in 2001 by Ross School of Business's Amy Wrzesniewski and Stern School of Business's Jane Dutton to describe the process people use to make a job their own. In their 2001 article for *The Academy of Management Review*, they define job crafting as "the physical and cognitive changes individuals make in the task or relational boundaries of their work" (p. 179). Job crafters change the task boundaries (what their job is physically) by altering the form or number of activities they engage in while doing the job (such as a file clerk developing a system of document filing that enables him to get his work done faster). Employees change the cognitive task boundaries by altering the way they see the job (for example, a fast-food fry cook thinking of herself as a "French fry culinary artist"). Finally, job crafters alter the relational boundaries of their jobs by exercising discretion over with whom they interact while doing the job (for example, a realtor choosing to work with clients and their families based on how well she gets along with them). See Table 23.1 for more examples of job crafting.

Job crafting has the ability to contribute to emotional well-being, which comprises the factors that make people happy. Martin Seligman of the University of Pennsylvania defines overall happiness in 2002's *Authentic Happiness* as pleasure, engagement (also known as *flow*), and meaning. Pleasure includes enjoyable experiences through the senses (such as great-tasting food) and higher pleasures (such as comfort and fun). Engagement, or *flow*, is the experience in which time stands still and a person feels completely at home, usually during activities the person likes doing (such as sports or painting). Meaning occurs when people pursue activities that connect them to a cause outside of themselves and that make a positive difference in the world (such as volunteering at a local orphanage). Taken together, these three components comprise overall happiness. In their 2004 article for the American Academy of Arts and Sciences' journal *Daedalus*, Robert Biswas-Diener and his colleagues also suggest that happiness can be specific to an area in life such as work,

Table 23.1 Forms of Job Crafting

Form	Example	Effect on Meaning of Work
1. Changing the type or number of job activities	Grant writers create a timeline for completing a grant proposal, adding or deleting tasks based on the deadline	Grant writers change the meaning of their jobs to be project managers who complete work in a timely manner
2. Changing the view of the job	Salespeople in a clothing store pick out an entire outfit based on the customer's height, hair, personality, and the occasion	Salespeople change their view of the job to see their role as that of personal wardrobe consultants with a focus on high-quality customer service
3. Changing the number and manner of interactions with others on the job	Market researchers coordinate their analysis tasks with the sales force to provide salespeople with relevant information	Market researchers view their data analysis as an important part of the entire marketing department's team performance

marriage, or school. While happiness and emotional well-being are often used interchangeably, in this chapter emotional well-being is comprised of overall happiness, job satisfaction, and meaning in life and work.

According to Seligman, one of the world's leading researchers of happiness, satisfaction in one's job requires a passionate commitment to work that uses one's top individual strengths in the service of a greater good. He recommends re-crafting work to use one's unique signature strengths to achieve organizational goals and to experience pleasure, engagement, and meaning. Seligman's recommendations for well-being in work, when combined with Wrzesniewski and Dutton's model, lead to a performance improvement intervention that enables employers to guide and facilitate the job crafting process in the direction of emotional well-being for the employee and improved performance for the organization.

Job crafting has the potential to benefit the organization when employees' re-crafted meaning, identity, and work patterns align with organizational objectives. Job crafting relates to the areas of job design, process redesign, and job and task analysis in that it involves changing the processes, procedures, tasks, and products of work. While the focus of job crafting is on increasing meaning in work and changing role or identity in the organization, a 2006 article by Paul Lyons suggests that the outcomes of job crafting improve organizational performance "through the provision of better services, processes, and/or products" (p. 91). Not only does job crafting have the potential to enhance the individual employee's emotional well-being, but it can benefit the organization as well.

All employees are potential job crafters, given the right individual and work contexts. Job crafting is most likely to occur when individual employees have the motivation to job craft and when perceived opportunities to engage in the crafting act present themselves. The general effects of job crafting are to change the individual's meaning of work and work identity, while maintaining a focus on alignment with organizational performance. *Work identity* refers to the way individuals define themselves at work. *Meaning of work* is the way individuals understand the purpose of their work or what is achieved by that work. Job crafting acknowledges the fact that, regardless of the job description, employees make a job fit who they are and the skills and abilities they bring to work. In essence, job crafting describes the process employees use to make jobs their own. When jobs enable employees to use their greatest strengths to serve a meaningful cause, employees are more likely to experience emotional well-being. Based on the work of Wrzesniewski and Dutton, Table 23.1 provides examples of the three forms of job crafting, as well as the effect of the re-crafted jobs on the meaning of work.

WHAT WE KNOW FROM RESEARCH

Job crafting finds its basis in both organizational theory and empirical research on crafting work. It is useful to examine the existing literature to create a theoretical context for the findings that job crafting is effective at improving performance and promoting emotional well-being in organizations.

The Theoretical Rationale for the Effectiveness of Job Crafting

The existing research on work and job design primarily focuses on ways in which supervisors and managers initiate changes in jobs and tasks according to Hackman & Oldham's 1980 book *Work Redesign*. Their job characteristics model provides the dominant theoretical framework that describes how workers judge their jobs to be satisfying and motivating based the objective features of the job; these objective characteristics include skill variety, task identity and significance, autonomy, and feedback. Wrzesniewski and Dutton go on to suggest that "the job design perspective puts managers in the role of job crafters" (p. 187).

On the other hand, the job crafting view emphasizes the proactive changes employees make to their own work. Other theories that support the idea that employees craft new jobs out of existing jobs include role innovation, role making, personal initiative, organizational citizenship behaviors, and task revision.[1] Salancik and Pfeffer's social information processing research from 1978 also provides a foundation for job crafting by predicting how people perform their jobs. Job crafting not only affects the way people complete their job tasks, but it also impacts the way people see their jobs.

We also know from theoretical research that people find more meaning in work that they feel is a "calling." Bellah and his colleagues in 1985 described the job-career-calling distinction for the meaning of work. People who view their work as a "job" see it as a means to an end that allows them to earn money, and consequently they need to enjoy their time away from work to find emotional well-being. When people view work as a "career," their job is performed out of a desire for higher social status and increased power, which results in improved self-esteem. In contrast, people who view their work as a "calling" perceive that their employment gives them fulfillment through work that is morally and socially meaningful.

Martin Seligman goes further to suggest in 2002 that people who view their work as a "calling" are happier: an essential component of emotional well-being in the workplace. He recommends re-crafting work to use one's greatest individual strengths to achieve organizational goals and to experience each of the three elements of overall happiness: pleasure, engagement (or *flow*), and meaning. Of these elements, Seligman says the "best understood aspect of happiness during the workday is having flow—feeling completely at home within yourself when you work" (p. 173). Mihaly Csikszentmihalyi, the pioneer in happiness research who coined the term *flow*, asserts in his 2003 book *Good Business* that "redesigning the workplace promises to lead to an enormous improvement in the 'bottom line' of human happiness" (p. 96). He declares that the "best strategy for creating such an organization is to provide the conditions that make it conducive for workers to experience flow" (p. 108). One way to facilitate the experience of *flow* is for workers to use their greatest strengths at work.

The theoretical literature provides a solid foundation for the value and use of job crafting. Now that we have grounded our discussion of job crafting in relevant theory, the following section provides an examination of the performance outcomes reported in empirical studies of job crafting. First, we will examine the outcomes of an empirical study of happiness interventions.

The Empirical Support for the Effectiveness of Job Crafting

A happiness study by Seligman and his colleagues in 2005 provides some of the strongest links between emotional well-being and the job crafting intervention. Across 477 participants, the researchers found that three happiness interventions increased happiness over time and decreased symptoms of being depressed. One of the two most effective exercises involved deploying an individual's strengths. The exercise, "using signature strengths in a new way" (p. 416), consisted of participants taking an online assessment of their strengths and receiving feedback on their top five strengths. They were asked to use one of these strengths in a new and different way every day for one week (although some continued the exercise even longer on their own). The resulting increase in happiness and decrease in depressive symptoms lasted six months. This exercise is the most similar to the job crafting intervention presented in this chapter and demonstrates the effectiveness of using an individual's signature strengths as a method to improve emotional well-being. These impacts seem to apply across industries, as illustrated by case study examples from Wrzesniewski and Dutton's 2001 research.

Wrzesniewski and Dutton provide six examples of job crafting to illustrate its process. The first is a study of hospital cleaning staff that reveals that cleaning workers crafted their jobs by viewing them as critical to healing patients and by carefully timing their tasks to increase efficiency. Next, hairdressers changed the relational boundaries of their jobs by getting to know their clients, making personal disclosures about themselves, and letting go of clients whose lack of self-disclosure led to unpleasant interactions. Similarly, restaurant cooks were found to change the task and cognitive boundaries of their jobs by decreasing their number of tasks and expanding their view of the job tasks to see them as an integrated artistic endeavor. Other examples show ways in which employees actively construct their own meaning of work and work identity.

In 2006, Lyons found through a mixed-method study of thirty-four office equipment sales representatives that 74 percent of respondents reported at least one attempt at job crafting (or shaping) in the previous year, usually involving changing task functions and relationships. Virtually all job crafting focused on improvements to benefit the customer, employee, and/or company. Of those who reported job crafting during their research interviews, 18 percent described over four separate attempts to shape their jobs. The study also found a strong relationship between the frequency of job crafting and the individual's own level of competitiveness, as measured by survey results.

Interestingly, research suggests that task interdependence (the degree to which employees need each other to get their work done) actually encourages the cognitive and relational aspects of crafting, while inhibiting the crafting of tasks. Brenda Ghitulescu's 2006 dissertation study examining 164 automotive workers and 661 special education teachers showed that work discretion and task complexity facilitate job crafting. Individuals' job crafting was found to enhance affective outcomes by increasing employees' levels of job satisfaction and commitment, while decreasing absenteeism and turnover. Job crafting also increased employees' effectiveness outcomes on quality and efficiency ratings. These individual effects extended to improve team productivity levels as well.

In summary, a review of the research suggests the value of offering a well-designed job crafting intervention. In the theoretical literature, the job characteristics model describes the types of job designs initiated by managers that make a job satisfying and motivating for employees. The job crafting literature describes the process employees engage in to make their jobs more satisfying and motivating on their own. Also presented is an empirical study that demonstrates the effectiveness of expressing one's signature strengths to improve emotional well-being. Employees who engage in job crafting are shown to increase their productivity as well. The job crafting intervention presented in this chapter combines job crafting with strengths expression to enable employers to actively manage the process employees use to make a job more satisfying and motivating so that employers can improve performance and well-being in their organizations.

WHEN TO APPLY

As has been discussed, all employees are potential job crafters; thus, it is important to understand the conditions under which job crafting is likely to be initiated by employees. It is also imperative for managers to understand when to get involved in this process and to apply a job crafting intervention (JCI).

The factors that enable job crafting are the motivation and perceived opportunity to shape work. First, we will examine *motivation*. Employees are motivated to job craft when they have a desire for personal control over their jobs. Motivation for job crafting also occurs when employees want to create a positive self-image in their work. Finally, employees are motivated to job craft when they want to fulfill a basic desire for human connection.

Next, we look for *perceived opportunities*. Employees perceive opportunities to job craft when they have a sense of freedom or discretion in their job tasks and how they complete them. Another condition that causes employees to perceive opportunities for job crafting occurs when job tasks require little task interdependence with co-workers. Job crafting opportunities also become apparent when employees have autonomy in their work (that is, freedom from close monitoring or supervision by management).

It is appropriate for managers to apply the job crafting intervention to improve performance when there is a change in performance measures or strategic goals. Job crafting is intended to align employees' tasks, relationships, and cognitive boundaries with the new performance goals. Managers should also encourage job crafting when they recognize that employees perceive that their needs are not being met in the job as it is currently designed. This can be evidenced by decreased productivity and increased job shopping activities (searching for new jobs or even applying for other positions), as Minnie Osteyee describes in her 1990 dissertation. Finally, management should initiate the JCI when the features of the job or occupation are "stigmatized" and job crafting is intended to create a positive work identity that boosts productivity, according to Wrzesniewski and Dutton, writing in 2001.

STRENGTHS AND CRITICISMS

Some advantages and disadvantages of job crafting are listed below:

Advantages

- People who experience more meaning in their work tend to exhibit more productivity, organizational commitment, engagement with their work, and organizational citizenship behaviors—going above and beyond the call of duty to help people in the organization or the organization itself.
- Encouraging job crafting enables managers to benefit from processes in which many employees already engage.
- Job crafters who change their work to use their signature strengths transform a "job" into a "calling," which in turn leads to improved emotional well-being.
- Emotional well-being in work typically results in increased job satisfaction and improved performance. It also has the potential to increase job tenure.
- Exercising signature strengths benefits nearly everyone involved—customers receive better service, managers gain a more productive employee, and the employee derives positive emotion.

Disadvantages

- Job crafting is largely improvisational and not visible to management in some cases, which removes some degree of managerial control. The more traditional job or process redesign may yield similar results for managers attempting to influence employees' job shaping activities directly.
- Workers who are unmotivated or who do not perceive opportunities to job craft are less likely to engage in the process.
- Job crafting can greatly improve person-job fit, but may not alleviate a lack of fit in other areas (person-group fit, person-vocation fit, and meaning-mission fit).[2]

RECOMMENDED DESIGN, DEVELOPMENT, AND IMPLEMENTATION PROCESS

The job crafting intervention (JCI) consists of assessing employees' strengths, communicating both strengths and performance goals with employees, and supporting employees in re-crafting their work within the boundaries of the employer's desired performance outcomes. Traditionally, job crafting is thought to be a process initiated and directed by the individual employee. This chapter introduces the JCI as a means for managers to become actively involved in this process to steer job crafting in the direction of the organization's performance goals. Recommendations for applying the job crafting intervention follow.

1. *Make the case for job crafting.* Introduce job crafting to decision-makers, supervisors, and employees. Describe the problems associated with lack of emotional well-being in work (such as increased absenteeism or turn-over). Note the benefits of job crafting and its success in reversing these trends. Provide the costs incurred by implementing the job crafting intervention (monetary costs of assessment materials and time needed to assess and train employees on their strengths). Also cite the most current incidences and associated costs of absenteeism and turnover within the organization.

2. *Assess and identify employees' signature strengths.* Strength tests—including the VIA Inventory of Strengths[3] (see viastrengths.org) and the StrengthsFinder Profile (see strengthsfinder.com)[4]—can accomplish this task. Managers who are familiar with the strengths research and who are highly skilled at assessing a person's signature strengths and how they can best use them may be able to identify the employee's strengths through qualitative interviews. Be sure to provide employees with an explanation of their assessment results and how their individual strengths can be deployed in the workplace.

3. *Match employees' job tasks to their signature strengths.* During the selection phase, choose employees whose signature strengths fit the work they will do. If the employer cannot find an applicant whose signature strengths fit the organization's objectives, then matching strengths to the job can be implemented gradually. With employees who have already been hired, Seligman (2002) recommends that law firms reserve five hours of the work week for "signature strength time" during which associates perform a non-routine assignment or cross-training that uses their individual strengths in the service of the firm's goals (p. 182). This incremental approach can be used in other occupational settings as well.

4. *Inform employees of performance measures and organizational goals.* Communicate clearly to ensure that employees have a thorough understanding of what performance outcomes are expected of them. Also, make sure that employees know about the cultural norms and preferred methods or styles for accomplishing tasks within the organization.

5. *Encourage employees to re-craft their current work to use signature strengths more often in furtherance of the organization's performance goals.* Once it is clear that employees understand the parameters

management has set, allow them freedom to re-craft their work within the scope of the organization and work unit's performance goals.

6. *Measure employee performance after the job crafting intervention has been implemented to determine whether management's goals are being met.* Evaluate employees' re-crafted job tasks and work patterns to determine whether the employees are meeting management's desired performance outcomes, or if their re-crafted work is ineffective in accomplishing the employer's goals.

7. *Take corrective action when necessary.* Realign employees' task and relational boundaries in cases in which they have been re-crafted in ways that prevent the desired performance.

CRITICAL SUCCESS FACTORS

As detailed in this chapter, both theory and empirical results suggest that job crafting can be an effective strategy for improving performance and enhancing employee well-being. The following are some critical success factors of note.

Social

- The factors that enable job crafting by employees should be in place (employees should feel motivated to engage in job crafting, and they should perceive opportunities for job crafting). If an employee feels no motivation to personalize his or her job, management will have to attempt to supply extrinsic incentives, recognition, or rewards to spur what is inherently an intrinsically motivated process.

- The perceived opportunities for job crafting occur when employees have autonomy in completing job tasks and there is low task interdependence in their work. According to Van der Vegt and Van de Vliert's 2002 article for the *Journal of Managerial Psychology*, this is very important for jobs in which employees must complete their work in teams, since task interdependence is embedded into jobs that are structured into teams. It is important to note Ghitulescu's finding that this task interdependence can encourage re-crafting relationships and cognitive aspects of the job, but it discourages the crafting of task boundaries. Thus, for managers who facilitate teams, it will be important to emphasize the use of job crafting to improve team relationships and cognitive boundaries.

Political

- Revised work patterns must be consistent with the performance and organizational goals that the employer has set for employees. Otherwise, the individual employees may feel very satisfied with the new design of their work, but they may not perform to the standards that the organization or work group requires from them. Both the individual and the employer's needs must be met by the re-crafted work.

Economic

- Reward systems and incentives must encourage individuals to reshape their work to meet performance goals. Giving employees bonuses for having completed a job crafting training, for instance, without regard for the job crafting activities they use after the training would not necessarily focus employees on meeting management's performance goals. Management should target rewards to re-crafted work that meets the employer's goals.

Legal

- Re-crafted job tasks must fulfill the fiduciary responsibilities of the position and of the organization. Managers should monitor employees' performance to ensure that the task boundaries, in particular, do not diverge from the duties that must be performed for the organization and the particular job.

Technical

- Technology should be used to communicate effectively the performance measures and strategic goals of the organization to individual employees. While computer-mediated communication may be effective for aspects of the job crafting process, face-to-face meetings may be helpful particularly when assisting employees in re-crafting relational boundaries to improve team performance.

Intercultural

- Culture influences the way people judge their own well-being and the avenues through which they achieve well-being. As such, individuals whose cultural background encourages them to fulfill their needs for control, connection with others, or positive identity through their work are more likely to job craft.

SUMMARY

This chapter examines the job crafting intervention as a tool for enhancing employees' emotional well-being in organizations. Employers can use the JCI to create work environments where employees use their best strengths to achieve emotional well-being in the workplace. This increased emotional well-being in turn leads to positive outcomes such as increased organizational commitment, organizational citizenship behaviors, and improved performance. Job crafting empowers employees to create work that expresses their own greatest strengths while fulfilling the organization's strategic and performance goals.

Notes

1. The idea that employees craft new jobs out of prescribed jobs can also be found in theories of role innovation (Schein, 1971;Van Maanen & Schein, 1979), role making (Graen & Scandura, 1987), personal initiative (Frese, Faye, Hilburger, Leng, & Tag, 1997), organizational citizenship behaviors (Organ, 1988, 1997), and task revision (Staw & Boettger, 1990). Job crafting also builds on the social information processing perspective (Salancik & Pfeffer, 1978) by predicting how people enact their jobs.

2. *Person-group fit*: This is defined as the compatibility of individuals and their work groups. See Amy Kristof's 1996 article "Person-Organization Fit" for a meta-analysis of fit literature. *Person-vocation fit*: Both people and occupations have personalities; person-vocation fit is the similarity between the two. This theory is based on Holland's (1985) RAISEC (realistic, investigative, artistic, social, enterprising, conventional) typology. *Meaning-mission fit*: Represents the compatibility between the personal meaning of the individual and the mission of the organization. I wrote on this concept in my 2006 dissertation work.

3. Peterson and Seligman created the VIA Inventory of Strengths to assess individual strengths. It can be found online at www.authentichappiness.org as well as in Seligman (2002). This is the strengths assessment used in the empirical happiness intervention research study.

4. Buckingham and Clifton (2001) created a helpful strengths assessment, the StrengthsFinder Profile. The newer version is available in StrengthsFinder 2.0 (Rath, 2007).

References

Bellah, R. N., Madsen, R., Sullivan, W. M., Swidler, A., & Tipton, S. M. (1985). *Habits of the heart: Individualism and commitment in American life*. New York: Harper and Row.

Biswas-Diener, R., Diener, E., & Tamir, M. (2004). The psychology of subjective well-being. *Daedalus*, *133*(2), 18–25.

Buckingham, M., & Clifton, D.O. (2001). *Now, discover your strengths*. New York: The Free Press.

Csikszentmihalyi, M. (2003) *Good business: Leadership, flow, and the making of meaning*. New York: Penguin Group.

French, M. L. (2006). The alignment between personal meaning and organizational mission among music executives: A study of happiness, job satisfaction, and responsibility toward employees. (Doctoral dissertation, Pepperdine University, 2006). *Dissertation Abstracts International*, *67*(11).

Frese, M., Fay, D., Hilburger, T., Leng, K., & Tag, A. (1997). The concept of personal initiative: Operationalization, reliability and validity of two German samples. *Journal of Occupational & Organizational Psychology, 70*(2), 139–161.

Ghitulescu, B. E. (2006). Shaping tasks and relationships at work: Examining the antecedents and consequences of employee job crafting. (Doctoral dissertation, University of Pittsburg, 2006). *Dissertation Abstracts International, 68*(01). UMI No. AAT 3251178. Retrieved December 31, 2007, from ProQuest Digital Dissertations database.

Graen, G. B., & Scandura, T. A. (1987). Toward a psychology of dyadic organizing. *Research in Organizational Behavior, 9*, 175–208.

Hackman, J. R., & Oldham, G. R. (1980). *Work redesign*. Reading, MA: Addison-Wesley.

Holland, J. L. (1985). Making vocational choices: A theory of vocational personalities and work environments (2nd ed.). Upper Saddle River, NJ: Prentice Hall.

Kristof, A. L. (1996). Person-organization fit: An integrative review of its conceptualizations, measurement, and implications. *Personnel Psychology, 49*(1), 1–49.

Lyons, P. (2006). Individual competitiveness and spontaneous changes in jobs. *Advances in Competitiveness Research, 14*(1), 90–98. Retrieved December 31, 2007, from ProQuest Database.

Mathieson, K., & Miree, C. E. (2003). Illuminating the invisible: IT and self-discovery in the workplace. In R. A. Giacalone & C. L. Jurkiewicz (Eds.), *Handbook of workplace spirituality and organizational performance* (pp. 164–180). Armonk, NY: M.E. Sharpe.

Organ, D. W. (1998). *Organizational citizenship behavior: The good soldier syndrome.* Lexington, MA: Lexington Books.

Organ, D. W. (1997). Organizational citizenship behavior: It's construct clean-up time. *Human Performance, 10*(2), 85–97.

Osteyee, M. L. (1990). Academic secretaries: Perspectives of how they influence and are influenced by a university environment as they seek job satisfaction. (Doctoral dissertation, Syracuse University, 1990). *Dissertation Abstracts International, 52*(04). UMI No. AAT 9126121. Retrieved December 31, 2007, from ProQuest Digital Dissertations database.

Rath, T. (2007). *StrengthsFinder 2.0: A new and upgraded edition of the online test from Gallup's now, discover your strengths*. New York: Gallup Press.

Salancik, G. R., & Pfeffer, J. (1978). A social information processing approach to job attitudes and task design. *Administrative Science Quarterly, 23*, 224–253.

Schein, E. H. (1971). Occupational socialization in the professions: The role of innovation. *Journal of Psychiatric Research, 8*, 521–530.

Seligman, M. E. P., Steen, T. A., Park, N., & Peterson, C. (2005). Positive psychology progress: Empirical validation of interventions. *American Psychologist, 60*(5), 410–421.

Seligman, M. E. P. (2002). *Authentic happiness: Using the new positive psychology to realize your potential for lasting fulfillment*. New York: The Free Press.

Staw, B. M., & Boettger, R. D. (1990). Task revision: A neglected form of work performance. *Academy of Management Journal*, *33*, 534–559.

Van der Vegt, G., & Van de Vliert, E. (2002). Intragroup interdependence and effectiveness: Review and proposed directions for theory and practice. *Journal of Managerial Psychology*, *17*(1/2), 50–67. Retrieved April 2, 2008, from ABI/INFORM Global database.

Van Maanen, J., & Schein, E. H. (1979). Toward a theory of organizational socialization. *Research in Organizational Behavior*, *1*, 209–264.

Wrzesniewski, A., & Dutton, J. E. (2001) Crafting a job: Revisioning employees as active crafters of their work. *The Academy of Management Review*, *26*(2), 179–201. Retrieved October 31, 2007, from ProQuest Database.

Recommended Readings

Baumeister, R. F. (1991). *Meanings of Life*. New York: The Guilford Press.

Csikszentmihalyi, M. (1997). *Finding flow: The psychology of engagement with everyday life*. New York: Basic Books.

Diener, E., & Lucas, R. E. (2000). Subjective emotional well-being. In M. Lewis & J. M. Haviland (Eds.), *Handbook of emotions* (2nd ed.) (pp. 325–337). New York: The Guilford Press. Retrieved November 10, 2004, from http://www.psych.uiuc.edu/~ediener/hottopic/paper2.html.

Frankl, V. E. (1968). *The doctor and the soul: From psychotherapy to logotherapy* (2nd ed.). New York: Alfred A. Knopf.

Frankl, V. E. (1984). *Man's search for meaning: An introduction to logotherapy* (3rd ed.) New York: Simon and Schuster.

Quinn, R. E., Dutton, J. E., & Spreitzer, G. M. (2004). *Reflected best self exercise: Assignment and instructions to participants*. Retrieved May 24, 2006, from http://www.bus.umich.edu/Positive/PDF/reflectedbest_ exercise_preview.pdf.

Torraco, R. J. (2005). Work design theory: A review and critique with implications for human resource development. *Human Resource Development Quarterly*, *16*(1), 85–109. Retrieved May 24, 2006, from ProQuest Database.

Wrzesniewski, A., McCauley, C., Rozin, P., & Schwartz, B. (1997). Jobs, careers, and callings: People's relations to their work. *Journal of Research in Personality*, *31*(1), 21–33.

PART SEVEN

EDITORS'
DISCUSSION

Motivation and self-concept, or the desire and belief that you will accomplish meaningful results, plays a critical role in the successful improvement of human and organizational performance. Motivation stretches far beyond printing slogans on banners, posters, and coffee mugs, or inviting motivational speakers annually to "rally the troops." It is a component of most every e-mail message, each meeting with your project team, and even the boundaries that are placed around how an individual's job is defined. Motivation and self-concept encompass a set of performance interventions that broadly provide the foundation for accomplishing useful and meaningful results.

Improving performance isn't just about improving workplace productivity or the financial bottom line of the organization; it can, and should, also lead to increased job satisfaction, longer retention, improved quality of life for employees, reductions in job-related stress, new social networks, and numerous motivation-related benefits. Performance interventions that improve motivation and self-concept are therefore closely associated with—and often part of—many other performance interventions that are spread throughout the Performance Pyramid.

Vision, missions, and objectives (see Part Two of this handbook), for example, motivate and inspire employees and organizational partners to achieve desired results. Likewise, succession planning (see Chapter Twenty-Nine), coaching programs (see Chapters Eleven and Twenty-Seven), incentive systems (see Chapter Eighteen), and other performance interventions can also have substantial motivation and self-concept components. Performance interventions that develop knowledge and skills (see Part Eight of this hand-book) are also frequently associated with, and often dependent on, motivation and self-concept. Accordingly, you will want to align and link all of these performance interventions in order to accomplish significant and sustainable results.

References and Resources from Editors' Contributions to Part Seven

American Institute of Stress: http://www.stress.org/job.htm

Vadri, Y., Wiener, Y., & Popper, M. (1989). The value content of organizational mission as a factor in the commitment of members. *Psychological Reports, 65*, 27–34.

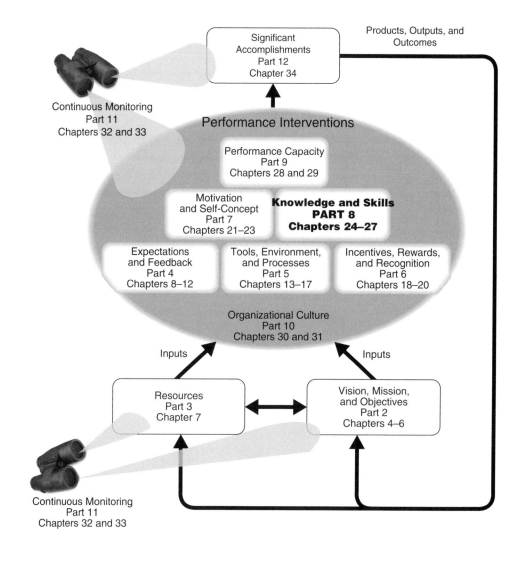

Continuous Monitoring
Part 11
Chapters 32 and 33

Significant
Accomplishments
Part 12
Chapter 34

Products, Outputs, and
Outcomes

Performance Interventions

Performance Capacity
Part 9
Chapters 28 and 29

Motivation
and Self-Concept
Part 7
Chapters 21–23

**Knowledge and Skills
PART 8
Chapters 24–27**

Expectations
and Feedback
Part 4
Chapters 8–12

Tools, Environment,
and Processes
Part 5
Chapters 13–17

Incentives, Rewards,
and Recognition
Part 6
Chapters 18–20

Organizational Culture
Part 10
Chapters 30 and 31

Inputs

Inputs

Resources
Part 3
Chapter 7

Vision, Mission,
and Objectives
Part 2
Chapters 4–6

Continuous Monitoring
Part 11
Chapters 32 and 33

KNOWLEDGE AND SKILLS

Starting in the Introduction, and throughout each of the subsequent parts and chapters of this handbook, we have emphasized the importance of systemic and comprehensive performance improvement. We have used Wedman's Performance Pyramid to organize various improvement activities in such a manner that significant results can be accomplished. Further, we have strived to link multiple levels of results using Kaufman's Organizational Element Model. These two models provide an essential linkage between the results that you intend to accomplish—societal outcomes, organizational outputs, and individual/team products—and the performance interventions that you select for your performance improvement system. We have also encouraged you to examine the numerous performance interventions associated with each component of the Performance Pyramid in order to create a system for improving performance that is holistic, rather than limited or fragmented.

Within holistic performance systems, you will commonly find performance interventions that focus on the development of knowledge and skills. Learning is, after all, a critical precursor to many improvements in performance. Whether you are building the capacity of employees to utilize new software systems through traditional classroom training or expanding the knowledge of managers in relation to strategic initiatives, the use of performance interventions that build knowledge and skills can be an important element of your improvement efforts.

Beyond knowledge and skills interventions that focus on the performance issues at the heart of your improvement effort (for instance, e-learning courses on the safe use of a networked computer application), the development of knowledge and skills also plays a fundamental role in the implementation of many other performance interventions. For example, if you are introducing a revised succession planning program (see Chapter Twenty-Nine) with the goal of reducing the transition period after managers retire, the performance intervention will require the development of knowledge and skills that support successful implementation. Organizational leaders may require information on how to use succession planning to effectively manage their units, or new communication skills may be required to promote the sharing of knowledge between retiring managers and the employees who will succeed them. In response, you would include some forms of knowledge and skills development (such as, e-learning, traditional training, mentoring, coaching) to support the introduction of performance interventions efforts.

Expanding Your Options

Traditional training—those ways of delivering training that have been used for many years. These usually focus on presentation, such as a lecture format, and take place within a classroom. They are distinguishable from newer or more hands-on training methods such as e-learning or simulations.

The performance interventions in the knowledge and skills component of the pyramid model are probably some of the most familiar and popular. Traditional classroom training, for instance, frequently represents the largest investment organizations make into building knowledge and skills—commonly their largest investment into improving performance as well. Training programs can, after all, be used to effectively build knowledge and skills and accomplish results. From courses on how to use Microsoft Access to workshops on team leadership, there are many appropriate and valuable uses for training; accordingly, there are many approaches to designing, developing, implementing, and evaluating training programs.

The contributing authors to this part of the book have selected performance interventions that offer you alternatives to traditional training. With e-learning, team learning, mentoring, coaching, and many other available choices, the chapters in this part are meant to expand your options for developing knowledge and skills. Examining your options is, after all, central to making useful and justifiable decisions about how to improve performance.

WHAT'S COMING UP

In Chapter Twenty-Four, Ryan Watkins examines e-learning as a performance intervention that can build knowledge and skills regardless of time zone or location. By removing these barriers, e-learning can offer the flexibility required to develop useful knowledge and skills that contribute to the improvement of performance. Sometimes e-learning can be used to directly build skills related to the performance issue, such as when you create an e-learning module on a new software application, while at other times you might choose e-learning to support the implementation of other performance technologies, such as restructuring (see Chapter Seven), performance management (see Chapter Twelve), or process improvement (see Chapter Seventeen).

e-Learning

Ryan Watkins

INTRODUCTION

In its many forms, e-learning has become an essential tool for the training and professional development services that shape many of today's businesses and public sector organizations. As a consequence, there is a growing recognition that an effective e-learning program can be a vital component to improving human performance. Whether e-learning in your organization includes just a limited number of vendor-purchased online courses or the year-around management of international professional development events delivered via satellite, e-learning can be a dynamic and valuable tool for performance improvement efforts. This is especially true when you want to help employees build knowledge and/or skills without the time and location limitations associated with traditional classroom training.

DESCRIPTION

The boundaries of what is and what is not "e-learning" are not easily defined since e-learning can range from self-paced online tutorials to instructor-led graduate courses at a university. Similarly, e-learning encompasses courses that make limited use of Internet tools such as e-mail as well as training programs that make intensive use of both Internet and satellite communications tools for synchronous (real time) learning activities. Thus, definitions of e-learning must remain broad and without the limitations associated with specific technologies or current delivery systems. Otherwise, definitions that define e-learning based on specific technologies would limit our perspectives to a small sample of potential tools. e-Learning can therefore be pragmatically described simply as learning events or activities that are facilitated, to some degree, by electronic media.

Expanding Your Options

On-the-job training (OJT)—employee training that takes place while the associated job or tasks are taking place. Often a professional trainer (or sometimes an experienced employee) acts as the instructor, and utilizes formal classroom training. Alternatively, e-learning (see this chapter) can be used to provide training on the job.

Based on businessdictionary.com definition (January 2009)

Like other learning-focused human performance interventions, e-learning can result in the development of knowledge and/or skills for building competence. Either in lieu of traditional classroom training or as a complement to classroom activities, e-learning can provide a variety of tools and resources for expanding your training intervention, both beyond the boundaries of the classroom as well as outside the often-limited time of traditional training. The flexibilities inherent to e-learning (such as potential time and location independence) can increase the prospective value of e-learning as a tool within your performance improvement system. From on-demand, self-paced instructional units that learners can access when they are on the job to real-time video conferences that link learners from around the world into an engaging hands-on course, e-learning can take on many forms to assist learners to accomplish desirable learning and performance objectives. Blended e-learning (combining the benefits of classroom instruction with e-learning opportunities) can further enhance your ability to increase the knowledge and/or skills of learners based on social, political, technological, and economic realities within your organization. Yet, all of these options can make e-learning programs and projects hard to manage and successfully implement within nearly any organization.

The success of an e-learning program or project therefore begins and ends with its alignment to desired learner performance. Finding the appropriate balance of e-learning options (for instance, what is the appropriate blend of online video content and interactive knowledge building through discussion boards?) and choosing the best e-learning technologies (such as learning management systems, course management systems, or satellite video conferencing tools) are just a few of many decisions that must be made in order to implement a successful e-learning initiative. From selecting analysis tools and systematically verifying the link between the performance and learning objectives to creating a change management plan that addresses the political, social, economic, and other critical success factors, the development of a robust e-learning effort requires the thorough integration of what we know about instructional design, human performance, learning, and information technologies.

WHAT WE KNOW FROM RESEARCH

As a relatively new field of practice within training and education, e-learning research is still building a body of foundational research that can provide validated knowledge to inform our decisions. Leveraging the research in instructional systems design, information technology management, adult learning, multi-media development, and other closely related disciplines, e-learning research is beginning to give us the valued guidance that is necessary for successful e-learning initiatives to be systematically developed within organizations. In 2006, as part of their annual *Review of Trends in Workplace Learning and Performance* for the American Society of Training and Development (ASTD), Ray Rivera and Andrew Paradise described the current state of e-learning as follows:

> "Organizations' investments from previous years in learning technologies are now paying off. e-Learning has reached a high level of sophistication, both in terms of instructional development and the effective management of resources. Many organizations with high-performing learning functions are able to attribute clear cost savings, efficiency gains in the learning function, increased content reuse, and decreased costs of learning development and delivery to successful technology investments.
>
> "Many organizations have achieved blended learning solutions that afford many of the benefits of classroom-based learning (e.g., personal attention, interaction with other learners) without the high costs frequently associated with live, instructor-led learning.
>
> "The use of technology to deliver learning was nearly the same in both samples, at 36.9 percent in [Bench Marking Forum] BMF organizations and 36.3 percent in BEST [Award recipient] organizations. At least 60 percent of technology-based learning was online in 2005, and almost 90 percent of online learning was self-paced."

Just as e-learning has grown in acceptance and use within organizations, research in e-learning has also expanded in order to provide guidance to the complex decisions that you will have to make in selecting, designing, developing, and implementing a useful e-learning program or project. The expansion of research from the limited media-comparison and case studies that constituted most of the initial research, studies in e-learning now include hypotheses associated with the pedagogical, human computer interaction, business model, strategic implementation, mobile learning, change management, and other implications of e-learning at the individual, organizational, and societal levels. From traditional experimental studies to complex meta-analyses of multiple research findings, the diversity of e-learning research today can be helpful in guiding many organizational decisions.

In this chapter I will cover just a few of the major research findings that can provide initial guidance in the development of a successful e-learning effort. In addition, at the end of this chapter are many links to valuable online repositories of e-learning research, as well as information on useful books, research manuscripts, and journal articles that can help guide your practice.

e-Learning Theories and Frameworks

As a specialized application of distance education, e-learning builds on the theories and research of distance education, adult learning, and related disciplines. These include, but are not limited to, theories related to the industrialization of education, constructivism, systems theory, and equivalency theory. Of the grounded theories, the one that will likely have the most impact on your design and development of e-learning is the theory of transactional distance developed by Michael Moore of Penn State University. The theory, as explained by Moore in his chapter for the 2007 *Handbook of Distance Education*, relates three characteristics that are unique to distance education (and as a consequence also unique to e-learning) and their ability to moderate the impact that physical and temporal distance could otherwise have on learning and learner performance. The three characteristics relate to structure, dialogue, and autonomy.

Structure, within the theory, consists of the elements of learning such as lessons, objectives, assessments, feedback, and other elements common to instructional design. From the perspective of transactional distance, the continuum that ranges from very structured training to unstructured training is a primary factor in learning when training is done outside the boundaries of the traditional classroom. Structure within these terms could be at the course, administrative, or programmatic levels. This structure of an e-learning course or program then moderates the impact on learning when it is combined with variables of dialogue and autonomy. Within the theory, dialogue represents more than mere communication or interactions; dialogue specifically refers to what Moore describes as ''a particular kind of interpersonal interaction, and it happens after a course is designed, within the environment determined by the course structure when teachers exchange words and other symbols with learners, aimed at the latter's creation of knowledge'' (p. 92).

Dialogue within this context then represents the specific use of e-learning communications for instructors to assist learners in the development of skills and knowledge, beyond interactions that may or may not have those aims. Dialogue, when integrated with the structure of the e-learning course, can moderate the transactional distance that could otherwise limit learning. In theory, as e-learning structure increases, you should find subsequent increases in the transactional distance of learners, while increases in dialogue have the opposite effect—decreasing the transactional distance. The theory does not, however, provide directions for striking the ideal balance of these characteristics, since it would vary widely from situation to situation, objectives to objectives, and organization to organization.

Expanding Your Options

Train-the-trainer—workshops that teach individuals instructional skills to enable them to become effective in training roles. This enables subject-matter experts within an organization to impart their own knowledge and skills effectively to others within the organization.

Based on kevineikenberry.com definition (January 2009)

Last, learner *autonomy* is added as the third moderating variable for transactional distance. In combination with structure and dialogue, the level of autonomy that each learner demonstrates in relation to a specific e-learning experience further moderates learning at a distance. In theory, as the transactional distance increases in e-learning, then greater learner autonomy is necessary for learning objectives to be achieved. Again, the theory of transactional distance does not provide specific guidelines on how to balance the three moderating variables but it does provide e-learning developers with a framework for examining how e-learning programs, projects, and courses can address transactional distance in order to improve the performance of learners.

When designing specific e-learning courses, learning theories and instructional design theories will similarly have substantial influence on the design and development of learning activities. You should use information processes models, teaching-learning conversations, motivation, learning styles, and other theories, models, and frameworks as your foundations when creating specific lessons, assessments, instructional strategies, and learning events. While e-learning may not have a large theory base of its own, yet, there are many instructional and learning theories that should be applied in order to ensure the success of your learners and e-learning efforts.

Media Comparison Studies

Media alone do not improve learning. From software applications to new hardware devices, e-learning tools are routinely compared to traditional classroom training in order to gauge their relative effectiveness. While results from this research vary moderately from study to study (as does the quality of the research), the consensus of research findings with various forms of e-learning technologies have concluded that, across-the-board, the introduction of new media, by itself, makes no significant difference in learning when compared to traditional classroom instruction. Based on work first reported by the University of Southern California's Richard Clark in his 1985 meta-analysis of decades of research, Thomas Russell, of North Carolina State University, has now collected hundreds of studies with various educational technologies that further demonstrate the conclusion that technology alone makes no significant differences in learning. Initially publishing 355 examples in his 1999 book and posting hundreds of studies online since then, Russell provides copious examples that lay bare the authenticity of the "no significant difference" role of media in learning.

From online tools (such as learning management systems, desktop video, or downloadable podcasts) to hardware devices (such as, laptops, iPods, or mobile phones), the media tools that are used to deliver instructional content for e-learning, likewise, do not improve learning on their own. This isn't to say that new media can't improve the efficiency of learning in your organization or that technologies can't be used to capture the interest and motivate learners. Rather, these conclusions simply validate that the use of new technologies (for example, moving classes to desktop video conferences or making the Power-Point slides from a recorded lecture available for download to an iPod) will not improve learning or performance by themselves. It is, instead, the use of media to create effective learning events around content that is valid and engaging that has the greatest influence on learning and performance. From timely training materials and motivational activities to engaging feedback on performance and appropriate instructional strategies, quality content can often be delivered through e-learning media to effectively and efficiently produce the desired learning.

Pairing e-learning technologies with appropriate performance and learning objectives is, therefore, critical to the successful of any e-learning program or project. As part of the many decisions that lead to this desired alignment of objectives and instructional opportunities, the match of appropriate technologies (for instance, streaming audio with PowerPoint slides or interactive discussion boards) with the desired results of the e-learning program or project is critical (although not sufficient for success). In reviewing your options, remember that, while media options give you many new and exciting techniques for delivering instruction, the media you select will not by itself improve learning.

Multi-Media Development

The design and development of effective e-learning materials adheres to a relatively small number of grounded principles. We know, for instance, that adding appropriate graphics to complement written words in instructional materials can improve learning. Noting the research in this area, e-learning expert Ruth Clark, suggests in the 2002 article "Six Principles of Effective e-Learning" that "the trick is to use illustrations that are congruent with the instructional message. Images added for entertainment or dramatic value not only don't improve learning but they can actually depress learning." For example, Roxana Moreno and Richard Mayer, professors of psychology at the University of California Santa Barbara, have studied the effectiveness of multi-media for over a decade. Through numerous research experiments Moreno and Mayer have researched the impact and influence of differing combinations of multi-media elements (audio, animations, text, etc.) to determine which foster the greatest positive influence on learning and performance. In a 2000 study that mixed and matched text, auditory, and animated instructional content regarding topics including meteorology and lightning, the results illustrated that learners performed better when instructional animations included concurrent auditory narrations rather than text narrations. Later research also indicated that, by reducing the competition between verbal (text) and non-verbal (animation) screen images, you can improve learning and performance. Fortunately, advances in technology (such as access to broadband Internet connections, improved audio compression software, and others) allow this research to be applied in the development of e-learning content.

While the multi-media tools that are commonly available in e-learning (such as, PowerPoint, web pages) offer us many options for easily adding graphics to our instructional materials, nevertheless, alone these tools will not improve learning or performance. But when paired with grounded instructional strategies based on research, they can help us create more effective training. This isn't to say, however, that a little knowledge of research findings can't be dangerous. Moreno and Mayer's research also indicates that, while the addition of audio explanation of especially complex or unfamiliar graphics can help improve learning, the addition of background music and sounds that are not related to the instructional content can actually reduce learning and performance. As you can see, the application of research findings to multi-media development can be rather specific, and you will want to refer to the research literature routinely to ensure that you are applying the grounded principles that will best ensure learning and performance.

In a 2004 article for the *Journal of Educational Psychology*, Mayer and his colleagues report on the impact of personalized content in multi-media instruction. Students in three research studies received either personalized or non-personalized versions of an animated lesson on the human respiratory system. Using active voice, personalized instruction in a conversational tone led to significant higher learner performance on assessments of knowledge transfer (but without significant differences on assessments of retention). As a consequence, when you develop e-learning content, you should consider how personalized messages may be of value in supporting the transfer of knowledge to the workplace in your organization.

However, even as recently as 2006, Slovenian researchers Eva Jereb and Branislav Smitek describe the many challenges of integrating research findings into the practice: "Multimedia design is currently created by intuition [citing Sutcliffe]. Given the complexity of multimedia interaction, it is [however] unlikely that a craft-style approach will produce effective interfaces." As you can see, it is important that multi-media elements of any e-learning program or project be designed, developed, and implemented through systematic and research-grounded processes. While technology decisions may often drive the multi-media options available to e-learning efforts, it is the various learning design decisions that will ultimately lead to its success or failure. Use research from e-learning, education, distance education, training, human computer interactions, and other related disciplines to ensure that your multi-media e-learning capitalizes on the strengths of new technologies while avoiding the pitfalls that plaque many e-learning programs.

e-Learning Communities and Virtual Teams

In their chapter within Michael Moore's 2007 *Handbook of Distance Education*, Randy Garrison of the University of Calgary and Walter Archer of University of Saskatchewan advocate that distance education has progressed beyond a preoccupation with the limited focus on organizational and structural barriers that characterized earlier research. In the same way, e-learning is also expanding the boundaries of its research beyond a preoccupation on new technologies. One of the most pragmatic of these research foci is the nurturing of learning communities in the design and development of e-learning programs and courses. Based around a community of inquiry framework (which includes social, cognitive, and teaching presence), research in learning communities has ignited developments in the use of group and team e-learning.

While not required for achieving the objectives of all e-learning programs, developing learning communities within your e-learning programs or courses can be useful for many instructional goals that include for example, complex team-driven tasks or leadership skills. In 1994, for instance, Maryam Alavi at the

University of Maryland found that, among MBA students, those who used technology in their group decision making reported higher levels of skill development and overall grades in the course. More recently, research led by Leslie Moller of the University of North Texas demonstrated that developing a learning community can have positive impacts on the motivation of learners. As Moller and her colleagues report in a 2005 article for the *Quarterly Review of Distance Education*, this motivation did not, however, seem to carry over into desired changes in attitude.

In application, research in e-learning communities has given us practical recommendation for guiding the development of online teams, creating learning activities for online learners, facilitating online group processes, and encouraging learners to increase their social and cognitive presence within e-learning courses. All of these can, and should, guide your development of effective e-learning, as well as knowledge sharing programs within your organization. For instance, Australian researchers Colin Baskin, Michelle Barker, and Peter Woods studied the development of group skills (such as managing risk, being assertive, facilitating group processes, or performing situated group roles) within teams using information and communication technologies (ICTs). Their research, with special emphasis on the group skills required in industry applications, illustrates how virtual teams develop in relation to Kirkpatrick's four levels of evaluation. Interestingly, their findings, reported in a 2005 issue of the *British Journal of Educational Technology*, indicate the ICT-rich environments can foster the development of group skills and support the transfer of group skills into industry practice.

From leading your decisions on how to develop virtual teams to increasing learner motivation in training, the development of learning communities within e-learning has become substantiated as a promising tool for improving learning and performance. Future research will hopefully define best practices in the development of online learning communities and provide further evidence as to their effectiveness in relation to various instructional and performance objectives. For the time being, this is an exciting area of research to watch develop.

In summary, research on e-learning can provide many valuable insights that can enhance your design, development, and implementation efforts. In addition, and potentially with greater importance, the findings of e-learning research can help steer you away from the potential misapplication of marketing materials disguised as research findings.

WHEN TO APPLY

e-Learning is routinely a valued element within a large set of human performance interventions. For instance, if the time required for new employees to reach desired levels of performance exceeds your desires, then you may want to use an e-learning solution in coordination with a mentoring program, a renewed recruitment strategy, and a job aid to assist managers in communicating performance expectations with new employees. With these valued components, e-learning can then provide both the orientation training for new employees as well as continuing access to just-in-time knowledge for applying desirable behaviors in the workplace.

e-Learning is not, however, a one-size-fits-all solution for human perform-ance issues. Learners are not always prepared with the necessary study skills to adequately develop skills through e-learning activities, nor are the cultures of all organizations supportive of learning that takes place outside of the training classroom. As a result, it is important to assess the readiness of both the organization and its employees for e-learning before selecting this intervention as a means for accomplishing results.

If your desired performance relies on knowledge and/or skills that are not present, then e-learning may be a useful human performance technology. Similarly, if performers require continuing access to training materials as they are updated, then an e-learning solution may be a good option as part of your performance improvement efforts. Determining whether e-learning is appropriate for improvement efforts is therefore a question closely tied to the performance (and learning) objectives that you have identified through sys-tematic needs assessment and analysis processes.

STRENGTHS AND CRITICISMS

Some strengths and criticisms of using e-learning for performance improvement efforts follow.

Strengths

- e-Learning doesn't restrict the development of knowledge and skills to any specific time or place.
- e-Learning can be effectively designed and developed using variations on the instructional design processes often applied for traditional classroom training.
- e-Learning can provide content in multiple and/or combined formats more efficiently than earlier training options.
- e-Learning can offer dynamic content that allows for greater learner interactions with the content (for example, hypertext or interactive animations).
- When designed appropriately, e-learning can offer engaging and inter-active learning opportunities with similar effectiveness as those of the traditional classroom.

Criticisms

- e-Learning may not be appropriate for learners who do not have the experience, skills, or confidence to learn in non-traditional formats.
- The up-front development costs will often exceed those of traditional classroom training.
- When poorly designed and developed, e-learning courses can be less effective than other training options.
- Technology, rather than learning theory, routinely drives decisions about which media options to use in e-learning.
- e-Learning can present instructors with new challenges that may be beyond their current skills or confidence.
- e-Learning content can overuse media options and be distracting to learners.

RECOMMENDED DESIGN, DEVELOPMENT, AND IMPLEMENTATION PROCESS

To get started with your e-learning initiatives, I recommend the following process:

1. Identify the needs (gaps in results) that are to be addressed through the set of performance interventions.

2. Identify the performance objectives (and related learning objectives) that will be used to guide the design and development of the e-learning program or project. These performance objectives should define the detailed results that are to be accomplished by the e-learning program or project, either independently or in coordination with other performance interventions. Objectives can then guide your decisions throughout the design, development, and implementation as well as inform your evaluations after implementation.

3. Determine the desired alignment of the e-learning program or project with the other performance improvement interventions (for more information, see my 2007 book *Performance by Design*). For example, will e-learning provide for desired learning objectives as part of a new employee orientation while job aids and mentoring will provide for continuing professional development? Verify this alignment early in the planning stage and then assess your adherence to this alignment throughout the design, development, and implementation processes; this will keep you from either drifting away from coordinated results or contributing results at the expense of other programs.

4. For identified performance objectives, complete a task analysis (for more information, see 1989's *Handbook of Task Analysis Procedures* by David Jonassen, Wallace Hannum, and Martin Tessmer). Likewise, for each derived learning objective complete an instructional analysis (see Walter Dick's classic *The Systematic Design of Instruction*, currently in its seventh edition). These analyses should provide you with detailed information on both how current results are being achieved as well as "best practice" information about how desired results can be accomplished in the future. Also, conduct analyses of the learners and the performance environment as inputs into the design of your e-learning program or project. Although you will want to avoid "analysis paralysis," you do want to enter the design and development processes with clear and detailed information on what learners must know and be able to do in order for performance objectives to be accomplished.

5. Based on the information you have collected, determine whether your e-learning program or project is more appropriate for rapid-design, traditional-learning, or strategic e-learning (see Table 24.1). Based on this classification, you can select appropriate instructional design and development frameworks (or models) for creating effective instructional content.

6. Based on the selected category of e-learning and the associated design framework (or model), develop an e-learning management plan. The plan should include pre-design, design and development, and post-development stages, with each stage including the tasks that must be completed in order for an effective e-learning program or project to be achieved. From identifying partners and generating team roles to determining critical deliverables and due dates, your management plan should provide a comprehensive guide to all stages of e-learning development.

7. Systematically manage each of the e-learning design, development, and implementation processes. In the design of any e-learning program or project, you will want to ensure that there is a systematic approach that links objectives, assessments, instructional strategies, media decisions, formative evaluation, implementation, and program evaluation. While rapid design and development may integrate and simultaneously execute several of these steps, the alignment of each is essential to the creation of e-learning materials that lead to learning and performance no matter which category of e-learning you are creating.

8. Verify throughout the design and development of your e-learning programs or courses that your processes remain focused on the performance objectives that are to be accomplished by learners. Technology changes, challenges, and opportunities can each distract from the design

and development efforts, leading your e-learning efforts away from the targeted performance improvements.

9. Complete a formative evaluation of your e-learning content and materials. Have representatives of the general learner population who will use the e-learning complete both early prototypes as well as finalized versions of the learning materials in order to assess their effectiveness, efficiency, motivating influence, and other characteristics. Individual and group formative evaluations should be used to ensure that adequate feedback for making improvements is received.

10. Coordinate the implementation of your e-learning products with the implementation of other performance technologies that are part of your performance improvement initiative. Synchronize the implementation of your e-learning products with the implementation of other performance technologies in order to ensure that the success of the e-learning programs do not come at the expense of the other performance technologies or the entire improvement system.

Table 24.1 Comparison of e-Learning Categories

Category Development	Timeframe Estimates	Budget for Development	Developed by	Design Resources
Rapid	< 3 weeks	Staff of one to three professionals and little or no budget	SMEs with templates and training professional guidance	*Rapid Instructional Design* by George Piskurich (2006); *Creating Successful e-Learning* by Michael Allen (2006)
Traditional	three to eleven weeks	$5,000 to $30,000 per instructional hour	Training professionals, such as instructional designers, instructors, course authors	*e-Learning and the Science of Instruction* by Ruth Clark & Richard Mayer (2007); *Designing Web-Based Training* by William Horton (2000); *Web-Based Training* by Margaret Driscoll (2002)

(Continued)

Table 24.1 (*Continued*)

Category Development	Timeframe Estimates	Budget for Development	Developed by	Design Resources
Strategic	12 + weeks	Often blended, costs can go higher	A cross-functional team that includes HR, instructional design, and others	*The Systematic Design of Instruction* by Walter Dick (2008); *Beyond e-Learning* by Marc Rosenberg (2005)

Based on Josh Bersin and Jennifer DeVries' 2004 article ''Rapid e-Learning: What Works.''

CRITICAL SUCCESS FACTORS

While the quality of content is essential to the success of an e-learning program, by itself it is not sufficient for success. Attribution of success must therefore be spread across several factors that each contribute to achievement of valuable results.

Social

- If you introduce e-learning into an organizational culture that has a tradition of classroom training, it can be challenging. Successful implementations of e-learning often require extensive change management strategies that address the motivation, attitudes, and confidence of employees to effectively use e-learning opportunities.

- Prepare learners with the necessary technical skills and study strategies. e-Learning is routinely new to learners and, while they may have a strong record of success in traditional training courses, they may require additional skills (such as critical reading, effective online group development, and communication skills) that are unique to e-learning courses.

- Within many e-learning programs or courses, you should create an interactive environment in which learners can engage with others to build and share knowledge.

Political

- Like other performance technologies, e-learning initiatives are most successful when they have a strong advocate within the organization's leadership. If you do not have the political capital to ensure the long-term success of the e-learning program or project, then identifying additional advocates in various parts of the organization may be necessary.

- Do not invest all of your political capital into a single e-learning technology. Technologies quickly come and go in e-learning, and therefore you will want to focus your performance improvement strategies about the accomplishment of performance objectives rather than the implementation of any specific hardware or software component.

Economic

- Secure long-term funding for e-learning is necessary since ongoing maintenance and improvements are essential. Too often e-learning projects are viewed (and consequently funded) as a short-term quick-fix rather than a strategic investment.
- Do not underestimate the time required for technical development and implementation, as well as the instructional design phases, of a successful e-learning program.

Legal

- Familiarize yourself with and avoid violating the copyright or privacy policies of your organization when implementing an e-learning solution.

Technical

- The technical implementation of e-learning greatly depends on the infrastructure already existing within your organization and the scope of your e-learning requirements. If you are implementing a new medium- or large-scale learning management system you should likely plan for twelve to eighteen months of technical development lead time before any courses can be made available.
- Verify that the information technology and/or technical helpdesk employees within your organization are familiar with the e-learning course and/or platform before releasing it to learners. Inevitably, there will be technical problems with any e-learning course or system, and consequently adequate technical support should be prepared.

SUMMARY

For many performance improvement initiatives where the development of knowledge and/or skills is required, e-learning can provide a valuable option to be considered when creating your improvement system. When paired with mentoring, motivation, new technology, or other performance interventions, e-learning can further provide unique opportunities to expand learning within your organization, without the traditional limitation of time and location that plague classroom training. The successful implementation of an e-learning program or project should not, however, be assumed. The successful design, development, and implementation of an e-learning initiative require systematic planning and execution.

Notes

- The executive summary of Rivera and Paradise's annual state of the industry report can be found at http://www.astd.org/NR/rdonlyres/791AD143-0F07-4A1F-A974-0149C5D3360D/0/SOIR_2006_Executive_Summary.pdf.

- Thomas Russell's online collection of research illustrating that technology alone makes no significant difference in learning can be found at http://www.nosignificantdifference.org.

- More information on the research of Richard Mayer can be found at http://www.psych.ucsb.edu/people/faculty/mayer/

- For an illustration of the relationships among education, distance education, e-learning, and even m-learning, see Georgiev, Georgieva, and Trajkovski, 2006.

References

Allen, M. W. (2006). *Creating successful e-learning: A rapid system for getting it right first time, every time.* San Francisco: Pfeiffer.

Alavi, M. (1994). Computer-mediated collaborative learning: An empirical evaluation. *MIS Quarterly, 18*(2), pp. 159–174.

Baskin, C., Barker, M., & Woods, P. (2005). When group work leaves the classroom does group skills development also go out the window? *British Journal of Educational Technology, 36*(1), 19–31.

Bersin, J., & DeVries, J. (2004). Rapid e-learning: What works. Retrieved July 17, 2007, from www.learn.com/files/pdf/111204_Rapid_E_learning(1).pdf

Clark, R. E. (1983). Reconsidering research on learning from media. *Review of Educational Research, 53*(4), 445–459.

Clark, R. E. (1985). Evidence for confounding in computer-based instruction studies: Analyzing the meta analyses. *Educational Communication and Technology Journal, 33*(4), 249–262.

Clark, R. E. (1994). Media will never influence learning. *Educational Technology Research & Development, 42*(2), 21–29.

Clark, R. E. (2002). Six principles of effective e-learning: What works and why. *e-Learning Solutions e-Magazine.* Retrieved June 20, 2007, from www.elearningguild.com/pdf/2/091002DES-H.pdf.

Clark, R., & Mayer, R. E. (2002). *e-Learning and the science of instruction: Proven guidelines for consumers and designers of multimedia learning.* San Francisco: Pfeiffer.

Dick, W. O., Carey, L., & Carey, J.O. (2004). *The systematic design of instruction.* Boston: Allyn & Bacon.

Driscoll, M. (2002). *Web-based training: Designing e-learning experiences.* San Francisco: Pfeiffer.

Garrison, D., & Archer, W. (2007). A theory of community of inquiry. In M. G. Moore & W. G. Anderson (Eds.), *Handbook of distance education.* Mahwah, NJ: Lawrence Erlbaum Associates.

Georgiev, T., Georgieva, E., & Trajkovski, G. (2006). Transitioning from e-learning to m-learning: Present issues and future challenges. SNPD2006. *Proceedings of the Seventh ACIS International Conference on Software Engineering, Artificial Intelligence, Networking, and Parallel/Distributed Computing,* pp. 349–353.

Jereb, E., & Smitek, B. (2006). Applying multimedia instruction in e-learning. *Innovations in Education and Teaching International, 43*(1), 15–27.

Jonassen, D. H., Hannum, W. H., & Tessmer, M. (1989). *Handbook of task analysis procedures.* New York: Praeger.

Horton, W. (2000). *Designing web-based training: How to teach anyone anything anywhere anytime.* Hoboken, NJ: John Wiley & Sons.

Mayer, R. E., Fennell, S., Farmer, L., & Campbell, J. (2004). A personalization effect in multimedia learning: Students learn better when words are in conversational style rather than formal style. *Journal of Educational Psychology, 96,* 389–395.

Mayer, R. E., Heiser, J., & Lonn, S. (2001). Cognitive constraints on multimedia learning: When presenting more material results in less understanding. *Journal of Educational Psychology, 93*(1), 187–198.

Moller, L., Huett, J., Holder, D.Young, J.et al. (2005). Examining the impact of learning communities on motivation. *Quarterly Review of Distance Education, 6*(2), 137–143, 182–184.

Moore, M. (2007). The theory of transactional distance. In M. G. Moore & W. G. Anderson (Eds.), *Handbook of distance education.* Mahwah, NJ: Lawrence Erlbaum Associates.

Moreno, R., & Mayer, R. (1999). Cognitive principles of multimedia learning: The role of modality and contiguity. *Journal of Educational Psychology, 91*(2), 358–368.

Moreno, R., & Mayer, R. (2000). A coherence effect in multimedia learning: The case for minimizing irrelevant sounds in the design of multimedia instructional messages. *Journal of Educational Psychology, 92*(1), 117–125.

Piskurich, G. M. (2006). *Rapid instructional design: Learning ID fast and right.* San Francisco: Pfeiffer.

Rivera, R., & Paradise, A. (2006). *State of the industry in leading enterprises.* Alexandria, VA: ASTD. Retrieved July 17, 2007, from http://www.astd.org/NR/rdonlyres/ 791AD143-0F07-4A1F-A974-0149C5D3360D/0/SOIR_2006_Executive_Summary.pdf.

Rosenberg, M. J. (2005). *Beyond e-learning: Approaches and technologies to enhance organizational knowledge, learning, and performance.* San Francisco: Pfeiffer.

Russell, T. L. (n.d.). No significant difference phenomenon website. Retrieved July 11, 2007, from http://www.nosignificantdifference.org/.

Russell, T. L. (1999). *The no significant difference phenomenon as reported in 355 research reports, summaries and papers.* Raleigh, NC: North Carolina State University.

Watkins, R. (2007). *Performance by design: The selection, design, and development of performance technologies that achieve results.* Amherst, MA: HRD Press.

Recommended Readings and Websites

Berge, Z. L., & Mrozowski, S. (2001). Review of research in distance education, 1990 to 1999. *The American Journal of Distance Education, 15*(3).

Carabajal, K., LaPointe, D., & Gunawardena, C. (2007). Group development in online distance learning groups. In M. G. Moore & W. G. Anderson (Eds.), *Handbook of distance education.* Mahwah, NJ: Lawrence Erlbaum Associates.

Dede, C., Dieterle, E.Clarke, J., Ketelhut, D., & Nelson, B. (2007). Media-based learning styles. In M. G. Moore & W. G. Anderson (Eds.), *Handbook of distance education.* Mahwah, NJ: Lawrence Erlbaum Associates.

Hannafin, M., Hill, J., Song, L., & West.R. (2007). Cognitive perspectives on technology-enhanced distance learning environments. In M. G. Moore & W. G. Anderson (Eds.), *Handbook of distance education.* Mahwah, NJ: Lawrence Erlbaum Associates.

Holmberg, B. (2007). A theory of teaching-learning conversations. In M. G. Moore & W. G. Anderson (Eds.), *Handbook of distance education.* Mahwah, NJ: Lawrence Erlbaum Associates.

Peters, O. (2007). The most industrialized form of education. In M. G. Moore & W. G. Anderson (Eds.), *Handbook of distance education.* Mahwah, NJ: Lawrence Erlbaum Associates.

Watkins, R. (2006). Proactive planning for success. *Distance Learning, 3*(2), 59–61.

Watkins, R. (2004). Aligning e-learning with strategic plans. *Distance Learning, 1*(5), 33–34.

Watkins, R. (2005a). *75 e-Learning Activities: Making Online Learning Interactive.* San Francisco: Pfeiffer.

Watkins, R. (2005b). Developing interactive e-learning activities. *Performance Improvement, 44*(5), 5–7.

Watkins, R., & Corry, M. (2007). *e-Learning companion* (2nd ed.). Boston: Houghton Mifflin.

http://www.elearningguild.com. e-Learning Guild

http://www.elearning-reviews.org/and http://www.wisc.edu/depd/html/artmonth3.htm. Reviews of recent research on e-learning.

EDITORIAL CONNECTIONS

As illustrated in Chapter Twenty-Four, e-learning is a valuable performance intervention that offers you flexibility that is not found in traditional classroom programs. By taking learning out of the classroom, e-learning can help find new ways to engage participants and support the transition from learning to application—especially when paired with electronic performance support systems (see Chapter Thirteen) or performance aids (see Chapter Fourteen). e-Learning also uses this flexibility to create an effective continuum that stretches from technology-enriched classroom training on one end to distance learning on the other—with blended learning filling the space between.

Expanding Your Options

Brown bag lunch sessions—training or educational presentations provided to an organization's members. Brown bag sessions were traditionally scheduled during lunchtime, with attendees being encouraged to bring their lunches with them.

The combination of different learning delivery formats, known as "blended learning," enhances e-learning by mixing and matching what can be done best in person with the strengths of other delivery formats. For instance, you may want to consider using online resources to build foundational skills before a short face-to-face workshop that focuses on the application of those skills through case study exercises. Many other mixes of technology-enriched learning also fall within the umbrella terms of e-learning and blended learning, of course.

As with all other performance interventions, e-learning may not be appropriate for all of your improvement efforts. Remember, no one solution is appropriate for all of the diverse performance issues of an organization. It is therefore all the more critical that you recognize the strengths and limitations of all performance interventions in order to make justifiable decisions about which will best achieve desired results. Just as you would want to independently consider the benefits and risks of incentives, rewards, recognitions as performance interventions, within the performance improvement domain of knowledge and skills you should assess, analyze, compare, and contrast a range of interventions that may be appropriate for your improvement effort.

While both traditional classroom training and e-learning frequently focus on the growth of individual knowledge and skills, the development of team learning is also a critical element in many improvement efforts. After all, when teams grow together—building shared knowledge and growing their skills to function as a team—they increase their capacity to accomplish significant and desired results. Similarly, teams can also expand their ability to move from a collection of individual tasks and achievements to the accomplishment of collective results as a team (that is, the whole is greater than the sum of the parts).

WHAT'S COMING UP

In Chapter Twenty-Five, Scott Schaffer examines the important role of cross-disciplinary teams in the development of knowledge and skills to improve performance. As you will read in the chapter, cross-disciplinary teams can be an effective intervention for accomplishing useful results on many levels. You can, for instance, use cross-disciplinary teams to build the knowledge and skills of individuals within the organization as they relate to specific performance issues. If, for example, logistical challenges are too inter-related to be parsed out to individuals (such as managing inventory, distribution, and labor), then you could use cross-disciplinary teams as an intervention to improve performance by transitioning these responsibilities from assorted individuals to a single team.

Expanding Your Options

Matrix management—an organizational or management structure that takes employees with similar skills and pools them around (typically) two functional tasks. For example, employees may have a role related to a specific product line, as well as a role related to a business process such as research, accounting, or sales that cuts across multiple product lines.

Based on wikipedia.org definition (January 2009)

In the same way, cross-disciplinary teams can be used to support the implementation of other performance interventions in your improvement effort. One application of this might involve using a team approach to implement a newly designed set of processes and procedures (see Chapter Seventeen). By working together as an interdisciplinary unit, individual members can benefit and learn from the experiences and knowledge of others on the team.

Expanding Your Options

Cross-training—training that cover several tasks within a department or organization.

Based on businessdictionary.com definition (January 2009)

In the chapter, Schaffer offers practical techniques and steps for effectively using teams to improve performance. Consider the value of integrating a cross-disciplinary team approach into your system of performance interventions: a team ability to accomplish significant results is frequently greater than the sum of individual member's capacity.

CHAPTER TWENTY-FIVE

Cross-Disciplinary Team Learning

Scott P. Schaffer

INTRODUCTION

Understanding how to support teams has become a matter of urgency for many organizations. Globalization has created information, communication, and technological challenges and opportunities that require collaboration. Much research on the power of team learning in such collaborations suggests ways to improve team learning processes and effectiveness. Using teams to improve organizational performance gained currency as part of the total quality movement, wherein activities are based on teamwork. A review of more than a hundred studies identified three major categories of team process: (1) identification and matching of individual goals and perceived interests and abilities with attributes of the team project; (2) formation of a group of individuals via project coordination, management, goal setting, leadership, resource provision, and several other such support systems; and (3) completion of a project and the related documentation requirements and reflection related to project satisfaction and success. While all teams theoretically move through these processes, there is great variation in the context or situations in which team work is performed. Performance support systems for teams should be focused on both individual and team performance and the related practices necessary to achieve results. An example of such as system is the cross-disciplinary team learning (CDTL) framework developed to guide designers of team performance systems, especially teams comprised of people from different disciplines and cultures.

DESCRIPTION

A cross-disciplinary or multi-disciplinary team is comprised of two or more individuals from different disciplines interacting to solve a complex, ill-structured problem. Such teams have many characteristics in common with groups, but groups, by definition, work on less complex and/or less enduring tasks. Teams from the same discipline may engage in similar processes as cross-disciplinary teams but have less potential for new knowledge creation, given their more narrow perspective. Cross-disciplinary team performance can thus be thought of as an extension of task completion to include innovation and organizational capacity building (see Part Nine of this handbook). Typically, such a team will be represented by different levels of technical expertise as well as non-technical expertise in areas such as sales, marketing, human resources, accounting, and so on. Many examples of such teams can be found in the design arena within software development and product design firms. An example of an innovative team in the manufacturing sector is nicely illustrated by Dorothy Leonard, who describes how a small steel company leverages the knowledge of its associates across technical, quality, and managerial functions to solve emerging problems. Cross-disciplinary teams are also naturally found in customer service environments, where content experts and sales associates are often teamed, and in healthcare, where physicians, nurses, physicians' assistants, and therapists may be part of a treatment team.

WHAT WE KNOW FROM RESEARCH

As organizations have become flatter, the horizontal relationships between workers and work functions have been the focus of much research. Famous for 1989's *Cooperation and Competition*, Johnson and Johnson's fundamental work related to cooperation within groups and the interdependence of group members. Studies of team work and high performance work organizations also increased dramatically as organizations began organizing work units and cells as part of their total quality management and process improvement efforts. Furthermore, Dorothy Leonard-Barton's research, published in 1995 as *Wellsprings of Knowledge*, focused on how organizations develop capacity to learn and innovate while solving problems highlighted the importance of knowledge building by high performing, cross-functional teams.

Expanding Your Options

Job rotation systems—job designs in which employees moved between two or more jobs in a planned manner. The goal is to expose the employees to different experiences and a wider variety of skills to enhance job satisfaction as well as provide cross-training.

Based on businessdictionary.com definition (January 2009)

Organizational learning theorists such as Peter Senge, Ikujiro Nonaka, and Hirotaka Takeuchi also propose that individual interaction is the basic unit of knowledge and that teamwork is the primary way to disseminate that knowledge throughout the organization. According to Peter Scholtes, Brian Joiner, and Barbara Streibel's *Team Handbook*, teams appear to be particularly effective, or at least more effective than individuals, when: a task is complex, creativity is needed, the path forward is not clear, efficient use of resources is required, fast learning is necessary, high levels of commitment are desirable, implementation requires cooperation with others, and the task requires cross-functional processes. What does a high-performing team look like? High-performing teams are extremely results-focused and often work with a high degree of autonomy and flexibility. Such teams may be formed to solve problems that emerge during large complex projects. Such teams may be called upon to redesign a process or develop a new product in response to customer requirements or a change in the availability of materials. High-performance teams are also formed proactively with a mandate to create new approaches to doing business.

Recognition of the power of team learning has resulted in a plethora of studies suggesting ways to improve team learning processes and effectiveness. A 2005 review of more than one hundred such studies led by psychology professor Daniel Ilgen and management professor John Hollenbeck at Michigan State University has identified three major categories of team process that consistently emerge: (1) identification and matching of individual goals and perceived interests and abilities with attributes of the team project; (2) formation of a group of individuals via project coordination, management, goal setting, leadership, resource provision, and several other such support systems; and (3) completion of a project and the related documentation requirements and reflection related to project satisfaction and success. While all teams theoretically move through these processes, there is great variation in the context or situations in which team work is performed. *Context* has been identified as a critical mediating factor in team performance. But how does a manager or team member understand the importance of context and the impact it has on performance? For an answer, we turn back to academia and collaboration research as well as the role of activity systems in defining context.

Within the academic community, computer-supported collaborative work (CSCW) emerged as a way to systematically examine the impact of emerging information and communications technologies on collaboration efforts in groups or teams. The CSCW movement eventually was subsumed more or less within the learning sciences and computer supported collaborative learning (CSCL). This evolution has created both opportunity and challenges relative to applying CSCL research findings to practice. A focus on collaborative learning and the group unit of analysis has been a step toward a better understanding of team collective thinking or team cognition. Examination of the team as unit of analysis has evolved from an emphasis on the social and cultural aspects of team systems. One example of this type of framework that has risen in popularity is the use of activity theory to describe team interactions from a socio-cultural systems point of view. The outcomes of an activity system are the result of interactions between people, the artifacts they create, tools they use, how they divide labor, the roles different members of the community (managers, customers, suppliers, consultants) play, and the rules under which teams and the community must operate.

Activity systems help to describe team context from a social and cultural point of view. Research situated within globally distributed teams of architecture, building construction, and engineering school at Stanford University help to explain team context from a cross-disciplinary learning point of view. These researchers studied how team learning evolved during a project and, especially, how (and if) team members from different disciplines interacted in innovative ways. Using descriptive and qualitative methods of data collection with large numbers of students, patterns of team learning they characterized as cross-disciplinary learning or CDL were identified. These patterns were summarized as (1) *islands of knowledge*, defined as individual problem solving focused on their own discipline-specific knowledge; (2) *awareness*, defined as recognition of the potential importance of other team members' discipline knowledge to the project; (3) *appreciation*, characterized by active listening, questioning, and concept development; and (4) *understanding*, characterized by team members active discussion about and use of the language of one another's discipline. As team members evolved toward understanding, Fruchter and Emery report in the 1999 *Proceedings of the Computer Support for Collaborative Learning* conference, projects became more innovative in design and that teams generated "new knowledge" that resulted in process improvements or in some cases whole new processes.

A framework for assessing and developing teams I created is shown in Figure 25.1. This cross-disciplinary team learning (CDTL) framework provides theoretical grounding for assessing team learning and performance requirements.

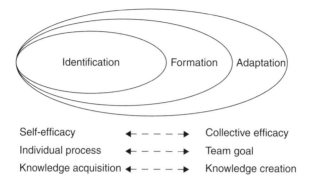

Figure 25.1 Macro-Level Cross-Disciplinary Team Learning Framework.

Performance support systems for teams should be focused on both individual and team performance and the related practices necessary to achieve results. The CDTL framework has been developed to guide designers of team performance systems, especially teams comprised of different disciplines and cultures. It includes the following elements: *Identification*, *Formation*, and *Adaptation*. The relationship between the elements is complex, dynamic, and non-linear. Behaviors, attitudes, and cognitions associated with each of the elements have been validated with over one thousand individuals and 350 cross-disciplinary, project-based teams in a university setting. Scales based on the framework were represented by statements describing each of the CDTL elements. These scales were certified by team learning experts as part of a content validation study. Questionnaire items based on the scales were administered to team members whose responses were then aligned with CDTL elements via factor analysis to validate the scales.

WHEN TO APPLY

While there is a high degree of complexity involved in supporting cross-disciplinary teams, many organizations have other performance improvement processes in place that can be leveraged to help keep teams on track. Employee selection and orientation training that emphasizes cooperation and a team approach would create conditions for successful team formation. Knowledge management systems (see Chapter Fifteen) that emphasize creation of new knowledge that can be spread to the rest of the organization help create a culture that promotes innovation. Such a culture is essential for cross-disciplinary teams that thrive on being able to draw from the knowledge and experiences of others. From a technology support perspective, existing performance support systems may be adapted to address team needs. Performance support systems often have extrinsic support features that may be readily used by teams to manage processes, communicate, or share information.

Establishing cross-disciplinary teams is critical for organizations that place a high value on innovative solutions and developing a capacity to learn and solve future problems. This tends to be the case for diverse teams working on relatively complex and long-term projects. These are typically product design and development teams but also could be implementation teams or smaller teams involved in managing caseloads over a long period of time. A definite trend in team research is a renewed focus on teams in customer service environments including healthcare. Teams put together for the purpose of completing a relatively routine or short-term task are not as likely to benefit greatly from an emphasis on team interaction. Teams are more likely to benefit from support based on CDTL when they are comprised of individuals from at least two different disciplines, when the project task(s) is sufficiently complex and of long enough duration, and when the development of long-term organizational learning capacity is part of the mission of the organization. In recognition of the fact that many organizations have little expertise with using teams, a summary of a few strengths and criticisms of cross-disciplinary teams follows.

STRENGTHS AND CRITICISMS

Strengths

- Teams are more effective than individuals when a project is complex and requires a creative solution.
- Cross-disciplinary teams produce a wider variety of creative, innovative solutions. The logic follows that organizations that nurture diverse teams develop the capacity to solve future problems or respond to opportunities, and research supports this contention to a degree.
- Forming teams with individuals from different disciplines greatly increases the number of divergent ideas generated during brainstorming and scoping/defining phases of a project.

Criticisms

- Evidence of the effectiveness of diverse teams is mixed. Literature shows that, while diverse teams are creative, they are also prone to inefficiencies and longer cycle times.

- While a culture of learning within an organization is necessary for capacity-building, organizational cultures that value task completion over innovation will generally not see the potential benefits of supporting cross-disciplinary learning processes.

WHEN TO APPLY

An old adage in the instructional design field suggests that understanding the task, the learner, and the context leads to effective learning experiences. Thus, it is not surprising that these factors are essential to understanding the design of support systems for cross-disciplinary team learning. Complex, ill-structured tasks or problems that have many possible solutions are ideal for cross-disciplinary teams that will naturally bring a variety of perspectives to the situation. Identification of individual behaviors, cognitions, and attitudes as the team evolves is critical to the design of learner feedback systems. In terms of context, the team socio-cultural system can be characterized as the tension between project outcomes, artifacts, tools, roles, customers-community, and organizational rules and guidelines.

The CDTL framework best addresses opportunities to leverage existing capability. For the most part, teams are made up of dedicated individuals who want to do a good job. The challenge may be that they have little experience working with others with different skill sets than their own. In the previously mentioned healthcare example, the performance challenge is that there are different levels of service that must be provided. A patient makes an appointment with a staff person, then is first seen by a nurse or practitioner, then is seen by a physician, then perhaps a specialist or therapist, and then follow up is provided again by the nurse practitioner. Ideally, one person would do all of this, but this is just not possible. From a performance improvement perspective, a challenge such as this requires much more than training to learn how to be a better team member. What is required is clear alignment of an organization's vision and team and individual performance goals. From a cultural point of view, organizations that value team and cross-disciplinary team learning and the collective expertise that is brought to bear on problems should communicate this value to others.

Guiding principles and related behaviors to support team learning have been developed to help transfer CDTL research to practical settings. Principles are meant to provide a crosswalk to competencies or skill sets that organizations may have already identified as important for team work. The design of task, learner, and context support, John Wedman has asserted since 2004, should be aligned with adequate resources to support team performance. A description of each principle is provided in Table 25.1.

Table 25.1 Principles of CDTL

Principles	Description
Support individual and team self-regulated learning	Individuals set personal goals for the project and monitor them relative to team goals. Team process goals are monitored relative to its cross-disciplinary evolution.
Expect teams to learn and perform across disciplines during projects	Specific guidelines for individual and team learning and performance are incorporated into the performance review process.
Reward team member provision of ongoing, experiential feedback	Peer feedback is supported with a documentation process that compensates high performers. Subsequent new knowledge generation is part of overall team performance evaluation.
Provide tools to manage, build, and share new team knowledge	New knowledge assets generated by the team are captured by collaboration systems that support information sharing and communications.
Incentivize teamwork that leads to innovation and capacity-building	Highlight accomplishments of high knowledge-generating, innovative teams with case studies, bonuses, and other recognition.

RECOMMENDED DESIGN, DEVELOPMENT, AND IMPLEMENTATION PROCESSES

Applying these principles in practice follows the basic CDTL processes identified in Figure 25.1. These overlapping and iterative processes are not linear but will be revisited throughout a project. The processes include:

1. *Identify individual and team goals and develop a system to monitor or track goal attainment.* This is similar to the analysis phase of the ADDIE model given that performance goals of the project must be identified and specific objectives for accomplishing tasks assigned. Performers also assess their levels of self-efficacy and overall readiness to effectively participate on the project. Ideally, individual development plans are incorporated into the overall performance system. From a team learning perspective, individuals begin the process of becoming aware of other team members' backgrounds and experiences.

2. *Form team roles, sub-teams, and support systems.* This phase incorporates elements of analysis, design, and development as team leaders and role players emerge and objectives for the project are continually clarified. Information and communications technologies that incorporate features that support critical reflection and peer feedback are selected and individuals are provided guidance in using these tools. As teams form, individuals become increasingly aware of and begin to appreciate the perspectives of team members from other disciplines.

3. *Adapt project processes and deliverables to reflect team knowledge.* In this phase, team members implement and test ideas and concepts based on their collective understanding of project and client requirements. This phase includes project completion and reflective evaluation of project success by team members and clients. Teams that have effectively learned from one another during the project through high-quality interactions would be expected to be more creative and innovative as reflected in the products and reusable knowledge generated during the project.

Supporting Technologies

A common challenge for many teams is identifying technologies to support cross-disciplinary work, which often requires high levels of collaboration and communication. While it is not likely that teams will be able or even want to develop their own tools, they may be in a position to recommend collaboration/communication tools, features, or requirements to the information technology function in their organization. Table 25.2 shows the alignment of CDTL

Table 25.2 CDTL Design Principles for Supporting Selection/Evaluation of Collaborative Software Applications

Support Systems/Tools	CDTL Design Prescriptions
Embedded implicit or explicit cues or scaffolds in tools such as journals, blogs, and other personal reflection spaces	Support individual and team goal setting and planning, guide individual and team self-reflection, facilitate individual and team self-observation of performance
Access to individual and team spaces and their interactions/contributions	Facilitate setting of individual and team learning and performance goals, and provide spaces for individual and team self-assessment. Support the inclusion

Support Systems/Tools	CDTL Design Prescriptions
	of team members' discipline-centered descriptions and profiles and promote awareness of team members' ongoing contributions
Smart links to customized, disciplined-based vocabularies and glossaries	Provide access to language tools; track team members' cross-disciplinary language adoption
Chat, discussions forums, and other communication tools with embedded mechanisms for reaching common agreement (techniques to close communication loops)	Support negotiation of cross-disciplinary perspectives and language and use of clear and concise communication among team members
Contextual comment boxes, voting tools, quality assurance and product/process satisfaction polls	Facilitate intra-team peer feedback; encourage client and community feedback; enable internal and external expert feedback; support feedback across teams
Include aural and visual cues of face-to-face discourse and provide examples of effective and ineffective ways of disagreeing and criticizing	Support effective interactions among team members; integrate different forms of discourse and knowledge representation
Discussion forums with branching and mapping features	Facilitate unified team areas for problem-centered discourse. Provide access to semantically structured knowledge maps and information repositories. Encourage team members to build on each other's work and ideas
Allow team members to create a community that connects actual, past, and prospective team members, experts, other project teams and stakeholders	Facilitate social networking
Collaborative writing/design tool with parallel access to chat or discussions	Provide facilities for simultaneous task allocation and articulation
Create collaborative meeting agendas, electronic meeting system, alternatives generation and voting, etc.	Support team decision-making processes

principles with the features of four commonly available collaboration tools or systems. This table also illustrates how these tools vary in their ability to support team practices thought to be critical to innovation. A particular challenge is for many teams to move beyond a project focus that emphasizes task completion to a focus on problem solving and user-centeredness. The latter requires interaction among individuals from multiple disciplines with a range of experience and expertise levels. Design principles for supporting teams shown in the table are tied to the performance support, social-cultural, and knowledge development systems that underlie the CDTL framework.

CRITICAL SUCCESS FACTORS

Much research has focused on identifying factors necessary for successful implementation of teams. These factors generally cluster into system factors and human factors. System factors relate to vision, management, performance measures, and political considerations, while human factors relate to knowledge and skills, leadership, and culture. These factors are briefly described below:

Vision

- Organizations that succeed because they "know what they know" and can act upon this knowledge have created both a top-down and bottom-up approach to innovation. Leaders who understand the importance of aligning resources with high-yield, hard-to-measure team learning processes must be willing to take risks. The payoff, more innovative products, services, and processes, is much easier to measure.

Management

- Great cross-disciplinary teams are not accidents. Planning, goal setting, and feedback systems are an integral part of the CDTL framework. Teams have difficulties when they fail to include reflection time in project schedules. Reflection helps managers see where more support is needed, when roles can be shifted, or how barriers to performance may be addressed.

Measures

- Clearly defined mission, vision, and goals understood and developed by team members strongly relate to successful teamwork. Teams with clearly defined missions are able to, in turn, define roles and clarify the importance of tasks to be completed. This team focus creates an expectation of success that is measureable and aligned with customer requirements.

Politics

- The identification and management of external relationships and their impact on team processes helps teams think systemically and value contributions of entities outside the team. Government, society, suppliers, customers, managers, and other teams all have potential influence on team process and outcomes. Seeing the process from the point of view of these entities can be a particular strength of a cross-disciplinary team.

Knowledge and Skills

- A key strength of cross-disciplinary teams is the breadth of knowledge and skills possessed by its members relative to homogeneous teams. This strength is represented in the team's collective problem-solving and creative abilities, as well as the potential array of technical skills integrated into overall team processes.

Leadership and Culture

- It is one thing to build tools and processes that can support teams and then hope they will use them. It is quite another to nurture a participatory culture that seeks out such tools to support innovation and creativity. Armed with a clear vision, goal, expectations, and potential rewards, cross-disciplinary teams become subcultures or micro-systems that have the potential to become viral and spread influence throughout an organization. This kind of contagion may have short-term side-effects but excellent long-term benefits.

SUMMARY

The relationship between teams and performance is complex. Evidence has shown that teams outperform individuals when tasks require complex, creative solutions. However, teams often underperform and are forced to isolate project tasks to complete them on time and within budget. In this chapter, we advocate for setting higher expectations and goals for teams, which necessitates rethinking team composition to assure diversity and cross-functionality. While teams comprised of multiple disciplines are desirable in many situations, such teams require performance support that is appropriate and targeted. The cross-disciplinary team learning framework provides a way forward for a learning function in an organization that uses teams to solve problems. The framework provides specific guidelines for supporting team systems, human resources, and enabling technologies with a focus on team results that are innovative and creative in their execution.

Note

For many examples of how activity systems are applied within the domain of human performance technology (HPT), see the 2007 special issue of *Performance Improvement Quarterly* focused on this topic. Furthermore, a chapter by Sasha Barab, Michael Evans, and Eun-Ok Baek in the 2004 *Handbook of Research on Educational Communications and Technology* is dedicated to the use of activity theory as a lens for examining group and team work within the performance improvement arena.

References

Barab, S. A., Evans, M. A., & Baek, E.-O. (2003). Activity theory as a lens for charactering the participatory unit. In D. H. Jonassen (Ed.), *International handbook on communication technologies* (Vol. 2, pp. 199–214). Mahwah, NJ: Lawrence Erlbaum Associates.

Fruchter, R., & Emery, K. (1999). Teamwork: Assessing cross-disciplinary learning. In C. Hoadley & J. Roschelle (Eds.), *Proceedings of the Computer Support for Collaborative Learning (CSCL) 1999 conference*. Stanford University, Palo Alto, California.

Ilgen, D. R., Hollenbeck, J. R., Johnson, M., & Jundt, D. (2005). Teams in organizations: From input-process-output models to IMOI models. *Annual Review of Psychology, 56*, 517–543.

Johnson, D. W., & Johnson, R. T. (1989). *Cooperation and competition: Theory and research*. Edina, MN: Interaction Book.

Leonard-Barton, D. (1995). *Wellsprings of knowledge: Building and sustaining the sources of innovation*. Boston: Harvard Business School Press.

Scholtes, P., Joiner, B., & Streibel, B. (1996). *The team handbook*. Madison, WI: Oriel Incorporated.

Senge, P. (1990). *The fifth discipline: The art and practice of the learning organization*. New York: Doubleday.

Wedman, J. F. (2004). *Welcome to exploring the performance pyramid*. Columbia, MO: University of Missouri. Retrieved February 10, 2009, from http://performance pyramid.missouri.edu/.

Recommended Readings

Engeström, Y. (1987). *Learning by expanding: An activity-theoretical approach to developmental research*. Helsinki: Orienta-Konsultit.

Guzzo, R. A., & Dickson, M. W. (1996). Teams in organizations: Recent research on performance and effectiveness. *Annual Review of Psychology 47*, 307–338.

Kelley, T., & Littman, J. (2001). *The art of innovation: Lessons in creativity from IDEO, America's leading design firm*. New York: Doubleday.

Koschmann, T. D. (1994). Toward a theory of computer support for collaborative learning. *Journal of the Learning Sciences, 3*(3), 219–225.

Lei, K. (2007). Cross-disciplinary team learning (CDTL) model: Development and validation. Unpublished doctoral dissertation, Purdue University.

Sawyer, R. K. (2007). *Group genius: The creative power of collaboration.* New York: Basic Books.

Schaffer, S. P., & Lei, K. (2007). Supporting collaborative problem solving in engineering design teams. Paper presented at the 36th ASEE/IEEE Frontiers in Education Conference, San Diego, CA.

Stahl, G. (2006). *Group cognition: Computer support for building collaborative knowledge.* Cambridge, MA: MIT Press.

 # EDITORIAL CONNECTIONS

Teams play an important role in many, if not most, organizational activities. Production teams, management teams, cross-disciplinary teams, and many others are common in organizations. Today, the roles for teams are also expanding with the development of less-formal networks and communities of practice that link together the task-orientation of teams with the benefits of networking.

Expanding Your Options

Tuition reimbursement system—an organizational policy of compensating employees for expenses accrued while engaging in educational endeavors that enhance the employee's skills and knowledge in a way that may be beneficial to the organization.

As a result, you can effectively use teams—in many different forms—to improve performance. Cross-disciplinary teams can, for example, directly address a specific performance issue in your organization, just as management teams can be used to support the application of other performance interventions. In all cases, consider the benefits of using teams to build knowledge and skills. Use cross-functional teams, for instance, as a way to build individual knowledge through interactions with peers from other functional units of the organization, or use production teams to generate improvements that stretch beyond the combined capacity of individual team members.

Just as you can use other performance interventions, such as training, e-learning (see Chapter Twenty-Four), or performance support (see Chapter Fourteen), the development of team knowledge and skills is critical to the improvement of performance. As with individuals, building the performance capacity of teams, units or groups, requires your attention. From mentoring of teams to webinars supporting team learning, you should build the knowledge and skills of teams to ensure their capacity to achieve desired results.

WHAT'S COMING UP

In Chapter Twenty-Six, mentoring is examined as a performance intervention for developing the knowledge and skills of individuals and teams within your organization. While often associated with the professional development of junior employees, mentoring can also be an equally effective intervention for building basic skills (for example, procurement, software) or the capacity to apply complex knowledge (for example, leadership, knowledge management, interpersonal communications). For that reason, mentoring can be a dynamic intervention within many improvement efforts, offering unique benefits for building knowledge and skills through mentoring relationships, rather than formal training.

CHAPTER TWENTY-SIX

Mentoring

Stella Louise Cowan

INTRODUCTION

The first mentor can be traced back to Greek mythology. King Odysseus requested that his wise and trusted friend Mentor serve as guide for the growth and development of his son Telemachus. The King was embarking on the Trojan War and recognized that in his absence Telemachus would need a surrogate father or patriarchal force in his life. Beyond Mentor's wisdom and trustworthiness, the King viewed Mentor as someone with the depth of life experiences, knowledge, and passion for teaching others that made for a perfect patriarchal force. Mentor was a teacher, adviser, encourager, and role model. Telemachus was the successor to the throne, and Mentor provided the classic combination of wisdom and support for a "junior" individual's advancement. Grooming Telemachus to be a worthy successor to the throne in Greek mythology can be viewed as the predecessor, in terms of offering an informal model, to guiding a mentee's upward career movement through today's organizational hierarchy.

The modern use of mentoring emerged from the recognition that junior members of the organization have needs early in their careers for guidance, support, and sponsorship in relationship to advancement. In terms of recent history, mentoring has been a frequent subject in popular management literature for more than three decades. Kathy Kram, a pioneer in mentoring research, published her classic *Mentoring at Work* in 1983. Her book laid the groundwork for the rise in studies on mentoring that followed over the next decades. From her empirical studies, Kram identified two primary mentor functions: career support and psychological support. Historically, mentoring has been predominately related to career support, in the form of outcomes for mentees, such as promotions, salary upgrade, and job fulfillment.

In addition, those categories of outcomes potentially acted as performance motivators for the mentee. The mentoring was typically one-on-one, with the mentor facilitating the mentee's career advancement. Career advancement is the velocity at which a person's career movement is occurring in conjunction with the level the person ultimately attains in the organization's job hierarchy. The psychological support refers to emotional and interpersonal outcomes such as enhanced self-esteem, confidence building, camaraderie, and counseling, that is, guidance, advice, and a listening ear. The types of support have not changed. However, much has changed over the years in how organizations use mentoring and view its importance. Mentoring is no longer synonymous only with career movement. Rather, it is associated increasingly with organizational strategies such as succession planning (see Chapter Twenty-Nine), talent management, diversity initiatives (see Chapter Thirty-One), and knowledge transfer.

Much has changed in the workplace over the years, particularly in the last decade. Mergers, acquisitions, off-shoring, downsizing, de-layering, and restructuring are arguably the rule, not the exception, in the workplace of the 21st century. These changes signify new directions in the structure, design of work, and strategic thrust of organizations. With these types of changes, the role of mentoring has evolved. The old model of the senior leader serving as the sage advisor/counselor orchestrating the career of a more junior individual in the organization no longer is the perfect fit for today's workplace reality.

Mentoring Formats

Alternatives forms of, and roles for, mentoring have gained momentum during the last decade. The types of mentoring formats have evolved to include lateral or peer mentoring, group mentoring, cross-cultural mentoring, distance or virtual mentoring, performance-based mentoring, and reverse or upward mentoring. Lateral or peer mentoring relationships can be used to focus on job-related skill development. Ida Abbott, attorney, author, and respected consultant to law firms and legal organizations on mentoring, provides a picture of performance-based mentoring in her 2000 book *The Lawyer's Guide to Mentoring*. As Abbott explains, performance-based mentoring is characterized by a highly structured process that focuses on performance outcomes. It can support mentees in understanding the requirements for success in the organization and connecting their performance and career goals to the business objectives of the organization.

A key function for reverse or upward mentoring is knowledge management. Reverse or upward mentoring can be used to transfer knowledge from a younger generation of employees to an older generation of employees. Baltimore-based author Donna Owens has contributed several articles to *HR Magazine*, including one in 2006 concerning virtual mentoring. In that article, Owens shares the experiences of several mentors, mentees, and practitioners responsible for administering an organization's program. She notes that distance or virtual mentoring allows for development across geographical distances. In addition, online mentoring has great utility in a global workplace where employees are on different sides of the country or the world. Finally, web-based distance mentoring can be appealing to younger generations that are more likely to be technophiles and comfortable communicating and building relationships using technology.

Another important distinction is the difference between informal and formal mentoring approaches. Informal mentoring can be described as guidance, support, and discussion that is casual and often social. Typically, no specific goals are defined and the relationship often occurs spontaneously or on an "as needed" basis. The mentor and the mentee may have met by "accident" and not as part of an organized effort to seek mentoring. The relationship evolves naturally, so it may run into inconsistency in terms of the number, length, and planned outcomes of mentor-mentee contacts. However, this does not mean that a mentor and her or his mentee cannot and should not formalize some goals for the experience. The mentor and mentee can choose to refine or change the goals at any time. The decision can be based on a number of factors, such as alterations in the development needs or priorities of the mentee, evolving organizational changes that impact structural hierarchy or create new options for career advancement strategies, and unanticipated resource or expert-availability issues relevant to a persistent roadblock to a particular goal.

Formal mentoring can be described as a structured, purposeful process for supporting career advancement, professional growth, or skill development. Traditionally, the mentoring relationship is arranged through an organizational matching process. However, there is a growing trend to integrate elements of the informal, spontaneous marching features with the arranged relationship. This can include conducting social events (for example, a networking breakfast or book circle luncheon) designed to initiate relationship building prior to the formal matching. Mentors and mentees would share information, such as career interests, hobbies, and work style, during these facilitated events and provide their matching preferences, if any. In the case of formal programs that have a designated time horizon, such as two years, overarching program goals are established to facilitate measurement of progress and success. Success can be the achievement of specific outcomes around factors such as the implementation of development plans, the time required to on-board or acclimate promoted leaders to their new level of work, integration of new hires into the organization, and so forth. In addition to the overarching program goals, mentees are expected to set individual goals or create a development plan.

The criteria or the decision process for selecting goals includes consideration of program structure (program length, frequency of contact between mentor and mentee, and so forth) the overarching purpose of the program (for example, career advancement, or skill development), alignment with the organization's strategic direction, divisional priorities, the mentee's personal preferences, the depth of a goal's potential results, budget constraints, and resources required to implement the goal. Resources can refer to people, technology, budget dollars, and knowledge. Finally, in formal programs, contacts or sessions between the mentor and the mentee are typically scheduled or planned relative to frequency, length, format, and even content.

Diversity-focused mentoring entails the purposeful arrangement of mentoring relationships across cultural dimensions such as gender or race, to mitigate inequities in the organization to address, for example, persistent barriers to promotion experienced by a racial minority group. A barrier in this example could be a tendency by leaders in an organization to champion/mentor non-minorities almost exclusively as high-potential talent for promotions or career advancement. As a result, members of the organization who are people of color do not have the benefit of a career champion (mentor) to influence perceptions about their potential and orchestrate opportunities (for example, lead on a high-visibility project) that can deepen job skills, confidence, and creditability. A cultural dimension, in this context, refers to the characteristic categorization of individuals into groups based on the broad, surface-level diversity factors or differences. Other cultural dimensions in this categorization include age, sexual orientation, and religion. However, race and gender are the most common cultural dimensions that encompass diversity-focused mentoring programs. Additionally, inclusion merits highlighting in light of its role as an underpinning element in diversity-focused mentoring. Inclusion, within this framework, refers to the disposition and ability to interact and work productively across cultural differences.

Mentoring, by an individual who is senior in job level or by a peer, can be used to support an organization's diversity initiatives (see Chapter Thirty-One) and address glass-ceiling issues. "Glass ceilings" refer to situations in which the upward career movement of a person qualified to be promoted is truncated at a lower level. The truncation is based on non-performance-related criteria or judgment influenced by stereotyping. The term is frequently associated with the challenges that women face in their efforts to advance their careers. A number of different situations can indicate a glass-ceiling issue. High turnover numbers in conjunction with low career advancement rates by women can signal that an organization has a glass ceiling issue. One example is the disproportionate representation of women in senior leadership positions at an organization. Another example is the lack of minority males in an organization's leadership pipeline for succession management.

The design for a mentoring program does not have to conform to a single format or purpose; the program can be an amalgam of several formats. For example, a program that addresses diversity issues does not have to focus solely on job promotion or career advancement. The program's design infrastructure can be constructed in a way to facilitate performance or skill-based outcomes, combine group with individually assigned mentoring, promote peer mentoring, and include a distinct coaching aspect.

DESCRIPTION

As discussed previously, the function of the mentor has expanded. Traditional definitions are limited, partly because they are bound within levels or hierarchies. A single mentor can wear many "hats," such as confidant in corporate political matters or new job orientation partner. Additionally, a mentee might require or benefit from more than one mentor (at the same time). Further, a different type of mentor might be needed at different "moments" in a mentee's career or development planning. This is especially true considering current elements that shape career environment, such as the dissolution of the psychological "contract" between employees and organizations. The psychological contract refers to employees' beliefs that a factor of the work-compensation exchange between them and the organization is employment security or permanency. Workers are more mobile; organizations are less predictable.

It is within this context (that is, the change in the career and employment contract) that the phenomenon of "development networks" or multiple developmental relationships has garnered increased attention. Kram proposed in 1985 that individuals depend on support from more than one person (mentor) regarding development for career advancement. She referred to this concept as "relationship constellations." Along with fellow researcher and mentoring scholar Monica Higgins, Kram expanded the original concept of relationship consternations in defining the developmental network perspective. Their 2001 article "Reconceptualizing Mentoring at Work" defines it as a collection of concurrently held relationships (people) that a mentee identifies at any point during his or her career arch that actively engage in developing the mentee for career advancement. Not all of these relationships (mentors) have to come from within the organization; that is, some can be external mentors (for example, from other companies, professional organizations, or the individual's social circle).

Noted researchers and contributors to the body of knowledge on mentoring and careers Suzanne de Jamasz, Sherry Sullivan, and Vicki Whiting describe a multiple mentor network in which mentees actively search for different guides and mentors who are in diverse places or levels in their career. In a 2004 article for *Academy of Management Executive*, they propose that, for career success in today's world, one mentor is not sufficient. The rapid, continuous emergence of new knowledge, for example, point to this. As de Jamasz and her colleagues explain, one mentor cannot possess all of the required knowledge. A constellation of mentors has great value, providing unique points of view; access to a broader range of experiences; the availability of multiple sources of knowledge and information; and increased opportunities for interactions that build confidence (for example, incidences of positive affirmation and reinforcement).

Mentor roles can range from the patriarchal figure to a co-worker who is a confidant and role model. Following are descriptions of several mentoring types:

- *Traditional.* The traditional mentor describes a person who is the all-knowing, influential senior leader orchestrating a junior member's upward career transitions. The mentor is a guardian and protector and typically in a position to broaden the mentee's exposure to upper leadership and is prominent in the organization at large.

- *Peer or Lateral.* The peer or lateral mentor describes a person who occupies a comparable position in the organization in terms of salary, status, and job scope. An additional aspect of the peer mentor relationship is the reciprocity factor—that is, both individuals can take turns at giving and receiving guidance and support.

- *Step Ahead.* The step-ahead mentor describes an expanded version of the peer mentor. Organizations are using the step-ahead mentor with new hires or newly promoted individuals. Mentoring researchers Ellen Ensher, Craig Thomas, and Susan Murphy explain that the step-ahead mentor is one who has several more years of experience than the mentee and in most instances is one or two steps further in his or her career. As they point out in a 2001 article for the *Journal of Business and Psychology*, mentees are socialized into the culture, and the step-ahead mentor benefits from practicing his or her feedback skills and gaining a sense of empowerment by supporting a colleague.

- *One Hierarchical Level Above.* The mentor who is one hierarchical level above the mentee describes a relationship in which the mentor is not necessarily a senior leader but is nonetheless in a position to offer a perspective and support from a level above.

- *Survivor.* The survivor mentor, as prominent mentoring scholars Lillian Eby and Angie Lockwood explain in a 2001 article, is a unique type of mentoring by a co-worker (in the same or another departmental) who has survived organizational staff reductions or a merger. Survivor mentors can share what they have learned about navigating change in the organization, bridge the gap between the old culture and the new direction in terms of the organization.

Types of Results That Can Be Expected

The results that can be expected from mentoring evolve around career enhancement; skill building and professional growth; talent management; and knowledge transfer include:

Career enhancement or satisfaction: Career-related results can be expected, particularly when the mentoring relationship is integral to or a component of an individual's overall career strategy. When this is the case, the mentor's spectrum of support includes intentional actions and advocacy to prompt the mentee's career advancement. Overarching career outcomes associated with high satisfaction include salary growth, job perks, speed of promotion, and engaging nature of work, among other elements. However, a career strategy is more than a "wish list" of future job promotions. It includes the planning and execution of professional development options. Career-related results can also be expected when mentoring has a role in management replacement planning. For example, a mentor guides a mentee through specific job experiences to increase his or her readiness for succession to a designated position, either a promotion or lateral, on the organization's replacement planning chart. The combination of being on a succession track and the attention, time, and emotional investment of the mentor can engender career satisfaction. A positive mentoring experience can boost confidence and self-esteem, as mentees are given feedback that is both developmental and affirming.

Skill building and professional growth. Skill building refers to increasing an individual's capacity to perform and get the desired results or outcomes in a specific area. Examples of development areas include project implementation, conflict management, presentation skills, or coaching others. Formal mentoring almost exclusively has some degree of a development perspective, meaning that mentees set goals and receive actionable feedback. It is common that through the mentoring relationship, mentees are exposed to or directed toward opportunities for professional growth such as participation in a local chamber of commerce international leadership consortium.

Talent development and commitment. A strategy for talent management is imperative for today's organizations. Talent management is the process of recruiting, on-boarding, and developing potential or rising talent. The overarching goal is to develop or hire the right talent and then align that talent with the right job at the right time, based on strategic business objectives. Talent management shares an intimate relationship with succession planning. Succession planning seeks to ensure the continuity of leadership by cultivating talent from within the organization, through planned, targeted development activities. It is that cultivation of talent that is realized as an outgrowth of mentoring. Assigning high potentials or individuals being groomed for promotion to mentors supports talent development. The mentors can, among other things, expose the "talent" to key people and unique opportunities, share wisdom about organizational politics, and so forth. An organization's grand strategy for succession planning (see Chapter Twenty-Nine) characteristically has a talent management prong. Commitment to the organization is another result that can be realized. As Ensher, Thomas, and Murphy point out, through socializing mentees to the organizational norms, mentors support reduced turnover rates and increased commitment to the culture.

Transfer of organizational knowledge. Knowledge is the components of information employees receive or exchange, process and generate to both do their jobs and innovate. The "sum" of the knowledge within the organization is its human capital. Knowledge management (see Chapter Fifteen) is critical to the organization's competitiveness. Knowledge management can be defined as the structure for acquiring, transferring, embedding, and using knowledge. Through mentoring, knowledge such as insight about clients, ideas, and thought processes can be transferred from the mentor to the mentee or vice versa in the case of upward mentoring. This is realized by virtue of a number of elements, including the framework for the mentoring relationship. The mentoring relationship provides a framework (meetings, purposeful interactions, actionable feedback, goal setting, and so forth) for mentors to impart knowledge. Additionally, the anticipated deficit in leadership due to growing number of retiring Baby Boomers has made mentoring a strategy for knowledge transfer. As discussed previously, succession planning focuses on leadership continuity. The exodus of retiring Baby Boomers challenges that continuity. The transfer of knowledge that occurs through mentoring, particularly when it is targeted and purposeful, supports mitigating that challenge.

WHAT WE KNOW FROM RESEARCH

Essential Factors Associated with Quality of Mentoring

The degree of satisfaction with a mentoring program or with the quality of the mentorship can depend on a number of essential factors. The factors can include voluntary versus involuntary participation, frequency of meetings or exchanges, input into the matching decision, and training or orientation. Understanding the influence of these factors provides essential information for mentoring program design. The University of South Florida's Tammy Allen, along with Lillian Eby of the University of Georgia and Ohio State University's Elizabeth Lentz, examined these types of factors in relationship to mentoring outcomes, for example, mentor and mentee satisfaction, career advancement, and psychological support. Their research, which looked at formal programs exclusively, sought to identify correlations between these individual factors and greater mentorship quality.

Matching. The matching strategy, in particular, can have a negative impact on the degree of satisfaction with the mentoring relationship, longevity of the relationship, and outcomes. Allen and colleagues report in their 2006 article for the *Journal of Applied Psychology* that the perception of input or influence into the matching process appeared to be a critical element for mentors and mentees. They indicated that this result was consistent with noted researcher Ralph Viator's 1999 finding that mentees who reported more input into the matching decision identified a greater satisfaction with the mentoring relationship. Allen and colleagues propose that, by perceiving a level of influence in the matching decision, mentors and mentees may put energy into the relationship before it is formally launched. As a result, both individuals are more inclined to push the relationship to its full potential. As they explained, this provides an answer for why perceived input into the matching strategy can be an essential factor of successful formal mentoring. Additionally, in those situations in which mentees perceived greater input into the matching decision, the mentees also indicated higher quality mentorship and role modeling.

Training. While Allen and her colleagues did not find a correlation between the mere receipt of training and mentorship quality, they did find that the quality of the training is associated with mentees reporting mentorship quality. In addition, the research revealed that the time spent in training had a positive relation to psychological mentoring. Allen and her team concluded that simply receiving training is not sufficient to produce a positive effect on mentoring behaviors. The quality of the training should be perceived as high. Another notable finding regarding training was that mentors related to mentors who reported that the training was of high quality. These mentors were more inclined to report that they provided psychological mentoring.

Proximity and Frequency of Interactions. Geographic distance can present a challenge to the development and maintenance of a mentoring relationship. Opportunities for interacting face-to-face can be limited or infrequent. Meetings or interactions are especially important early in the relationship during the building of interpersonal connections, trust, and mutual comfort with sharing. The "space" that exists when mentors and mentees are in different departments is also a variable relative to proximity. That space can be represented by lack of real knowledge or connection to the other individual's department or communication silos (barriers) between departments, for example. Allen and colleagues propose that when mentors and mentees are in the same department, the mentor's familiarity and understanding of the department may make it easier for the mentor to provide career support and guidance.

In terms of the results of their research, Allen, Eby, and Lentz found that proximity and interaction frequency had a moderate correlation to mentoring behaviors and quality. They suggest that organizations should not be preoccupied with pairing mentors and mentees across different geographic locations.

Results Associated with Formal Mentoring

Eby and Lockwood's 2001 study, mentioned earlier, consisted of a qualitative investigation into the reaction of mentees and mentors to participation in a formal mentoring program. The study confirmed the benefits of mentoring relative to several areas. The study also identified a number of problems, reported by both mentor and mentees associated with their experiences during the mentoring process.

Mutual Learning Most Common Benefit. The most common mentoring outcome reported by both mentors and mentees was learning. Both groups defined learning as understanding the organizational components and obtaining varied points of view on work issues. A common theme among the comments submitted by mentees regarding learning was the increase in knowledge or perspective on how other divisions operate. Learning was realized on both sides of the mentoring equation, which increased the value of mentoring.

Psychological and Career Support Were Prominent for Mentees. Mentees reported several benefits unique to them, including coaching, psychological support (for instance, camaraderie, affirmation, acceptance, and counseling), visibility within the organization, and sponsorship for promotions. An example of coaching was described as "thinking through a situation together." Support for career planning was reported by mentees as a benefit of the mentoring relationship. This included the mentee having dialogue with his or her mentor regarding specific next steps for career advancement. Networking opportunities were also reported as a benefit of the mentoring relationship. Other benefits were reported including enhanced job performance.

Developing Personal Relationship Prominent for Mentors. Mentors reported that it was pleasant becoming acquainted with their mentees and that the experienced proved to be satisfying on a personal level. Some mentors also reported personal gratification and managerial skills as benefits of mentoring. Personal gratification refers to the emotional fulfillment and pride a mentor feels regarding the progress of his or her mentee.

Problems. Mismatches were the most common problem reported by both mentors and mentees. Some of the reasons they reported their pairing or relationship as a mismatch were lack of common experiences or interests with each other, age disparity, and personality differences. Scheduling challenges were also cited by both groups as a problem. Not surprisingly, the percentage of mentors reporting scheduling as a problem was higher than that of mentees.

Some mentees felt the mentoring program did not yield particular outcomes or benefits that they expected.

Themes for Program Improvement. The most frequently reported theme for improvement was the need to communicate the program objectives with greater clarity. Close behind that theme was the need for improved matching and expanded opportunities to share the mentoring experience after the matching occurs (such as bringing program participants together in a group meeting). Other recommendations included clarifying the participants' roles and more effectively integrating the program into the organization's culture.

Mentoring and New Business Start-Ups

Australian researchers Lea Waters, Marita McCabe, Dennis Kiellerup, and Steven Kiellerup conducted a 2002 examination into the impact of formal mentoring on the success of the new business ventures and self-esteem of mentees. Waters and her colleagues selected the subject of their research in response to what the authors referred to as a "call" to mentoring researchers to redirect their focus from established organizations to emerging organizations. They pointed to the new reality where the career movement of individuals does not follow a predictable path in a single organization, but moves through many organizations over the individual's lifetime.

The objective assessment of business-related outcomes, meaning profits, revealed that neither career support nor the psychological function of mentoring had a significant correlation to the amount of profits. However, Waters and her team warned that the conclusions required caution, given the myriad of economic factors that affect profit. When perceived business success is used as the outcome, career-related support is more closely linked to success than psychological support is. Psychological support was shown to have a stronger relationship to enhancing self-esteem. It should be noted that the mentees' perception of success was affected by the frequency of contact with their mentors and not supported in the raw data on profitability.

Value and Likely Results

Allen and colleagues propose that, by perceiving a level of influence in the matching decision, mentors and mentees may put energy into the relationship before it is formally launched. As a result, both individuals are more inclined to push the relationship to its full potential. As they explained, this provides an answer for why perceived input into the matching strategy can be an essential factor of successful formal mentoring. Additionally, in those situations in which mentees perceived greater input into the matching decision, the mentees also indicated higher quality mentorship and role modeling. This gives insight into the design principles for formal mentoring programs. It is obviously essential to view the matching strategy as a lynchpin to success. Matching should include an element of perceived participant input, such as opportunities to get acquainted, before the program launch, and identify preferred choices for a mentoring partner. The preferred choices would be understood as one element among several others, such as gender mix, in the selection criteria.

Waters and colleagues cited several differences between a new business start-up and the organizational setting. For instance, they indicated that the title and political statue of the mentor has very limited relevance in the new business start-up situation. They suggest the nature of the function will differ. Even though a business start-up presents a different context from an organizational setting, there is synergy between the two relative to program design points that can be extracted from the results of the research. For instance, a list of managerial skills required in today's dynamic, rapidly changing business environment would arguably include entrepreneurial thinking. Managers, and in many cases individual contributors, are called upon to think like they own the business or function for which they are responsible. This can include elements such as growing the customer base, launching new services, and reducing expenditures. Within this context, the approach, type of advice, identification of resources, and so forth required by a mentor in the business start-up situation has congruence with mentoring a manager in the organizational setting.

Some Details on the Research Studies

Eby and Lockwood's Study. The participants were from two different organizations with formal mentoring programs. The organizations represented the telecommunications and community-based health industries. The mentees selected for the program were high-potential employees. Program goals were designated as: to expand the mentees' exposure across the organization, support career development, and develop leader skills. Mentors and mentees were paired across different business units.

Participants responded to interview questions that were part of a program evaluation project. One-on-one interviews were conducted by telephone with mentors and mentees. The design and purpose of the interview questions included gaining an understanding of what mentors and mentees perceived as the benefits of mentoring. Responses in the interviews were classified into themes by two individuals with consideration knowledge of the mentoring literature and process. The two individuals independently created and coded a list of schemes from the responses. A final scheme was developed by comparing the two independent schemes

Waters, McCabe, Kiellerup, and Kiellerup's Study. Participants were selected based on the viability of their preliminary plan for establishing a new business. Mentors were individuals who had achieved success in their own business. The primary focus of the program was to support mentees in fully developing their business plans.

WHEN TO APPLY

The overarching factor regarding appropriateness is whether or not the mentoring program has a connection to the organization's overall strategy for leveraging its human capital within the context of staying competitive and highly viable. In this context, human capital refers to the sum of the intellectual, relationship with internal and external clients, and creative value of the organization's people. Mentoring falls under the realm of "people" strategies relative to the strategies executed by an organization to achieve business excellence. People strategies involve tactics and approaches for which the focal point for realizing results is the actions, new behaviors, and heightened contributions of people (employees). Non-people-related strategies, meaning those involving organizational processes, technology, and policies, are viewed as more directly connected to achieving business excellence. Tactics for leveraging human capital where the involvement of mentoring is appropriate include on-boarding new leaders; developing new skills as a result of process or technology changes; developing rising talent or high potentials; supporting organizational change; managing organizational knowledge; and transitioning leaders as they move upward.

When Mentoring Is Appropriate

The essential question is whether or not mentoring is aligned with the organization's business goals. A notable amount of traction is being gained by mentoring as an on-boarding tactic to socialize individuals to the culture and better position them for success. On-boarding can be for individuals new to the organization, new to the role of leadership, or transitioning to a new level of leadership. With the rapid pace of change, new leaders, in particular, can have a short horizon for moving from new to their roles to mastery of the functions and responsibilities of the roles. Using mentors to on-board new leaders in order to reduce incidents of derailment associated with the relentless pressure to master the role functions is a savvy application option for implementation. Organizations want new leaders to be socialized (introduced, acquainted with the norms, made aware of informal communication and decision channels, and so forth) into the leadership subculture and positioned for success as expediently as possible. The leadership subculture refers to that part of the organization's overall culture that is unique to or of greater significance among the leadership population. Culture refers to the values, viewpoints, and assumptions held by members of the organization. In addition, it encompasses the formal and informal protocols and organizational channels that members use to interact and achieve goals.

In a formal program or a program that is a part of a bigger leadership development picture, a mentor can facilitate a purposeful indoctrination of the mentee to the work environment, work flow, team dynamics, and internal and external clients. A development process can be designed whereby the mentor is the lynchpin who creates opportunities, such as assignments, structured meetings, or job shadowing, for the mentees to learn about key factors such as their teams and what they will need to do meet objectives. Leaders promoted and therefore transitioning to a higher level of accountability, influence, and political implications can also benefit from on-boarding facilitated by a mentor. A mentor who has already navigated the territory serves to direct the mentee toward those situations and people who will enhance performance at the new level. That could entail such actions as attending a pivotal board meeting or strategizing around establishing a relationship with a client who is perceived as difficult.

Mentoring is appropriate as a facet of a broader solution to address the need for new process or people skills brought about by organizational changes. An example of a broader solution is an organization-wide skills-based training and development architecture. It is common for such a learning architecture to include classroom training, learning event, e-learning, and performance-support tools to address both the core and evolving skill development needs. Both performance-based and peer mentoring fit situations that involve skills development. For example, peers who are early adopters or high performers who have acquired competency in the new skills can serve as mentors. Depending on the complexity of the new skills, mentoring groups are a viable option following formal training to reinforce the learning and support implementation of the new skills. In the group setting, there is not as much opportunity for individual attention or input. The mentees share the arena and therefore the mentor's attention.

Mentoring can play an integral role in developing rising talent or high potentials. Assigning a mentor to an individual identified as a rising talent signifies that the individual's professional growth is important and will be addressed from an organizational perspective in an intentional way. For example, the mentor's guidance is targeted at fast-tracking the mentee's readiness for assuming higher leadership or professional accountability, as well as increased hierarchical stature.

An important thrust of knowledge management is the acquisition, transfer (from one organizational member to another), and embedding or institutionalization of information, practices, new learning, strategies, and so forth. Mentoring is appropriate for the transfer of knowledge because it provides a framework for sharing or imparting information from one individual (the mentor) to another (the mentee) or from one individual to a group of others. It is a feasible avenue for promoting organizational learning. This can be achieved through the didactic conversations between the mentor and mentee, identification of skills that the mentee desires to work on, sharing of ideas, and the reinforcement of new learning. An example of an option used for knowledge management is a "community of practice." A community of practice refers to an informal collection of individuals who come together to work on a shared concern. A community of practice shepherded by a group mentor (expert, senior leader, connector to resources) who is focused on a new implementation, for example, provides a structured means for reinforcing and transferring learning. A peer network of customer service trainers, spearheaded by an experienced, high-performing lateral mentor, formed for the purpose of extracting opportunities from lessons learned and integrating best practices is another example. In this context, the term "spearheaded" entails leading, providing development counsel, and directing the focus.

When Mentoring Is Not Appropriate

Mentoring is not appropriate as a stand-alone solution to address diversity or glass ceiling issues. It can certainly support an organization's efforts to improve career opportunities for women and minorities. However, a persistent imbalance, on the negative side, in the growth opportunities, rate of promotion, and the active recruitment of women and minorities is a systemic problem in the organization that requires a holistic approach. The organization has to consider a broad array of human resource interventions in these cases. Such interventions include training, behavioral modeling by top leadership that exemplifies equity on promotional considerations, a recruitment strategy that respects inclusion, and a talent management strategy that does not ignore the often less visible or cultivated talent—notably women and minorities.

Mentoring is not appropriate as a "reward" based on favoritism or designated for the select few. In other words, it is not a "reward" exclusively for some, as opposed to dictated by what is most strategic for the organization. The sponsorship, attention, and benefits of a mentor engenders a sense of "being special" in the mentee. This is a positive outcome of mentoring and, as discussed previously, contributes to job satisfaction and retention. However, creating mentoring opportunities/matches, as in formal programs, should not be reduced to a status symbol or perceived in a way that is divisive. Mentoring should appear as accessible, under equitable circumstances, even though not everyone in the organization will be mentored. This is not to say that mentoring cannot be viewed as a reward, as in the case of assigning mentors to rising talent or high potentials. Additionally, informal mentoring matches occur spontaneously through mutual attraction and common interests.

Mentoring is not appropriate when the process is not valued by the organization's culture—particularly not valued by leadership. In this context "valued" refers to the perspective that mentoring is important, can make a difference, and is worth the effort required. Additionally, valuing mentoring is congruent with valuing employee and leadership development. If the culture does not value mentoring or development, then there should be a concerted effort to raise the perception of mentoring in the organization's culture. Creating a value proposition for mentoring is a step in the right direction, that is, illustrating how mentoring can impact performance, retention, diversity initiatives, and so forth. Indicators that the culture does not value mentoring include the following circumstances:

- Resistance by leadership to carve out time for developing staff; leaders do not make it a priority, habitually reschedule or cancel time set for development discussions, or express a view that development planning is not a lynchpin activity in which they need to engage;

- A lack of promotion of development as an organizational imperative; the organization does not have processes such as talent management, development-based pay, employee training curriculums for specific jobs or competencies, or an expressed philosophy regarding the value of employee development;

- Limited or no programs that facilitate development, for example, a training curriculum beyond job skills training or on-site college courses;

- Low organization score on an employee satisfaction survey relative to opportunities and support for employee development; and/or

- Data from employee exit interviews identify lack of development support as a factor in decisions to exit the organization.

An ideal situation would be to connect mentoring to performance management (see Chapter Ten) by including it in the mentor's performance goals. Time spent mentoring would be expected and rewarded.

Application in Relation to Other HPT Interventions

As discussed previously, a junior member of the organization receiving career support from a senior leader/member in the organization was traditionally the predominate focus of mentoring. Even though mentoring has expanded in both types of mentors (for example, lateral) and the focus of mentoring relationships (for example, performance-based), career support has remained on the development spectrum. Additionally, it is most common for individuals who seek out mentors to do so for the overall purpose of career sponsorship and advancement. These factors point to a natural connection or relationship between mentoring and career development. Ensher and colleagues point out that positive career outcomes from both formal and informal mentoring have been shown by a number of researchers, including Daniel Turban and Thomas Dougherty 1994 study into protégés' personalities, and William Whitely and Pol Coetsier's 1993 investigation into mentoring's impact on early career outcomes. For example, researchers have identified notable income advances and accelerated promotion rates as two such positive factors experienced by employees with mentors, as compared to those without mentors.

Career results from mentoring can be both intrinsic, such as higher satisfaction with the workplace, and extrinsic, such as job advancement. Mentoring can provide more than support for career advancement. Another outcome traditionally associated with mentoring is the psychological support that comes from the attention and guidance the mentee receives from the mentor. Mentoring can be employed as an intervention to affect motivation and self-concept (see Part Seven of this handbook). Psychological support has a connection to building self-confidence and motivation. An individual's self-concept and degree of motivation can affect productivity and job satisfaction.

Mentoring can also be a learning and development intervention, in support of building skills and knowledge. In today's flatter, more participative organizations, the use of mentors to facilitate development is a savvy tactical approach. One avenue for achieving this is through mentoring that focuses on job-related skill development. The mentor and mentee create a skill development worksheet to use as a roadmap for achieving the desired outcomes. The idea of the development worksheet or contract is to break down a particular skill into performance components in order to form a framework for the mentoring actions. The worksheet is basically an action planning tool that is goal-focused. If the skill being developed is project management, for example, the mentor and mentee would determine the individual performance components on which the mentor will provide support.

The mentor does not have to provide support for development on every aspect of the skill. Examples of components that the mentor and mentee can agree on for skill or performance improvement relative to project implementation are using project management templates or software effectively; breaking the project down into components or deliverables that are actionable and results-focused; identifying/describing project milestones that signify progress explicitly; meeting deadlines consistently for completing components and reaching milestones; and addressing roadblocks expediently and effectively. This refers to using the right strategy to eliminate or impede the roadblocks.

The mentee would seek advice, counsel, connection to key resources, and so forth, as he or she worked on building competency in the skill area. The key question is: What does the mentee need to do, know, or practice to build competency in each component of the skill? This is where identifying the broad performance components of the skill, such as the ones in the preceding bullets, fits into the equation. Which of the components can be best developed in the mentoring format versus, for example, classroom training or a job aid? (See Chapter Fourteen.) Mentoring can be a better option, for instance, when one-on-one transfer/sharing of experience, feedback as an instructional tool, and sponsorship for on-the-job application—to name several factors—provide appropriate conditions for development. Additionally, consider the skill being developed in the context of the mentee's bigger development picture. Do this by creating a hierarchy of the mentee's development needs. Place those needs that are most essential to high performance at the top of the hierarchy. Another option is to consult, as applicable, the mentee's career, training, succession, or professional development plan.

Finally, the types of functions mentors perform in career, learning and development, or skill development (performance-based) mentoring situations can be classified as follows:

- Sharing, for example, experience, point-of-view, resources, tools, personal lessons learned, or stories;

- Advising or recommending, for example, an activity, resource, expert, or action;

- Reviewing, for example, work, progress on development actions, or the outcome of a contact with an expert;

- Facilitating goal setting, for example, using a framework such as SMART (specific, measurable, action-oriented, realistic, and time-bound) to help the mentee create goals that have substance;

- Tailoring opportunities in a purposeful way (for example, stretch assignments); monitoring progress on those opportunities and using them as a springboard for discussions;

- Confidence building, for example, providing feedback that expresses confidence in the mentee or is motivational; making the mentee feel special by virtue of the time and attention he or she receives from the mentor; and

- Network building, for example, targeted connection to individuals with influence, status or power.

STRENGTHS AND CRITICISMS

Other Options Available to Accomplish Intended Goals

Before discussing the strengths and criticisms, it would be valuable to examine other options available to accomplish the intended outcomes of mentoring. While mentoring certainly has a range of applications, other options are available to accomplish the same or similar outcomes. Classroom training and learning events such as "brown bags" or "lunch-and-learns" offer viable alternatives for skill or knowledge building. Mentoring is a longer-term situation than training or learning events. The framework of mentoring is a relationship between the participating parties that is unlike the relationship between trainees and facilitators. In fact, at the foundation of mentoring is the development over time of the professional and personal relationships between the mentor and mentee. Development of the relationships involves engendering understanding, trust, sense of connection, and so forth. On the other hand, brown bags and lunch-and-learns are typically forty-five- to sixty-minute informal sessions or gatherings for a "slice" of education/information about a topic (for example, three keys for effective career planning). The dissemination of information rather than relationship building and sponsorship is the focus. The presenter can be an outside guest/expert or an internal resource; time for questions and answers should be included. Brown bags and lunch-and-learns are a well-suited choice for the reinforcement of learning concepts to a broad number of individuals following a training class. They are also viable as a choice for cascading information or a personal enrichment topic, such as stress management, throughout a division or the whole organization. Finally, by virtue of bringing people together around a shared interest, brown bags and lunch-and-learns can be conducive to such outcomes as peer sharing and networking.

Mentoring can be described as an intense, personal relationship, as opposed to a stand-alone, formal interaction. This can be particularly true of a mentoring relationship that continues for a long period of time. The mentor can make learning more targeted and personal. However, classroom training programs that are more experiential in their design provide an incubator for internalizing concepts and building skill. *Experiential* refers to training activities that simulate the real-world application of the learning points. This allows for experiencing and applying the desired learning. Classroom training or learning events are the suitable choice when inter-group dynamics are foundational to the learning. For example, hearing divergent ideas on case studies, role playing, and engaging in learning games are integral to achieving the performance objectives of a course in consultative salesmanship.

As discussed previously, mentoring has been closely associated with career advancement during its history. The mentor as an advocate and promoter of an individual's/mentee's career has been a common phenomenon. Mentoring is not the only strategy available in this regard. A formal, structured career planning program, integrated with the organization's human resources function, can also accomplish such outcomes as career advancement. The structured career program can include such aspects as resume writing workshops, job preview events (see Chapter Eight), college tuition reimbursement, advance promotion pools for managerial jobs, and so forth. Mentoring can provide a more personal one-to-one career advocacy experience, as opposed to the more turnkey structured career planning process. The structured career program is a viable choice when an organization wants to improve employees' perceived as well as accrual equity regarding career advancement support. It can also cover a broader swath of employees across the organization, as compared to what one-on-one or group mentoring alone can accomplish. In the case of either the structured career program or mentoring program, employees have to be self-directed (not passive) to experience the full advantages of these processes.

Strengths

Mentoring as a process has a number of overall advantages. At the top of the list is certainly its capacity for promoting learning and development without the formality or administration of scheduling classes. Mentoring can be used to extend learning beyond the classroom walls. Additionally, learning and development can be two-way, as mentor and mentee learn from each other. An example of this two-way learning exchange is the mutual increase in cultural awareness that can develop from a cross-cultural mentoring relationship. In the one-on-one mentoring relationship in particular, mentees benefit from concentrated, individual time with a benefactor for their development or career progression. The mentees, for example, receive advice, debrief experiences, or engage in lessons-learned discussions, identify key learning options, become socialized to the norms of the organization's culture, and pre-strategize for upcoming experiences. The convergence of these factors can accelerate attainment of outcomes related to career advancement or skill building. Further, closer ties can be built between the mentor and mentee, resulting in a longer, more meaningful relationship. In these closer, longer relationships, the mentor is able to gauge the positive impact of his or her mentoring more readily, which can act as an internal reward for the mentor.

Mentoring can enhance an organization's strategy for retaining talent through the guidance, psychological support, and the cultural navigation role that leaders or senior work colleagues, as mentors, can play. In addition, with sharing, interacting, and communicating being integral to the mentoring process, mentoring can be a natural vehicle for knowledge transfer and relationship building.

Mentoring is flexible in terms of offering a number of formats, including one-on-one, group, and distance/virtual, to accommodate the situation, organizational environment, or need. Group mentoring, for example, provides an opportunity for a broader scope of feedback and teaching, that is, feedback and teaching from mentor as well as fellow mentees. This occurs as mentors facilitate group mentoring sessions and engage mentees in sharing their stories, lessons, expertise, and so forth. A peer mentoring network or process provides an effective means for on-boarding or orientating new work team members, project team members, or newly hired employees.

Criticisms

Matching mentor to mentee is more of an art than science; forced matching can be disastrous and can impede positive outcomes such as career movement or skill improvement. Pairs matched through a formal process may be less at ease or have less identification with each other. Eby and Lockwood point out that pairs who connect on an informal basis have a mutual appeal for the relationship. Mismatches can occur from assigned matches and mentors and mentees request a "separation" or simply stop participating. Organizations are frequently unprepared for handling failed mentor-mentee matches. They fail to identify, communicate, and administer policy regarding this issue.

Time is another factor that warrants discussion. Fast pace and long hours that signify today's work world can make it difficult to find sufficient time for exchanges between mentor and mentee. This situation also discourages some mentors from participating voluntarily. Time can be essential to successful development, guidance, and planning. A substantive discussion regarding the goals the mentee wants to accomplish during the mentoring relationship requires back-and-forth dialogue and decision making. This process is an essential part of guidance and planning. In addition, it lays the foundation for development. Time should be allocated during the first two meetings/interactions, for example, for the content of the goals to be crystallized. Face-to-face or virtual, such as email, telephone, or teleconference, interactions are necessary to cultivate the mentoring relationship, in particular the career or skill development aspects.

Approaches to mentoring program design can benefit from more focus on the new generation (Millennials) entering the workforce. Diane Thielfoldt and Devon Scheef, experts on understanding generational differences in the workplace, provide perspective on mentoring the new generations. Their 2004 article "Generation X and the Millennials" paints a picture of the different generations in the workplace and how to mentor them. Millennials enter the workplace with an intimate relationship with technology, a unique socialization style (banding together/teaming, social networking across boundaries and geography, and so forth), a respect for job levels/titles, and expectations that the workplace is a structured environment. In terms of how they should be mentored, a formal mentoring relationship in a group setting, with designated meetings and mentors with an in-charge attitude, may be best suited for Millennials.

Another population or group that does not receive proper attention in the design of mentoring programs is lower-level employees. The issue is that lower-level employees are often excluded in mentoring programs. Programs typically focus on the leadership or high-potential population. This is especially true regarding formal mentoring programs in which the mentor is a more senior member of the organization and career mentoring is involved. Organizations fail to make a concerted effort to leverage the full depth of the organization's membership when identifying potential mentees.

The importance of determining the right balance between structure and fluidity can be overlooked. Structure refers to such components as goal setting, minimum number of meetings, forms, and program duration or timeframe, such as twelve months. Too much structure can impede the process or be very labor-intensive to administer. Too much fluidity can dilute the process because essential information may not be tracked effectively and problems not addressed expediently.

RECOMMENDED DESIGN, DEVELOPMENT, AND IMPLEMENTATION PROCESS

There are four basic phases for implementing a program.

1. Foundation
2. Infrastructure
3. Launch
4. Monitoring and Evaluation

Foundation

Canadian researchers Ronald Burke and Carol McKeen, both frequent contributors to the literature on mentoring, describe three essential questions to address when designing a mentoring program. The first is: "What is the goal of the program?" Another way of asking this is: "What benefits can be realized from a mentoring program?" The answers to these questions illuminate the business need or performance gap that the mentoring program can address. Examples of needs include reducing the time new first-line leaders must spend getting oriented to their role and achieving mastery of the role's functions or glass ceiling issues that contribute to turnover and low engagement in the organization's female and minority population. The program goal can be, for example, to improve the professional and career advancement process for emerging management talent through targeted, personalized facilitation of role function and political skill development. When refining or finalizing the goal, ensure the program client, sponsors, or stakeholders are involved in the review and approval.

Determining the goal is critical and doing so leads to the next essential question proposed by Burke and McKeen: "How will the program's goals be attained?'' Answering this question is synonymous with developing the program infrastructure. It is in the foundation phase that the preliminary work required to develop the infrastructure occurs. The primary facets of the infrastructure are the matching process, orientation or training, and communication. Identify potential matching criteria (for example, personal preference; cross-function; cross-race; cross-gender; program goals; skills or knowledge needs; development needs; or personality) by using instruments to assess communication and collaboration style and to mentor self-perceived strengths. The criteria should be based on the focus of the program. For example, if the focus is on diversity, arranging mentoring pairs across gender or race would be important. If the focus is on eliminating knowledge silos, then matching pairs from different functions is important. Eliminating silos refers to facilitating the dissemination and utilization of knowledge across functions or divisions. If the focus is career advancement, then attention should be given to creating mentoring matches whereby the mentor is at a level to facilitate career movement. Burke and McKeen point out that matches have a higher probability of being successful when mentees have significant input into who will be their mentors. Create opportunities, virtual or face-to-face, for mentees and mentors to get acquainted. Orientation or training is the other component of the infrastructure that should be given attention. During the foundation phase, an outline of the orientation or training content is sufficient.

What processes (formal or informal) are already in place to address the gap or need? Who owns/is responsible for the processes? Can you use/leverage any of these processes? For example, if the information technology (IT) division has an evolving leader program wherein individuals with potential for management positions are identified and systematically nurtured professionally, data, people resources, and systems from this process could be shared. It is not unusual for divisions within an organization to have their own facsimile of a leader development process. The programs are not necessarily formal or highly structured. Such processes are particularly evident when an organization does not have a systematic, organization-wide management development or succession program. It is strategic to identify division- or department-created leader develop and/or mentoring processes that are in existence. This can be accomplished through a survey; communication at council or committee meetings (for example, an organization-wide training council); working with human resources (HR) through interviewing HR business partners or liaisons assigned to the organization's various divisions; and so forth. HR business partners or liaisons are HR practitioners whose focus is to support the division to which they are assigned achieve its strategic initiatives. They are focused more on the strategic aspect of HR services, such as conducting and analyzing divisional talent audits, as opposed to the transactional aspect. An example of a transactional service is setting up candidates for job interviews.

Assess the people and technology resources needed to implement and administer the program. The prominent factors involved in determining the resources needed are the size, which relates to the number of mentors and mentees that will be involved; the duration; and the complexity of the program. Additional key factors include the scope of training or orientation for mentors and mentees; the matching process (for example, paper-based, matching by committee or technology-enabled); the extent to which any processes will be automated; whether the organization's existing communication vehicles can be leveraged, how evaluation will be handled, and what processes will be set in place to handle questions (Q & A). Examples of communication and Q & A processes requiring limited or no day-to-day human administration once launched include a homepage on the organization's intranet with answers to frequently asked questions, several profiles or audio interviews of successful mentoring pairs on the intranet or in the organization's newsletter; cascading information through a series of succinct articles or memos about ways to get the most out of mentoring; and webcasts on aspects of mentoring such as goal setting, managing time, communication expectations, and so forth. The webcasts can be archived and retrieved by program participants when, and as often as, needed. The foundation phase presents an opportunity to scrutinize the feasibility of these types of tactics for development and implementation at a later stage. Of course, budgetary constraints are the final arbiter in decisions regarding which tactics to employ.

Creating a plan for building program advocacy is another key part of the foundation phase. A letter from top leadership promoting participation in the mentoring program is one tactic for building advocacy. The final essential question proposed by Burke and McKeen is: "Is top leadership supportive of the program?" A program sponsor or champion can be an important asset. Contact top leaders who through their words and/or actions are proponents of programs such as mentoring, employee development, or leader development. Enlist their support to influence their peers regarding the value of a mentoring program. Consult with these leaders to develop communications, in their names, that promote the program. Develop a "graphic model" linking the mentoring process and outcomes to the organization's strategic direction and cultural imperatives to support the discourse between leaders regarding mentoring. Create a "fact sheet" about mentoring—for example, who else does it among the organization's customers and among other leading organizations; why they do it; what it is; what it is not; and so forth.

It is evident that the foundation phase covers essential aspects of building a successful mentoring program, including establishing the program goal, outlining the infrastructure, and garnering sponsorship. The key implementation points of the phase can be summarized as follows:

- Start by identifying the overarching goal of the program;
- Pinpoint the business need, performance gap, or cultural gap the program is expected to address, for example, get new leaders up to peak performance faster, improve cross-gender sensitivity, and so forth;
- Engage the requesting client, stakeholders, or sponsors in refining or finalizing the program's overarching goal;
- Identify the target population for program participation, for example, new managers, high potentials, individuals on a succession plan, and new hires;
- Determine whether any processes already exist within the organization that can address the need that the mentoring program will fulfill; consider whether these processes can be leveraged;
- Determine how matching will be performed; identify the matching criteria; and
- Outline the orientation or training content.

Infrastructure

During the infrastructure phase, the program infrastructure is developed more fully. The infrastructure consists of the matching process, orientation or training, and communication.

Matching. There are several avenues for matching. Allowing for naturally occurring pairs to form a relationship is one avenue. In this approach, mentors and mentees are brought together socially to allow them to get acquainted and find a preliminary match. They can also choose an individual they already know and have an affinity for engaging in a developmental relationship with. Additionally, mentees can be provided with tips and resources on how to find a mentor and initiate a relationship. Technology-enabled matching can also facilitate naturally occurring pairs in forming relationships. Eve Tahmincioglu describes the use of technology for matching at Dow Chemical and at Wyndham International, Inc., in a 2004 article for *Workforce Management*. The mentee enters the qualities he or she would like in a mentor into a searchable a database containing mentor profile information. Examples of information that can be in the database include: experience, leadership style, approach to mentoring, and self-identified strengths. A list of names of potential mentors, in rank order with the closest match at the top, is generated based on the mentee's input. The mentee and potential mentor arrange to meet in person and solidify the match or decide whether or not it is the right fit. When mentors and mentees are dispersed geographically, technology-enabled matching is a viable option. Additionally, technology-enabled program administration can save money, time, and labor.

Matching can also be accomplished by a committee or top leadership decision-makers based on program goals. The caution is that matching that does not include any level of involvement by the mentors and mentees is more likely to result in mismatched pairs. This can be mitigated by involving participants in the selection process. That can be achieved by allowing participants to complete personality style profiles that are used in the matching decision. Participants can also submit names of individuals with whom they would prefer to be paired for inclusion in the matching decision making.

Orientation or Training. The learning design for the orientation or training for participation in the mentoring program should be completed in this phase. Both mentors and mentees need to be prepared for succeeding. It is important to ensure they understand the value of the program to them and to the organization, their roles, the tools available to them to support the process, and so forth. A three- to four-hour orientation or training session is typically sufficient. Recommended content for the session includes:

- Purpose and definition of mentoring at the organization;
- An icebreaker activity to generate conversation between participants, encourage exchange of ideas or information, and help lower any anxiety about participating in the orientation session;
- Role, responsibilities, and expectations of the participants;
- Connection to the organization's performance, succession, or leader development system, if a connection exists;
- Tools, such as job aids or learning contracts or career planning work-sheets, question-and-answer email box, and so forth;
- Skills for effective mentoring; primary areas for skill building include establishing rapport, time management, giving and receiving feedback, and translating feedback into action planning;
- Steps for setting learning, career, or networking goals to accomplish during the mentoring relationship;
- Setting boundaries in the mentoring relationship, relative to scheduling time, confidentiality, and discussion topics; and
- Skill practice opportunities; that is, role playing the mentor and mentee's conversation in the initial meeting, training simulations for giving actionable feedback, mock development planning exercises, and so forth.

Develop or purchase easy-to-apply performance-support tools (see Chapter Fourteen) for helping mentors and mentees maximize the benefits of the mentoring relationship. Mentoring expert Ida Abbott's booklet ''Being an Effective Mentor: 101 Practical Strategies for Success,'' is a good example of such a performance-support tool. The strategies describe actionable steps for such important elements as preparing for and conducting the first meeting, setting goals, effective communication, and facilitating the mentee's learning. Abbott also has a companion tool for mentees that provides practical suggestions for making the mentoring relationship a success, including key points for forming a mentoring mindset. The schedule for when training will occur should also be developed during this phase.

Communication. If mentoring is a new initiative, then communication can be particularly important. However, the degree to which the organization chooses to make the mentoring program transparent to the culture determines the extent of the communication plan. The transparency factor can be related to organizational politics, the organization's past experience with implementing similar changes, or organizational norms that dictate taking a low-key approach to introducing new programs. Budget limitations, whether or not the program is organization-wide, and the size of the program can also impact the communication plan.

The overall purpose of communication is to inform, influence, and promote the mentoring initiative in the organization. The audiences involved should be those individuals or populations directly affected by the initiative as participants, decision-makers, or program architects. These include potential mentors and mentees, sponsors, stakeholders, and upper leadership. For example, in the case of mentoring that focuses on leadership development, the potential mentors and mentees can be the entire leadership population. In the case of mentoring that focuses on diversity, the potential mentees can be female and minority leaders identified as high potentials.

Communication is not limited to the written form, such as a letter or e-mail. Communication can encompass lunch meetings, town halls, panel discussions, Future Searches (see Chapter Four), and so forth. Town halls or lunch meetings can be used to introduce the program to mentors and mentees. These types of meetings can serve a dual purpose. They are an ideal arena for program participants to hear the same information and messages at the same time and a social setting for participants to network and get acquainted. A panel discussion is an ideal option for communicating different vantage points relative to the mentoring process. Those vantage points can include panel members who represent past participation in a program, HR, program sponsorship, and program administration. The panel can present information such as specific talking points, and it can conduct a Q & A segment. Talking points for these communication events should include how the program works, why it is valuable to both the organization and the individual, and how it fits into the organization's strategic picture. An e-mail communication, electronic distribution of a program pamphlet or PowerPoint slideshow, or inter-office distribution of a paper-based pamphlet can serve the same purpose. When the participant population numbers are substantial or geographically dispersed, an electronic communication is a more feasible option.

Launch

The infrastructure phase involves development and design. At the conclusion of the infrastructure phase, the matching strategy, orientation, training plan, and communication plan should be ready to implement. During the launch phase the components of the infrastructure are implemented or executed. The focus of the launch phase is implementation and promotion. The schedule for launching the program components should be based on factors such as the length of the program, whether or not the program has a designated time horizon (for example, twelve months), and the program's connection to the implementation of other initiatives such as succession planning. The matching strategy can be executed prior to orientation and training. The advantage of this approach is that activities can be included in the orientation session that facilitate the matched pairs becoming acquainted or developing a level of social comfort with each other. However, matching can initiate and continue after orientation. The advantage of this approach is that activities allowing participants to provide input into the matching can be integrated during the session or sessions.

An example of such an activity is "rapid roundtable" where mentors are rotated every ten minutes from table to table, where they share highlights from their stories/biographies with a table of mentees. Typically, the rotation continues for two or three complete rounds, time permitting and depending on the size of the group. Mentees are encouraged to ask questions and take notes. Mentors' complete biographies can be made available as a handout at the end of the session and/or online if the mentoring program has a homepage on the organization's intranet. After the orientation session, mentees select their top three choices for mentor. The mentees' preferences are included in the matching decisions, with the understanding that not everyone can receive his or her first choice. Of course, elements in addition to the rapid roundtable activity are used to support mentees in making their choices. Personality, communication, or work style assessments can be administered to provide participants with additional insight into both themselves and potential mentoring partners. This can be achieved during the orientation through learning activities focused on interpreting the categories of results/styles. Orientation and training should occur prior to the first meetings/exchanges between the mentors and mentees, since the purpose is to prepare participants for the program. In the case of informal mentoring, this cannot always be accomplished because mentoring is occurring spontaneously outside of implementation boundaries.

It is recommended that mentors and mentees be brought together periodically for education, dialogue, and reinforcement of key information. The sessions do not have to be in person. In some cases participants in the mentoring program are dispersed geographically, making meeting in person impossible. Using technology such as teleconferencing is a viable option in these cases.

Strategize ways the program can be promoted. Recommendations for promotion include an article in the corporate newsletter, information sessions, announcement at leadership meetings or other training workshops, and a welcome reception hosted by program sponsors.

Monitoring and Evaluation

Monitoring the progress of mentors and mentees is an important program facet. Data and feedback on the program's progress are necessary in order to make timely, appropriate adjustments if issues arise. Equally essential, the data can be used to identify the need for future changes and improvements for the mentoring program. Particular attention should be directed toward what the data reveals regarding setting and pursuing goals, the value of feedback or input such as recommendations for improvement, clarity around roles and expectations, and personal satisfaction with the relationship. These factors are central for an effective process.

Specifically, data should be collected regarding the program process and the mentoring relationship. Program process refers to the structural components such as the value of the training, the mechanisms for finding answers to questions, the support tools provided, and so forth. The mentoring relationship encompasses the interpersonal relationship and the psychological and developmental support. Such support includes committing time for the relationship, emotional engagement with the mentoring partner, giving and receiving developmental feedback, mutual confrontation of roadblocks to success, satisfaction with the mentoring experience, and so forth. In this context, aspects of emotional engagement include receptivity to the process, genuine interest in the mentee's development/success, and trust-building behaviors. Progress can be tracked through periodic evaluations, an end-of-program evaluation, interviews, focus groups, and the number of successful matches. Exit interviews with mentors and mentees are also an option to debrief the mentoring experience.

Developing policy is another element of monitoring and evaluation. The organization's policy regarding the management of complaints, the dissolution of mentoring pairs that are not working, and the re-pairing of individuals should be determined. The policy manual can also include the program goals, the scope for the program, eligibility for the program, expectations of the participants, and key points regarding confidentiality. Finally, any program disclaimers should be included in the policy. A common disclaimer in mentoring program policies is one that advises mentees that participation in the program does not in any way guarantee job promotion. Make the policy document available to all participants in the program by distributing it during the training, for example.

CRITICAL SUCCESS FACTORS

Formulating a clearly defined reason or goal for the existence of the program is perhaps the foremost critical success factor. Be very clear on the purpose of the mentoring program and how it aligns with the organization's strategic direction. In addition, ensure that program objectives are articulated with clarity to all program stakeholders, that is, program leaders, administrators, sponsors, and participants. View the design and implementation of the program from a holistic perspective. Carefully consider, within the context of the organization's structure and culture, any social, political, legal, or intercultural factors.

It is also important for the organization to assess the depth and breadth of any culture-related barriers that could impede success. Examples of such cultural barriers are listed and described below:

- *Impact of a secret versus an open process.* A secret process means the mentoring program is not publicized and that only select individuals are invited to participate. In addition, the criteria for selection of participants are not widely shared. Even if an organization feels justified in opting for a secret process, it does not mitigate the impact on trust and inclusion. Employees can see the program as designated for the few or inequitable. If the program is designated for a particular group, such as managers, it is better to communicate that openly.

- *Effect of distance mentoring on participation and relationship building.* It is strategic to consider geographic distance if it will be a factor for engaging in mentoring relationships in the organization. Prepare for possible challenges. Incorporate mentors and mentees in leveraging the available technology such as e-mail, videoconferencing, e-journal (blog), and so forth. In addition, sharing a photo, short biography (a document or audio file), and/or commitment statement on an organization's intranet can help participants develop comfort with self-disclosure in the virtual world.

- *Questionable commitment of budget and people to sustain the program.* Without a solid budget, it is difficult to launch and, more importantly, sustain a formal program. It behooves the program designers to secure (through their organization's processes) budgetary and personnel support before launching.

- *Impact of low-trust culture on participant's comfort with confidentiality.* Implementing mentoring in a culture with issues related to trust runs the risk of failure. The mentoring experience is built around a personal relationship between two people in which communication, sharing, and self-disclosure are critical ingredients. It can be challenging to promote a program or cultivate mentoring relationships in a culture of low trust or fear.

Additionally, make sure both mentees and mentors receive some type of orientation to the program. Training that does not encompass the relevant content points for preparing mentors and mentees for the process, or is a one-time event when reiteration is needed, can jeopardize the level of success. Mentors and mentees need to understand their roles, what is expected of them, the value of the program, program policies, how to access and program resources, relationship-building techniques, and so forth.

Matching mentors with the right mentees is a lynchpin of the process. This even holds true for informal programs whereby mentors and mentees form their own matches. Do not force a match that is not working. Have a process in place to help mentors and mentees handle matches that do not work, such as a trial period for determining whether or not the mentee and mentor are able to solidify the match. At the conclusion of the trial period, mentees and mentors would be matched in new pairs, providing individuals were available for the re-matching. Another option can be to provide assessment and guidance from a mentoring program administrator on ways to improve the relationship before dissolving it. Of course, marked differences in personality or communication style can be impossible to surmount. However, issues related to time, such as finding time to meet or maximizing the time together, lend themselves to suggestions for improving the situation. This is not intended to imply that there is a magic elixir, if you will, for solving issues between mismatched pairs; there is not. The salient point is that tactics can be implemented for time management, such as scheduling meetings ahead of time, starting each meeting or exchange with a progress review, meeting or communicating virtually (e-mail, voice mail, text messaging), focusing on the quality not the amount of time spent together, and preparing ahead for any discussion or meeting. Finally, when possible, collect some data on why the match did not work. Seek answers to questions such as: Did the mentee want too much time? Was the mentor hard to reach? Did the mentor initiate or participate in defining expectations for the mentoring relationship?

The mentoring pairs should be encouraged to acknowledge and agree on the boundaries of confidentiality regarding what can and cannot be shared from their discussions. For instance, sharing client-sensitive policy decisions or personal information that was discussed would be a breach of confidentiality. The mentor and mentee can agree not to share confidential information with each other. However, that approach can impose limitations on the scope of the issues that the pair chooses to address.

References

Abbott, I. O. (2000). *The lawyer's guide to mentoring*. Washington, DC: National Association for Law Placement, Inc.

Allen, T. D., Eby, L. T. & Lentz, E. (2006). Mentorship behaviors and mentorship quality associated with formal mentoring programs: Closing the gap between research and practice. *Journal of Applied Psychology*, *91*(3), 567–578.

Burke, R. J., & McKeen, C. A. (1989). Developing formal mentoring programs in organizations. *Business Quarterly*, 53, 76–80.

de Jamasz, S. C., Sullivan, S. E., & Whiting, V. (2003). Mentor networks and career success: Lessons for turbulent times. *Academy of Management Executive*, *17*, 78–91.

Eby, L. T., & Lockwood, A. (2004). Protégés and mentors' reactions to participating in formal mentoring programs: a qualitative investigation. *Journal of Vocational Behavior*, *67*, 441–458.

Ensher, E. A., Thomas, C., & Murphy, S. E. (2001). Comparison of traditional, step-ahead, and peer mentoring on protégés' support, satisfaction, and perceptions of career success: A social exchange perspective. *Journal of Business and Psychology*, *15*(3), 419–438.

Higgins, M., & Kram, K. (2001). Reconceptualizing mentoring at work: a developmental network perspective. Academy of Management. *The Academy of Management Review*, *26*(2), 264–288.

Kram, K. E. (1985). *Mentoring at work: Developing relationships in organizational life*. Lanham, MD: University Press of America.

Owens, D.M. (2006). Virtual mentoring. *HR Magazine*, *51*, 105–107.

Tahmincioglu, E. (2004, December). Logging on to link mentors, protégés: Keyword: matchmaking. *Workforce Management*, pp. 63–65.

Thielfoldt, D., & Scheef, D. (2004, August). Generation X and the millennials: What you need to know about mentoring the new generations. *Law Practice Today*. Retrieved May, 16, 2008, from http://www.abanet.org/lpm/lpt/articles/mgt08044.html.

Turban, D. B., & Dougherty, T. W. (1994). Role of protégé personality in receipt of mentoring and career success. *Academy of Management Journal*, *37*(3), 688–702.

Viator, R. E. (1999). An analysis of formal mentoring programs and perceived barriers to obtaining a mentor at large public accounting firms. *Accounting Horizons*, *43*, 37–53.

Waters, L., McCabe, M., Kiellerup, D., & Kiellerup, S. (2002). The role of formal mentoring on business success and self esteem in participants of a new business start-up program. *Journal of Business and Psychology*, *17*(1), 107–121.

Whitely, W. T., & Coetsier, P. (1993). The relationship of career mentoring to early career outcomes. *Organizational Studies*, *14*, 419–441.

EDITORIAL CONNECTIONS

Mentoring, as described in Chapter Twenty-Six, comes in a variety of formats, including lateral or peer mentoring, group mentoring, cross-cultural mentoring, distance or virtual mentoring, performance-based mentoring, and reverse or upward mentoring. Thus, mentoring interventions can vary in their focus, size, target group, and/or communication techniques. Performance-based mentoring might, for instance, focus on the improvement of individual performance in one or more specific areas, while at the same time building constructive relationships between junior and senior staff. Alternatively, an upward mentoring intervention might focus on knowledge sharing between retiring staff and current staff, thus being closely tied to succession planning (see Chapter Twenty-Nine).

As a result, mentoring can be a very dynamic, connecting element in your performance improvement system. The flexibility of format makes mentoring a valuable performance intervention in most organizations. Mentoring can used to support everything from motivation and self-concept to expectations and feedback. By building relationships around the accomplishment of results, mentoring is often a well accepted and appreciated performance intervention that contributes substantially to an organization's culture (see Chapters Thirty and Thirty-One).

WHAT'S COMING UP

Executive leadership coaching, as described in Chapter Twenty-Seven, also offers many of the performance benefits of mentoring, although with a slightly different focus. As the name of the intervention suggests, executive leadership coaching focuses on the development of leadership knowledge and skills by building the relational prowess of organizational executives. As Daniel White describes in the chapter, the impact of leadership successes and failures is amplified by several magnitudes when the decisions are those of organizational executives. Consequently, the development of leadership skills within the ranks of executives is a key activity for improving performance.

CHAPTER TWENTY-SEVEN

Executive Leadership Coaching

Daniel White

INTRODUCTION

Organizations invest in developing leaders because of their potential for powerful impact. Their words and deeds have an influence on all around them. The things they say become amplified as if spoken through a loudspeaker. Because of their power, their accomplishments as well as their missteps are often exaggerated in the eyes of others. Their actions and decisions affect people and the organization in a variety of ways. For example, they provide vision and strategic direction that can lead the organization down successful or ruinous paths. They maintain important relationships with members that can be inspiring, neutral, or demoralizing. They can stimulate learning and innovation or foster stagnant adherence to the status quo. They serve as moral exemplars encouraging either ethical or corrupt business practices. They serve as role models for people who emulate their actions and attitudes, whatever they may be. Because of the tremendous impact inherent in leadership roles, investing in the development of leaders can have a sizable effect on an organization, its members, and, of course, the leaders themselves.

Leadership is filled with challenges. Leaders need to integrate vision, strategy, people, and systems in order to build a successful organization. They need to balance several seemingly contradictory approaches, such as influencing versus being influenced, delegating versus making decisions, rewarding versus holding people accountable, and many others. Deciding which approach best suits each situation requires wisdom, insight, and judgment. Developing these abilities takes talent, perceptiveness, and effort. This chapter describes a process for helping leaders develop these abilities.

In their 1995 *The Leadership Challenge*, James Kouzes and Barry Posner define leadership as "the art of mobilizing others to want to struggle for shared aspirations" (p. 30). How do leaders learn this art of mobilizing others to want to struggle? Most learn through some combination of personal experience, observation of role models, and formal training. Organizations support experiential learning by moving leaders into new roles and providing them with stretch assignments. In these experiences, they try out a variety of actions, observe the outcomes, and re-use the ones that work.

Expanding Your Options

Project post-mortem—review of a project analyzing all aspects of it, from conception to completion. It focuses on achievement of goals, mistakes made, and lessons learned for future improvement.

Leaders also learn through observation and study. For example, watch mentors and role models to learn their techniques. Additionally, they attend formal training programs and read books and articles to learn and practice new skills. They try out techniques of their mentors, authors, and trainers, and, over time, become skillful leaders.

Coaching: An Individualized Approach to Leadership Development

Coaching provides another way to develop leadership skills. Its goal is to accelerate the leader's development. It compresses the leader's formation of concepts, experimentation, behavioral learning, practice, and feedback into an intensive, multi-month, developmental experience. By using this regular and intense focus over an extended time period, coaching speeds learning time, enabling leaders to learn and change behavior in months rather than years.

Since the mid-20th century, leadership training emphasized the generic skills and practices of leadership, practices that all leaders could use. In the last two decades, organizational psychologists have recognized that many leadership practices are rooted in the individual, that is, they are successfully applied, or not, based on an individual's personality. Their style, beliefs, and values shape the way they lead and either enhance or inhibit their ability to lead. Coaching has evolved as a way to leverage this individual component of leadership. It differs from other developmental approaches by this intense focus on the individual.

Coaching also gives leaders experience in self-development. When people develop and change behavior they generally pass through a series of predictable phases. As they progress through the phases of change, they learn how to move from being unaware of the need for change (pre-contemplation) to thinking about change (contemplation) to preparation for change to acting on the change and to maintenance of the change. (See the Phases of Behavioral Change section later within this chapter.) They learn how to observe their behavior, recognize its impact, reflect on their underlying thought processes, and alter their behavior. The self-development skills they learn through coaching become a foundation for their continuing development throughout their careers.

Coaching also brings hope and the possibility of change into people's lives. Leaders recognize that change is possible. When they engage in personal change, they counter the routine and cynicism that can arise from working in a competitive, political workplace. Coaching can bring out the best in people by building a realistic optimism about what is possible.

Expanding Your Options

Experimentation—using new methodologies for problem solving or carrying out business processes.

DESCRIPTION

Goals and Expected Results of Coaching

The goal of leadership coaching is to facilitate behavior change that enables both the leader and the organization to become more successful. It is expected that these behaviors will be visible to others and have real, measurable impact on the organization. Some of the most frequently selected behavioral goals include providing feedback, influencing, resolving disagreement, delegating, communicating strategy, and developing people. It is most important that the behavior change goal fits the individual client as well as the organization's needs and culture (see Chapter Thirty).

The leader and coach determine the behavior change goals early in the coaching process. They begin by assessing the leader's style and practices. They gather this information about the client from a variety of sources. The coach can interview or survey a sample of the client's stakeholders to learn about their perceptions of the leader's behavior patterns. (This process is called 360-degree feedback because it gathers the perceptions of people senior to, parallel to, and direct reports to the designated leader; see Chapter Nine). 360-degree feedback generally provides an accurate assessment of the leader as perceived by stakeholders. Personality assessment instruments can clarify their motivations and preferred modes of acting. The coach and client interpret the assessment information, then use it to identify specific, behaviorally oriented goals. These goals become the client's development plan, which serves as the focus of the coaching process.

The Coaching Process

Because behavior change requires a good deal of commitment, energy, and focus, coaches tend to advise leaders to select only one, two, or three behavioral goals to work on within the coaching engagement. A majority of coaching engagements last for approximately six months, with weekly or bi-weekly sessions of one to one-and-a-half hours. They then spend the rest of their time together understanding, developing, practicing, and refining new behaviors. The coaching engagement can be broken down into four broad phases:

1. *Introduction*—to each other and to the coaching process;
2. *Assessment*—of strengths and development needs;
3. *Selection of a development plan*—choosing one or two critical, new leadership practices; and
4. *Development*—learning, practicing, and refining the new practices.

Introduction. The coaching process begins with the coach and client getting to know each other and agreeing on a structure for the coaching process, for example, frequency and length of meetings, confidentiality and progress reporting, and an overview of the coaching activities.

Assessment. Next, they begin the assessment process. The coach may introduce a process for gathering feedback from others about how they perceive the client. This is usually done through 360-degree interviews or a 360-degree leadership assessment instrument. The coach may also introduce a personality assessment exercise, such as the Myers-Briggs Type Instrument or other instrument. Coaches generally select instruments based on a few criteria: the instrument(s) that they are most familiar with, the instrument(s) that fit the client's situation best, and the instrument(s) that are used in the client organization. Together, they integrate all this information into an expanded view of the leader. They will examine the behavioral descriptions from the 360-degree feedback and look to the personality assessment both for the motivations and preferences underlying these behaviors, as well as for consistency of the behaviors with their assessed style.

Selection of a Development Plan. As the coach and client interpret the assessment information, they first look to deepen the client's self knowledge. They interpret the 360-degree feedback for the consistent patterns of how the client is perceived by others. They study the personality profile, relating this information to the client's self-perceptions and the coach's perceptions about the client. They also discuss the client's self-perceptions, motivations, beliefs, and values, seeking to integrate all this information into a detailed picture of the client. They then use this to identify the client's strengths and one, two, or three development needs. (Since behavior change takes a great deal of concentration and self-awareness, coaches select a small number of development areas to help them manage their energy and maintain the client's focus on the most important changes. Too many goals make it less likely that real, lasting change will take place.) It is interesting to note, as Prochaska, Norcross, and DiClemente point out in their 1994 book *Changing for Good*, that with many people, their strengths and development needs are direct opposites of each other, often resulting from over-using the strength. For example, a leader who steps in and gets personally involved when problems arise might not be very empowering or trusting of people to handle problems when they arise.

Development. Once the coach and client have identified a development plan, they begin by enabling the client to develop skill and comfort with new behaviors. They examine the old behavior patterns by talking about how the client acts in certain situations. Then they invent and practice new behaviors, first in the safety of the coaching room, then within the workplace. The client practices and refines the new behaviors until he or she becomes competent and comfortable with them.

The Process of Behavioral Change—Cognitive-Behavioral Coaching

The coaching approach described in this chapter has its roots in both behavioral and cognitive psychology pioneered by Aaron Beck in the 1970s. The cognitive-behavioral approach begins with the recognition that people are sense-making animals who both interact with and interpret their environments. When the coach works with the client's interpretations, he or she draws upon cognitive psychology. When the coach works on the client's interactions, he or she draws on behavioral psychology. A skilled coach continually looks to relate the client's interpretations with his or her actions, hence cognitive-behavioral coaching.

Coaches do this because the key principle underlying cognitive-behavioral coaching is the causal relationship between a person's interpretations and his or her actions. The way a person thinks about a particular situation guides his or her behavior in that situation. For example, I will act differently if I believe a bear is approaching my campsite than if I think my son is approaching. Cognitive psychologists refer to these situationally based thinking patterns as mental models or structures of interpretation. A person's mental model of a particular situation determines his or her behavior in that situation. Expressed formulaically:

$$\text{Mental model}_1 \rightarrow \text{Behavior}_1$$

Or "mental model *one* drives behavior *one*." After a key behavior has been selected, the coach helps the client to understand the nature of the mental model that is driving the behavior and to recognize how the model influences the behavior. One way of creating this understanding is to ask the client to think about a situation in which he or she uses the behavior, then to describe the thoughts that immediately precede the behavior. Through talking about relevant mental models, the client becomes aware of what thoughts led him or her to engage in the critical behavior.

Since making a behavior change takes considerable energy and time, succeeding at it requires considerable motivation. Identifying a motive for the change becomes an important step for the client. One way to find this motivation is to examine the impact of the critical behavior. Often the impact of the current behavior is not pleasing to the client, or to others. For example, a client who does not delegate may be experiencing an under-performing, under-motivated team, as well a personal work overload. By focusing on these impacts of his or her own behavior, the client can decide that he or she doesn't like this impact and wants it to change.

We could express this as:

$$\text{Mental model}_1 \rightarrow \text{Behavior}_1 \rightarrow \text{Impact}_1$$

Or "mental model *one* drives behavior *one* which leads to impact *one*." After acknowledging the undesirability of the current situation, the coach can ask the client what impact would be more desirable. The coach can then move the conversation to exploring this new, more desirable impact.

$$\text{Mental model}_1 \;\rightarrow\; \text{Behavior}_1 \rightarrow \text{Impact}_{1\,(\text{undesirable})}$$
$$\downarrow$$
$$\text{Impact}_{2\,(\text{desirable})}$$

Talking about a new impact, whether it is a more motivated team or more respect from senior management, can serve as the seed for a motivation to change. Exploring a more desirable impact and recognizing that it is truly possible can motivate the client to want to invest energy into making the change.

The next task for the coach and client is to determine what type of new behavior will lead to the new impact.

$$\text{Mental model}_1 \rightarrow \text{Behavior}_1 \rightarrow \text{Impact}_{1\ (\text{undesirable})}$$
$$\downarrow$$
$$\text{Behavior}_2 \leftarrow \text{Impact}_{2\ (\text{desirable})}$$

At first blush, the new behavior may seem obvious. For example, delegating more can lead to a more motivated team. But it can be challenging to develop and put into practice the specific, new behaviors that fit both the client and the situation. The client may find it relatively easy to delegate tasks, but have difficulty delegating decisions, because it comes into conflict with an existing mental model. The old mental model might say something like, "These are the decisions that I should make because I am the most knowledgeable and have the best judgment."

Now the coach will need to extend the roadmap back to the mental model arena. The coach and client can re-examine the old mental model that is preventing the practice of the new behavior and explore new mental models that would better support the new behavior.

$$\text{Mental model}_1 \rightarrow \text{Behavior}_1 \rightarrow \text{Impact}_{1\ (\text{undesirable})}$$
$$\downarrow$$
$$\text{Mental model}_2 \leftarrow \text{Behavior}_1 \leftarrow \text{Impact}_{2\ (\text{desirable})}$$

In the example above, the coach might ask the client whether he could imagine a way that his staff could become knowledgeable enough for him to trust their decisions.

The Phases of Behavioral Change

To the client, the process of change can feel like a journey into an unknown territory. Most people have never taken this trip before and benefit from a guide who can point out the milestones and landmarks letting them know how far they have come and how far they still have to go. A coach who understands the experience of behavior change can provide this road map. The phases of change model can serve as this valuable coaching tool. The phases model is based on research by James Prochaska and colleagues, whose research demonstrates that all people who make successful behavioral change pass a series of distinct phases on their way to long-term change. Each phase is characterized by its own new awareness, level of commitment, and unique emotions, thoughts, and activities.

Understanding the phases of change helps the coach and client determine the agenda and pace of the coaching process. By understanding the client's location in the sequence of phases, the coach can select a strategy that helps the client progress. The phases can serve as a road map for the coach and client, reminding them of where they are, where they've been, and where they need to go next. Awareness of the phases helps the coach stay on the same page as the client, while still nudging the client through the change progress.

1. *Pre-contemplation*—In this initial phase, clients are largely unaware of the need for change and have no intention of changing behavior. If they are aware of problems, they tend to blame them on others, wishing that other people would change. Some of the thoughts and emotions of a person in pre-contemplation are denial, blame, believing that change is not a priority, avoidance, anger, hopelessness, defensiveness, resistance, feeling that "I'm fine," lack of awareness of an issue, and resentment. Because leaders who are in pre-contemplation attribute the causes of problems to others, they generally do not initiate their own coaching. It is usually their manager or human resources manager who initiates it.

   The main coaching strategies in pre-contemplation are to build trust and rapport with the client and to begin examining the process of

   $$\text{Behavior}_1 \rightarrow \text{Impact}_{1 \ (\text{undesirable})}$$

   and to contemplate the desirability of a different impact. If the client can imagine a different, more desirable impact, this can become the motivator to engage in the change process. The coach can facilitate envisioning this by asking the client about his or her feelings about the current situation, then reflecting on the client's dissatisfactions. As the client builds an awareness of a different impact, he or she begins moving into the contemplation phase.

2. *Contemplation*—In this phase clients are aware of an opportunity or problem and of their behavior that contributes to it. They are seriously considering grappling with the behaviors that contribute to the problem. They have not yet made a commitment to take action, usually because the effort seems overwhelming or because they feel positively about some aspect of their contributory behavior. The thoughts and emotions in the contemplation phase include a sense of possibility, speculation about different impacts (what might be), questioning about what it might take to get there, a sense of doubt, confusion, or conflict, or even feeling overwhelmed by the apparent enormity of the change that lies ahead of them. Clients may say, "I've acted this way for forty years and I don't think I can change."

The coaching strategies in contemplation include examining Behavior$_1$ and the situations in which the client uses it. To deepen the client's understanding of Behavior$_1$, the coach can ask questions such as:

- "When do you do it?"
- "When do you not do it?"
- "With whom do you do it?"
- "What happens just before it?"
- "What is rewarding about doing it?"
- "What does it feel like to not do it?"

To examine the client's thinking, the coach can ask:

- "What are your beliefs about the situation? About yourself in this situation? About others in this situation?"
- "What is your prior, similar experience and how did you interpret it?"

The coach can also ask about for the client's feelings about the situation and his or her behavior. As clients better understand the situation, their behavior, and mental models, they become ready to identify an alternate behavior, one that will lead to the more desirable impact. Even if a client defends current behavior as "tough but right," the coach can ask about the impact of the behavior and whether the client might wish for a more satisfying or productive impact. The key here is to open up possibilities, not to debate leadership philosophies. When the client begins to contemplate different outcomes, he or she can begin the preparation phase.

3. *Preparation*—Clients intend to take action soon. They are planning new behaviors and anticipating trigger situations. They may have already made attempts to modify their behavior, but these attempts might have been sporadic and only partially effective. In the preparation phase, clients demonstrate their desire to move ahead by planning steps and by exploring, brainstorming, inventing new behavioral options, and keeping their motivation by anticipating new outcomes. The coach accelerates the client's development in this phase by helping him or her invent new behaviors, by finding role models who are skilled at the behaviors, and by practicing the new behaviors to increase skill and comfort. The coach also helps the client modify mental models by talking about and labeling new thoughts and emotions that will support the new behavior.

4. *Action*—When the client has practiced enough to develop some skill and comfort with the new behavior and mental model, he or she is ready to put it into action in the workplace. In the action phase, clients are taking

concrete steps to change their behavior. The action may inspire both excitement and anxiety in them. If they have prepared well, they are behaviorally and emotionally ready for action. As they are trying out the new behavior, clients often feel a sense of satisfaction and pride at actually implementing the change. The main coaching strategies in the action phase are to give action assignments and to debrief them by asking about the new behavior, its impact, and the client's accompanying thoughts and emotions. The coach wants to reinforce the client's successful experience, thought, emotion, and to examine what did not work well, so as to make alterations. Coaches ask questions to strengthen and deepen awareness of the new behavior. And because behavior change takes time, they plan more action trials. When a client has developed an initial level of mastery and confidence, he or she is ready to move into the maintenance phase and to terminate the formal coaching process.

5. *Maintenance and termination*—In this phase, clients are working to consolidate their gains, reinforce the new behaviors and attitudes, and prevent a relapse into the old patterns. The goal in the maintenance phase is to "hard-wire" the new behaviors and mental models into memory. To accomplish this, the coach will review and label the successful behaviors and support thoughts and emotions. Since the coach will be leaving the formal relationship soon, clients seek other people for feedback and support and discuss upcoming opportunities to continue to use the new behaviors. Finally, the coach will want to end the process elegantly by offering some level of continued contact and by expressing, as appropriate, confidence, optimism, and encouragement.

Coaching Skills

Questioning. In the coaching process the coach uses a variety of skills to enable the client to reflect, learn, and progress. The coaching skills are primarily conversational and interpersonal. If the two primary modes of conversation are questioning and advocating, (as Peter Senge points out in the 1990 classic *The Fifth Discipline*) then, in coaching, questioning is the more valuable mode because it invites learning. Questions seek to move beyond what is already known to generate new knowledge. Good questions enable clients to make their thinking processes visible and to describe the mental models, beliefs, and values that drive their behavior.

Determining What to Ask. The coach can use questions to guide the conversation. The coach can ask a question that will ask the client to explore his or her last statement more deeply. Or the coach can ask a different question that will move the conversation to a new topic. The coach uses his or her knowledge and intuition to decide between these two directions.

A coach's understanding of behavioral learning and the phases of change is the first guiding principle of questioning. They use this knowledge like a road map to decide whether to deepen the client's experience in a phase or move to a new phase. They formulate questions that facilitate the client's learning and self-awareness; then, when the client has sufficiently experienced a phase, they formulate questions that lead the client through the next predictable phase of behavior change.

In using questions to navigate the road map, the coach might ask about any of the themes in the cognitive behavioral model. The coach could ask about a current behavior, the thoughts and emotions underlying current behavior, the impact of current behavior, a more desired impact, an alternate behavior, or new thoughts or emotions that could drive an alternate behavior.

The second principle of questioning is to use listening and empathy to deepen the clients' awareness of what they are thinking or feeling in a given moment. The coach acts as a mirror to reflect back to the client. In using the questions and listening as a mirror, the coach could ask about the facts or meaning of what the client is describing or the emotions he or she seems to be experiencing. Or the coach could simply ask a question that follows what the client has just said.

Listening. The coach balances listening with an open mind with listening around a hypothesis. The coach listens intently to both the facts and the feelings that the client is expressing. Effective listening requires being open and interested in what the client is saying, as well as trying to understand the client's ideas, perceptions, and experiences. To do this the coach needs to suspend his or her own judgment and preconceptions and try to see the world from the client's perspective.

To be of greatest value, the coach also needs to listen to the client through the filter of his or her own experience. The coach forms hypotheses about the client and how the client thinks, acts, and affects others. The coach uses his or her own mental models about leadership, human behavior, and organizational politics to hypothesize about the client's process of mental models → behaviors → impacts. They also think about what a new process might be. They listen to seek information to explain, confirm, or disconfirm their hypotheses. To listen most productively, the coach needs to balance open-minded listening with hypothesis-driven listening. It is important that coaches become aware of their own biases and filters so they don't unconsciously distort their perceptions of clients. This self-awareness leads both to more open-minded listening and more accurate hypotheses.

Questioning and listening are valuable because they enable the client to define the content of the coaching conversation. This is particularly important because clients learn best when they form their own interpretations and provide their own answers. Yet there are times when the coach needs to advocate a position, offer advice, or teach a new skill. The best times to advocate are when clients ask for help, since this is when they will be most receptive to the coach's suggestion. If the coach believes that the client would benefit from a suggestion or a different interpretation, he or she can volunteer an idea. Here it is best to ask the client for permission to advocate; for example, "Can I offer a suggestion here?" or "You might say something like this in that situation. . . . "

People learn mostly from experience. Therefore listening to the coach relate a story about another client's experience or about the coach's own experience can be a powerful way for the client to indirectly experience new options. Stories are most useful when clients identify with the main character of the story and the challenge resembles their own challenge. A coach who chooses the appropriate moments, selects the right story, and tells it well can accelerate the client's learning process.

Sometimes the client needs to learn a new skill, like how to give negative feedback or how to express disagreement without appearing disagreeable. Occasionally clients can figure out how to do this on their own. But often, they need some guidelines or behavior models from the coach. In these situations the coach needs to act like a trainer, using a step-by-step approach, describing a specific behavior, and modeling this behavior. Once the client understands the new skill intellectually, it is extremely important to give him or her an opportunity to practice. As with formal training, practice is valuable because it gives clients a chance to try out the behavior on their own, in the safety of the coaching room, with an opportunity for immediate feedback.

WHAT WE KNOW FROM RESEARCH

Leadership coaching is a new profession. Writing about coaching began to appear in the late 1980s, and research began in the late 1990s. Most of the research has been small studies conducted about coaching programs in organizations. Only a few research studies have involved larger samples (of one hundred or more participants) and control groups.

Manchester, an executive coaching firm, studied one hundred executives. As reported in a 2001 article for *The Manchester Review* by Joy McGovern and her colleagues, their twelve-month study yielded an average of 5.7 times the initial investment in a typical six-month executive coaching assignment, or a return of more than $100,000 on an outlay of approximately $17,500. Their stakeholders rated their success in achieving their behavior change goals at 85 percent in a post-coaching assessment. The executives reported the following types of improvements in their organizations:

- Productivity (53 percent of executives reported improvements);
- Quality (48 percent);
- Organizational strength (48 percent);
- Customer service (39 percent);
- Reducing customer complaints (34 percent);
- Retaining executives who received coaching (32 percent);
- Cost reductions (23 percent); and
- Bottom-line profitability (22 percent).

They also reported these improvements in their relationships and organizational climate:

- Working relationships with direct reports (reported by 77 percent of executives);
- Working relationships with immediate supervisors (71 percent);
- Teamwork (67 percent);
- Working relationships with peers (63 percent);
- Job satisfaction (61 percent);
- Conflict reduction (52 percent);
- Organizational commitment (44 percent); and
- Working relationships with clients (37 percent).

When asked about what made the coaching effective, the Manchester respondents identified these success factors:

- The coach-client relationship;
- Quality of feedback;
- Quality of assessment; and
- Manager's support.

Another outcomes study reported by Olivero, Bane, and Kopelman in a 1997 issue of *Public Personnel Management* involved coaching among managers within the public sector. This study evaluated executive coaching as a follow-up to leadership training, with a comparison group receiving only the training, without coaching. The study compared the two groups, a coaching plus training group and a training only group. The coaching plus training group showed productivity increases of 88 percent, almost four times higher than the training-only group.

A third study by La Salle University's James Smither and his colleagues in 2003 studied over four hundred leaders who worked with coaches, comparing them to a comparison group of over seven hundred leaders without coaching. The coaching group showed these differences from the comparison group:

- Set more specific goals for their departments;
- More often, solicited ideas for improvement from their supervisors; and
- Received improved (17 percent higher) performance ratings, as measured through multi-source feedback from direct reports and supervisors.

Another study of the effectiveness of coaching was conducted by Carol Gegner of Executive Coaching and Consulting Systems as part of her master's thesis at the University of San Francisco in 1997. The study focused on the executive's perception of the coaching process. A survey using a 5-point Likert scale revealed the following results, in a post-coaching-only study. (Percentages indicate reported improvements in coaching engagements ranging from three months to three years.)

- Gained a better understanding of others—94 percent;
- Understanding how my actions impact others—94 percent;
- Applied my learning to future choices—92 percent;
- Challenged my own actions—90 percent;
- More sensitive to others—85 percent;
- Maintained my goals achieved in coaching—83 percent;
- Applied the feedback to other areas of life—83 percent;
- Stretched my abilities to new heights—81 percent;
- Encouraged others to achieve—81 percent;
- Developed better relationships—81 percent; and
- Developed a better balance in life—71 percent.

In a 2003 study conducted by consulting psychologist Karol Wasylynshyn, eighty-seven executive coaching clients whom she coached over a span of sixteen years were interviewed. The three most substantial results reported by these clients were:

- Sustained behavior change —65 percent;
- Increased self-awareness—48 percent; and
- More effective leadership—45 percent.

These five studies all support the hypothesis that coaching facilitates sustained behavior change, in spite of their methodological limitations. In many instances, coaching results in meaningful and valuable behavior change, possibly more change than interpersonal skills training and other human resource interventions.

Certainly more research on leadership coaching is needed. More outcome studies with randomized experimental and control group and pre- and post-coaching assessments would provide even more solid data. Additionally, more research on the coaching techniques and coach characteristics would lead to improved coach training and supervision. But for a very young profession, the research supports the promise of coaching and should enhance its credibility and continued use in leadership development.

WHEN TO APPLY

When Coaching Is Most Effective

The goal of coaching is to help leaders to develop new skills or broaden their perspectives in a variety of situations. Based on my experience and informal conversations with more than sixty other coaches, the three most common situations for employing coaching are

- Leaders new in position (external hire, promotion, new assignment);
- Leaders with limited interpersonal or leadership effectiveness; and
- Experienced leaders facing new challenges.

Leaders New in Position. When a leader assumes a new position, he or she faces the natural challenges of being a newcomer. Along with the newness, the leader is expected to learn quickly and make some visible impact. Coaching can accelerate this learning and adaptation process.

For an external hire, the culture, the strategy, the people, the procedures, and even the industry might be unfamiliar. The approaches that worked in their previous jobs may not work in their new ones. They need to learn the new environment, build new relationships, determine what behaviors will work best, and develop these behaviors, all fairly quickly. Coaching can be a big help in deciphering the new culture and developing the new behaviors.

Similarly, when someone is promoted to a new position, new behaviors and perspectives are needed. One client who moved from managing ten people to managing forty-five people faced this challenge. His transition from managing technical contributors to managing managers called for a different management style and less involvement with the details of the department's work.

Additionally, as the new manager of a large department with many resources, he found himself under attack from peers who wanted to control his resources. So he needed to find a way of protecting his department from these aggressions.

Leaders with Limited Interpersonal or Leadership Effectiveness. Many coaching assignments focus on developing effective interpersonal skills. Leadership is a very interpersonal job. As John Kotter reports in his 1999 classic *On What Leaders Really Do*, executives spend much of their day in conversation. Leaders need to be skilled at influencing, listening, learning, teaching, and interpreting spotty information. They have to build trust and develop excellent relationships with a wide variety of people, including direct reports, peers, senior managers, customers, and other stakeholders. Developing and balancing these relationships requires tact, empathy, assertiveness, negotiation, political savvy, and cultural sensitivity. Many leaders use coaches to help them develop the high level of relationship skills required by their roles.

For some, the challenge lies in managing direct reports, relating to them in ways that bring out their motivation and best efforts. For others, peer relationships are their biggest challenge. In today's team environments, some struggle with representing one's own ideas while staying open to the ideas of others. A coach can help these leaders to manage people, listen, negotiate, and collaborate.

The third arena for interpersonal skills lies in "managing up." As leaders move to more senior positions, their managers have less time to devote to them. In most organizations, senior management has its own subculture. Leaders learning to manage up must figure out the optimal ways of relating to their managers. They need to empathize with their managers and understand their managers' goals to determine the level of detail, frequency of communication, and communication style that are most appropriate. A coach can help them find this optimal managing-up style.

Experienced Leaders Facing New Challenges. It is particularly challenging to leaders when their organizations encounter a changed environment, change strategy, or enter new markets. A new organizational strategy means that the organization will need to act differently. And this means that the leaders will need to act differently. They will have to specify new behaviors for the members, then teach and reinforce these new behaviors. For example, a biotechnology company was making a transition to being a pharmaceutical research organization. Their goal shifted from identifying and selling promising technologies to discovering safe, effective, and novel drugs. Their old biotech strategy called for employees to identify novel mechanisms and collect small amounts of scientific data to demonstrate the value of these mechanisms to larger companies. In their new strategy, employees had to do much more thorough research, not just in identifying novel targets and in proving their importance, but also in developing and refining drugs that would act effectively and safely on these targets to cure a disease. To be successful, the organization's leaders had to act as empowering coaches, helping scientists to determine the next, most valuable series of experiments, to understand and respond to the competitors' work, and to work more effectively in interdisciplinary teams. These leaders used a coach to help them become scientific leaders rather than senior scientists.

Coaching is also particularly valuable for leaders faced with tricky interpersonal situations. Leaders facing conflicts with colleagues will benefit from coaching, as will leaders who need to manage conflict among direct reports. Coaching can help leaders strategize about how to deal with colleagues with whom they are in conflict or in facilitating a resolution among their direct reports.

There are two situations in which coaching is not particularly effective. The first is with a client who either doesn't want to consider change or work with a coach. No matter how skilled the coach or how compelling the reason to change, the impetus for change still rests mainly with the client. The client must recognize the value of the change and invest the energy trying out new behaviors and in questioning existing mental models. If the client never embraces this commitment, the process does not work. Many clients begin the process with uncertain commitment, then increase their commitment as the process progresses. A client who never commits stays in the pre-contemplation phase and never progresses. These clients continue to defend their current patterns, avoid questioning their behavior, and blame others for any negative impact. After one or two months of continuing, unwavering resistance, a skilled coach will recognize the situation, share his or her observations with the client, and propose ending the engagement. A variation on the light bulb joke is relevant here:

Q. How many coaches does it take to change a light bulb?

A. None. The light bulb has to want to change.

The second less-than-promising situation is when coaching is used as a last resort prior to termination. Sometimes organizations have decided to terminate a leader. The leader may have alienated large numbers of people and lost the credibility to influence anyone. The organization may use coaching to give the person a last chance before termination. Often, however, in these situations there is too much water under the bridge. Perceptions have hardened, and there is nothing the leader can do to rebuild his or her reputation. More cynically, the organization expects the leader to fail and is using coaching to demonstrate that they tried to help the leader as part of their defense against possible wrongful termination litigation. A skilled coach will recognize this, share his or her views with the organization, and consider turning down the assignment.

Common Development Themes in Coaching

The coaching process generally focuses on one or two areas of behavior change. Some common themes in the development plans of coaching clients include:

- *Delegation and empowerment*—Giving others the opportunity to make decisions; delegating technical work; and focusing on leadership work;
- *Influencing*—Discovering how to appeal to the interests of others and to different organizational subcultures;
- *Providing feedback*—Sharing observations on others' work, both positive and constructive feedback, especially for newer leaders;
- *Developing people*—Engaging in the patient, step-by-step process of helping people develop skills;
- *Communicating clearly and succinctly*—Describing complex topics in understandable ways;
- *Listening*—Truly tuning into others and taking their ideas seriously; and
- *Collaborating*—Finding out how to merge ideas with others, especially with people from different disciplines or with different ideas.

Each of these developmental needs can become the focus of a coaching engagement. The coach and client would follow the processes described earlier in this chapter. They would use the assessment data to determine the development need; find a compelling motivation to change; examine the client's current behaviors and mental models; explore alternative behaviors and mental models; rehearse them and practice them in the workplace; and debrief and continue applying them until they become new habits.

STRENGTHS AND CRITICISMS

Strengths

Why is coaching so effective? The author's conversations with approximately forty other executive coaches and clients identified these strengths of leadership coaching.

Customization. Leadership coaching is an individualized learning process that is customized to one leader. The coach and client work at understanding the client's style, values, and specific workplace challenges. They use these unique characteristics to guide the coaching process and make sure that the new behaviors and mental models are congruent with and adoptable by the client. They also examine the client's job, the stakeholders, and the organization's mission and strategy and culture and use this information to ensure that the client's behavior fits their environment as comfortably and smoothly as a tailor-made suit.

Repetition. As Joseph LeDoux reports in 1996's *The Emotional Brain*, neuroscience suggests that as people learn new behaviors they develop new neural connections in their brains. Repetition of a new behavior is thought by some to create and deepen these neural pathways. With enough practice and repetition, the brain develops and strengthens these neural connections to the point that the new behaviors become comfortable habits.

Coaching engagements that last for several months provide this repetition and practice of the new behaviors. It is especially important for the coach to recognize this principle and provide ample opportunity for behavioral practice and verbal reminders. This repetition factor also supports limiting the number of new behaviors in the client's development plan.

Time for Reflection. Another strength of coaching is the time and safety it provides for reflective practice. Busy executives have little time to reflect on their conversations, meetings, and decisions. Without that reflection it is hard to learn and grow from experience. If nothing else, coaching provides time for leaders to examine important situations, their thought processes, actions, and impacts. With regular reflection, many leaders can teach themselves how to alter their behavior to become more effective.

Safe Place for Experimentation. Coaching also provides a safe place to experiment with new behaviors and approaches. With just their trusted coaches in the room, leaders can try out new behaviors, notice what they feel like, and get feedback from a coach. They can try things that might be too risky to try in the workplace. They can make mistakes and revise them until they invent their own best ways of handling challenging situations.

Balance of Support and Challenge. One of the most important and difficult coaching roles is the skillful balancing of support and challenge. The coach supports the client by communicating a belief in the client's talents and capabilities. This support bolsters the client's confidence and ability to try new approaches.

The coach also challenges the client by pointing out behaviors and thought processes that are producing undesirable impacts. Many leaders receive little constructive feedback, especially from direct reports. The feedback leaders do receive is often at the level of result, omitting an analysis of the leader's behaviors that might have led to that result or alternative behaviors that might have caused a different result. Because of this, challenges from the coach represent a unique and valuable perspective for the client. Because most coaches are trained in psychology and leadership, they can delve more deeply into a leader's behaviors and mental processes, helping the person to develop the patterns that are most effective.

Criticisms

Possible Isolation. The greatest weakness of coaching is directly related to its strength. The individualized nature of coaching and its focused dialogues between the coach and client do not directly involve others. The leader can become isolated from the rest of the organization. Coaching may create significant change in the individual leader, but leave out the other stakeholders. The individual may change, but if others do not change, the system can remain the same and eventually even pull the leader back to old patterns.

Needing Help Seen As a Sign of Weakness. The other weakness of coaching is its potential for having a negative connotation among accomplished professionals. In some organizations anyone needing help of any sort can be seen as a sign of weakness or poor performance. Even though the process of self-reflection and behavioral change takes a great deal of wisdom, courage, and intelligence, coaching can have a questionable status in a rugged individualist, macho culture.

The coach, HR professionals, client, and senior leadership can do a lot to position coaching as positive and developmental. They can demonstrate their belief in leadership coaching and its value to the organization. They can be open about their coaching experience and sell it as supportive to the organization's strategy and culture.

Varying Styles and Quality of Coaching. Coaching is a new profession, emerging as an important practice only in the last twenty years. While the availability and quality of training, standards, and certification for coaches has grown considerably, there is no uniform licensing for coaches. Anyone can hang a shingle and get work if he or she is skillful enough at selling him- or herself.

The purchasers of coaching have been getting more sophisticated. As they become more experienced, they are asking coaches about their experience in both coaching and leadership and their coaching process. They are also expecting regular progress reports and looking for the behavior changes that they expect from a professional coaching engagement.

RECOMMENDED DESIGN, DEVELOPMENT, AND IMPLEMENTATION PROCESS

There are two types of leadership coaching commonly used in organizations: short, training-based coaching and longer, multi-session coaching. In the shorter version, coaching is provided as an adjunct to a leadership training program. The training program includes a 360-degree feedback instrument. (There are many commercial leadership assessment instruments that can be added to the leadership training. Some can even be customized to fit the competencies, strategy, and culture of an organization.) A coach spends one to three hours with each participant, interpreting the feedback and using it to compose a development plan. This training-based coaching gives each participant an individualized learning experience, with a small investment of time and money. It lacks the deeper analysis and repetition of a six- or nine-month coaching engagement. But it can be an effective way to introduce coaching into an organization. Leaders generally have a positive and valuable experience with the coach, and some become interested in working with a coach in a longer-term program.

Some organizations introduce full-service leadership coaching by beginning with one or more of their senior leaders. Since senior leaders have the greatest impact, coaching them has the most visible effects. And since coaching is often effective, the senior leaders will recommend coaching to their middle managers as a way to accelerate their development. Working with seniors also builds the credibility and desirability of coaching throughout the organization.

Other organizations may put their toes in the coaching waters by starting with a valued manager who faces some interpersonal challenges. If the coaching is able to help this leader develop, the organization may find it useful enough to offer to several other leaders.

The first phase in introducing coaching involves selling coaching to leadership, as an HR professional would sell any other new program. Pilot-testing coaching with selected leaders and communicating their experiences can enhance receptivity.

Selecting and matching coaches is another important component of a coaching program. This includes identifying a small number of skilled coaches. Successful coaching experience is the most important criteria. The two most important competencies for coaches are the ability to counsel and facilitate behavior change and an understanding of leadership, that is, "the art of mobilizing others to want to struggle for shared aspirations." Along with these skills, a familiarity with the culture and industry can be a real plus because the leadership practices that are effective in one organization may be ineffective in another. For example, successful leadership practices in a multi-national bank differ from those in a technology firm or a university. Some HR professionals who select coaches also look for a coach who has a good personality fit with a particular client, although many coaches are skillful enough to adapt their styles to different clients.

As with any project, it is important to contract at the beginning of the engagement. The sponsor will want to define the length of the engagement (three, six, or nine months), the fee, and invoicing process. Progress reporting is another important and potentially tricky process. In leadership coaching there are essentially two clients, the individual leader and the organization. The coach needs to meet the needs of both. Skilled coaches have figured out how to maintain a level of confidentiality with the individual client, while reporting progress to the organization. Generally, the coach will ask the leader to share his or her development plan with at least the immediate manager. Then the coach will share with the manager and/or the HR manager top-line information about the client's progress on the behavior changes. The coach will keep confidential the more personal information such as the client's motivations, mental models, emotions, and disappointments.

Evaluation can be conducted in a number of ways. The simplest comes from the coach and client debriefing their attempts at behavior change and examining observed impact. A higher level of objectivity can be achieved by conducting an abbreviated 360-degree feedback process near the end of the coaching assignment. A quick, online survey can be designed asking about the client's progress on his or her one, two, or three development areas. A pre-coaching and post-coaching survey can be conducted and compared to evaluate progress.

Coaching can be employed to enhance other interventions:

- It can be employed in conjunction with leadership training.
- It can be used as part of a strategic and/or culture change initiative to facilitate behavior change of leaders and, eventually, behavior change in the entire organization.
- It can be used as part of orientation and integration of new leaders (on-boarding).
- It can be used as part of leadership team building to facilitate behavior change that results in better teamwork or to enable the team to lead the organization more effectively.
- It can be used in succession planning (see Chapter Twenty-Nine), to provide feedback and developmental support in preparing leaders for future assignment(s).
- It can enhance a performance management process to help leaders implement the development plan that has been articulated in their performance reviews.

CRITICAL SUCCESS FACTORS

The primary success factor of coaching is observable behavior change. To reach this goal, there are several characteristics of a successful coaching process. They include:

- Excellent rapport and trust between coach and leader;
- An articulated, agreed-on development plan, defining desirable behavior changes and their potential impact;
- Feedback from stakeholders;
- Involvement of the leader's manager;
- Identification of the client's motivators for making the change;
- Examination of current behaviors, mental models, emotions, and motivators driving old behavior;
- New observations, perspectives, attitudes (mental models) by the leader;
- Trial, practice, and revision of new behaviors by the leader, especially practice in the workplace; and
- The client's progression through stages of contemplation, preparation, action, and maintenance.

When these elements are in place, the coaching engagement is usually successful.

SUMMARY

Coaching is a unique and powerful method for enhancing the performance of leaders. Much of its effectiveness comes from the one-on-one relationship between the leader and coach, their intense focus on a small number of behavioral and mind-set changes, and the opportunity for practice over a period of time. Coaching increases the leader's self-awareness, both behavior and thinking process, which enables the person to continue his or her development beyond the end of the formal coaching process.

The early research on coaching supports its effectiveness. Coaching produces measurable behavior change in a variety of different environments and populations. The research has also begun to identify the characteristics and techniques of the coach that facilitate successful coaching engagements.

Coaching is a new discipline that has evolved by drawing from many of the social and natural sciences. At its core, coaching uses concepts and approaches from counseling, behavioral, cognitive, and social psychology. It also uses concepts from adult learning, leadership studies, organizational behavior, cultural anthropology, psychotherapy, and neuroscience. It will continue to evolve as coaches experiment, learn, and conduct research.

Coaching integrates well with many other interventions. The synergies with leadership training, assessment and feedback, performance management, and succession planning have already been established. Some coaches have been combining coaching with team learning (see Chapter Twenty-Five), defining it as peer coaching. Others have been using coaching in conflict resolution and even e-learning. Coaching has already established itself as a valuable tool for developing leaders. It will continue to evolve as coaches, leaders, and organizations explore ways to make it even more effective and integrated.

Notes

- The leaders' challenges described in the Introduction to this chapter are based on the author's interpretation of the McKinsey & Co. 7 S Model. http://www.valuebased management.net/methods_7S.html

- Some examples in this chapter come from the Leadership Versatility Index, Kaplan DeVries, Inc., 2006

References

Gegner, C. (1997). Coaching: Theory and practice. Unpublished master's thesis. University of San Francisco.

Kotter, J. (1999). *On what leaders really do.* Boston: Harvard Business School Press.

Kouzes, J., & Posner, B. (1995). *The leadership challenge.* San Francisco: Jossey-Bass.

LeDoux, J. (1996). *The emotional brain.* New York: Simon and Shuster.

McGovern, J., Lindemann, M., Vergara, M., Murphy, S., Barker, L., & Warrenfeltz, R. (2001). Maximizing the impact of executive coaching: Behavioral change, organizational outcomes, and return on investment. *The Manchester Review, 6,* 3–11.

Olivero, G., Bane, D., & Kopelman, R. (1997). Executive coaching as a transfer of training tool: Effects on productivity in a public agency. *Public Personnel Management, 26,* 461–469.

Prochaska, J., Norcross, J., & DiClemente, C. (1994). *Changing for good.* New York: William Morrow.

Senge, P. (1990). *The fifth discipline: The art and practice of the learning organization.* New York: Doubleday, Random House.

Smither, J., London, M., Flautt, R., Vargas, Y., & Kucine, I., (2003). Can working with an executive coach improve multi-source feedback ratings over time? A quasi-experimental field study. *Personnel Psychology, 56,* 23–44.).

Wasylyshyn, K. (2003). Executive coaching: An outcome study. *Consulting Psychology Journal: Practice and Research, 55,* 94–106.

Recommended Readings

Argyris, C. (1993). *Knowledge for action: A guide to overcoming barriers to organizational change.* San Francisco: Jossey-Bass.

Beck, A. T. (1976). *Cognitive therapy and the emotional disorders.* New York: International Universities Press.

Blanchard, K., & Johnson, S. (1981). *The one minute manager*. New York: Berkeley Press.

Bolton, R. (1979). *People skills*. New York: Simon and Shuster.

Bush, M. W. (2004). Client perceptions of effectiveness in executive coaching. In I. Stein, F. Campone, & L. Page (Eds.), *Proceedings of the Second ICF Coaching Research Symposium* (pp. 30–37). Washington, DC: International Coach Federation,

Culbert, S. (1996). *Mind-set management*. New York: Oxford University Press.

Dunn, P., & Stober, D. (2004). Client's perception of change as a result of a coaching relationship. Poster presentation at the 112th Annual Convention of the American Psychological Association, July 28, 2004, Honolulu, Hawaii.

Goleman, D. (1995). *Emotional intelligence*. New York: Bantam Books.

Hernez-Broome, G. (2004). Impact of coaching following a leadership development program: Coaching is key to continued development. In I. Stein, F. Campone, & L. Page (Eds.), *Proceedings of the Second ICF Coaching Research Symposium* (pp. 88–94). Washington, DC: International Coach Federation.

Isaacs, W. (1999). *Dialogue and the art of thinking together*. New York: Doubleday.

Kennedy, E. (1988). *On becoming a counselor*. New York: Continuum.

Kotter, J. (1988). *The leadership factor*. New York: The Free Press.

Kouzes, J., & Posner, B. (1995). *The leadership challenge*. San Francisco: Jossey-Bass.

Lepsinger, R., & Lucia, A. (1997). *The art and science of 360 degree feedback*. San Francisco: Jossey-Bass.

Lew, S., Wolfred, T., Gislason, M., & Coan, D. (2003). Executive coaching project: Evaluation of findings. In I. Stein & L. Belsten (Eds.), *Proceedings of the First ICF Coaching Research Symposium* (pp. 62–69) Mooresville, NC: Paw Print Press.

Lombardo, M., & Eichinger, R. (2004). *For your improvement* (4th ed.). Minneapolis, MN: Lominger.

Luthans, F., & Peterson, S. (2003). 360-degree feedback with systematic coaching: Empirical analysis suggests a winning combination. *Human Resources Management*, *42*, 243–256.

O'Neill, M. B. (2000). *Executive coaching with backbone and heart*. San Francisco: Jossey-Bass.

Peltier, B. (2001). *The psychology of executive coaching*. Philadelphia: Brunner-Routledge.

Prochaska, J., Norcross, J., & DiClemente, C. (1994). *Changing for good*. New York: William Morrow.

Rosenberg, M. (1999). *Non-violent communication*. Encinitas, CA: Puddle Dancer Press.

Rowan, J. (1990). *Sub-personalities*. New York: Routledge.

Satir, V. (1978). *Your many faces*. Berkeley, CA: Celestial Arts.

Schön, D. (1983). *The reflective practitioner*. New York: Basic Books.

Senge, P. (1990). *The fifth discipline: The art and practice of the learning organization.* New York: Doubleday, Random House.

Thach, E. (2002). The impact of executive coaching and 360 feedback on leadership effectiveness. *Leadership and Organization Development Journal, 23,* (pp. 205–214).

Vygotsky, L. (1986). (rev. ed.). *Thought and language.* Cambridge, MA. MIT Press.

Watzlawick, P. (Ed.). (1974). *The invented reality.* New York: Norton.

White, D. (2003, April). Repairing damaged work relationships in R&D. *Research-Technology Management.*

White, D. (1996, September). Stimulating innovative thinking. *Research-Technology Management.*

White, D. (1997). Career development of technical professionals. (1997) In A. Pickman (Ed.), *Special challenges in career management.* Mahwah, NJ: Lawrence Erlbaum Associates.

White, D. (2006). *Coaching leaders.* San Francisco: Jossey-Bass.

Zaleznik, A. (1989). *The managerial mystique.* New York: HarperCollins.

PART EIGHT

EDITORS'
DISCUSSION

Just as many performance interventions can be used to improve performance—each addressing different components of the Performance Pyramid model—there are numerous activities within the area of knowledge and skills development that you can use to build performance capacity within your organization. Many times these will be performance interventions that directly target performance issues, such as training or mentoring focused on individual or team productivity. At other times you may want to use knowledge- and skills-building interventions to support the introduction of other performance interventions, such as using cross-disciplinary teams (see Chapter Twenty-Five) to build capacity around a knowledge management initiative.

Likewise, performance interventions associated with the development of knowledge and skills can be valuable for individual, team, and/or organizational performance issues. Often, differing applications of the same intervention (such as, e-learning, mentoring, or traditional classroom training) can actually be used at one or more of these levels within the improvement effort. For instance, in order to improve performance, you may find that a mix of process improvement (redesign or reengineering), new incentives, and more immediate feedback on performance is required. In addition, you might then want to consider a combination of team mentoring and short e-learning tutorials as performance interventions for building individual and team knowledge and skills around process improvement, incentives, and feedback. While the e-learning tutorials address individual skills development, team mentoring may be the appropriate intervention for building team-level knowledge.

In most performance improvement situations, knowledge and skill development interventions will be among the most well accepted of incumbent interventions. Traditional classroom training remains the dominate knowledge- and skill-building intervention in most organizations—widely used to address (appropriately or inappropriately) almost any performance problem. You can—and should—therefore use this familiarity with learning activities to your advantage when striving for a more systemic approach to performance improvement. By integrating multiple and varied interventions into your improvement plans (along with other traditional or non-traditional knowledge- and skill-building activities), you can highlight the necessary, but not sufficient, role that knowledge and skills play in the improvement of performance.

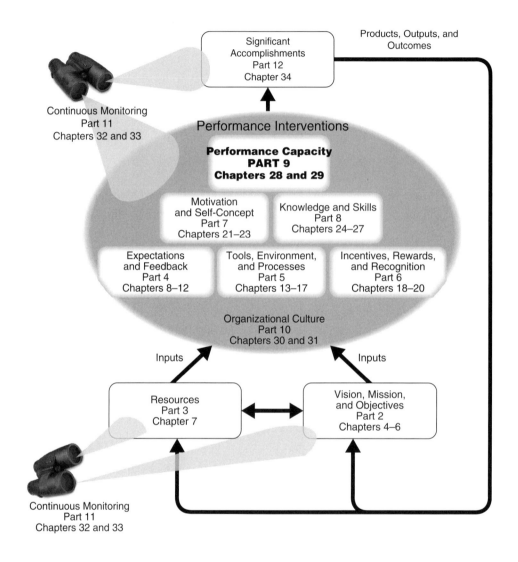

Products, Outputs, and Outcomes

Significant Accomplishments
Part 12
Chapter 34

Continuous Monitoring
Part 11
Chapters 32 and 33

Performance Interventions

**Performance Capacity
PART 9
Chapters 28 and 29**

Motivation and Self-Concept
Part 7
Chapters 21–23

Knowledge and Skills
Part 8
Chapters 24–27

Expectations and Feedback
Part 4
Chapters 8–12

Tools, Environment, and Processes
Part 5
Chapters 13–17

Incentives, Rewards, and Recognition
Part 6
Chapters 18–20

Organizational Culture
Part 10
Chapters 30 and 31

Inputs

Inputs

Resources
Part 3
Chapter 7

Vision, Mission, and Objectives
Part 2
Chapters 4–6

Continuous Monitoring
Part 11
Chapters 32 and 33

PERFORMANCE CAPABILITY

A s you may have noticed, in the illustrations of the Performance Pyramid throughout this handbook the Performance Capability block is positioned at the top. This is not intended to suggest that the interventions associated with performance capability are more important or of greater value than the interventions or other components within the pyramid. As John Wedman points out in Chapter Three, the pyramid shape illustrates that you must build a solid foundation of performance interventions, each contributing and support- ing the others in the accomplishment of significant results—none being of greater importance or value than the others since a complete performance system is necessary to achieve results.

Any block of the pyramid, then, could actually be "at the top." In some applications of the model, Knowledge and Skills may rest at the top of the pyramid; while in other instances, Expectations and Feedback or Motivation and Self-Concept may be at the top—supported by the other components (or blocks) of the model.

However, for purposes of structuring this handbook, one component had to be selected to sit atop the pyramid, and Performance Capability was selected. Performance Capability represents the general ability of the individuals and teams—as well as the organization itself—to accomplish significant and desired results. In other words, do individuals and teams—as well as the organization as a whole—have the necessary attributes (or capacity) for producing and deliv- ering required results?

677

Closely associated to Resources within the Performance Pyramid model, Performance Capability focuses on the human capital elements that are required to achieve results. Thus, while interventions concerning resources focus on the availability and quality of raw materials, financial capital, organizational structures, and equipment required for accomplishing desired results, performance capability interventions focus on the ability of people to produce significant accomplishments.

Expanding Your Options

Competency models—group the characteristics that lead to outstanding performance in a given job, role, or function in order to define what is required for achieving desired results.

Based on wikipedia.org definition (January 2009)

As a consequence, numerous performance interventions are associated with performance capability that you should consider when striving to improve performance. For example, recruitment programs and new interviewing techniques might be valuable performance interventions for ensuring that new employees have the necessary capacity to accomplish desired results. Capacity, in this context, includes such attributes as the aptitude to learn complex tasks, motivation to take on challenging tasks, physical ability to work long hours, and talent to lead others by example. At the other end of the spectrum, early or phased retirement interventions might also be valuable tools for ensuring that your organization is the "right size" for expansions or contractions within your industry and taking advantage of new opportunities—thus ensuring that the organization itself is capable of achieving desired results.

Improving performance capability is essential to achieving results. Although many of the associated interventions are often delegated to human resource departments, they are also a valued component of any improvement system. After all, if you set high performance expectations (see Part Four of this handbook) and support those expectations with a system of performance interventions (mentoring, rewards, feedback systems, performance aids and e-learning, among others) then you'll want the individuals and teams—as well as the organization itself—to have the capacity to accomplish desired results. Therefore, work with your human resources department to make certain that programs being used to attract and retain high-performing employees, for example, are adequately aligned with other performance interventions you are planning to implement.

WHAT'S COMING UP

In Chapter Twenty-Eight, Judith Hale describes how outsourcing can be used to effectively manage the capacity of your organization to accomplish desired results. As with all performance interventions, of course, outsourcing is not necessarily the one, single solution for all performance problems. Outsourcing, or the moving of tasks that have traditionally been completed by internal staff to external providers, nevertheless offers a valuable option for adding flexibility and agility to the human capital resources of your organization. When used appropriately, it can be a vital tool for ensuring that your team, unit, or organization is capable of accomplishing significant results.

CHAPTER TWENTY-EIGHT

Outsourcing

Judith A. Hale

INTRODUCTION

This chapter explains what outsourcing is, why it is used as a strategy to either reduce or avoid costs while rapidly increasing resource capability and capacity, and how to increase the odds of successful implementation. Outsourcing is the strategic decision to procure products and services from external resource providers—vendors or contractors—instead of developing or providing those products and services through the use of internal resources. Organizations have historically hired external providers to augment their internal staff; however, the practice was not always called outsourcing. Today the term outsourcing refers to the practice of relying solely on external vendors, that is, replacing rather than augmenting staff with external resources. It is associated with the elimination of job families previously internal to organizational operations, such as those used to operate customer call centers, perform transactional tasks such as payroll, and create electronic learning programs and materials. The term off-shoring refers to the outsourcing of job families to vendors located in another country. Backsourcing, reports the Institute for Corporate Productivity's David Wentworth in a 2008 feature for *HR World*, is a new term that is being used to describe the process of bringing outsourced services back in-house. What distinguishes outsourcing from simple contracting is that it is a strategic decision not to invest in improving internal capability but instead to leverage the capability of external providers for the long term. This chapter describes a seven-step process for increasing the odds that such outsourcing will be an effective intervention.

DESCRIPTION

Like any intervention, outsourcing should solve some problem or capitalize upon an opportunity. The problem or opportunity that outsourcing typically addresses is usually one of how to more cost effectively and quickly acquire additional people, find people with different expertise, or institute a more sophisticated infrastructure. Outsourcing can help organizations reduce or avoid costs for personnel, personnel development, and capital expenses while allowing them to rapidly increase their current capacity or capability. Organizations have two choices, as illustrated below. They can retool and invest in their own people's capability and infrastructure, including those who work in learning and performance, or they can contract to buy capability from outside vendors.

Solution Choices

- Retool or invest to increase
  - People's capability
  - Technology's capability
  - Facilities
- Use external resources to
  - Reduce the number of full-time employees or avoid adding full-time staff.
  - Buy expertise.
  - Gain access to technology.

The problems that outsourcing is typically hoped to solve are excessive costs, insufficient capability, and inadequate capacity. Organizations use outsourcing to help them be more cost-competitive by either reducing or avoiding costs while increasing their technological and workforce capability and capacity. For example 63 percent of the 301 companies that responded to the Wentworth's survey said they outsourced to cut costs. Companies use outsourcing for:

- Cost savings gained through the use of less costly resources, such as people located in other countries, more energy efficient facilities, or facilities located in geographies with lower taxes.
- Cost avoidance gained by eliminating employment costs normally incurred with full-time employees, such as Workers' Compensation,

retirement and health care benefits, vacations, and the investment in training to increase the skills of the current workforce.

- Increased capability and capacity gained through hiring firms that have the people with the required skill sets, the latest technology, and adequate facilities.

What Is Outsourced

The typical functions that are outsourced include:

- *Customer, technical, and sales support usually done by call centers.* The assumption is that vendors can provide capable and less costly call center staff because the centers are off-shore, where they have access to lower-cost personnel. However, the organization must cover the cost of training the vendor's call center staff and keeping them current in new products, changes in regulation, and so forth.

- *After-market product installation, servicing, repair, and maintenance, usually done by dealers, distributors, and product support firms.* The assumption is that after-market partners have people with the skills required to do the work. The organization, however, usually provides ongoing product training to the vendor.

- *Manufacturing of products or sub-assembly of products, and the warehousing and distribution of products.* The assumption is that there are savings in leveraging the capabilities of companies that specialize in these activities.

- *Human resources tasks such as recruitment, payroll, and the administration of benefits and health and wellness programs, usually done by large vendors that specialize in these areas and who have already established call centers to answer employees' questions.* The assumption is that these jobs are or can be scripted with clear procedures so that it is cost effective to train outsiders to do the work.

- *Learning and development, including libraries, instructional development, course registration and recordkeeping, tracking continuing education units (CEUs), delivery (both instructor led and electronic), and the printing and duplication of learning materials.* The assumption is that it is more cost-effective to leverage other companies' libraries, learning technologies, and instructional design and instructor skills.

For example, Amgen, a pharmaceutical company, outsourced its customer support function. Its vendors help customers work through the maze of health insurance red tape to get funding for long term use of prescription drugs. The vendors may also contact doctors to promote the use of specific drugs to treat chronic illnesses. In this situation, the company avoids hiring and training personnel in how to read and work through the fine print in insurance policies and, instead, leverages the skills of a vendor that specializes in this work. Allstate and SC Johnson also outsource their call centers. Allstate also outsourced some of its human resource functions. CDW and Cisco outsourced their small account receivables and payables.

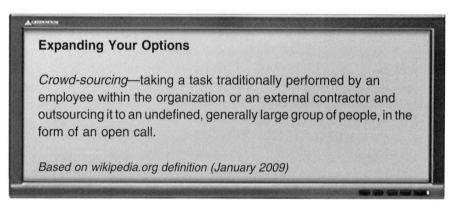

Expanding Your Options

Crowd-sourcing—taking a task traditionally performed by an employee within the organization or an external contractor and outsourcing it to an undefined, generally large group of people, in the form of an open call.

Based on wikipedia.org definition (January 2009)

Another example is the outsourcing of the training and development function. For example, Walgreens outsourced it sales training and some instructional design. It also uses contract trainers. Allstate outsourced its training and development and the management of its learning management system. Caterpillar outsourced the development of its e-learning curricula. As shown in the list below, there are two market pressures for outsourcing the development of training programs and materials. Many organizations require more training and performance support tools because of the need to retool workers in response to new technologies, regulation, products, and jobs. Those organizations may be unwilling to hire more instructional designers or invest in their development. Perhaps finding a shortage of qualified instructional designers, some organizations may look to outsourcing as a logical solution. As I relate in my book *Outsourcing Training and Development* from 2006, on the supplier side, vendors are attracted to the amount of money being spent on training and performance support.

Economic Drivers

- Consumer Side—new technologies, regulation, products, and jobs that fuel the need for:
  - More training or performance support tools.
  - More capable workforce.
  - Capital investments.

- Supplier Side—the amount of money being spent on training:
  - That is increasing the number of training providers.
  - That is attracting an influx of venture capital to fund start-up training providers.

The Argument to Outsource

The argument to outsource ranges from a desire to focus on the organization's core competencies to a desired to grow without capital investments as shown below.

So the organization can:

- Focus on core competencies.
- Leverage others' capability and capacity.
- Improve its ratios, specifically revenue per employee.
- Better manage its training costs.
- Lower its fixed costs such as facilities.
- Avoid capital investments in equipment and facilities.

What Types of Results Can Be Expected

The typical results expected from the decision to outsource are (1) cost savings by reducing the need for staff and by eliminating the need to make capital investments in facilities and equipment and (2) a rapid increase in capability and capacity by procuring external expertise (Hale, 2006). Whether or not these results are fully realized depend on a three variables: (1) the availability of capable vendors with the required expertise, (2) the willingness to expend the required effort to manage the vendor relationship, and (3) the risk and cost associated with using vendors or contractors compared with doing the work internally. Outsourcing training and development, for example, requires the contractor to have instructional designers capable of producing learning programs for both classroom and electronic delivery formats. It also requires those designers to have deep knowledge of the company's products, processes, and practices or have direct access to those that do. One way this is addressed is by requiring the contractor to hire the organization's instructional design and training staff as part of its agreement because the training staff has subject-matter expertise. If this is not done, then both the company and the contractor have to absorb the cost of facilitating access to subject-matter experts and reviewing materials for content accuracy. Another cost and risk to outsourcing is the potential loss or compromise of intellectual property related to product design and marketing strategies. Therefore, when a company chooses to outsource its training, it must absorb the cost of assuring its intellectual property is protected.

WHAT WE KNOW FROM RESEARCH

There is little research on the effectiveness of results of outsourcing; however, there are case studies and anecdotal evidence of both good and bad outsourcing. David Wentworth gives some reasons why organizations have ended their outsourcing arrangements. "It's not just cost overruns, disappointing results and changing strategies that are causing companies to bring HR processes back in-house," relates Wentworth in 2008, "sometimes it's just plain old poor quality." When reading about organizations' experiences, pay attention to who is telling the story and question their motivation. This is especially appropriate when attending conferences and listening to speakers talk about the virtues and sins of outsourcing. For example, if the article or presentation is co-authored, consider how new the engagement is, as there might not have been sufficient time to realize the full benefits or hidden shortcomings of the business relationship. Ask what the business problem being solved was and what the metrics of success were. Pay attention to how much effort the organization put into sustaining, managing, and providing oversight. Be a critical consumer.

When Not to Outsource

When contemplating outsourcing, the organization should, as part of its due diligence, do a cost/benefit analysis and a risk analysis. Outsourcing is a reasonable solution when the organization lacks the internal capability to do certain work without further investment. Such was the experience of many organizations with the need to more cost-effectively train a global workforce. In this case, using an electronic learning delivery system made sense, as advancements in learning technology made it possible to reach a dispersed multi-language workforce through the Internet and intranet. However, this required new skill sets for the learning professionals and an investment in learning technologies.

Unfortunately, some organizations lack experience developing electronic learning materials or the electronic infrastructure to do it cost-effectively. Using vendors that had such experience and had the latest learning technologies simply made sense. This was the challenge Caterpillar faced when it wanted to train some 45,000 technicians worldwide who worked for its dealers, distributors, and large industrial customers. The rapid advancements in learning technology also discouraged many organizations from making premature investments; instead some thought it wiser to leverage the technology invest-ments already made by vendors.

However, the reliance on external resources must not compromise or put at risk the organization's intelligence about it products, processes, or marketing strategy. Training and performance functions are frequently the keepers of the organization's history and product intelligence, particularly if they are respon-sible for the creation of technical training and performance support. Subject-matter experts are typically assigned to help create technical training pro-grams. When the training function is outsourced, even if the external provider is required to hire the organization's subject-matter experts who serve as trainers and instructional designers, history and technical expertise may be lost in the long term. For example, one organization that outsourced its training function required the vendor to hire its trainers and instructional designers who were subject-matter experts in the product. However, once the former employees went to work for the vendor, there was no mechanism to keep them current on new product developments as they lost contact with research and development. The vendor's business model was to keep people billable and to not invest in its own staff's development. The result was that the organization lost history, product intelligence, and the ability to keep its subject-matter experts current.

RECOMMENDED DESIGN, DEVELOPMENT, AND IMPLEMENTATION PROCESS

What follows is seven-step process that is designed to increase the odds that outsourcing is the appropriate intervention and done effectively. The process is shown in Figure 28.1.

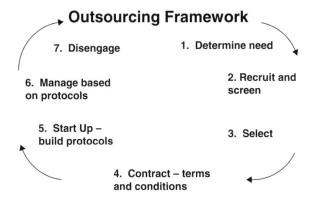

Figure 28.1 Outsourcing Framework.

Define the Need and the Gap

It is important to be clear on what problem outsourcing is expected to solve. For example, one problem may be that work is not being done, either because people lack the time or the capability. Another problem might be a desire to redeploy people to more valuable work instead of using them in their current roles. Ask what is not happening now because internal resources lack the capability to do it or whether it would be better to redeploy those internal resources to more value-adding work. The decision to outsource or not weighs the value or importance of the work being done, the capability of the staff doing the work, and the tradeoff of staff continuing to do the work compared to doing other work. Figure 28.2 illustrates the factors to consider for deciding whether and what to outsource.

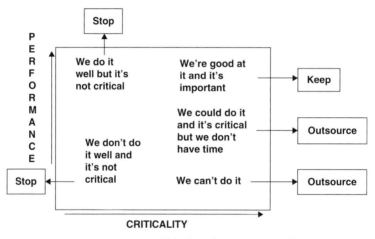

Figure 28.2 Factors to Consider When Deciding If and What to Outsource.

The need to outsource usually falls into one of three categories

1. Too much work exists for the current staff if additional employees are not hired. In this case, the desire is to *supplement* staff or resources by hiring external resources to do what internal staff does not have the time to do. The use of external vendors may be a short-term solution, unnecessary once the need is satisfied.

2. New work that requires new skills or technologies. In this case the desire is to *augment* staff or resources by hiring external resources to do what internal staff cannot because of the lack the resources or

capability. Outsourcing in such cases may be either short term or long term, depending on whether or not the need is ongoing or a one-time situation.

3. There is a better use for staff, or it is too costly to keep them. In this case the desire is to *replace* or *eliminate* staff or resources and to hire external resources to do the work that staff does. Staff may then be redeployed or let go.

The products of determining the need and gap are the baseline, metrics, and risk assessment. The baseline describes the current capability, capacity, productivity, costs, and so forth. The metrics are used to judge or measure the effectiveness of the outsourcing decision during evaluation. The risk assessment identifies what has to be done to protect the organization from loss of intellectual property or capability to compete in the future. Collectively, this information helps formulate exactly what services or tasks to outsource, what expertise is required of the vendor, and what to include in the contract.

Recruit and Screen Possible Providers

Once the problem is defined, agreed to, and quantified, the next step is to identify possible vendors. This can be done by issuing a request for qualification (RFQ) or by perusing trade shows and polling other organizations. The RFQ should include some background on the organization, instructions on how to respond, and a general description of the goods and services being sought. It should also ask about vendors and their:

- Experience with similar work (similar tasks, technology, or industry experience; former employees or competitor experience; and so forth);

- Business model (general contractor versus subcontractor, full-service provider versus specialist, use contractors versus full-time employees, hire the organization's employees, work on-site versus work at own site, and so forth); and

- Qualifications of personnel (technical expertise, language proficiency, security clearances, willingness to travel, ability to work on-site, available full or part-time to do the assignment, and so forth).

Vendors' past experience, business model, and access to capable staff will affect the cost of their services and how quickly they can be up and running (Hale, 2006). Depending on the nature of the work to be outsourced, this is also the time to ask potential vendors about:

- Performance bonds—a form of insurance that protects the company in case the vendor fails to deliver in a timely fashion or to the qualify level required;

- Disaster recovery—a way to protect data and resources in the case of a natural disaster like a flood or hurricane. Examples include having redundant systems or off-site storage of data;

- Commitment to use disadvantaged businesses as subcontractors—an agreement to hire or purchase goods from minority or women-owned companies;

- An intent to hire former staff—an agreement to offer staff whose jobs are being eliminated an opportunity to work for the vendor;

- The use of software in the public domain—an agreement to use software that is not proprietary to the vendor, which in turn allows the company to access any future updates without relying on the vendor. This is especially important when the relationship with the vendor ends; and

- Certificates of insurance—these are similar to performance bonds, however, they refer to workers' compensation, automotive insurance, and professional liability. The purpose is to protect the company should the vendor default on legal obligations such as paying employment taxes or the vendor has an accident while on the company's property or while doing work for the company.

The intent is to narrow the field to only viable vendors who have proven capability to do the work that is required.

Select the Best Provider

Next, a request for proposal (RFP) should be issued that includes some background on the organization, instructions on how to respond, a budget range, and the selection criteria. As a rule of thumb, the criteria might include availability, commitment to hire former staff, past experience doing similar work, and the ability to commit an adequate number of qualified specialists. Depending on the nature of the work to be outsourced, it may also contain requirements about ownership of any products created, including intellectual and real properties. The responses to the RFPs provide a list of criteria by which to compare vendors and select the best qualified one.

Develop the Contract. Once the decision is made as to which vendor to use, the next step is to develop the contract. Contracts typically have two parts: the "master agreement" and the "addenda." Even though contracts are developed by legal departments, it is best if everyone understand the intent behind each provision. The addenda specify the deliverables and are intended to be added or modified as the work progresses and new work is required. The master agreement, however, is relatively unchanging. It contains the general provisions or rules of engagement as shown below:

Contract Elements
- Master agreement—applies to all work
  - Gets the vendor into the accounts payable system.
  - Describes the deliverables in general.
  - Describes the accountability, role, and responsibilities of the vendor's personnel.
  - Describes what is and is not to be included in fees.
- Addenda—applies to specific deliverables

Most of the master agreement is boilerplate; however, some parts apply particularly to outsourcing, specifically the provisions about service level measures, quality level measures, dispute resolution, and flexibility.

Master Agreement
- General provisions or rules of engagement
  - Confidentiality agreement
  - Exit clause
  - Efficacy of operations
  - Financial stability
  - Indemnification clause
  - Governance
  - Liability
  - Reporting requirements
  - Timeliness
  - Termination
  - Safety
  - Service level agreement
  - Quality level
  - Dispute resolution
  - Flexibility

Service level and quality level measures are the standards used to judge the adequacy of the service and the quality of the work done. Specifying these standards is especially important if there is a dispute, and pre-defining how service and quality will be measured at the start increases the odds the relationship will be successful. Service level measures include the number and qualifications of the people assigned to do the work, a commitment for people being available to do the work, the timeliness of the work, the hours of operation, and an agreement to follow the reporting rules or rules of engagement. Quality level measures are the standards that will be used to judge the adequacy and utility of the work produced. They might include a commitment to follow industry standards, conduct usability tests, get signoffs as to the accuracy and completeness of any work, commitment to follow pre-defined work procedures and protocols, and the like.

Dispute resolution explains the protocols or guidelines to follow when there is a problem. The protocols include items like who should be told when there is a disagreement, when the other side should be informed, and how the message should be sent. The protocols might also explain who has the authority to mediate a dispute and whether a neutral venue is required, such as arbitration, if the parties cannot resolve the dispute themselves. Flexibility is putting language into the contract that allows both sides to take advantages of emerging technological advancements and be able to respond to regulatory changes, evolving customer expectations, and new developments in the marketplace. The products of these provisions are a contract that supports a relationship that works for both parties.

Start-Up

About the time the contract is signed (ideally even beforehand), the organization should think about how it wants to provide oversight. Protocols are oversight rules that help make explicit assumptions about how the relationship will work. In the world of outsourcing, the common protocols include:

- How the parties will communicate with one another, such as weekly meetings or conference calls, who will attend, who is copied, and so forth;
- Who has authority to make major and minor modifications to the project plan, and who is to be informed when changes are made;
- Who has authority to commit resources (people, dollars, space, and equipment);
- How requests for investment in new technology or capital resources will be handled;
- How frequently and to whom actual time and dollar usage will be reported and compared to budget and plan;
- How a change in staffing will be handled; and
- How to address disputes, problems, the need for new or different resources, and the like.

The question of who owns any intellectual property used during the execution of the project or created by the vendor as a result of the work should be answered, either as a provision in the contract or through a protocol. The protocols are living documents that should help avoid misunderstandings and facilitate communication, speedy decisions, and flexibility so the work is done within budget, on time, and to standard.

Before the work gets fully underway, a vendor orientation should be conducted to review the service and quality level standards, the reporting process, and protocols. This is also the time to create a vendor profile that includes contact information for all personnel involved in the project. If the vendor is going to work on-site, it may be necessary to also arrange for badges, pass codes, work space, and equipment. If the vendor is to hire staff on behalf of the contracting organization, offers have to be made, salaries negotiated, and terms of agreement created. If the work is to be done off-site or off-shore, protocols should be created for transfer of products (intellectual and real). The products are a useful set of procedures or guidelines for working together.

Manage the Relationship Based on the Protocols

Once the relationship is underway, the vendor has to produce deliverables to standard and the organization has to provide oversight. A mistake organizations make is assuming their involvement is not necessary once the contract is signed. Their involvement is crucial throughout the term of the agreement. Vendor management is a role requiring its own skill set that includes diplomacy, negotiation, mediation, confrontation, and project management. Other chapters in this handbook address some of the skills and processes used to establish and maintain effective working relationships with stakeholders and other vested parties. A product of effective oversight is a successful relationship that satisfies the goals that were used as the basis for the decision to outsource.

Disengage

Contracts by definition come to an end. Even if the organization wants to renew the relationship with the vendor, both parties will want to renegotiate the terms of engagement, the nature of the deliverables, and the scope of the work. Disengagement is also the time to revisit who owns what, which party has the rights to the products produced, the adequacy of the plan, and whether or not the outsourcing solution produced the desired outcomes. The products of ending a relationship should include best practices, lessons learned, and a deeper understanding of the people and financial resources required to produce worthy work to standard.

CRITICAL SUCCESS FACTORS

Organizations that have not had success with outsourcing typically did not take the time to manage the relationship or fully understand what was required to produce the work or provide the service. Increasing the likelihood of successful outsourcing requires a number of commitments, including:

- Being clear and in agreement about what the expected benefits of outsourcing are;

- Deciding in advance what you will use as evidence that the relationship was worth the time and money;

- Setting a baseline in terms of what it takes in terms of resources and dollars to currently do the work internally. Without a baseline it is difficult to judge what was gained from the relationship;

- Selecting vendors whose business models support the needs of the organization and whose values complement that of the organization;

- Structuring the contract so that it benefits both parties, and being sure to include provisions for taking advantage of new developments and changing needs;

- Together building work protocols that facilitate communication, collaboration, and problem solving;

- Putting energy into the relationship.

- Working at making it work; and

- Celebrating efficiencies, innovation, collaboration, and interim goal accomplishments.

SUMMARY

Outsourcing is a strategy for using external resources. Specifically, it is designed to optimize the expertise of others, avoid unnecessary development of internal capability and capacity, and allow organizations to deploy the organization's resources on work best done internally. Making the relationship work is not easy. It requires commitment by both parties.

References

Hale, J. (2006). *Outsourcing training and development: Factors for success*. San Francisco: Pfeiffer.

Wentworth, D. (2008). Backsourcing—Bringing HR processes back in-house. Retrieved May 18, 2009, from http://www.hrworld.com/features/trendwatcher-backsourcing-072508/.

Recommended Readings and Websites

Brown, D., & Wilson, S. (2005). *The black book of outsourcing: How to manage the changes, challenges, and opportunities*. Hoboken, NJ: John Wiley & Sons.

Dominquez, L. (2006). *The manager's step-by-step guide to outsourcing*. New York: McGraw-Hill.

Greaver, M. (1999). *Strategic outsourcing: A structured approach to outsourcing decisions and initiatives*. New York: AMACOM.

Hale, J. (2006). *Outsourcing training and development: Factors for success*. San Francisco: Pfeiffer.

Power, M., Desouza, K., & Bonifozi, C. (2006). *The outsourcing handbook: How to implement and create a successful outsourcing process*. London: Kogan Page.

newsletter@i4cp.com. TrendWatcher, an online newsletter published by the Institute for Corporate Productivity.

www.outsourcingtraining.com. The Outsourcing Training website reports the latest outsourcing activities and facts and figures. This website is sponsored by the large training consulting firms.

www.whitehouse.gov/omb. To find guidelines that can help you formulate an argument for and against outsourcing, check the A-76 Guidelines. Once on the home page, go to the section titled circulars.

 EDITORIAL CONNECTIONS

The value of outsourcing, from a performance improvement perspective, often lies in its ability to provide flexibility or agility to the human capital resources of an organization. As a result, many times outsourcing is a useful performance intervention when the demand for an organization's services or products is growing faster than it is capable of meeting. By outsourcing tasks to external providers, organizations can often free up internal employees' time and resources, allowing them to focus on the accomplishment of core business results. Alternatively, outsourcing can also offer the flexibility that an organization requires when there are dips or declines in demand since outsourced work can often be discontinued. When demand re-stabilizes, you can then determine whether tasks should remain with an external provider or if "backsourcing" is an option for bringing the tasks back within the organization.

Expanding Your Options

Recruitment—the process of sourcing, screening, and selecting people for a job at an organization or firm, or for a vacancy within an organization.

Based on wikipedia.org definition (January 2009)

Expanding Your Options

Retention—a systematic effort by an organization to create and cultivate an environment that encourages current employees to remain employed within the organization; using policies, incentives, rewards, compensation, benefits, and other tools to address the diverse desires and motivations of current employees.

Based on wfnetwork.bc.edu definition (January 2009)

WHAT'S COMING UP

Another pragmatic intervention for managing the performance capability of your organization is succession planning. Often likened to workforce planning or talent management interventions, succession planning manages the premeditated transition as experienced employees leave an organization. Hillary Leigh examines the applications of succession planning in Chapter Twenty-Nine, offering useful insights and guidance for how to create a system for succession planning that effectively improves performance.

Succession Planning and Management

Hillary Leigh

INTRODUCTION

Set in Christmastime 1183 A.D., James Goldman's play *The Lion in Winter* tells a story of Henry II, King of England, as he struggles to choose an heir among his sons, John, Geoffrey, and Richard. It is a story of intrigue, with each character plotting with and against the others, in an effort to outwit the others and achieve their individual desires. Among Henry's goals is his desire to continue the legacy that he and his father before him built.

In the opening scenes, Henry responds to his mistress' query about the importance of his successor: "I've got to know before I die. I've built an empire and I've got to know it's going to last. I've put together England and I've added to it half of France. I am the greatest power in a thousand years. And after me comes John. If I can't leave this state to John, I've lived for nothing." (p. 6).

While a work of historical fiction, the story of Henry suggests that, when an organization is doing well, succession itself is about the protection of its past legacy and perpetuation of that success into the future. As an issue that essentially boils down to survival, succession has the potential to be contentious and deeply personal. The role of succession planning and management (SPM) in an organization that is achieving desired results then is to plan for and manage succession in a way that assures the existence of suitable and adequately prepared successors and smooth transition into their new roles, thereby reducing the uncertainty and turbulence that surround succession's inevitable occurrence and increases the likelihood of continued survival and success for the organization. SPM plays a different role in organizations that are struggling, where succession marks a visible deviation from past direction. In both cases, effective succession planning and management involves answering these general questions:

- What roles are critical to the organization's achievement of desired results?
- Which employee(s) are likely to meet the requirements of these roles?
- What development opportunities exist to prepare these employees more fully?
- How can the transition be managed in a way that reduces uncertainty?

This chapter attends to subtleties within these general questions and discusses strategies for designing effective succession planning and management systems.

DESCRIPTION

A common conception of succession planning is that it is about getting "the right people, in the right place, at the right time." Left there, the definition begs the questions, "What do you mean by '*right*'?" and "How do you accomplish this?" For this reason, succession planning and management seems a more appropriate label for the processes by which those employees who hold critical positions in the organization are identified, prepared, and transitioned for the purpose of ongoing or improved organizational results. This definition includes several important elements, including the issue of time: SPM is about proactive planning for the future, but it is also oriented to the here-and-now in its emphasis of management. The specific activities of identification, preparation, and transitioning will be discussed at later points in the chapter, but it is worthwhile to note that SPM's degree of focus upon key people, or leaders, within an organization is a point of disagreement among authors on the subject.

Expanding Your Options

Acquisitions—a corporate action in which an organization buys most, if not all, of the target organization. Acquisitions are often made as part of an organization's growth strategy thereby improving the organization's capacity to accomplish desired results.

Based on investopedia.com definition (January 2009)

For instance, in the 1994 edition of his book *Effective Succession Planning*, William Rothwell defines SPM as "any effort designed to ensure the continued effective performance of an organization, division, department, or work group by making provision for the development and replacement of key people over time." In a more recent 2002 article, he expands on that, saying that SPM is a "strategy that can help an organization meet its continuing need for people at all levels in all occupational groups." This characterization—that of SPM being an intervention associated with all job levels within an organization—is in marked contrast to discussions about succession planning in the media (which often deal with the replacement of chief executives) or even the notion of succession underpinning the story of Henry that began this chapter. What then is succession planning? Is it a strategy solely aimed at the development and replacement of leaders or is it concerned with all job levels?

Maybe making the distinction is quibbling over semantics, but given the possible costs associated with SPM, defining it as a strategy most concerned with leadership roles is appropriate, and more importantly, useful. This is because it acknowledges that people who perform as leaders within organizations have different characteristics than those who perform at front-line job functions. An example of this is illustrated in research reported in 2004 by Anthony Patti, Lillian Fok, and Sandra Hartman from the University of New Orleans (UNO). Their study surveyed pairs of managers and front-line employees at fifty-six organizations in the southern United States and found that managers reported higher levels of benevolence, compliance with change, facilitation of organizational goals, and desire for growth.

Of course, it is important to consider this research from the perspective that it is not the case that serving in a leadership role causes these differences. Rather, people who have these characteristics may be more likely to end up in management roles. A second consideration is that the findings depend upon the reported opinions of individuals about themselves, so they are a more accurate indicator of what they *believe to be true* of themselves and not necessarily what is *actually true* of them. Setting these limitations aside, the UNO findings support a somewhat straightforward but important conclusion: leaders are different from front-line workers and, by extension, if there are differences between individuals in these groups, then strategies for identifying and developing those who will replace them ought to also be different.

This argument might well be affectionately termed a "different strokes for different folks" justification for proposing alternative strategies for developing leaders than for the rest of the talent pool. However, a second reason justifies separate definitions and approaches to increasing workforce capacity at different job levels within an organization; namely that an important characteristic of a leader is that he or she is responsible and often accountable for achieving results within the organization. Perhaps even more importantly, leadership practices are also commonly associated with the actual performance of the whole organization rather than a distinct division or unit. This point is illustrated by the findings of a 2006 study of manufacturing organizations in the United States, Great Britain, France, and Germany by economists Nicholas Bloom of Stanford University and John Van Reenen of the London School of Economics. Once the impact of country and industry were controlled for, the authors found that leadership practices have a strong influence on organizational performance.

Given the higher stakes for having the right people in key roles within the organization, the tactics employed in identifying, developing, and transitioning them into their job roles ought to require more rigorous justification than required for their front-line counterparts. Similar SPM processes can be used at all levels of an organization; assuming the costs-to-potential-benefit ratios make sense.

Succession planning and management are related to a number of other interventions aimed at increasing the capacity of an organization's workforce, including talent management initiatives, workforce planning, leadership development, traditional employee selection practices, replacement planning, and career counseling. For the purposes of comparison, simplified (perhaps overly so) definitions of these interventions are shown in Table 29.1.

Clearly, SPM has commonalities with each of these interventions but can be distinguished according to several criteria, including (1) the scope of job functions that are covered by the program, (2) the impetus for initiating the intervention, (3) orientation to planning, and, to a lesser extent, (4) specific practices employed in the effective design, development, and implementation of the initiative.

It is useful to look at each criterion as a continuum and examine where each intervention falls on it. For instance, SPM interventions target a smaller amount

Table 29.1 Some Definitions

Intervention	Definition
Talent management	Ongoing processes of developing and retaining employees at all job levels within an organization
Leadership development	General development of employees who show promise for taking on leadership roles within an organization
Employee selection	Coordinated efforts to identify, recruit, and hire talent external to an organization
Career counseling	Guidance provided to individual employees about development for the purposes of accomplishing their own career goals
Replacement planning	Transitory development of an employee for the purposes of filling a single vacancy

of an organization's workforce than large-scale approaches to talent management, have far more proactive reasons for initiation than traditional selection and employment practices, and take a longer-range approach to planning than replacement planning strategies. Admittedly, some of these distinctions may merely be an issue of semantics; for instance, the issue of the scope of SPM strategies is far from settled in the research literature and will be discussed in greater detail later in this chapter.

In a final introductory note on SPM's relationship to other workforce capacity interventions, it typically incorporates elements of these other interventions and, depending on the size of the organization and its commitment to building capacity, they are often executed alongside one another. SPM can, for example, be effectively integrated with performance interventions such as coaching, mentoring, change management, outsourcing, and many other systematic efforts to improve performance (see Chapters Twenty-Seven, Twenty-Six, Sixteen, and Twenty-Eight, respectively).

Expanding Your Options

Mergers—the combining of two or more organizations, usually through a mutual agreement, by offering the stockholders ownership in the united organization.

Based on investopedia.com definition (January 2009)

It might be easy to forget that interventions are designed to intervene between some aspect of the here-and-now in an effort to affect change in the future. As such, it can be helpful for the performance consultant to think of an intervention as a stimulus with predictable consequences or results. Leader succession, especially that of an organization's chief executive officer, has been linked to changes in organizational performance. Of course, our world is more complicated than controlled research environments, making it necessary to study additional factors in the succession context such as current performance, organizational size, and age, as well as successor characteristics. In regard to succession planning and management programs themselves, they are recommended in situations in which:

1. Turnover (or predicted turnover) is high in critical leadership positions,

2. Candidate search and recruitment costs are high, and

3. Extended vacancies exist in key leadership roles.

WHAT WE KNOW FROM RESEARCH

Knowledge about what works best in the design, development, and implementation of a particular intervention can be derived from multiple sources including both research and practice. This section will briefly discuss evidence in light of both of these areas; however, it acknowledges the complex nature of succession planning and management and posits that it is more useful to view SPM programs as a *set of interventions*, many of which are also discussed in this volume. Therefore, the review places primary emphasis on the nature of succession and factors in the context that may affect it. It then examines knowledge about SPM in the context of key decisions within it: selection of potential leaders, what activities are used to develop them, and strategies for managing transition. Finally, it presents findings from research and practice on the application of SPM and its effectiveness in the workplace.

Succession Theory

Theoretical research on succession is relevant because it answers questions about why coordinated efforts to succession planning and management are worthwhile. In the early 1960s, Oscar Grusky, now professor emeritus at UCLA's Department of Sociology, asserted that succession was worthy of study because succession itself is inevitable and, when it does occur, develops an environment of uncertainty. While a foundation for much of the contemporary research on succession, Grusky's major theories of succession sprang from research on succession in a surprising place: baseball organizations. The resulting theories are generally referred to as the common sense, vicious circle, and ritual scapegoating theories of succession. Simplified explanations of these theories are as follows:

- *Common sense—*   Succession causes positive changes in performance.
- *Vicious circle—*   Performance and succession change are inter-related.
- *Ritual scapegoating—*   Succession has little or no effect on performance and is merely a symbolic act of finger-pointing.

Since Grusky's seminal publications in 1960 and 1963, succession research has attempted to test these theories and determine the extent that other contextual factors are associated with succession and what effects they have upon an organization's performance. Additionally, research examines targeted issues within the processes of succession planning and management.

The Selection Decision

Typically, research on CEO succession examines the consequences of a succession event and reports mixed results. A 2006 article for *Organization Science* journal by Qing Cao, Likoebe Maruping, and Riki Takeuchi notes that more recent research on CEO succession seeks to disentangle the complex relationship between CEO succession and firm performance. These types of studies examine the effects of issues such as whether or not the prior CEO left voluntarily, the organization's performance prior to succession, the extent of change that is occurring in the organization's environment, and finally, the internal/external decision.

The internal/external selection decision involves deciding whether a suitable candidate already exists within the organization or if an external search for potential candidates ought to be performed. Clearly, this decision is closely associated with aspects of replacement planning. Depending on one's definition of SPM, it can be viewed as a critical decision or, in the case of external recruitment, as a failure of the SPM program itself. This perspective is illustrated in Jeremy Smerd's 2007 examination of CEO succession at Merrill Lynch and Citigroup in the trade publication, *Workforce Management*; here decisions to search for external candidates are described as a failure of each organization's board to plan for a void in the CEO role and as disregard for the succession plan. Research bearing on the issue of the internal/external decision is less clear-cut about the extent to which this actually represents a failure of planning or simply part of an open planning process.

The distinction between an internal candidate and an external candidate may seem a straightforward matter of whether or not the potential candidate is already employed by the organization. But another important issue is the contextualized meaning of the internal/external decision: Does the decision signal change or continuation of current strategies? This is an important aspect of Turkish researcher Ayse Karaevli's investigations into CEO "outsiderness" and its consequences for organizational performance.

Karaevli studied ninety firms in the United States' airline, inorganic chemicals, and paint industries between 1972 and 2002. The research, published in a 2007 issue of *Strategic Management Journal*, involved the review of 140 CEO succession events and several performance indicators (return on assets, return on sales, and shareholder returns) for three-years following each succession. The research focused on linking the organizational results after CEO succession with the degree to which the new CEO was an outsider (as a measure of experience in that particular firm and industry). The study also considered issues such as the turbulence of the environment, the performance of the organization prior to the succession, the age and size of the organization, and CEO successor characteristics (such as age and educational background).

The findings of this study indicated that selecting an outsider CEO (again, as determined by tenure in the company and the industry) is warranted in very uncertain situations, for instance when the organization is experiencing dramatic growth in market share or, conversely, when the organization is performing poorly. A somewhat counter-intuitive finding is also supported by the study's data: when a CEO is hired from the outside organization, concurrent changes to senior-level leaders yield better organizational performance, supposedly as a function of lack of hostility and resistance to change. The application of this research suggests that there is no straightforward "yes or no" answer to the question of hiring a CEO; rather the answer appears to be "it depends."

As far as other leadership roles are concerned, most succession planning research distinguishes between the "heir apparent approach," which identifies and develops one successor, and "pooled" approaches that select and develop a group of high-potential candidates. More recent conventional wisdom advocates pooled approaches over heir apparent tactics. In a series of recommendations for SPM in small and family-owned business (FOBs), Donald Levitt suggests in a 2005 *Journal for Quality and Participation* article "keeping many irons in the fire" due to the potentially demoralizing effect of heir apparent approaches on other members of the work team. In illustration of this point, Bernard Nickels, of the U.S. Office of Personnel Management, led a 2006 evaluation of the long-running Presidential Management Fellows Program. Within this twenty-seven-year-old program that attracts and identifies a pool of graduate-level students for leadership within federal agencies, nomination (versus self-identification) was strongly associated with accomplishment, especially when the nominating body had extensive understanding of the program and its criteria. These findings suggest that the development activities employed in SPM initiatives alone are not enough to ensure high performance, but that who is selected (and how this process occurs) are equally important.

Development Strategies

Another factor that is integral to effective succession planning and management is the actual opportunities and strategies that are used to develop those that are selected for the program. According to a 2005 article for the *Journal of Administrative Management* by Robert Kovach of the RHR International consulting firm, this is the "real work" of succession planning and where programs often fail.

In regard to more formalized approaches to development, SPM programs may include study in a university program. Of course, participants in these activities perceive varying degrees of relevance and satisfaction related to professional development. For instance, Joy Mighty and William Ashton of the University of New Brunswick studied graduates of a twelve-year-old management development program. In general, graduates of the program were satisfied with the program and found the curriculum to be relevant to their work environment. Furthermore, 10 percent of the graduates reported having moved up to levels of middle and senior management (of note, given the maturity of the program, the authors expected this to be higher, but given that approximately 76 percent of the graduates were women, Mighty and Ashton suggest in their 2003 article "Management Development: Hoax or Hero?" that the low percentage of graduates' advancement may relate to issues of gender in the workplace [see Chapter Twenty-Six] and a "glass ceiling"). Admittedly, these findings are only related to one university program and are therefore not generalizable to other university programs. A similar statement might be made about the effectiveness of corporate training courses and programs.

Succession planning and management are often connected to small firms and family-owned businesses. In her study of small, growing firms in Wales, Sally Sambrook raises a solid argument: because there are not natural successors in small firms that are not family-owned, succession planning is even more critical than in those that are family-owned. The study itself was small, as it analyzed succession planning in only three firms. Her in-depth analysis, reported in a 2005 issue of *Journal of Small Business and Enterprise Development*, discovered that advancement in small firms generally occurred within a particular area in the firm rather than across different business units; thus specialists were created. The actual development of potential successors involved informal learning and hands-on work with activities delegated by the incumbent leader that stretched the skills of potential successors to the point of allowing for failure as an opportunity for learning.

Of course, planning to allow for failure is difficult to negotiate, but the recommendation of integrating development activities is a theme demonstrated by several of the studies discussed in this chapter. For example, Paul Bernthal and Richard Wellins of Development Dimensions International discovered through their 2006 research that while formal training was the most commonly used development activity, special projects assignments (such as working on a task force) were seen as the most valuable. Mark Busine and Bruce Watt note in a 2005 article for *Asia Pacific Journal of Human Resources* that these projects are typically lengthy assignments requiring six months to two years of involvement (and therefore, development).

Essentially, the effectiveness of development activities included in SPM programs depend upon their direct linkage to business needs and the functions that support them. Apart from that, the development activities differ very little from other types of interventions aimed at increasing the capacity of an organization's workforce.

Managing Exit Strategies and Transition

As a succession event occurs, it is critical to consider exit strategies for the predecessor and means for a smooth passing of the reins to the successor. These considerations are issues that are often discussed in family-owned businesses, report Raveendra Chitoor and Ranjan Das in their 2007 article for *Family Business Review*, where decisions are sometimes seen as family decisions, rather than business decisions. According to a 2006 *Human Resource Management Review* article by Rodger Griffeth, David Allen, and Rowena Barrett, succession in family-owned businesses revolves around two issues: ownership and leadership. While changes in either can occur coincidentally, it is not always the case, and each has implications for the other. In their review of the research on factors that affect the retention of a successor between generations in FOBs, the authors found a number of factors that affect a potential successor's desire to take over. Not surprisingly, a number of these deal with issues in the family itself and not the nature or performance of the business alone. Among those that have a positive effect are (1) a positive relationship between the parent and the successor, (2) the ability of the parent to relinquish power, (3) the extent of separation between business and family roles of the parent, (4) trust and respect despite generational differences, (5) positive childhood experiences working in the business, and (6) senses of loyalty and responsibility to and pride in one's family (as well as general harmony within it).

Aside from the issue of whether or not intergenerational transfer occurs in a family-owned business, the literature in this area often describes guidelines for formulating an exit strategy for the predecessor. In FOBs, these guidelines may deal directly with maintenance of wealth for the predecessor (which necessitates the involvement of a certified public accountant [CPA] or someone who is knowledgeable about tax law); however, if one extends this line of thinking to other organizations, then the predecessor's personal desires and motives ought to be given consideration, as well as his or her reason for leaving, as these may well impact the overall transition process.

Application of Succession Planning in the Workplace

Bernthal and Wellins, mentioned earlier, performed a series of benchmarking studies that illustrate trends, approaches to, and issues for the development of leaders and planning for their succession. The first study was conducted in 1999, a second in 2001, and a third in 2003. Their fourth and most recent iteration, the Leadership Forecast Study, was carried out in 2005 and 2006. This study surveyed 4,559 leaders from more than nine hundred organizations in forty-two countries; of these organizations, 63 percent employed more than one thousand people. The study's objectives were related to aspects of both leadership development and succession planning. Therefore, the study sought to identify the usage and utility of leadership development practices, describe differences in perceptions of leadership from multiple perspectives (organizational level, departmental job function), and associate specific leadership practices with improved organizational performance. Several of the Leadership

Forecast Study findings are particularly relevant to a description of current application of succession planning programs in organizations:

- The usage of succession planning programs remained fairly unchanged between 2003 and 2005. During these years, 54 percent and 55 percent (respectively) of organizations reported having a succession planning program in place. Furthermore, those organizations that do have succession planning programs in place expect an increase of positions filled by talent within the organization.

- Succession planning programs that include front-line management functions appear to be on the rise; with 25 percent of the organizations' reporting front-line coverage by their succession planning programs. However, efforts are generally focused on senior leaders within an organization. Over the course of the study series, succession planning programs focusing on senior leaders increased 9 percent. Moreover, filling senior leadership positions is perceived to be difficult and 66 percent of the HR professionals who participated in the study believe that it will become increasingly difficult to do so in the future.

- While a little more than half of the organizations utilized succession planning programs, these programs were not viewed as effective by HR professionals. Moreover, a little more than one-third of the organizations' HR professionals viewed their succession planning practices as ineffective.

- Involvement of the most senior organizational leader as well as line managers to identify potential candidates and make objective assessments of potential candidates' on-the-job performance and readiness for promotion are strongly associated with the success of new leaders who are identified, developed, and transitioned through succession planning.

Before moving to a discussion of the applications of SPM, it is worthwhile to note that a good portion of the research reviewed in this section focused on special cases of succession planning and management , such as CEO succession, small firms, and family-owned businesses, mainly because succession is widely discussed in these types of situations. The extent to which these findings are applicable to other contexts is unclear, and the reader is therefore cautioned to consider the applicability of the findings to other contexts and leadership roles.

The Effectiveness of SPM Initiatives

Admittedly, the benefits of an SPM initiative seem to be self-evident. Intuitively, leaders play an important role in achieving organizational results and it therefore seems like a good idea to take a proactive and coordinated effort to replacing them. It should not be surprising to find studies of the effectiveness of SPM initiatives that predominately include the perceptions of employees

---

Additional Findings from Practice

Based on their practical consultancy experience, DDI's Mark Busine and Bruce Watt provide the following guidelines for SPM programs:

- Incorporating project assignments into developmental activities;
- Considering employees' personal motivations and career goals;
- Using objective measures of current performance and readiness;
- Sharing information with potential leaders;
- Clearly defining position requirements;
- Linking succession planning program to organizational strategy;
- Creating a program that is adaptable to changes in organizational strategy;
- Involvement and visible support from senior leaders;
- Involving front-line managers to identify a pool of potential candidates;
- Utilizing the expertise and support of human resource staff;
- Sharing accountability at all levels in the organization;
- Including formal training and university programs as a component of development efforts;
- Incorporating mentoring or coaching programs as a component of development efforts;
- Including the development of direct reports as a performance expectation of leaders;
- Establishing a timeline for the program; and
- Using electronic planning and tracking systems.

---

within the organization. In addition to many of the studies already discussed in this chapter, Tracy Taylor and Peter McGraw's 2004 study of SPM programs within organizations in Australia found that such program had a positive impact on: (1) CEO involvement, (2) senior management support, (3) line management involvement with potential candidates, (4) integrated development opportunities, and (5) linkage of program with business strategies. These positive effects, it should be noted, however, were exclusively judged and reported by human resource personnel.

In a 2001 study that departs from solely measuring satisfaction or general adoption of SPM initiatives, Tung-Chun Huang attempted to determine the effects of implementing an SPM program on human resource outcomes (morale, job satisfaction, and job turnover rate) in Taiwanese corporations (this included an analysis of the sophistication of the SPM initiative itself). In general, SPM initiatives had no effect on organizational results; however, there were differences in organizational achievement as the level of sophistication of a program increased. Huang says in an article for the *International Journal of Manpower* that there are two important implications for these findings: (1) the design, development, and implementation of an SPM initiative must be undertaken *very carefully*, and (2) if the SPM program is not problem-based or "decorative" then it is probably better to have no program at all.

The next section examines applications of SPM and factors to consider when deciding whether or not to use the intervention.

WHEN TO APPLY

A problem-oriented approach to improving organizational results suggests a number of indications that a succession planning and management program is warranted, including frequent turnover in critical job functions, high costs for candidate searches, and extended periods of search for candidates. Other circumstances that might suggest examining the appropriateness of a scaled-down targeted approach to SPM include a high proportion of leaders performing multiple critical job functions, periods of rapid growth or low organizational performance, and anticipated or projected resignation of critical leaders.

On a large scale, this is currently true in the United States, where a potential mass exodus of the working population looms large as those born after World War II—the baby boomers—begin to reach retirement age. "Doomsday" predictions ought to be tempered by recent findings from the Department of Labor's Health and Retirement Study, suggesting that baby boomers are more likely to retire gradually (reducing work hours or transitioning into alternative careers). Of course, on a smaller scale, gaps in critical leadership positions may be due to any number of reasons besides retirement, including promotions, transfers, consolidations, and voluntary or involuntary resignations. The latter suggests that succession planning may supplement one of the more aggressive approaches to performance improvement: the pink slip.

Because SPM involves the ongoing development of leaders, it is worth noting that SPM requires an ongoing commitment of cost-effective resources to support the effort. While SPM programs should be flexible enough to accommodate changes in strategic direction, the long-range nature of their practices depend upon the continued provision of financial and human resources.

As alluded to throughout this chapter, succession planning is closely related to a number of other interventions that focus on recruiting and building capacity within an organization, such as leadership development, talent management, replacement planning, and traditional recruitment and employee selection practices. Traditional recruitment and employee selection practices are utilized when a position is already vacant or when the incumbent employee has indicated an intention to leave the organization. Replacement planning is usually focused on individual job roles and, as its name suggests, emphasizes maintaining the status quo. Talent management is very closely related to succession planning, except that it basically extends the process to all job functions within the organization. At first glance, leadership development is hardly distinguishable from succession planning. In regard to leadership development, it is useful to distinguish between identifying potential leaders and the general development of skills and the activity of grooming an individual for a particular position—although leadership development is often involved in succession planning programs (especially those that emphasize building capacity from within the organization).

STRENGTHS AND CRITICISMS

Some strengths and criticisms of succession planning are listed below.

Strengths

- Succession planning targets the development of those employees within the organization who are likely or expected to take on leadership roles within the organization. This targeted approach may reduce the costs of training and development (especially if training is integrated into current project assignments).
- Succession planning may reduce or eliminate the costs of external searches for candidates.
- Succession planning can also provide systematic procedures and policies during times of turbulent change in an organization and, on a more individual level, ease transitions for incumbent leaders who are leaving voluntarily and are concerned for the future success of the organization.

Criticisms

- Succession planning usually involves "tapping" the next generation of leaders; there is always the risk that, instead of having the process based on the organization's needs and the potential leader's relevant leadership characteristics, the decision will be based on nepotism or favoritism.
- Succession planning that merely emphasizes organizational fit and general competencies could build a leadership team that is overly homogenous and may increase "group-think."

- Succession planning depends on accurate identification of the future capacity needs of an organization. At its worst, it may rely upon the static view that tomorrow is merely an extension of today and that the skills, knowledge, attitudes, and abilities required of tomorrow's leaders will be the same as those required of today's leaders. A more conservative statement of this risk is that, at the very least, succession planning depends on the accuracy of predictions about what *might* be the case in the future.

RECOMMENDED DESIGN, DEVELOPMENT, AND IMPLEMENTATION PROCESS

Given the complicated nature of succession, the reader might be wise to view the following steps for designing, developing, and implementing an SPM intervention as general heuristics and considerations rather than a cookbook formula for success. Furthermore, these steps are intended to be scalable to the size of the initiative and the organization.

1. If it hasn't already been done, establish a results-oriented strategic plan for the organization.

2. Ensure that everyone working in the organization knows what results they are responsible for and how their work contributes to the achievement of organizational results.

3. Determine the level of coverage for the succession program:

   - Prioritize leadership job functions based on their criticality and how essential they are to achieving the organizational results. The more direct the linkage, the more important it is to consider a succession plan for the job function.

   - Determine what resources are available to support the program. This should not only be a function of budgetary considerations, but also should factor in the current costs of recruitment, selection, and training for these positions when vacancies arise.

4. Break down the components of the job functions included in the SPM program. Explicate the results that are expected of the performer, as well as what skills, knowledge, attitudes, and abilities are required to meet these expectations. Also consider what specific challenges are associated with the job function. This will not only assist in identifying prior experience that is required to perform the job, but also prepare potential candidates for the realities of performing it.

5. Identify potential leaders based on a set of straightforward criteria that consider both past performance and future potential. In 2003, Robert Rogers and Audrey Smith recommended in a DDI report that criteria include the employee's past performance, interpersonal skills, motivation to lead, fit with organizational values and culture, and ability/willingness to learn. The criteria should be consistently applied to all job functions included in the program. Remember that the size of this pool will vary depending on the size of the organization and the level of coverage for the program.

6. Assess both the strengths and development opportunities of potential leaders.

7. Create a menu of development opportunities, including internal training, mentoring, university coursework, and special work projects.

8. Utilize incumbent leaders and human resource staff to conduct meetings with individuals within the potential leaders' pool to design an individualized maintenance and development plan.

9. Provide feedback to potential leaders about their progress on their maintenance and development plan.

10. Create strategies for exit and transition that involve both the incumbent leaders and those who will succeed them.

11. Evaluate the intervention on an incremental but ongoing basis. As appropriate, this should involve collection of data as described in the following list of indicators. This list is prepared chronologically rather than by order of importance and should not be considered all-inclusive.

   - The ratio of potential leaders to outgoing leaders
   - Number of maintenance and development plans
   - Progress/achievement on maintenance and development plans
   - Overall tenure of key leaders
   - Average tenure of key leaders
   - Perceptions of leaders, potential leaders, and subordinates about the extent to which leaders are prepared to do their jobs
   - Perceptions of both predecessors and successors about the extent that the SPM program prepared successors to take on their new roles
   - Relevant individual, departmental, and organizational results
   - Percentage of vacancies filled by program participants
   - Average length of vacancies
   - Overall costs of recruitment

- Average costs of recruitment per vacancy
- Program costs
- Comparisons and trends of these indicators to data collected warranting an SPM intervention (prior to when it was initiated)

CRITICAL SUCCESS FACTORS

Several factors are critical to the success of an SPM intervention.

Alignment
- On the front end of the process, an SPM program must be clearly and directly aligned with the organization's strategy. If this criterion is not satisfied, then any SPM effort is typically misguided and most likely subtracting value from the organization.

Roles
- The decision about what roles ought to be included in the program is important. Not only should the most critical roles in the organization be covered by the program but the amount of resources committed to the program must also match the amount of resources required to support it.
- In the same way, job roles must be well-defined; this can be a challenge for organizations in which "job creep" has slowly moved people away from doing what is detailed in their job descriptions. The responsibilities, competencies, and characteristics required of potential leaders guide the development process and therefore must be specifically explicated.

Social
- There are also several social factors related to implementing an SPM program, including open communication about what is going to happen or is currently happening during the process and direct, visible support of the intervention by senior leaders within the organization.
- Given the nature of SPM, this point is critical to avoid (when possible) the appearance of "force-outs" and, ultimately, to support the proactive nature of SPM.

Time
- The practical issue of time is a factor in the success of an SPM intervention. If a successor is identified from within the organization, there must be enough time for that person to develop the knowledge, skills, attitudes,

and abilities to perform the job effectively before an incumbent leaves the organization.

Economic and Legal Aspects

- There are concerns for the economic and legal aspects of SPM, especially in small and family-owned businesses, where the incumbent is concerned not only with the ongoing success of the organization, but also his or her own personal livelihood. To this end, the involvement of legal and accounting professionals is advised.

Selection

- There are also several potential pitfalls to avoid. These include issues related to the selection of the successor; it is important to communicate to those potential leaders in the development pool that they are not guaranteed advancement.

- It must be the case that advancement always depends on candidates' ability to meet the needs of a position and deliver the required results, and this point must be clearly communicated to potential leaders.

SUMMARY

Succession is inevitable and, depending on the environment preceding it, changes in leadership that occur as a result of it have different meanings. The role of succession planning and management in both environments is (1) to reduce uncertainty through the appropriate identification, selection, and preparation of potential leaders and (2) to allow for smooth passing of the organizational reins to successors. Along with consideration of these issues through key decisions in the process, this chapter provided practical steps for the design, development, implementation, and evaluation of SPM initiatives. As with any intervention, the reader is cautioned to consider both the application of an SPM intervention and the general guidelines provided here based on their utility for closing a performance gap within an organization's context.

Notes

- A report and micro-level analysis of the Heath and Retirement Study may be found at http://www.bls.gov/osmr/abstract/ec/ec060120.htm.

- For additional discussion of how performance and interventions can subtract value from an organization, refer to D. M. Brethower and K. Smalley (1998) *Performance-Based Instruction: Linking Training to Business Results*. San Francisco: Pfeiffer.

References

Bernthal, P., & Wellins, R. (2006). Trends in leader development and succession. *Human Resource Planning, 29*(2), 31–40.

Bloom, N., & Van Reenen, J. M. (2006). Measuring and explaining management practices across firms and countries. *NBER Working Paper No. W12216* Retrieved on August 24, 2008, from http://ssrn.com/abstract = 902568.

Busine, M., & Watt, B. (2005). Succession management: Trends and current practice. *Asia Pacific Journal of Human Resources, 43*(2), 225–236.

Cao, Q., Maruping, L. M., & Takeuchi, R. (2006). Disentangling the effects of CEO turnover and succession on organizational capabilities: A social network perspective. *Organization Science, 17*(5), 563–576.

Chitoor, R., & Das, R. (2007). Professionalization of management and succession performance—A vital linkage. *Family Business Review, 20*(1), 65–79.

Goldman, J. (2004). *The lion in winter.* New York: Random House Trade.

Griffeth, R. W., Allen, D. G., & Barrett, R. (2006). Integration of family-owned business succession with turnover and life cycle models: Development of a successor retention process model. *Human Resource Management Review, 16*(4), 490–507.

Grusky, O. (1960). Administrative succession in formal organizations. *Social Forces, 39*(2), 105–115.

Grusky, O. (1963). Managerial succession and organizational effectiveness. *American Journal of Sociology, 62*, 21–31.

Huang, T. (2001). Succession management systems and human resource outcomes. *International Journal of Manpower, 22*(7/8), 736–747.

Karaevli, A. (2007). Performance consequences of new CEO "outsiderness": Moderating effects of pre- and post-succession contexts. *Strategic Management Journal, 28*, 681–706.

Kovach, R. (2005, October/November). Cultivating the next generation of leaders. *Journal of Administrative Management*, pp. 22–25.

Levitt, D. (2005). Family business forum: Developing the next generation. *The Journal for Quality and Participation, 28*(3), 16–18.

Mighty, E. J., & Ashton, W. (2003). Management development: Hoax or hero? *The Journal of Management Development, 22*(1/2), 14–31.

Nickels, B. J., Sharpe, J. P., Bauhs, K., & Holloway-Lundy, A. (2006). The presidential management fellows program: Lessons learned during 27 years of success. *Human Resource Management Review, 16*, 324–339.

Patti, A. L., Fok, L. Y., & Hartman, S. J. (2004). Differences between managers and line employees in a quality management environment. *The International Journal of Quality and Reliability Management, 21*(2/3), 214–230.

Rogers, R., & Smith, A. (2003). *Finding future perfect senior leaders: Spotting executive potential.* Pittsburgh, PA: Development Dimension International.

Rothwell, W. J. (1994). *Effective succession planning: Ensuring leadership continuity and building talent from within*. New York: AMACOM.

Rothwell, W. J. (2002). Putting success into your succession planning. *The Journal of Business Strategy, 23*(3), 32–37.

Sambrook, S. (2005). Exploring succession planning in small, growing firms. *Journal of Small Business and Enterprise Development, 12*(4), 579–594.

Smerd, J. (2007). Heirs not apparent. *Workforce Management, 86*(21), 1–2.

Taylor, T., & McGraw, P. (2004). Succession management practices in Australian organizations. *International Journal of Manpower, 25*(7/8), 741–758.

Recommended Readings and Websites

Andrews, K. Z. (2001). The performance impact of new CEOs. *MIT Sloan Management Review, 42*(2), 14.

Bernthal, P., & Wellins, R. (2005). *Leadership forecast 2005-2006: Best practices for tomorrow's global leaders*. Pittsburgh, PA: Development Dimensions International.

Bernthal, P., & Wellins, R. (2003, 2001, 1999). *The leadership forecast: A benchmarking study*. Pittsburgh, PA: Development Dimensions International.

Bickford, D. J. (2001). The journey from heir apparent to CEO: Win, wait, or walk? *The Academy of Management Executive, 15*(4), 137–138.

Gamson, W., & Scotch, N. (1964). Scapegoating in baseball. *American Journal of Sociology, 70*, 69–72.

Giambatista, R. C., Rowe, W. G., & Riaz, S. (2005). Nothing succeeds like succession: A critical review of leader succession literature since 1994. *The Leadership Quarterly, 16*, 963–991.

Johnson, J. E., Costa, L. L., Marshal, S. B., Moran, M. J., & Henderson, C. S. (1994). Succession management: A model for developing nursing leaders. *Nursing Management, 25*(6), 50. Retrieved October 19, 2007, from the ProQuest database.

Kaiser, R. B., Hogan, R., & Craig, S. B. (2008). Leadership and the fate of organizations. *American Psychologist, 63*(2), 96–110.

Rothwell, W. J. (2005). (2nd ed.). *Effective succession planning: Ensuring leadership continuity and building talent from within*. New York: American Management Association.

Schaffer, R. H. (1997). Planning for succession. *Journal of Management Consulting, 9*(3), 9–11.

http://www.talentmgt.com/succession%5Fplanning/: Talent management

PART NINE

EDITORS'
DISCUSSION

Interventions for managing performance capability can be applied at the individual, team, or organizational levels. In Chapters Twenty-Eight and Twenty-Nine, the authors examined outsourcing and succession planning as interventions to help manage the capacity of organizations to accomplish desired results. Similarly, numerous performance interventions can be used to manage the individual or team performance capabilities. For example, recruitment programs are often effective tools for ensuring that the individuals brought into the organization have the necessary capacities to achieve results. Likewise, employee retention programs are a valuable resource for ensuring that high-performing individuals and teams within your organization remain

Expanding Your Options

Interviewing—process in which a potential employee is evaluated by an employer for prospective employment in the organization. It typically precedes the hiring decision and is used to evaluate the candidate's capacity to achieve desired results as well as the organization's capability to meet the candidate's desires.

Based on wikipedia.org definition (January 2009)

there. Both recruitment and retention programs are most effective when closely associated with incentives (see Chapter Eighteen), rewards and recognition (see Chapter Nineteen), compensation (see Chapter Twenty), workforce planning, mentoring (see Chapters Twenty-Two and Twenty-Six), job previews (see Chapter Eight), and other performance interventions that reflect the components of a holistic performance system.

The capacity to accomplish results, or performance capability, should not be overlooked as a key component of your performance improvement system. If the individuals and teams within your organization, or for that matter the organization itself, do not have the necessary capability or capacity to accomplish results, then even well-intentioned performance interventions will not produce substantial and sustainable results. These are, however, often difficult conversations to have within organizations, since most of us want to believe that we are capable of achieving desired results. Nevertheless, the fact remains that if individual employees do not have the capacity to accomplish results, then changes must be made. Analyze your organization's capacity for achieving results at the individual, team, and organizational levels, and then examine the various performance interventions that can be used to improve the performance capabilities.

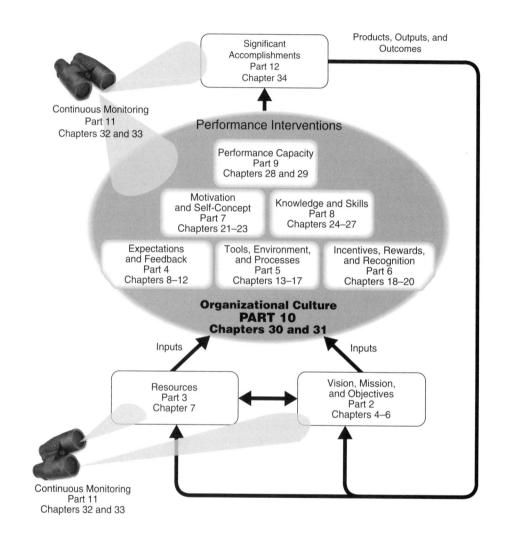

Products, Outputs, and Outcomes

Significant
Accomplishments
Part 12
Chapter 34

Continuous Monitoring
Part 11
Chapters 32 and 33

Performance Interventions

Performance Capacity
Part 9
Chapters 28 and 29

Motivation
and Self-Concept
Part 7
Chapters 21–23

Knowledge and Skills
Part 8
Chapters 24–27

Expectations
and Feedback
Part 4
Chapters 8–12

Tools, Environment,
and Processes
Part 5
Chapters 13–17

Incentives, Rewards,
and Recognition
Part 6
Chapters 18–20

**Organizational Culture
PART 10
Chapters 30 and 31**

Inputs

Inputs

Resources
Part 3
Chapter 7

Vision, Mission,
and Objectives
Part 2
Chapters 4–6

Continuous Monitoring
Part 11
Chapters 32 and 33

ORGANIZATIONAL CULTURE

Behind the scenes of all organization performance is its culture. Whether it is the production of computer components or providing consulting services to financial institutions, results happen within the context of organizational culture. In most cases, this includes the integration of the diverse cultures from multiple organizations such as suppliers, partners, clients, communities, and others. Because of this, your efforts to improve performance must attend to both the internal culture of your organization and also to the influences of cultures of outside organizations.

The culture of an organization is created by the individuals within the organization and influenced significantly by those they interact with external to the organization. Organizational culture is a fluid construct that is continually changing and shifting. In your organization, for example, you may also find that distinct divisions or units (or even informal networks of people) all have unique cultures, and these cultures interact with one another on a daily basis. In the same way, cultures of external organizations, such are clients or suppliers, also influence the cultures within your organization. All of this creates systems that are both very complex—and at the same time essential—to the success of any efforts to improve performance.

Although in many instances an organization's culture is tough to define or pin down due to its complexity, culture is essential to the success of improvement efforts. Culture, including everything from professional expectations to social relationships, strongly influences how performance interventions are implemented and their sustainability over time. Without cultural support, improving performance is an uphill battle that rarely leads to desired results.

Organizational culture, as discussed in many contexts in the past several decades, strongly influences most aspects of a performance system. Within the Performance Pyramid model, for instance, culture provides the conditions under which other components of the performance system interact and accomplish results (see Chapter Three). Performance interventions, such as those to improve expectations and feedback, relate to other interventions, like those associated with motivation and self-concept, within the context of the organization's culture. Consequently, the impact of any and all performance interventions is moderated by the culture of the organization.

It is equally true that performance interventions play an important role in shaping organizational cultures. As discussed in Chapter Sixteen, efforts to improve performance bring change to organizations; change that has to be managed in order to ensure success. These changes also impact the culture of an organization; some changes lead to negative reactions and other changes have positive influences on the advancement of the culture in support of the performance goals of the organization.

Performance interventions associated with organizational culture are, however, typically not as direct or precise as interventions examined in other parts of this handbook. Most often, cultural interventions work indirectly to influence or support the achievement of results, rather than striving for direct or immediate performance impacts. For example, after completing an assessment of your organization's culture, you may find that customs or traditions have developed around formal one-hour meetings; therefore, all meetings become scheduled for one hour, even if less or more time is required. While policy changes or tutorials on how to manage meetings could have some impact on the length of meetings, if you cannot change the cultural norms that support one-hour meetings, then few improvements in performance will occur—and those improvements will likely be temporary at best.

Changing behavior often requires changes in the culture—changes that either support desired behavior or counter undesired ones. In most situations, however, cultures do not respond as we might hope to direct attempts to change their characteristics. Just try moving the coffeepot from the break room to the hallway, or having people leave their doors open while they are in their offices, and you'll find that changing culture is tough work. Changing the cultural norms of an organization is most often achieved more reliably through indirect influence, rather than direct intervention.

Indirect influence on organizational culture comes through the relationship between your comprehensive performance system and the organization's culture. The relationship between the two is reciprocating. While performance interventions (from mentoring and incentives to knowledge management and succession planning) may rely on organization culture to support their imple-mentation and success, an organization's culture likewise relies on performance interventions to shape its future. Whereas one direct activity or intervention may build resistance to change, the combined influence of performance inter-ventions from a holistic performance system can begin to guide the culture of an organization. Thus, an organization's culture can be influenced by your improvement activities—just as the organizational culture will influence the design and implementation of your improvement efforts.

WHAT'S COMING UP

In Chapter Thirty, Boise State University's Anthony Marker provides the foundation for understanding how culture can impact your efforts to improve performance and how your efforts can influence the culture. This foundation is the starting place for managing the complex relationship of organizational culture to performance improvement.

Organizational Culture

Anthony Marker

INTRODUCTION

We all probably have a good idea of what culture is. After all, each of us is a member of many cultures, such as family cultures, ethnic cultures, religious cultures, national cultures, occupational cultures, organizational cultures, and others. Whenever people are together long enough to have shared experiences—successes and failures—they develop assumptions, values, and beliefs that influence their behavior and guide their future decisions. These are the basis for the cultures that surround us and provide a context for nearly all that we do. No wonder then, that those of us who are interested in improving human performance should be interested in culture, specifically that within an organization. This chapter examines what organizational culture is, how we can analyze it, and what its impact may be on human performance.

DESCRIPTION

Organizational culture is sometimes defined as our shared values, the way we do things around here, or the rituals and stories we share when bringing someone new into the organization. However, Edgar Schein, a recognized academician and consultant with over forty years of experience in the areas of organizational culture and change, reminds us in his 1999 book *The*

Corporate Culture Survival Guide that these informal definitions point to the manifestations of culture, but do not go to the "level where culture really matters." That is to say, none of those initial definitions goes deep enough to provide a reliable guide for maintaining or transforming an organization's culture, or even for recognizing which of our interventions will be accepted or rejected.

Culture is a property of any group that has been together long enough to have shared experiences leading to successes, failures, or both. Cultures can be found at all hierarchical levels and in organizations of all sizes—from small work groups to entire industries. Individuals in such groups are affected, and their behavior is shaped, by the values, norms, and beliefs of the group. But when it comes to a specific organization, how can we recognize its culture? To help with this task, Schein proposes a culture continuum based on visibility. He breaks the continuum into three levels, beginning with the most visible.

Level 1—Artifacts

Artifacts are highly visible. They are those manifestations of the culture that can be observed with the senses while walking around an organization's premises. Artifacts consist of the sights, sounds, smells, and textures that can be identified and counted. They are also perhaps the least useful for diagnosing the true cultural characteristics, because they can be a reflection of what is *wanted* rather than of what *exists*. In other words, you can see *what* is presented but you do not know *why* these particular characteristics are on display.

Level 2—Espoused Values

Espoused values are at least partially visible. They are the things that people *say* they value. Sometimes, these statements can be found in written records that detail the organization's values, ethics, vision, goals, and philosophy. But records are not enough. To gain an understanding of the organization's espoused values, you must also talk to people and ask questions about what you observe. You may then see inconsistencies between the artifacts and the espoused values. Regardless of what you find at this level of analysis, Schein advises refraining from assuming that you now know an organization's culture. You still need to dig deeper.

Level 3—Basic Underlying Assumptions

Underlying assumptions are largely invisible. They consist of the basic norms, values, and beliefs developed through shared experience. Those that lead to success are reinforced; those that lead to failure are eventually extinguished. Yet most of these underlying assumptions are unconscious and, therefore, invisible to the organization's members and, without careful investigation, also to those who try to understand the culture. Uncovering culture at this third level takes considerable effort and skill.

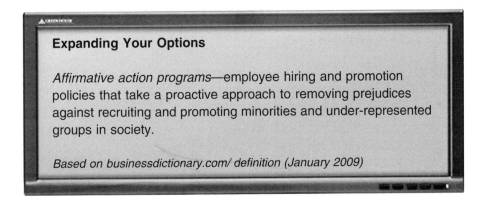

Expanding Your Options

Affirmative action programs—employee hiring and promotion policies that take a proactive approach to removing prejudices against recruiting and promoting minorities and under-represented groups in society.

Based on businessdictionary.com/ definition (January 2009)

Why Culture Matters to Performance Improvement (PI) Practitioners

When we speak of human performance interventions, it is common to hear the term "systemic" used. This is a positive development for the field. It means practitioners have begun to look holistically at performance problems and corresponding interventions meant to address them. While several holistic factors such as environmental requirements, resource availability, and organizational goals may impact implementation of any performance-improving intervention, one of the most important holistic variables is organizational culture.

Organizational culture may be hard to define in operational terms, but despite its elusive nature, most PI practitioners know that when interventions are not aligned with the culture, they run the risk of being cast aside. As Kotter and Heskett suggest in their 1992 book *Corporate Culture and Performance*: "When the cultures are our own, they often go unnoticed—until we try to implement a new strategy or program which is incompatible with their central norms and values. Then we observe, first hand, the power of culture" (p. 3). This seems true regardless of how strong other factors—funding, leadership, expertise, resources, and commitment—may be in support of that intervention.

Odom, Boxx, and Dunn assert in a 1990 article for *Public Productivity & Management Review* that: "The pervasiveness of an organization's culture requires that managers recognize the underlying dimensions of their organization's culture and their impact on employee satisfaction and commitment, work-group cohesion, strategy implementation, and organizational performance" (p. 157).

And finally, Schein reminds us: "Culture matters. It matters because decisions made without awareness of the operative cultural forces may have unanticipated and undesirable consequences."

WHAT WE KNOW FROM RESEARCH

In *Corporate Culture and Performance*, Kotter and Heskett reviewed the research on organizational culture. Their focus was on corporations and came to the following four conclusions:

1. *Corporate culture can have a significant impact on long-term economic performance:* They found that organizational cultures that fostered equal attention to all primary stakeholder groups (customers, stockholders, and employees) and that emphasized leadership from managers at all levels of the organization's hierarchy outperformed corporations that didn't have that focus by a "huge margin." The impressive performance disparity is shown in Table 30.1.

2. Corporate culture will probably be an even more important factor in determining the success or failure of organizations in the future. They found that less-adaptive or non-adaptive cultures are "performance degrading" cultures that have a negative impact on financial returns. This is so for a number of reasons, the primary being that this type of culture works against strategic adaptation when conditions change. Since the rate of change has only increased in the time since Kotter and Heskett wrote, their conclusion that adaptive cultures will have an advantage is probably even truer today.

3. *Corporate cultures that hinder long-term financial performance are not rare:* Kotter and Heskett concluded that, despite having intelligent and talented people as members, cultures that restrain long-term financial performance are more common than we might expect. They suggest that such restraining cultures arise easily—especially when members of the organization feel the organization is performing well—and encourage behavior that hinders performance. Once such cultures are in place, they exhibit an inertia that makes it difficult to change course. One reason for this inertia and the resulting negative effect on performance is that the culture tends to be invisible to those who live within it. Hence, it becomes an unaware support for the existent power structure which is threatened by the proposal of any substantial change.

4. *Although difficult to change, corporate cultures can be altered to enhance performance:* Kotter and Heskett finally conclude that while extremely complex and time-consuming, culture change is possible—given the right leadership (as differentiated from management). One difficulty in making such a change is that what constitutes a good or desirable culture is situationally dependent. Hence it is hard to know for any specific organization exactly what kind of cultural change should be the goal.

The literature offers few descriptions of successful cultural transformations.

Table 30.1 Performance Disparity Between Corporate Cultures Emphasizing vs. Lacking Leadership from Managers

Factors Studied over an Eleven-Year Period	Corporate Cultures Emphasizing a Balanced Stakeholder Focus and Distributed Leadership	Corporations Lacking Those Cultural Characteristics
Revenue Increase	682 percent	166 percent
Workforce Expansion	282 percent	36 percent
Stock Price Growth	901 percent	74 percent
Net Income Improvement	756 percent	1 percent

Results reported in Kotter and Heskett, 1992, p. 11.

More recently, Jesper Sørensen proposed in 2002 that strong organizational cultures may be good at incremental change, but when environments are volatile—and most business environments today arguably match this description—and change is more constant or dramatic, then the benefits of a strong organizational culture may disappear.

In summary, while there is some evidence that cultures can be altered, it is debatable whether they can be wholly transformed. What this and subsequent research, such as that of Cameron and Quinn in 1999, suggests is that, even though specific traits of an organization's culture can impact organizational performance, there is no single best culture for any industry or area. However, it does seem that high-performing cultures tend to be those that are well aligned with their mission, vision, goals, and strategies as well as with existent environmental constraints. Hence, organizational cultures that are flexible and highly adaptive are likely to provide performance advantages in the current, fast-changing environment.

WHEN TO APPLY

When is it appropriate to pay attention to organizational culture? In fact, there are very few occasions during a performance improvement process when you can afford to ignore culture. That said, there are certainly times when it is more important to plug what you know about organization culture into your equation. Here are some of those times.

When Guiding Principles Are Being Devised or Revised

Most organizations, whether they are small "mom and pop" businesses or large multinational corporations, have high-level principles that guide decision making. Sometimes these guiding principles are explicit and communicated clearly to the organization's members. At other times, they are merely implied. In both cases, these principles guide leaders at all levels in making decisions, whether these decisions deal with something as high-level as acquiring another company or with something as mundane as choosing pencils and pens. And, whatever the level, the guiding principles need to be aligned with the culture. Hence, two occasions when a PI practitioner should take the culture into particular account are when *devising* and when *revising* the guiding principles.

It is not unusual to find organizations that are still working with implied guiding principles. This is particularly true of fledgling organizations with few employees. The guiding principles in such situations are often only visible through the behavior and decisions of the organization's leadership. However, as organizations grow and become more specialized, there tends to be less face-to-face contact between people across levels. When this happens, those leading the organization often find it necessary to formalize the guiding principles—to *devise* them—for the first time. Anyone who has engaged in this process knows that it can be unexpectedly complex and often involves a long drawn-out process of negotiation.

In addition to taking culture into consideration when an organization is devising its first guiding principles, the PI practitioner may be dealing with an organization that has long-established, explicit principles and, because of problems with external adaptation or internal integration, may have to *revise* those principles. On such occasions, the PI practitioner should understand the existing culture.

Whether devising or revising, those involved need to ascertain that the guiding principles align with the culture—with the values, beliefs, and norms of the organization's members. If instead there is misalignment, those in leadership roles must recognize the challenge, and perhaps the danger, of going against the culture and plan accordingly.

When Mergers and Acquisitions Occur

Another common scenario during which culture can play a large role is when two organizations merge or when one organization acquires another. Even when the two organizations are in the same line of business, it is unusual to find completely compatible cultures. When such cultural mixing happens, it can have a serious negative impact on productivity in both organizations. Mixing cultures is tricky because, as we have seen, culture isn't merely a matter of decision making but instead also involves the values, norms, beliefs, and even the artifacts that members of the organization hold dear. Forcing change, even if eventually possible (and organizational ecologists still argue this issue), is painful. One culture normally ends up swallowing the other and becoming dominant.

For instance, during the "tech boom" of the late 1990s, a large Chicago corporate consulting organization acquired a mid-sized consulting company in Boston. The Chicago firm's culture was fast-paced and focused on the bottom line. It had made several prominent acquisitions over a few years and was outwardly oriented and somewhat scattered. It made the Boston acquisition based on the prospect of gaining entry to a new market segment, paying little attention to how the two companies would fit together. By contrast, the Boston firm's culture was based on close relationships, both internally and externally. It was focused on providing quality services to a select clientele. Needless to say, the two cultures did not mix well. Within a few weeks of the acquisition, many members of the Boston firm left to find employment at places better matched to the culture they were used to. This posed a serious problem for the Chicago firm. They had purchased a services company based heavily on the knowledge and skills of its members. As those members disappeared, so did the value of their investment.

Mixing cultures can work with planning and with a bit of luck. However, there are other times when, no matter how much preparation is put into mixing two or more cultures, they may behave like oil and water—they mix for a time, but if you turn your attention away from them, they revert back to their original nature.

When Interventions Are Underway

Human performance technology (HPT) interventions—by their very nature—introduce something new or change an existing aspect of the organization. When this occurs, the intervention affects and is affected by the organizational culture.

One of the enduring tools used by PI practitioners is Thomas Gilbert's Behavior Engineering Model (BEM), which he published in 1978 (see Chapter Two). The BEM classifies causes for performance problems into two categories: those having to do with the environment and those having to do with the individual. These can be visualized as the two rows of a table (Table 30.2). The two broad categories can then be divided into three types of problems (seen as columns): Information, Tools, and Motivation. The result is a 2 by 3 matrix for analyzing causes for performance problems. The interventions PI practitioners recommend in order to address performance problems nearly always fall cleanly into one of the six cells of the BEM. Interventions in any one of those cells are subject to the influence of organizational culture. For this reason, Wedman's Performance Pyramid integrates the elements of Gilbert's model with organizational culture, providing a holistic structure for this handbook (see Chapter Three).

Table 30.2 The Behavior Engineering Model

	Information	*Instrumentation*	*Motivation*
Environment	• Data • Feedback	• Capacity • Tools • Resources	• Consequences • Rewards • Incentives
Person	• Knowledge • Skills	• Capacity	• Motives

Adapted from Gilbert, 1978

For instance, changes to an organization's reward structure (environment ×
motivation) will be impacted by the organization's culture—its values, norms,
and beliefs. These determine what it is important to reward. Any attempt to put
into place a system that rewards behavior counter to those values is likely to
cause problems, either with the intervention or within the organization. Likewise, changes to the availability or form of information to employees (environment × information) should fit in with the value of information-sharing in the
organization. If an organization is run by managers who like to keep a close hold
on information, then an intervention that proposes sharing information is likely
to be resisted or to wither from lack of managerial support.

In all cases, the interventions we create in order to improve performance exist
in a cultural context. If the intervention supports and is supported by the existing
organizational culture, it has a greater chance for success. On the other hand, if
that intervention opposes the existing culture, it may face serious challenges.

When Recruitment and Retention Are Means of Renewal

When organizations are trying to renew themselves, they often do so by
recruiting and hiring people who exhibit the traits of the new approach. The
hope is that, by bringing in people with new perspectives, values, and orientations, the existing culture can be coaxed to change, that this "new blood" will
pull the rest of the organization along. However, such attempts, especially in
isolation from other organizational factors, rarely seem to work.

Geary Rummler warned as early as 1990 that pitting a good performer against
a bad system will result in the system winning almost every time. So it goes
when an organization brings someone in to change the culture. The result is
likely to be a new employee who is exhausted and miserable from spending all
of his or her time and energy fighting through the obstacles of the existing
culture and who, as a consequence, has little time to do the tasks for which he or
she was hired. Even when a number of employees are hired for the same reason,
they are likely to find the road slow and difficult unless the system is changed to
favor the new culture they are supposed to represent.

The other side of this issue is that of retention. In trying to change culture, organizations may inadvertently alienate existing employees unless they actively work to bring those employees along with them into the new orientation. While doing so is likely to be difficult, ignoring the cultural implications may result in even more serious impact to the business down the road.

STRENGTHS AND CRITICISMS

The PI practitioner should be aware of the advantages and disadvantages of dealing with a strong culture, as well as of doing a cultural analysis.

Strengths of a Strong Culture

- A strong organizational culture—and one that is aligned with the internal and external environmental requirements—can provide conditions for organizational-level performance improvements on measures such as workforce expansion and increased shareholder value.
- A strong, aligned culture allows an organization to focus more tightly on its stated priorities.
- A strong, aligned culture can allow for faster decision making and can function with fewer levels of managerial hierarchy.

Criticisms of a Strong Culture

- Strong organizational cultures can be surprisingly resistant to change, even in the face of a clear need or threat.
- The stronger the culture, the more difficult it is to change. Any cultural transformation is complex and requires strong and committed leadership, a well-communicated vision, and time. It also requires removing support for the old culture while establishing support for the new, desired culture. The stronger the culture, the more difficult it is to meet these requirements.
- Experience with one strong organizational culture may blind PI practitioners to the unique attributes of the current organization and cause them to forget that there is no one "best" culture.

Strengths of Cultural Analysis

- A well-done cultural analysis can help PI practitioners shape and/or propose interventions that have a better chance of being successfully implemented. This, in the end, translates into value added for the client.

Criticisms of Cultural Analysis

- Cultural analysis often requires time-consuming qualitative methodologies. Because it takes time, it is often cut short. Then, based on inadequate or faulty data, PI practitioners and organizational leaders may make costly mistakes.

- A cultural analysis that ends at the artifact level may do more harm than good. Artifacts—those manifestations of culture that are on the surface and most visible—can lead a PI practitioner to believe he or she can understand a culture just by walking around the organization's premises and observing activities and interactions. However, a true understanding of the culture of an organization requires digging deep, not only to uncover the basic assumptions and values held, but also to find the reasons they exist.

RECOMMENDED CULTURAL ANALYSIS PROCESS

Those looking for a recommended process on how to transform an organizational culture will not find it here. The transformation of an organizational culture is a strategic-level intervention that should be left to the experts; it is complex, time-consuming, and potentially very costly if done poorly. The focus here is on how to conduct a cultural analysis. The goal is to provide PI practitioners with a reliable process for discovering alignment issues in order to identify obstacles and opportunities that may impact their interventions.

Collecting Data: Surveys vs. Interviews

As discussed earlier, various methodologies (see Chapter Thirty-Three) have been used to research organizational culture, from highly quantitative approaches to highly qualitative ones. Because PI practitioners are often pressed for time at the beginning of a project, it may be tempting to use quantitative approaches such as surveys. Schein is fairly clear that a quantitative approach will not uncover the aspects of culture that are most useful, asserting that surveys "do not reach the tacit shared assumptions that may be of importance in your organization." He gives a few reasons for this:

- Until you start investigating and gathering data, you don't know what to ask, and *Catch 22*
- Asking people in an organization about their shared phenomena is "inefficient and possibly invalid." (Schein, 1999, p. 61)

Basic assumptions are buried beneath the surface, and surveys, by their very nature, do not allow for a follow-up to a response with a timely "Well, why is that?" On the other hand, qualitative approaches do lend themselves to such follow-up and, hence, are more appropriate for getting at underlying cultural values. Among the qualitative approaches that can be used are interviews and focus groups. Both of these approaches allow for asking *why* to get to the origins of a value or belief. One example of such an approach is the "5-Why" kaizen technique, discussed at length in Masaaki Imai's 1986 book. Those who use this approach are advised to ask "why" five times in order to get to the root cause of a problem. This technique lends itself well to cultural analysis.

Process

Few, if any, qualitative inquiries into organizational culture will follow a step-by-step process without deviation. However, a general guide for the PI practitioner may be helpful.

1. *Define the Business Problem:* In all likelihood, if you are doing an organizational culture study, you are doing it in the context of an unresolved organizational problem. As with any performance intervention, it is crucial to identify that problem up-front and keep it visible while you are collecting data. In fact, the business problem should guide the data collection. Collecting data that has no bearing on the business problem is likely to be looked on by the client as a waste of precious time and financial resources.

2. *State Your Goals and Objectives:* Once you have identified the problem, clarify the project goals and objectives. This will go a long way toward keeping your data collection on track.

3. *Identify Artifacts:* Identify and catalogue cultural artifacts. Schein provides a list of artifacts that includes the following (p. 67):

   - Dress codes;
   - Levels of formality;
   - Physical work spaces (layout, lighting, windows, common areas, etc.);
   - Customization of work spaces;
   - Hours and mode of work (in office, telecommute, strict use of time clocks);
   - Balance between work and family life;
   - How decisions are made;
   - How information and knowledge are shared and communicated;
   - Jargon, uniforms, and other badges or forms of identification;
   - Rites and rituals; and
   - How disagreements and conflicts are handled.

   You may want to use a table similar to Table 30.3 to collect your data so that it will match the data you collect in your environmental analysis.

4. *Identify the Espoused Values:* If the espoused values, or what we *say* the culture is or should be, are different from what they really are, note that. You can find evidence of these in formal communications like mission

statements, strategy documents, safety posters, job aids, computer "splash" screens or home pages, and other documents meant for internal and/or external consumption. You can also find evidence in informal communications with organizational members.

5. *Identify the Shared Tacit Assumptions and Values:* Seek to identify stories of successes and failures in the organization that are passed on through organizational lore. Who were the heroes? Who were the disappointments? What did they do to be remembered that way?

6. *Compare for Alignment:* Once you have collected examples of the three levels of cultural evidence, compare them to the problem. Look for contradictions and signs of misalignment. For instance, if the organization professes to put worker safety as a top priority, look at the systems that foster or inhibit safe work practices such as performance criteria, reward structures, tool allocations, or other support structures. If the organization actually supports its espoused values, then you have likely found evidence of alignment. However, if the organization asserts that it values one thing while supporting an alternative (perhaps opposite) value, then you have identified misalignment. Recognizing instances of alignment or misalignment will help point to potential obstacles or opportunities for particular interventions or implementation strategies.

Table 30.3 Sample of a Cultural Data Collection Matrix

Artifacts	Espoused Values	Basic Assumptions and Beliefs	Misalignments and Contradictions Opportunities and Obstacles
External Environment	Community involvement; Community planning and layout; Religious artifacts; Ethnic artifacts	Espoused societal or community assumptions and values; External regulations	Basic societal and/or community assumptions and values that impact the organization
Organization	Work hours; Work/family balance; Power hierarchies; Workspace design and allocation; Information sharing; Org charts	Statements of Mission, Vision, Strategy, Goals, Policies, Organization Performance Measures	Underlying assumptions and beliefs about successes and failures of the organization as a whole; Stories; Heroes
Job/Process	Meetings (length, formality, content);	Scheduling; Process improvement	Underlying assumptions and

Artifacts	Espoused Values	Basic Assumptions and Beliefs	Misalignments and Contradictions Opportunities and Obstacles
	Evidence of standardization; Communication patterns	approach; Flexibility; Degree of cross-functional integration; Job/process measures	beliefs about successes and failures of processes and tasks; Stories; Heroes
Worker	Individualization of workspace; Work routine; Dress; Formality of relationships; Daily rituals; Communication preferences	Individual work/task priorities; Work ethic; Degree of conformity to org. values	Underlying assumptions and beliefs about successes and failures of individuals; Stories; Heroes

Note: This is meant merely to be suggestive, not definitive.

Using Cultural Analysis in the HPT Model

How does a cultural analysis fit into the HPT model? PI practitioners may find useful applications of cultural data in several stages of the model (see Chapter One).

Organizational Analysis. Organizational analysis is the first phase of the HPT model. During organizational analysis, PI practitioners typically collect data about an organization's mission, vision, strategy, and goals, which are good sources of information about the organization's espoused values. Because you are already collecting information that is closely connected to the organization's culture, it makes sense to start your cultural analysis in this phase.

Environmental Analysis. Environmental analysis involves collecting data concerning the opportunity or problem being addressed. This analysis suggests collection of data at four levels, from the lowest to the highest: worker, job/process, organization, and environment. If you map the cultural data to these levels (using a table like the one in Table 30.3), you are likely to identify useful patterns across the various data sets.

Gap Definition. The definition of the performance gap is a statement of the difference between *what is* (the current state of the opportunity or problem) and *what is desired* (the optimal state of the opportunity or problem). The creation of this gap statement provides another opportunity to look for alignment problems. How do the current and desired states align, or misalign, with what you have learned about the organizational culture?

Cause Analysis. During the cause analysis phase, look for places to tackle root causes of a problem. This will enable you to recommend interventions that will efficiently and effectively address the business problem or opportunity that started you down this road in the first place. Cultural misalignments can create obstacles to performance. For instance, if management says it values teamwork but, in actuality, it fosters competition among team members, that knowledge might suggest an intervention point.

Intervention Selection, Design, and Development. The selection, design, and development of interventions is likely to be closely tied to implementation and the eventual success or failure of the intervention. This is, perhaps, one of the two most important phases in which a solid understanding of organizational culture can make a big difference. Understanding an organization's culture can provide you with insight into which interventions are likely to work and how significant the results they produce will be. It is far better to understand how your costly intervention will be received *before* you have developed it than it is to wait until after the development process is underway, or worse, completed.

Implementation. Although implementation appears near the end of the HPT process, it should be planned for early. Through foresight, you may be able to eliminate or lessen implementation obstacles and, in the process, save time and money and avoid potential embarrassment with the client. Your foresight will be better if you understand the organization's culture. Such an understanding can provide early warning signs about how a planned intervention will be accepted or resisted.

Evaluation. Like implementation, evaluation appears at the end of the HPT process, but a careful examination of the model shows that it is related to each of the model phases. Much of what PI practitioners do to add value to an organization is to plan for and carry out evaluations. Organizations tend to reward desirable behaviors and punish undesirable ones. How they decide between the two is often based on some form of evaluation. What they choose to measure and evaluate is usually based on their basic assumptions and values. By understanding the culture, you can better understand "what counts" and, therefore, what to measure and how to evaluate.

In summary, an understanding of organizational culture—and the alignments or misalignments of that culture as they are expressed in the organization—integrates well with the HPT process.

CRITICAL SUCCESS FACTORS

Since PI practitioners are often directly responsible for the outcome of traditional PI interventions—for example, e-learning, job redesign, mentoring (see Part Seven of this handbook)—they should be familiar with the critical success factors for these endeavors. Although PI practitioners are unlikely to be *responsible* for maintaining or transforming a culture, since they may well be *involved* in the process should it occur, they can also benefit from knowing what the critical success factors are for culture-related interventions.

Maintaining a Culture

When our organizational culture is suited to our goals, strategies, and environmental conditions, we work to maintain or even strengthen it. The thinking is: Why mess with success? Adherence to such a status quo is easiest when the organization is a bureaucracy. After all, bureaucracies are defined by standardization and codification, and it is relatively easy to standardize processes, procedures, hierarchy, and similar aspects of the organization. But when we standardize a process or a procedure (in essence, specific behaviors), we tend to confine it and restrict its flexibility, and many of today's organizations exist in a rapidly changing environment wherein flexibility is a critical asset. So the question becomes: How do we "maintain" something that itself needs to be flexible?

Provide Standard Principles for Behavior. One approach is to standardize, not through direct control of behavior, but through principles that guide behavior. For example, as a manager, I might order you always to buy a number 2 pencil of Brand X. By giving you a fixed standard, I control your behavior and the outcome of that behavior. However, if business is moving quickly and conditions are changing, you may see that a number 2 pencil of Brand X is not the best purchase for the situation. In my absence, what can you do? You need the flexibility to respond to the changed situation. You need not a standard of how-to-behave, but a standard principle upon which your behavior can be based. Instead of ordering you to buy a number 2 pencil, I might offer the principle that writing devices purchased must be handheld, or inexpensive, or make clear marks, or other criteria. Given the principle, you are free to decide what number and brand is best. In fact, you are free to decide whether something other than a pencil is best. You have flexibility.

Hire for Cultural Alignment. Another approach to maintaining or strengthening an existent culture has to do with the selection of new employees. Should you recruit people who have the skills needed and try to acculturate them after they arrive, or should you hire people who fit your cultural profile and provide them with skills training? Since people vary along a continuum on both skills and cultural fit, this is rarely an either/or choice. However, it is worth noting that some organizations with strong cultures—cultures they view as essential to their success or even survival—often hire for cultural alignment, expecting that it is easier to train for missing skills than it is to change an individual's values. Schein supports this approach and lists it first among the four mechanisms he recommends for reinforcing an existing culture:

- Hire new members for cultural fit;
- Reward behavior that matches cultural assumptions;
- Punish behavior that defies cultural assumptions; and
- Create and maintain training, indoctrination, mentoring, and socialization programs that expose newcomers to the culture and mix those newcomers with old timers steeped in the desired culture.

Transforming an Organizational Culture

Can organizational cultures be transformed? It seems clear that they can be altered, but the experts disagree on whether or not they can be completely transformed. However, regardless of what the experts say, new internal or external demands sometimes demand that some degree of cultural transformation occur. Even partial transformation may positively impact an organization's competitive position and survivability. With that in mind, what might you, the PI practitioner, do to help an organization make this kind of transition?

Create Urgency. Organizational cultures come to exist because a group of people has been successful in adhering to certain assumptions and values. In turn, the culture helps to define the group, to bind its members together, and to promote success. As such, culture is a powerful force to maintain things as they are. Hence, proposals to change the culture *on purpose* are likely to be met with strong resistance, if not totally ignored. What is needed, then, is some sense of urgency, the kind of urgency that usually comes from a threat to the organization's survival. Threats can be economic, political, technological, legal, moral, ethical, environmental, or social. Without such a serious threat—and sometimes even with— efforts at cultural transformation are likely to be difficult, if not impossible.

Tip the Anxiety Balance Toward Survival. Any effort to change something as foundational as an organization's culture is cause for a high level of anxiety among the group's members. The reason? Changing cultural assumptions means giving up beliefs and values that have proven successful in the past for a new set of assumptions that may or may not work. It means giving up the known for the unknown. Even under the best of conditions, such a change requires more than a fair share of trust and faith. You can help if you can "tip the anxiety balance." If group members feel more anxiety about the group's or organization's survival than they do about the uncertainties of transformation, they are more likely to accept the change. An analogy is that if the ship is on fire and in serious danger of sinking, even in high seas, passengers are likely to give the lifeboats a try. However, there is a danger in this approach. If you tell people their ship is on fire and about to sink, and you offer no alternative, your words are likely to have a negative impact. The same is true with an organization's members who are told that their survival is in question. If you offer them no alternative (no "lifeboat"), then the negative impact on morale, productivity, and retention is likely to be disastrous. The point here is that, if the organization is in trouble, make sure the people know it and provide them with a clear and reasonable alternative.

Have a Clear Vision of the Future. Knowing where you are going is an important component of arriving at the desired destination. Just as it is critical for instructional designers to know the desired outcomes of a training program in order to design suitable instruction, so it is critical for those involved in the transformation of an organization's culture to have some idea of the desired end-state. As much as possible, cultural transformation goals should be clear, attainable, and well communicated.

Involve Employees to Gain Buy-In. It is far better to engage the organization's members as active participants in the change than it is to inflict a cultural transformation on them without their active involvement. Change determined and managed entirely from "on high" often feels like a punishment for those below. To get increased acceptance and buy-in, employees should be involved early in the process, and their involvement should be maintained throughout the entire transformation. A caution: organizational members are quick to detect disingenuous attempts to solicit their participation, so it is important that they see and feel that their involvement contributes and is taken seriously by the organization's leadership.

Provide Needed Training. One source of anxiety resulting from cultural transformation efforts comes from people not knowing whether their current knowledge and skills will be up to the new expectations. Training programs can show them how their current knowledge and skills will transfer to the new culture and/or provide them with the new knowledge and skills required. In either case, such programs can go a long way toward increasing psychological safety and removing one obstacle to acceptance of the change.

Provide Scaffolding. Related to educational and training programs, mechanisms for coaching (see Chapters Eleven and Twenty-Seven), mentoring (see Chapters Twenty-Two and Twenty-Six), and other informal scaffolding measures can provide psychological safety nets during the transformation, while at the same time reinforcing the desired cultural assumptions and corresponding behavior.

Align Structure. Hierarchical organizational structures favor managerial behavior that emphasizes control and political decision making. Flatter or matrix types of organizational structures (see Chapter Seven) enable shared decision making and distribute authority throughout the organization. As already discussed, one type of structure is not inherently better than another; it is only better in relation to the demands of the internal goals and the external environmental conditions. The goal is to create a structure that will foster and promote the type of organizational culture you are trying to achieve.

Align Systems. While transforming an organization's culture may take place primarily in the hearts and minds of the organizational members, the support structure for that transformation is largely in the organizational system. If the necessary tools are not provided to enable the change, people are being asked to work with the wrong tools—a sure recipe for resistance, resentment, and poor performance. Taking a cue from Gilbert's behavior engineering model and Wedman's Performance Pyramid, make sure that the organizational systems dealing with (1) information and communication, (2) tools and resources, and (3) compensation, rewards, and punishment support the desired culture.

Address the WIIFM Factor. Many factors might lead an organization's members to accept or resist the transformation to a new culture, and we have already touched on several of these. However, one additional factor worth noting is the WIIFM (What's in it for me?) factor. Many organizations, when they make major changes, justify those changes by listing such benefits as increased organizational productivity, reduced costs, reduction in inventory requirements, or increased environmental capital. All of these emphasize how the *organization* will benefit from the transition, but none of them say how the *people* involved will be affected. Any change is likely to impact an organization's members personally, and often not for the better. Changes may alter valued relationships with other employees, require changes in work habits or routines, alter skills sets needed, devalue something people are good at, and value something they don't yet know how to do. Change can have a number of influences on individuals. By examining, anticipating, and making a good-faith effort to address the individual WIIFM factors, PI practitioners can significantly ease the pain members feel, as well as their resistance to the new culture.

SUMMARY

This chapter examined what organizational culture is, how you can analyze it, and what its impact may be on human performance. Here are some takeaways:

- Organizational culture provides context for all other issues.
- Organizational culture is more than what is visible on the surface.
- Misalignment can cause far-reaching problems.
- Organizational cultural impacts the practice of HPT.
- Analyzing an organizational culture is challenging.

References

Cameron, K. S., & Quinn, R. E. (1999). *Diagnosing and changing organizational culture.* Reading, MA: Addison-Wesley.

Gilbert, T. F. (1978). *Human competence: Engineering worthy performance.* New York: McGraw-Hill.

Imai, M. (1986). *Kaizen: The key to Japan's competitive success.* New York: McGraw-Hill.

Kotter, J. (2006). Leading change: Why transformation efforts fail. In J. V. Gallos (Ed.), *Organizational development* (pp. 239–251). San Francisco: Jossey-Bass.

Kotter, J., & Heskett, J. L. (1992). *Corporate culture and performance.* New York: The Free Press.

Odom, R. Y., Boxx, W. R., & Dunn, M. G. (1990). Organizational cultures, commitment, satisfaction, and cohesion. *Public Productivity & Management Review, 14*(2), 157–169.

Ouchi, W. (1985). Organizational culture. *Annual Review of Sociology, 11*, 457–483.

Rummler, G. A., & Brache, A. P. (1990). *Improving performance: How to manage the white space on the organizational chart.* San Francisco: Jossey-Bass.

Schein, E. (1999). *The corporate culture survival guide.* San Francisco: Jossey-Bass.

Sørensen, J. B. (2002). The strength of corporate culture and the reliability of firm performance. *Administrative Science Quarterly, 47*(1), 70–91.

Recommended Readings

Cook, S. D. N., & Yanow, D. (1993). Culture and organizational learning. *Journal of Management Inquiry, 2*(4), 373–390.

Deal, T. E., & Kennedy, A. A. (2000). *Corporate cultures: The rites and rituals of corporate life.* New York: Basic Books.

Dean, P. J. (1999). Designing better organizations with human performance technology and organization development. In H. Stolovitch & E. Keeps (Eds.), *Handbook of human performance technology: Improving individual and organizational performance worldwide* (2nd ed., pp. 321–334). San Francisco: Jossey-Bass.

Denison, D. (1996). What is the difference between organizational culture and organizational climate? A native's point of view on a decade of paradigm wars. *The Academy of Management Review, 23*(3), 619–654.

Gallagher, R. S. (2003). *The soul of an organization: Understanding the values that drive successful corporate cultures.* New York: Dearborn Trade Publishing.

Gallos, J. V. (2006). Reframing complexity: A four-dimensional approach to organizational diagnosis, development and change. In J. V. Gallos (Ed.), *Organizational Development* (pp. 344–362). San Francisco: Jossey-Bass.

Jones, B. B., & Brazzel, M. (Eds.). (2006). *The NTL handbook of organizational development and change: Principles, practices, and perspectives.* San Francisco: Pfeiffer.

Kunda, G. (1992). *Engineering culture.* Philadelphia: Temple University Press.

Leibler, S. N., & Parkman, A. W. (1999). Human resources selection. In H. Stolovitch & E. Keeps (Eds.), *Handbook of human performance technology: Improving individual and organizational performance worldwide* (2nd ed., pp. 351–372). San Francisco: Jossey-Bass.

Lineberry, C. S., & Carleton, R. J. (1999). Analyzing corporate culture. In H. Stolovitch & E. Keeps (Eds.), *Handbook of human performance technology: Improving individual and organizational performance worldwide* (2nd ed., pp. 335–350). San Francisco: Pfeiffer.

Sales, M. J. (2006). Understanding the power of position: A diagnostic model. In J. V. Gallos (Ed.), *Organizational development* (pp. 322–343). San Francisco: Jossey-Bass.

Schein, E. (1999). Cultural change. In D. Langdon, K. S. Whiteside, & M. M. McKenna (Eds.), *Intervention resource guide: 50 performance improvement tools* (pp. 125–130). San Francisco: Pfeiffer.

 # EDITORIAL CONNECTIONS

The individuals who comprise an organization have multiple and continually changing factors influencing their performance. From events at home and relationships with co-workers to their experiences within the organization and their career aspirations, employees' performance is pushed and pulled on a daily basis. Consequently, the cultures that develop within organizations are equally complex. From interpersonal relationships to longstanding organizational norms, the cultures that exist within an organization significantly shape how people perform their jobs and the results that they accomplish.

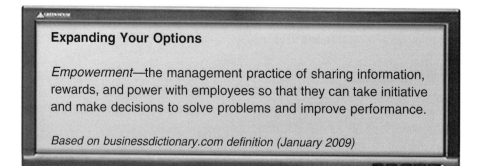

Expanding Your Options

Empowerment—the management practice of sharing information, rewards, and power with employees so that they can take initiative and make decisions to solve problems and improve performance.

Based on businessdictionary.com definition (January 2009)

Despite this complexity, you will want to work on developing an organizational culture that supports your improvement efforts, as well as an improvement effort that shapes your organization's culture around performance. Chapter Thirty offers useful guidance in better analyzing and understanding the cultures that exist within your organization, as well as their potential influence on your improvement efforts.

WHAT'S COMING UP

Next, in Chapter Thirty-One, Tyrone Holmes examines "Diversity and Cultural Competence" (and more specifically diversity training) as a performance intervention for accomplishing significant results through changing an organization's culture.

Diversity and Cultural Competence

Tyrone A. Holmes

INTRODUCTION

In 2005, the Society for Human Resource Management facilitated a study exploring diversity activities within organizations. This study found that two-thirds of the organizations surveyed offered diversity training for their employees. Although such initiatives may be as widely utilized as this study established, they do not always function effectively as tools for improving both individual and organizational performance. Many organizations fail to take critical steps before and after a training event to make sure that educational content is transferred to the workplace in a way that meaningfully enhances performance.

This chapter describes a three-phase performance-based diversity training model designed to solve this problem. The model outlines steps that must be taken before, during, and after a diversity event. When implemented, these steps ensure that the diversity training initiative has a positive, measurable impact on employee performance.

DESCRIPTION

The United States in the 21st century is one of the most culturally diverse countries in the world. Whether examining age, ethnicity, race, language, or religion, we are more likely than ever to find ourselves in increasingly diverse organizational settings, working with culturally different individuals. Evron Esen reports in a 2005 study for the Society for Human Resource Management that diversity has contributed to a substantial increase in the number of organizations that implement diversity activities, including formal training and education. These initiatives, of course, are useful to the organization only if their educational content translates into performance-enhancing practices in the organization. All too often, inadequate steps taken in the transition process may lead to the effects of the training being lost.

Unfortunately, not all of these initiatives have had a meaningful impact on overall performance (for example, see Taylor Cox's 2001 *Creating the Multicultural Organization* as well as Hayles and Russell's 1997 book *The Diversity Directive*). One reason for this is that many organizations fail to take the requisite steps before and after an educational event to ensure the training is transferred to the workplace in a way that positively enhances performance. My performance-based diversity training model, discussed at length within Pfeiffer's 2006 training *Annual*, seeks to address this problem by emphasizing three fundamental principles:

1. The success of any diversity training event must be defined in terms of employee performance. Other measures such as participant reaction to the training program may be utilized, but are insufficient to determine overall program success.

2. The diversity training event itself, while important, is not enough to facilitate a substantive and sustained increase in employee performance. Other program elements that take place before and after the training event will have a considerable impact on program success.

3. The most effective way to ensure that the diversity training event leads to improved performance is to specifically plan for that performance well in advance of the training program.

The performance-based diversity training model describes the implementation of specific steps in three phases of the process: activities that occur pre-training, those that take place during the training event, and post-training activities. These enable an organization to ensure that the training has a positive impact on individual and organizational performance. The steps in the three phases are

Pre-Training Activities
- Clarify the benefits of the diversity training;
- Define post-training performance expectations;
- Communicate these performance expectations to the trainees; and
- Identify support and reinforcement activities to complement the training.

The Training Event
- Implement the diversity training using skills-based learning strategies.

Post-Training Activities
- Implement the support and reinforcement activities already identified to enable practical application of the newly acquired skills;
- Evaluate the impact of the diversity training on individual and organizational performance; and
- Provide additional learning opportunities for continued growth.

Detailed descriptions of the various implementation steps for each phase are given in the following sections.

WHAT WE KNOW FROM RESEARCH

Diversity programs are well established within the American workplace. In Esen's study, it was found that organizations engage in a wide variety of diversity-related activities. These include employee leave to observe religious or cultural holidays, diversity recruitment and retention activities, diversity-related community outreach, and diversity-focused business policies and decisions. Two of every three organizations, says Esen, offer some form of diversity education. This education covers a variety of subject areas such as anti-discrimination, diversity awareness, cultural awareness, diversity management, and diversity knowledge/skills development. Shawn Fegley's 2006 follow-up study for the Society for Human Resource Management reiterates that typically diversity training is provided for employees at all organizational levels.

Performance-focused diversity practices, including educational programs, have the potential to provide many benefits for individuals and organizations. Pertinent studies that support this claim include Cox (1994) and Kossek, Zonia, and Young (1997). These include improved individual and organizational performance, enhanced customer service, and an improved bottom line. Moreover, an in-depth exploration of such benefits can be found in a 1997 report by Cox and Beale, in a study by Hayles and Russell from 1997, and within a 2001 research study sponsored by the Society for Human Resource Management and *Fortune* magazine. Improved individual and organizational performance refers to measurable increases in employee productivity and work quality, enhanced team performance, improved organizational processes, and enhanced workforce quality. Evidence for such assertions have been reported at least as early as Charlan Jeanne Nemeth's 1985 study "Dissent, Group Process, and Creativity" and, earlier, in Robert Ziller's contribution to *Experimental Psychology* from 1972.

Schreiber and Lenson's 2001 *Multicultural Marketing* and Cox's *Cultural Diversity in Organizations* from 1994 both refer to enhanced customer service as an increased ability to connect with and serve a diverse customer base. This can be reflected in greater sales in multicultural markets, reduced customer complaints, and increased market share. It also applies to internal customers such as employees, and can be seen in better attitude and morale. Improved organizational bottom line refers to increased revenues, reduced costs, and enhanced organizational value and profitability. This can be apparent in a variety of organizational measures such as increased sales, stock value, and retention (especially among underrepresented group members), reduced cost-per-hire, and decreased turnover. It can also be reflected in a reduction in racial and sexual harassment and associated legal costs. (Further discussion of these issues can be found in various works, including Cox; Cox, and Beale; Cox and Blake; and Hayles and Russell.)

While diversity programs offer much potential for individual and organizational performance improvement, Cox, as well as Rynes and Rosen, report that such practices as diversity training and education are not always effective and often fail to achieve desired results. Indeed, as has been described by the University of Michigan's Taylor Cox Jr. in his 2001 book *Creating The Multicultural Organization,* several reasons exist for this lack of success, particularly as it applies to the training event itself:

1. *Participants and training facilitators with different expectations regarding the diversity training and its outcomes.* A common problem with diversity training is the separation between participant expectations and actual program content. For example, participants may be expecting to learn about a specific cultural group, but the facilitators focus on teaching listening and communication skills. This disconnect between participant expectations and program reality makes it more difficult to transfer the training back to the workplace and emphasizes the need to clarify expectations with participants prior to the training event.

2. *Participants unprepared prior to implementation of the diversity training program.* Along the same lines, diversity training effectiveness can be greatly diminished if participants are not prepared prior to the educational event. For example, some training programs require meaningful participant interaction and personal disclosure to be successful. Participants need to be clear as to how this will take place so that they can be aware of and can understand the implications.

3. *Insufficient training time to accommodate the diversity program objectives and training situation.* Another major reason for ineffective diversity training is a lack of sufficient time to achieve training program objectives. For example, if the purpose of the training program

is to increase knowledge relative to a specific topic (for example, rituals and customs in a particular country), training time can be relatively short. Conversely, if the training is designed to modify behaviors and develop specific skill sets, substantially more time is needed. Training may be best when spread over multiple sessions.

4. *Failure to disseminate enough pertinent information during the diversity training session.* One less common problem with diversity training is a failure to supply sufficient content during the educational session. Because diversity training often utilizes highly interactive instructional methods to facilitate small- and large-group discussions, there may be little time for information to be disseminated through lecture. While a focus on group interaction is very useful, there should be several segments of lecture provided by the facilitators who are, presumably, content experts who can facilitate the knowledge-transfer process.

5. *Inappropriate group size to be able to achieve specified objectives.* Groups that are either too large or too small can inhibit training program effectiveness. For example, if the focus of the training is on skills development through behavioral modeling, then group size must be relatively small so that participants can view the behavioral model, practice the skill, and receive feedback on their performance. Conversely, if the objective of the training session is to disseminate information, larger groups can be utilized.

6. *Facilitators who cannot successfully handle the sensitive subject matter inherent in most diversity training programs.* Another cause of unsuccessful diversity training is the use of ineffective session facilitators. Simply stated, diversity training is one of the more difficult forms of training to implement. Trainers must be able to effectively open the training in a way that creates buy-in to the process. This is true for any type of educational process but can be especially difficult in a diversity session because discomfort, skepticism, and even outright hostility may be exhibited by some participants. The trainer must be able to handle sensitive subject matter, deal with problem participants and difficult emotional issues, and facilitate the session using a variety of instructional techniques (lecture, case study, and role play). Finally, the facilitator must be able to close the session in a way that facilitates the transfer of educational content to the workplace.

WHEN TO APPLY

The performance-based diversity training model can be applied to a wide variety of diversity programs and interventions. This includes both instructor-led activities such as classroom, online, and remote formats and self-paced learning formats such as print, CD-ROM, and online. To demonstrate its application, three examples are provided below. The first example in Table 31.1 applies the model to an online diversity recruitment program where the goal is to help participants develop the tools and resources needed to recruit high-quality, culturally diverse candidate pools. In this example, the key steps include defining post-training performance expectations for the learners, the training intervention, and measures that can be used to evaluate training program effectiveness.

Table 31.1 Diversity Recruitment Training Example

Goal: To provide participants (people directly responsible for employee recruitment) with a variety of tools and resources that allow them to increase the quality and diversity of candidate pools.

Pre-Training Activities	The Training Event	Post-Training Activities
Performance Expectations: Use the Internet to identify sources of high quality, culturally diverse candidates. Apply four types of networking to increase the quality and diversity of candidate pools. Apply specific criteria to evaluate the organization's strengths and weaknesses with regard to employee recruitment and retention.	**The Training Program:** A series of four, one-hour online training modules that describe the criteria that candidates use when deciding whether to accept a particular job; identify sources of high quality, culturally diverse candidates; demonstrate the use of Internet recruitment techniques, and provide participants with an overview of the four types of networking.	**Training Evaluation:** The impact of the diversity recruitment training on learner performance will be evaluated by applying the *candidate pool diversity percentage* metric (number of diverse candidates divided by total number of candidates). This provides an indication of how effective participants are at increasing the diversity of candidate pools.

The second example, presented in Table 31.2, applies the model to a classroom-based diversity skills training program with a focus on the multicultural communication and conflict management competencies. Here, the focal points include behavioral performance expectations, a description of the training intervention, and potential support and reinforcement activities for the participants as a follow-up to the training program.

Table 31.3 demonstrates the model as applied to a classroom-based performance coaching program. The primary objective of this training session is to help trainees develop the specific skills needed to facilitate performance

Table 31.2 Diversity Skills Training Example

Goal: To help participants develop the skills and knowledge needed to communicate, resolve conflict and solve problems in culturally diverse environments.

Pre-Training Activities	The Training Event	Post-Training Activities
Performance Expectations: Eliminate words, gestures and phrases that break down communication and offend others. Use *active listening* to successfully understand and respond to the needs of others. Use the *conflict mediation* process to successfully resolve day-to-day conflicts in a timely manner.	**The Training Program**: Five, four-hour training sessions on the competencies of diversity, multicultural communication, and conflict resolution. Primary emphasis will be on the use of behavioral modeling to demonstrate effective use of the skills, to facilitate participant skill practice, and to provide positive and constructive feedback regarding participant performance.	**The Support and Reinforcement Activities**: Performance expectations will be directly tied to the formal performance appraisal process. Trainees will serve as third-party conflict mediators within the organization. Trainees will have monthly meetings to discuss progress in the three performance areas.

improvement conversations such as those providing positive and constructive feedback when dealing with a diverse range of employees. The focus of this program is on articulating on-the-job performance expectations, describing training program content, and identifying the metric that will be used to evaluate training program effectiveness.

STRENGTHS AND CRITICISMS

The model has both strengths and limitations, as listed below:

Strengths

- The model provides a systematic framework for the design, facilitation, and evaluation of a performance-focused diversity training program. This should clarify the implementation process for program designers and facilitators.
- Because of the systematic framework, the model provides a means to connect a diversity training program with other organizational initiatives and strategies (for example, an organization's strategic plan).

- The model clarifies and reinforces an understanding of performance expectations for trainees prior to, during, and after the training event. It enables participants and facilitators to have similar expectations regarding program content and objectives.

- The model applies techniques and processes that facilitate long-term skill development and on-the-job application. This includes an appropriate blend of interactive learning and lecture.

- The model provides a framework for the successful use of diversity measures and metrics that can be used to evaluate training program effectiveness.

Table 31.3 Performance Coaching Training Example

Goal: To help participants (managers and supervisors) develop the skills and knowledge needed to facilitate successful performance improvement conversations with a diverse range of employees.

Pre-Training Activities	The Training Event	Post-Training Activities
Performance Expectations: Provide positive and constructive feedback to employees on a continuous basis. Assist each employee with the development of a career plan. Identify organizational barriers to employee success, and develop a plan to address each barrier.	**The Training Program:** Three, four-hour training sessions that describe the three primary behaviors of coaching, introduce the three-step feedback model, and utilize behavioral modeling to facilitate participant skill practice.	**Training Evaluation:** The impact of the performance coaching training on learner performance will be evaluated using the *turnover* metric (number of terminated employees divided by the average employee population) and examining the results on a demographic basis. This provides an indication of how effective the organization is at retaining diverse employee groups.

Criticisms

- Applying the model requires a sizable time commitment. In addition to the typical activities that take place during training program development such as needs assessment and training program design, this process requires identification of program benefits, clarification of post-training behavioral expectations, communication of expectations prior to implementation of the training, and identification of additional support and reinforcement activities. While these all benefit the educational process, program facilitators will have to spend a respectable amount of time carrying out these steps.

- Applying the model may carry a sizable financial and human resource cost. To successfully implement a performance-based diversity training initiative, several individuals with a variety of skill sets will be needed. For instance, instructional system developers may be required to design the training event. Program facilitators may be required to facilitate the training program (if it is an instructor-led program). Individuals with assessment expertise will be needed to identify measures and metrics that can be used to evaluate program effectiveness. Prior to the training event, the participants should be notified about the program and the behavioral expectations that will be placed upon them. This may necessitate some discussion in a format that will take the participants away from their jobs. Altogether, this can result in a considerable cost for the organization.

RECOMMENDED DESIGN, DEVELOPMENT AND IMPLEMENTATION PROCESS

The performance-based diversity training model describes three phases in the diversity training initiative. Specific steps must be taken at each of these phases to maximize the impact of the training on performance at both the individual and organizational levels.

Before the Diversity Training Event

The most important component of the diversity training process involves those actions that are taken prior to the training event. The success of any training intervention will be determined by how effectively one clarifies the benefits of diversity training, defines performance expectations, communicates these expectations to learners, and identifies support and reinforcement activities that can be applied after the completion of the training.

1. *Clarify the benefits of diversity training.* The first step in the process is to clarify the benefits of the training for the learners, their managers, and the organization as a whole, what David Forman refers to in his 2004 article for *Performance Improvement* journal as "The Triple Win." Before effectively designing a training program, one must be clear about what each of the parties will gain from the experience. For example, if a performance coaching program for supervisors is to be facilitated, the trainees may benefit from developing skills that will improve their ability to manage the performance of a diverse range of employees. This in turn can lead to rewards such as promotional opportunities and salary

increases. The participants' managers can benefit by developing a talent pool of supervisors who will be ready to fill leadership positions that will open in the near future. They will also profit from having employees who are performing at higher levels due to more effective performance coaching. Advantages to the organization include improvements to its human capital and leader performance. Likewise, if a multicultural customer service training program is to be facilitated, trainees can benefit from developing skills that will allow them to successfully manage difficult service problems with a diverse range of customers. Managers benefit from the reduction of customer service complaints across various demographic groups, and the organization gains by having more satisfied customers.

2. *Define performance expectations.* According to Robert Gagné (1985) and John Keller (1983), it is critical to communicate post-training performance expectations to the learners. In a 2004 article for *Performance Improvement* journal, I describe how one effective way to do this is to focus on diversity competencies. The term *diversity competencies* describes the specific skills, abilities, and behaviors needed to function effectively in culturally diverse settings. Examples of these described in Table 31.4 include *self-awareness, diversity knowledge, multicultural communication, conflict management, empowering environments, professional development, recruitment and selection,* and *coaching and mentoring.* These competencies can be used to define performance expectations in concrete behavioral terms. For example, if the focus of training is recruitment and retention, participants can be expected to create a list of nontraditional recruiting sources and use them in their next job search (recruitment and selection). If, instead, the training aims to create more culturally inclusive work environments, then the learners may be expected to review organizational policies for bias and make modifications as needed (empowering environments). To achieve a training objective of reducing participant biases, a performance expectation may include identifying a personal bias or prejudice and create an action plan for reducing its impact (self-awareness).

3. *Communicate performance expectations to learners.* Once performance expectations have been defined, these must be communicated to the learners *prior to the training event.* This will enable them to be clear about expectation and benefits from the outset, as well as to begin the training process with specific goals in mind. As Keller explains in his 1983 article "Motivational Design of Instruction," this can have the added benefit of increasing the learner's interest in the diversity training.

4. *Identify support and reinforcement activities.* Once the diversity training is complete, there must be activities that support and reinforce the skills

developed during the session. Learners should be provided with continuous opportunities to apply their new skills on the job. Gagné (1985) and Keller (1983) reiterate this, going on to emphasize that, if trainees are not provided a chance to apply these new skills, they will likely lose them. There are numerous ways such opportunities can be provided. For example, if a group of supervisors has completed performance coaching training, the members should be given a chance to provide positive and constructive feedback and to create performance plans for employees as soon as their training is complete. Likewise, if an organization's expatriate employees have participated in a multicultural communication course, they should have opportunities to apply their newly developed skills in cross-cultural interactions as soon as possible. Participants should also have an opportunity to receive feedback on their performance and to receive continuous on-the-job practice.

Table 31.4 Diversity Competencies

Competency	Behavioral Description
Self-Awareness	Values diversity, respects differences, and attempts to learn about the culturally different. Aware of personal strengths, weaknesses, and styles. Has insight regarding personal biases and prejudices and actively seeks to reduce them.
Diversity Knowledge	Possesses knowledge of diverse cultures and groups, including variations in communication and learning styles. Understands how various issues of diversity affect the workplace and the work environment.
Multicultural Communication	Communicates effectively with people who are culturally different and actively attempts to interact with people who are different from him- or herself. Actively attempts to apply a wide range of communication strategies and skills to successfully interact with a diverse range of people.
Conflict Management	Can effectively resolve personal and organizational conflicts, including those that are diversity based, using a variety of conflict management techniques.
Empowering Environments	Actively works to create an environment in which all individuals are treated respectfully and fairly and have the opportunity to excel. Challenges biased and discriminatory attitudes and behaviors.
Professional Development	Takes part in ongoing education and development activities including those that are diversity-based. Establishes effective professional networks.

(Continued)

Table 31.4 (*Continued*)

Competency	Behavioral Description
Recruitment and Selection	Consistently recruits high-quality, culturally diverse candidate pools and makes valid selection decisions. Utilizes appropriate recruitment methods and sources to maximize candidate pool quality and diversity.
Coaching and Mentoring	Consistently develops effective mentoring and coaching relationships with various staff members, including culturally different individuals.

The Training Event

In my article for *Performance Improvement* journal, I suggested that diversity training programs may focus on modalities emphasizing knowledge, skills, and/or awareness. Knowledge is the cognitive domain that focuses on learning information, concepts, and theories that contribute to effective performance. Skills—typically the most relevant learning domain in terms of workplace performance—refer to developing behaviors and abilities needed to perform at the highest level possible. Awareness is the affective learning domain that involves learning about oneself and the impact that one's behavior, attitudes, and values have on overall effectiveness. Paul Pedersen's 1994 *Handbook for Developing Multicultural Awareness* reiterates these principles.

In 1998, Dana McDonald-Mann noted five basic methods that are included in both classroom sessions and workshop-based skills training. These are lecture, case study, role play, behavioral modeling, and self-assessment activities. Lectures and case studies can have the greatest impact on the *knowledge* domain. Lectures can be used to present content-specific information to a large group of people over a relatively short period of time. They can also incorporate two-way interaction through the use of small-group discussions. Applying lectures in brief segments can be an effective means of disseminating important diversity information and facilitating the knowledge-transfer process. However as noted by Ruth House in the 1996 edition of *The ASTD Training and Development Handbook*, it is important to be mindful that lecture works best in an interactive format that engages participants in discussions and exploration of disseminated information.

Case studies (see Chapter Thirty-Three) present participants with a specific organizational situation or scenario. The participants review the situation, the outcome, and the behavior of the individuals involved to determine whether alternative actions might have yielded a superior result. These can be effective at provoking thought, facilitating discussion, and enhancing overall knowledge.

Case studies offer several educational advantages for diversity training. They are specific and offer real situations in which participants can become active learners rather than passive observers. They facilitate team problem solving and decision making and help participants understand that a diverse group of people can see the same situation in very different ways. Case studies can also improve listening and cross-cultural communication skills through the facilitation of group discussion with a diverse array of individuals. Julius Eitington's 2002 book titled *The Winning Trainer* explores the various merits of case studies.

Role plays and behavioral modeling are the most effective ways to facilitate skill development and behavior change. S. Thiagarajan's chapter in ASTD's 1996 *Training and Development Handbook* concerning instructional games, simulations, and role plays illustrates how role plays are highly interactive exercises in which participants act out characters assigned to them in a specific scenario. Each trainee is provided with the opportunity to practice skills that have been learned during the educational program. Because of the practice component involved, role plays are very effective at helping participants develop new skills, learn new information, and change attitudes.

Behavioral modeling, a technique based on Albert Bandura's well-known 1986 theory of social learning, enhances the effectiveness of role-playing. It provides participants with an opportunity to observe the effective facilitation of a behavior or skill (that is, the behavioral model), to practice the desired behavior, and to receive feedback on performance. Of all the skills-based training methods, behavioral modeling is arguably the most important since it provides the learner with an opportunity to observe the desired behavior and to continuously practice the behavior in a relatively safe environment. For a more detailed explanation of role playing and behavioral modeling, Eitington's *The Winning Trainer* is again an invaluable resource.

Finally, skills-based training can also have a positive impact on the *awareness* domain by incorporating self-assessment activities. Self-assessment activities consist of paper-and-pencil inventories that evaluate the respondent's current status and functioning in a specific area such as communication skills or coaching effectiveness. These inventories give workshop participants insight into their attitudes and behaviors and the impact these have on performance. This in turn allows participants to modify their behavior in ways that will increase their overall effectiveness.

After the Training Event

If the pre-training activities have been well-facilitated and the skills-based diversity training program has been well-implemented, the post-training activities are relatively simple. Specifically, there are three matters that should be addressed to ensure that the training content is transferred to the workplace in a way that positively impacts performance:

1. *Implement support and reinforcement activities.* As previously discussed, once back on the job, it is very important for trainees to be provided with the opportunity to apply their newly acquired skills. Therefore, a plan should be created that describes how these support activities will be implemented for each training participant. For example, if human resources staff participate in a diversity recruitment workshop, they should be afforded the opportunity to apply their newly developed skills and knowledge in organizational staffing processes as soon as the training session is complete. This will require the support and active involvement of the participants' managers, who will be identifying the potential reinforcement activities and providing performance feedback on an ongoing basis.

2. *Evaluate the impact of the training on individual and organizational performance.* Much has been written on training evaluation and the various tools and methodologies that can be used to facilitate the assessment process. Donald Kirkpatrick's 1998 book *Evaluating Training Programs* is one such resource for more information on this topic. However, for our purposes, the approach is relatively simple. Evaluation should address two basic questions. First, are the training participants applying their new skills in a way that improves individual, and potentially, organizational performance? Second, have the participants met the performance expectations defined prior to the facilitation of the diversity training program? Both of these questions can be addressed through the administration of an organization's formal performance management system. In other words, the observations of the participants' managers will be crucial in determining the overall effectiveness of the training program.

3. *Provide additional learning opportunities.* Finally, if the training participants have had a positive, performance-enhancing learning experience, then it may be viable to provide additional developmental opportunities to support their learning. This can be done through a variety of methods such as classroom training, developmental assignments (on-the-job training), developmental relationships (coaching and mentoring; see Chapters Eleven, Twenty-Six, and Twenty-Seven), or self-directed learning activities (using the Internet, CD-ROM, or distance learning; see Chapter Twenty-Four).

CRITICAL SUCCESS FACTORS

To maximize the chances for success when applying the performance-based diversity training model, three steps that should be emphasized:

1. *Be clear about what accomplishments (products, outputs, and outcomes) are desired.* The process should begin with a clear articulation of the purpose of the educational process. This includes defining specific objectives, benefits, and performance expectations. Most importantly, this should occur well in advance of the training event and be formally communicated to the trainees.

2. *Verify that the training is connected to the organization's strategic objectives.* For instance, if one of the organization's goals is to increase sales revenue, the diversity training should have a direct impact on achieving this goal. This might be done through a program that teaches participants to connect with multicultural markets. If an organizational goal is to improve employee retention, this can be addressed through a training program that helps participants create culturally inclusive environments. In any case, how the diversity training initiative will assist the organization in achieving one or more of its strategic objectives should be able to be communicated.

3. *Make sure there is appropriate leadership support for the training and development initiative.* In their book on best practices in leadership development, Giber, Carter, and Goldsmith (2000) emphasize that one commonality among successful programs is the support and involvement of senior management. This can take several forms, including verbal reinforcement of the importance of the training initiative, active participation in the training sessions and use of senior managers as program faculty if a train-the-trainer approach is utilized.

SUMMARY

Diversity training holds great promise for improving individual and organizational performance. Although the reality has not lived up to this promise, by applying the performance-based diversity training model described in this chapter, organizations can greatly increase their chances of facilitating diversity training programs that have a positive impact on individual performance and overall organizational effectiveness.

References

Bandura, A. (1986). *Social foundations of thought and action: A social cognitive theory.* Upper Saddle River, NJ: Prentice-Hall.

Cox Jr., T. (2001). *Creating the multicultural organization: A strategy for capturing the power of diversity.* San Francisco: Jossey-Bass.

Cox, T. (1994). *Cultural diversity in organizations: Theory, research & practice.* San Francisco: Berrett-Koehler.

Cox, T., & Beale, R. L. (1997). *Developing competency to manage diversity: Readings, cases & activities*. San Francisco: Berrett-Koehler.

Cox, T., & Blake, S. (1991). Managing cultural diversity: Implications for organizational competitiveness. *The Executive, 5*(3), 45–56.

Eitington, J. E. (2002). *The winning trainer: Winning ways to involve people in training*. Woburn, MA: Butterworth-Heinemann.

Esen, E. (2005). *2005 workplace diversity practices*. Alexandria, VA: Society for Human Resource Management.

Fegley, S. (2006). *2006 workplace diversity and changes to the EEO-1 process*. Alexandria, VA: Society for Human Resource Management.

Forman, D. C. (2004). The triple win: The missing link in improving the effectiveness of training programs. *Performance Improvement, 43* (5), 20–26.

Gagné, R. (1985). *The conditions of learning* (4th ed.). New York: Holt, Rinehart and Winston.

Giber, D., Carter, L., & Goldsmith, M. (2000). *Best practices in leadership development handbook*. San Francisco: Pfeiffer.

Hayles, R., & Russell, A. M. (1997). *The diversity directive: Why some initiatives fail & what to do about it*. Alexandria, VA: American Society for Training and Development.

Holmes, T. A. (2006). Connecting training to performance. In E. Biech (Ed.), *The 2006 Pfeiffer annual: Volume 1, training* (pp. 197–204). San Francisco: Pfeiffer.

Holmes, T. A. (2004). Designing and facilitating performance-based diversity training. *Performance Improvement, 43*(5), 13–19.

House, R. S. (1996). Classroom instruction. In R. L. Craig (Ed.), *The ASTD training and development handbook* (4th ed.). New York: McGraw-Hill.

Keller, J. M. (1983). Motivational design of instruction. In C. M. Reigeluth (Ed.), *Instructional-design theories and models: An overview of their current status*. Mahwah, NJ: Lawrence Erlbaum Associates.

Kirkpatrick, D. L. (1998). *Evaluating training programs: The four levels* (2nd ed.). San Francisco: Berrett-Koehler.

Kossek, E. E., Zonia, S. C., & Young, W. (1997). The limitations of organizational demography: Can diversity climate be enhanced in the absence of teamwork? In M. N. Ruderman, M. W. Hughes, & S. E. Jackson (Eds.), *Selected research on work team diversity* (pp. 121–152). Washington, DC: American Psychological Association and the Center for Creative Leadership.

McDonald-Mann, D. G. (1998). Skill-based training. In C. D. McCauley, R. S. Moxley, & E. Van Velsor (Eds.), *The center for creative leadership: Handbook of leadership development* (pp. 106–126). San Francisco: Jossey-Bass.

Nemeth, C. J. (1985). Dissent, group process, and creativity. *Advances in Group Process, 2*, 57–75.

Pedersen, P. (1994). *A handbook for developing multicultural awareness* (2nd ed.). Alexandria, VA: American Counseling Association.

Rynes, S., & Rosen, B. (1995). A field survey of factors affecting the adoption and perceived success of diversity training. *Personnel Psychology, 48,* 247-270.

Schreiber, A. L. & Lenson, B. (2001). *Multicultural marketing: Selling to a new America.* Lincolnwood, IL: NTC Contemporary Publishing Group.

Society for Human Resource Management and *Fortune.* (2001). *Impact of diversity initiatives on the bottom line.* Alexandria, VA: Society for Human Resource Management.

Thiagarajan, S. (1996). Instructional games, simulations, and role-plays. In R. L. Craig (Ed.), *The ASTD training and development handbook* (4th ed.). (pp. 517–533). New York: McGraw-Hill.

Ziller, R. C. (1972). Homogeneity and heterogeneity of group membership. In C. G. McClintock (Ed.), *Experimental psychology* (pp. 385–411). New York: Holt, Rinehart and Winston.

Recommended Readings

Holmes, T. A. (2005). How to connect diversity to performance. *Performance Improvement, 44*(5), 13–17.

Holmes, T. A. (2005). Value-added diversity consulting. In E. Biech (Ed.), *The 2005 Pfeiffer annual: Volume 2, consulting* (pp. 219–228). San Francisco: Pfeiffer.

Johnson, R. L., & Simring, S. (2000). *The race trap: Smart strategies for effective racial communication in business and in life.* New York: HarperCollins.

Rasmussen, T. (1996). *The ASTD trainer's sourcebook: Diversity, create your own training program.* New York: McGraw-Hill.

Wildermuth, C. (2005). *Diversity training (ASTD Trainer's Workshop Series).* Alexandria, VA: ASTD Press.

PART TEN

EDITORS'
DISCUSSION

A s with other interventions associated with organizational culture, diversity and cultural competence have a reciprocating relationship with culture. The diverse culture of an organization influences the success of the intervention as much as the intervention can have an influence on the culture of the organization. Thus, the development of diversity training as a perform-ance intervention is best done within the context of a comprehensive perform-ance system. Therefore, you can employ diversity training—along with other performance interventions such as career mentoring (see Chapter Twenty-Two), realistic job previews (see Chapter Eight), and managerial coaching (see Chapter Eleven)—to shape your organization's culture. You can also use these same performance interventions to support diversity and cultural competence initiatives within your organization.

Expanding Your Options

Collaboration—involves a cooperative arrangement in which two or more parties work jointly to achieve a common objective.

Based on businessdictionary.com definition (January 2009)

These relationships between various performance interventions and organizational culture clearly illustrate the importance of using a systemic approach to performance improvement and the accomplishment of results. By moving beyond single solutions (such as training, mentoring, or incentives alone) to include sets of interventions that address all components of the Performance Pyramid model, you are better able to create a supporting relationship between culture and interventions. Such a mutually beneficial relationship that is required to accomplish significant results—results at the individual, team, organizational, and societal levels of Kaufman's Organizational Elements Model.

When striving to improve the accomplishment of results, the important role of organizational culture should not be under-valued. An organizational culture that supports the achievement of desired results is a necessary component of any performance system; without this you are continually fighting an uphill battle. While organizational cultures are amazingly resilient to attempts to change them and few direct interventions have lasting impacts, you can shift the culture of your organization through holistic performance systems that focus on the achievement of desired results at multiple levels—individual, team, organizational, and societal. Use numerous and varied performance interventions from all components of the Performance Pyramid to create the necessary culture for success.

References and Resources from Editorial Contributions to Part Ten

Kaufman, R. (2006). *Change, choices, and consequences: A guide to mega thinking and planning.* Amherst, MA: HRD Press.

Kaufman, R. (2006). *30 seconds that can change your life: A decision-making guide for those who refuse to be mediocre.* Amherst, MA: HRD Press.

Kaufman, R., Oakley-Brown, H., Watkins, R., & Leigh, D. (2003). *Strategic planning for success: Aligning people, performance, and payoffs.* San Francisco: Jossey-Bass.

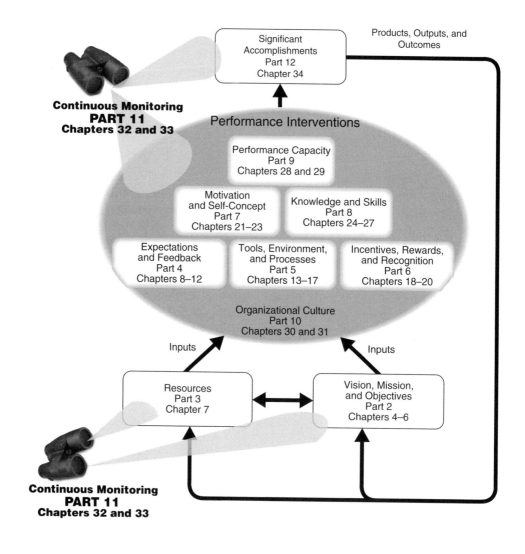

Products, Outputs, and Outcomes

Significant Accomplishments
Part 12
Chapter 34

Continuous Monitoring
PART 11
Chapters 32 and 33

Performance Interventions

Performance Capacity
Part 9
Chapters 28 and 29

Motivation and Self-Concept
Part 7
Chapters 21–23

Knowledge and Skills
Part 8
Chapters 24–27

Expectations and Feedback
Part 4
Chapters 8–12

Tools, Environment, and Processes
Part 5
Chapters 13–17

Incentives, Rewards, and Recognition
Part 6
Chapters 18–20

Organizational Culture
Part 10
Chapters 30 and 31

Inputs

Inputs

Resources
Part 3
Chapter 7

Vision, Mission, and Objectives
Part 2
Chapters 4–6

Continuous Monitoring
PART 11
Chapters 32 and 33

PART ELEVEN

CONTINUOUS MONITORING

Improving performance in your organization requires a focus on accomplishing significant and sustainable results. Accordingly, improvement efforts also require continuous monitoring of performance—not quick fixes or one-size-fits-all solutions. Not deciding what to do based on marketing brochures or new gadgets. Not solutions in search of problems. Sustained improvements in performance require longitudinal projects that typically begin with a needs assessment to identify performance gaps and opportunities, leading to the selection and implementation of an appropriate system of performance interventions. Once concluded, these tasks are followed by continual performance monitoring (often, for example, through annual or semi-annual needs assessments) to ensure that the improvement efforts have prolonged positive impacts.

Too often, especially when trying to improve performance, activities that worked in one organization (or in another part of the same organization) are viewed as solutions to the challenges being faced by all others. You may have seen this with the broad application of management by objectives, quality management, process re-engineering, or other such fads of recent decades. Clearly, it is not that these were ineffective performance interventions: each was and is actually quite effective under certain circumstances. Nevertheless, from lagging sales to slowing staff productivity, the complex challenges that face organizations are rarely the same, and so the performance interventions that will improve results will differ. Needs assessments have become an essential tool for deciding what improvement activities should be used based on the results desired.

767

Expanding Your Options

Quality management programs—a data-driven method for ensuring that all organizational activities are effective and efficient. Quality management can be considered to have three main components: quality control, quality assurance, and quality improvement. Quality management programs focus not only on product quality, but also on the means to achieve it.

Based on wikipedia.org definition (January 2009)

Use the systematic steps of a needs assessment to identify opportunities to make improvements based on facts and information, rather than on assumptions. Use assessments to prioritize your needs based on the cost to improve performance versus the cost of not improving performance; then let what you find out guide your decisions about what to do next. In other words, decide what results you seek before you determine what processes (mentoring, coaching, training, motivational workshop, knowledge management) will best achieve those results.

This distinction between results and processes (or ends and means) also helps you distinguish between what people in your organization may "want" (for example, new computers, new managerial structures, mentoring relationships with peers, and so forth) and what are their true "requirements" (for example, sufficient financial reports for making decisions, inputs that meet design specifications, timely feedback on performance). As the previous examples illustrate, within the context of performance "needs" are gaps in results rather than deficiencies in resources. Pragmatically, this distinction between needs and wants (or ends and means) offers a continual focus on accomplishing results, guiding all of your performance improvement decisions. Conducting a needs assessment, therefore, guides you through challenging decisions and provides justifications for the many choices you will make along the way.

At its most basic, a needs assessment is simply the comparison of where you are (in terms of performance and results) and where you seek to be. Thus, a needs assessments is an effective tool for analyzing the differences between the accomplishments to which your organization aspires (for instance, zero defects or damage) and the results that are currently being achieved (three of every one thousand products are returned due to defects or damage)."Needs" are then most effectively defined by this same gap between current and desired results.

Roger Kaufman and others recommend that needs be assessed at multiple levels of the organization, including individual, organizational, and societal. His

Organizational Elements Model can be applied for establishing strategic direction at these same levels, a needs assessment can identify gaps between the desired results of the strategic direction and the current achievements for the corresponding levels (see the model in Figure P.11.1 below).

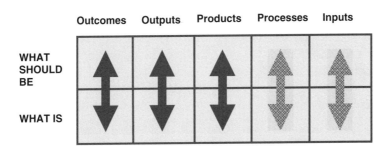

Figure P11.1   Kaufman's Organizational Elements Model Applied to a Needs Assessment.

Because needs assessments help inform decisions, they can be used *proactively* to identify opportunities to improve performance, *reactively* in response to the consequences of less-than-desirable results, or *continuously* as an integrated component of an improvement program. This makes needs assessments a valuable tool for decision-makers at all levels of an organization and in almost any role. From those wanting to improve individual performance or working to create a new initiative within an organization, to those charged with developing complex programs with external partners or improving the outcomes of long-running organizational undertakings, needs assessments can be used to either formally or informally guide decisions. Whether the assessment is proactive, reactive, or continual, the processes are best applied to inform performance-related (or results-focused) decisions.

Needs assessment can also help you avoid missteps. Often, the simple answers to your professional challenges don't provide solutions that are justifiable or ethically responsible. Roger Kaufman is well known for suggesting that for every performance problem there is a solution that is simple, straightforward, acceptable, understandable . . . and *wrong*. For instance, human resource professionals commonly receive managers' requests for new or additional training on a variety of organizational topics. From software applications to communication skills, training is often seen by managers as the sole solution to performance problems. And while training may initially seem to be a reasonable solution, an informed decision requires that additional information be considered before rushing ahead with any single solution. Quite often, organizational challenges are not linked to any single cause, such as inadequate knowledge or skills of employees.

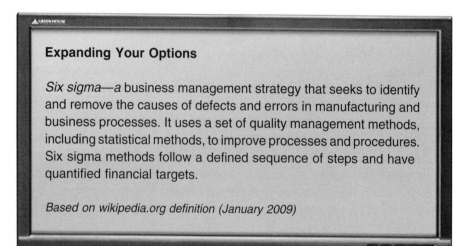

Expanding Your Options

Six sigma—*a* business management strategy that seeks to identify and remove the causes of defects and errors in manufacturing and business processes. It uses a set of quality management methods, including statistical methods, to improve processes and procedures. Six sigma methods follow a defined sequence of steps and have quantified financial targets.

Based on wikipedia.org definition (January 2009)

Systems of performance interventions focus on building the capabilities of individuals and the capacity of the organization to accomplish significant and sustainable results. These multi-activity systems are typically used to change behavior and improve results. Thus, needs assessments can guide decision-makers in evaluating complex *needs* (or performance gaps) in order to identify sets of solutions that address the systemic issues of performance, rather than only one or two symptoms.

WHAT'S COMING UP

In Chapter Thirty-Two, James Altschuld and Traci Lepicki offer pragmatic guidance for how to manage a successful needs assessment. Focusing on the implementation team—a needs assessment committee—as a hallmark of this performance intervention, the chapter provides poignant guidance for any needs assessment.

CHAPTER THIRTY-TWO

Needs Assessment

James W. Altschuld
Traci L. Lepicki

INTRODUCTION

Lucky you: you have been asked to lead a needs assessment! But what next? Whether you are internal to the organization or an external consultant, you are probably familiar with the concept of *need* and what is meant by the assessment of needs. After all, most of us have heard of Abraham' Maslow's hierarchy of needs. Perhaps you have even participated in or led an assessment before.

Nevertheless, after thinking about the activity a little more—particularly if you are asked to head the effort—questions like the following may begin to keep you up at night:

- How do we get started?
- Who is going to work with me on this project?
- Will we have to send questionnaires to all employees?
- What questions should we ask the people concerned?
- How will we analyze information we get from managers?

And this is just the beginning. A 2004 article by Jim Altschuld for *Performance Improvement* journal contends that if a needs assessment (NA) is viewed just as a set of methods (such as planning, asking, analyzing, etc.), then the likelihood of success is sharply reduced. Although methods are important, the results of any NA should be a blueprint for organizational improvement. This is an underlying perception that is essential for maximum effect. With this goal in mind, NA may indeed be a significant undertaking—particularly if you are facilitating or coordinating it. Consequently, even more questions may start to make your evenings restless:

- Who is behind the NA request?
- Does everybody involved understand what *needs* are (and are not) and what it takes to examine them?
- How do we get the NA project started?
- If the uncovered needs require serious individual and/or organizational changes, are the staff and administrators ready and motivated to act?
- Given office politics, what are the boundaries of the assessment, are some data sources off limits, and/or are others not easily accessible?
- What sacred cows or organizational traditions might present obstacles? For example, could some part of the company or agency be adversely affected by the results of your work?
- Could jobs be lost or changed dramatically? If so, might individuals or groups be reluctant to provide data or answer surveys?

All of these questions present challenges, since they relate to the social environment surrounding a NA. Addressing such concerns is as important as defining the appropriate methods for your project.

The intent of this chapter is to describe NA as a tool for improving human performance and to provide an overview of the assessment process. Importance will be placed on the needs assessment committee (NAC), a working group that forms the focal point of the effort so that unnecessary expenditures of resources and staff time can be minimized. The chapter begins with the basic concepts of *needs* and NA, and later NA is contrasted with needs sensing and needs analysis. Then the text shifts toward how to get the assessment started and moving forward in your specific circumstances. This is consistent with the view that many NAs, when complete, are not well utilized and do not have the impact that they should on the organization. Many end up in binders left to gather dust on office bookshelves, often because they simply did not begin with the pragmatic idea that they were a guide for organizations to improve and change.

DESCRIPTION

What Is a Need?

In its simplest form, a *need* is a measured discrepancy between the current state (what is) and the desired one (what should be). Without data about both states and the ability to contrast them, it is not possible to have a defined *need*. Surprisingly, until recently many NAs did not investigate both conditions, instead tended to focus more on solutions people wanted for their problems. Needs indicate the size and direction of existing gaps and, when compared and prioritized, they serve as input for actions to alleviate underlying problems. While this discrepancy definition implies quantification ($x - y = z$), most assessors advocate the use of mixed methods (including qualitative ones) for a full understanding of *needs*.

Several practical examples of needs are provided in Table 32.1. Needs might be assessed globally (as in health care in Rows a and b of Table 32.1) or locally within an organization (as in the case of the senior health care center in Row c). For the former, follow-up NA questions might include: What are the health consequences of these situations? For the latter, questions may include: Do personnel have the skills to meet state service standards? What skill updates might be required for them to perform their jobs appropriately?

Table 32.1 Examples of Need Discrepancies (What Is vs. What Should Be)

Area	What Is	What Ideally Should Be
a. Health	30 percent of U.S. population is overweight	100 percent at or near a reasonable weight for age, height, gender, and body build
b. Senior Health	Significant numbers of senior women in certain groups are not getting regular mammograms	100 percent or close to 100 percent will take the test on a regular basis
c. Senior Health Care Center Workforce	Senior population likely to increase to 20 percent in the next twenty to twenty-five years, leaving inadequate numbers of appropriately trained staff for health care centers. Current expected growth in qualified staff (nurses, doctors, mental health counselors, and others) is only 5 percent in the next five years.	Given the pent-up need and the time necessary for specialized training of qualified staff, should grow by 15 percent in the five years.
d. Wealth	John currently earns $100,000 annually.	John wants to win the lottery and be worth $2,000,000.

Adapted from Altschuld and Lepicki, California Aging Workshop, 2007

Needs might be short-term (current costs of medical procedures related to being overweight) or long-term (the challenges of an overweight population). This continuum of short-term to long-term *needs* will influence your NA processes and procedures.

Last, it should be noted that the entry in Row d of the table is present only as an illustration of a *want*. While the difference in John's present and desired wealth is a discrepancy, it would be considered by most people to be a *want* rather than a need and it inappropriately incorporates a solution (winning the lottery) into the discrepancy.

Are There Levels of Needs?

Yes, all needs are not the same. In their best-selling 1995 book on needs assessment, Belle Ruth Witkin and Jim Altschuld wrote about the three levels of individuals who can experience needs.

Level 1 are the ultimate receivers of goods and services. These can be patients in hospitals, consumers or purchasers of products, students in schools, those in need of mental health counseling, etc.

Level 2 consists of those who provide services and goods for Level 1. These include teachers in schools, health care workers, sales personnel, and company trainers who keep staff up-to-date with the latest technologies.

Level 3 is comprised of the managers, the administration, and the support necessary to enable work to be accomplished, as well as available finances and other similar entities. This level forms the structure or system that enables the supply chain, allowing Level 2 to deliver its wares to Level 1.

What frequently and appropriately happens in many NAs is that, by identifying the needs of Level 1, those of Levels 2 and 3 tend to become more obvious. On the other hand, misguided NAs may place too much stress on the training of staff or, for example, looking at performance or organizational problems at Levels 2 and 3. This may cause Level 1 to become forgotten, and this subverts the systemic approach required for a successful NA. After all, the function of institutions, agencies, and businesses is to make certain that they provide for Level 1 stakeholders—to ensure that what Level 2 and 3 staff members are doing positively impacts the needs of the ultimate receivers of goods and services. That is the *raison d'etre*.

What Is Needs Assessment?

A needs assessment is a formal process to obtain information on the two states (current versus desired), compare them, identify gaps, and arrive at needs-based priorities for organizational actions. Causal analyses of needs are often part of the endeavor. NAs begin when a group feels that it has problems that must be explored in depth. In 1972 Bradshaw classified these as "felt" needs, as opposed to "normative, comparative, or expressed" needs. This group perception of felt needs leads to a study that concludes with priorities and plans for change and/or new directions. As NA concludes it evolves into needs analysis (see the "When to Apply" section of this chapter for elaboration of this activity).

What Is a Needs Assessment Committee (NAC)?

A needs assessment committee is a critical component of any NA. It is a working committee consisting of members selected for their commitment to the task, the ability to cooperatively contribute to the deliberations, the technical skills they bring that meet the demands of the NA, and, most notably, for formal and informal influence on decisions within the organization. The NAC, while generally maintaining a constant core, can be a fluid group, with new members coming and going throughout the NA. The committee may especially benefit by the addition of different members when the NA proceeds to planning programs for prioritized needs.

Given its role in the NA, the NAC is very important. It guides the design of the assessment and instruments to be used, the actual collection of data, analysis and interpretation, and reporting conclusions drawn to the organization. It plays a vital role in communicating what has been learned about needs, and recommends pertinent actions to be taken. Ideally, the NAC should incorporate nine to twelve people who then may be divided into subcommittees. Very large groups (twenty or more) require more management and resources and therefore should only be used for large-scale needs assessments. The NAC is often facilitated by an external consultant, but at certain points in the process it may be more appropriate to switch to an internally directed committee. In either case, the leader of the NAC must strive to keep the team on task and moving forward throughout the NA.

What Results Can Be Expected from an NA?

A needs assessment is a focused institutional self-study of problematic issues that should be examined because improvement of performance appears warranted. For example, can our company's goods and services be better than they are today, or are there difficulties in the work environment (such as training, communication, work flow, etc.) that are reducing performance? NA outcomes, then, include clarification on organizational priorities, identification of strengths and weaknesses, recognition of the causes underlying needs, discovery of new ways to do things, and recommendations of interventions to be used for improving performance. NA ties into organizational activities such as short- and long-term strategic planning (see Part One of this handbook) and evaluation of programs (see Chapter Thirty-Four), quality control, performance management (see Chapter Twelve), human resource management, performance improvement, and monitoring management information systems data (see Chapters Ten and Thirty-Three). It may affect organizational culture (see Part Ten of this handbook) in relation to how people learn and use information through knowledge management (see Chapter Fifteen). Consider the example in Exhibit 32.1 for an outcome of an NA.

Exhibit 32.1 A Technically Successful NA

One of the authors led a team conducting an assessment of nationwide needs for a training organization in a major and quite specialized technical field. Surveys were distributed to businesses about current and future needs in the area of concern. Based on the results and on a review of the literature, current and future training possibilities were identified and suggested for organizational review, prioritization, and action.

The survey was of high quality, the results were useful, but the NA was essentially a failure. What went wrong was that management changed during the study and the new leadership simply placed little or no faith in what had been contracted before their time. Since NA is successful only if it leads to performance improvements, this NA could not attain its goal because its recommendations were never implemented.

Interestingly, two years after dismissing the study, the same issues uncovered by the needs assessors arose again. One member of the leadership group then noted that they had missed millions of dollars of potential work by not listening to the suggestions of the NA. The assessment was a technical success—but nonetheless a failure.

WHAT WE KNOW FROM RESEARCH

In a short chapter such as this, it would neither be useful nor feasible to have a comprehensive extensive review of the literature on needs assessment, analysis, sensing, causal analysis, and related topics from theoretical and empirical research perspectives. Nevertheless, many of the principles that cut across strategies for human performance interventions and improvement should guide your NA activities and are worthy of some discussion.

Organizations are idiosyncratic, and what works in one company or institution might not (and probably will not) work well in another. This notion has been advanced by several noted researchers and practitioners, including Ethan Sanders and Julie Ruggles in 2000 and Harold Stolovitch and Erica Keeps in 2002. There is no Holy Grail, no magic elixirs or panaceas for improving performance. Every intervention, including NA, will have to be tempered and adjusted to the contours and context of local situations if they are to be successful.

Expanding Your Options

Root cause analysis (RCA)—problem solving method aimed at identifying the foundational—or root—causes of performance problems or events. A root cause analysis attempts to address performance problems by identify and then correcting or eliminating the causes, rather than treating the symptoms.

Based on wikipedia.org definition (January 2009)

This theme is echoed throughout this chapter and book alike, so when you look at techniques and ideas, be aware of their strengths and weaknesses and how they might be adapted for a particular organization. Don't buy into them automatically and blindly. Although the authors' stance on NA processes is clear and direct, it can always be adapted and modified as required. Likewise, consider when to sequence NA activities in the broader umbrella of improvement efforts. For example, should a NA follow a performance analysis (see Figure 1.3 in Chapter One), as proposed by Allison Rossett in her 1999 book *First Things Fast*, leading to a more informed assessment? Is a formal NA with questionnaires and focus groups really the best way to go? Might something else (such as causal analysis, developing a training package, changing policies or incentives, for example) be better and more beneficial? Ultimately, the extent and timing of the NA must be best tailored to your circumstances.

A second idea that emerges from the literature, especially from the work of Sanders and Ruggles, is that many disciplines, fields, and areas of study have contributed to scholarship constituting the basis for improving performance. While there is overlap, there are also differences, as well as subtly unique emphases. In this regard, consider the contributions of Joe Harless and Tom Gilbert, both pioneers in the field of human performance technology (HPT). Their early works—*An Ounce of Analysis* from 1975 and *Human Competence* from 1978—serve as a foundation for later thinking. Still it is difficult to create a unifying structure around the enterprise to capture a gestalt of performance improvement. This is both a rich (challenging) aspect of improving human performance and a troublesome one at the same time, and this observation is especially relevant to NA.

Numerous models, frameworks, and approaches are available for assessing needs, so many in fact, that in 1998 this handbook's co-editors inventoried and analyzed many of these. Organizations would benefit by reviewing these NA strategies for similarities and differences, as well as looking at case studies and pertinent research in the area of concern. Two of the more well known and complementary approaches come from Roger Kaufman and colleagues, whose work in needs assessment goes back to 1981 and earlier, and Belle Ruth Witkin and Jim Altschuld (whose 1995 *Planning and Conducting Needs Assessments* was updated by Jim Altschuld and David D. Kumar in 2009 as *The Needs Assessor's Handbook*).

In Kaufman's approach, described by Ryan Watkins and John Wedman in 2003, needs occur between results: discrepancies between desired (what should be) accomplishments and current (what is) achievements. Further, gaps in results can occur at any point along a continuum:

- **Mega level:** Results (and therefore needs) for which the primary client and beneficiary is society as a whole.
- **Macro level:** Results (and therefore needs) for which the primary client and beneficiary is the organization.
- **Micro level:** Results (and therefore needs) for which the primary client and beneficiary are individuals and groups within the organization.

Importantly, the *system* and *systemic* dimensions of Kaufman's thinking in the continuum align closely with the three phases of NA underlying Witkin and Altschuld's framework. Their emphasis lies in the process and procedures for conducting the NA as outlined below. This approach generalizes to human performance and is the basis for the remaining sections of this chapter.

- *Phase 1.* Pre-assessment focuses the NA and deals almost entirely with existing data and information relative to the needs area.
- *Phase 2.* Assessment is based on the premise that if Phase 1 does not produce enough information, new data will have to be collected. Also in this phase, the causes of needs will be explored.
- *Phase 3.* Post-assessment occurs when there is compelling evidence for high-priority needs. Concrete action plans are prepared to counter the problems and their underlying causes.

Apart from the two approaches to NA discussed here, there are many other others frameworks, such as B. J. Cohen's 1981 model for needs assessment related to the distribution of social service resources; Robert Fiorentine's explanation of similar principles in 1994; Kavita Gupta's and her colleagues' 2007 guide to NA; and Allison Rossett's 1987 discussion of assessment within training. The goal, thus, is to explore models and procedures (in conjunction with research and case studies done in organizations or agencies similar to yours) in order to determine how well they align. What kinds of procedures and tools do they recommend? How expensive was their NA? What processes might be best for what the organization is considering? A quick search of the literature can yield large dividends.

The third and final issue that is commonly addressed in the NA literature is where NA falls within a performance initiative. Most researchers and expert practitioners advocate that in the beginning of any improvement process there should be some form of needs assessment, needs analysis, discrepancy identification, and/or an analogous strategy. At a 2005 presentation for the U.S. Army's Training and Doctrine Command, Richard Clark referred to the determination of gaps—the very basic definition of need—when he outlined a very useful approach to performance improvement. After all, a tenet of HPT is that a systematic process of collecting "what is" and "what should be" data and identifying and clarifying gaps is essential for thinking about possible organizational actions.

WHEN TO APPLY

How do you determine whether a *needs assessment*—or *needs sensing* or *needs analysis*—is the best approach for your organization? Often, and somewhat incorrectly, these terms are used interchangeably. Although *need* is the common thread, some distinctions exist between these processes.

Needs sensing is the process involved in collecting opinions about possible needs while not actually measuring gaps. It is characterized in surveys or interviews by questions that do not directly lead to a discrepancy. Key leaders may, for example, be interviewed about perceptions that will be affecting an organization. These are then summarized to identify trends across responders. In a survey they may be asked to indicate the extent to which a statement represents a *need*, but they do not rate the two conditions (current versus desired) that define it. Needs sensing is, nevertheless, a reasonable process that may uncover *needs* but does not deal with "what is" and "what should be," whereas a needs assessment does.

Needs analysis is often mistaken for needs assessment. In 1988, Sara Russell Rodriguez of the Oklahoma State Department of Health noted that this was inappropriate since one cannot analyze something before it is identified, which is exactly what NA does. Needs analysis must be preceded by NA. When a need has been detected and possible causes determined, analysis commences (examining causal factors and potential solutions). Thus the two entities are discrete, yet intertwined, having a distinct temporal relationship.

In normal usage there is frequently slippage in terminology, and the three terms become intermingled. Since the processes are sometimes used together to improve performance, this is not always a problem. That being said, however, the position advocated here is that it is valuable to discuss the concepts and illustrate their unique qualities—but to remember that NA views discrepancies as the absolute heart of the matter.

For the most part, when an organization is encountering problems or recognizing that it must change or rethink what it does, that is the ideal time for NA to be undertaken. Market share being lost, clients not using services, the competitive edge dropping, or the climate in the organization not being productive, are all examples of what might impel a decision to conduct a NA, which in turn can lead to performance interventions discussed elsewhere in this book.

STRENGTHS AND CRITICISMS

Some of the strengths and criticism of using needs assessment are listed below:

Strengths

- NA is a structured, systematic procedure for identifying and thinking through needs with the purpose of organizational change and action.
- If done in a fairly receptive environment, characterized by the willingness of administrators and workers to look at and carefully weigh new directions and ideas, a NA can be a cathartic experience.
- The use of existing data can reduce NA costs, particularly if the NAC consists of members who are familiar with sources of existing data.
- As part of a systematic process for problem analysis, the NAC allows for fluidity in member composition, thereby providing a voice to multiple stakeholders. The NAC members eventually become strong advocates of the efforts of the committee.

Criticisms

- NA can require a significant investment of time and resources.
- Managing a NAC can be complicated and it will often take time for the team to gel. This may be further complicated by new members joining and others leaving the committee.
- External consultants or several internal individuals can often move faster than large committees, which require more facilitation and management.

- It is sometimes difficult for committees to reach consensus.
- People can be action oriented while NAs take more of a deliberation stance, looking at problems in depth before thinking about their resolution.

RECOMMENDED DESIGN, DEVELOPMENT, AND IMPLEMENTATION PROCESS

The three-phase model seems daunting if all of its steps are religiously followed in the precise order that they are presented here. Hence, it should be used in a flexible manner. Below are the steps per phase:

Phase 1—Pre-Assessment

1. Develop the focus for the assessment.
2. Establish the NAC that is responsible for the remainder of the steps within this phase.
3. Sort out the values driving the assessment.
4. Identify and locate existing resources and information for the need area.
5. Arrive at consensus regarding recommendations for the organization and its decision-makers.

In this phase, one of the following three decisions will be made:

- There is enough available information to say that the need is not important and does not warrant further data collection or effort from the organization;
- Information is insufficient for making recommendations, and it is necessary to create new sources of data. (Be careful as this may entail sizable commitments of funds and time.)
- There is sufficient information, and the organization should move forward to Phase 3 and begin planning to resolve the identified needs.

The criticality of Phase 1 cannot be overstated. It relies heavily on previous internal studies, archived materials, reports by external groups, and information derived from routinely kept databases. It represents an inexpensive investment by the organization. Phase 2 commonly requires more financial resources to facilitate.

Phase 2—Assessment

1. Identify discrepancies at Levels 1, 2, and 3. This can be done via a variety of data-collection methods, as shown Table 32.2. Some tend to be better suited for one phase than another. Mixed methods are usually part of the methodological landscape.

2. Prioritize discrepancies.

3. Conduct causal analysis of needs.

4. Identify preliminary solution criteria and possible solution strategies.

Table 32.2 An Overview of Needs Assessment Methods

Data Type	Comments/Description	Information Generated
Archival		
• Records/logs Social indicators Census data Epidemiological studies Test data Information derived from databases Other existing sources	• Data exists usually in databases or records In some instances, it may be possible to initiate new record-keeping Existing data may not exactly match the intent of the needs in question	• Mostly quantitative data about the current (what is) status of target groups Sources may reveal ideas about causes contributing to needs Some databases/records include comments necessitating qualitative analyses and interpretation
Communicative– Noninteractive		
• Written questionnaires Critical incident technique Mailed Delphi surveys Web-based surveys Observations	• Methods rely primarily on structured instruments or forms Surveys mostly have scaled questions with perhaps a few open- ended questions Observations may follow detailed protocols or permit more freedom in describing phenomena	• While some of the data may be quantitative in nature, it comes from values, judgments, and opinions of those providing responses and perspectives
Communicative– Interactive		
• Public hearings Community group forums Nominal group techniques (NGT)	• Procedures involve the use of small or large groups with varying degrees of interaction	• Highly qualitative data that is summarized into themes and reoccurring concepts

Focus group interviews (FGI) Cyber or virtual FGI Interviews Key informant interviews DACUM process Scenario discussions	Group leadership is especially critical to the success of the procedures and the results produced	Data will be about perceptions, opinions, judgments, and values Information might be about consensus on goals, courses of action, causes, priorities, and the like

Analytic

• Fishbone diagrams Cause and consequence analysis Quality function deployment (QFD) Fault tree analysis (FTA) Success mapping Task analysis Risk assessment Trend analysis Cross impact analysis Force field analysis	• Processes that examine solution strategies and causes or risks associated with needs and/or ways to resolve them Results might be shown in graphs or diagrams emanating from the analytic process	• Problems that might lead to the failure of a solution strategy Guidance in choosing a strategy with a high likelihood of resolving a need (with other information from NA, makes for a more comprehensive understanding of needs)

Adapted from Altschuld and Kumar, 2009

Phase 3—Post-Assessment

1. Make final decisions to resolve needs and select solution strategies.
2. Develop action plans for solution strategies, communicating plans, and for building support.
3. Implement and monitor plans.
4. Evaluate the overall NA endeavor (document with an eye to revisit and reuse).

CRITICAL SUCCESS FACTORS

Success in doing what has been proposed in the three phases of a NA depends on social, cultural, political, legal, technical, and economic factors. These include choosing the right members of the NAC, the technical and facilitation skills necessary for the assessment, the organizational context, politics within and external to the organization, the time and resources available, the ability of a group to rapidly develop a focus for the endeavor, the availability and accessibility of information pertinent to the area of concern, the clarity of the charge to the NAC, and other assorted issues. Consequently, the NAC is the key to the overall success of the needs assessment.

Many NA articles and reports, explicitly or implicitly indicate that some sort of a NAC-like group is operating; especially in Phase 1 activities. As Marjorie L. Budd emphasized in 1996, NAC helps embed the assessment into the organization's human resource development policies. This ensures that it is on target with organizational problems, as highlighted by Steve McGriff in 2003. A guiding mechanism like this is present in subtle fashion in a 2000 case study by Elwood F. Holton and his colleagues, as well as in Russell Westcott's 1995 chapter in ASTD's *Conducting Needs Assessment*, "A Quality Systems Needs Assessment."

What is meant by success? Let's scrutinize Exhibit 32.2.

Exhibit 32.2 The NAC at Work

Altschuld and Witkin, in their 2000 book *From Needs Assessment to Action*, described the involvement of a NAC in reshaping the performance evaluation system for staff members in a large college. The dean of the college knew of problems in the performance evaluations of staff, but did not have a clear understanding of the specifics of these. She recruited two well-known faculty members, seven influential members of the staff, as well as the head of the business office, to form an investigative group. This group was given capacity to seek assistance (such as training) from the university's office of human resources. In effect, this small group of ten members became the NAC.

What can we learn from the makeup of this NAC and what it did for Phase 1, 2, and 3 activities? See Tables 32.3 and 32.4.

Table 32.3 Desirable Characteristics of NAC Members

Desired Abilities	Actual Abilities	Comments
Social Skills	Working well with others. Good work orientation. Willing to state opinions and to consider those of others. Not interested in playing power games.	These skills are absolutely critical for successful NACs. Nearly all members were thought of as proactive and fair.
Organizational Influence	Faculty generally well thought of by other faculty, administration, and staff. Staff perceived in the same way.	Staff members were the informal opinion leaders and in some instances the formal ones.

| | Group would not be seen as just pursuing the dean's interests. All members were quite knowledgeable about the college. | One faculty member led a unit, and the other was noted (moderately positively) for outspokenness. Everyone had been in the college for a long time. |
| Technical skills | One faculty member was good with databases and flowcharts, the other in evaluation and instrument design. Many of the staff members had spreadsheet and database skills. | The skills coupled with outside technical assistance were more than sufficient for the NA. |

Table 32.4 Overview of NAC Activities in the Three Phases

Phase and Key Activities	*Results*
Pre-Assessment	
Initial get-acquainted and discussion meetings. Dean explained general charge but left committee to decide its own direction. HR personnel provided some articles/ materials for the group to read. Information was obtained about what other colleges do. Group members informally interviewed a few staff and administrators.	Dean was correct that evaluation was haphazard, uneven, and/or not done at all. Despite the word "evaluation," there seemed to be readiness for investigation of needs and recommendations for change. Committee decided to conduct a survey of staff and to continue collecting and reviewing information about performance evaluation.
Assessment	
Staff survey conducted throughout the entire college along with additional interviews. Review of sources was ongoing. Based on what was learned, the NAC began to consider options for personnel evaluation and what it might	NAC was active in all interviews, survey design and implementation, and subsequent analysis and interpretation. Periodically, the NAC communicated with staff and dean but plotted its own direction.

(Continued)

<table>
<tr><td colspan="2" align="center">Table 32.4 (Continued)</td></tr>
</table>

Phase and Key Activities	Results
take to implement across need Levels 1, 2, and 3.	Role playing was especially good because it helped the committee think
NAC, via playing negative and positive roles, began to look at causes and possibilities with a new system.	about the range of positions and the human side of the equation.
A plan was developed with a timeline and pilot test/evaluation before full-scale use of new assessment procedures.	
Plan included an extensive communication process across the college with members of the NAC being the prime communicators.	
Post-Assessment	
A four-component (planning, coaching, feeding back, evaluating) system was explained to all college units over several months by NAC faculty and staff.	The NAC as the purveyor of the system was helpful in getting real "buy-in." Numerous unanticipated problems arose (lack of up-to-date position descriptions, issues in obtaining
Via the communication process, input was sought and led to refinements before implementation.	feedback for certain types of positions, etc.) that pointed toward modifications.
The NAC continued to meet and integrate information from the expanded interactions.	Overall outcome is still visible long after initial committee work.
Pilot trials were carried out and further changes made.	
NAC felt that it should continue with the evaluation and more changes but with less involvement than in the first year.	

The NAC worked on this project involving performance evaluation problems for a year, with the expectation that it would continue on in a less-intense manner, into a second year. The dean picked the NAC members well, and while giving a general charge to the group, she moved aside so that it had free reign to define its processes and procedures. If this had not been done, the assessment would have been very top-down and probably would have resulted in less significant outcomes.

During the first few months, the group met about every two weeks with self-determined assignments (for both faculty and staff) completed in the interim. The commitment was evident with almost 100 percent attendance at the meetings. As an estimate, there may have been as many as twelve to fifteen formal meetings, with most occurring at the start of the process. Assignments were done, even though they required extra effort for each member, beyond his or her typical duties. The NAC in this case epitomized a working and policy-making board at the same time. The leader from the business office shared in this commitment, and the human resource members also came to embody the spirit of it. Undoubtedly, this overall mindset must exist for success in any NA endeavor.

Consider Table 32.4 within Exhibit 32.2. Numerous instances of success are noted, with many stemming from the collaborative dynamics of the NAC itself. Without going into every nuance, several key elements are highlighted below.

In Phase 2, as the NAC was becoming more focused on a possible solution strategy, it conducted a fun role-playing session in which favorable and unfavorable reactions to the evaluation strategy under consideration were explored. Members divided into two groups, with one being those who would be adverse to the plan and the second being enthusiastic endorsers of the new procedures. Given the topic, it was obviously easier to be in the former.

This was a tremendous change of flow for the committee, with members really owning their imagined roles. By doing this exercise, the NAC saw features of its ideas that needed more attention. This activity could easily be applied to many NAs in highly varied organizations. It could even be videotaped for use in disseminating solution strategies.

As noted in the post-assessment phase in Table 32.4, another element that stood out was the dissemination or selling of the new system. The administration in Exhibit 32.2 did not participate in this. Instead, in teams of two committee members went to units within the college to briefly describe how recommendations were developed and how they conceptualized conducting a pilot test. The teams explained that what was being proposed was itself in process and would be expected to evolve and improve. They led discussions and asked for more input, which they received.

Thus, in a moderate period of time spanning less than a year and using "volunteered" participants, the NAC went from a vague perception of a need to the initial use of a new system for more than four hundred employees. The system had provisions for coaching staff and promoting growth besides just evaluating work. The NAC therefore went beyond its original responsibility of designing and installing an evaluation to achieve the more valuable result of fostering improvement college-wide. Such an outcome occurs only when a NAC has independence from a heavy controlling force and in the absence of fear of change on the part of administrators and personnel.

In this example, the quality and success of the effort across the three phases is supported by the fact that the system recommended by the committee has now been used for ten consecutive years. The three-phase process can therefore be a viable one—provided that it tends to follow what happened in this case. If it is too controlled or does not have the enthusiastic backing of all segments of the organization, it just will not work as well as it did in this instance. Without openness and willingness to change, it is doubtful that an NA will be effective, and the model will not be so utilitarian.

It is important to note here, however, that not all NAs work as well as the one described above. For instance, the first example depicted an assessment that did not have an impact on the organization conducting it. This point underscores the fact that Phase 1 and the nature of the NAC are critical elements for conducting assessments resulting in organizational improvement.

SUMMARY

In a brief review of NA studies, Altschuld and Kumar's *The Needs Assessor's Handbook* points out that very few would be considered completely in accord with the two schema of NA discussed in the chapter. Does that mean that they are not useful or representative of real-world practice? Our view is that this just reflects what was stated in the previous paragraph and how people must adjust in the NA landscape. It is better to have guiding frameworks than not. They organize thought processes and establish the boundaries of the playing field.

Needs assessment is a systematic process that provides guidance for making organizational improvement decisions. Different models and approaches to NA should be reviewed for their strengths and weaknesses as related to your specific organizational context. In general, a needs assessment committee is vital to a successful assessment. In addition, it is important to be flexible. If any model or approach is too involved for your local situation, choose what might work in the specific setting and adapt it as appropriate. Consider what is feasible and will lead to positive change. Models are not straitjackets to be forcefully applied. They are heuristic devices; see them in that light!

References

Altschuld, J. W. (2004). Emerging dimensions of needs assessment. *Performance Improvement*, *43*(1), 10–15.

Altschuld, J. W, & Kumar, D. D. (2009). *The needs assessor's handbook: Book 1 the needs assessment kit.* Thousand Oaks, CA: Sage.

Altschuld, J. W., & Witkin, B. R. (2000). *From needs assessment to action: Transforming needs into solution strategies.* Thousand Oaks, CA: Sage.

Bradshaw, J. (1972, March 30). The concept of social need. *New Society*, *496*, 640–643.

Budd, M. L. (1996). HRD/Organization Alignment Model. http://govinfo.library.unt.edu/npr/library/book/Appendix%20A.htm

Cohen, B. J. (1981). Do you really want to conduct a needs assessment? Philadelphia: Management and Behavioral Science Center, University of Pennsylvania.

Clark, R. E. (2005, February). Human performance technology (HPT). Presentation at TRADOC VTC.

Fiorentine, R. (1994). Assessing drug and alcohol treatment needs of general and special populations: Conceptual, empirical, and inferential issues. *Journal of Drug Issues*, *24*(3), 435–452.

Gilbert, T. F. (1978). *Human competence: Engineering worthy performance.* New York: McGraw-Hill.

Gupta, K., Sleezer, C. M., & Russ-Eft, D. F. (2007). *A practical guide to needs assessment.* San Francisco: Pfeiffer.

Harless, J. H. (1975). *An ounce of analysis.* Newnan, GA: Harless Performance Guild.

Holton, E. F., Bates, R. A., & Naquin, S. S. (2000). Large-scale performance-driven training needs assessment: A case study. *Public Personnel Management*, *29*(2), 249–265.

Kaufman, R., Stakenas, R. G., Wager, J. C., & Mayer, H. (1981). Relating needs assessment, program development, implementation, and evaluation. *Journal of Instructional Development*, *4*(4), 17–26.

McGriff, S. (2003). ISD Knowledge base/analysis: Needs assessment. http://www.sjsu.edu/depts/it/mcgriff/kbase/isd/analysis.html

Rodriguez, S. R. (1988). Needs assessment and analysis: Tools for change. *Journal of Instructional Development*, *11*(1), 25–28.

Rossett, A. (1987). *Training needs assessment.* Englewood Cliffs, NJ: Educational Technology Publications.

Rossett, A. (1999). *First things fast: A handbook for performance analysis.* San Francisco: Pfeiffer.

Sanders, E. S., & Ruggles, J. L. (2000). HPI soup: Human performance improvement. *Training and Development 54*(6), 26–37.

Stolovitch, H. D., & Keeps, E. J. (2002, March 19). Stop wasting money on training. *Toronto Sun.*

Watkins, R., Leigh, D., Platt, W., & Kaufman, R. (1998). Needs assessment: A digest, review, and comparison of needs assessment literature. *Performance Improvement Journal, 37*(7), 40–53.

Watkins, R., & Wedman, J. (2003). A process for aligning performance improvement resources and strategies. *Performance Improvement, 42*(9), 9–17.

Westcott, R. (1995). A quality systems needs assessment: Formations in metal, inc. In J. J. Phillips & E. F. Holton, III (Eds.), Conducting needs assessment (pp. 267–281) Arlington, VA: ASTD.

Witkin, B. R., & Altschuld, J. W. (1995). *Planning and conducting needs assessments: A practical guide*. Thousand Oaks, CA: Sage.

 EDITORIAL CONNECTIONS

A needs assessment can provide essential information on the relative value, worth, or costs associated with gaps between current and desired results. As such they are an important tool for pragmatically applying the strategic direction of your organization, as well as setting priorities that guide decisions throughout your improvement process. By defining performance problems in measurable terms and prioritizing needs based both on the cost to meet the need and the cost of ignoring it, needs assessments provide essential information for making valuable decisions before, during, and after any improvement effort. Rarely, however, can these decisions be made without the input of new data and information—or looking at data and information from new perspectives.

Expanding Your Options

Quality control tools—cause-and-effect diagrams (which identify possible causes for an effect or problem and categorize ideas), check sheets (structured forms for collecting and analyzing data), control charts (graphs used to study how a process changes over time), histograms, Pareto charts (bar graphs showing which factors are more significant), scatter diagrams, and stratification (which separates data gathered from a variety of sources so that patterns can be seen).

Based on asq.org/learn-about-qualitydefinition (January 2009)

As a consequence, needs assessments are closely associated with processes for collecting data and information. From focus groups to surveys and interviews to performance observations, numerous tools and techniques can be used to collect useful performance information. Each has strengths, and each has weaknesses; therefore you will want to choose wisely whenever gathering information to inform the improvement of performance.

WHAT'S COMING UP

In Chapter Thirty-Three, Anne Marrelli offers a comprehensive examination of the most commonly used data collection techniques used in improving human and organizational performance. The chapter also provides practical guidance for how to select the most appropriate techniques for your improvement efforts. This is a chapter that you will likely want to return to many times as you choose the most appropriate ways to gather useful information for informing decisions during all phases of your improvement effort.

CHAPTER THIRTY-THREE

Data Collection

Anne F. Marrelli

INTRODUCTION

The collection of data is an essential step in the systematically identifying and analyzing of performance improvement opportunities and selecting, designing, and justifing interventions to address them. Data collection is also vital in evaluating the efficacy of the interventions after they are implemented, as well as identifying obstacles to overcome or modifications that are required to increase their effectiveness. There are two prerequisites to collecting useful data: (1) basic knowledge of research and data analysis methods and (2) knowledge of a variety of data collection instruments. Understanding research and analysis concepts and principles will help you plan the research design, sampling strategy, and data analysis procedures. Familiarity with a range of data collection methods will enable you to select the instruments that will best provide the information you need to answer your specific research questions.

This chapter provides an overview of ten different types of instruments. Each overview includes a description of the method, and a summary of its strengths and criticisms. The chapter also discusses factors to consider in selecting data collection methods and fundamental guidelines for the application of these methods.

WORK SAMPLES

Description and Application

The work sample method of data collection is the systematic collection and review of products created on the job in the normal course of work. Examples include written documents such as reports, memos, or letters; tangible products such as a bowl created by a potter, a training course developed by an instructional designer, or a poster created by a graphic designer; and routine work records such as audiotapes of a customer service representative's conversations with clients or computer records of a data-entry clerk's output.

Strengths

- Work samples provide direct evidence of performance and therefore offer strong validity. Unlike data collection methods such as surveys and focus groups in which data is based on the reports of people, the data is not filtered through employees' perceptions.

- Work samples are unobtrusive measures that do not require direct interaction with the individuals under study. They therefore are not susceptible to the changes in behavior that may occur when individuals know they are being observed.

- Because the review of work samples does not require the presence of workers, scheduling and coordination of participants is not required.

- Video and audio recordings expand the collection of work samples to intangible behaviors such as interactions with others.

- Because samples of routine work are studied, employees do not need to take time away from work to participate in the data collection effort, as they do in focus groups, surveys, and interviews, nor do they need to be motivated to participate.

Criticisms

- The collection of an adequate number of work samples can require significant administrative coordination and time.

- It can be difficult to ensure that the work samples obtained are truly representative of the employees' output. Especially in situations in which individuals choose the work samples they provide, as in asking job candidates to provide samples, the samples may not be representative of the individual's usual products.

- The review of work samples can be expensive and time-consuming, especially when highly trained reviewers are required.

- Employees can be uncomfortable about handing over their work for review. They may suspect that the collection is a prelude to layoffs or punitive performance evaluations. Strong sponsorship of the data collection by a respected and trusted executive and abundant communication can overcome this reservation. However, in many cases, it is not necessary to inform employees that their work is being reviewed because the work they produce is the property of their employer and the review is not focused on individual outcomes.

OBSERVATION

Description and Application

In using observation methods, data is collected by systematically watching employees as they perform their jobs and documenting their behaviors. Well-conducted observation can provide valuable qualitative and quantitative information about the employee, the job, and the work environment. Observations often yields data that cannot be obtained through paper- or interaction-based methods such as questionnaires or interviews and focus groups. Observations may be conducted by a trained observer or via video or audio recordings.

Strengths

- Many of the nuances of work behavior that are missed in paper- and interview-based techniques can be readily perceived in observations. The impact of actually seeing people at work often provides the performance technologist with a deeper level of understanding of the job, its context, and challenges than is possible with other methods.

- Both verbal and non-verbal behavior can be observed.

- Interactions of job incumbents with colleagues, managers, and customers can be observed to create a full, rich perspective of behavior and the work environment not possible in other data collection methods.

- Many people in an organization trust observation data more than data collected via other methods because they see the observations as direct measures of actual work behavior. Observations can therefore facilitate buy-in for organizational initiatives.

- Observation can be adapted to many different situations.

- Observation can measure constructs such as racial prejudice through their demonstration in behavior that cannot be accurately measured with other data collection methods.

Criticisms

- Observation is an expensive and time-consuming data collection method. Especially with more complex jobs, an observer may need to spend many hours over many days to develop a comprehensive understanding of the job.

- The quality of the data depends heavily on the skill, objectivity, and sensitivity of the observers, who need to be carefully trained to produce accurate reports. If the observers are not properly trained, the data collected may be unreliable because of the biases of the observer, poor recording techniques, or rating errors such as leniency or central tendency errors.

- The presence of an observer may modify the employee's typical behavior.

- Employees may object to being observed. If there are strong objections, they may purposely alter their usual behavior.

- It can be difficult to interpret the observations, especially when the work observed involves intangible tasks such as problem solving.

SURVEYS

Description and Application

In surveys, data is collected by asking a selected group of people a set of questions on a topic of interest. Survey items may query people on their experiences, future plans, attitudes, values, choices, opinions, or perceptions. The set of questions with accompanying instructions is often called a questionnaire. The questions are presented individually to each subject in person, print, electronically, or via telephone. If the survey is administered in print, it may be distributed and completed in a group setting or mailed to respondents and returned via postal mail or fax. Electronic surveys may be distributed and completed on a touch-screen kiosk, on a diskette or via e-mail, the Internet, or an organization's intranet. Telephone surveys may be conducted by a live caller or via interactive voice response in which the participant listens to pre-recorded questions and then indicates the selected responses via a touch-tone phone.

The number of questions asked in a survey may vary from one to a hundred or more. For example, some organizations distribute monthly surveys of four or five questions to check the progress of a new intervention. Others may administer annual surveys of employee satisfaction that consist of 150 or more questions. The survey may be distributed to an entire population (termed a census survey) or to a representative sample of the population (termed a sample survey).

Several question formats are used in surveys, including multiple-choice questions, rating scales, ranking scales, checklists, and open-ended questions. Often a survey will be divided into sections and a different format will be used for each section.

Strengths

- Information can be easily and economically collected from large groups of geographically dispersed people.

- Respondents may complete print and electronic surveys at a time and place that are convenient for them.
- Surveys allow for broad representative input and can build consensus for the study results.
- The survey questionnaires can be customized for subgroups of respondents.
- Anonymous surveys can encourage candid responses.
- Multiple-choice or rating-type questions yield quantitative data that can be easily summarized, analyzed, and reported.
- Surveys offer flexibility for both assessing attitudes and collecting facts.

Criticisms

- The data collected are limited to what can be obtained through direct, straightforward questions. Open-ended questions can be included, but respondents may be reluctant to write in detail. Thus, it can be difficult to obtain in-depth information. One cannot aid respondents' thinking process by posing impromptu probing questions, as is possible in interviews and focus groups.
- The quality of the data collected is heavily dependent on the specific experiences of the respondents as well as their awareness, perceptions, honesty, and memory.
- Some people are bored with surveys or object to their impersonal nature and therefore respond carelessly.
- There is no mechanism to check for individual respondents' understanding of the questions or that they know enough to respond appropriately. (This can be partially mitigated through pilot testing the survey.)
- Unless respondents have a strong motivation to complete the survey, response rates may be low. Hence it can be challenging to secure a representative sample of the population.
- It can be difficult to summarize and analyze the responses to open-ended questions.

WORK DIARIES

Description and Application

In a work diary, or work log, participants document how they spend their work days, listing both their activities and start and stop times for each. They may be asked to make entries for several hours, days, weeks, or months, depending on the needs of the study and the complexity and variety of the job. For a simple, routine job, a one-day log may be adequate to capture all work activities, whereas it may require several weeks, or even months, of documentation to identify the full range of activities for a complex job or a job with cyclical responsibilities.

For the days selected for inclusion in the work diary study, participants may be asked to note their activities for the entire day, as in the manager's example in Exhibit 33.1, or only during certain portions of the day such as the first hour of work, the morning, or after the end of the formal work day. In some studies, participants are asked to document what they are doing at a defined time interval, such as every fifteen minutes or every hour.

A wide range of media can be used to produce work diaries. The traditional approach is to ask participants to write their tasks by hand in a paper log. Alternative methods using a computer include creating a diary in a word processing program, making entries in a diary on the web, or sending periodic reports via e-mail messages. Voice-based approaches include telephoning participants at specific intervals and asking them what they are doing or requesting that participants call in and leave voice mail messages at certain times of day. Voice mail is especially useful in situations in which the workforce is mobile and may work at several different locations over the course of the study. Another approach is to ask participants to record their diaries on

---

Exhibit 33.1   A Sample Work Diary

August 29, Monday

Time	Activity
8:00 – 8:15	Briefly reviewed e-mail and planned work for the day in my planner.
8:15 – 8:45	Prepared agenda for tomorrow's staff meeting.
8:45 – 9:00	Read and sorted my mail.
9:00 – 9:30	Met with direct report to review her draft development plan. Made suggestions.
9:30 – 9:50	Read and responded to my e-mail.
9:50 – 10:15	Met with direct report for an individual update. Discussed her goal progress and provided feedback on yesterday's presentation.
10:15 – 10:30	Took shuttle to main building.
10:30 – 12:00	Participated in weekly management meeting.
12:00 - 1:00	Ate lunch at cafeteria then took return shuttle.
1:00 – 4:10	Worked on writing our section's quarterly report. Was interrupted ten times by employees asking questions and five times by phone calls.
4:10 – 5:30	Received urgent call from my boss. Met with him to help him prepare for a meeting tomorrow with senior executives on our new talent management plan.
5:30 – 6:30	Made minor revisions to the talent management plan, then made copies for tomorrow's meeting.

audiotape. Videotaped diaries are yet another technique. A video camera can be set up for each participant. At the requested intervals, each participant turns on the camera and describes the work accomplished. Alternatively, a camera operator can film the participant at work and ask the participant to describe the work.

Strengths

- Work logs are easy for most people to understand and complete.
- The lists of activities offer both an excellent overview of a job and in-depth insights into job responsibilities and challenges. They can cover the full range of job behaviors.
- Work diaries illustrate the daily rhythm of the job that can be especially valuable and is difficult to obtain through other methods of data collection.
- The data obtained from work diaries is typically trusted as accurate by leaders and employees in an organization, and thus they may be more inclined to accept the results of studies in which this method is employed.
- Work diaries do not require the direct involvement of the performance technologist with the participants and thus are not susceptible to the behavior changes that often occur when people know their behavior is being observed. However, if self-recording is used, participants may not accurately report their activities.
- The work diaries are completed individually by each participant, and so they do not require coordination and scheduling of meetings, which can often be a time-consuming task.
- Work diaries may be used for almost any job from unskilled to highly skilled, complex positions.
- The availability of various modes of reporting, including paper, online, voice, audio, and video, make it possible to offer reporting formats compatible with participants' preferences and needs.

Criticisms

- Many people will quickly tire of continuously making entries in a log. They need to be highly motivated to maintain the logs. However, motivation can be increased by offering rewards for completion, explaining how the log can help the individual identify ways to streamline his or her own work, or requiring completion as part of the daily work tasks. Minimizing the span of time when diary entry is required will also reduce tedium.
- Participants may be reluctant to report their daily activities, perhaps fearing they will face negative consequences for revealing their actual work behavior. Assurances of confidentiality, and anonymity if possible, will be helpful in assuaging their fears.

- As in any self-report data collection technique, reporting errors are common. People may forget to document all their activities or may not fully or accurately describe them.
- As with most qualitative data, it is time-consuming and challenging to summarize and analyze the data collected.

CASE STUDIES

Description and Application

The case study is a data collection method in which in-depth descriptive information about specific entities, or cases, is collected, organized, interpreted, and presented in a narrative format. The case study report is essentially a real-life story. The subject of the case may be an individual, a family, a neighborhood, a work group, a classroom, a school, an organization, or any other entity. A case study may also focus on social or natural events such as new supervisors' first six months on the job, employees' reactions to the acquisition of their organization by another company, or community response to a natural disaster. As a data collection approach, it is widely applied in sociology, anthropology, psychology, education, and medicine and offers much potential value to performance technology. Case studies offer rich perspectives and insights that can lead to in-depth understanding of variables, issues, and problems. The renowned Swiss developmental psychologist Jean Piaget, for example, based his theories of childhood intellectual development on the study of two cases: his own children.

Implementation of a case study approach involves a unique degree of interaction for participants, the researcher, and the research audience. The researcher collaborates closely with the participants to collect the data, then selects and structures the ideas to include in the report, developing themes, highlighting some ideas, subordinating or eliminating others, and finally connects the ideas and embedding them in a narrative context. In this process, the researcher communicates the personal meanings of events and relationships as voiced both by the participant and by the researcher. Based on the audience's prior experience and personal knowledge, they in turn shape what they read.

Strengths

- When involvement is important to the success of a research or performance improvement project, case studies are a good choice for a data collection method. They promote participation and buy-in because participants are typically directly involved in providing information through interviews, focus groups, or other means. Participants also have the opportunity to offer their own interpretation of events and feel good about being the center of attention.

- Case studies are very useful for collecting outcome data when there are no acceptable, valid, or reliable measures of the phenomenon being studied, for example, creativity and self-esteem. These are goals of many development programs, but currently there is a lack of good measures, especially those that are sensitive to incremental changes before and after completion of a program. Case studies are a useful way of documenting changes experienced by participants rather than depending on standardized instruments that may not be sensitive to the uniqueness of the situation at hand.

- Case studies are valuable in exploratory research in areas for which there is little previous work and not much is known about the phenomenon of interest.

- Case studies add depth and detail to quantitative data such as surveys. They flesh it out and give it life. The quantitative data identifies the areas of focus, and the qualitative data gives substance to those areas of focus.

- The deep and personal perspectives obtained through case studies can identify issues and performance problems that are not easily uncovered through other methods of data collection.

- A rich case study leads the reader first to awareness, then to understanding to facilitate the construction of knowledge, as if he or she actually experienced the events described.

- A methodological strength of case studies is their flexibility. New areas of information that were not foreseen in the original research plan can be discovered and explored. Unlike surveys or other measuring instruments that cannot be changed once they are distributed, in a case study the researcher can expand or reduce the topics addressed and revise the questions asked as he or she works through the data collection process and uncovers important points.

- Case study research is appealing and can be interesting for both the researcher and the reader of the researcher's work. The information collected about the idiosyncratic experiences of real people and the narratives written to document those experiences are engaging because they are essentially stories about our fellow human beings, an endlessly fascinating topic for most people.

Criticisms

- Value judgments and philosophical decisions are important in communicating the results of case study research. Assessment of the meaning of the data also depends heavily on the researcher's knowledge of the entity or event studied and the enveloping social context. Although this is true in many research methods, case studies provide more discretion to decide which information to include in the case study and how to present and interpret it. It is important to note that this subjectivity is not purely a disadvantage because the flexibility and personal nature of case studies make them vibrant and rich sources of data.

- Because case studies are, by definition, detailed examinations of specific persons or entities, the number of cases that can be included in a study is small. Generalizability to a larger group is therefore limited.

- Case studies require a high level of analytical ability and writing skill to successfully integrate and document the information obtained from multiple sources of data.

- Case studies are labor- and time-intensive, both in data collection and in writing the case study narrative.

PROCESS MAPPING

Description and Application

Process mapping is the step-by-step documentation of the actions taken by workers as they create a product or provide a service. The maps depict the inputs, the performers, the sequence of actions the performers take, and the outputs of a work process in a matrix or flow chart format, usually combining both words and simple graphics. The maps may also include the elapsed time required to perform each step, the feedback the performers receive, conditions of work, consequences, and other elements. Process mapping is typically conducted by a facilitator working with a small group of employees who are highly knowledgeable about the process. This group often includes the process owner, top performers, and representatives of each work group that participates in the process. Process mapping is also known as system task analysis, process task analysis, process diagramming, and work mapping.

Expanding Your Options

Action triggers—events that occur (such as, performance dropping below desired levels) and cause consequent actions to be performed (such as, the initiation of a pre-defined performance improvement intervention).

Based on archive.groundworkopensource.com definition (January 2009)

A process map may focus on the actions of an entire organization, a business unit, a division, a function, a work group, or an individual performer. If the process involves a complex entity such as a business unit, a series of maps may be produced beginning at the highest level (for example, the business unit) and then proceeding to lower levels (such as a division and work group). A simplified example of a process map for catalog telephone orders is shown in Exhibit 33.2.

Exhibit 33.2 Catalog Telephone Order Process Map

Performer	Process Steps			
Customer	1. Calls service center and is routed to first available associate	2. Tells associate the catalog numbers of items selected		
Sales Associate		3. Enters order into computer system as customer talks		
Picker		4. Receives batch of orders with item numbers via computer	5. Fills each order by picking items from warehouse shelves and placing in tub	6. When has picked twenty-five orders, brings them to Packing	7. Enters the twenty-five order completions in computer
Packer				8. Packs and labels each order and delivers to Shipping
Shipper				9. Enters orders as "shipped" in computer and loads on truck

Strengths

- Process mapping helps the performance technologist develop a systems view of a situation because the map highlights the interactions of several individuals or work groups and how the work of one entity is affected by the work of another.

- Creating the map guides one through a step-by-step, thorough appraisal of a performance situation.

- The mapping technique can be adapted to studying the work of entire organizations or business units, functions, work groups, or individuals.

- As much or as little detail as is needed can be collected.

- Process mapping requires a small investment of time and employee involvement to collect a large amount of valuable data.

- Employees are often comfortable describing their work processes and do not hesitate to provide candid information.

- The completed process maps can also serve as effective educational and communication tools.

- Process mapping offers high validity and reliability. It provides straight-forward data that requires minimal interpretation.

Criticisms

- Process mapping typically is based on input from only a small group of employees. However, wider input can be achieved by circulating the draft map for review and feedback to a larger group.

- It requires a high level of facilitation skill to guide a group through the process mapping exercise.

- Persons who do not like working with detail can find it very difficult to sustain their focus through the four to eight or more hours usually required to create a process map.

- As with most data collection methods, the quality of the data collected depends heavily on the accuracy of the information provided by participating employees.

LITERATURE REVIEWS

Description and Application

A literature review consists of the identification, reading, summarization, and evaluation of previously published articles, books, reports, or Internet entries on a topic of interest. The review may also encompass unpublished documents such as dissertations, manuals, or personal correspondence. There are four dimensions to consider in planning a literature review: the genre of literature (academic, professional, business, or government); the types of sources (primary or secondary); the time period reviewed; and the extent of coverage (comprehensive or selected sources). The objective of the literature review will determine the choices made for each dimension.

Strengths

- Literature reviews are versatile. They can be conducted for almost any topic and can provide both overview and in-depth information.

- Literature reviews are relatively inexpensive and efficient. A large amount of data can be collected quickly at minimal cost.

- No scheduling or coordination is involved. The cooperation of others is not required.

- The only resources needed are a good library or online database and a competent reviewer.

- Literature reviews are an excellent first step in a project because they provide a conceptual framework for further planning.

Criticisms

- An effective literature review requires a high level of skill in identifying resources, analyzing the sources to identify relevant information, and writing a meaningful summary.

- Literature reviews are limited to collecting information about what has happened in the past, and usually within organizations other than the researcher's own workplace. They cannot provide data about actual current behavior.

INTERVIEWS

Description and Application

In interviews, an individual responds orally to questions asked orally by one or more persons. Interviews may be conducted face-to-face or via telephone or videoconferencing. In a structured interview, the interviewer asks a series of pre-planned questions that are asked of all interviewees. The interviewee may be asked to select one of several choices provided or may be asked to respond in his or her own words. In unstructured interviews, each interviewee may be asked different questions or no response choices are provided. The interviewers are free to develop their own questions based on the interviewees' particular characteristics or experiences or their responses to previous questions. Many interviews combine the structured and unstructured techniques. For example, in selection interviews, interviewers often begin by asking the job candidate a series of pre-planned questions about their education and experience that are asked of all candidates, but then tailor subsequent questions to further probe the individual candidate's responses.

Strengths

- Through the personal interaction with the interviewee, the interviewer can build rapport and trust and thus promote the sharing of candid information that the interviewee would not provide in a survey or focus group.
- Questions can be tailored to the characteristics and circumstances of individual interviewees.
- The interviewer can probe for more detail, clarity, and context of the information the interviewee offers or expand the scope of the interview to include topics that arise.
- In face-to-face interviews, the interviewer can observe body language, gestures, and tone of voice that reveal feelings and attitudes toward both the interview itself and the topic of discussion.
- The personal connection inherent in interviews helps build buy-in for organizational initiatives and social programs.

Criticisms

- Interviews are expensive and time-consuming.
- Skilled interviewers are required to obtain high-quality data.
- It can be difficult to accurately and fully record the interviewee's responses.
- The qualitative data obtained may be difficult and laborious to analyze.
- Because interviews are essentially interpersonal interactions, there is much potential for bias both in how the interview is conducted and in how the interviewee responds. Characteristics of the interviewer and the interviewee, situational variables, and the interaction of these may affect interview outcomes. For example, a female interviewee may respond differently to a female interviewer than she would to a male interviewer on some topics.
- Some people find interviews threatening and will not provide candid information.
- It can be difficult or impossible to determine the accuracy of the information provided by the interviewee.

FOCUS GROUPS

Description and Application

A focus group is a small-group discussion in which participants respond to a series of questions on a single topic. A skilled facilitator meets with five to twelve people to collect in-depth qualitative information about the group's ideas, perceptions, attitudes, or experiences on the defined topic. Focus groups are sometimes called "group interviews" because they are an extension of individual interviews. The purpose of interviews is usually to obtain detailed, in-depth information. In focus groups, there is the additional goal of stimulating group members' thinking through the contributions of others. Creative ideas, new perspectives, insightful hypotheses, and nuances of the topic are voiced that any one individual might not have considered.

Focus groups generally provide qualitative data about feelings, attitudes, perceptions, or ideas rather than independently verifiable, objective data such as facts and figures. They are often used as a source of preliminary data to form the foundation for more intensive research efforts such as individual interviews or surveys. Focus groups are frequently chosen as a data collection method in organizational change initiatives because, in addition to the data collected, they generate feelings of involvement and buy-in among participants that increase enthusiasm and willingness to work for improvement.

Strengths

- Focus groups can result in rich, in-depth qualitative information and insights on the inner workings of an organization that are not easily obtainable through other data collection methods.

- Participants can build on each other's ideas to provide a broad perspective that cannot be obtained in individual interviews.

- The rapport that develops among group members and the facilitator frequently stimulates participants to contribute more and deeper information than they would in an individual data collection technique such as an interview or survey.

- The flexibility of focus groups allows unexpected ideas to be explored.

- A large amount of data can be collected relatively inexpensively and quickly.

- Substantially less planning and preparation time are required for focus groups than for other group data collection methods such as surveys.

- Focus groups can facilitate support for organizational improvement efforts through personal participation and involvement.

Criticisms

- The collection of useful data requires participant trust. Focus groups may not be an effective method of data collection in organizations when there is low trust or in cultures in which a single misstep can hinder one's career. Group members may withhold information or contribute only what they believe others want to hear.

- Compared to individual interviews, the researcher cannot easily build a personal relationship with each participant. Rather, the facilitator strives to create a comfortable environment so that participants are willing to openly share their thoughts with each other.

- Focus groups can be difficult to schedule and organize because they require the physical presence of selected people in the same place at the same time.

- The quality of the data collected may vary with the analytical ability and experience of group members.

- It can be difficult and labor-intensive to analyze the large amount of qualitative data collected in focus groups.

- The quality of the group discussion and the usefulness of the data depend heavily upon the skill of the facilitator.

- Unless the facilitator is very skillful, more assertive individuals often tend to dominate the discussion, and members who are not good collaborators can frustrate the group.

- The data may be negatively impacted by "group think," such as confining thinking to one perspective.

- The employee time and lost productivity involved in participating in focus groups can be costly to an organization, especially when highly paid employees participate.

CRITICAL INCIDENTS

Description and Application

Critical incidents are narrative descriptions of important events that occurred on the job. Critical incidents document the work context, the specific situation that arose, the persons who were involved, what each person did and said, and the results. The incidents may be confined to a particular topic or may cover the breadth of work experience. Critical incidents can be collected through several different methods, including focus groups, individual interviews, surveys, and work diaries. They are typically one to a few paragraphs in length.

Strengths

- Critical incidents provide dramatic demonstrations of the impact of behavior. They spark interest in a report or presentation because they give real-life examples. They provide the human story behind research findings or organizational decisions.

- When the data is collected through an anonymous survey approach, critical incidents allow the performance technologist to obtain emotion-laden data about individuals' private thoughts, feelings, and actions while protecting their identity.

- Critical incidents provide rich, in-depth data at a lower cost than observations.

- They are easy to develop and administer.

- Many people enjoy sharing stories of their work experiences. They like to feel that they are being heard and that their experiences are important. Therefore, it is usually not difficult to persuade people to participate in a data collection effort.

- Critical incidents can measure abstract constructs such as motivation through their demonstration in reported behavior.

Criticisms

- In critical incidents, reports of behavior are filtered through the lenses of individuals' perceptions, memory, honesty, and biases and, therefore, may not be entirely accurate.

- It can be time-consuming and laborious to summarize and analyze the data.

- It can be difficult to convince people to share their critical incidents through a survey because they are reluctant to expend the effort required to write their own stories. More labor-intensive and expensive interviews and focus groups are often more successful approaches.

RECOMMENDED DESIGN AND DEVELOPMENT PROCESS

To achieve accuracy and reliability in the collection of your data, it is recommended that you use more than one method of collecting information. All research methods have weaknesses and strengths. In their classic text *Unobtrusive Measures*, Eugene Webb, Donald Campbell, Richard Schwartz, and Lee Sechrest emphasize the importance of using multiple methods that have *different* methodological weaknesses. This will ensure that the strengths of one supplement the weaknesses of another. Choosing methods with complementary strengths and weaknesses provides a fuller picture of the problem or opportunity you are studying and consequently affords a sounder basis for your conclusions. For example, survey questions are often based on in-depth data previously collected in interviews, focus groups, or observations. Surveys are a good way to verify the generalizability of the data collected with these methods because surveys are less expensive to administer to a large group of respondents. Conversely, interviews, focus groups, and observations can be used as follow-ups to surveys in order to probe more deeply into the initial information collected.

The data collected in different instruments also illuminates multiple facets of the issue and therefore provides deeper and broader insights. If data from multiple sources reveals the same root causes, you can have greater confidence in the accuracy and comprehensiveness of the information. The data, and therefore your performance improvement project, will also possess more credibility with stakeholders.

When you are selecting data collection methods, it is important to carefully consider the eight questions below.

1. Will the Instrument Answer Your Research Questions?

The first and most important step in any data collection effort is to clearly and specifically define the questions you want to answer. Why are you collecting the data? What do you hope to learn? The method you select must supply the information required to answer your particular questions. Some methods may be expedient but will not provide accurate information. For example, if you want to know the turnover rates in an organization over the past three years, a review of personnel records would be a good choice, but a focus group would not be.

2. From What Sources Do You Plan to Collect Information?

An instrument will only provide the information you need if you use it to obtain data from the appropriate people or other source. For example, a survey could be a good choice to collect information about employees' levels of proficiency in specific competencies, but only if you distribute the survey to the people who are in a position to provide accurate information. A common mistake in competency assessment is to ask employees to assess their own proficiency through a survey. Research has consistently shown that people do not accurately assess their own level of competency. A 2004 study of flawed self-assessment by David Dunning, Chip Heath, and Jerry Suls attests to this. Competency self-assessment information collected from employees in a survey is very likely to be inaccurate. However, if instead managers are asked to rate their employees' proficiency in specific competencies in a survey instrument, they may be better able to provide accurate information.

3. Does the Method Align with Your Research Design?

Consider which methods will provide the data you need to make the inferences or comparisons required to answer your research questions. Are you seeking the current perceptions of employees? Are you comparing two work units that perform similar functions? Are you studying employees before and after participation in a training program? Do you want to find out whether there is a relationship between employee satisfaction and certain supervisor behaviors? Or are you exploring changes over time in the organization? For example, if you want to find out whether frequent individual meetings between employees and their supervisors are related to employees' trust in their supervisors, a focus group will supply general information, but it cannot provide the quantitative data required to compute a correlation coefficient to definitively answer your research question. A survey with a numerical rating scale would be a better choice in such an instance.

4. Will the Method Provide Valid Data?

Determine whether the instrument will accurately measure the behavior, perceptions, outcomes, or other factors you need to measure. The closer the measurement is to the target behavior, the greater the accuracy. For example, if you are trying to identify problems that are leading to poor quality work, it is likely that you will collect more accurate information if you view actual samples of the work than if you interview employees to ask them about the mistakes they make.

5. Will the Method Provide Reliable Data?

Consider whether the method will provide consistent information. Ask yourself whether, if you took a second measurement, would you get the same results? For example, it is important to recognize that an instrument such as a survey that measures people's perceptions may provide very different results depending on when it is administered because events may alter their perceptions.

6. Is the Method Practical?

Choose methods that are suitable for your organization, the situation, and the people from whom you plan to collect data. Also consider the resources available to you such as time, money, and staff. For example, although you may feel that individual interviews with managers and executives are the optimal approach to collecting the information you need, you may not have the time or staff to conduct the interviews within the project timelines. Organizational acceptance of your chosen method is another key variable to consider. For example, in some organizations, employees have been surveyed so frequently in the past that many will no longer willingly complete a survey.

7. What Data Analysis Options Do You Have?

At the same time as you are deciding which data collection methods to use, you also need to decide how you will analyze the data. The method and analysis are interdependent. You must plan how the collected data will be analyzed before you make a final choice of data collection methods. The methods provide different data types (qualitative or quantitative) and content (numerical ratings, one-word answers, paragraph-length narrative text), and you will have to assess whether the type and content will allow you to perform the analyses required to answer your research questions. Also consider the expertise and resources you have available for data analysis. For example, work diaries provide large quantities of detailed, qualitative data about work tasks, which can be time- and labor-intensive to analyze. A higher degree of expertise is also required to accurately interpret the data. If you have limited time and staff and no experience in qualitative data analysis, work diaries would be a poor choice for you.

8. What Methods Have Been Used Successfully in the Past?

A good way to select appropriate data collection methods is to learn from the work of other performance technologists. Review studies on your topic reported in journals. Talk to experienced colleagues to discover which methods have been successfully used to obtain the kind of data you need with the type of population you are studying. Focus on the benefits, problems, and pitfalls experienced. Not only will you avoid potential problems, but you will increase your professional knowledge base.

CRITICAL SUCCESS FACTORS

Several planning and implementation guidelines that are critical to the success of all methods are described below.

Sampling
- In most performance improvement projects, only a sample of the target employees, cases, or events are included in data collection, although the results are generalized to all. In this situation, you will need to select a representative sample for participation in data collection. The entities included in the sample should be representative of the larger population on the key characteristics most relevant to the study.
- If a sample of employees will participate in focus groups designed to assess employees' perceptions of the compensation package offered by the organization, it would be important that the participants be representative of all the employees in terms of work function, job level, work location, years of work experience, and perhaps, gender and racial category.

- Basic research methods textbooks will provide valuable guidance for readers not familiar with sampling strategies.

Scheduling

- Prepare a schedule for the data collection effort, including instrument development, testing, actual data collection, and data analysis.
- Build in extra time because it almost always takes much longer than what might be expected. In fact, it is even recommended that you double your best time estimate.
- If you will be collecting data directly from people, as in focus groups, interviews, or surveys, scheduling their participation at a time convenient for them is likely to increase your response rates.
- For focus groups and interviews, invite at least 20 percent more people than actually needed. For surveys, you may need to invite double or triple the number of respondents required for a representative sample.
- Invite people to participate at least two weeks in advance, and then send a reminder a few days before the event, restating the purpose and benefits of the data collection, the location, time, and place and expressing appreciation for their participation.

Pilot Testing

- It is essential to conduct at least one pilot test of your instruments in conditions as close as possible to the actual data collection. The purposes of pilot testing are to determine whether revisions are needed to the content of the instrument and instructions, to estimate the time required to complete the data collection, and to test the data recording procedures. For example, in a nationwide survey recently managed by the author, the research team conducted pilot tests with employees in three different government agencies. As a result of the pilot tests, a few questions were eliminated, two were added, and several others were revised. The time the employees took to complete the pilot survey was clocked, and this was used to estimate the average time required for completion. After these revisions to the survey, a second round of pilot testing was conducted to test the web-based system for administering the survey and recording the data.
- In addition to pilot testing the collection and recording of data, it is also important to carefully plan and test data analysis techniques before beginning to collect actual data. This enables you to preview the types of results you will receive, try out your chosen analysis techniques, and identify potential problems.

Training

- Provide hands-on training and abundant practice to staff members who will be collecting the data, summarizing it, or analyzing it.

- Do not assume that because someone has collected similar data in the past, he or she can do it well in the current study. Each study has unique requirements. Training to mastery is necessary to ensure proficiency.

Ethical Issues

- It is good practice to discuss the potential ethical issues of data collection with an institutional review board or other committee that approves data collection efforts within the organizations involved.

- It is also important to review the ethical standards of your profession before making decisions about the data collection tools you will employ and the data you will collect. These standards are usually available from professional associations.

- The employees asked to participate in the data collection effort should be informed of the purpose of data collection, how the information will be used, their role, whether participation is voluntary, how long it will take, and whether their responses will be anonymous or confidential. If the data will be available for their review, participants should be told how they can obtain the results.

SUMMARY

In addition to the data collection methods discussed in this chapter, there are other methods worth exploring, such as written and performance-based assessments, content analysis, and sociometric tools such as network analysis. The Recommended Readings section that follows provides information on these data collection methods as well as more detailed information on the ten methods described here.

References

Dunning, D., Heath, C., & Suls, J. M. (2004). Flawed self-assessment: implications for health, education, and the workplace. *Psychological Science in the Public Interest, 5*(3), 69–106.

Webb, E. J., Campbell, D. T., Schwartz, R. D., & Sechrest, L. (2000). *Unobtrusive measures* (rev. ed.). Thousand Oaks, CA: Sage.

Recommended Readings

Flick, U. (2006). *An introduction to qualitative research* (3rd ed.). Thousand Oaks, CA: Sage.

Gilbert, T. F. (1996). *Human competence: engineering worthy performance* (2nd ed.). Silver Spring, MD: International Society for Performance Improvement.

Hammond, S. A. (1998). *The thin book of appreciative inquiry* (2nd ed.). Plano, TX: The Thin Book Publishing Co.

Kraut, A. I. (1996). Introduction: an overview of organizational surveys. In A. I. Kraut (Ed.), *Organizational surveys* (pp. 1–14). San Francisco: Jossey-Bass.

Langdon, D. (1999). Process mapping. In D. Langdon, K. Whiteside, & M. McKenna (Eds.), *Intervention resource guide* (pp. 311–317. San Francisco: Pfeiffer.

Langdon, D. (2000). *Aligning performance: Improving people, systems, and organizations*. San Francisco: Pfeiffer.

Leigh, D. (2006). SWOT Analysis. In J. A. Pershing (Ed.), *Handbook of human performance technology: Principles, practices, and potential* (3rd ed.) (pp. 1089–1108). San Francisco: Pfeiffer.

Liebert, R. M., Poulos, R. W., & Strauss, G. D. (1974). *Developmental psychology*. Upper Saddle River, NJ: Prentice-Hall.

Marrelli, A. (2004). The performance technologist's tool box: Surveys. *Performance Improvement, 43*(10), 38–44.

Marrelli, A. (2005). The performance technologist's tool box: Critical incidents. *Performance Improvement, 44*(10), 40–44.

Marrelli, A. (2005, August). The performance technologist's tool box: Literature reviews. *Performance Improvement, 44*(7), 40–44.

Marrelli, A. (2005). The performance technologist's tool box: Observations. *Performance Improvement, 44*(2), 39–43.

Marrelli, A. (2005). The performance technologist's tool box: Process mapping. *Performance Improvement, 44*(5), 40–44.

Marrelli, A. (2005). The performance technologist's tool box: Work samples. *Performance Improvement, 44*(4), 43–46.

Marrelli, A. (2007). The performance technologist's tool box: Collecting data through case studies. *Performance Improvement, 46*(7), 39–44.

Marrelli, A. (2007). The performance technologist's tool box: Work diaries. *Performance Improvement, 46*(5), 44–48.

Marrelli, A. (2007). The performance technologist's tool box: Unobtrusive measures. *Performance Improvement, 46*(9), 43–47.

Marrelli, A. (2008). The performance technologist's tool box: Focus groups. *Performance Improvement, 47*(4), 39–45.

Marrelli, A., Hoge, M., & Tondora, J. (2005). Strategies for competency modeling. *Administration & Policy in Mental Health, 32*(5-6), 533–561.

Marrelli, A. F. (1998). Ten evaluation instruments for technical training. In D. L. Kirkpatrick (Ed.), *Another look at evaluating training programs* (pp. 58–65). Alexandria, VA: American Society for Training and Development.

Morrell-Samuels, P. (2002, February). Getting the truth into workplace surveys. *Harvard Business Review, 80*(2), 111–118.

Patton, M. Q. (2002). *Qualitative research and evaluation methods* (3rd ed.) Thousand Oaks, CA: Sage.

Pelto, P. J., & Pelto, G. H. (1978). *Anthropological research: The structure of inquiry* (2nd ed.). Cambridge, England: Cambridge University Press.

Pershing, J. L. (2006). Interviewing to analyze and evaluate human performance technology. In J. A. Pershing (Ed.), *Handbook of human performance technology: principles, practices, potential* (pp. 780–794). San Francisco: Pfeiffer.

Phillips, J. J. (1991). *Handbook of training evaluation and measurement methods* (2nd ed.) Houston, TX: Gulf.

Phillips, J. J. (1997). *Return on investment in training and performance improvement programs.* Houston, TX: Gulf.

Rogowski, R. (2005). On the path to excellence: Effective benchmarking through the case study method. *Performance Improvement, 44*(7), 21–25.

Rogelberg, S. G., Church, A. H., Waclawski, J., & Stanton, J. M. (2002). Organizational survey research. In S. G. Rogelberg (Ed.), *Handbook of research methods in industrial and organizational psychology* (pp. 141–160). Malden, MA: Blackwell.

Rubin, H. J., & Rubin, I. S. (1995). *Qualitative interviewing: The art of hearing data.* Thousand Oaks, CA: Sage.

Stake, R. E. (2005). Qualitative case studies. In N. K. Denzin & Y. S. Lincoln (Eds.), *The Sage handbook of qualitative research* (3rd ed.) (pp. 443–466). Thousand Oaks, CA: Sage.

Swanson, R.A. (1994). *Analysis for improving performance: tools for diagnosing organizations and documenting workplace expertise.* San Francisco: Berrett-Koehler.

General Methods

Clardy, A. (1997). *Studying your workforce: Applied research methods and tools for the training and development practitioner.* Thousand Oaks, CA: Sage.

Denzin, N. K., & Lincoln, Y. S. (2005). *The Sage handbook of qualitative research* (3rd ed.) Thousand Oaks, CA: Sage.

Patton, M. Q. (2002). *Qualitative research and evaluation methods* (3rd ed.). Thousand Oaks, CA: Sage.

Assessments

Shrock, S., & Coscarelli, W. (2007). *Criterion-referenced test development: Technical and legal guidelines for corporate training and certification* (3rd ed.) San Francisco: Pfeiffer.

Case Studies

Stake, R. E. (1995). *The art of case study research.* Thousand Oaks, CA: Sage.

Yin, R. K. (2008). *Case study research: Design and methods.* Thousand Oaks, CA: Sage.

Content Analysis

Gilmore, E. R. (2006). Using content analysis in human performance technology. In J. A. Pershing (Ed.), *Handbook of human performance technology: Principles, practices, potential* (pp. 819–836). San Francisco: Pfeiffer.

Krippendorff, K. (2008). *The content analysis reader.* Thousand Oaks, CA: Sage.

Focus Groups

Krueger, R. (2008). *Focus groups: A practical guide for applied research.* Thousand Oaks, CA: Sage.

Stewart, D. W., Shamdasani, P. N., & Rook, D. W. (2006). *Focus groups: Theory and practice* (2nd ed.). Thousand Oaks, CA: Sage.

Interviews

Campion, M. A., Palmer, D. K., & Campion, J. E. (1997). A review of structure in the selection interview. *Personnel Psychology, 50*(3), 655–702.

Rubin, H. J., & Rubin, I. S. (1995). *Qualitative interviewing: The art of hearing data.* Thousand Oaks, CA: Sage.

Literature Reviews

Cooper, H. M. (1998). *Synthesizing research: A guide for literature reviews.* Thousand Oaks, CA: Sage.

Galvan, J. L. (2006). *Writing literature reviews: A guide for students of the social and behavioral sciences.* Glendale, CA: Pyrczak.

Pan, M. L. (2004). *Preparing literature reviews.* Glendale, CA: Pyrczak.

Network Analysis

Knoke, D., & Yang, S. (2007). *Social network analysis* (2nd ed.). Thousand Oaks, CA: Sage.

Process Mapping

Langdon, D. (2000). *Aligning performance: Improving people, systems, and organizations.* San Francisco: Pfeiffer.

Surveys

Dillman, C. A. (2000). *Mail and internet surveys: The tailored design method.* Hoboken, NJ: John Wiley & Sons.

Fink, A. (2008). *How to conduct surveys* (4th ed.). Thousand Oaks, CA: Sage.

Gillham, B. (2008). *Small-scale social survey methods.* New York: Continuum.

PART ELEVEN

EDITORS'
DISCUSSION

Improvements in human and organizational performance cannot be sustained when performance is viewed solely from the perspective of a single point in time. In today's dynamic organizations, performance is always in flux—performance that is down today may be up in a few months. As a consequence, to be most effective, improvement efforts must take a longitudinal perspective on performance; systematically collecting data and information over time to adequately identify, prioritize, and make decisions related to performance needs (that is, gaps in results). This allows for adjustments in performance interventions to be made based on valid data – rather than assumptions or impulses. The continuous monitoring of performance, through recurring needs assessments and other data collection efforts, can then inform your decisions today, tomorrow, next month, and into the future.

Expanding Your Options

Customer surveys—a data collection tool used to gather information from customers or clients in order to learn about expectations, whether they are being met, general satisfaction, as well as recommendations for improvements.

Based on qualitydigest.com definition (January 2009)

Your ability to accurately and routinely collect useful information for informing decisions is essential to the success of any improvement initiative. As the achievement of desired results improves, there is no time to rest on past successes. Rather, this is the ideal time to reexamine needs and start preparing the next system of performance improvement activities. Continue to use needs assessment data and information to (1) make decisions about which performance interventions to select, (2) monitor the successful implementation of interventions, (3) assess the ongoing impact of performance interventions, and (4) build the foundation for longitudinal impact evaluations that will measure the long-term success of your improvement efforts.

Continuous monitoring of performance ensures the sustainable accomplishment of results. Nevertheless, the monitoring of results is seldom included in project plans or budgets. Many organizations—through policies, incentives, and leadership decisions—often inhibit the continuous monitoring of performance improvements. Frequently, for instance, successful project managers are promoted or moved to the next project before significant results are achieved. The ensuing leadership vacuum (see Chapter Seven) often leads to a reduction in performance associated with the project.

Consequently, it is important that you build continual monitoring of performance—either through recurring needs assessments or other data collection processes—into the design and budget of your improvement system. From complete needs assessments every two years to monthly performance checks (see Chapter Ten), you can use a range of activities to systematically and regularly monitor results—most of which require few resources once the routine is established. The data and information from continuous monitoring efforts can then be used to address emerging performance issues or further refine performance interventions.

References and Resources from Editorial Contributions to Part Eleven

Kaufman, R. (2006). *Change, choices, and consequences: A guide to mega thinking and planning*. Amherst, MA: HRD Press.

Kaufman, R., Oakley-Brown, H., Watkins, R., & Leigh, D. (2003). *Strategic planning for success: Aligning people, performance, and payoffs*. San Francisco: Jossey-Bass

Watkins, R. (2007). *Performance by design: The systematic selection, design, and development of performance technologies that produce useful results*. Amherst, MA: HRD Press.

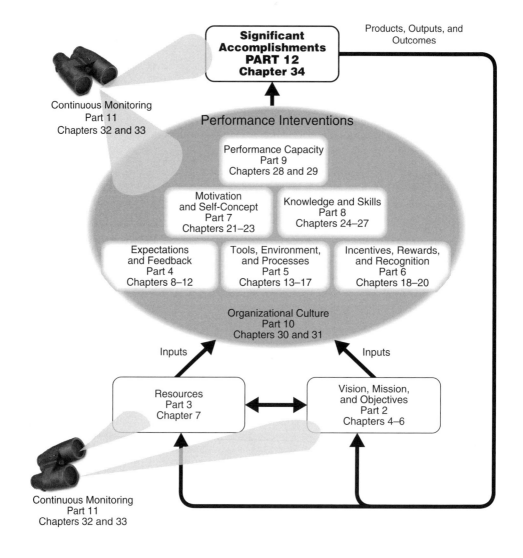

Significant
Accomplishments
PART 12
Chapter 34

Products, Outputs, and
Outcomes

Continuous Monitoring
Part 11
Chapters 32 and 33

Performance Interventions

Performance Capacity
Part 9
Chapters 28 and 29

Motivation
and Self-Concept
Part 7
Chapters 21–23

Knowledge and Skills
Part 8
Chapters 24–27

Expectations
and Feedback
Part 4
Chapters 8–12

Tools, Environment,
and Processes
Part 5
Chapters 13–17

Incentives, Rewards,
and Recognition
Part 6
Chapters 18–20

Organizational Culture
Part 10
Chapters 30 and 31

Inputs

Inputs

Resources
Part 3
Chapter 7

Vision, Mission,
and Objectives
Part 2
Chapters 4–6

Continuous Monitoring
Part 11
Chapters 32 and 33

Significant
Accomplishments

Performance improvement efforts, from beginning to end, should focus on the achievement of results. From defining the strategic direction of your organization in terms of results to be accomplished (see Part One of this handbook), to comparing motivation and self-concept performance interventions (see Part Seven of this handbook), to the continual monitoring of performance (see Part Eleven of this handbook), your focus must remain on the accomplishment of significant and sustainable results. This focus should guide all of your decisions and performance interventions, thereby ensuring that everything your organization uses, does, produces, and delivers leads to beneficial outcomes.

Accordingly, Roger Kaufman's three levels of results (societal outcomes, organizational outputs, and individual/team products) provide a practical framework for guiding performance improvement efforts. Use the three levels described in Part One of this handbook to initially define a pragmatic strategic direction for your organization—aligning internal and external performance expectations. Following this, apply the three levels when comparing numerous performance interventions to ensure that results at all levels will be accomplished.

Organizational results are dependent on individual and team results. A corollary is that external clients and partners (as well as society as a whole) depend on organizations to deliver outputs that contribute value. Upon completing the systemic-loop, individuals then rely on the societal value of their contributions to give their work meaning or worth. All three levels of results are interrelated and mutually dependent systems, providing a comprehensive framework for guiding your performance improvement decisions.

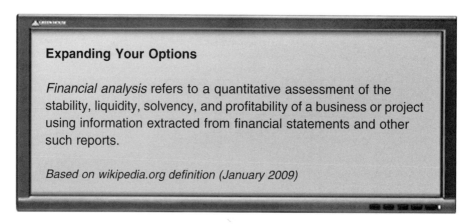

Expanding Your Options

Financial analysis refers to a quantitative assessment of the stability, liquidity, solvency, and profitability of a business or project using information extracted from financial statements and other such reports.

Based on wikipedia.org definition (January 2009)

WHAT'S COMING UP

Nevertheless, even with a continual focus on accomplishing meaningful results, measuring the success of your improvement efforts is the only way to know the impact of your activities. In Chapter Thirty-Four, Patti and Jack Phillips offer insights and recommendations on how to measure the accomplishment of results through pragmatic Return On Investment (ROI) analysis. As they describe it, ROI analysis is an integral and vital component of any evaluation; closely aligning evaluations at Kirkpatrick's Levels 1, 2, 3, and 4. ROI analysis provides practical information regarding the success of an improvement initiative within the context of other results indicators.

CHAPTER THIRTY-FOUR

Return on Investment

Patti P. Phillips
Jack J. Phillips

INTRODUCTION

Measuring the success of human performance interventions takes on a variety of forms. Both qualitative and quantitative data, as well as financial and non-financial data, are necessary to report the complete story of success. The need for data that satisfy the taste of various stakeholders has positioned the ROI Methodology as a leading technique to measure human performance technology (HPT) success. The methodology is used to evaluate program success in private-sector, public-sector, and non-profit organizations.

While return on investment (ROI) is the ultimate measure developed through the ROI Methodology, it is only one of six measures. Whether working with e-learning, coaching, leadership, or process improvement initiatives, this approach to accountability develops results important to all stakeholders.

DESCRIPTION

The nature and scope of program *value* is changing. With functions supporting human capital moving under the realm of the chief financial officer (CFO) and the popular press pouncing on functions designed to support and develop human resources, it is no wonder that the types of results reported have shifted from activity-based to results-based.

In the past, program, project, or process success was measured by activity: number of people involved, money spent, days to complete. Little consideration was given to the benefits derived from these activities. Nevertheless, more often today than in the past, *value* is defined as monetary benefits compared with costs. The following examples illustrate how organizations from a variety of industries, sectors, and countries report value for programs in which they invest:

- Apple Computer calculated the ROI for investing in process improvement teams.
- Sprint/Nextel developed the ROI on its diversity program.
- The Australian Capital Territory Community Care agency forecast the ROI for the implementation for a client relationship management (CRM) system.
- Accenture calculated the ROI on a new sales platform for its consultants.
- Wachovia developed the forecast ROI and actual ROI for its negotiations program.
- Le Meridien Hotels calculated the ROI of a training program of conference coordinators.
- The cities of New York, San Francisco, and Phoenix showed the monetary value of investing in projects to reduce the number of homeless citizens on the streets.
- CVS Caremark Pharmacy Operations conducted an ROI study on an electronic documentation tool.
- A major U.S. Department of Defense agency developed the ROI for a master's degree program offered by a major university.
- Codelco conducted an ROI initiative to evaluate multiple human performance improvement initiatives including an employee retraining program.

In response to this shift from process to results, many people argue that there is too much focus solely on economic value. But it is economics, or money, that allows organizations and individuals to contribute to the greater good. Organizations and individuals have choices about where they invest resources. For monetary resources to be put to best use, they must be allocated to programs, processes, and projects that yield the greatest return. Italian economist Vilfredo Pareto demonstrated this in his work with economic efficiency. Pareto optimality is the ultimate measure of efficient use of resources—when resources are allocated to best use and no further reallocation takes place. But when resources do need to be shifted, the determination should be made using a common measure. The ultimate normalizing factor is money; which makes it a pragmatic proxy for assessing at least one important characteristic of *value*.

Once a measure is converted to money, then measures and program outcomes can be compared in the same terms. However, it is only when a comparison between program monetary benefits and program costs is made that objective and equitable decisions about resources occur. This is the ultimate benefit of the ROI Methodology—providing program owners and clients a tool by which they can allocate resources using a common metric that has been used for centuries.

Decisions being made about programs and projects do not always involve resource allocation. Many stakeholders can use information explaining how they can improve their programs so they achieve greater results. Some stakeholders want data to understand how they can better support the implementation of a program. Other stakeholders want data that tell them what has been invested. And some stakeholders just want a good story. Stakeholders may include consumers, taxpayers, shareholders, executives, participants, managers, supervisors, community groups, unions, and others. Each stakeholder defines value based on his or her perspective, and thus the data they require to make decisions about programs and resources can be unique.

This requirement for data beyond the cost-benefit comparison has been a concern for economists and accountants for years. Charles T. Horngren's 1982 *Cost Accounting* text clearly states that to report ROI at the exclusion of other performance measures is insufficient. This is another benefit of the ROI process described in this chapter; the process generates data important to all stakeholders. Categorized into five levels of program results, the data reported represent the chain of impact that occurs as people are involved in training, performance improvement, coaching (see Chapter Eleven), leadership development, knowledge management (see Chapter Fifteen), career development counseling, and any type of effort designed to change what people do (see Chapter Sixteen)—and more specifically what they accomplish.

The results achieved through the implementation of the ROI process go well beyond an economic metric and process improvement data. By implementing the process routinely and using the resulting data, program and project owners can:

- *Align* programs and processes to the business by designing and evaluating them with the ultimate economic need in mind.
- *Improve* processes overall, using the data derived through evaluation to change the way they do their business.
- *Justify* or enhance budgets using data that resonate with key decision-makers.
- *Build* partnerships that support the transfer of knowledge, skills, and information to the workplace, by engaging in dialogue initiated by evaluation results versus hearsay.
- *Earn* a seat at the table by speaking the language of the business.

This chapter introduces the ROI Methodology and describes how it is can be used to report HPT success.

WHAT WE KNOW FROM RESEARCH

Peter Rossi, Howard Freeman, and Mark Lipsey define *evaluation research* in their 1999 text as efforts to place value on events, things, processes, or people. Similarly, in *The Training Evaluation Process*, David Basarab and Darrell Root suggest *program evaluation* is a systematic process by which data are collected and converted into information for measuring the effects of a program, helping in decision making, documenting results to be used in program improvement, and providing a method for determining the quality of a program. These definitions of evaluation have never resonated with professionals of human performance improvement disciplines as clearly as they do today. The past two decades have seen a shift in these disciplines to renew and enhance their focus on results. Today, "show me the money" is the mantra of senior executives and other stakeholders. In order to respond to this cry, learning and performance improvement professionals must ensure that they are providing the data and information stakeholders need to make decisions, including how best to allocate resources.

The most fundamental measure used to allocate resources is either the benefit-cost ratio (BCR) or return on investment percentage (ROI). These metrics have been used for centuries to show the ultimate profitability of a program, process, or initiative. But when used in isolation of other measures of performance, they limit the evaluator's ability to determine the quality of a program or to make recommendations for improving performance.

In response, researchers and practitioners have developed a variety of approaches to show value and improve programs. The ROI Methodology, developed and introduced to the training industry by Jack Phillips in the early 1970s, has become a standard approach to evaluation in many organizations. Because it is systematic in nature, grounded in theory and practice, and driven by a set of conservative standards, the approach develops credible information that describes the value of programs and supports in decision making as it relates to programs and resources. Today, the ROI Methodology is used to measure the success of training programs, performance improvement interventions, human resources programs, meetings and events, marketing campaigns, and quality initiatives. In addition, the process is applied to programs in higher education, government agencies, and the social sector.

Evaluation Frameworks and Processes

A variety of approaches exist to evaluating and showing the contributions of human performance improvement programs. For example, utility analysis—

grounded in economics, finance, and psychology—is finding new applications as organizations seek practical approaches for placing value on their investments in people. While the works of Herbert Brogden, and Lee Cronbach and Goldine Glaser in the 1940s and 1960s remain the basis for much of the current research in utility analysis, Wayne Cascio (2000), Michael Sturman (2003), and John Boudreau and his colleagues (1999), among others, have applied utility analysis to calculate job performance contribution in monetary terms to the cost of programs.

Other valuation methods from economics and finance have also found their place as tools for evaluating human performance improvement programs. Cost-benefit analysis is a classic approach to determining the economic feasibility of programs and initiatives. Based on the theoretical frameworks of welfare economics and public finance, the original intent of cost-benefit analysis was to ensure optimum level of efficiency in allocating resources. Used primarily as a tool to make investment decisions (for example, Do we invest in a park for the community? Do we invest in a parking lot? Do we invest in a new sales person? Do we invest in technology?), the benefit-cost ratio is also reported post-program as a metric reporting success with an investment. The fundamental BCR calculation is:

$$\text{BCR} = \frac{\text{Program Benefits}}{\text{Program Costs}}$$

From accounting and business finance the human performance improvement field gets return on investment (ROI). ROI is the most common measure for value-added benefits. Like its cousin, cost-benefit analysis, ROI compares the monetary benefits of programs to the cost of those programs. Traditionally, ROI focused on a historical look at investment success; however, it is commonly used to forecast the potential return on investing in a program or project. The fundamental ROI calculation is:

$$\text{ROI} = \frac{\text{Net Program Benefits}}{\text{Program Costs}} \times 100$$

Both cost-benefit analysis and ROI provide us with tools to show the ultimate success of investing in programs and projects. It is only by placing benefits and costs in monetary terms that the two can be equally compared. These measures give senior executives and administrators a measure of learning success compara-ble to measures of success used for other investments. No other measures give us an opportunity to compare the contribution of human performance interventions to the contribution of other investments in the same terms. But to ensure a credible explanation of how the economic contribution evolved and that good decisions are made about programs, additional information is needed.

The classic approach to evaluating success with training investments gives us this additional information. In the 1950s Don Kirkpatrick introduced the training industry to four steps (now referred to as four levels) to training evaluation. This logical approach of presenting training results has been used by hundreds of organizations and critiqued and debated by hundreds of researchers. Regardless of one's opinion of Kirkpatrick's four levels, the framework is the most often cited and serves as the basis for other similar works. For instance, as early as 1994 Roger Kaufman and John Keller suggested a five-level framework of evaluation that builds on the earlier work of Don Kirkpatrick.

Other approaches to evaluating interventions focused on human performance improvement include Warr, Bird, and Rackham's 1970 four-level CIRO (context, input, reaction, and outcome) approach to program evaluation. Daniel Stufflebeam's CIPP (context, input, process, and product), first introduced in the 1960s, has also been a staple in education evaluation over the decades. Robert Brinkerhoff's 2003 six-stage evaluation and success case method are well recognized and widely used. Holton's 1996 inquiry into the four-level evaluation model has also made an important contribution to measurement and evaluation within learning and performance improvement programs. Together, these and other researchers have provided a variety of approaches to evaluating learning and performance improvement initiatives.

In the 1970s, Jack Phillips conducted the first ROI study on an educational program. But at the time there was no evidence of ROI's application to training. The program under study was a cooperative education program. To develop his study, Phillips combined the theories of cost-benefit analysis and ROI with Kirkpatrick's four steps to evaluation, along with standards to support replication and credible, usable output. It was at this point that the Phillips five-level framework and ROI Methodology evolved. Today it reaches well beyond the training field into performance improvement, human resources, quality, marketing, meetings and events, volunteer programs, and others. Table 34.1 compares the features of cost-benefit analysis/ROI, Kirkpatrick, and Phillips' ROI process.

Measures Captured at Each Level

The debate regarding the use of the Kirkpatrick/Phillips approach to developing and categorizing evaluation results continues. But the flow of the framework presents a logical approach to decision making as investments are made. Figure 34.1 represents what Phillips and Phillips refer to at the learning value chain, representing a chain of impact that occurs as participants engage in an intervention, react to it, acquire knowledge/skills/information, apply that knowledge, and as a consequence observe improvement in key business measures. By converting the improvement in the measures to money and comparing that monetary benefit to the program costs, stakeholders can easily see whether the benefits of the program outweigh the investment.

As the figure shows, this chain of impact begins with "inputs" or indicators, what Phillips and Phillips refer to as Level 0. These inputs do not represent

Table 34.1 Comparison of CBA/ROI, Kirkpatrick, and Phillips

	Kirkpatrick's Four Levels	Phillips' Five Levels	CBA/ROI
Measure Participant Reaction	✓	✓	
Measure Learning	✓	✓	
Measure Application/Behavior	✓	✓	
Measure Impact/Results/Benefits	✓	✓	✓
Measure ROI		✓	✓
Isolate the Effects of the Program		✓	
Determine Program Costs		✓	✓
Convert Benefits to Monetary Value		✓	✓
Identify Intangible Benefits	✓	✓	✓

results, but are an important part of the measurement mix, as they are a clear indication of the activity and costs involved in delivering and implementing human performance improvement programs. Each level of evaluation (Levels 1 through 5) presents a different type of measure, ensuring data important to all stakeholders are developed through the evaluation process.

Uses of Data Generated by the ROI Methodology

The concern many researchers have with the concept of these levels revolves around the utility (or lack thereof) of the various measures taken at each level. Warr, Allan, and Birdi's 1999 article for the *Journal of Occupational and Organizational Psychology* addressed this issue by testing the relationships among various levels. While an association among measures was not necessarily the intent of the original four levels, receipt of useful information at each level is an imperative.

Evaluation without use leads to another activity with which the human performance improvement professional is burdened. Evaluation that provides useful information, however, gives the human performance improvement professional a process by which change and decisions can be made. Table 34.2 presents some uses of data at each level. It is important to note that the uses presented represent only a sample and they are dependent on the measures taken and analysis conducted with those measures.

Each level of evaluation has an important role in ensuring human performance improvement programs achieve their objectives, show value, and improve

Level	Measurement Focus	Typical Measures
0. Inputs and Indicators	Inputs into the program including indicators representing scope, volumes, costs, and efficiencies	Types of Topics, Content Number of Programs Number of People Hours of Involvement Costs
1. Reaction and Planned Action	Reaction to the program including the perceived value of the project	Relevance Importance Usefulness Appropriateness Intent to Use Motivational
2. Learning	Learning how to use the content and materials, including the confidence to use what was learned	Skills Knowledge Capacity Competencies Confidence Contacts
3. Application and Implementation	Use of content and materials in the work environment, including progress with implementation	Extent of Use Task Completion Frequency of Use Job Contribution Actions Completed Success with Use Barriers to Use Enablers to Use
4. Business Impact	The consequences of the use of the content and materials expressed as business impact measures	Productivity Revenue Quality Time Efficiency Customer Satisfaction Employee Engagement
5. ROI	Comparison of monetary benefits from the program to program costs	Benefit/Cost Ratio (BCR) ROI (%) Payback Period

Figure 34.1 The Learning Value Chain.

Adapted from P. P. Phillips and J. J. Phillips. (2007) *The Value of Learning: How Organizations Capture Value and ROI.* San Francisco: Pfeiffer, p. 17.

Table 34.2 Uses of Evaluation Data at Each Level.

Level of Evaluation	Potentials Use of Data
Level 1: Reaction and Planned Action	Improve program delivery and design
	Change learning environment
	Develop facilitators and project managers
	Improve participant selection process
	Predict, explain, and improve learning outcomes
	Predict, explain, and improve application outcomes
	Forecast ROI
Level 2: Learning	Identify subject-matter masters versus non-masters
	Determine knowledge change
	Select job candidates
	Change program delivery and design
	Predict, explain, and improve application outcomes
	Forecast ROI
Level 3: Application and Implementation	Improve program delivery and design
	Change learning transfer strategy
	Build relationships with participant supervisors/ managers
	Alter processes inhibiting learning transfer
	Improve alignment between program and business measures
	Predict, explain, and improve business impact results
	Forecast ROI
Level 4: Business Impact	Show contribution of program to the business
	Explain linkage between program and business results
	Build relationships with participant supervisors/ managers
	Build relationships with other stakeholders in the performance improvement process
	Explain ROI results

(*Continued*)

Table 34.2 (*Continued*)

Level of Evaluation	Potentials Use of Data
Level 5: ROI	Show contribution of program to the business
	Compare program benefits versus program costs
	Compare results with other investments
	Allocate resources based on contribution
	Predict future program contribution

over time. The data developed at each level also provide the program owner valuable information that will help them and other stakeholders make decisions about programs. The ultimate measure of program success, ROI (Level 5), provides stakeholders a common metric by which they can determine the contribution of human performance interventions and compare the contribution of one intervention to that of another. But to report this one simple metric in isolation of the other measures would represent an incomplete story. Hence, the acceptance and use of the ROI Methodology by human performance improvement professionals in their effort to report program results, including ROI.

WHEN TO APPLY

The ROI Methodology generates data categorized along the five-level framework described in the previous section. While the process and standards are applicable regardless of to which level of evaluation you intend to use to evaluate a program, and any program can be evaluated up to and including ROI, there are some considerations to keep in mind when deciding which programs should be evaluated all the way through ROI (Level 5).

1. *Need for the evaluation.* If a program or project is being evaluated to understand how well a facilitator is performing based on feedback from his or her performance coach, Level 1 evaluation will suffice. However, if an evaluation is conducted to understand the extent to which the initiative is contributing to business performance and the results should exceed the cost of the initiative, then the evaluation should go to Level 5—ROI.

2. *Need for the program.* The need for the program is one of the strongest drivers of the evaluation. Program objectives serve as the basis for the evaluation. Program objectives should therefore represent the requirement for the program and the program should be designed around those required results. If these elements are in place, the level to which an evaluation is conducted is evident.

3. *Program profile.* Programs evaluated to Level 4 (business impact) and Level 5 (ROI) are usually large, expensive, strategically focused programs and initiatives. Such programs may be an executive development program intended to provide leaders an opportunity to enhance their leadership skills, or a change initiative designed to centralize operations to improve efficiencies, or the implementation of a new technology, or a sales training designed to increase sales to new customers. Programs evaluated at Levels 1 and 2 are often low-cost or they are frequently compliance programs that must be deployed regardless of their cost or their impact. Although organizations can evaluate compliance programs to Levels 4 and 5, and some do, this is typically limited to cases in which non-compliance has been a costly issue.

4. *Stakeholder requirements.* Executives, senior managers, and front-line supervisors have their reasons for asking for data and information. Routinely, these stakeholders make decisions about programs and the resources to be allocated to those programs. Therefore, they require information to make useful and justifiable decisions. If the information is unavailable, they will either make the decision anyway, or ask for it. This need for data often influences the level to which an organization evaluates programs or projects.

In a study we conducted in 2003 with public sector organizations, respondents identified nine criteria—in order of importance—that determine whether or not they would evaluate a program to Levels 4 and 5. While the criteria may be ranked differently, the same criteria are used to select programs for Level 4 and 5 evaluation in private-sector and non-profit organizations.

Rank 1. Important to strategic objectives

Rank 2. Links to operational goals and issues

Rank 3. Expensive program

Rank 4. Comprehensive needs assessment conducted

Rank 5. Top executive interest

Rank 6. High visibility

Rank 7. Significant investment in time

Rank 8. Involves large target audiences

Rank 9. Expected to have a long life-cycle

Research describes a variety of approaches to evaluating human performance improvement interventions. Kirkpatrick's four-level framework serves as the basis for many of these approaches. The missing elements of Kirkpatrick's four-level framework were the cost-benefit comparison, a process model, and standards to ensure replication and usability of data. Jack Phillips built upon Kirkpatrick's work to develop the ROI Methodology. This process provides data important to all stakeholders, including the ultimate measure of success, ROI. Combined, the data generated through the ROI process tells the complete story of program success and provides an opportunity to improve programs based on results. While conducting an ROI study is doable for all types of programs, evaluation up to ROI (Level 5) typically reserved for the 5 to 10 percent of the programs targeting strategic business needs.

STRENGTHS AND CRITICISMS

Some strengths and criticisms of the methodology include:

Strengths

- ROI Methodology generates six types of data categorized along the five-level framework to provide a balanced approach to measurement and results.
- ROI Methodology follows a step-by-step process model, including a step to isolate the effects of the program, ensuring consistent and credible results.
- ROI Methodology is guided by standards, or twelve guiding principles, to ensure reliability in application.
- ROI Methodology has a wide application of use as demonstrated by over one hundred published case studies and many more unpublished case studies.
- ROI Methodology, when implemented to its fullest, can create a sustainable evaluation practice, aligning programs, projects, and initiatives to the business for as little as 3 to 5 percent of a learning or performance improvement function's budget.

Criticisms

- ROI Methodology can be a resource-consuming approach to evaluation when implementation is not planned appropriately.
- Data generated through the ROI Methodology can be misused if not appropriately presented.
- Too much focus can be placed on the single ROI metric, rather than the complete results.
- ROI Methodology requires skills that learning and performance improvement professionals may not be comfortable applying.
- ROI Methodology is sometimes viewed as a job performance review tool rather than a program or process improvement tool.

RECOMMENDED DESIGN, DEVELOPMENT, AND IMPLEMENTATION PROCESS

The ROI process follows ten steps that occur in four phases: evaluation planning, data collection, data analysis, and reporting. Figure 34.2 presents the ten-step process model.

Evaluation Planning

1. If they do not already exist, develop program objectives at each level of evaluation. Use the needs assessment data that originally justified the development of the program as a basis for documenting objectives. Objectives should reflect the results requirements of stakeholders, beginning with the highest level of need. Specific objectives serve as the basis for the evaluation, describing what will be measured and defining success of the measurement. Objectives should be identified at each of the five evaluation levels (see our 2008 book *Beyond Learning Objectives*).

2. Plan your evaluation and gather baseline data. Planning is one of the most important steps in evaluation. Deciding how you plan to collect data, analyze data, and to whom to report data at the outset sets the stage for successful implementation. Gathering baseline performance data for program objectives during the planning stage prevents you from having to do so later. When baseline data are unavailable, the evaluation can still take place, but the research question changes from "What change in performance in the measures occurs before, during, and after the program?" to "What is the performance in the measures during and after the program?" or, if the program is already complete, then "What is the performance in the measures after the program?"

Data Collection

3. Collect Levels 1 and 2 data during program implementation. These data, while they can be collected post-program, are important early in the implementation process because with these data immediate changes to the program can be made to perpetuate a successful, sustainable application. You can collect these data with surveys, questionnaires, tests, performance assessments, and other routinely applied evaluation instruments.

4. Collect Levels 3 and 4 data after program implementation. Change in behavior and resulting impact on the business occurs after the knowledge, skills, and/or information presented during a program are applied routinely. A variety of tools are available to capture these data. Surveys and questionnaires (see Chapter Thirty-Three) are probably the most

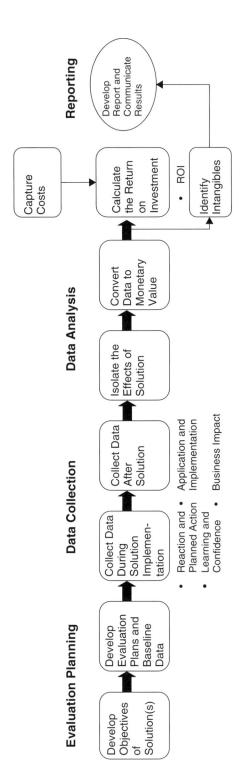

Evaluation Planning

Develop Objectives of Solution(s)

Develop Evaluation Plans and Baseline Data

Data Collection

Collect Data During Solution Implementation
- Reaction and Planned Action
- Learning and Confidence

Collect Data After Solution
- Application and Implementation
- Business Impact

Data Analysis

Isolate the Effects of Solution

Convert Data to Monetary Value

Capture Costs

Calculate the Return on Investment
- ROI

Identify Intangibles

Reporting

Develop Report and Communicate Results

Figure 34.2 The ROI Methodology Process Model.

© 2008 ROI Institute, Inc. Used with permission

popular because they are inexpensive and easy to administer. But for initiatives such as executive coaching (see Chapter Twenty-Seven), an action plan may be more appropriate. Likewise, feedback on behavior using a 360-degree feedback instrument are ideal for some performance interventions but not others (see Chapter Nine). Also, don't forget case studies, interviews, and focus groups (see Chapter Thirty-Three) as potential performance measures. Level 4 data can be captured with some of the same tools as Level 3 data, as well as other performance records where the business measures (see Chapter Ten) are routinely housed (such as annual reports or quarterly profit and loss reports).

Data Analysis

5. If you want to report valid results, the first required step is to isolate the effects of your program. Multiple factors can influence improvement in business measures, so it is important to report only the contribution of the program being evaluated. There are a variety of techniques to help you do this. Credible and proven methods for doing this are based on decades of work for organizations employing the ROI Methodology. As Phillips and Aaron suggest in their book *Isolation of Results: Defining the Impact of the Program*, while a control group method is the ideal from a scientific standpoint, it is also often the least feasible for certain programs and organizations. Other options are available including trend line analysis and forecasting methods.

   On occasion, conditions, time, and resources do not allow for such analysis. A fall-back technique is an estimation process, whereby the estimates are gathered from the most credible source(s) and adjusted for error. Estimating your program's contribution is not a technique you will want to use all of the time—preferably you should use a more robust approach whenever possible. But when the die is cast and someone asks "How do you know your program contributed to the results?" estimations can help you get to the answer.

6. If you want to report ROI, you first must convert your Level 4 business impact measures to monetary values. Techniques to convert measures to money are vast. Very likely, there are standard values available in your organization for some measures. If not, other techniques include historical costs, experts within and outside your organization, databases galore, statistical models, and there is always the estimation process (see Chapter Ten). According to Phillips and Burkett, there are two considerations when you are trying to convert a measure to money: "Can you do it with minimum resources?" and "Will the stakeholder(s) perceive the value as credible?" If the answer to either question is no, report the improvement in the Level 4 business impact measure as intangible.

7. Identify the intangible benefits of the program. Intangible benefits are those Level 4 business impact measures we choose not to convert to monetary values. These are derived through the evaluation process, but we choose not to include them in the ROI calculation. This does not mean they are more or less important than the ROI; rather, by reporting them we complete the story of program success.

8. Tabulate the program costs—all of them. The cost of your program or process is more than the contract amount you agreed to pay the consultant; it's more than the budget line item for that program. Fully loaded costs are included in the ROI denominator. Cost categories include analysis, design, development, implementation, and evaluation. For example, the analysis costs would include design and development of data collection instruments, time to collect and analyze data, and time of respondents to provide data. Delivery costs would include materials, facilities, participant time involved, facilitator time involved, and travel and lodging, among other costs. Jack Phillips and Lizette Zuñiga, in their book *Costs and ROI*, provide details as to the costs to include when calculating ROI.

9. Calculate the ROI. Use of the ROI Methodology generates multiple types of data. The ultimate measure of program and process success, ROI puts into one metric all the profit, cost savings, and cost avoidances gained by a program. Then by comparing those gains to the cost of the program, you can immediately see from an economic perspective how well you did. The formulae are simple: For the benefit-cost ratio, take your program benefits and divide by cost. For the ROI, take your net program benefits and divide by costs, then multiply by 100.

Reporting

10. Communicate the results of your ROI study. Evaluation without communication is a worthless endeavor. However, when results are communicated properly, evaluation can prove to be a powerful influence. There are four primary audiences to whom ROI results should be communicated: participants, participants' supervisors, your team, and the client. The final detailed report should serve as your record and as evidence to the stakeholders that you followed a credible process. It will also serve you well if you evaluate a similar program in the future. Other tools to communicate results include websites, blogs, newsletters, meetings, conferences, and networking events.

This methodology is guided by twelve guiding principles or standards that ensure consistent application. Table 34.3 presents the standards and what they mean.

Table 34.3 ROI Methodology: Twelve Guiding Principles.

Guiding Principle	Meaning
1. When a higher level of evaluation is conducted, data must be collected at lower levels.	Tell the complete story of program success.
2. When an evaluation is planned for a higher level, the previous level of evaluation does not have to be comprehensive.	Conserve resources for the higher level of evaluations.
3. When collecting and analyzing data, use only the most credible sources.	Keep it credible.
4. When analyzing data, choose the most conservative alternative for calculations.	Keep it conservative.
5. At least one method must be used to isolate the effects of the solution.	Give credit where credit is due.
6. If no improvement data are available for a population or from a specific source, it is assumed that little or no improvement has occurred.	Make no assumptions for non-respondents.
7. Estimates of improvements should be adjusted for the potential error of the estimate.	Adjust for error in estimates.
8. Extreme data items and unsupported claims should not be used in ROI calculations.	Omit the extremes.
9. Only the first year of benefits (annual) should be used in the ROI analysis for short-term solutions.	Report first year benefits only.
10. Costs of the solution should be fully loaded for ROI analysis.	Account for all costs.
11. Intangible measures are defined as measures that are purposely not converted to monetary values.	Report intangible benefits.
12. The results from the ROI Methodology must be communicated to all key stakeholders	Communicate and use your evaluation data.

CRITICAL SUCCESS FACTORS

The ROI Methodology is a widely accepted approach to measuring and reporting success of any type of HPT initiative. To make it work in your organization, consider the following critical success factors.

Methodological

- Follow the twelve guiding principles. These standards were developed to ensure credibility by keeping assumptions conservative.

- Begin thinking evaluation and ROI before launching the program or process. Clarify program needs beginning with the highest level of needs. Develop program objectives at each level of evaluation reflecting those needs.

- Plan your evaluation. Complete the data collection plan, ROI analysis plan, and project plan.

Cultural

- Assess your organization's readiness for ROI. Some organizations do not have pressure to show value for programs and processes. If you fit this description, then don't worry about ROI. But if your organization has experienced failed programs, if senior management is concerned about resource allocation, if you have a large budget and a lot of programs, or if you just want to be accountable for the funds you're asked to manage, then you may be ready for ROI.

- Select data collection and data analysis techniques that work for you. Some organizations are e-based through and through. If this is the case, electronic survey instruments may be a good tool for collecting data. Other organizations forbid that another survey instrument be administered. If this is the case, use data collection tools such as focus groups and interviews. If your organization will not allow you to offer a program to one group and purposefully withhold it from another group, then you know you can't use control groups as a technique for isolation, so look to other techniques. The point is to consider your culture and use the tools that work for your culture. There is no one best way to collect and analyze data. You must look at the program, your resources, and the culture in which you work. The ROI process described in this chapter gives you that flexibility.

Social

- Educate others in the ROI Methodology. There is still a great deal of misunderstanding about the ROI Methodology. By educating others through workshops, presentations, and briefings, the application of the methodology will go much smoother and others will see how the approach fits into the organization and how data will be used. One of the biggest fears of ROI is that the results will describe performance of individuals. That is not the intent—it is all about program and process improvement. Once people understand what it is and why it is important, the acceptance of ROI grows.

- Educate potential respondents on the evaluation process. A big mistake that is often made in collecting data is administering a questionnaire to unsuspecting respondents. Tell participants of a program or project that the evaluation is going to take place, how it is going to take place, and what questions they will be asked to answer. You will not only get better responses, but more of them!

Political

- Identify an ROI champion. This is a person to whom you will look for guidance on the process as well as guidance through the organizational scrutiny. Identify someone who is an advocate and supporter of learning and performance improvement initiatives, but also has the political clout to help you get the funding and audience to begin pursuing the ROI Methodology.

- Build relationships and support from front-line supervisors. Front-line supervisors, those supervisors of participants of your programs and processes, can be your worst enemy and your greatest ally. You need them to not only support your programs, but also to support your evaluation process. They will be a source of data for you in some circumstances. The more they are engaged in the evaluation process, the more they will learn about the learning and performance improvement process.

Economic

- Balance accuracy and cost. Manage the investment in evaluation. You never want to spend more on evaluation than on the program itself. An ROI study should only cost you 5 to 10 percent of the total program cost. Guiding principle 2 of our ROI standards tell us that when you evaluate to the higher levels, you don't have to be comprehensive at the lower levels. The higher levels of evaluation provide more important data to the client. So spend the resources on reporting results that resonate with the client. This does not mean skipping the lower levels; those data are important too. But it does mean using your resources wisely.

- Use shortcuts at the higher levels of evaluation. When evaluating programs, you need the best data given your time and resource constraints. Sometimes estimates are the way to go. As mathematicians Derrick Niederman and David Boyum say in their book *What the Numbers Say*, "Educated guessing will sometimes be a more efficient use of your time than painstaking research." Be able to explain why you take the steps you take so you can put the results into context.

Legal

- Use the ROI Methodology as a process improvement tool, not a job performance assessment tool.

Technical

- Build capacity. There are a variety of skills required for successful evaluation with which a learning and performance improvement professional may not be comfortable. This does not mean you should run out and take an online statistics course. But it does mean that, in order to sustain the ROI process as the basis for your evaluation practice, you need to either have or know where to acquire the knowledge, skills, and information necessary to support successful application. A variety of sources are available to you, many of which are represented in this book.

- Utilize software tools. The good news about the ROI Methodology is that there are many software tools to help you get started. In the Notes section, you will see tools available to help you implement the ROI Methodology.

SUMMARY

ROI is an important metric when measuring HPT success. Comparing program benefits to costs is an imperative, particularly for expensive, strategically positioned programs. While it is the ultimate measure of program success, it is important to report ROI in the context of other measures of performance. Evaluation is about improving processes as well as reporting value. Thus, it is important to report results relevant to all stakeholders, thereby influencing their decision-making process with regard to the program or project.

Notes

- A variety of case studies describing the application of the ROI Methodology have been published in case books offered through ASTD, SHRM, Pfeiffer, Berrett-Koehler, and the ROI Institute. A list of these publications can be found at http://www.roiinstitute.net/publications/books/.

- For an interesting application of utility analysis on human resource interventions see Michael Sturman's 2003 examination of the method within the hospitality industry.

- A simple explanation of cost-benefit analysis can be found at http://management.about.com/cs/money/a/CostBenefit.htm.

- There are a variety of myths about the use of ROI in measuring human performance improvement success. For information that dispels many of these myths, see Patti

Phillips' *ROI in Performance Improvement: Myth Versus Reality*, located at http://knol.google.com/k/patti-phillips-phd/roi-in-performance-improvement-myth/ftwrrl7ik2kk/2#.

- The uses of evaluation data generated at each level of evaluation are only as good as the questions asked, how they are asked, and how they are analyzed. First and foremost, the right questions must be asked the right way. There are a variety of resources available to help human performance improvement professionals write the appropriate questions at each level. To begin your understanding of what questions to ask at each level see Phillips and Phillips (2007a, 2007b), Phillips and Phillips (2008), as well as KnowledgeAdvisors at http://www.knowledgeadvisors.com. To begin developing skill in writing questions right, see Fink (2002), Devellis (2003), and Fowler (1995).

- Historically, programs and processes targeting human performance improvement were developed with learning outcomes and occasionally behavioral outcomes in mind. To ensure a program or process is designed to drive business measures to the point that the monetary value of improvement in those measures exceed the costs, objectives should be developed at all levels of the evaluation. For additional information on developing objectives at Levels 1, 2, 3, 4, and 5, see Phillips and Phillips (2008).

- A variety of case studies may be downloaded at http://www.roiinstitute.net/tools, including *Nation's Hotel: Measuring ROI in Business Coaching* (how actions plans have been used to capture Level 4 data), *Retail Merchandise* (how control group arrangement was used to isolate the effects of sales training), and *Healthcare, Inc.* (how trend line analysis was used to isolate the effects of a sexual harassment prevention program).

- Samples of planning documents can be found at http://www.roiinstitute.net/tools/.

- The single step most often ignored in evaluating programs is the isolation step. Some researchers tend to ignore it when a control group arrangement is inappropriate. The unfortunate thing is that, when this step is ignored, you can't answer the fundamental question "How do you know it was your program that caused the results you are reporting?" There is no absolute answer to this question, but there are processes available that will allow you to take the most conservative approach to answering it. For more on isolating the effects of a program to results see Phillips and Aaron, 2008.

- Converting data to money is easier than you might think. To learn more, including the five steps to convert a measure to money, see Phillips and Burkett, 2008.

- A cost summary profile is available at http://www.roiinstitute.net/tools/. Download this tool and start developing cost profiles for your programs.

- To assess your organization's reading for ROI, download a simple survey found at http://www.roiinstitute.net/tools/.

- For a good, easy reference to statistics, see the *Electronic Statistics Textbook* at http://www.statsoft.com/textbook.

- A variety of software tools are available to support application of the ROI Methodology in learning and performance improvement. See Knowledge-Advisors and Gaelstorm.

- For other tools that support the ROI Methodology targeting large meetings and events, you may use to launch initiatives or recognize employees, see Meetings Metrics and iDNA.

References

Anthony, R. N., & Reece, J. S. (1983). *Accounting text and cases*. New York: Irwin.

Basarab, D. J., & Root, D. K. (1992). *The training evaluation process*. Boston: Kluwer Academic Publishers.

Brinkerhoff, R. O. (2003). *The success case method: Finding out quickly what's working and what's not*. San Francisco: Berrett-Koehler.

Brinkerhoff, R. O., & Apking, A. M. (2001). *High-impact learning*. San Francisco: Berrett-Koehler.

Brinkerhoff, R. O., & Dressler, D. (2002, July). Using evaluation to build organizational performance and learning capability: A strategy and a method. *Performance Improvement*. *41*(6), 14–21.

Brogden, H. E. (1949). When testing pays off. *Personnel Psychology, 2*, 171–183.

Boudreau, J. W., Sturman, M. C., Trevor, C. O., & Gerhart, B. (1999). The value of performance-based pay in the war for talent. Center for Advanced Human Resource Studies Working Paper #99-06, School of Industrial and Labor Relations: Cornell University.

Cascio, W. F. (2000). *Costing human resources: The financial impact of behavior in organizations* (4th ed.). Cincinnati, OH: South-Western College Publishing.

Cronbach, L. J., & Glaser, G. C. (1965). *Psychological tests and personnel decisions* (2nd ed.). Urbana, IL: University of Illinois Press.

Fink, A. (2002). *The survey kit* (2nd ed.). Thousand Oaks. CA: Sage.

Fowler, F. J. (1995). Improving survey questions: Design and evaluation. *Applied Social Research Methods Series, 38.*

Gaelstorm. http://gaelstorm.com/. Retrieved June 2008.

Hammonds, K. H. (2007, December 19). Why we hate HR. *Fast Company.*

Holton, E. F. (1996). The flawed four-level evaluation model. *Human Resource Development Quarterly, 7*, 5–21.

Horngren, C. T. (1982). *Cost accounting*. Upper Saddle River, NJ: Prentice Hall.

iDNA. http://www.idnausa.com/approach/measurable_results.php. Retrieved June 2008.

Kaufman, R., & Keller, J. M. (1994, Winter). Levels of evaluation: Beyond Kirkpatrick. *HRD Quarterly, 5*(4), 371–380.

Kearsley, G. (1982). *Costs, benefits, & productivity in training systems*. Reading, MA: Addison-Wesley.

Kirkpatrick, D. L. (1975). Techniques for evaluating training programs. In D. L. Kirkpatrick (Ed.), *Evaluating training programs* (pp. 1–17). Alexandria, VA: ASTD.

Kirkpatrick, D. L. (1994). *Evaluating training programs: The four levels*. San Francisco: Berrett-Koehler.

KnowledgeAdvisors. http://www.knowledgeadvisors.com/.

Meetings Metrics. http://www.meetingmetrics.com/. Retrieved June 2008.

Mishan, E. J. (1960, June). A survey of welfare economics, 1939-59. *The Economic Journal, 70*(278), 197–265.

Musgrave, R. A. (1969, September). Cost-benefit analysis and the theory of public finance. *Journal of Economic Literature, 7*(3), 797–806.

Nas, T. F. (1996). *Cost-benefit analysis*. Thousand Oaks, CA: Sage.

Niederman, D., & Boyum, D. (2003). *What the numbers say: A field guide to mastering our numerical world*. New York: Broadway Books.

Phillips, J. J. (1995, Summer). Corporate training: Does it pay off? *William & Mary Business Review*, pp. 6–10.

Phillips, J. J. (1997). *Handbook of training evaluation and measurement methods* (3rd ed.). Boston: Butterworth Heinemann.

Phillips, J. J., & Aaron, B. C. (2008). Isolation of results: Defining the impact of the program. In P. P. Phillips & J. J. Phillips (Eds.), *Measurement and evaluation series*. San Francisco: Pfeiffer.

Phillips, J. J., & Phillips, P. P. (2007). *Show me the money*. San Francisco: Berrett-Koehler.

Phillips, J. J., & Phillips, P. P. (2008). *Beyond learning objectives: Develop measurable objectives that link to the bottom line*. Alexandria, VA: ASTD.

Phillips, P. P. (2003). Training evaluation in the public sector. Doctoral dissertation. The University of Southern Mississippi, Hattiesburg. International Development.

Phillips, P. P., & Burkett, H. (2008). Data conversion: Calculating the monetary benefits. In P. P. Phillips & J. J. Phillips (Eds.), *Measurement and evaluation series*. San Francisco: Pfeiffer.

Phillips, P. P., & Phillips, J. J. (2007). *The value of learning*. San Francisco: Pfeiffer.

Phillips, P. P., & Zuñiga, L. (2008). Costs and ROI. In P. P. Phillips & J. J. Phillips (Eds.), *Measurement and evaluation series*. San Francisco: Pfeiffer.

Rossi, P. H., Freeman, H. E., & Lipsey, M. W. (1999). *Evaluation: A systematic approach* (6th ed.). Thousand Oaks, CA: Sage.

Schneider, C. (2006, February 16). The new human-capital metrics: A sophisticated crop of measurement tools could take the guesswork out of human resources management. *CFO Magazine*.

Sibbett, D. (1997). *Harvard Business Review*, 75 years of management ideas and practices 1922–1977. *Harvard Business Review*.

Stufflebeam, D. (1983). The CIPP model for program evaluation. In G. Madeus, M. Scriven, & D. Stufflebeam (Eds.), *Evaluation models: Viewpoints on educational and human service evaluation* (pp. 117–142). Boston: Klewer Nijhoff.

Sturman, M. C. (2003, April). Utility analysis: A tool for quantifying the value of hospitality human resource interventions; utility analysis can be used to assess the effectiveness of human resource interventions (among other uses). http://www .allbusiness.com/accommodation-food-services/546109-1.html. Retrieved August 2008.

Swanson, R. A., & Holton, E. F. (1999). *Results: How to assess performance, learning and perceptions in organizations*. San Francisco: Berrett-Koehler.

Warr, P., Allan, C., & Birdi, K. (1999). Prediction: Three levels of training outcome. *Journal of Occupational and Organizational Psychology, 72*, 351–375.

Warr, P. B., Bird, M., & Rackham, N. (1970) *Evaluation of management training*. London: Gower Press.

Recommended Readings

DeVellis, R. F. (1999). Scale development: Theory and applications (2nd ed.). In *Applied Social Research Methods Series, 26*. Thousand Oaks, CA: Sage.

Phillips, J. J., & Phillips, P. P. (2008). *Beyond learning objectives*. Alexandria, VA: ASTD.

Phillips, J. J., & Phillips, P. P. (2008). *ROI in action*. San Francisco: Pfeiffer.

Taleb, N. N. (2007). *The black swan: The impact of the highly improbable*. New York: Random House.

Whyte, J. (2004). *Crimes against logic: Exposing the bogus arguments of politicians, priests, journalists, and other serial offenders*. New York: McGraw-Hill.

PART TWELVE

EDITORS' DISCUSSION

Measuring the accomplishment of significant results cannot be an after-thought when improving performance. From the first conversations, you should focus all decisions and performance interventions on the achievement of meaningful performance that aligns all that your organization uses, does, produces, and delivers with the accomplishment of results for clients and society. If the alignment of these results guides all of your decisions, linking the strategic objectives of your organization with the performance interventions that you implement, then the likelihood of achieving desired results is much greater.

Expanding Your Options

Balanced scorecards—used in strategic management to identify, monitor, and improve various internal functions and their resulting external results. Balanced scorecards measure performance and assist in accomplishing results through performance feedback. Scorecards generally identify measures related to (1) learning and growth, (2) business processes, (3) customers, and (4) finance.

Based on answers.com definition (January 2009)

ROI analysis provides a vital tool for assessing results. As with any analysis procedure, ROI analysis can grow out of control through complex calculations and differing perspectives regarding the attribution of results within performance interventions. Nonetheless, ROI analysis can also be done in pragmatic ways that inform future decisions without debilitating the process through "analysis paralysis." Use ROI analysis when it makes sense: when the results of the analysis will be used to guide future decisions on improving performance. In the same way, manage the scope of your ROI analysis to ensure that you are not using a $1,000 analysis to measure the impact of a $10 performance intervention.

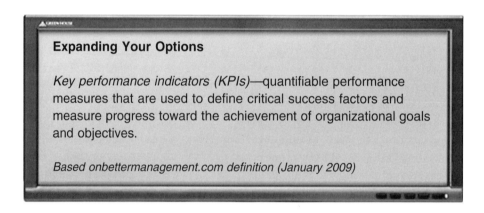

Expanding Your Options

Key performance indicators (KPIs)—quantifiable performance measures that are used to define critical success factors and measure progress toward the achievement of organizational goals and objectives.

Based onbettermanagement.com definition (January 2009)

Likewise, ROI analysis is not the only performance intervention that you can use to measure significant accomplishments. Many of the data collection and needs assessment techniques described in Chapters Thirty-Two and Thirty-Three can also provide valuable information regarding the achievements of individual improvement interventions, and systemic performance improvement initiatives. Impact evaluations, cost-effectiveness analysis, and cost-consequences analysis are also useful performance interventions for measuring success. All of these approaches focus on measuring results and providing information that can guide your future decisions.

References and Resources from Editorial Contributions to Part Twelve

Kaufman, R. (2006). *Change, choices, and consequences: A guide to mega thinking and planning.* Amherst, MA: HRD Press.

Kaufman, R., Oakley-Brown, H., Watkins, R., & Leigh, D. (2003). *Strategic planning for success: Aligning people, performance, and payoffs.* San Francisco: Jossey-Bass.

Kaufman, R., Watkins, R., & Sims, L. (1997). Cost-consequences analysis: A case study. *Performance Improvement Quarterly, 10*(2), 7–21.

Watkins, R. (2007). *Performance by design: The systematic selection, design, and development of performance technologies that produce useful results.* Amherst, MA: HRD Press.

Watkins, R., Leigh, D., Foshay, R., & Kaufman, R. (1998). Kirkpatrick plus: Evaluation and continuous improvement with a community focus. *Educational Technology Research and Development, 46*(4), 90–96.

EDITORS' EPILOGUE

From the manufacture of plastic injection mold die to the preparation of financial reports, the results produced by individuals, teams, and organizations are the essential ingredients of society. Financial, social, technological, political, legal, manufacturing, and numerous other institutions all rely on integrated systems of performance. The results produced by one person act as inputs to the work of another; likewise, the deliverables of one organization contribute to the achievements of many other organizations. Consequently, performance—the accomplishment of valued results—is the foundation of all organizational activities. Organizations must achieve results that add value to the society in which they exist, just as individual employees must achieve results that add value to the organizations in which they work.

Improving performance that is improving the accomplishment of results, thereby becoming a vital activity within all organizations. Numerous performance interventions can be used to achieve desired results. Efforts to improve performance, nevertheless, must focus on the achievement of results rather than on the processes, procedures, tools, techniques, or interventions that can be used to achieve results. While it is often tempting to quickly identify solutions to performance problems, these rapid decisions about what to do—without a strong grounding in what results must be achieved—frequently lead to disappointment and even disaster.

Deciding what results should be accomplished is not always an easy task. After all, within complex systems there are typically multiple perspectives—leading to questions of which results should be accomplished and how they should be prioritized. In response, we have used Roger Kaufman's Organizational Elements

Model throughout this handbook as a guide for differentiating and aligning results. The model distinguishes three types of results (societal outcomes, organizational output, and individual/team products), but it does not presume that any one type is more important than another. Within a system it is the *alignment* of results that is essential to success. Thus the model provides a framework for aligning all that your organization uses, does, produces, and delivers with valuable outcomes for your external societal partners.

Multiple performance interventions can, and should, then be assessed, compared, and contrasted based on their ability to improve results at one or more of the three levels—thus contributing to the success of the whole system. Alignment from the results to be accomplished to the improvement activities that are available is vital to the successful improvement of performance. In spite of this, training interventions have historically been the solution for most performance issues—whether the issue is the introduction of new software applications or the declining productivity of sales staff. Training interventions—like any other single solution—rarely achieve the significant and sustainable improvement in results. Systems of improvement activities, from training and mentoring to performance aids and job crafting, are typically required to improve the achievement of individual, team, or organizational results.

Throughout this handbook, therefore, we have emphasized the importance of first defining the results to be accomplished before selecting the interventions to achieve those results. Connected this with the fundamental perspective that systems of integrated performance interventions are necessary to achieve sustainable improvements in performance. We have used Wedman's Performance Pyramid model to provide a theoretical and visual structure for how practical improvements can be made in your organization. The Performance Pyramid illustrates the important linkages between the results to be accomplished and the interventions we can use to achieve them, as well as the interdependent relationships that exist between the foundational components of a performance system.

Although it could be tempting to assume that the pyramid model imposes a hierarchy among performance interventions (for example, Knowledge and Skill interventions versus Expectations and Feedback interventions), this is not the case. The components within the model could actually be redistributed in many different ways; with Incentives, Rewards, and Recognition being at the top in some instances and Motivation and Self-Concept at the top in others. As a heuristic, the pyramid suggests that you must build a foundation of improvement activities that address many aspects of performance in order to accomplish significant results. Thus, you ought not simply choose performance interventions from the various chapters within this handbook; rather you should build a comprehensive and coordinated set of improvement activities that address the complete performance system.

In the Introduction to this volume, we presented the following four goals for this handbook:

Goal 1: The handbook should expand your perceptions of the possibilities; helping you find numerous performance interventions can be used to improve performance.

Goal 2: The handbook should embrace performance improvement as a pragmatic science that seeks to accomplish valuable results for individuals, teams, organizations, and all of society through evidence-based practice.

Goal 3: The handbook should represent an interdisciplinary approach to improving performance, drawing on fields and disciplines that are not typically represented adequately in literature or practice.

Goal 4: The handbook should be a user-friendly guide that practitioners, students, researchers, and others can all use, regardless of their experience or academic training.

Thanks to our talented contributing authors, who artfully crafted chapters that are both research-based and yet very practical, we believe that the *Handbook of Improving Performance in the Workplace, Volume Two: Selecting and Implementing Performance Interventions* provides a broad perspective on how many different performance interventions can be used to accomplishment significant results. The interventions included in chapters of this handbook, as well as those mentioned in the Expanding Your Options features, represent improvement activities from many different disciplines—from management and organization development to human resources and instructional design. In the end, we believe that we have achieved our goals and created a handbook that you will find useful in improving performance and accomplishing significant results that contribute to your organization and society. We hope that you agree.

References and Resources from Editors' Epilogue

Kaufman, R. (2006). *Change, choices, and consequences: A guide to mega thinking and planning.* Amherst, MA: HRD Press.

Kaufman, R. (2006). *30 seconds that can change your life: A decision-making guide for those who refuse to be mediocre.* Amherst, MA: HRD Press.

Kaufman, R., Oakley-Brown, H., Watkins, R., & Leigh, D. (2003). *Strategic planning for success: Aligning people, performance, and payoffs.* San Francisco: Jossey-Bass.

Watkins, R. (2007). *Performance by design: The systematic selection, design, and development of performance technologies that produce useful results.* Amherst, MA: HRD Press.

Watkins, R., & Wedman, J. (2003). A process for aligning performance improvement resources and strategies. *Performance Improvement Journal, 42*(7), 9–17.

Wedman, J., & Graham, S. W. (1998, Fall). The performance pyramid. *The Journal of Continuing Higher Education, 46*(3), 8–20.

ABOUT THE EDITORS

Ryan Watkins, Ph.D,. is an associate professor at the George Washington University in Washington, D.C. He is an author of the best-selling *e-Learning Companion: A Learner's Guide to Online Success* (Houghton Mifflin, 2005, 2007), *Performance by Design: The Systematic Selection, Design, and Development of Performance Technologies* (HRD Press, 2006), and *75 e-Learning Activities: Making Online Courses Interactive* (Pfeiffer, 2005). In addition, he has co-authored three other books on organizational planning and more than sixty articles on instructional design, strategic planning, needs assessment, distance education, and performance technology. Watkins is an active member of the International Society for Performance Improvement (ISPI) and was a vice president of the Inter-American Distance Education Consortium (CREAD). He frequently offers workshops and consulting services on needs assessment, performance improvement, and e-learning. In 2005 Watkins was a visiting scientist with the National Science Foundation. For more information, visit www.ryanrwatkins.com or needsassessment.org.

Doug Leigh, Ph.D., is an associate professor of education at Pepperdine University's Graduate School of Education and Psychology. He earned his doctorate in instructional systems from Florida State University, where he served as a technical director of projects with various local, state, and federal agencies. His current research, publication, and consulting interests concern cause analysis, organizational trust, leadership visions, and alternative dispute resolution. Doug is co-author of *Strategic Planning for Success: Aligning People, Performance, and Payoffs* (2003) and *Useful*

*Educational Results: Defining, Prioritizing, and Accomplish*ing (2001). He is also a two-time chair of the American Evaluation Association's needs assessment topic interest group and past editor-in-chief for the International Society for Performance Improvement's journal, *Performance Improvement*. A lifetime member of ISPI, Doug has most recently served as chair of its research committee. For more information, visit www.dougleigh.com or needsassessment.org.

ABOUT THE CONTRIBUTORS

James W. Altschuld is Professor Emeritus in educational research and evaluation at The Ohio State University. He has published extensively on needs assessment and has co-written two books on the topic, with a series of five now underway. Currently, he serves as the evaluator for the Ohio Science and Engineering Alliance.

Rona S. Beattie is professor and head of the Division of People Management and Leadership at Glasgow Caledonian University in the U.K. Her e-mail address is r.beattie2@gcal.ac.uk.

Shelley A. Berg is a senior instructional designer in the financial services industry. She has a master's degree in instructional and performance technology from Boise State University. Berg has experience in international and domestic training, performance management, and call center management. Berg's recent research has been in the areas of informal learning and the use of employee engagement surveys as a performance improvement tool. Her bachelor's degree is in organizational communication from the University of Wisconsin-Eau Claire. She can be reached via e-mail at ShelleyAnnBerg@yahoo.com.

Jim Breaugh is a professor of management and of psychology at the University of Missouri–St. Louis. He is a Fellow of the Society for Industrial and Organizational Psychology. He has written extensively on the topic of employee recruitment. He consults regularly with organizations on issues concerning employee recruitment and selection.

Dr. Marty Bray works as a professor of instructional systems technology at the University of North Carolina at Charlotte specializing in issues surrounding the delivery of instruction via the Internet. In addition to his work at the university, Dr. Bray consults with businesses to help them develop online training systems that are uniquely suited to their business needs. He received his doctorate from Indiana University in instructional systems technology. Prior to earning his doctorate, he was a teacher and media coordinator in the public schools of North Carolina. He may be reached at mbray@email.uncc.edu.

Steven J. Condly, Ph.D., is senior associate at HSA Learning & Performance Solutions LLC. He has worked with organizations such as Intel, DaimlerChrysler, Coffee Bean & Tea Leaf, the International Association of Fire Fighters, and the Building Owners and Managers Institute International on such issues as employee performance; the design, development, and validation of test and survey instruments; computer science education; and employee motivation and incentive systems. Dr. Condly is the recipient of several grants and awards related to his work and research, including the ASTD's 2004 Research Award for his meta-analysis article regarding incentives. He can be reached at scondly@gmail.com.

Seung Youn (Yonnie) Chyung, Ed.D., is an associate professor of the Department of Instructional and Performance Technology at Boise State University. She received an Ed.D. in instructional technology from Texas Tech University and has been teaching at Boise State since 1996. She teaches graduate courses in foundations of instructional and performance technology, evaluation methodology, and e-learning principles and practices. She has published her research reports in the *American Journal of Distance Education*, the *Journal of Education for Business*, the *Journal of Experimental Education*, the *Journal of Workplace Learning, Performance Improvement Journal, Performance Improvement Quarterly*, and *Quarterly Review of Distance Education*. Chyung is the author of two books: *Foundations of Instructional and Performance Technology* (2008) and *Training Professionals' Web Design Toolkit* (2004), published by HRD Press. She is a frequent presenter at the annual conference of the International Society of Performance Improvement. She can be reached via e-mail at ychyung@boisestate.edu.

Stella Louise Cowan is currently a leadership development consultant in the Human Performance Department at Blue Cross and Blue Shield of Michigan. Cowan is also an adjunct professor in Spring Arbor University's School of Graduate and Professional Studies. She has over fifteen years of experience in training and organizational development. This includes ten years designing and delivering training and performance solutions for Blue Cross and Blue Shield of

Michigan. Stella has also held positions as employee development manager for Blue Care Network, senior learning and performance consultant for Plante and Moran, and learning systems consultant for Development Dimensions International (DDI). Cowan is the author of several application-focused training workbooks designed to support the development of front-line leaders. She has a master's degree in education (with a focus in training and development) from Wayne State University. She can be contacted at indybridge@msn.com.

John Donovan, Ph.D., is an associate professor at Rider University in the Management and Human Resources Department within the College of Business Administration. He received his Ph.D. in industrial and organizational psychology from University at Albany, State University of New York. Dr. Donovan's published research and work presented at international conferences has focused on the effects of feedback on employee motivation and goal setting, methods of employee selection, and the design of organizational training programs. Beyond the academic world, John has experience in designing and implementing employee assessment programs (including 360-degree feedback systems), executive coaching, and facilitating strategic alignment within organizations.

James T. Driggers is currently the Science of Learning Branch Head for the Naval Education and Training Command. He is in the final course of his studies at Old Dominion University in Norfolk, Virginia, working toward completion of a doctorate in instructional design and technology. Driggers received his bachelor's in occupational education from Southern Illinois University in Carbondale in 1985, his master's in elementary education from Old Dominion University in Norfolk, Virginia, in 1992, and his Certificate of Advanced Studies in Educational Administration from the George Washington University in Washington, D.C., in 2003. He can be reached at jtdrigers@msn.com.

Andrea D. Ellinger is a professor of human resource development at the University of Texas at Tyler in the College of Business and Technology. Her e-mail address is Andrea_Ellinger@uttyler.

Alexander E. Ellinger is a professor of marketing and supply chain management at the University of Alabama. His e-mail address is aellinge@cba.ua.edu.

Marvin Faure is a management consultant specializing in change management, motivation, and leadership, bringing twenty-five years of leadership experience to the service of his clients. As a coach and consultant to executive management, he leads frequent strategy workshops and leadership retreats. Prior to launching MindStore in Switzerland, Faure held successive positions as an officer in the British Navy, field engineer in the oil industry, sales executive in manufacturing,

HR executive in services and organization development consultant in the software industry. He has traveled extensively and has lived in more than ten countries in Africa, Asia, Australasia, and Europe. He holds a first degree in engineering science from Cambridge University, England, and an MBA from INSEAD, France. He can be contacted at marvin.faure@mindstore.ch or www .mindstore.ch.

Michelle French is an assistant professor in the Business Administration Department at Mount St. Mary's College in Los Angeles. She teaches courses in management, organizational behavior, and leadership. She earned her doctoral degree in organizational leadership from Pepperdine University. Dr. French's current research interests include meaning-mission fit and the relationship of well-being to work. She can be reached via e-mail at mfrench@msmc.la.edu.

Jessica Jean Frumkin is a Ph.D. student in the instructional technology program at Wayne State University. She has supplemented her education with real-world experience, working with small businesses, higher education facilities, and Fortune 500 companies. She has presented at the International Society for Performance Improvement on evidence-based design, incentive systems, the Fortune 500, and serious games. Frumkin's area of research is non-contingent based motivation in the workplace and how it relates to organizational performance. For more information, please visit www.insparked.com.

Ingrid Guerra-López, Ph.D., is an associate professor at Wayne State University in Detroit and director of the Institute for Learning and Performance Improvement. She is also an associate research professor at the Sonora Institute of Technology in Mexico and principal of Intelligence Gathering Systems. She consults nationally and internationally in the area of performance improvement and management, particularly as it relates to performance measurement, evaluation, and tracking. She is the author of five evaluation and assessment books, approximately one dozen book chapters related to performance improvement, and over two dozen articles in performance, management, and human resource journals. Her research is currently focused on performance measurement systems and their impact on decision making and organizational effectiveness.

David G. Gliddon, Ph.D., serves as faculty in the School of Business at Colorado Technical University and the CTU Institute for Advanced Studies. He received his Ph.D. in workforce education and development with a specialization in training and human resources from Penn State University. He received his master's in human resource administration with a specialization in human resource development from the University of Scranton and his bachelor's in psychology with a specialization in business and a minor in philosophy from Penn State University. Dr. Gliddon received the 2005 Colorado Technical University Faculty Service Award and is chair of the Library Committee. He has provided executive consulting to director and VP-level clients, achieving a multitude of successes in state-wide strategic curriculum development projects in Pennsylvania; nation-wide compensation, EEO, and employee relations projects; and global performance management, staffing, training, and HRIS project implementations. He can be contacted via his e-mail address, david. gliddon@ctuonline.edu, or by visiting his professional profile on www.isoil.org or www.davidgliddon.com.

Bea Griffith-Cooper, M.Ed., served the healthcare industry for over sixteen years as a consultant, adviser, trainer, mentor, and change agent before moving into academia. In 2006 she and a partner started LearnSmith Associates, LLC, a human resource development and statistical research consulting business. In 2008 she had the opportunity to join Ferris State University's Faculty Center for Teaching and Learning as an instructional designer, faculty resource, and adjunct faculty member. Griffith-Cooper's daily focus is supporting faculty to develop and improve their teaching and learning practices. Currently, she is the lead designer on a university-wide initiative to build Ferris State's first non-clinical doctorate. She graduated from Vanderbilt University's Peabody College with her master's of education in human resource development in 1999. From her graduate studies in human and organizational development, she draws on a wide range of interventions from multiple disciplines, including instructional systems design, organizational development, human resource management, and behavioral psychology. Griffith-Cooper has published *The Theory of Variation: Making Sense of Process Improvement Data* and *Introduction to Profound Knowdedge* (a workshop manual and course pack). She has co-authored an article in *Performance Improvement*.

Judith A. Hale, Ph.D., CPT, is the author of *Outsourcing Training and Development* (2006), *The Performance Consultant's Fieldbook: Tools and Techniques for Improving Organizations and People* (2nd ed., 2007), *Performance-Based Management: What Every Manager Should Do to Get Results* (2003), *Performance-Based Evaluation: Tools and Techniques for Measuring the Impact of Training* (2002), and *Performance-Based Certification: How to Design a Valid, Defensible, Cost-Effective Program* (2000). She is a contributing author to *The Handbook of Performance Technology* (3rd ed.; 2006). She has dedicated her professional career to helping management develop effective and practical ways to improve individual and organizational performance. She is known for making sense out of confusion and helping others stay focused on what matters. She is able to explain complex ideas so people understand their relevance and how to apply them. Dr. Hale was awarded a B.A. from Ohio State University, an M.A. from Miami University, and a Ph.D. from Purdue University.

Debra Haney, Ph.D., CPT, is the supervisor of the Human Performance Improvement Department for the Naval Education & Training Command, U.S. Navy, where she coordinates performance improvement projects. She has consulted in knowledge management, performance improvement, and training for over fifteen years to Fortune 500 corporations, governmental, and higher education organizations. Dr. Haney is a national member of ISPI and ASTD, has presented at national conferences, and has published numerous articles and book chapters. She has an M.S. in instructional design from Indiana University and a B.A in business administration. She may be reached at deb.haney@earthlink.net.

Robert G. Hamlin is Emeritus Professor and chair of human resource development at the University of Wolverhampton in the U.K. His e-mail address is r.g. hamlin@wlv.ac.uk.

Christine D. Hegstad, Ph.D., is president and CEO of MAP Professional Development Inc., a consulting firm dedicated to helping busy professionals create meaningful careers and purposeful lives. A frequent keynote speaker and trainer, Dr. Hegstad has worked with Fortune 500 companies such as Wells Fargo and Pioneer Hi-Bred International, as well as a variety of small firms, associations, universities and not-for-profits. Her work has been featured in *Human Resource Development Quarterly* and *Human Resource Development International,* her signature series of guidebooks, and in a variety of newspapers and magazines. To learn more, please visit Dr. Hegstad on the web at www .meaning-and-purpose.com.

Tyrone A. Holmes, Ed.D, is the president of T.A.H. Performance Consultants, Inc., a full service human resource development consulting firm specializing in the enhancement of individual and organizational performance. As a dynamic speaker, trainer, consultant, and coach, Dr. Holmes has helped countless individuals enhance their ability to communicate, resolve conflict, and solve problems in culturally diverse settings. He has created and copyrighted numerous training systems and speaks on a variety of communication, diversity and wellness topics. Dr. Holmes is certified as a personal trainer through the American Council on Exercise. He is also certified as a level 2 (expert) cycling coach through USA Cycling. For more information, visit Dr. Holmes' website at www.doctorholmes.net. You can also e-mail him at tyrone@doctorholmes.net.

Sandra Janoff has led meetings with Marvin Weisbord for decades in the business, community, education, health care, and science and technology sectors. They co-direct the international Future Search Network and are co-authors of *Future Search: An Action Guide* (2nd ed.; 2000) and *Don't Just Do Something, Stand There!* (2007). They have managed Future Searches in Africa, Asia, Europe, India, and North and South America and trained more than thirty-five hundred people worldwide in using their principles. Janoff is a psychologist and consultant. She was a staff member in Tavistock conferences sponsored by Temple University in Philadelphia and The Tavistock Institute of Human Relations in Oxford, England. She also has run training workshops in systems-oriented group dynamics. Sandra taught mathematics and chemistry from 1974 to 1984 in an experimental high school and ran workshops in Pennsylvania schools on alternative practices in education. She is co-author with Yvonne Agazarian of "Systems Thinking and Small Groups" for the *Comprehensive Textbook of Group Psychotherapy*. Her research on the relationship between moral reasoning and legal education was a lead article in the *University of Minnesota Law Review*.

Karyl King, PMP, has eighteen years of leadership in project management, specifically in developing project management methodologies in the new product development and healthcare industries. She has extensive experience in leading and working collaboratively with team members to complete projects in new product development, quality enhancement, rapid tooling, and information technology development, using the Toyota lean methodology for process improvement. She is currently a project manager at Spectrum Health, leading innovation projects through the What I.F.? Innovation Lab. King graduated from Davenport University with her bachelor in general business degree in 2000. She currently serves on the board for the West Michigan Project Management Chapter. She has co-authored an article, "The Partnership Between Project Management and Organizational Change: Integrating Change Management with Change Leadership," in *Performance Improvement*.

Eugene Kutcher, Ph.D., is an assistant professor of management at Rider University's College of Business Administration, where he teaches courses in organizational behavior, human resources, and employee selection and training. Dr. Kutcher received his Ph.D. in industrial/organizational psychology from Virginia Tech and has published articles related to management decision making, work-family conflict, and job interview dynamics. In the corporate context, he has experience creating assessments of employee knowledge and skills and designing and evaluating training and development programs.

Miki Lane, Ph.D., CPT, is a senior partner for MVM Communications a leading Canadian developer, producer, and deliverer of performance improvement products and services. He was an author and part editor of both the first and second *Handbook of Human Performance Technology* (1999, 2003). His current book, written with MVM colleagues, is *Stepping Up: A Roadmap for New Supervisors*. He frequently presents at the national ISPI conferences and has served in leadership positions both locally and internationally. He has twice served on the ISPI Board. He was on the instructional design team that won the Outstanding Instructional Product/Intervention of the Year Award from ISPI. Dr. Lane also received the ISPI award for an outstanding performance aid in 2000. He was recognized for his service to ISPI as recipient of the 1999 Distinguished Service Award. In 2002 he received his Certified Performance Technologist certification from ISPI. He can be reached at mml@mvmcommunications.com.

Doug Leigh, Ph.D., is an associate professor of education at Pepperdine University's Graduate School of Education and Psychology. He earned his doctorate in instructional systems from Florida State University, where he served as a technical director of projects with various local, state, and federal agencies. His current research, publication, and consulting interests concern cause analysis, organizational trust, leadership visions, and alternative dispute resolution. Dr. Leigh is co-author of *Strategic Planning for Success: Aligning People, Performance, and Payoffs* (2003) and *Useful Educational Results: Defining, Prioritizing, and Accomplish*ing (2001). He is also a two-time chair of the American Evaluation Association's needs assessment topic interest group and past editor-in-chief for the International Society for Performance Improvement's journal, *Performance Improvement*. A lifetime member of ISPI, Dr. Leigh has most recently served as chair of its research committee. For more information, visit www.dougleigh.com or needsassessment.org.

Hillary Leigh is a doctoral student in Wayne State University's instructional technology program. Her research interests include evidence-based intervention selection and justification for the field of performance improvement. Her dissertation topic relates to practitioners' usage of scientific and artistic evidential sources when selecting an intervention. On the practical side, she has consulted with healthcare, educational, and retail organizations to select, develop, implement, and evaluate a variety of instructional and non-instructional interventions.

Traci L. Lepicki is a program manager at the Center on Education and Training for Employment at The Ohio State University. Her work focuses on adult basic education learners and designing programs to meet the needs of such individuals and those who provide services to them.

Sally Lollie is an active and progressive practitioner of performance improvement and organization efficiency/effectiveness. She has more than twenty years of experience consulting and working inside organizations competing in health-care, automotive, manufacturing, financial services, hospitality, and retail. As a management consultant, Lollie specializes in bottom-line operational improvements, strategic planning, improving employee satisfaction, leadership development/coaching and change initiatives. With a background in organizational management and industrial engineering technology, she has co-authored and constructed numerous initiatives and projects that have resulted in successful enterprise-wide transformations. Lollie regularly presents at conferences about performance improvement, systems integration, and organization change projects using case studies from financial, healthcare, manufacturing, and hospitality organizations. She has guest lectured before members of the International Society for Performance Improvement, the American Society for Training & Development, Credit Union National Association, Manufacturer's Association, and American Healthcare Management Association and numerous state and regional associations across the country. Lollie coaches executives to conduct initiatives or leads the effort for them. You can reach her at pci.slollie@yahoo .com or by phone at (586) 945-9946.

Steven J. Lorenzet, Ph.D., is the associate dean and an associate professor of human resource management in the College of Business Administration at Rider University. He is the former director of Rider's MBA program. His research interests include training and development, leadership, and work motivation. His research has received multiple awards, including the Citation of Excellence from Emerald Management Reviews. Dr. Lorenzet is also an active consultant, with experience in the pharmaceutical, legal, military, financial, and academic industries. He received his Ph.D. in organizational studies (human resource management and organizational behavior) from the University at Albany, State University of New York.

Anthony (Tony) Marker, Ph.D., is an assistant professor for the Instructional and Performance Technology Department at Boise State University. He holds a Ph.D. from Indiana University and is a Leadership in Energy and Environmental Design (LEED) Accredited Professional. He teaches graduate courses in performance technology, evaluation, needs assessment, organizational culture, and sustainability. His research interests include the state of research in HPT, change management, and finding ways for HPT practitioners to create and promote socially and environmentally sustainable interventions. Dr. Marker can be reached at anthonymarker@boisestate.edu.

Anne F. Marrelli, Ph.D., is a research psychologist for the U.S. Merit Systems Protection Board in Washington, D.C. She and her colleagues conduct research studies to assess the soundness of Federal merit employment systems and make recommendations to the President, Congress, and other Federal decision makers for its improvement. Dr. Marrelli's former employers include American Express, Hughes Electronics, Educational Testing Service, and the County of Los Angeles. She earned M.S. and Ph.D. degrees in educational psychology from the University of Southern California. Dr. Marrelli is the author of numerous journal articles, book chapters, and technical reports. She may be reached at anne .marrelli@mspb.gov.

Frank Nguyen, Ed.D., is an assistant professor in educational technology at San Diego State University. For the past ten years, he has developed learning and performance solutions for various Fortune 500 companies. He is co-author of *Efficiency in Learning* (Pfeiffer, 2006) and has written various articles on e-learning, instructional design, and performance support. Nguyen earned master's and doctoral degrees in educational technology from Arizona State University. He may be contacted at www.frankn.net.

Tahir M. Nisar is a reader (associate professor) in organizational behavior and HR at the University of Southampton, UK. He has written numerous articles on executive compensation published in both academic and practitioner journals, including the *Journal of Financial Services Research*, the *Journal of Labor Research* and *Performance Improvement*. Nisar has also co-authored a book, *Investor Engagement* (Oxford University Press, 2007), and edited a special issue of *Management Decision* on the influence of finance on company management practices.

Patti P. Phillips, Ph.D., is president and CEO of the ROI Institute and an adjunct professor in the University of Southern Mississippi Ph.D. in Human Capital Development program, where she teaches workforce analysis, survey, design, and qualitative research. She works with organizations in the private and public sectors as they implement the ROI Methodology. Prior to her work with the ROI Methodology, she enjoyed a thirteen-year career in a large electric utility. Today, as author and speaker on the topic of ROI, Patti participates in conferences around the world as keynote presenter, workshop facilitator, and panelist. She can be heard over the Internet as she participates in webcasts hosted by a variety of journals and associations. Phillips holds a Ph.D. in international development from the College of Business and Economic Development at the University of Southern Mississippi, a master's degree in public and private management from Birmingham-Southern College, and a bachelor's degree in education from Auburn University. For more information, visit www .roiinstitute.net.

Jack J. Phillips, Ph.D., chairman of the ROI Institute, is an expert on accountability, measurement, and evaluation and is developer of the ROI Methodology.

He provides consulting services for Fortune 500 companies and major global organizations. The author or editor of more than fifty books, he has conducted workshops and presented at conferences in forty-four countries. His expertise in measurement and evaluation is based on more than twenty-seven years of corporate experience. He has served as training and development manager at two Fortune 500 firms, senior human resource officer at two firms, president of a regional bank, and management professor at a major state university. He holds undergraduate degrees in electrical engineering, physics, and mathematics; a master's degree in decision sciences from Georgia State University; and a Ph.D. in human resource management from the University of Alabama. For more information, visit www.roinstitute.net.

Christine Prigmore is a performance consultant for Handshaw Inc. in Charlotte, North Carolina. She focuses on the human side of e-learning and web-based training. She manages the instructional design process, seeing projects through the needs assessment, analysis, and design phases. After training programs are implemented, she evaluates learner performance against the original business goals. As a part of the performance consultant role, she co-invented Handshaw's Learning Content Management System, nogginware™. Prigmore is an active member of the International Society for Performance Improvement and has presented at the Carolinas' ISPI chapter on the subject of learning content management systems. Previously, she has worked in the technical training industry as an operations manager and account representative. She received her BS/BA in finance from the University of Florida and is currently working toward her master's of education in instructional systems technology at the University of North Carolina at Charlotte. She may be reached at Chris.prigmore@handshaw.com.

Jennifer Rosenzweig is an organizational consultant to companies large and small. Her practice emphasizes business growth by taking a systems view and tapping into the potential of the people in the organization. Her areas of expertise include instructional design, motivation, communications, leadership development and the application of positive change techniques. Her work history has spanned many industries, including the automotives and telecommunication. Before becoming the principal of Libera Consulting, she was a consultant in the incentives industry and spent many years leading teams that developed custom learning solutions. Jennifer has two master's degrees, one in performance improvement and instructional design from the University of Michigan–Dearborn, and another in positive organizational development from Case Western Reserve University. She is currently pursuing a Ph.D. in organizational consulting. She can be contacted at jrosenzweig @liberaconsulting.com.

Scott P. Schaffer is an associate professor in the educational technology program at Purdue University and an affiliated faculty member at the Regenstrief Center for Healthcare Engineering, where he studies applications of learning and performance technologies within various healthcare contexts. Schaffer has several years of consulting experience with a wide variety of organizations and focuses mainly on assessment and evaluation challenges. He has written and spoken widely on these topics, with more than seventy-five articles and presentations to his credit. Schaffer is currently working on a book about innovation in teams which he hopes to complete in 2009. He can be reached at schaffer3999@gmail.com.

Marcey Uday-Riley, MSW, CPT, is a partner in IRI Consultants, a Detroit-based consulting practice. As a practitioner with over twenty-five years' experience, she supports organizational transformation through the improvement of organizational and business processes and the development of leadership skills and employee capability. In addition to actively working on multiple client engagements, Uday-Riley is a frequent presenter both in the United States and internationally for such organizations as ISPI, ASTD, Mid America Human Resource Symposium, and the International Association of Personnel in Employment Security. She has been an adjunct professor or guest lecturer at Oakland University in Michigan, the University of Michigan–Dearborn, and Eastern Michigan University. In addition, she has been published in several journals. For more information, e-mail meur@mindspring.com or www.iriconsultants.com.

Darlene Van Tiem, CPT, CPLP, Ph.D., is an Associate Professor Emerita, coordinator of graduate-level performance improvement and instructional design, School of Education, University of Michigan–Dearborn and adjunct faculty, Capella University, mentoring doctoral dissertations and independent studies. Previously, she was human resources training director at AT&T (Ameritech) Yellow Pages (responsible for Michigan, Ohio, Indiana, and Wisconsin); curriculum manager for General Motors Technical Curriculum, including training GM suppliers, through General Physics Corporation. Van Tiem is 2009–2010 president of ISPI. She is lead author, with Jim Moseley and Joan Dessinger, of two award-winning ISPI companion books: *Fundamentals of Performance Technology: A Guide to Improving People, Process, and Performance* (2nd ed.) and *Performance Improvement Interventions: Enhancing People and Performance Through Performance Technology*. She has also published over fifty journal articles and chapters and presented approximately fifty juried presentations for professional associations. She holds an M.S.A. from Central Michigan University, an M.Ed. from Marygrove College, an M.A. from Michigan State University, and a Ph.D. from Wayne State University. Contact her at dvt@umich.edu.

Lya Visser, Ph.D., is director of Human Resource Development at the Learning Development Institute (USA & France). She has a rich experience in working in distance education and has explored e-learning themes and issues on different continents and in a variety of exiting circumstances. Her professional interest is in the development of effective learning systems. Her research and publication interests are in the areas of learner support, critical thinking and motivation and communication. Visser holds a doctoral degree in educational science and technology from the University of Twente, The Netherlands.

Ryan Watkins is an associate professor at the George Washington University in Washington, D.C. He is an author of *Performance by Design: The Systematic Selection, Design, and Development of Performance Technologies* (HRD Press, 2006), *75 e-Learning Activities: Making Online Courses Interactive* (Pfeiffer, 2005), and the best-selling *e-Learning Companion: A Learner's Guide to Online Success* (Houghton Mifflin, 2005, 2007). In addition, he has co-authored two books on educational planning and more than sixty articles on instructional design, strategic planning, needs assessment, distance education, and performance technology. In 2005 Watkins was a visiting scientist with the National Science Foundation. For more information please visit www.ryanrwatkins.com or www.how2elearn.com.

John Wedman is professor and director of the School of Information Science and Learning Technologies at the University of Missouri. Wedman's background includes significant experience in business/industry, government, higher education, and K–12 schools. He founded three small businesses dedicated to training design and evaluation and performance improvement. Much to the amazement of his university colleagues, he often uses his business/industry experiences to bring for-profit approaches to his work in higher education. Wedman is the lead developer of the Performance Pyramid framework and associated needs assessment tools, all of which can be found at the website for this book.

Marvin Weisbord and Sandra Janoff have led meetings for decades in the business, community, education, health care, science, and technology sectors. They co-direct the international Future Search Network and are co-authors of *Future Search: An Action Guide* (2nd ed.; 2000), and *Don't Just Do Something, Stand There!* (2007). They have managed Future Searches in Africa, Asia, Europe, India, and North and South America and trained more than thirty-five hundred people worldwide in using their principles. Weisbord consulted with business firms and medical schools from 1969 to 1992. He was for twenty years a partner in Block Petrella Weisbord, Inc., and a member of NTL Institute. He is a fellow of the World Academy of Productivity Science. He also received a

Lifetime Achievement Award in 2004 from the Organization Development Network, which voted his book *Productive Workplaces* (1987) among the five most influential books of the past forty years. He also wrote *Organizational Diagnosis* (1978), *Discovering Common Ground* (1992), and *Productive Workplaces Revisited* (2004).

Daniel White is a leadership coach and organization development consultant. He works with clients to strengthen their ability to manage people, lead organizations, collaborate, and innovate. Prior to his role as a coach and organization development consultant, White served as director of organization and executive development at CitiGroup. There he implemented original approaches to leadership training and organization effectiveness and championed two major culture change efforts that enabled rapid business growth. As a consultant, he has worked with organizations such as Johnson & Johnson, Pfizer, Schering Plough, Siemens, Bristol-Myers Squibb, Regeneron, Lundbeck USA, CitiGroup, JP MorganChase, The New York Stock Exchange-Euronext, Standard & Poors, Dow Jones, Prudential, UBS, CIT, Rothschild, Societe Generale, R.R. Donnelley, *The New York Times*, Reuters, MTV, Universal Music, Columbia University, American Institute of Architects, and the New York City schools. He teaches the executive coaching course in the NYU master's degree program in human resources management. He can be reached at dwdiscover @aol.com.

Frank S. Wilmoth is presently the director for learning excellence with Prudential Real Estate and Relocation Services. Over the past eighteen months, he and his team have partnered with Harold Stolovitch Associates in the development of a performance based, blended learning solution that Wilmoth's learning team could then deliver to six hundred new associates joining the company's new Global Relocation Center in Scottsdale, Arizona. Prior to joining Prudential, he had a full and distinguished military career with the U.S. Army, where he gained extensive experience as both a professional trainer and leader during the Persian Gulf War. He culminated his military career with service as a senior curriculum developer, instructor, and department chair at the Army's Command and General Staff College. Wilmoth holds a master of science degree in logistics management from Florida Institute of Science and a master of education degree in instructional systems technology from the University of North Carolina at Charlotte. Frank may be reached at FSWil@aol.com.

NAME INDEX

SUBJECT INDEX

Page references followed by *fig* indicate an illustrated figure; followed by *t* indicate a table.

Pfeiffer Publications Guide

This guide is designed to familiarize you with the various types of Pfeiffer publications. The formats section describes the various types of products that we publish; the methodologies section describes the many different ways that content might be provided within a product. We also provide a list of the topic areas in which we publish.

FORMATS

In addition to its extensive book-publishing program, Pfeiffer offers content in an array of formats, from fieldbooks for the practitioner to complete, ready-to-use training packages that support group learning.

FIELDBOOK Designed to provide information and guidance to practitioners in the midst of action. Most fieldbooks are companions to another, sometimes earlier, work, from which its ideas are derived; the fieldbook makes practical what was theoretical in the original text. Fieldbooks can certainly be read from cover to cover. More likely, though, you'll find yourself bouncing around following a particular theme, or dipping in as the mood, and the situation, dictate.

HANDBOOK A contributed volume of work on a single topic, comprising an eclectic mix of ideas, case studies, and best practices sourced by practitioners and experts in the field.

An editor or team of editors usually is appointed to seek out contributors and to evaluate content for relevance to the topic. Think of a handbook not as a ready-to-eat meal, but as a cookbook of ingredients that enables you to create the most fitting experience for the occasion.

RESOURCE Materials designed to support group learning. They come in many forms: a complete, ready-to-use exercise (such as a game); a comprehensive resource on one topic (such as conflict management) containing a variety of methods and approaches; or a collection of like-minded activities (such as icebreakers) on multiple subjects and situations.

TRAINING PACKAGE An entire, ready-to-use learning program that focuses on a particular topic or skill. All packages comprise a guide for the facilitator/trainer and a workbook for the participants. Some packages are supported with additional media—such as video—or learning aids, instruments, or other devices to help participants understand concepts or practice and develop skills.

- *Facilitator/trainer's guide* Contains an introduction to the program, advice on how to organize and facilitate the learning event, and step-by-step instructor notes. The guide also contains copies of presentation materials—handouts, presentations, and overhead designs, for example—used in the program.

• *Participant's workbook* Contains exercises and reading materials that support the learning goal and serves as a valuable reference and support guide for participants in the weeks and months that follow the learning event. Typically, each participant will require his or her own workbook.

ELECTRONIC CD-ROMs and web-based products transform static Pfeiffer content into dynamic, interactive experiences. Designed to take advantage of the searchability, automation, and ease-of-use that technology provides, our e-products bring convenience and immediate accessibility to your workspace.

METHODOLOGIES

CASE STUDY A presentation, in narrative form, of an actual event that has occurred inside an organization. Case studies are not prescriptive, nor are they used to prove a point; they are designed to develop critical analysis and decision-making skills. A case study has a specific time frame, specifies a sequence of events, is narrative in structure, and contains a plot structure—an issue (what should be/have been done?). Use case studies when the goal is to enable participants to apply previously learned theories to the circumstances in the case, decide what is pertinent, identify the real issues, decide what should have been done, and develop a plan of action.

ENERGIZER A short activity that develops readiness for the next session or learning event. Energizers are most commonly used after a break or lunch to stimulate or refocus the group. Many involve some form of physical activity, so they are a useful way to counter post-lunch lethargy. Other uses include transitioning from one topic to another, where "mental" distancing is important.

EXPERIENTIAL LEARNING ACTIVITY (ELA) A facilitator-led intervention that moves participants through the learning cycle from experience to application (also known as a Structured Experience). ELAs are carefully thought-out designs in which there is a definite learning purpose and intended outcome. Each step—everything that participants do during the activity—facilitates the accomplishment of the stated goal. Each ELA includes complete instructions for facilitating the intervention and a clear statement of goals, suggested group size and timing, materials required, an explanation of the process, and, where appropriate, possible variations to the activity. (For more detail on Experiential Learning Activities, see the Introduction to the *Reference Guide to Handbooks and Annuals*, 1999 edition, Pfeiffer, San Francisco.)

GAME A group activity that has the purpose of fostering team spirit and togetherness in addition to the achievement of a pre-stated goal. Usually contrived—undertaking a desert expedition, for example—this type of learning method offers an engaging means for participants to demonstrate and practice business and interpersonal skills. Games are effective for team building and personal development mainly because the goal is subordinate to the process—the means through which participants reach decisions, collaborate, communicate, and generate trust and understanding. Games often engage teams in "friendly" competition.

ICEBREAKER A (usually) short activity designed to help participants overcome initial anxiety in a training session and/or to acquaint the participants with one another. An icebreaker can be a fun activity or can be tied to specific topics or training goals. While a useful tool in itself, the icebreaker comes into its own in situations where tension or resistance exists within a group.

INSTRUMENT A device used to assess, appraise, evaluate, describe, classify, and summarize various aspects of human behavior. The term used to describe an instrument depends primarily on its format and purpose. These terms include survey, questionnaire, inventory, diagnostic, survey, and poll. Some uses of instruments include providing instrumental feedback to group members, studying here-and-now processes or functioning within a group, manipulating group composition, and evaluating outcomes of training and other interventions.

Instruments are popular in the training and HR field because, in general, more growth can occur if an individual is provided with a method for focusing specifically on his or her own behavior. Instruments also are used to obtain information that will serve as a basis for change and to assist in workforce planning efforts.

Paper-and-pencil tests still dominate the instrument landscape with a typical package comprising a facilitator's guide, which offers advice on administering the instrument and interpreting the collected data, and an initial set of instruments. Additional instruments are available separately. Pfeiffer, though, is investing heavily in e-instruments. Electronic instrumentation provides effortless distribution and, for larger groups particularly, offers advantages over paper-and-pencil tests in the time it takes to analyze data and provide feedback.

LECTURETTE A short talk that provides an explanation of a principle, model, or process that is pertinent to the participants' current learning needs. A lecturette is intended to establish a common language bond between the trainer and the participants by providing a mutual frame of reference. Use a lecturette as an introduction to a group activity or event, as an interjection during an event, or as a handout.

MODEL A graphic depiction of a system or process and the relationship among its elements. Models provide a frame of reference and something more tangible, and more easily remembered, than a verbal explanation. They also give participants something to "go on," enabling them to track their own progress as they experience the dynamics, processes, and relationships being depicted in the model.

ROLE PLAY A technique in which people assume a role in a situation/scenario: a customer service rep in an angry-customer exchange, for example. The way in which the role is approached is then discussed and feedback is offered. The role play is often repeated using a different approach and/or incorporating changes made based on feedback received. In other words, role playing is a spontaneous interaction involving realistic behavior under artificial (and safe) conditions.

SIMULATION A methodology for understanding the interrelationships among components of a system or process. Simulations differ from games in that they test or use a model that depicts or mirrors some aspect of reality in form, if not necessarily in content. Learning occurs by studying the effects of change on one or more factors of the model. Simulations are commonly used to test hypotheses about what happens in a system—often referred to as "what if?" analysis—or to examine best-case/worst-case scenarios.

THEORY A presentation of an idea from a conjectural perspective. Theories are useful because they encourage us to examine behavior and phenomena through a different lens.

TOPICS

The twin goals of providing effective and practical solutions for workforce training and organization development and meeting the educational needs of training and human resource professionals shape Pfeiffer's publishing program. Core topics include the following:

    Leadership & Management

    Communication & Presentation

    Coaching & Mentoring

    Training & Development

    E-Learning

    Teams & Collaboration

    OD & Strategic Planning

    Human Resources

    Consulting